THE CRIMINAL JUSTICE SYSTEM AND WOMEN

Offenders, Victims, and Workers

Second Edition

THE CRIMINAL JUSTICE SYSTEM AND WOMEN

Offenders, Victims, and Workers

SECOND EDITION
Edited and Compiled
by

Barbara Raffel Price
Natalie J. Sokoloff

McGraw-Hill, Inc.

New York   St. Louis   San Francisco   Auckland   Bogotá   Caracas
Lisbon   London   Madrid   Mexico City   Milan   Montreal   New Delhi
San Juan   Singapore   Sydney   Tokyo   Toronto

This book was set in Palatino by The Clarinda Company.
The editors were Phillip A. Butcher and Bridget Isacsen;
the production supervisor was Leroy A. Young.
The cover was designed by Carla Bauer.
Arcata Graphics/Martinsburg was printer and binder.

THE CRIMINAL JUSTICE SYSTEM AND WOMEN
Offenders, Victims, and Workers
Second Edition

4 5 6 7 8 9 0 AGM AGM 9 0 9 8 7

ISBN 0-07-050779-1

Library of Congress Cataloging-in-Publication Data

The criminal justice system and women: offenders, victims, and
  workers / edited and compiled by Barbara Raffel Price, Natalie J.
  Sokoloff.—2nd ed.
      p.   cm.
    Includes bibliographical references.
    ISBN 0-07-050779-1
    1. Sex discrimination in criminal justice administration—United
States.   2. Female offenders—United States.   3. Women—United
States—Crimes against.   I. Price, Barbara R.   II. Sokoloff,
Natalie J.
  HV6791.C754   1995
  364.973′082—dc20   94-21320

ABOUT THE EDITORS

BARBARA RAFFEL PRICE is a graduate of Smith College and holds an M.A. and Ph.D. from The Pennsylvania State University. She is Dean of Graduate Studies and Professor of Criminal Justice at John Jay College of Criminal Justice, The City University of New York. A former Vice President of the American Society of Criminology, she is a Fellow of both the American Society of Criminology and the Western Society of Criminology and Trustee-at-Large of The Academy of Criminal Justice Sciences. Dr. Price is Vice Chair of the Alliance of Nongovernmental Organizations of Crime Prevention at the United Nations. She is the author of several books, including *Police Professionalism: Rhetoric and Action,* and numerous articles on women and law enforcement.

NATALIE J. SOKOLOFF is Professor of Sociology at John Jay College of Criminal Justice, The City University of New York, and is a member of the doctoral faculty in Sociology, Criminology, and Women's Studies at the Graduate Center of The City University of New York. In 1994 she also was appointed a scholar of the Institute for Teaching and Research on Women at Towson State University (Towson, Maryland), part of the University of Maryland system. Formerly associated with the New York State Division for Youth in its research evaluation program and the Mount Sinai School of Medicine in its Department of Community Medicine (New York City), she holds a bachelor's degree (magna cum laude) from the University of Michigan, a master's degree from Brown University, and a Ph.D. from The City University of New York, Graduate Center. Professor Sokoloff is the author of

Between Money and Love: The Dialectics of Women's Home and Market Work (Praeger, 1980), *The Hidden Aspects of Women's Work* (coeditor, Praeger, 1987), and *Black Women and White Women in the Professions: Occupational Segregation by Race and Gender, 1960–1980* (Routledge, Chapman, Hall, 1992). She has published widely in numerous journals, including *Social Problems, Justice Professional, Quest: A Feminist Quarterly,* and *Current Perspectives in Social Theory,* as well as in several anthologies on women and work.

ABOUT THE CONTRIBUTORS

Sharyn L. Roach Anleu lectures in sociology at the Flinders University of South Australia. She completed her undergraduate and master of arts degrees at the University of Tasmania (Hobart) and received a Ph.D. in sociology from the University of Connecticut in 1986. Anleu's current research is on the legal regulation of new reproductive technologies and the entry of women into the legal profession. She authored *Deviance, Conformity and Control* (Longman Cheshire) and has published in *Sociology, Gender and Society, Work and Occupations,* and the *Australian and New Zealand Journal of Sociology.*

Regina A. Arnold is Associate Professor of Sociology at Sarah Lawrence College, where she teaches courses on deviance and criminology theory. She holds an M.A. and a Ph.D. in sociology from Bryn Mawr College. Her major research interests are female deviance and crime and the criminal justice system, with work focusing specifically on women in prison.

Joanne Belknap is an Associate Professor of Criminal Justice at the University of Cincinnati. Her research has focused on women victims of male violence and women workers in the criminal justice system. She testified before the Independent Commission to the Los Angeles Police Department (the "Christopher Commission") regarding the Rodney King case and gender issues related to police brutality. She is working on a book on women and crime. Her Ph.D. is from Michigan State University.

Angela Browne, a social psychologist specializing in violence, is in the Public Sector Division of the Department of Psychiatry at the University of Massachusetts Medical Center. In 1987 she wrote *When Battered Women Kill.* Her current research is on the correlates of homelessness for women and children.

Jane Caputi teaches in the American Studies Department at the University of New Mexico in Albuquerque. She is the author of *The Age of Sex Crime,* a feminist analysis of the atrocity of serial sex murder, and collaborated with Mary Daly on *Webster's First New Intergalactic Wickedary of the English Language.* Her new book on the cultural implications of the invention of nuclear technology is entitled *Gossips, Gorgons, and Crones: The Fates of the Earth.* She is currently writing a book with Ann Scales on sexual representation, culture, and the law called *The Pornography of Everyday Life.*

Meda Chesney-Lind, Ph.D., is Director of Women's Studies at the University of Hawaii at Manoa and Vice President–elect of the American Society of Criminology. The author of over fifty monographs and papers on women and crime, she has written *Girls, Delinquency and Juvenile Justice* with Randall G. Shelden. She was awarded the American Society of Criminology's Michael J. Hindelang Award for the "outstanding contribution to criminology, 1992," and also received the Paul Tappen Award from the Western Society of Criminology.

Richard Curtis is a Principal Research Associate at National Development and Research Institutes, Inc., in New York City, where he is completing work on a study of social factors and HIV risk among intravenous-drug users. He was formerly a Senior Research Associate at the Vera Institute of Justice in New York City, where he conducted an ethnographic study of the New York City Police Department's Tactical Narcotics Team. His M.A. is from Teachers College, Columbia University.

Kathleen Daly is Visiting Associate Professor of Sociology at the University of Michigan. She received her Ph.D. from the University of Massachusetts in 1983, taught at the State University of New York at Albany in 1982–1983, and was a member of the faculty at Yale University from 1983 to 1992. Her book *Gender, Crime, and Punishment* is forthcoming from Yale University Press.

Kathleen J. Ferraro is an Associate Professor of Justice Studies and Women's Studies at Arizona State University. She holds a Ph.D. in sociology from Arizona State University and has spent most of her career examining issues related to violence against women. Her current research focuses on the problems of homeless people in Arizona.

Michelle Fine is a Professor of Social Psychology at The City University of New York, Graduate Center. Among her most recent books are *Disruptive Voices* (University of Michigan Press) and *Beyond Silenced Voices* (coeditor with Lois Weis, SUNY Press).

Cheryl Gomez-Preston was a police officer in the Detroit Police Department. Because of her experience there, she founded the Association for the Sexually Harassed (ASH).

Linda Gordon is the Florence Kelley Professor at the University of Wisconsin. She is the author of *Woman's Body, Woman's Right* and *Cossack Rebellions: Social Turmoil in the 16th Century Ukraine.* Her history of family violence, *Heroes of Their Own Lives,* won the Joan Kelly Prize of the American Historical Association for 1988. She recently published an anthology, *Women, the State and Welfare,* and a book on the history of welfare is forthcoming.

Drew Humphries has a Ph.D. in criminology from the University of California, Berkeley, and is an Associate Professor of Sociology at Rutgers University, Camden, New Jersey. She has published in the areas of female victimization, crime and the media, the political economy of crime, the history of social control, and maternal crack/cocaine use.

Andrew Karmen is an Associate Professor in the Sociology Department of John Jay College of Criminal Justice of The City University of New York. He earned his Ph.D. in sociology in 1977 from Columbia University. He is the author of a textbook, *Crime Victims: An Introduction to Victimology* (2d ed., Brooks/Cole, Pacific Grove, California, 1990), and coeditor of a reader, *Deviants: Victims or Victimizers* (Sage, Newbury Park, California, 1983). Other subjects he has written about include agents provocateurs inciting political violence, the use of deadly force by police, the Rosenberg atom spy case, the link between drug addition and crime, auto theft, and vigilantism.

Dorie Klein is a researcher at the Western Consortium for Public Health, Berkeley, California, where she has recently completed a study of perinatal women and substance use. She was formerly the director of Court Services for Alameda County, California, where she has worked on developing jail alternatives. She co-organized the 1991 International Feminist Conference on Women, Law and Social Control, and she has published on women, crime, victimization, and justice. Her Ph.D. Crim. is from the University of California, Berkeley.

Eileen Leonard is Professor of Sociology and Director of Women's Studies at Vassar College. She authored *Women, Crime and Society: A Theoretical Critique of Criminology* (Longman, Inc., 1982) and has published articles and book reviews relating to women, crime, and imprisonment.

Catharine A. MacKinnon is a professor of law at the University of Michigan Law School. She is a graduate of Smith College and Yale Law School and has a Ph.D. in political science from Yale. She has published on constitutional law, including political theory, feminism, Marxism, and jurisprudence. Her books include *Sexual Harassment of Working Women, In Harm's Way: The Pornography Civil Rights Hearings,* and *Women's Lives, Men's Laws.*

Lisa Maher is a criminology graduate student at Rutgers University. Her doctoral research is on women and drugs. She has published widely in this area.

Coramae Richey Mann, Professor of Criminal Justice at Indiana University, Bloomington, received her Ph.D. in sociology from the University of Illinois, Chicago. Her research is on those oppressed by the juvenile and criminal justice systems: youth, women, and racial/ethnic minorities. Professor Mann is the author of articles, chapters, and three books: *Female Crime and Delinquency, Unequal Justice: A Question of Color,* and *Women Murderers: Deadliest of the Species?*

Susan E. Martin is a health scientist administrator at the Prevention Research Branch of the National Institute of Alcohol Abuse and Alcoholism. She was formerly at the Police Foundation, where she studied the status of women in policing. Her research also includes studies of sentencing, offender rehabilitation, child abuse, drunk driving, and hate crimes. She is the author of *Breaking and Entering: Policewomen on Patrol* and is working on a book on women as professionals in criminal justice. She received her Ph.D. in sociology from American University.

Nancy A. Matthews has been a Lecturer in Sociology at the University of California, Los Angeles. The article in this book is extracted from her Ph.D. dissertation, "Stopping Rape or Managing Its Consequences? State Intervention and Feminist Resistance in the Los Angeles Anti-Rape Movement, 1972–1987" (Univeristy of California, Los Angeles).

Imogene L. Moyer is on the faculty of the Criminology and Women's Studies Departments at Indiana University of Pennsylvania. She has a Ph.D. in sociology from the University of Missouri and is the author of *The Changing Roles of Women in Criminal Justice.* Her research is on women's prisons, police processing of women/minority offenders, child abuse, women in academia, and feminist criminology.

Christine E. Rasche is an Associate Professor of Criminal Justice and the Director of Criminal Justice Programs for the University of North Florida, where she has also served as the Director of Women's Studies. She received her Ph.D. in sociology from Washington University in St. Louis. Her research has focused on women and crime, with particular emphasis on battered women, domestic homicide, and women in prison. She has been appointed by the governor of Florida to serve as a clemency reviewer for cases of women murderers in prison for killing their abusers.

Ruthann Robson is on the faculty of City University of New York School of Law, where she teaches courses on feminist legal theory, sexuality and the law, family relations, and constitutional law. She has written numerous law review articles on the possibilities of a specifically lesbian legal theory as well as a book, *Lesbian (Out)law: Survival Under the Rule of Law.*

Diana E. H. Russell is a Professor Emeritus of Sociology, Mills College, Oakland, California. She obtained a Postgraduate Diploma from the London School of Economics and a Ph.D. from Harvard University. She is the author, editor, or coeditor of 11 books, including *The Politics of Rape, Crimes against Women* (with Nicole van de Ven), *Rape in Marriage, Sexual Exploitation,* and *The Secret Trauma* (for which she received the 1986 C. Wright Mills Award). Her current research will be published in *Telling Men's Secrets: South African Incest Survivors Speak Out.*

Lynn Hecht Schafran is an attorney and the director since 1981 of the National Judicial Education Program to Promote Equality for Women and Men in the Courts, a project of the NOW Legal Defense and Education Fund in cooperation with the National Association of Women Judges. She advises state and federal task forces on gender bias in the courts throughout the country. She is a graduate of Smith College and the Columbia University School of Law.

Dorothy Moses Schulz, a former police captain, is an Assistant Professor of Criminal Justice at John Jay College of Criminal Justice, The City University of New York. She holds a Ph.D. in American civilization from New York University. The author of numerous articles on police topics, she is working on a book on the history of women in U.S. policing and researching issues surrounding the employment of women in police departments in Caribbean countries.

Diana Scully is an Associate Professor of Sociology and Director of Women's Studies at Virginia Commonwealth University. She is currently President of the Southeastern Women's Studies Association.

Her research is on the politics of women's health care (*Men Who Control Women's Health: The Miseducation of Obstetrician-Gynecologists*) and sexual violence against women (*Understanding Sexual Violence: A Study of Convicted Rapists*).

Cassia Spohn is Professor of Criminal Justice and an Isaacson Professor at the University of Nebraska at Omaha. She recently coauthored a book, *Rape Law Reform: A Grassroots Movement and Its Impact*, with Julie Horney. Her research has examined the impact of rape law reform, racial disparity in sentencing, and the factors that influence judges' sentencing decisions.

Darrell Steffensmeier is Professor of Sociology at The Pennsylvania State University, University Park. His research includes the sociology of law, organized crime, and the structural covariates of crime (including race, gender, and age). His recent book, *The Fence: In the Shadow of Two Worlds*, was the recipient of the 1987 Award for Outstanding Scholarship from the Society for the Study of Social Problems. During 1990 and 1991 he served as project director of the *1990 Report—Organized Crime in Pennsylvania: A Decade of Change*. He is currently conducting an NSF-sponsored study of men and women lower-court judges in Pennsylvania.

Jacqueline Trescott is a freelance writer.

Nanci Koser Wilson (B.A. and M.A. in sociology from the University of Kansas, Ph.D. in sociology from the University of Tennessee) is a member of both the Criminology and the Women's Studies faculties and Coordinator of the Doctoral Program at Indiana University of Pennsylvania. Wilson, a pioneer in the study of women and crime, was cofounder of the American Society of Criminology's Division on Women and Crime. Her more recent research interests are in the areas of ecological crime, ecofeminism, and environmental ethics and law.

CONTENTS

WOMEN WORKERS IN THE CRIMINAL JUSTICE SYSTEM

Introduction by Barbara Raffel Price and Natalie J. Sokoloff

EPILOGUE

PREFACE

In the time since the first edition of this book was published,* much has changed. While women have made some remarkable strides in the United States and throughout the world, many traditional forms of repression remain, and new forms have emerged. Today women play a greater role in the American criminal justice system, but that system still does not treat women well. Many more women from diverse backgrounds are now lawyers, judges, police, and corrections officers. And feminists' lobbying efforts have strengthened laws dealing with some of the crimes against women, such as rape, battering, sexual harassment, and stalking. Yet other laws and the attitudes of those empowered to carry out the laws have done much new damage to women. The years have been marked by increased female incarceration, addiction, and poverty. In spite of the time-honored fact that men are almost always the perpetrators of violent, aggressive crimes, the rate of women's incarceration increased dramatically during these intervening years, more than double that of men.

Several factors were responsible: the increased poverty of women over the last decade; major structural shifts in U.S. capitalism and the world economy; a more punitive criminal justice system less inclined to use alternatives to incarceration for first offenders; a decline in differential treatment and judicial discretion at sentencing as a result of new mandatory sentencing laws; an increase in drug use and addiction among women; a powerful conservative mind-set that attributed

---

*For the first edition of this book, see Barbara Raffel Price and Natalie J. Sokoloff (eds.), *The Criminal Justice System and Women: Women Offenders, Victims, and Workers.* Clark Boardman Company Ltd., New York, 1982.

criminality to amoral, evil self-will; and the largely ignored forces of racism and sexism in the context of advanced monopoly capitalism.

We want the reader to obtain a broad perspective on women in the criminal justice system—as offenders, as victims of crime, and as working members of the system. We hope to show how women affect and are affected by crime and the criminal justice system. In the time that has passed since publication of the first edition of this book, much, other than the treatment of women offenders, has changed. A substantial amount of research has been conducted on women in the criminal justice system, and hence most of the chapters in this book are new; only one chapter (Chapter 2) from the first edition is repeated here. It is followed by an afterword to put the original material into perspective in relation to the current situation.

While we have retained the original format (three parts, one each on offenders, victims, and workers), which has proved to be highly popular with our readers and other writers, we are fortunate to have more original chapters written specifically for this edition than did the first volume. There have been many new developments in feminist and multicultural scholarship, as well as in criminological research and writing, since we published our first book on women and the criminal justice system.* Therefore, we invited leading scholars to write original essays for this edition. In this way we endeavored to provide the reader with the most current thinking on many aspects of women and the criminal justice system.

In the intervening period since the first edition was published, many new courses on women and crime have been incorporated into college curricula. And more doctoral theses have been written on women and crime. The intellectual growth of and greater familiarity with a wide variety of feminist thinking have become evident. All these factors— more research, more education, and the increasing influence of a multicultural feminist perspective—have helped to gain broader recognition of the deep biases in the United States against women and minorities, which, as this book takes as its primary theme, are also embedded in the nation's criminal justice system.

THEMES OF THE BOOK

The readings have been selected to illustrate several important themes common to women's involvement in different ways throughout the criminal justice system. Paramount in the planning of this new edition was our objective that students be able not only to explore the roles of women as offenders, victims, and workers but also to understand

---

*One of these developments was the creation of a scholarly journal devoted to some of the newest and best research on women and the criminal justice system. The journal, *Women & Criminal Justice,* appeared in 1989 under the editorship of Clarice Feinman.

and question socially structured systems through which women from diverse sectors of U.S. society participate. Readers also should seriously consider ways in which women participate not only in perpetuating but also in changing the system.

This book addresses broad issues surrounding the criminal justice system as it pertains to women. It identifies issues that are only slowly being recognized as central to understanding how and why the system operates in relation to women. For example, the section on women offenders does not stop with the simple notion that women are not free of criminal behavior, including the commission of violence, although, as noted above, the majority of criminal aggression is male. The book, and all of Part One in particular, raises questions as to *why* women become criminal. Why do they break the law? Who created those laws and in whose interest? What pressures lead women to commit certain types of crimes and not others? Are women more or less protected by the laws than men? If women are less well protected, what are the causes of unequal protection?

In the search for answers to these and many other questions, the criminal justice system must be viewed as a set of institutions that are very much part of the larger society. As such, the system reflects and perpetuates society's material conditions, values, attitudes, and biases. Where society is sexist, racist, and classist, the criminal justice system will be likewise. Thus, the major theme of this book is a focus on sexism, racism, and class bias as they affect women offenders, victims, and practitioners. Discrimination takes many forms; one of these has been the failure to protect women from physical harm, including murder by those with whom they are or have been involved. For example, women continue to be harassed and tormented by former husbands, lovers, and even would-be lovers. Persistent harassment can impede a woman's ability to lead a normal life, including leaving her home, going to work, and escorting her children to school. After considerable pressure from women's groups, from survivors of harassment and battering, and from others, many states have passed antistalking laws that provide for criminal sanctions (beyond those available through the often ineffectual orders of protection) against men intent on harming women who have rejected them. In regard to occupational discrimination, women in growing numbers are entering traditional male fields, such as policing and corrections. Full acceptance, as we observed in the first edition of this book, is still not established. The values, attitudes, structures, and practices that perpetuate work discrimination need to be exposed so that remedies may be found and women and minorities can function to their full capacities. Not only will they then have access to better-paying and more prestigious work, but they may also be expected to advance in the organization so that their leadership will reform the way police and corrections officers function in their roles as social control agents. This is an obviously contradictory situation for women and minority men.

The purpose of the criminal justice system is to assure the physical safety of the community by controlling people's behavior, judging the accused, and punishing the guilty. An elaborate structure of rules and enforcers of these rules (police, courts, and corrections) has been developed to make people comply with society's standards. As the book focuses on women, the poor, and minorities, it identifies issues unique to them, including their disadvantaged status within the context of the criminal justice system. First, as offenders, women and minorities—especially poor minority women—are judged by different standards than white men (for example, many more drug-offending women than men are sentenced to prison as first-time offenders), women and minorities are convicted and punished for different behavior, and as ex-offenders women have different needs when returning to society. Second, women are victimized by crimes in different ways than men and have different needs as victims and survivors of male violence. And third, access to positions in the criminal justice system is different for women and minorities than for white men.

The readings describe how sexism, racism, and the class structure associated with capitalism have harmful effects on women and minority men in the criminal justice system. *Sexism* is defined as the socially organized cultural beliefs, practices, and institutions that result in systematic male superiority and male domination over women as a group. Sexism means that women are treated on the basis of their socially defined "female nature." Moreover, the patriarchal relations of male domination operate in different ways with different groups of people under particular historical experiences. *Racism* is similar; the term refers to the socially organized attitudes, policies, and institutions that result in systematic domination of one racial/ethnic group over another. Finally, *capitalism* refers to the economic and political ways in which private ownership of productive property and the production of services and goods are organized in the interest of profit making for the relatively few. In each case a group—women, racial minorities, or poor and working-class people—is severely disadvantaged in the daily course of life. It is especially important to understand how these social forces of class, race, and gender operate *simultaneously* as they impact on all people's lives—including the lives of the oppressed and the privileged.*

The underlying causes of discrimination against and mistreatment of large segments of society are easier to describe than to change. The

---

*Patricia Hill Collins, *Black Feminist Thought*, Routledge, Chapman, Hall, New York, 1990.

writers contributing to this book are aware that there are neither easy answers nor quick solutions. This book and the represented writers also recognize that there is a need for thorough analysis of the social interaction of gender, class, and race—as well as sexual orientation, age bias, and the like—if we are to work effectively on the problems of women and minorities in relation to the criminal justice system.

In this regard, there have been changes since the publication of the first edition of this book. First, there is a growing consensus that change will not come about without a close collaborative relationship between scholars and researchers on the one hand and social activists on the other. Second, there is today a growing respect for the potential that a varied feminist analysis offers, particularly as it uncovers new ways of examining both legal and social science questions. It is both exciting and challenging to see that criminology is beginning to draw on feminist and multicultural theories and research emerging in other disciplines and to apply these insights and perspectives to the fields of crime, justice, and the law.

But some things in this second edition remain the same: the articles continue to draw on feminist scholarship as we find it today. As seen in the chapters of this book, feminist theory is eclectic in nature, with tremendous possibilities for growth. Because there has not been premature closure on epistemological, theoretical, or methodological grounds, authors do not necessarily share a paradigm or explanatory framework. Whether the outcome in the long term will or ought to be a shared "standpoint" remains to be seen.

ORGANIZATION OF THE BOOK

This book is divided into four sections: "Theories and Facts about Women Offenders" (Part One), "Women Victims of Crime" (Part Two), "Women Workers in the Criminal Justice System" (Part Three), and the Epilogue.

In Part One the topic of women offenders is presented first by examining theories about female criminality. In asking why women commit crimes, it is necessary to first consider some basic notions about criminal law. Law is defined in this book as a set of rules that control behavior through negative sanctions, and crime is understood as socially constructed behavior. With these definitions in mind, Chapter 1 explores how law is created and changed, as well as how law has affected and been affected by women from diverse racial and class backgrounds. Following Chapter 1, several authors discuss issues of crime causation, especially in reference to women and girls (Chapters 2, 3, 4, 7, and 8). Chapter 6 describes women offenders once they are convicted. Chapter 5 analyzes official crime statistics in order to describe the types of crimes women most frequently commit.

Chapters 9 and 10 deal with the important topic of women and drugs. It is, in large part, the political economy of drugs, drug addiction, the drug culture, and repressive social policies that have greatly expanded the female prison population and caused tremendous personal pain to women and their children. Throughout this section, the systemic ways in which patriarchy, capitalism, and racism affect women involved in the criminal justice system are explored.

Part Two examines women victims and survivors of male crime. The introduction to this section is a new, original essay written by Andrew Karmen (as was the introduction in the first edition). Karmen, who specializes in victimology, constructs three different paradigms to explain victimization. In so doing he lays a foundation for the chapters that follow on specific forms of victimization. Chapters 11 and 12 discuss issues pertaining to the crime of rape. Chapters 13 through 15 cover different aspects of battering and domestic violence with an analysis of why women do not escape violence by leaving home, the special problems domestic violence presents to women of color, and the role of the criminal justice system in protecting battered women. Two other chapters on violence against women discuss femicide (Chapter 16) and violence against lesbians (Chapter 19). Finally, two chapters in this section focus on practices that seriously victimize women physically and psychologically—incest (Chapter 17) and sexual harassment (Chapter 18)—with the latter describing the evolution of legal thinking concerning this relatively newly recognized form of victimization.

Part Three considers women as working members of the criminal justice sytem. The introduction provides an overview of how women influence the entire criminal justice system by their efforts on behalf of women offenders and victims, by their determination to work as practitioners within the criminal justice system, and by their challenges to the sexism, racism, and class bias that they encounter within the system. The first three chapters (20 through 22) in this section cover the courts, judges, and lawyers. First, Chapter 20 documents the increasing evidence substantiating bias against women and minorities in the courts; then Chapters 21 and 22 explore the different roles that women and minority judges and lawyers might assume in an effort to eliminate discrimination. Next, Chapters 23 through 25 turn to law enforcement and women in police work. In Chapter 23 the reader is presented with an original essay on the history of policewomen, whose presence has always been unacceptable in the dominant male police culture. Chapters 24 and 25 discuss the sexism and racism that many women police systematically face within their own departments. Corrections officers experience similar hardships in their work, and this is discussed in Chapter 26, along with the special approach that women bring to work. Chapters 27 and 28 present topics not generally thought of as the core of criminal justice but which we consider very important for students to consider. Chapter 27 addresses the faculty and curriculum that prepare students for careers in criminal justice, and Chapter 28 describes the importance of collaboration between researchers and service providers.

The Epilogue, on the future, consists of a single essay that should be seen as a beginning, not as an end. In this original essay, a leading feminist criminologist, Kathleen Daly, suggests directions for future work for all women and men concerned with social justice. The Epilogue should be particularly relevant for today's students of criminology and criminal justice. It urges all of us to have the courage to take the steps needed to transform the system in both little and big ways and to foster broad-scale social change that deals with sexism, racism, and the criminal justice system. The remaining chapters for this section are yet to be written. We leave that challenge to our readers.

ACKNOWLEDGMENTS

We feel that special acknowledgments are in order for those women who have been important to us personally and important to the movement in transforming the sexist, racist, and classist nature of our criminal justice system. This book is for Inez Garcia, Joan Little, Yvonne Wainrow, and Desi Woods, all imprisoned for protecting themselves against male attackers; for Kitty Genovese, Greta Rideout, Diane Williams, Carmita Wood, and Anita Hill, all victims of male assaults and intimidations; for Rhonda Copelon, Eleanor Holmes Norton, Constance Baker Motley, Kris Glen, Patricia Williams, Sonia Sotomayor, Felicia Spritzer, and Luz Santana, and all women working for change in the criminal justice system. This book is also for our mothers, sisters, daughters, and sons, and most especially our students, who have been invaluable in teaching us about the criminal justice system and women.

We want to thank John Jay College of Criminal Justice of The City University of New York, President Gerald W. Lynch of the college and Provost Basil Wilson, and our colleagues and students for providing the kind of environment that promotes interdisciplinary analysis and a continuing quest for knowledge. It was in such a setting that almost 15 years ago the two editors of this book originally came together over their concern for women in the criminal justice system. As should be clear from our earlier book, each editor contributed her unique skills and expertise; both are equally responsible in the production of this volume.

We wish to make special note of our appreciation to the scholars who wrote chapters specifically for this book: Dorie Klein, Eileen Leonard, Meda Chesney-Lind, Darrell Steffensmeier, Coramae Richey

Mann, Lisa Maher, Richard Curtis, Andrew Karmen, Dorothy Moses Schulz, and Kathleen Daly. Those who were especially helpful at different stages of our work were Meda Chesney-Lind, Drew Humphries, Nancy Jurik, and Carrie Menkel-Meadow.

We want to thank our editor at McGraw-Hill, Phil Butcher, for his wisdom in signing us up quickly so that we could spend all of our time on the content of this volume. He made it possible for Cybele Eidenschenk, and later Bridget Isacsen and Laura Warner, to assist us and for Susan Caringella-MacDonald (Western Michigan University), Helen Eigenberg (Old Dominion University), Edna Erez (Kent State University), Donna Hale (Shippensburg University), Eleanor M. Miller (The University of Wisconsin–Milwaukee), Susan Miller (Northern Illinois University), Dianne Post (Arizona State University), and Alissa Pollitz Worden (State University of New York at Albany), to provide insightful and constructive reviews. There are many authors whom we wanted to include in the book but space did not permit. We are especially grateful to those scholars who prepared material that, owing to length requirements, we were unable to include. These are Frances Bernat, Lynne Goodstein, and Evan Stark.

We are very indebted to Lydia Latchinova for her continually competent assistance in all aspects of the book's preparation. With her help, this book was completed on schedule.

For their continuing sustenance and encouragement, and for their willingness to assume many of the time-consuming household tasks essential to the creation of this volume, we are indebted to Robert Price and Fred Pincus. And for his inspiration to his mother and willingness to share her with the larger process of social change and the work that needed to be done to finish this book, we are grateful to Josh Pincus-Sokoloff.

Natalie J. Sokoloff
Barbara Raffel Price

THE CRIMINAL JUSTICE SYSTEM AND WOMEN

Offenders, Victims, and Workers

Second Edition

PART ONE

THEORIES AND FACTS ABOUT WOMEN OFFENDERS

This section of the book provides the reader with recent scholarship on female offenders. Specifically, this new scholarship is feminist in its focus. Feminist scholarship encompasses a number of common themes, including (1) focusing on the social construction of knowledge and how, most typically, it is male-defined; (2) examining how scientific research is strongly influenced by the power relations of gender, race, and class; (3) challenging deterministic thinking that holds that who we are (i.e., our gender) is "determined" by our biology; and (4) studying gender relations in such a way that questions are raised about its taken-for-granted nature in society.

Feminist scholarship today is best characterized as a *set of perspectives*, representing a continuum of feminist thought. Each perspective has a theoretical framework that is linked to different assumptions about the causes of gender inequality and women's oppression. These perspectives also result in important differences in strategies for social change. Historically, the most common frameworks have included those of liberal, radical, Marxist, and socialist feminists. (For an early review of this literature, see Sokoloff, 1980; Jaggar, 1983. For a more recent discussion of this literature and its relationship to women and crime, see Daly and Chesney-Lind, 1988.)

It will help the reader to be aware of the basic thesis of each of these major feminist perspectives. *Liberal feminism,* the most mainstream of the perspectives, stresses the importance of equality of women with men within the existing political and social structures in society. From this perspective, the cause of gender inequality is identified as cultural attitudes with regard to gender role socialization. For example, liberal feminists (Adler, 1975; Adler and Simon, 1979) argued, in relation to crime, that more women were turning to crime as attitudes toward gender equality changed in society and greater employment opportunities in the legal and illegal worlds emerged. In contrast, *radical feminism* identifies male dominance and control as the cause of gender inequality and the essential set of social relations that must be eliminated from all social institutions. Man's control of women's sexuality and the norm of heterosexuality are identified as at the core of women's oppression. For example, it was the radical feminists who transformed our understanding of the crime of rape from that of sexuality and uncontrollable male sexual needs to one of systemic violence against women.

Marxist feminism views women's oppression as a function of class relations in a capitalist society. This approach sees the elimination of class oppression as a necessary (although no longer sufficient) prerequisite to the reduction of oppression against women. Women face a double burden in this analysis: they are oppressed economically both in low-wage jobs in the labor market and by their unpaid family responsibilities centered on reproductive labor (childbearing, child care, and housework). A Marxist feminist would argue that the persistently lower crime rates of women are due to their marginalization in relation to the means of production. Petty theft and shoplifting are, therefore, among the typical female crimes.

Socialist feminists combine the Marxist and radical feminist perspectives and identify as the causes of gender inequality and women's oppression both patriarchy and capitalism in public as well as private spheres of life. (Other forms of socially structured inequality such as racism and heterosexism are equally important to the socialist feminist analysis.) The obvious example here is the crime of prostitution, in which women are understood to have limited control over both their sexual and economic life; moreover, in a patriarchal capitalist society much prostitution among poor young women is related to both the prior sexual, physical, and economic abuse in their private life and the limited opportunities and ongoing abuse in their public life.

These four major paradigms are presented here in only a very rough format. Students should be aware that within each of these four perspectives there are many differences. And beyond that, new intellectual insights and developments are continually occurring. Thus, feminist theory is made up of many different threads and is on the cutting edge of developing new ways of understanding women's lives and changing their relationship to crime and criminality.

Moreover, because the dominant voice of American feminism traditionally has been white, middle-class, first-world, and heterosexual, other feminist perspectives reflecting diverse racial, ethnic, cultural, and sexual orientations (such as African-American, Latina, Asian-American, Jewish, and lesbian) have begun to emerge in both feminist scholarship and the study of crime. Clearly, race, ethnicity, and class are equally as important as gender in understanding men's as well as women's relationship to the criminal justice system. Unfortunately, in criminology as in the larger society, when we think of gender, we usually think only of women (not men and women), and when we talk about race, we focus only on racial/ethnic minorities (not minorities and whites). Feminist scholarship challenges these uncritically accepted assumptions.

Two questions persistently asked by feminist scholars (for a review of this literature, see Daly and Chesney-Lind, 1988) in the field of criminology have been (1) Do theories of men's crimes apply to women—and if not, how and why not? and (2) How can we explain the fact that women are far less likely than men to be involved in criminal activity? What implications does this have for the study of crime—for both men and women? Further, women scholars of color have challenged how myths of gender expectations and socially structured inequality impact differently on white women and various groups of women of color in the study of female offenders (e.g., see Lewis, 1981; Young, 1986; Arnold, Chapter 8 herein).

Since the publication of the first edition of this volume in 1982, the contributions of various feminist perspectives to the study of criminology and specifically to the study of female offenders have grown steadily. Two areas are of particular significance. The first contribution is in theory and research. Work is in progress, for example, on building a firm theoretical foundation for explaining crime causation that directly addresses female criminality. This effort, which has accelerated during the past decade, is clearly established in several chapters in Part One, especially those by Dorie Klein (Chapter 2), Eileen Leonard (Chapter 3), and Meda Chesney-Lind (Chapters 4 and 6), as well as in the Epilogue of the book, written by Kathleen Daly.

Feminist scholars have made the case and incorporated into their research the principle that not all women are the same (see Moraga and Anzaldua, 1981; hooks, 1984; Collins, 1990; Andersen and Collins, 1992; Klein, Chapter 2 herein). Because the social conditions and experiences of women's lives vary according to their position in the race and class as well as gender systems of society, they must be examined and understood as such. In this book we have sought to put this concept into practice by examining gender issues in conjunction and in conflict with race and class (Sokoloff and Price, Chapter 1; Mann, Chapter 7; Arnold, Chapter 8; Humphries et al., Chapter 10).* Further, feminist research does not limit inquiry to an analysis of aggregate data (Steffensmeier, Chapter 5; Chesney-Lind, Chapters 4 and 6) but also engages in dialogue with subjects so that women's realities are used to create new theories as well as to provide the context for cold statistics (Arnold, Chapter 8; Maher and Curtis, Chapter 9; Humphries et al., Chapter 10).

The second area of important contributions concerns practical reforms and social policy changes. Here, in spite of strong opposition and some setbacks from conservative political forces, particularly in the 1980s, the accomplishments have been impressive. These have included elimination of some laws that imposed harsher or indeterminate sentences on women but not men and improvement of some of the conditions in prisons such as expanded medical care, educational opportunities, and a few in-prison nurseries for newborns. Many of these improvements in prison, and to some extent in jail life, are the outcome of hard-fought struggles by prison reformers to provide women inmates with the same opportunities for self-improvement while incarcerated as are available for men. However, attaining parity with incarcerated men is often a double-edged sword. First, conditions and services in men's prisons are typically far from adequate. Second, in an attempt to gain parity with men, women prisoners have ended up with far more prison cells than improved conditions or programs (see Chesney-Lind, Chapter 6). And finally, as bad as things are in prison, the ultimate tragedy is that life in prison is sometimes better than outside (Clines, 1993). Thus the needs of women inmates must be understood in the context of the broader class, race, and gender structures of our society: these women are predominantly poor, from racial/ethnic minorities, in ill health, and poorly educated, with limited skills; they are responsible for the care of one to three children, have alcohol and drug problems, and were likely to have been physically and/or sexually victimized as youngsters and adults. How they end up in prison is discussed throughout the first section of this book.

In the United States today there continues to be a backlash to the women's liberation movement, to its objectives, and a particularly harsh reaction to its successes (Faludi, 1991). The backlash can be seen, in part, in the sharply increased rate of incarceration of women—particularly poor and minority—despite a decrease in female violent offenses. And it can

---

*While sexual orientation is important, literature on crimes by and against lesbians, as well as the treatment of lesbians by the criminal justice system, is abysmally lacking.

be seen in the periodic revival of the myth that a new and more dangerous type of female criminal has emerged as a result of the women's movement.

In the chapters that follow in Part One we examine many of these issues as we focus on women offenders. In particular, we place the issues surrounding female criminality in the context of a society where true equality for women, racial/ethnic minorities, and the poor has yet to become a reality. Part One, "Theories and Facts about Women Offenders," consists of 10 chapters covering the law, theoretical analyses of crime causation, delinquency, arrest data, incarcerated women, the effects of race and class, and specific offenses for which women are arrested or otherwise controlled by social service agencies or the state: drug possession and sales, petty theft, prostitution, and drug use during pregnancy.

Because the field of women and crime has changed so much in the past decade and because so much new research has been done, only one of the original chapters (Klein, Chapter 2) from the first edition was retained, and it has been supplemented by an afterword written specifically for this edition. A second piece, by Steffensmeier (Chapter 5), has been thoroughly updated. Chapter 1, which was written by the editors and which appeared in the earlier edition, has been substantially rewritten to reflect the current situation as we see it now. Five of the chapters in Part One are original essays written for this edition. Chapters 8 and 10 are reprints of important recent articles: the first, by Arnold, is about the relationship between black women's victimization and criminalization; the second, by Humphries et al., describes the state's intrusion into the lives of women who are pregnant while using illegal drugs. These chapters represent the cutting edge of research and theory on women offenders.

Chapter 1 provides the context for Part One by discussing the historical, political, and social processes that influence the development of law and their underlying class, race, and gender biases. It further shows the reader how the early sexism that governed law, albeit constantly changing, still is with us today. Finally, it raises serious questions about the ability of the law to deliver fairness and justice to women, minorities, and the poor—particularly poor minority women.

In Chapter 2 Klein gives a clear picture of the sexism embedded in past theories of criminality and goes on in her afterword to identify the challenges facing feminist researchers today. These include establishing the scientific basis of theories of crime, questioning the gender and race biases inherent in scientific research and scholarship, and establishing a new definition of crime.

Chapter 3 flows directly from Chapters 1 and 2. Here Leonard closely examines the well-known and accepted sociological theories of criminality: Merton, Becker, Sutherland, Cloward and Ohlin, and the like. Her analysis reveals how they fail to include gender and therefore fail to explain female criminality. She indicates to the reader how new theory needs to be organized to take into account not only gender but also race, class, and culture. In so doing, she argues for a "general theory" of criminality that ultimately can be used to explain both male and female crime.

Part One next turns its attention in Chapter 4 to the juvenile justice system and discusses what girls who get entangled with the law face. Although this book is primarily about adult women, it is important for the reader to have some understanding of female delinquency. Almost one-fifth of adult women in jail had juvenile records (Bureau of Justice Statistics, 1992). Through identifying similarities for juveniles and adults in the criminal justice system, we can further our general understanding and ability to bring about reform. Chesney-Lind describes a system steeped in sexism and suggests that the juvenile justice system is a major force in women's oppression. As Leonard has shown for theories of crime about adult women, Chesney-Lind points out the inadequacy of existing delinquency theories for explaining offending by girls.

The reader is given a detailed look in Chapter 5 at the amount and types of crime women are currently committing. Steffensmeier finds very little change over time in female arrest rates for the most serious, violent crimes of homicide, aggravated assault, and robbery. When shoplifting and minor thefts are eliminated from the seven index crimes—the most serious according to the FBI—female arrest rates show only a small increase. Yet the percentage increase in the female prison population was higher than the increase in the male population each year between 1980 and 1989 (Greenfeld and Minor-Harper, 1991). In fact, between 1980 and 1990, the number of women in prison increased from 13,420 to 44,234, and the number of men skyrocketed from 316,401 to 730,141 (Greenfeld and Minor-Harper, 1991; Jankowski, 1992).

Chapter 6 considers possible causes for this extraordinary growth in the number of women imprisoned. Chesney-Lind concludes that the system is imprisoning more women than in the past for drug offenses (for example, about 1 in 10 were jailed for drugs in 1983, while this was true for 1 in 3 in 1989) (Bureau of Justice Statistics, 1992), that mandatory sentencing laws have reduced the amount of discretion previously available to judges, and that women have been caught up in a conservative punishment-oriented era in general. Evidence is emerging of some judges' discomfort with these mandatory sentencing statutes for drug offenses (Treaster, 1993). While 31 percent of women in state prisons were serving their first sentence and were not previously sentenced to probation, jail, youth facilities, or prison, only 18 percent of males were serving a first conviction (Greenfeld and Minor-Harper, 1991). Clearly, the system is more punishment-prone for women than men. Another factor in the disproportionate growth of the female prison population is the increase in women entering prison with severe mental illness as a result of the closing of mental hospitals. In New York State, the only maximum security prison for women has tripled its severely mentally ill prisoners in the last five years (Clines, 1993). These facts about incarcerated women support the book's theme of a sexist criminal justice system.

In Chapter 7 Mann describes how the criminal justice system has been widening its net where women of color are concerned, particularly African-American and Latina women. Using new data from three states—California, Florida, and New York—Chapter 7 provides an analysis of arrest, pretrial, and sentencing trends. Mann demonstrates pervasive racism throughout the criminal justice system in the three states, which together incarcerate almost one-third of the nation's imprisoned women.

In Chapter 8 the reader learns more of ways in which institutionalized race, class, and gender oppression turn a group of black female victims into criminals. Arnold introduces the concept of structural dislocation to explain how young African-American girls end up as criminals and are imprisoned. On the basis of extensive in-depth interviews, she describes how girls, seeking to actively resist their victimization at home within the family, run away, thereby severing ties with support structures of family, school, and ultimately work (dislocation). By refusing to accept or participate in their own victimization, these young women are labeled and processed first as status offenders or juvenile delinquents, later as criminals. Eventually, they replace the lost support of the family with a deviant street culture (relocation), and this choice often leads to periods of crime and imprisonment.

Maher and Curtis describe, in Chapter 9, the results of their detailed ethnographic interviews with women who are part of the world of drugs, poverty, and street-level prostitution. They challenge the simplistic connection all too often made between drugs and crime by showing how women's incarceration for drugs has risen dramatically as their rates for violent crime have declined. As Klein did in Chapter 2, Maher and Curtis argue for a shift in focus from changing the individual woman sex worker to understanding and changing the economic and social *context* of drugs and violence in a neighborhood in social and economic decline where these women must live their lives. The reader hears directly from the women who become involved in violent incidents. Most often these women become the target of violence rather than the initiator. This chapter, as well as Chapter 6, firmly responds to the new female violent offender myth that emerges periodically.

Part One ends with Chapter 10, which reports on criminalizing pregnancy. During the 1980s prosecutors attempted to control women's bodies by accusing the women of either drug trafficking or child abuse because they used drugs during pregnancy. By the 1990s social conditions changed so that the focus moved to punishing these women through the family court rather than the criminal court. Given that such policies have disproportionately affected poor and minority women, the reader may question how racial and class biases affect the patriarchal social control of women and their bodies. (For an overview of "The Criminalization of a Woman's Body," see two special issues of *Women & Criminal Justice,* 1991, 1992.) This chapter takes the reader full circle back to Chapter 1, in which we point out that the law is not static while remaining race-, class-, and gender-biased. Who makes the law, who interprets the law, and in whose interest the law operates are always critically important issues when women, minorities, and the poor are under consideration.

Taken together, these 10 chapters provide both a theoretically challenging and empirically powerful picture of women offenders in the United States. While we would encourage the reader to read the selections in the order presented, other orders may well be appropriate; the editors are confident that each essay stands on its own and makes a valuable contribution to our store of knowledge about women and crime.

The reader should be aware that Part One does not cover all the topics related to women, crime, and justice. For example, other issues of significance to consider are gender and white-collar crime (e.g., Daly, 1989; Maher and Waring, 1990;), prostitution (Barry, 1979; Bell, 1987; Jenness, 1990; Chancer, 1993), women who commit homicide and other acts of violence (e.g., Fortune, Vega, and Silverman, 1980; Kowalski, Shields, and Wilson, 1985; Simpson, 1991), AIDS and other health issues (e.g., Clark and Boudin, 1990; Waring and Smith, 1991), women partners of male prisoners (e.g., Fishman, 1990), mothers in prison and their children (e.g., Baunach, 1985), and the varied perspectives of women from different racial/ethnic communities (e.g., Latina, Asian, and Native American) on all these topics. We invite our readers to turn to other literature and to participate in the research process to increase both the body of knowledge and the resources necessary for activism and change in the area of women, crime, and justice.

REFERENCES

Adler, Freda. 1975. *Sisters in Crime: The Rise of the New Female Criminal.* New York: McGraw-Hill.

———, and Rita James Simon (eds.). 1979. *The Criminology of Deviant Women.* Boston: Houghton-Mifflin.

Andersen, Margaret L., and Patricia Hill Collins (eds.). 1992. *Race, Class, and Gender: An Anthology.* Belmont, Calif.: Wadsworth.

Barry, Kathleen. 1979. *Female Sexual Slavery.* Englewood Cliffs, N.J.: Prentice-Hall.

Baunach, Phyllis Jo. 1985. *Mothers in Prison.* New Brunswick, N.J.: Transaction Books.

Bell, Laurie (ed.). 1987. *Good Girls/Bad Girls: Feminists and Sex Trade Workers Face to Face.* Seattle: Seal Press.

Bureau of Justice Statistics. 1992. *National Update,* vol. 1, no. 4. NCJ-135722. Washington, D.C.: U.S. Department of Justice.

Butterfield, Fox. 1992. "Are American Jails Becoming Shelters from the Storm?" *The New York Times* (July 19): E4.

Chancer, Lynn. 1993. "Prostitution, Feminist Theory, and Ambivalence: Notes from the Sociological Underground." Paper given at the American Sociological Association Meetings, Miami.

Clark, Judy, and Kathy Boudin. 1990. "Community of Women Organize Themselves to Cope with the AIDS Crisis: A Case Study from the Bedford Hills Correctional Facility," *Social Justice,* 17 (2): 90–109.

Clines, Francis X. 1993. "Tough Matriarch, Easy Touch and Good Listener," *The New York Times* (April 24): 25, 28.

Collins, Patricia Hill. 1990. *Black Feminist Thought.* New York: Routledge, Chapman, Hall.

Daly, Kathleen. 1989. "Gender and Varieties of White-Collar Crime," *Criminology,* 24 (4): 769–793.

———, and Meda Chesney-Lind. 1988. "Feminism and Criminology," *Justice Quarterly,* 5 (December): 497–538.

Faludi, Susan. 1991. *Backlash: The Undeclared War against American Women.* New York: Crown.

Fishman, Laura T. 1990. *Women at the Wall: A Study of Prisoners' Wives Doing Time on the Outside.* Albany: SUNY Press.

Fortune, Edith P., Manuel Vega, and Ira J. Silverman. 1980. "Study of Female Robbers in Southern Correctional Institutions," *Journal of Criminal Justice,* (8): 317–325.

Greenfeld, Lawrence A., and Stephanie Minor-Harper. 1991. *Women in Prison.* Bureau of Justice Statistics. Washington, D.C.: U.S. Department of Justice.

hooks, bell. 1984. *Feminist Theory: From Margin to Center.* Boston: South End.

Jaggar, Allison. 1983. *Feminist Politics and Human Nature.* Totowa, N.J.: Ballanheld Harvester.

Jankowski, Lewis W. 1992. *Correctional Populations in the United States, 1990.* NCJ-134946. Bureau of Justice Statistics. Washington, D.C.: U.S. Department of Justice.

Jenness, Valerie. 1990. "From Sex As Sin to Sex As Work: COYOTE and the Reorganization of Prostitution As a Social Problem," *Social Problems,* 37 (August): 403–420.

Kowalski, G. S., A. L. Shields, and D. G. Wilson. 1985. "The Female Murderer: Alabama 1929–1971," *American Journal of Criminal Justice,* vol. 10 (Fall): 75–90.

Lewis, Diane. 1981. "Black Women Offenders and Criminal Justice: Some Theoretical Considerations," in Marguerite Warren (ed.), *Comparing Female and Male Offenders.* Beverly Hills, Calif.: Sage.

Maher, Lisa, and Elin J. Waring. 1990. "Beyond Simple Differences: White-Collar Crime, Gender and Workforce Position," *Phoebe,* 2 (1): 44–54.

Mann, Coramae Richey. 1990. "Black Female Homicide in the United States," *Journal of Interpersonal Violence,* 5 (June): 176–201.

Moraga, Cherrie, and Gloria Anzaldua (eds.). 1981. *This Bridge Called My Back: Writings by Radical Women of Color.* New York: Kitchen Table/Women of Color Press.

Paltrow, Lynn M. 1990. "When Becoming Pregnant Is a Crime," *Criminal Justice Ethics,* 9(1) (Winter/Spring): 41–48.

Simpson, Sally. 1991. "Caste, Class, and Violent Crime: Explaining Difference in Female Offending," *Criminology,* 29 (1): 115–135.

Sokoloff, Natalie J. 1980. *Between Money and Love: The Dialectics of Women's Home and Market Work.* New York: Praeger.

Treaster, Joseph B. 1993. "Two Judges Decline Drug Cases, Protesting Sentencing Rules," *The New York Times* (April 17): 1, 27.

Waring, Nancy, and Betsey Smith. 1991. "The AIDS Epidemic: Impact on Women Prisoners in Massachusetts—An Assessment with Recommendations," *Women & Criminal Justice*, 2 (2): 117–143.

Young, Vernetta. 1980. "Women, Race and Crime," *Criminology*, 18 (1): 26–34.

———. 1986. "Gender Expectations and Their Impact on Black Female Offenders and Victims," *Justice Quarterly*, 3 (September): 305–327.

CHAPTER 1

THE CRIMINAL LAW AND WOMEN

NATALIE J. SOKOLOFF / BARBARA RAFFEL PRICE

ABSTRACT

Too often, books and articles dealing with offenders—including those focusing on women—fail to take into account the historical, political, economic, and social relations that influence the development of laws. Laws determine who will be defined as criminal and which behavior is an offense. Many changes in the law have occurred since the first edition of this book was published in 1982. These include mandatory sentencing, especially for drug offenses—a change that is important in explaining increases in the U.S. prison population, comprising primarily the poor and racial/ethnic minorities.

Despite such important changes, the key questions of this chapter remain as important today as they were earlier. Offenders still become offenders because they break certain laws (and are caught). But who makes these laws? In whose interest? At what expense to certain groups, such as women, workers, poor people, people of color, and gays and lesbians? Which kinds of laws affect women most? How do they impact differently on women depending on their racial/ethnic and class backgrounds or sexual orientation? How well are the laws enforced? What kinds of laws are women most likely to break? And how does a sexist legal system—which is simultaneously racist, class-biased, and heterosexist—treat women lawbreakers?

Criticisms of criminal justice injustices are often voiced; only the naive would assert that the criminal justice system provides equal justice. It would also be simplistic to claim that a major overhaul of the system is likely in the foreseeable future, but feminist theory and policy can challenge the existing system. Through the development of new race- and class-conscious feminist theory and research, a revitalized criminology can emerge which will help to build a more rational and equitable system.

Our society is complex, and the causes of crime are deep-seated. There are no simple explanations, and there are no simple solutions to prevent or control crime. Nevertheless, reforms are in order. But to effect realistic reforms that address the system's most serious weaknesses, society must understand *why* an institution premised on "equal justice for all" perpetrates injustices, *how* the system perpetuates these injustices, and *what* needs to be done to maximize the system's strengths without sacrificing its ideals. Finally, and perhaps most important, we must begin to understand that the future integrity of the system depends as much on broad-based and systemic social change as on reform efforts within criminal justice.

This book addresses one of the more serious and blatant failings of the criminal justice system: its treatment of women. Of interest here are women offenders, women who break the law; women victims, women who are harmed by others who break the law; and women professionals and paraprofessionals who are employed to carry out the law. Before any discussion of women who break laws and become criminals in the process, the law itself needs careful scrutiny.

First, let us begin by asking who is responsible for making the laws under which women are convicted. Why have these laws been made? In whose interest were these laws created? Which groups of women are more likely to be punished for violating these laws? Second, rather than looking solely at an individual lawbreaker's motivation, behavior, or immediate social environment, let us examine some of the ways in which society is organized to promote the conditions that cause behavior defined as criminal in this society. Third, let us examine the context for understanding criminal law in relation to women, with an emphasis on the relationship between criminal, civil, and administrative law and their differential impact on women.

This chapter is based on the premise that the legal system, like the criminal justice system, operates under the class, race, and gender biases inherent in the larger society. How this impacts women offenders is the special concern of this chapter and is a question that prepares the reader for the chapters that follow in this section. The problems that women face within the legal system are neither specific nor intrinsic features of that system. Rather, they are related to broader issues in American life—sexism, racism, and capitalism—that are reflected in the organization and administration of the legal system itself. In this regard, the reader should be aware that problems arise if "women as a group" are simplistically treated as a monolithic entity. Clearly, not all women share the same interests, problems, goals, political commitments, or life experiences. But gender cannot be understood apart from the systems of domination and subordination of race, ethnicity, class, and homophobia that impact on how the law affects different groups of women—and men.

To foster a better understanding of these concerns about the law and its relationship to

---

This article was written expressly for inclusion in this text.

women, this chapter considers the following basic issues: (1) the law: What is it? Who makes it? Who is affected by it? (2) types of law, (3) theories of crime causation affecting the development of the law, (4) women under the law, and (5) social movements and the criminal justice systems.

THE LAW

What Is It?

Law, in the broadest sense, is a set of formalized and codified rules that govern people's behavior and carry negative sanctions for violation. Laws are enacted norms; they are explicitly brought into being by legislation written by elected public officials and frequently generated by various interest groups. Public agencies (police, judiciary, and corrections) have been created to enforce the laws as they are written. As Hart (1968) argues, the technique of criminal law consists primarily in announcing certain standards of conduct and attaching unpleasant consequences to acts (or omissions) violating those standards, thereby hoping to motivate people to conform. The penalties imposed by the criminal law are more serious than the negative sanctions that face violators of informal social norms. These legal penalties may include fines, probation, imprisonment, and—in some states—death.

As the criminal law is now organized, it is applied primarily to individuals rather than to corporations. This is due, in part, to the fact that the legal system is grounded in the protection of private property and the accumulation of private and corporate profits, as much as in the physical security of individual citizens. In fact, the criminal law was developed to apply to individual human behavior and motivation. An emphasis on individual responsibility and accountability is embedded in our culture.

Though some harms done by corporations, many of which cause illness or death, have been subjected to civil actions, criminal prosecutions, or the hybrid "civil penalties," punishment has usually been in a monetary form (Stone, 1975; Coleman, 1989). Not only is corporate crime far more costly than street crime, but many of these crimes are very violent indeed, killing and crippling far more people than all street crimes put together (Reiman, 1990; Ermann and Lundman, 1992). Several examples of how the law impacts upon individuals in contrast to corporations are instructive.

On the one hand, if an individual is found to have murdered another person, s/he will probably be imprisoned, and may even be executed. On the other hand, although it has been proved that cigarette smoking as well as secondary smoke leads to cancer, which, in turn, often leads to death, the tobacco industry continues to thrive. Likewise, even though research and the experience of women have found that the silicone gel in breast implants is linked to a variety of immune system diseases, and even though medical researchers alerted the manufacturers to the hazards as early as 1978, it was not until 14 years later that the federal government banned its use pending further study (Hilts, 1992). And criminal charges have not been filed against companies, such as Dow Corning, producing these dangerous products (Kessler, 1992). In fact, the toughest sanctions do not punish offenders but instead try to stop further criminal action or reduce damage already done (Coleman, 1989). Of course, tobacco companies are now required to supply warnings with their products. If consumers continue to smoke, it is at their own risk. The federal government's ban on silicone gel implants comes too late for many women who have developed immune system diseases (Hilts, 1992). But does this truly absolve these industries of guilt when cigarette smokers succumb to lung disease or when women become ill or die from silicone gel implants?[1] When a person is murdered, is the murderer's guilt any less because of society's constant warnings that citizens must protect themselves against violent crime? Even though intent is a key element in the case of one individual killing another, the examples given here are disconcerting.

Although the deterrent effect of criminal sanctions is often debated, there is no doubt that the possibility of punishment does not overly intimidate corporations (Mokhiber, 1989). This is in part because corporations are never certain if they will be accused of wrongdoing; in part because, unlike most individuals who are accused of crimes, corporations experience little stigmatization when taken to court; and in part because the punishments, when applied, are weak when compared with the profits to be made by disregarding the law. So, when one group of corporate offenders was fined $1.8 million for antitrust crimes, this was a "mere pittance" for doing business, since they made about $2 billion in profits from these crimes. And such fines are often tax-deductible (Simon and Eitzen, 1993)!

One further issue is that the requirement of *mens rea*—i.e., that for some crimes the state must demonstrate that an actor intended to behave in a manner defined as illegal—makes prosecuting a large corporation difficult, if not impossible. The law works well to protect corporations' property rights; it works far less well to protect people from the harmful impact of their often admittedly unintended acts (Coleman, 1989; Reiman, 1990). Typically, intent must be found in an identifiable high officer of the corporation—hardly an easy charge to prove.

In these and other ways, the law defines which behavior will be punished, how it will be punished, and who will be punished. In so doing, the law protects what those in power value most.

Who Makes the Law?

Women, racial/ethnic minorities, the poor, and working-class people benefit far less from the law than others in society. Who, after all, makes the law? Rich white men— and those who work in their interest—are most influential in creating laws. The intent of framers of the law was to protect not only men but men's property (Beard, 1935; Zinn, 1980). Much of the criminal law is written by state legislatures and the U.S. Congress, whose members are overwhelmingly male. In 1993 the House had only 48 women members (11 percent) out of a total of 435 seats; the Senate had 6 women senators out of 100. The state legislatures have slightly more women, averaging 16.9 percent, but there is great variation from state to state.

Both mainstream and radical political theorists have observed that the state, and thus the legal system, and its criminal laws operate in the interests of the dominant class in a capitalist society. In the United States the dominant class is the wealthy business class. Those who write the laws either belong to or represent this dominant class—whether a Democrat or a Republican is President. When Jimmy Carter was President, the majority of senators owned at least a quarter million dollars in stocks and assets, while at least 22 of the 100 senators were millionaires (*U.S. News & World Report*, 1980). Under Ronald Reagan's more openly "pro-business" administration, four out of five Cabinet-level officials were at least half-millionaires, and more than half (10 of 17) were millionaires (*New York Times*, 1981). When George Bush became President in 1989, three of his initial Cabinet members had a combined worth of $250 million. And although President Bill Clinton's Cabinet was less wealthy, it, too, included nine millionaires (Vaughn, 1993).

The concentration of corporate, financial, and banking power, and of the concomitant political power, in relatively few hands is a critical consideration in a realistic analysis of the criminal law. The 4,000 largest corporations (far less than 1 percent) hold 77 percent of all corporate assets and receive more than 90 percent of all profits made by U.S. corporations (Sherman, 1991; Coleman, 1989). Likewise, the top 1 percent of households (834,000) had greater wealth than the bottom 90 percent of Americans (84 million households) (Nasar, 1992). This is largely related to the fact that less than 1 percent of the population owns half of all corporate stock, three-fifths of all business assets, and three-fourths of all bonds and trusts (Kennickell and Woodburn, 1992).

In short, it has been argued by some that

> . . . the law became the ultimate means by which the state secures the interests of the governing class. Laws institutionalize and legitimize property relations. It is through the legal system, then, that the state explicitly and forcefully protects the interests of the capitalist class. Crime control becomes the coercive means of checking threats to its economic arrangements. . . . The state did not appear as a third party in the conflict between classes [as pluralists have argued], but arose to protect and promote the interests of the dominant economic class, which owns and controls the means of production. (Quinney, 1975:290.)

Although some individuals who participate in making the laws have come from the poor and working classes, as well as from racial/ethnic minorities, the system of lawmaking is controlled by those with vested interests in private property and directed toward the protection of individual and corporate wealth or those who represent those interests.

It is important to remember that despite the alliance between the wealthy business class and the legal system (see Miller, 1978 and Domhoff, 1990, for a discussion of corporate and government interlocks), the law is not static. Challenges are constantly made by those who believe the ruling elite are indifferent to or in conflict with their interests. For example, the working class has won many rights and labor reforms previously denied them under the law, such as the right to strike and the right to unionize. In addition, even elite factions come into conflict on certain issues. For instance, while the insurance industry has often supported car safety regulation, the automobile industry has fought vehemently against it.

Who Becomes a "Criminal"?

The law, created in large part by and for the dominant class in society, defines which behavior is punishable and thereby determines which groups of people are most likely to be punished.

In our society people are most commonly arrested for crimes against property (burglary, larceny), crimes against the public order (prostitution, gambling, narcotics possession, disorderly conduct, vagrancy), and crimes against persons (assault, murder). Those most likely to be arrested and convicted of these crimes are poor and working-class people, who are also disproportionately members of racial/ethnic minority groups.

A recent example of how laws are created that impact differentially on groups by race, class, and gender is demonstrated by the "war on drugs." This "war" created (via legislation and the courts) a large, new wave of criminals—people convicted of possessing or selling small amounts of drugs. Others commit crimes to support their drug habits. The harsh laws were enacted to prevent the top levels of the drug world from distributing deadly drugs throughout the country. However, these state-created crimes have impacted especially severely on "small-time" women offenders. In 1989, "women were more likely than men . . . to be jailed on drug charges" (BJS, 1991b); more than one-third of all women in local jails were accused or convicted of drug offenses (BJS, 1992a), and about 60 percent of the women in federal custody were serving sentences for drug offenses (Smith, 1990). And, as we know, the majority of women in prison are poor, black, and Hispanic women (BJS, 1991c).

Other state-created drug crimes (via prosecution) include the criminalization of women's bodies. Women in at least 24 states have been arrested and prosecuted after their newborn babies tested positive for drugs (Lewin, 1992). Although the rate of drug use by pregnant, poor black women and the rate of drug use by more privileged, pregnant white women were the same in a Florida study, black women were reported to the authorities for their drug use 10 times more often than white women (Chasnoff, Landress, and Barrett, 1990).

Class, then, is a key consideration in understanding crime data. People from lower socioeconomic backgrounds are much more likely to be found guilty and receive harsher sentences than those from higher socioeconomic backgrounds. In fact, the favorable treatment of middle- and upper-class people is found to exist at all stages of the criminal justice process, including arrest, preliminary hearing, pretrial release, pretrial detainment, trial, sentence, and parole. The poor are less likely to have a private attorney, to have reasonable bail set, to have a jury trial, to have the case dismissed or to be acquitted, to receive probation or a suspended sentence, and, if convicted, to receive a relatively short sentence (Nagel and Weitzman, 1972; for reviews of recent literature, see Coleman, 1989; Reiman, 1990; Beirne and Messerschmidt, 1991).

According to the American Correctional Association (1990), almost three-fourths (73 percent) of all women in jails and prisons had previous work experience in low-level sales,

services, and clerical work; and half (54 percent) of them held an average of one to three jobs a year prior to incarceration. Their wages were extremely low: almost half (48 percent) would have earned an annual full-time salary between $6,720 and $13,000—*if* they worked full-time (i.e., their highest hourly wage was between $3.36 and $6.50). It is not surprising that 60 percent had received welfare assistance before their arrest. Less than half of all female offenders had a high school education.

People from poorer socioeconomic classes are more likely than wealthier people to be involved in behavioral patterns that have a greater probability of being handled officially as criminal in our system—behaviors that result in charges of drunkenness, assault, disorderly conduct, burglary, and robbery (Reiman, 1990). In contrast, middle- and upper-class people tend to be involved in activities not normally dealt with by the criminal justice system, even though they may be defined as crimes. For example, although criminal laws extend to white-collar activities such as fraud, tax evasion, misuse of funds, illegal political contributions, criminal antitrust practices, and an estimated 70,000 to 80,000 deaths caused by faulty products or exposure to dangerous chemicals, both white-collar offenders and corporations typically face only the less demanding civil penalties, a leniency grossly out of proportion to the corporate crime wave.

And corporate offenders are not likely to be apprehended (Reiman, 1990; Ermann and Lundman, 1992). Sufficient resources are rarely allotted to federal and state agencies to enforce regulations affecting corporations. The U.S. Environmental Protection Agency (EPA) offers an example of the problem. This agency is responsible for enforcing regulations on toxic waste dumping by manufacturers, which often causes serious harm to people and the environment. However, the EPA, with 17,856 employees (*World Almanac*, 1992), has only 63 criminal investigators to cover the entire country (according to EPA's personnel records).

In asking who becomes a criminal, bias against racial/ethnic minorities also must be understood. The condition of blacks in relation to the law and at each stage of the criminal justice process is significantly worse than it is for whites (see Nagel and Weitzman, 1972; Jaynes and Williams, 1989, Chap. 9; Hutchinson, 1990). As the task force investigating racism in the New York State Court System recently declared, "there are two justice systems at work in the courts of New York State, one for whites and a very different one for minorities and the poor" (quoted in Gray, 1991). A New Jersey state task force likewise found widespread racism in that state's court system: blacks were more likely to be arrested, less likely to be released on bail or to see members of their own race in the courtroom and jury box, less confident in the courts and less likely to use the courts to settle disputes, and more likely to be the target of a death penalty hearing when charged with murder, especially if the victim was white (Sullivan, 1992).

Recent studies of mandatory sentencing in three midwestern states showed that sentencing of blacks has become much tougher than that of whites. Judge Gerald Heaney (1991) found that after new mandatory sentencing rules went into effect in 1989, the average length of sentence for blacks rose 55 percent (from 3.8 to 5.9 years), while for whites it rose only 7 percent (from 2.9 to 3.1 years). His analysis of 1989 national data among the age group with the highest crime rate (18 to 35 years old) revealed that blacks served an average of 6.9 years, compared with 4.3 years for Hispanics and 4.5 years for whites. Moreover, the U.S. Sentencing Commission (1991) found that white defendants are better able than blacks to plea-bargain their way out of tough mandatory prison sentences for drug

crimes. Even after taking into account arrest records and aggravating circumstances surrounding the crimes, the commission found that racial disparities in mandatory sentencing remained.

Looking at minority women in particular reveals the harsh realities of race and gender discrimination (see Mann, Chapter 7 herein). According to Morgan-Sharp's (1992) review of the literature, both race and gender bias appear throughout the criminal justice process, where the poor, minorities, and women are heavily disadvantaged. She finds that race and gender are directly related to arrest; pretrial treatment, such as bail setting; and differential sentencing in both presentencing recommended by probation officers and judicial decisions. She also points to the negative effects of race and gender in prison location, prison staff, availability of prison programs, and biases in parole boards and their decisions against minority women. These results, she argues, reflect the relative powerlessness of women and minorities in American society.

Racism is not unique to the criminal justice system; it springs from the fabric of American society. Studies have reported discrimination against blacks in education (Blackwell, 1981; Kozol, 1991), employment and wages (Passell, 1991; Swoboda, 1991), government contracts (Labaton, 1991), housing (Noah, 1991; Vobejda, 1992), banking (Quint, 1992), the media (Johnson, 1992), and even shopping (Williams, 1991). This sad reality is reflected in the fact that a much larger number of young black men 20 to 29 years old (610,000, or almost one-fourth) are under some type of formal control by the criminal justice system (either in jail or prison or on probation or parole) than are in college (436,000) (Mauer, 1990). The racial distribution of prison inmates is but one indicator of the impact of racism: male prisoners are 45.3 percent black and 12.6 percent Hispanic (Maguire and

Flanagan, 1991); women prisoners are 46.1 percent black and 11.7 percent Hispanic (BJS, 1991c). Yet, blacks constitute only 12.3 percent of the general population and Hispanics 8.1 percent (U.S. Bureau of the Census, 1991). In some states, like New York, more than three-fourths of all women arrested are black (52.8 percent) or Hispanic (23.2 percent) (See Mann, Chapter 7 herein). Over time, not only have black arrest rates been higher than white, but the gap has been widening (Jaynes and Williams, 1989, Chap. 9).

Who Becomes a Victim?

Despite recent attempts at crime control, and despite the common belief that it is the white middle and upper classes that are most likely to be victims of street crime, the data show that poor and minority groups living in urban areas are the most common victims of violent crime. For example, there are 4.5 robberies for every 1,000 whites but 13 for every 1,000 blacks and 8.4 for every 1,000 members of other races (BJS, 1991a). Murder, aggravated assault, armed robbery, and forcible rape happen most often to blacks, who, both male and female, have higher rates of victimization than whites (Whitaker, 1990).

Adjusted homicide rates show that the black murder rate was almost six times the rate for whites. Homicide rates were highest for black males (52.3), followed by black females (12.3), white males (7.9), and white females (2.9) (Whitaker, 1990). According to several reports, in 1990, blacks are not only 10 times more likely to be murdered than whites but also 40 percent more likely to be burglarized, 50 percent more likely to be robbed, and 25 percent more likely to be assaulted (Hutchinson, 1990).

For minority women racism is compounded by sexism. According to Uniform Crime Reports (UCR) data, black and Latina women are more likely to suffer crimes of violence than white women. In addition, black women are 1.5 times more likely to be raped than other women (Bowker, 1981); yet black rape victims are believed less often by the police than white rape victims (Robin, 1982). Victimization data also tell us that men and women are most likely to be victimized by people of the same gender or from the same social class and racial background. However, women are victimized more by men than by other women. Victimization also appears related to being away from the home and family, but in the same neighborhood (for fuller discussion, see Karmen, Introduction to Part Two of this book). Yet, once again, the "general" findings do not fully apply to women: many crimes against women (e.g., rape and assault) occur in the home and with known assailants (Timrots and Rand, 1987). This may explain why women have a higher fear of crime, even though official data show young men to be at greatest risk of violent victimization (Stanko, 1992; Young, 1992). While violent crime is declining in this country, violent crime against men is declining more rapidly than that against women. The Justice Department reports that the violent crime rate against men declined 20 percent from 1973 to 1987, while rates of violent victimization of females changed little (Lewin, 1991).

This chapter began by asking what is law and who makes it. The discussion proceeded from a general definition of law to a discussion about who becomes a criminal and who is victimized. It was demonstrated that women did not do very well—they are underrepresented in the making of the law, yet badly overrepresented in harms done to them. Women, along with poor people and minorities, have been historically underprotected by the law and seem far less able to obtain equitable treatment before the criminal law. A brief discussion of the different types of law follows.

TYPES OF LAW

Laws can be distinguished by their sources. These may be legislatures, courts, or administrative agencies; we speak correspondingly of statutory, case, and regulatory (or administrative) law. Laws can also be distinguished by the relationship between the wrongs they address and the remedies they provide. In *criminal law* the state brings an action against a person (whether individual or corporation); the remedy sought is punishment for the harm done. In *civil law* a complainant, either a public entity or a person, brings an action against a defendant; the remedy sought is compensation to the complainant for the harm done; punitive damages may be awarded as well. In *administrative law* agencies may bring actions against persons; the remedy sought is compliance with agency regulations. These actions are to be distinguished from those brought by the state or with the state's concurrence to punish persons who have committed crimes defined by regulatory agencies. In addition, courts may impose penalties for noncompliance with their rulings and their codes of conduct, e.g., perjury.

Statutory Law, Case Law, and Regulatory Law

When legislative action is taken, typically at the state, federal, or local jurisdictional level, the result is *statutory law,* or the criminal codes. When court decisions and opinions are handed down, *case law*—a body of precedents that influences subsequent interpretations of the law—results. Constitutional law has been particularly useful in seeking remedies where women are concerned. The 14th Amendment of the U.S. Constitution provides for due process and equal protection of the law. So, for example, women in prison are now able to challenge the conditions of their confinement, which include unequal opportunities (for job training, schooling, medical care, etc.) in comparison with opportunities for their male counterparts in prison.

When government agencies, like the Equal Employment Opportunity Commission (EEOC), are empowered by legislatures to write rules and regulations binding on specific persons and organizations, the result is *regulatory* and *administrative law.* For example, in 1986 the Supreme Court ruled that severe or pervasive sexual harassment of an employee by a supervisor constituted a violation of federal law (Faison, 1991). The EEOC, as a regulatory agency, monitors compliance with and brings charges against those accused of violating Title VII of the 1964 Civil Rights Act, where sexual harassment is viewed as a form of job discrimination.

Criminal and Civil Law

Civil law is the body of law concerned with resolving private conflicts, particularly those concerning private property, such as conflicts over contracts, divorce, and child support. Criminal law, by contrast, is assumed to deal with crimes against the state, rather than against an individual person or corporation— even though the act may have been committed against an individual. This is because criminal law applies to acts that are considered so serious and important to the general welfare that the state must take action to preserve public order. Thus the state initiates the prosecution. In some cases the victim may bring a civil action against the defendant as well. Thus criminal and civil law overlap, although there are important distinctions between them.

What this means in practical terms is that if an individual threatens another person on the street for his or her money, holds up a bank, or shoplifts, s/he will be punished as a criminal if caught and convicted. If, however, an automobile company makes a car with faulty parts and people are injured or killed, typically the company is sued for civil but not criminal damages; that is, the company is fined or reprimanded, but no one in the corporation is seen as responsible (as a "criminal"), and no one is incarcerated.

Further, in criminal law if an individual or corporation has been harmed, the wrong is interpreted as a "social wrong," a crime against society. In this case, the state musters all its force and brings suit against the violator; that is, the force and legal machinery are deployed in the interest of the "victim." In civil law, however, the state interprets a violation as a private wrong against an individual, and therefore it is the individual's duty to seek redress by taking his or her case to the courts. Typically, the penalty is some kind of "reprimand" or fine.

In this discussion of the distinction between criminal law and civil law, it becomes obvious that the criminal law tends to work against specific groups (typically the less powerful), while the civil law operates more typically to the advantage of powerful interest groups or corporations. Again, how these two bodies of law affect women demonstrates our point. For example, there is a tendency to restrict attention to acts done *by* individual women and currently defined in criminal codes, such as prostitution, shoplifting, and writing checks with insufficient funds. There is little discussion, on the other hand, about harms which are done by corporations and professionals *to* large groups of women but which are not defined as criminal. Such harms include brown lung disease among female cotton mill workers, the production of medical devices (especially birth control pills and intrauterine devices) that endanger health and often life, and questionable medical procedures (e.g., half of all hysterectomies have been found to be medically unnecessary). These are serious, often life-threatening abuses against women that are not considered crimes against women by the law. Federal regulators tend to choose the less burdensome civil enforcement and generally opt for the civil injunction and fines that at the corporate level are meaningless. The government does not assign significant personnel either to enforce existing law where criminal law could apply or to review ways to enact laws and protect the public where the law does not yet apply. When violence is done against both women and men by powerful individuals and corporations, then, the use of formalized criminal law is rare.

In short, criminal law tends to focus on individual street crime or organized crime. Pervasive corporate crime that is harmful to vast numbers of people is more likely to be covered under the less punitive civil or administrative law in this country. Most of the laws enacted as a result of the political efforts of the civil rights and women's movements, such as affirmative action hiring and equitable educational opportunities, fail to extend significantly the criminal law. Cases of discrimination in employment and education admission normally come under civil and administrative law. The institution or corporation responsible for a violation is generally liable, at best, for victim compensation, possible loss of federal monies, or, most likely, a court order directed toward compliance. Thus, even where there is a punitive penalty, the offender often risks incurring the penalty rather than changing and conforming to the law. Stone (1975) points out that even cease-and-desist orders involve only monetary threats, since the corporation, university, or government agency is not imprisonable.

The limitations of criminal law are far-reaching, particularly for women, who are systematically discriminated against. Consider as a last example the fact that legislation was passed in the 1970s banning discrimination against women employees and students in educational institutions receiving federal funds. Despite thousands of complaints of discrimination, there has not been a single instance in which funds have been withheld by the federal government from a university or college found to be engaging in gender discriminatory practices. Thus, the violator is never punished with imprisonment or any severe sanction.

THEORIES OF CRIME CAUSATION

The law and the penalties prescribed for violations of the criminal law reflect particular theories of crime causation (see Beirne and Messerschmidt, 1991; Traub and Little, 1980). The three most common theories, the first two of which justify and interpret the law, are the classical school, the positivist school, and the school of radical or Marxist criminology.

The two great systems of early criminological theory were classicism and positivism: a debate between "free will" and "determinism"; between punishment that "fits the crime" and punishment that "fits the criminal"; in fact, between punishment and rehabilitation of the criminal. Although modern criminology is largely positivist, the conservative era dominating the last two decades of the twentieth century has led to many crime policies based on the rational calculus of classical criminology. So complete has been the triumph of positivism over classicism that even neoclassical criminology—which emerged as a compromise solution to the extremes—has developed in positivist terms (Beirne and Messerschmidt, 1991).

The classical approach holds that people have "free will," are responsible for their acts, and generally will behave rationally, thus avoiding punishment where foreseeable by abiding by the law. Accordingly, law clearly states both penalties and crimes (supposedly making punishment severe enough to encourage right behavior), anticipating the

general compliance of the public. Law must be certain and punishment must be swift, according to the classical school, so that people will be clear about the relationship between their acts and punishment. The trend to incarcerate women for minor drug offenses, often with lengthy sentences, is an example of classical theory in action.

Positivists, by contrast, state that criminal behavior is determined—whether biologically or socially. It is caused by measurable factors, such as brain characteristics, body structure, specific physical features, gender, and even the social environment. While the members of the positivist school denied "free will," emphasizing "scientific" causes, especially hereditary factors early on, they considered criminals legally and socially responsible for their acts (Cohn, 1976).. Positivists established the idea of examining and changing the criminal to locate the cause of the crime. Though early positivism emphasized biological causes, it did not rule out as causal factors society and its institutions—the family, religion, and the school. Women were readily "explained" when they came into conflict with the law as victims of their own unique biology, which made them irrational, irresponsible, or both (see Klein, Chapter 2 in this book).

Positivists held that the purpose of punishment is rehabilitation; in their "medical models" punishment and treatment are indistinguishable. Positivists would have the law focus on the offender's resocialization—psychological help or job training—whatever is needed to turn the offender into a law-abiding citizen. In explaining crime causation, the positivist school—especially the more contemporary sociological theorists—also pointed to inequality of social forces including socialization, citing lack of socially structured opportunities in life (e.g., see Merton, 1938, 1969). The implication for women was that they should be rehabilitated or resocialized so that they

can "fit in" to society according to the prevailing norms. The traditional role of women
in society was not questioned. Women's prisons typically trained prisoners, if they were
trained at all, in basic homemaking skills and
some rudimentary sex-stereotyped occupational skills: cooking, cleaning, sewing, laundry, beauty care, typing, and, more recently,
word processing. As Feinman (1982) showed,
women not only were trained to "fit in" to
society as "perfect ladies" but, in the process,
were prepared to be housemaids for middle-
and upper-class women.

Different responses result from the two
theories. The case of drug-using, pregnant
women provides a clear example of how theory influences practice in the criminal justice
system. The classical approach, seen in several jurisdictions, is to criminalize the woman's behavior and prosecute her for "delivering" drugs to a fetus or her "unborn child."
Positivists would insist that the woman enter
drug treatment, attend courses on prenatal
nutrition and child-care workshops, etc. Both
schools of thought would try to change the
woman, make her meet their standards of
behavior rather than change her world.

These two theories, classicism and positivism, have been the ones most commonly
used to explain crime by men, with notable
inattention to issues of gender. Criminologists within these traditions accepted the
legal or state definitions of crime. For them,
crime causation was located in the individual
offender, who was understood as pathological, abnormal, or deviant. When positivism
predominated the thinking of decision makers in the criminal justice system (1960s and
1970s), the conclusion was drawn "that ill-
adjusted individuals in conflict with society,
in other words, 'deviants,' must be psychologically 'rehabilitated' by the criminal justice
system" (Klein and Kress, 1976).

Influenced by the women's movement,
women in the 1970s insisted that they be

included in research and analysis in the criminal justice system. But the result was not
new theory; rather, women were mostly
"added on" to existing theories (see Sokoloff,
1980, for an example of how this applies to
research on women and work). Thus, female
criminality historically has been seen as
resulting from women's innate biological or
psychological characteristics. Social and economic factors were rarely noted; even when
they were recognized, the ultimate explanation reverted to the individual woman: akin
to the "victim-blaming" approach discussed
by Karmen (see Introduction to Part Two of
this book). In short, a woman's biological or
reproductive capacities were identified as the
defining characteristics on which her criminality (as well as her normality) depended.
Though mainstream criminology today recognizes social conditions (especially poverty,
racism, and unemployment) as significant, it
still tends to focus on developing different
coping mechanisms to help the incarcerated
woman to function better in society as it
is now structured, rather than challenging
social structures to rearrange opportunities
for all in society.

In contrast to the above theories, which
accept the confines of the existing social system, radical or Marxist criminology, which
emerged in the 1970s, attributes much crime
to injustices in the organization and production of criminal law. It focuses on ruling-class
control of all major institutions (e.g., business,
legislatures, courts) and the social relations
between the rich and powerful and the working class and poor. Radical criminology maintains that those in power create the legal
code—in their own interest—defining some
acts as serious crimes while ignoring others
or reducing them to violations of administrative regulations. As Beirne and Messerschmidt (1991: 505) argue: "Using Marxist
social theory, radicals have developed theories that give priority to historical and struc-

tural analyses of crime that focus on economic relationships, class struggle, capital accumulation, and the role of the reserve army of labor."

Although radical criminology recognizes that street crime is a serious matter requiring legal attention, it does not focus its analysis on developing strategies to deter individual criminals,[2] as the two earlier theories did. Rather, this school is concerned with how the political economic system itself promotes the conditions (poverty, unemployment, etc.) that cause typical street criminal behavior (Platt, 1974; Beirne and Messerschmidt, 1991). At the same time, radical criminology emphasizes that the system ignores, in large part, the economic and social exploitation of workers, minorities, and poor people by factory owners, big business, government officials, and others in power.

Radical criminology calls for a transformation of the entire political economic system. This approach argues for changing the criminal justice and legal systems by changing the underlying social relations between dominant and subordinate groups in society, particularly between the business class and the working class; here the dominant/subordinate relations between whites and racial/ethnic minorities as well as between men and women are noted but are of secondary importance.

With regard to women, a radical or Marxist analysis tries to understand the impact of women's economic dependence in the family on their formally labeled criminal behavior.[3] It maintains that women's inferior economic and political status causes some women to resort to crime to support themselves and their children. Finally, rather than trying to change the women and their criminal behavior, Marxist criminologists draw attention to changing social, economic, and political causes of crime.

As pointed out earlier, feminist theory is not specifically a criminological theory but, rather, is increasingly visible in criminologists' research and thinking. While criminology has yet to experience the full impact of feminist theory (Daly and Chesney-Lind, 1988; also see Daly, the Epilogue herein), feminist demands and activism have had a widespread impact, most notably on the crimes of rape and wife/woman battering. (For a review of feminist theories as they affect criminology, see Beirne and Messerschmidt, 1991.) Feminist thought embraces a variety of perspectives. The most common are liberal, radical, Marxist, and socialist (Sokoloff, 1980; Jaggar, 1983). Most recently, different groups of women of color have become influential in feminist theory and practice (e.g., Baca Zinn et al., 1986; Collins, 1990; Dill and Baca Zinn, 1994; Arnold, Chapter 8 in this volume). All encompass a common view of the importance of understanding women's oppression; each argues for a different set of strategies for social change favorable to women. Some feminist scholars believe that further theoretical development and research will transform traditional criminological theory, helping us both to finally understand female criminality (and victimization) and to explain male criminality more completely (see Leonard, Chapter 3; Klein, Chapter 2; and Daly, the Epilogue).

WOMEN UNDER THE LAW

How does the system of criminal and civil law relate to women in the United States? Women have historically been treated in the law as property, first of their fathers and then of their husbands. It was not until the twentieth century that women acquired independent legal rights in western societies. In the United States it was not until 1971 that the Supreme Court ruled that women were to be interpreted as persons under the Constitution (*Reed v. Reed*, 404 U.S. 71, 92 S. Ct. 251, 30 L.Ed.2nd 225, 1971). Until 1971, courts considered a woman's rights and responsibilities to be determined by her status as wife and mother (Freeman, 1989). The concept of *mens rea*, mentioned above, is applicable here, since the law often required the state to prove a person intended to do an act before it could prosecute. Women were once not viewed as mentally capable of intending to do anything; they were seen as too childlike. Thus they were exempted from the penalties that many laws imposed. However, this "chivalrous" attitude meant that some women—most notably white and middle-class—received special treatment, but only when it suited men and always at the expense of women's independence. Women from poor, working-class, and slave origins were never afforded such "chivalrous protections" (Klein and Kress, 1976).

While today women increasingly are seen as equal before the law, the fact that women in the United States have always been defined in the law primarily by their patriarchal relation to the home as wife and mother has had important consequences for how they are treated in the larger society. For example, only in 17 states, in the District of Columbia, and on federal lands does the law state that there is no exemption for husbands from conviction for raping their wives; all other states have laws that permit some marital rape exemptions (NCWFL, 1991). This is the case in spite of estimates which suggest that at least 600,000 wives are sexually assaulted each year by their husbands.

Ideas about the proper role of women in society are not static: women have fought hard throughout history to better their conditions. In the legal system in particular, women have long sought changes that would improve their lives. However, the members of the legal system are for the most part men. Thus, even if many laws were not sexist, the fact that those who make the laws (federal and state legislators, government administra-tors, and judges) and those who enforce the laws (police and courts) are overwhelmingly male affects in major ways how women are thought of and treated by the legal system. Even when the criminal law does not formally discriminate against women, in practice—as the law operates in the processing of women from police to courts to jails—the law very often does discriminate.

An excellent example of such discriminatory treatment is the processing of female juveniles apprehended for status offenses. A status offense is one that allows the state to intervene in a juvenile's life for behavior that, if done by an adult, would not be prosecutable. Running away from home, incorrigibility, and being in danger of falling into vice are examples of status offenses. Historically, girls have been much more likely than boys to be brought into juvenile court for status offenses (the status offense of being a runaway is 63 percent female) (see Chesney-Lind, Chapter 4 in this book). Girls were often punished more severely than youngsters who committed more serious property crimes or even some violent offenses. The girls were punished for sexual "promiscuity" and other trivial offenses. Although the number of girls in detention and training centers dropped by 40 percent in the 1970s following a federal law on deinstitutionalization of status offenders, the numbers began to creep up again in the 1980s. At the same time that institutionalization in the juvenile justice system was decreasing, the incarceration of juveniles in mental health facilities doubled, suggesting a transfer of girls from one system of social control to another. The wording of the statutory law may not discriminate against girls, but the way the law is carried out often does.

The creation and differential application of the law to the detriment of women has been discussed in this section. Attention has been given to the way in which the law is particularly disadvantageous to poor, working-class, and racial/ethnic minority women. More work is needed on how the law negatively impacts on lesbians, too. In the past women have been viewed by the law as incompetent, childlike, and in need of protection; males were seen as their protectors and financial caretakers. Husbands and wives were even treated as "one" under the law—and that "one" was the male. Finally, the double standard of morality based on biological determinism was built into the legal process itself. The myth of purity prevailed: women criminals were said to offend because they were women; for them chivalry gave way to vengeance.

Sadly, too little has changed; the law is still harsher toward women than men. Women in jail are less likely than men to have a juvenile record and less likely to have been convicted of a crime in the past. Almost one out of three female inmates in jail had never been convicted previously compared with one out of five males (BJS, 1992b). For those in prison the statistics are remarkably similar: 31 percent of the women but only 18 percent of the men in prison were serving a first sentence (BJS, 1991c).

SOCIAL MOVEMENTS AND THE CRIMINAL JUSTICE SYSTEM

Criminal laws that are sexually discriminatory have gradually been modified or eliminated at the state and federal levels. This is in large part due to the legacy of the U.S. civil rights and women's movements in the mid-twentieth century.

The civil rights movement grew out of the struggle by blacks to overcome the laws and customs that segregated blacks from whites, thereby keeping blacks from gaining economic and political equality. The dominant force in the black liberation movement between the mid-1950s and mid-1960s was the civil rights struggle. Through marches,

demonstrations, sit-ins, boycotts, speeches, political lobbying, community organizing, and often-times massive arrests and beatings, two major pieces of legislation—the Civil Rights Act of 1964 and the Voting Rights Act of 1965—emerged that gave black women and men the legal tools to fight for their civil rights. While blacks have made some important gains in access to schools and employment, the underlying economic and political structure of our society continues to be organized on the basis of race, class, and gender inequality.

The women's movement followed on the heels of and modeled many of its tactics on those developed by the civil rights movement. Ironically, a ban on discrimination against women was added to Title VII of the Civil Rights Act of 1964 at the last minute by conservative congressmen in an attempt to defeat the bill. Although this ultimately backfired, women had so little political power at that time that the Equal Employment Opportunity Commission (EEOC) established under law to enforce Title VII ignored the provision on gender (Freeman, 1989). Soon after, the women's movement became highly visible through several national organizations, the National Organization for Women (NOW) being the largest and most influential mainstream one. The successes of the women's movement include obtaining new legislation, decreasing discriminatory laws and practices in the public and private sectors, and educating the public about the harmful effects of gender discrimination.

Pressure on Congress has resulted in federal legislation prohibiting gender discrimination in employment, education, credit, insurance, taxes, pensions, and some areas of the military. However, the enforcement of these laws has been seriously jeopardized in cities and regions across the country because of restricted public budgets and, despite more liberal trends in the 1990s, the persistence of conservative decision makers in positions of power. Their political strength has resulted since the 1970s in reduced federal protection in civil rights laws generally and a movement toward severely weakening affirmative action. Thus law itself has retreated in some areas and fails to protect adequately women and minorities. It may well be that a perception of many in this country that the women's movement was "too successful" has produced a powerful backlash—to the detriment of all women (Faludi, 1991).

Increasing the number of women from a variety of racial/ethnic and class backgrounds in positions of recognition and power has been of crucial importance to our society. However, this increase in number—despite the backlash—does not guarantee the needed changes in the underlying structures of power in society. As Kopkind (1992:123) has argued, despite increasing numbers of women political candidates (what he calls "femalization"), especially among Democrats in the 1992 elections, and therefore in the Congress and the Senate, "real feminization has hardly begun. Properly understood, that entails radical changes in the patriarchal relations, affecting class, race, the military establishment and the corporate economy."

This section has described two separate social movements in the United States, each working for specific objectives—greater equality of women and minorities, especially black Americans. Each has the potential to improve the conditions of women offenders, victims, and workers in the criminal justice system.

CONCLUSION

In this chapter the reader has been introduced to the criminal law as it relates to women, racial/ethnic groups, and the poor and working classes. The chapter began by explaining the law in terms of the purposes

it serves. This led to an explanation of what acts are defined as criminal, with a focus on the groups most affected by the law and the groups most likely to be either victims of crime or victims of the law itself. Theories developed to explain crime were identified as traditional rationales that have served to justify legal definitions of crime; the school of radical or Marxist criminology was singled out as the only theory of crime causation that generally locates the causes of criminal behavior not in the individual offender but in the political and economic arrangements of a capitalist society, which is simultaneously based on race and gender inequality. The impact of the law in relation to minority groups generally and women specifically was then explained, and the chapter concluded with a brief look at social movements that have arisen in response to this society's inequitable system of law and justice.

The basic theme of this chapter is that the law is not simple, value-free, or static. As you read through the other chapters in this book, it is important that you ask how the conditions of gender, race, class, and sexual orientation in the larger society affect what happens to women in the criminal justice system. Consider what can be done to challenge these historically specific social structures that undergird all aspects of our society, including the relationship between diverse groups of women and the criminal justice system.

NOTES

1. Despite recent government attempts to control cigarettes or compensate victims of illnesses due to silicone breast implants, no one is talking about bringing criminal charges against these manufacturers or heads of corporations.
2. More recently, a newer tradition of left realism has emerged to deal more thoroughly with

issues of street crime (see DeKeserdy and MacLean, 1991).

3. To be sure, Marx did not discuss women and crime. Also, gender and race inequality may exist under a variety of political/economic conditions. The position here is that women's relationship to crime in the United States occurs in a patriarchal, racist society under contemporary conditions of monopoly capitalism.

REFERENCES

American Correctional Association. 1990. *The Female Offenders: What Does the Future Hold?* Washington, D.C.: St. Mary's.

Baca Zinn, Maxine, Lynn Weber Cannon, Elizabeth Higginbotham, and Bonnie Thornton Dill. 1986. "The Costs of Exclusionary Practices in Women's Studies," *Signs,* 11 (2): 290–303.

Beard, Charles. 1935. *An Economic Interpretation of the Constitution of the United States.* New York: Macmillan.

Beirne, Piers, and James Messerschmidt. 1991. *Criminology.* San Diego: Harcourt Brace Jovanovich.

Blackwell, James. 1981. *Mainstreaming Outsiders: The Production of Black Professionals.* Bayside, N.Y.: General Hall.

Bowker, Lee (ed.). 1981. *Women and Crime in America.* New York: Macmillan.

Bureau of Justice Statistics (BJS). 1991a. *Criminal Victimization, 1990.* NCJ-130234. Washington, D.C.: U.S. Department of Justice.

———. 1991b. *National Update 1* (1) (July). Washington, D.C.: U.S. Department of Justice.

———. 1991c. *Women in Prison.* Washington, D.C.: U.S. Department of Justice.

———. 1992a. *Women in Jail, 1989.* NCJ-134732. (March). Washington, D.C.: U.S. Department of Justice.

———. 1992b. *National Update 1* (4) (April). Washington, D.C.: U.S. Department of Justice.

Chasnoff, Ira, Harvey Landress, and Mark Barrett. 1990. "The Prevalence of Illicit-Drug or Alcohol Use during Pregnancy and Discrepancies in Mandatory Reporting in Pinellas County, Florida," *New England Journal of Medicine,* vol. 322 (April 26): 1202–1206.

Cohn, Alvin. 1976. *Crime and Justice Administration.* Philadelphia: J. B. Lippincott.

Coleman, James William. 1989. *The Criminal Elite: The Sociology of White Collar Crime,* 2d ed. New York: St. Martin's.

Collins, Patricia Hill. 1990. *Black Feminist Thought.* New York: Routledge, Chapman, Hall.

Daly, Kathleen, and Meda Chesney-Lind. 1988. "Feminism and Criminology," *Justice Quarterly* 5 (December): 497–538.

DeKeserdy, William, and Brian MacLean. 1991. "Exploring the Gender, Race and Class Dimensions of Victimization: A Left Realist Critique of the Canadian Victimization Survey," *International Journal of Offender Therapy and Comparative Criminology,* 35 (2): 143–161.

Dill, Bonnie Thornton, and Maxine Baca Zinn (eds.). 1994. *Women of Color in U.S. Society.* Philadelphia: Temple University.

Domhoff, William. 1990. *The Power Elite and the State.* New York: Ade Gruyter.

Ermann, M. David, and Richard J. Lundman (eds.). 1992. *Corporate and Governmental Deviance.* New York: Oxford University.

Faison, Seth. 1991. "Sexual Harassment New as a Legal Issue," *The New York Times* (October 7): A14.

Faludi, Susan. 1991. *Backlash: The Undeclared War against American Women.* New York: Crown.

Feinman, Clarice. 1982. "Sex Role Stereotypes and Justice for Women," in Barbara Raffel Price and Natalie J. Sokoloff (eds.), *The Criminal Justice System and Women.* New York: Clark Boardman.

Freeman, Jo. 1989. *The Politics of Women's Liberation: A Case Study of an Emerging Social Movement and Its Relation to the Policy Process.* New York: David McKay.

Gray, Jerry. 1991. "Panel Says Courts are 'Infested with Racism,'" *The New York Times* (June 5): B1.

Hart, H. L. A. 1968. "Prolegomenon to the Principles of Punishment," in *Punishment and Responsibility.* New York: Oxford University.

Heaney, Gerald W. 1991. "The Realities of Guideline Sentencing: No End to Disparity," *The American Criminal Law Review,* 28 (2): 71. Washington, D.C.: Georgetown University Law Center.

Hilts, Philip J. 1992. "Strange History of Silicone Held Many Warning Signs," *The New York Times* (January 17): 1, 8.

Hutchinson, Earl Ofari. 1990. *The Mugging of Black America.* Chicago: African American Images.

Jaggar, Allison. 1983. *Feminist Politics and Human Nature.* Totowa, N.J.: Ballanheld Harvester.

Jaynes, Gerald David, and Robin Williams Jr. 1989. *A Common Destiny: Blacks and American Society.* Washington, D.C.: National Academy Press, chap. 9.

Johnson, Kirk A. 1992. "Can We Talk about Race?" *Extra!* (July/August): 6–7.

Kennickell, Arthur B., and R. Louise Woodburn. 1992. "Estimation of Household Net Worth Using Model-Based and Design-Based Weights." Publication Series, MS 138, Board of Governors of Federal Reserve System, Washington, D.C. 20551. (April.)

Kessler, Glenn. 1992. "Dow Knew for Years of Implant Troubles," *New York Newsday* (February 11): 5, 89.

Klein, Dorie, and June Kress. 1976. "Any Woman's Blues: A Critical Overview of Women, Crime, and the Criminal Justice System," *Crime and Social Justice,* 5 (Spring/Summer): 34–49.

Kopkind, Andrew. 1992. "Sisters Start Doing It for Themselves," *The Nation* (August 3/10): 121, 123, 124.

Kozol, Jonathan. 1991. *Savage Inequalities.* New York: Crown.

Labaton, Stephen. 1991. "Few Minority Companies Get Contracts in Savings Bailout," *The New York Times* (June 4): A1, D16.

Lewin, Tamar. 1992. "Drug Verdict over Infants Voided," *The New York Times* (July 26): 13.

———. 1991. "Violent Crime in the U.S.," *The New York Times:* 5.

Maguire, Kathleen, and Timothy J. Flanagan (eds.). 1991. *Sourcebook of Criminal Justice Statistics 1990.* U.S. Department of Justice, Bureau of Justice Statistics. Washington, D.C.: U.S. Government Printing Office.

Mauer, Marc. 1990. *Young Black Men and the Criminal Justice System: A Growing National Problem.* Washington, D.C.: Sentencing Project.

Merton, Robert K. 1938, 1969. "Social Structure and Anomie," in Donald R. Cressey and David A. Ward (eds.), *Delinquency, Crime and Social Process.* New York: Harper & Row, 254–284.

Miller, Judith. 1978. "Interlocking Directorates Flourish," *The New York Times* (April 23): D23.

Mokhiber, Russell. 1989. "Crime in the Suites," *Greenpeace,* vol. 14 (September/October): 14–17.

Morgan-Sharp, Etta F. 1992. "Gender, Race, and the Law: Elements of Injustice," *The Justice Professional,* 6 (Winter): 86–93.

Nagel, S., and Lenore Weitzman. 1972. "Double Standard of American Justice," in *Transaction: Social Science and Modern Society* (18): 18–25, 62.

Nasar, Sylvia. 1992. "Fed Gives New Evidence of 80's Gains by Richest," *The New York Times* (April 21): A1.

National Center on Women and Family Law (NCWFL). 1991. *Marital Rape Exemption.* New York: NCWFL.

New York Times. 1981. "Financial Reports Show that 10 Members of Cabinet Are Worth $1 Million or More." (January 26): 24.

New York Times. 1990. "Hispanic People Victimized More by Crime, Study Says." (January 16): A22.

Noah, Timothy. 1991. "Blacks Face Housing Discrimination in Most Cases, According to HUD Study," *Wall Street Journal* (August 30): B33.

Passell, Peter. 1991. "Blacks' Setbacks by Association," *The New York Times* (August 28): D2.

Platt, Tony. 1974. "Prospects for a Radical Criminology in the United States," *Crime and Social Justice,* 1 (Spring–Summer).

Quinney, Richard. 1975. *Class, State and Crime: On the Theory and Practice of Criminal Justice.* New York: Longman.

Quint, Michael. 1992. "Tracking Bias in Banks," *The New York Times* (February 16): 12F.

Reiman, Jeffrey H. 1990. *The Rich Get Richer and the Poor Get Prison: Ideology, Class, and Criminal Justice,* 3d ed. New York: Wiley.

Robin, Gerald D. 1982. "Forcible Rape: Institutionalized Sexism in the Criminal Justice System," in Barbara Raffel Price and Natalie J. Sokoloff (eds.), *The Criminal Justice System and Women: Offenders, Victims, Workers.* New York: Clark Boardman, 241–261.

Sherman, Howard J. 1991. "Monopoly, Prices, and Profits: The Concentration of Economic Power in the U.S.," in Berch Berberoglu (ed.), *Critical Perspectives in Sociology: A Reader.* Dubuque: Kendall/Hunt, 55–68.

Simon, David R., and D. Stanley Eitzen. 1993. *Elite Deviance*, 4th ed. Boston: Allyn and Bacon.

Smith, Brenda V. 1990. Testimony before the Select Committee on Children, Youth and Families Regarding Improved Drug Treatment for Pregnant Alcohol and Drug-Dependent Women (May 17). Washington, D.C.: National Women's Law Center.

Sokoloff, Natalie J. 1980. *Between Money and Love: The Dialectics of Women's Home and Market Work*. New York: Praeger.

Stanko, Elizabeth M. 1992. "The Case of Fearful Women: Gender, Personal Safety and Fear of Crime," *Women & Criminal Justice*, 4 (1): 117–135.

Stone, Christopher D. 1975. *Where the Law Ends*. New York: Harper & Row.

Sullivan, Joseph F. 1992. "Widespread Bias Found in Court System," *The New York Times* (August 7): B5.

Swoboda, Frank. 1991. "GAO Finds Job Training Discrimination," *Washington Post* (July 17): A21.

Timrots, A., and M. Rand. 1987. Bureau of Justice Statistics Special Report: Violent Crime by Strangers and Non-strangers. Washington, D.C.: U.S. Department of Justice.

Traub, E., and C. Little. 1980. *Theories of Deviance*, 3d ed. Itasca, Ill.: Peacock.

U.S. Bureau of the Census. 1991. *Statistical Abstract of the United States: 1991*, 111th ed. Washington, D.C.

U.S. News & World Report. 1980. "The Millionaire Contingent in Congress" (March 17): 4.

U.S. Sentencing Commission. 1991. "Special Report to Congress: Mandatory Minimum Penalties in the Federal Court Justice System." Washington, D.C.

Vaughn, Doug. 1993. "The Clinton Cabinet: Affirmative Action for the Ethically Challenged," *CovertAction Quarterly*, 44: 12–18, 55–56.

Vobejda, Barbara. 1992. "Neighborhood Racial Patterns Little Changed," *Washington Post* (March 18): A7.

Whitaker, Catherine J. 1990. *Black Victims*. NCJ 122562. Bureau of Justice Statistics. Washington, D.C.: U.S. Department of Justice.

Williams, Lena. 1991. "When Blacks Shop, Bias Often Accompanies Sale," *The New York Times* (April 30): A1, A14.

The World Almanac and Book of Facts 1991. 1992. New York: Pharos Books.

Young, Vernetta. 1992. "Fear of Victimization and Victimization Rates among Women: A Paradox?" *Justice Quarterly*, 9 (3): 419–441.

Zinn, Howard. 1980. *A People's History of the United States*. New York: Harper & Row.

THE ETIOLOGY OF FEMALE CRIME: A REVIEW OF THE LITERATURE

DORIE KLEIN

ABSTRACT

Chapter 2 begins with a major excerpt from Dorie Klein's now classic article on women offenders, which is followed by a contemporary afterword written specifically for this second edition of the book. In both cases, Klein's work ties in with many points made in Chapter 1 on the classist, racist, and sexist assumptions embedded in the literature on female criminality—yesterday and today.

In 1973 Klein, then a graduate student, published "The Etiology of Female Crime: A Review of the Literature," which was reprinted in the first edition of this book. In it, she argued that past theories of women's criminality depended on the idea that their criminal behavior was a result of their biology (meaning their sexuality) or their individual psychological problems. Thus, strategies for rehabilitating the offender focused on individual adjustment (meaning gender-appropriate behavior) to the socially acceptable "legitimate world." She noted that the then contemporary writers were also guilty of the same undocumented, poorly researched work as earlier criminologists. Klein ended her essay by questioning the impact of the political economy, racism, and sexism on the causes and definitions of female crime and called for social change of the broader society instead of focusing on the rehabilitation of the individual female offender.

In her "Afterword," Klein brings the reader up to date on feminist thinking in criminal justice in order to convey a sense of what has transpired since she wrote her groundbreaking essay two decades ago. In it, Klein describes what she sees as the three major challenges facing feminist criminology today. They are (1) a continuing search for the scientific basis of theories of crime, (2) a reexamination of the gender and racial biases in social science, and (3) the development of a new definition of crime. Each area presents formidable challenges to students, researchers, and ultimately, policy makers. As students of criminology, consider what you might be able to contribute to furthering this effort through your class discussions and research papers.

The criminality of women has long been a neglected subject area of criminology. Many explanations have been advanced for this, such as women's low official rate of crime and delinquency and the preponderance of male theorists in the field. Female criminality has often ended up as a footnote to works on men that purport to be works on criminality in general.

There has been, however, a small group of writings specifically concerned with women and crime. This paper will explore those works concerned with the etiology of female crime and delinquency, beginning with the turn-of-the-century writing of Lombroso and extending to the present. Writers selected to be included have been chosen either for their influence on the field, such as Lombroso, Thomas, Freud, Davis and Pollak, or because they are representative of the kinds of work being published, such as Konopka, Vedder and Somerville, and Cowie, Cowie and Slater. The emphasis is on the continuity between these works, because it is clear that, despite recognizable differences in analytical approaches and specific theories, the authors represent a tradition to a great extent. It is important to understand, therefore, the shared assumptions made by the writers that are used to laying the groundwork for their theories.

The writers see criminality as the result of *individual* characteristics that are only periph-

From *Crime and Social Justice: Issues in Criminology,* Fall 1973, pp. 3–30. Copyright © Crime and Social Justice, P.O. Box 4373, Berkeley, California, 94704. Reprinted by permission from *Social Justice.*

erally affected by economic, social and political forces. These characteristics are of a *physiological* or *psychological* nature and are uniformly based on implicit or explicit assumptions about the *inherent nature of women.* This nature is *universal,* rather than existing within a specific historical framework.

Since criminality is seen as an individual activity, rather than as a condition built into existing structures, the focus is on biological, psychological and social factors that would turn a woman toward criminal activity. To do this, the writers create two distinct classes of women: good women who are "normal" non-criminals, and bad women who are criminals, thus taking a moral position that often masquerades as a scientific distinction. The writers, although they may be biological or social determinists to varying degrees, assume that individuals have *choices* between criminal and noncriminal activity. They see persons as atomistically moving about in a social and political vacuum; many writers use marketplace models for human interaction.

Although the theorists may differ on specific remedies for individual criminality, ranging from sterilization to psychoanalysis (but always stopping far short of social change), the basic thrust is toward *individual adjustment,* whether it be physical or mental, and the frequent model is rehabilitative therapy. Widespread environmental alterations are usually included as casual footnotes to specific plans for individual therapy. Most of the writers are concerned with *social harmony* and the welfare of the existing social structure rather than with the women involved or with women's position in general. None of the writers come from anything near a "feminist" or "radical" perspective.

In *The Female Offender,* originally published in 1903, Lombroso described female criminality as an inherent tendency produced in individuals that could be regarded as biological atavisms, similar to cranial and facial features, and one could expect a withering away of crime if the atavistic people were prohibited from breeding. At this time criminality was widely regarded as a physical ailment, like epilepsy. Today, Cowie, Cowie and Slater (1968) have identified physical traits in girls who have been classified as delinquent, and have concluded that certain traits, such as bigness, may lead to aggressiveness. This theme of physiological characteristics has been developed by a good number of writers in the last seventy years, such as the Gluecks (1934). One sees at the present time a new surge of "biological" theories of criminality; for example, a study involving "violence-prone" women and menstrual cycles has recently been proposed at UCLA.[1]

Thomas, to a certain degree, and Freud extend the physiological explanation of criminality to propose a psychological theory. However, it is critical to understand that these psychological notions are based on assumptions of universal *physiological* traits of women, such as their reproductive instinct and passivity, that are seen as invariably producing certain psychological reactions. Women may be viewed as turning to crime as a *perversion of* or *rebellion against* their *natural feminine roles.* Whether their problems are biological, psychological or social-environmental, the point is always to return them to their roles. Thomas (1907; 1923), for example, points out that poverty might prevent a woman from marrying, whereby she would turn to prostitution as an alternative to carry on her feminine service role. In fact, Davis (1961) discusses prostitution as a parallel illegal institution to marriage. Pollak (1950) discusses how women extend their service roles into criminal activity due to inherent tendencies such as deceitfulness. Freud (1933; Jones, 1961) sees any kind of rebellion as the result of a failure to develop healthy feminine attitudes, such as narcissism, and Konopka (1966) and Vedder and Somerville (1970) apply Freudian thought to the problem of female delinquency.

The specific characteristics ascribed to women's nature and those critical to theories of female criminality are uniformly *sexual* in their nature. Sexuality is seen as the root of female behavior and the problem of crime. Women are defined as sexual beings, as sexual capital in many cases, physiologically, psychologically and socially. This definition *reflects* and *reinforces* the economic position of women as reproductive and domestic workers. It is mirrored in the laws themselves and in their enforcement, which penalize sexual deviations for women and may be more lenient with economic offenses committed by them, in contrast to the treatment given men. The theorists accept the sexual double standard inherent in the law, often noting that "chivalry" protects women, and many of them build notions of the universality of *sex repression* into their explanations of women's position. Women are thus the sexual backbone of civilization.

In setting hegemonic standards of conduct for all women, the theorists define *femininity,* which they equate with healthy femaleness, in classist, racist and sexist terms, using their assumptions of women's nature, specifically their sexuality, to justify what is often in reality merely a defense of the existing order. Lombroso, Thomas and Freud consider the upper-class white woman to be the highest expression of femininity, although she is inferior to the upper-class white man. These standards are adopted by later writers in discussing femininity. To most theorists, women are inherently inferior to men at masculine tasks such as thought and production, and therefore it is logical that their sphere should be reproductive.

Specific characteristics are proposed to bolster this sexual ideology, expressed for example by Freud, such as passivity, emotionalism, narcissism and deceitfulness. In the discussions of criminality, certain theorists, such as Pollak, link female criminality to these traits. Others see criminality as an attempt away from femininity into masculinity, such as Lombroso, although the specifics are often confused. Contradictions can be clearly seen, which are explained by the dual nature of "good" and "bad" women and by the fact that this is a mythology attempting to explain real behavior. Many explanations of what are obviously economically motivated offenses, such as prostitution and shoplifting, are explained in sexual terms, such as prostitution being promiscuity, and shoplifting being "kleptomania" caused by women's inexplicable mental cycles tied to menstruation. Different explanations have to be made for "masculine" crimes, e.g., burglary, and for "feminine" crimes, e.g., shoplifting. Although this distinction crops up consistently, the specifics differ widely.

The problem is complicated by the lack of knowledge of the epidemiology of female crime, which allows such ideas as "hidden crime," first expressed by Pollak (1950), to take root. The problem must be considered on two levels: women, having been confined to certain tasks and socialized in certain ways, are *in fact* more likely to commit crime related to their lives which are sexually oriented; yet even nonsexual offenses are *explained* in sexual terms by the theorists. The writers ignore the problems of poor and Third World women, concentrating on affluent white standards of femininity. The experiences of these overlooked women, who *in fact* constitute a good percentage of women caught up in the criminal justice system, negate the notions of sexually motivated crime. These women have real economic needs which are not being met, and in many cases engage in illegal activities as a viable economic alternative. Furthermore, chivalry has never been extended to them.

The writers largely ignore the problems of sexism, racism and class, thus their work is sexist, racist and classist in its implications. Their concern is adjustment of the woman to society, not social change. Hence, they represent a tradition in criminology and carry along a host of assumptions about women and humanity in general. It is important to explore these assumptions and traditions in depth in order to understand what kinds of myths have been propagated around women and crime. The discussions of each writer or writers will focus on these assumptions and their relevance to criminological theories. These assumptions of universal, biological/psychological characteristics, of individual responsibility for crime, of the necessity for maintaining social harmony, and of the benevolence of the state link different theories along a continuum, transcending political labels and minor divergencies. The road from Lombroso to the present is surprisingly straight.

LOMBROSO: "THERE MUST BE SOME ANOMALY. . . ."

Lombroso's work on female criminality (1920) is important to consider today despite the fact that his methodology and conclusions have long been successfully discredited. Later writings on female crime by Thomas, Davis, Pollak and others use more sophisticated methodologies and may proffer more palatable liberal theories. However, to varying degrees they rely on those sexual ideologies based on *implicit* assumptions about the physiological and psychological nature of women that are *explicit* in Lombroso's work. Reading the work helps to achieve a better understanding of what kinds of myths have been developed for women in general and for female crime and deviance in particular.

One specific notion of women offered by Lombroso is women's physiological immobility and psychological passivity, later elaborated by Thomas, Freud and other writers. Another ascribed characteristic is the Lombrosian notion of women's adaptability to surroundings and their capacity for survival as being superior to that of men. A third idea discussed by Lombroso is women's amorality: they are cold and calculating. This is developed by Thomas (1923), who describes women's manipulation of the male sex urge for ulterior purposes; by Freud (1933), who sees women as avenging their lack of a penis on men; and by Pollak (1950), who depicts women as inherently deceitful.

When one looks at these specific traits, one sees contradictions. The myth of compassionate women clashes with their reputed coldness; their frailness belies their capacity to survive. One possible explanation for these contradictions is the duality of sexual ideology with regard to "good" and "bad" women.[2] Bad women are whores, driven by lust for money or for men, often essentially *"masculine"* in their orientation, and perhaps afflicted with a touch of penis envy. Good women are chaste, "feminine," and usually not prone to criminal activity. But when they are, they commit crime in a most *ladylike* way such as poisoning. In more sophisticated theory, all women are seen as having a bit of both tendencies in them. Therefore, women can be compassionate *and* cold, frail *and* sturdy, pious *and* amoral, depending on which path they choose to follow. They are seen as rational (although they are irrational, too!), atomistic individuals making choices in a vacuum, prompted only by personal, physiological/psychological factors. These choices relate only to the *sexual* sphere. Women have no place in any other sphere. Men, on the other hand, are not held sexually accountable, although, as Thomas notes (1907), they are held responsible in *economic* matters. Men's sexual freedom is justified by the myth of masculine, irresistible sex urges. This myth, still worshipped today, is frequently offered as a rationalization for the existence of prostitution and the double standard. As Davis maintains, this necessitates the parallel existence of classes of "good" and "bad" women.

These dual moralities for the sexes are outgrowths of the economic, political and social *realities* for men and women. Women are primarily workers within the family, a critical institution of reproduction and socialization that services such basic needs as food and shelter. Laws and codes of behavior for women thus attempt to maintain the smooth functioning of women in that role, which requires that women act as a conservative force in the continuation of the nuclear family. Women's main tasks are sexual, and the law embodies sexual limitations for women, which do not exist for men, such as the prohibition of promiscuity for girls. This explains why theorists of female criminality are not only concerned with sexual violations by female offenders, but attempt to account for even *nonsexual* offenses, such as prostitution, in sexual terms, e.g., women enter prostitution for sex rather than for money. Such women are not only economic offenders but are sexual deviants, falling neatly into the category of "bad" women.

The works of Lombroso, particularly *The Female Offender* (1920), are a foremost example of the biological explanation of crime. Lombroso deals with crime as an atavism, or survival of "primitive" traits in individuals, particularly those of the female and nonwhite races. He theorizes that individuals develop differentially within sexual and racial limitations which differ hierarchically from the most highly developed, the white men, to the most primitive, the nonwhite women. Beginning with the assumption that criminals must be atavistic, he spends a good deal of time comparing the crania, moles, heights, etc. of convicted criminals and prostitutes with those of normal women. Any trait that he finds to be more common in the "criminal" group is pronounced an atavistic trait, such as moles, dark hair, etc., and women with a number of these telltale traits could be regarded as potentially criminal, since they are of the atavistic type. He specifically rejects the idea that some of these traits, for example obesity in prostitutes, could be the *result* of their activities rather than an indicator of their propensity to them. Many of the traits are depicted as "anomalies," such as darkness and shortness, and characteristic of certain racial groups, such as the Sicilians, who undoubtedly comprise an oppressed group within Italy and form a large part of the imprisoned population.

Lombroso traces an overall pattern of evolution in the human species that accounts for the uneven development of groups: the white and nonwhite races, males and females, adults and children. Women, children and nonwhites share many traits in common. There are fewer variations in their mental capacities: "even the female criminal is monotonous and uniform compared with her male companion, just as in general woman is inferior to man" (Ibid.:122) due to her being "atavistically nearer to her origin than the male" (Ibid.:107). The notion of women's mediocrity, or limited range of mental possibilities, is a recurrent one in the writings of the twentieth century. Thomas and others note that women comprise "fewer geniuses, fewer lunatics and fewer morons" (Thomas 1907:45); lacking the imagination to be at either end of the spectrum, they are conformist and dull . . . not due to social, political or economic constraints on their activities, but because of their innate physiological limitations as a sex. Lombroso attributes the

lower female rate of criminality to their having fewer anomalies, which is one aspect of their closeness to the lower forms of less differentiated life.

Related characteristics of women are their passivity and conservatism. Lombroso admits that women's traditional sex roles in the family bind them to a more sedentary life. However, he insists that women's passivity can be directly traced to the "immobility of the ovule compared with the zoosperm" (1920:109), falling back on the sexual act in an interesting anticipation of Freud.

Women, like the lower races, have greater powers of endurance and resistance to mental and physical pain than men. Lombroso states: "denizens of female prisoners . . . have reached the age of 90, having lived within those walls since they were 29 without any grave injury to health" (Ibid.:125). Denying the humanity of women by denying their capability for suffering justifies exploitation of women's energies by arguing for their suitability to hardship. Lombroso remarks that "a duchess can adapt herself to new surroundings and become a washerwoman much more easily than a man can transform himself under analogous conditions" (Ibid.:272). The theme of women's adaptability to physical and social surroundings, which are male initiated, male controlled, and often expressed by saying that women are actually the "stronger" sex, is a persistent thread in writings on women.

Lombroso explains that because women are unable to feel pain, they are insensitive to the pain of others and lack moral refinement. His blunt denial of the age-old myth of women's compassion and sensitivity is modified, however, to take into account women's low crime rate:

Women have many traits in common with children; that their moral sense is deficient; that they are revengeful, jealous. . . . In ordinary cases these defects are neutralized by piety, maternity, want of passion, sexual coldness, weakness and an undeveloped intelligence (Ibid.:151).

Although women lack the higher sensibilities of men, they are thus restrained from criminal activity in most cases by lack of intelligence and passion, qualities which *criminal* women possess as well as all *men*. Within this framework of biological limits of women's nature, the female offender is characterized as *masculine* whereas the normal woman is *feminine*. The anomalies of skull, physiognomy and brain capacity of female criminals, according to Lombroso, more closely approximate that of the man, normal or criminal, than they do those of the normal woman; the female offender often has a "virile cranium" and considerable body hair. Masculinity in women is an anomaly itself, rather than a sign of development, however. A related notion is developed by Thomas, who notes that in "civilized" nations the sexes are more physically different.

> What we look for most in the female is femininity, and when we find the opposite in her, we must conclude as a rule that there must be some anomaly. . . . Virility was one of the special features of the savage woman. . . . In the portraits of Red Indian and Negro beauties, whom it is difficult to recognize for women, so huge are their jaws and cheekbones, so hard and coarse their features, and the same is often the case in their crania and brains (Ibid.:112).

The more highly developed races would therefore have the most feminized women with the requisite passivity, lack of passion, etc. This is a *racist* and *classist* definition of femininity—just as are almost all theories of *femininity* and as, indeed, is the thing itself. The ideal of the lady can only exist in a society built on the exploitation of labor to maintain the woman of leisure who can *be* that ideal lady.

Finally, Lombroso notes women's lack of *property sense*, which contributes to their criminality.

> In their eyes theft is . . . an audacity for which compensation is due to the owner . . . as an individual rather than a social crime, just as it was regarded in the primitive periods of human evolution and is still regarded by many uncivilized nations (Ibid.:217).

One may question this statement on several levels. Can it be assumed to have any validity at all, or is it false that women have a different sense of property than men? If it is valid to a degree, is it related to women's lack of property ownership and nonparticipation in the accumulation of capitalist wealth? Indeed, as Thomas (1907) points out, women are considered property themselves. At any rate, it is an interesting point in Lombroso's book that has only been touched on by later writers, and always in a manner supportive of the institution of private property.

THOMAS: "THE STIMULATION SHE CRAVES"

The works of W. I. Thomas are critical in that they mark a transition from purely physiological explanations such as Lombroso's to more sophisticated theories that embrace physiological, psychological and social-structural factors. However, even the most sophisticated explanations of female crime rely on implicit assumptions about the *biological* nature of women. In Thomas' *Sex and Society* (1907) and *The Unadjusted Girl* (1923), there are important contradictions in the two approaches that are representative of the movements during that period between publication dates: a departure from biological

Social-Darwinian theories to complex analyses of the interaction between society and the individual, i.e., societal repression and manipulation of the "natural" wishes of persons.

In *Sex and Society* (1907), Thomas poses basic biological differences between the sexes as his starting point. Maleness is "katabolic," the animal force which is destructive of energy and allows men the possibility of creative work through this outward flow. Femaleness is "anabolic," analogous to a plant which stores energy, and is motionless and conservative. Here Thomas is offering his own version of the age-old male/female dichotomy expressed by Lombroso and elaborated on in Freud's paradigm, in the structural-functionalist "instrumental-expressive" duality, and in other analyses of the status quo. According to Thomas, the dichotomy is most highly developed in the most civilized races, due to the greater differentiation of sex roles. This statement ignores the hard physical work done by poor *white* women at home and in the factories and offices in "civilized" countries, and accepts a *ruling-class* definition of femininity.

The cause of women's relative decline in stature in more "civilized" countries is a subject on which Thomas is ambivalent. At one point he attributes it to the lack of "a superior fitness on the motor side" in women (Ibid.:94); at another point, he regards her loss of *sexual freedom* as critical, with the coming of monogamy and her confinement to sexual tasks such as wifehood and motherhood. He perceptively notes:

> Women were still further degraded by the development of property and its control by man, together with the habit of treating her as a piece of property, whose value was enhanced if its purity was assured (Ibid.:297).

However, Thomas' underlying assumptions in his explanations of the inferior status of women are *physiological ones*. He attributes to men high amounts of sexual energy, which lead them to pursue women for their sex, and he attributes to women maternal feelings devoid of sexuality, which lead *them* to exchange sex for domesticity. Thus monogamy, with chastity for women, is the *accommodation* of these basic urges, and women are domesticated while men assume leadership, in a true market exchange.

Why, then, does Thomas see problems in the position of women? It is because modern women are plagued by "irregularity, pettiness, ill health and inserviceableness" (Ibid.:245). Change is required to maintain *social harmony*, apart from considerations of women's needs, and women must be educated to make them better wives, a theme reiterated throughout this century by "liberals" on the subject. Correctly anticipating a threat, Thomas urges that change be made to stabilize the family, and warns that "no civilization can remain the highest if another civilization adds to the intelligence of its men the intelligence of its women" (Ibid.:314). Thomas is motivated by considerations of social integration. Of course, one might question how women are to be able to contribute much if they are indeed anabolic. However, due to the transitional nature of Thomas' work, there are immense contradictions in his writing.

Many of Thomas' specific assertions about the nature of women are indistinguishable from Lombroso's; they both delineate a biological hierarchy along race and sex lines.

> Man has, in short, become more somatically specialized an animal than women, and feels more keenly any disturbance of normal conditions with which he has not the same physiological surplus as woman with which to meet the disturbance. . . . It is a logical fact, however, that the lower human races, the lower classes of society, women and children show something of the same quality in their superior tolerance of surgical disease (Ibid.:36).

Like Lombroso, Thomas is crediting women with superior capabilities of survival because they are further down the scale in terms of evolution. It is significant that Thomas includes the lower classes in his observation; is he implying that the lower classes are in their position *because* of their natural unfitness, or perhaps that their *situation* renders them less sensitive to pain? At different times, Thomas implies both. Furthermore, he agrees with Lombroso that women are more nearly uniform than men, and says that they have a smaller percentage of "genius, insanity and idiocy" (Ibid.:45) than men, as well as fewer creative outbursts of energy.

Dealing with female criminality in *Sex and Society* (1907), Thomas begins to address the issue of morality, which he closely links to legality from a standpoint of maintaining social order. He discriminates between male and female morality:

> Morality as applied to men has a larger element of the contractual, representing the adjustment of his activities to those of society at large, or more particularly to the activities of the male members of society; while the morality which we think of in connection with women shows less of the contractual and more of the personal, representing her adjustment to men, more particularly the adjustment of her person to men (Ibid.:172).

Whereas Lombroso barely observes women's lack of participation in the institution of private property, Thomas' perception is more profound. He points out that women *are* property of men and that their conduct is subject to different codes.

> Morality, in the most general sense, represents the code under which activities are best carried on and is worked out in the school of experience. It is preeminently an adult and male system, and men are intelligent enough to realize

that neither women nor children have passed through this school. It is on this account that man is merciless to woman from the standpoint of personal behavior, yet he exempts her from anything in the way of contractual morality, or views her defections in this regard with allowance and even with amusement (Ibid.:234).

Disregarding his remarks about intelligence, one confronts the critical point about women with respect to the law: because they occupy a *marginal* position in the productive sphere of exchange commodities outside the home, they in turn occupy a marginal position in regard to "contractual" law which regulates relations of property and production. The argument of differential treatment of men and women by the law is developed in later works by Pollak and others, who attribute it to the "chivalry" of the system which is lenient to women committing offenses. As Thomas notes, however, women are simply not a serious *threat* to property, and are treated more "leniently" because of this. Certain women do become threats by transcending (or by being denied) their traditional role, particularly many Third World women and political rebels, and they are *not* afforded chivalrous treatment! In fact, chivalry is reserved for the women who are least likely to ever come in contact with the criminal justice system: the ladies, or white middle-class women. In matters of *sexual* conduct, however, which embody the double standard, women are rigorously prosecuted by the law. As Thomas understands, this is the sphere in which women's functions *are* critical. Thus it is not a matter of "chivalry" how one is handled, but of different forms and thrusts of social control applied to men and women. Men are engaged in productive tasks and their activities in this area *are* strictly curtailed.

In *The Unadjusted Girl* (1923), Thomas deals with female delinquency as a "normal" response under certain social conditions, using assumptions about the nature of women which he leaves unarticulated in this work. Driven by basic "wishes," an individual is controlled by society in her activities through institutional transmission of codes and mores. Depending on how they are manipulated, wishes can be made to serve social or antisocial ends. Thomas stresses the institutions that socialize, such as the family, giving people certain "definitions of the situation." He confidently—and defiantly—asserts:

> There is no individual energy, no unrest, no type of wish, which cannot be sublimated and made socially useful. From this standpoint, the problem is not the right of society to protect itself from the disorderly and antisocial person, but the right of the disorderly and antisocial person to be made orderly and socially valuable. . . . The problem of society is to produce the right attitudes in its members (Ibid.:232–233).

This is an important shift in perspective, from the traditional libertarian view of protecting society by punishing transgressors, to the *rehabilitative* and *preventive* perspective of crime control that seeks to control *minds* through socialization rather than to merely control behavior through punishment. The autonomy of the individual to choose is seen as the product of his environment which the state can alter. This is an important refutation of the Lombrosian biological perspective, which maintains that there are crime-prone individuals who must be locked up, sterilized or otherwise incapacitated. Today, one can see an amalgamation of the two perspectives in new theories of "behavior control" that use tactics such as conditioning and brain surgery, combining biological and environmental viewpoints.[3]

Thomas proposes the manipulation of individuals through institutions to prevent antisocial attitudes, and maintains that there is no such person as the "crime prone" individual. A hegemonic system of belief can be imposed by sublimating natural urges and by correcting the poor socialization of slum families. In this perspective, the *definition* of the situation rather than the situation *itself* is what should be changed; a situation is what someone *thinks* it is. The response to a criminal woman who is dissatisfied with her conventional sexual roles is to change not the roles, which would mean widespread social transformations, but to change her attitudes. This concept of civilization as repressive and the need to adjust is later refined by Freud.

Middle class women, according to Thomas, commit little crime because they are socialized to sublimate their natural desires and to behave well, treasuring their chastity as an investment. The poor woman, however, "is not immoral, because this implies a loss of morality, but amoral" (Ibid.:98). Poor women are not objectively driven to crime; they long for it. Delinquent girls are motivated by the desire for excitement or "new experience," and forget the repressive urge of "security." However, these desires are well within Thomas' conception of *femininity*: delinquents are not rebelling against womanhood, as Lombroso suggests, but merely acting it out illegally. Davis and Pollak agree with this notion that delinquent women are not "different" from nondelinquent women.

Thomas maintains that it is not sexual desire that motivates delinquent girls, for they are no more passionate than other women, but they are *manipulating* male desires for sex to achieve their own ulterior ends.

> The beginning of delinquency in girls is usually an impulse to get amusement, adventure, pretty clothes, favorable notice, distinction, freedom in the larger world. . . . The girls have usually become "wild" before the devel-

opment of sexual desire, and their casual sex relations do not usually awaken sex feeling. Their sex is used as a condition of the realization of other wishes. It is their capital (Ibid.:109).

Here Thomas is expanding on the myth of the manipulative woman, who is cold and scheming and vain. To him, good female sexual behavior is a protective measure—"instinctive, of course" (1907:241), whereas male behavior is uncontrollable as men are caught by helpless desires. This is the common Victorian notion of the woman as seductress which in turn perpetuates the myth of a lack of real sexuality to justify her responsibility for upholding sexual mores. Thomas uses a market analogy to female virtue: good women *keep* their bodies as capital to sell in matrimony for marriage and security, whereas bad women *trade* their bodies for excitement. One notes, of course, the familiar dichotomy. It is difficult, in this framework, to see how Thomas can make *any* moral distinctions, since morality seems to be merely good business sense. In fact, Thomas' yardstick is social harmony, necessitating *control*.

Thomas shows an insensitivity to real human relationships and needs. He also shows ignorance of economic hardships in his denial of economic factors in delinquency.

> An unattached woman has a tendency to become an adventuress not so much on economic as on psychological grounds. Life is rarely so hard that a young woman cannot earn her bread; but she cannot always live and have the stimulation she craves (Ibid.:241).

This is an amazing statement in an era of mass starvation and illness! He rejects economic causes as a possibility at all, denying its importance in criminal activity with as much certainty as Lombroso, Freud, Davis, Pollak and most other writers.

FREUD: "BEAUTY, CHARM AND SWEETNESS"

The Freudian theory of the position of women is grounded in explicit biological assumptions about their nature, expressed by the famous "Anatomy is Destiny." Built upon this foundation is a construction incorporating psychological and social-structural factors.

Freud himself sees women as anatomically inferior; they are destined to be wives and mothers, and this admittedly an inferior destiny as befits the inferior sex. The root of this inferiority is that women's *sex organs* are inferior to those of men, a fact *universally* recognized by children in the Freudian scheme. The girl assumes that she has lost a penis as punishment, is traumatized, and grows up envious and revengeful. The boy also sees the girl as having lost a penis, fears a similar punishment himself, and dreads the girl's envy and vengeance. Feminine traits can be traced to the inferior genitals themselves, or to women's inferiority complex arising from their response to them: women are exhibitionistic, narcissistic, and attempt to compensate for their lack of a penis by being well-dressed and physically beautiful. Women become mothers trying to replace the lost penis with a baby. Women are also masochistic, as Lombroso and Thomas have noted, because their *sexual* role is one of receptor, and their sexual pleasure consists of pain. This woman, Freud notes, is the *healthy* woman. In the familiar dichotomy, the men are aggressive and pain inflicting. Freud comments:

> The male pursues the female for the purposes of sexual union, seizes hold of her, and penetrates into her . . . by this you have precisely reduced the characteristic of masculinity to the factor of aggressiveness (Millett, 1970:189).

Freud, like Lombroso and Thomas, takes the notion of men's activity and women's inactivity and *reduces* it to the sexual level, seeing the sexual union itself through Victorian eyes; ladies don't move.

Women are also inferior in the sense that they are concerned with personal matters and have little social sense. Freud sees civilization as based on repression of the sex drive, where it is the duty of men to repress their strong instincts in order to get on with the worldly business of civilization. Women, on the other hand,

> have little sense of justice, and this is no doubt connected with the preponderance of envy in their mental life; for the demands of justice are a modification of envy; they lay down the conditions under which one is willing to part with it. We also say of women that their social interests are weaker than those of men and that their capacity for the sublimation of their instincts is less (1933:183).

Men are capable of sublimating their individual needs because they rationally perceive the Hobbesian conflict between those urges and social needs. Women are emotional and incapable of such an adjustment because of their innate inability to make such rational judgments. It is only fair then that they should have a marginal relation to production and property.

In this framework, the deviant woman is one who is attempting to be a *man*. She is aggressively rebellious, and her drive to accomplishment is the expression of her longing for a penis; this is a hopeless pursuit, of course, and she will only end up "neurotic." Thus the deviant woman should be treated and helped to *adjust* to her sex role. Here again, as in Thomas' writing, is the notion of individual accommodation that repudiates the possibility of social change.

In a Victorian fashion, Freud rationalizes women's oppression by glorifying their duties as wives and mothers:

It is really a stillborn thought to send women into the struggle for existence exactly the same as men. If, for instance, I imagined my sweet gentle girl as a competitor, it would only end in my telling her, as I did seventeen months ago, that I am fond of her, and I implore her to withdraw from the strife into the calm, uncompetitive activity of my home. . . . Nature has determined woman's destiny through beauty, charm and sweetness . . . in youth an adored darling, in mature years a loved wife (Jones, 1961:117–118).

In speaking of femininity, Freud, like his forebearers, is speaking along racist and classist lines. Only upper and middle class women could possibly enjoy lives as sheltered darlings. Freud sets hegemonic standards of femininity for poor and Third World women.

It is important to understand Freudianism because it reduces categories of sexual ideology to explicit sexuality and makes these categories *scientific*. For the last fifty years, Freudianism has been a mainstay of sexist social theory. Kate Millett notes that Freud himself saw his work as stemming the tide of feminist revolution, which he constantly ridiculed:

> Coming as it did, at the peak of the sexual revolution, Freud's doctrine of penis envy is in fact a superbly timed accusation, enabling masculine sentiment to take the offensive again as it had not since the disappearance of overt misogyny when the pose of chivalry became fashionable (Millett, 1970:189).

Freudian notions of the repression of sexual instincts, the sexual passivity of women, and the sanctity of the nuclear family are conservative not only in their contemporary context, but in the context of their own time. Hitler writes:

> For her [woman's] world is her husband, her family, her children and her home. . . . The man upholds the nation as the woman upholds the family. The equal rights of women consist in

the fact that in the realm of life determined for her by nature, she experience the high esteem that is her due. Woman and man represent quite different types of being. Reason is dominant in man. . . . Feeling, in contrast, is much more stable than reason, and woman is the feeling, and therefore the stable, element (Ibid.:170).

One can mark the decline in the position of women after the 1920's through the use of various indices: by noting the progressively earlier age of marriage of women in the United States and the steady rise in the number of children born to them, culminating in the birth explosion of the late forties and fifties; by looking at the relative decline in the number of women scholars; and by seeing the failure to liberate women in the Soviet Union and the rise of fascist sexual ideology. Freudianism has had an unparalleled influence in the United States (and came at a key point to help swing the tide against the women's movement) to facilitate the return of women during the depression and postwar years to the home, out of an economy which had no room for them. Freud affected such writers on female deviance as Davis, Pollak and Konopka, who turn to concepts of sexual maladjustment and neurosis to explain women's criminality. Healthy women would now be seen as masochistic, passive and sexually indifferent. Criminal women would be seen as *sexual* misfits. Most importantly, *psychological* factors would be used to explain criminal activity, and social, economic and political factors would be ignored. Explanations would seek to be *universal*, and historical possibilities of change would be refuted.

DAVIS: "THE MOST CONVENIENT SEXUAL OUTLET FOR ARMIES . . ."

Kingsley Davis' work on prostitution (1961) is still considered a classical analysis on the subject with a structural-functionalist perspective. It employs assumptions about "the organic nature of man" and woman, many of which can be traced to ideas proffered by Thomas and Freud.

Davis sees prostitution as a structural necessity whose roots lie in the *sexual* nature of men and women; for example, female humans, unlike primates, are sexually available year-round. He asserts that prostitution is *universal* in time and place, eliminating the possibilities of historical change and ignoring critical differences in the quality and quantity of prostitution in different societies. He maintains that there will always be a class of women who will be prostitutes, the familiar class of "bad" women. The reason for the universality of prostitution is that sexual *repression*, a concept stressed by Thomas and Freud, is essential to the functioning of society. Once again there is the notion of sublimating "natural" sex urges to the overall needs of society, namely social order. Davis notes that in our society sexuality is permitted only within the structure of the nuclear family, which is an institution of stability. He does not, however, analyze in depth the economic and social functions of the family, other than to say it is a bulwark of morality.

> The norms of every society tend to harness and control the sexual appetite, and one of the ways of doing this is to link the sexual act to some stable or potentially stable social relationship. . . . Men dominate women in economic, sexual and familial relationships and consider them to some extent as sexual property, to be prohibited to other males. They therefore find promiscuity on the part of women repugnant (Ibid.:264).

Davis is linking the concept of prostitution to promiscuity, defining it as a *sexual* crime, and calling prostitutes sexual transgressors. Its origins, he claims, lie not in economic hardship, but in the marital restraints on sexuality.

As long as men seek women, prostitutes will be in demand. One wonders why sex-seeking women have not created a class of male prostitutes.

Davis sees the only possibility of eliminating prostitution in the liberalization of sexual mores, although he is pessimistic about the likelihood of total elimination. In light of the contemporary American "sexual revolution" of commercial sex, which has surely created more prostitutes and semi-prostitutes rather than eliminating the phenomenon, and in considering the revolution in China where, despite a "puritanical" outlook on sexuality, prostitution has largely been eliminated through major economic and social change, the superficiality of Davis' approach becomes evident. Without dealing with root economic, social and political factors, one cannot analyze prostitution.

Davis shows Freudian pessimism about the nature of sexual repression:

> We can imagine a social system in which the motive for prostitution would be completely absent, but we cannot imagine that the system will ever come to pass. It would be a regime of absolute sexual freedom with intercourse practiced solely for pleasure by both parties. There would be no institutional control of sexual expression. . . . All sexual desire would have to be mutually complementary. . . . Since the basic causes of prostitution—the institutional control of sex, the unequal scale of attractiveness, and the presence of economic and social inequalities between classes and between males and females—are not likely to disappear, prostitution is not likely to disappear either (Ibid.:286).

By talking about "complementary desire," Davis is using a marketplace notion of sex: two attractive or unattractive people are drawn to each other and exchange sexual favors; people are placed on a scale of attractiveness and may be rejected by people above them on the scale; hence they *(men)* become frustrated and demand prostitutes. Women who become prostitutes do so for good pay *and* sexual pleasure. Thus one has a neat little system in which everyone benefits.

> Enabling a small number of women to take care of the needs of a large number of men, it is the most convenient sexual outlet for armies, for the legions of strangers, perverts and physically repulsive in our midst (Ibid.:288).

Prostitution "functions," therefore it must be good. Davis, like Thomas, is motivated by concerns of social order rather than by concerns of what the needs and desires of the women involved might be. He denies that the women involved are economically oppressed; they are on the streets through autonomous, *individual* choice.

> Some women physically enjoy the intercourse they sell. From a purely economic point of view, prostitution comes near the situation of getting something for nothing. . . . Women's wages could scarcely be raised significantly without also raising men's. Men would then have more to spend on prostitution (Ibid.:277).

It is important to understand that, given a *sexual* interpretation of what is an *economic* crime, and given a refusal to consider widespread change (even equalization of wages, hardly a revolutionary act), Davis' conclusion is the logical technocratic solution.

In this framework, the deviant women are merely adjusting to their feminine role in an illegitimate fashion, as Thomas has theorized. They are *not* attempting to be rebels or to be "men," as Lombroso's and Freud's positions suggest. Although Davis sees the main difference between wives and prostitutes in a macrosocial sense as the difference merely between legal and illegal roles, in a personal sense he sees the women who *choose* prostitution as maladjusted and neurotic. However, given the universal necessity for prostitution, this analysis implies the necessity of having a perpetually ill and maladjusted class of women. Thus oppression is *built into* the system, and a healthy *system* makes for a sick *individual*. Here Davis is integrating Thomas' notions of social integration with Freudian perspectives on neurosis and maladjustment.

POLLAK: "A DIFFERENT ATTITUDE TOWARD VERACITY"

Otto Pollak's *The Criminality of Women* (1950) has had an outstanding influence on the field of women and crime, being the major work on the subject in the postwar years. Pollak advances the theory of "hidden" female crime to account for what he considers unreasonably low official rates for women.

A major reason for the existence of hidden crime, as he sees it, lies in the *nature* of women themselves. They are instigators rather than perpetrators of criminal activity. While Pollak admits that this role is partly a socially enforced one, he insists that women are inherently deceitful for *physiological* reasons.

> Man must achieve an erection in order to perform the sex act and will not be able to hide his failure. His lack of positive emotion in the sexual sphere must become overt to the partner, and pretense of sexual response is impossible for him, if it is lacking. Woman's body, however, permits such pretense to a certain degree and lack of orgasm does not prevent her ability to participate in the sex act (Ibid.:10).

Pollak *reduces* women's nature to the *sex act*, as Freud has done, and finds women inherently more capable of manipulation, accustomed to being sly, passive and passionless. As Thomas suggests, women can use sex for ulterior purposes. Furthermore, Pollak suggests that women are innately deceitful on yet another level:

> Our sex mores force women to conceal every four weeks the period of menstruation. . . .

They thus make concealment and misrepresentation in the eyes of women socially required and must condition them to a different attitude toward veracity than men (Ibid.:11).

Women's abilities at concealment thus allow them to successfully commit crimes in stealth.

Women are also vengeful. Menstruation, in the classic Freudian sense, seals their doomed hopes to become men and arouses women's desire for vengeance, especially during that time of the month. Thus Pollak offers new rationalizations to bolster old myths.

A second factor in hidden crime is the roles played by women which furnish them with opportunities as domestics, nurses, teachers and housewives to commit undetectable crimes. The *kinds* of crimes women commit reflect their nature: false accusation, for example, is an outgrowth of women's treachery, spite or fear and is a sign of neurosis; shoplifting can be traced in many cases to a special mental disease—kleptomania. Economic factors play a minor role; *sexual-psychological* factors account for female criminality. Crime in women is *personalized* and often accounted for by mental illness. Pollak notes:

> Robbery and burglary . . . are considered specifically male offenses since they represent the pursuit of monetary gain by overt action. . . . Those cases of female robbery which seem to express a tendency toward masculinization comes from . . . [areas] where social conditions have favored the assumptions of male pursuits by women. . . . The female offenders usually retain some trace of femininity, however, and even so glaring an example of masculinization as the "Michigan Babes," an all woman gang of robbers in Chicago, shows a typically feminine trait in the modus operandi (Ibid.:29).

Pollak is defining crimes with economic motives that employ overt action as *masculine*, and defining as *feminine* those crimes for *sexual* activity, such as luring men as baits.

Thus he is using circular reasoning by saying that feminine crime is feminine. To fit women into the scheme and justify the statistics, he must invent the notion of hidden crime.

It is important to recognize that, to some extent, women *do* adapt to their enforced sexual roles and may be more likely to instigate, to use sexual traps, and to conform to all the other feminine role expectations. However, it is not accidental that theorists label women as conforming even when they are *not*; for example, by inventing sexual motives for what are clearly crimes of economic necessity, or by invoking "mental illness" such as kleptomania for shoplifting. It is difficult to separate the *theory* from the *reality*, since the reality of female crime is largely unknown. But it is not difficult to see that Pollak is using sexist terms and making sexist assumptions to advance theories of hidden female crime.

Pollak, then, sees criminal women as extending their sexual role, like Davis and Thomas, by using sexuality for ulterior purposes. He suggests that the condemnation of extramarital sex has "delivered men who engage in such conduct as practically helpless victims" (Ibid.:152) into the hands of women blackmailers, overlooking completely the possibility of men blackmailing women, which would seem more likely, given the greater taboo on sex for women and their greater risks of being punished.

The final factor that Pollak advances as a root cause of hidden crime is that of "chivalry" in the criminal justice system. Pollak uses Thomas' observation that women are differentially treated by the law, and carries it to a sweeping conclusion based on *cultural* analyses of men's feelings toward women.

> One of the outstanding concomitants of the existing inequality . . . is chivalry, and the general protective attitude of man toward women. . . . Men hate to accuse women and thus indirectly to send them to their punishment, police officers dislike to arrest them, district attorneys

to prosecute them, judges and juries to find them guilty, and so on (Ibid.:151).

Pollak rejects the possibility of an actual discrepancy between crime rates for men and women; therefore, he must look for factors to expand the scope of female crime. He assumes that there is chivalry in the criminal justice system that is extended to the women who come in contact with it. Yet the women involved are likely to be poor and Third World women or white middle-class women who have stepped *outside* the definitions of femininity to become hippies or political rebels, and chivalry is *not* likely to be extended to them. Chivalry is a racist and classist concept founded on the notion of women as "ladies" which applies only to wealthy white women and ignores the double sexual standard. These "ladies," however, are the least likely women to ever come in contact with the criminal justice system in the first place.[4]

THE LEGACY OF SEXISM

A major purpose in tracing the development and interaction of ideas pertaining to sexual ideology based on implicit assumptions of the inherent nature of women throughout the works of Lombroso, Thomas, Freud, Davis and Pollak, is to clarify their positions in relation to writers in the field today. One can see the influence their ideas still have by looking at a number of contemporary theorists on female criminality. . . .[5]

Crime defined as masculine seems to mean violent, overt crime, whereas "ladylike" crime usually refers to sexual violations and shoplifting. Women are neatly categorized no matter *which* kind of crime they commit: if they are violent, they are "masculine" and suffering from chromosomal deficiencies, penis envy, or atavisms. If they conform, they are manipulative, sexually maladjusted and promiscuous. The *economic* and *social* realities of crime—the fact that poor women commit crimes, and that most crimes for women are property offenses—are overlooked. Women's behavior must be *sexually* defined before it will be considered, for women count only in the sexual sphere. The theme of sexuality is a unifying thread in the various, often contradictory theories.

CONCLUSION

A good deal of the writing on women and crime being done at the present time is squarely in the tradition of the writers that have been discussed. The basic assumptions and technocratic concerns of these writers have produced work that is sexist, racist and classist; assumptions that have served to maintain a repressive ideology with its extensive apparatus of control. To do a new kind of research on women and crime—one that has feminist roots and a radical orientation—it is necessary to understand the assumptions made by the traditional writers and to break away from them. Work that focuses on human needs, rather than those of the state, will require new definitions of criminality, women, the individual and her/his relation to the state. It is beyond the scope of this paper to develop possible areas of study, but it is nonetheless imperative that this work be made a priority by women *and* men in the future.

NOTES

1. Quoted from the 1973 proposal for the Center for the Study and Reduction of Violence prepared by Dr. Louis J. West, Director, Neuropsychiatric Institute, UCLA: "The question of violence in females will be examined from the point of view that females are more likely to commit acts of violence during the premenstrual and menstrual periods" (1973:43).

2. I am indebted to Marion Goldman for introducing me to the notion of the dual morality based on assumptions of different sexuality for men and women.

3. For a discussion of the possibilities of psychosurgery in behavior modification for "violence-prone" individuals, see Frank Ervin and Vernon Mark, *Violence and the Brain* (1970). For an eclectic view of this perspective on crime, see the proposal for the Center for the Study and Reduction of Violence (footnote 1).

4. The concept of hidden crime is reiterated in Reckless and Kay's report to the President's Commission on Law Enforcement and the Administration of Justice. They note:

   "A large part of the infrequent officially acted upon involvement of women in crime can be traced to the masking effect of women's roles, effective practice on the part of women of deceit and indirection, their instigation of men to commit their crimes (the Lady MacBeth factor), and the unwillingness on the part of the public and law enforcement officials to hold women accountable for their deeds (the chivalry factor)" (1967:13).

5. See original publication's discussion of earlier writers' impact on contemporary (1960s) theorists.

REFERENCES

Bishop, Cecil. *Women and Crime*. London: Chatto and Windus, 1931.

Cowie, John, Valerie Cowie and Eliot Slater. *Delinquency in Girls*. London: Heinemann, 1968.

Davis, Kingsley. "Prostitution." *Contemporary Social Problems*. Edited by Robert K. Merton and Robert A. Nisbet. New York: Harcourt Brace and Jovanovich, 1961. Originally published as "The Sociology of Prostitution." *American Sociological Review* 2(5) (October 1937).

Ervin, Frank, and Vernon Mark. *Violence and the Brain*. New York: Harper and Row, 1970.

Fernald, Mabel, Mary Hayes and Almena Dawley. *A Study of Women Delinquents in New York State*, New York: Century Company, 1920.

Freud, Sigmund. *New Introductory Lectures on Psychoanalysis*. New York: W. W. Norton, 1933.

Glueck, Eleanor and Sheldon. *Four Hundred Delinquent Women*. New York: Alfred A. Knopf, 1934.

Healy, William, and Augusta Bronner, *Delinquents and Criminals: Their Making and Unmaking*. New York: Macmillan and Company, 1926.

Hemming, James. *Problems of Adolescent Girls*. London: Heinemann, 1960.

Jones, Ernest. *The Life and Works of Sigmund Freud*. New York: Basic Books, 1961.

Konopka, Gisela. *The Adolescent Girl in Conflict*, Englewood Cliffs, N.J.: Prentice-Hall, 1966.

Lombroso, Cesare. *The Female Offender*. (Translation). New York: Appleton, 1920. Originally published in 1903.

Millett, Kate. *Sexual Politics*. New York: Doubleday and Company, 1970.

Monahan, Florence. *Women in Crime*. New York: I. Washburn, 1941.

Parsons, Talcott. "Age and Sex in the Social Structure." *American Sociological Review* 7 (October 1942).

Parsons, Talcott, and Renée Fox. "Illness, Therapy and the Modern 'Urban' American Family." *The Family*. Edited by Norman Bell and Ezra Vogel. Glencoe, Ill.: The Free Press, 1960.

Payak, Bertha. "Understanding the Female Offender." Federal Probation XXVIL (1963).

Pollak, Otto. *The Criminality of Women*. Philadelphia: University of Pennsylvania Press, 1950.

Reckless, Walter, and Barbara Kay. *The Female Offender*. Report to the President's Commission on Law Enforcement and the Administration of Justice. Washington, D.C.: U.S. Government Printing Office, 1967.

Sarbin, Theodore R., and Jeffrey E. Miller. "Demonism Revisited: The XYY Chromosomal Anomaly." *Issues in Criminology* 5(2)(Summer 1970).

Schwendinger, Herman and Julia. "The Founding Fathers: Sexists to a Man." *Sociologists of the Chair*. New York: Basic Books, 1973.

Spaulding, Edith. *An Experimental Study of Psychopathic Delinquent Women*. New York: Rand McNally, 1923.

Thomas, W. I. *Sex and Society*. Boston: Little, Brown and Company, 1907.

Thomas, W. I. *The Unadjusted Girl*. New York: Harper and Row, 1923.

Vedder, Clyde, and Dora Somerville. *The Delinquent Girl*. Springfield, Ill.: Charles C. Thomas, 1970.

West, Dr. Louis J. *Proposal for the Center for the Study and Reduction of Violence*. Neuropsychiatric Institute, UCLA (April 10, 1973).

Zelditch, Morris, Jr. "Role Differentiation in the Nuclear Family: A Comparative Study." *The Family*. Edited by Norman Bell and Ezra Vogel. Glencoe, Illinois: The Free Press, 1960.

AFTERWORD

TWENTY YEARS AGO . . . TODAY*

"The Etiology of Female Crime: A Review of the Literature," written two decades ago, ended in a call for "a new kind of research on women and crime—one that has feminist roots and a radical orientation . . . that focuses on human needs, rather than those of the state, [and that] will require new definitions of criminality, women, the individual and her/his relation to the state." At that time, in 1973, there was a new women's movement, paralleling other international and domestic liberation movements. It consisted of thousands of women forming groups, reading the few books or articles available, demonstrating, writing, and swapping pamphlets. At the School of Criminology at the University of California, Berkeley, where I was studying, there flourished a radical, oppositional criminology, determined to remake the field in the image of the movements of the time: prisoners' rights, community control of the police, and decriminalization of victimless offenses.

---

*This Afterword was written expressly for inclusion in this text.

The presence of a critical mass of politically active women graduate students, at a time when few criminologists were female, allowed us to share and build on what little knowledge we had.[1] At that time there were no professional ethnographies of women lawbreakers, no recent theoretical readings in criminology that centered on women or gender, no studies of female prisoners that did not focus on their homosexuality or "affective" needs.

For a term paper, I decided to take what had been written on the causes of women's offenses and scrutinize it for its unexamined assumptions about women offenders.[2] Writing up what I found, I wondered naively, angrily, how, in our era and given the women's movement, such stereotypes about women could be taken seriously. The paper appeared in the special issue devoted to women by the School's journal (*Issues in Criminology*, 1973).

In the years since, the feminist critique of mainstream academic disciplines has exploded in volume and advanced light-years in depth, and interest in the issues of women, crime, victimization, and justice has also grown. Today "Etiology" may strike one as a long-ago first step, the passionate reaction of a beginner armed with the rhetoric of a young movement.

But have the concerns and hopes voiced in "Etiology" been met, or vanished with time? I would suggest neither; rather, they have been expressed in numerous ways and in the process gone through sea changes. In this Afterword, I will pose the challenge for feminist criminology in three areas which trace a common history to "Etiology" and hold importance for the future: the scientific basis of theories, the gender and racial bias in science, and the definition of crime. The common thread of my discussion is a simple premise: It is time to move away from considering "the feminist question in criminology" and toward exploring "the criminology question in feminism" (see Bertrand, 1991, paraphrasing Harding). Specifically, how can feminist insights into gender, power, and knowledge help us critically examine our understanding of crime, criminality, and victimization?

1. The debates over the scientific basis of theories of women's and men's behaviors have continued fiercely over two decades, although with new twists and turns around questions of biology and psychology.

Most recently, feminist philosophical and scientific critiques have argued that for many traditional European-identified thinkers, including Lombroso and his followers, femaleness was associated with biology or nature (e.g., primitive, irrational, nurturing), in contrast to male civilization. What is especially radical about these recent critiques is that they do not merely challenge the gender assignment of certain constructs, as earlier feminist work did (e.g., femaleness as a Lombrosian primitive). Rather, they question the very validity of these dichotomies: nature *versus* civilization, emotion *versus* reason, developed *versus* undeveloped world, female *versus* male (see Benhabib and Cornell, 1987; Nicholson, 1990; Sunstein, 1990).

The contemporary feminist argument is this: a quality that appears natural or biological must not be exclusively assigned to a gender; this very quality may be a historical ideological construction rather than an eternal objective truth. Woman herself is a constructed "Other," in Simone de Beauvoir's classic phrase, who by definition exists only in contrast to man. This is much like the criminal, who cannot exist without the contrast of the law-abiding citizen. Women, like minority-group members, criminals, and other relatively less powerful "Others," tend to be perceived in the dominant culture more one-dimensionally, more restrictively, than their opposites. Hence one finds the origins of the stereotyping of female offenders in traditional criminology, as discussed in "Etiology."

In contemporary criminology, on the other hand, there is now agreement that differences in women's and men's behaviors are social rather than natural, just as there is agreement that the sources of criminality are social rather than natural. Very few criminologists today argue that prostitution or shoplifting emerges out of women's nature or that violence is hormonal. More generally, few theories of criminality are based on nature. To this extent, criminology has moved away from overt biologism.[3] However, criminological work on women continues to focus on their experiences or qualities as they exist in comparison with those of men: in other words, the differences between the genders. Moreover, much work on women focuses uncritically on sexuality: first, as a natural, as opposed to a social, force, and second, as a female, rather than male, concern. Furthermore, in nearly all criminology, maleness remains the universal, femaleness the special case.

During the years, feminists have also wrestled with theoretical psychological perspectives on gender and sexuality, reexamining Freudianism with a far more sophisticated eye (certainly more so than mine in 1973!). One objective, among others, has been to understand how and why women and men are in fact made, as opposed to being born. The spotlight has been on such "gender factories" as families, although much of the psychoanalytic theorization is limited in its relevance to affluent populations in modern Western societies.

Within feminist and critical criminology, there is much distrust of psychology as the discourse used in "blaming the victim" and in the practices of social control. Within radical and critical feminism in general, there is

similar distrust of psychological approaches to gender domination, such as those that put primacy on sex roles. Structurally oriented and Marxist-influenced feminisms have instead focused on large-scale institutional and cultural aspects of life, such as the division of paid and unpaid labor.

Yet today there is interest in exploring people's personal choices as well as their structural constraints: in other words, in deepening our understanding of the subjective relations between an individual and society. For example, there has been the intriguing and much-debated work of Carol Gilligan (1982) on differences in women's and men's views of morality. One question now being asked of any psychological theory of gender is not so much what is its specific content, but upon what scientific basis is it making psychological claims about gender differences? Is a psychological theory, for example, implicitly biological (e.g., resting on women's childbearing capacity), psychoanalytic, culturally bound (e.g., based on women's childrearing role), or structural?

Much mainstream criminology today, like the positivist correctionalism of the past, is psychological in orientation, focusing on the personal characteristics of known offenders and victims. Only recently has this criminology shown any likelihood of drawing upon feminist work, with recent attention paid to the possibilities of investigating why certain forms of criminality are disproportionately male behaviors.

In the 1970s and early 1980s, many feminist scholars in different fields, abandoning biology and psychology, searched for the social roots of women's oppression, which cuts across many eras and cultures. Most argued that whatever the causes of patriarchy, they were due to the structuring of gender rather than either to the biological fact of sexual difference or to differential psychological development alone.[4]

Some feminist scholars have recently called for abandoning the search for the primary universal social cause of sexism, not because the search has failed but because, they argue, there is no such thing. Rather, they argue, there are diverse, geographically specific, historically varying causes and fragmented standpoints inclusive of gender and other (ethnic, class, sexual) forces (Nicholson, 1990).

This brings us to the contemporary feminist argument I noted at the outset, which states, at its most extreme, that it is not just the dualism of femininity/masculinity that is socially constructed but femaleness/maleness itself. It is not the existence of two genders that generates sexism but the other way around; in other words, women and men are not just made, but made up. Not only is there no essential woman's nature, as traditionalists (and some feminists) have believed. And not only is there no universal female experience, as most feminists have heretofore argued, in their advocacy of sisterhood. That we divide humans into two genders is a social artifact, according to this radical new argument, and the way this division happens differs enormously across eras and societies.

This approach to the study of gender, and hence of sexism with all its institutional and ideological facets, parallels schools of thought that view many taken-for-granted concepts and problems as socially constructed rather than as naturally occurring or arising spontaneously in society. One particular example is race, and another is crime. What this approach suggests is not that real experiences around gender, race, or crime do not exist. It means that how we label and explain these experiences involves fluid choices rather than inevitabilities. There are no essences to such concepts as woman or man, black or white, criminal or victim, other than what we attach to them. What it means to be a woman or man, black or white, a criminal or victim

changes dramatically with time and varies tremendously across cultures.

After acknowledging that something is socially constructed, there is still much to be done. Sexism, no more than racism or crime, cannot be "deconstructed" away by academic analysis such as the aforementioned. We want to know how and, if possible, who and why, and, above all, what to do about it. This practical urgency will require the continuous generation of "feminist roots and a radical orientation" for criminology as it considers specific victimizations and injustices.

2. A second, related aspect of the feminist critique concerns the question of whether science and expertise are fundamentally gendered and racially based.

Within criminology, the necessary first steps of this critique, including those begun in "Etiology," were to challenge traditional assumptions about women, redirect the search for the causes of women's behaviors to their circumstances and experiences, and implicitly hold out the desirability of a fuller range of experiences and behaviors open to all, regardless of gender.

But the next steps were to explore whether science and philosophy are masculine in an even more profound sense than merely male-dominated and male-oriented. Only recently has feminism undertaken critiques of both science and law as gendered in method and philosophical base as well as in overt content (Benhabib and Cornell, 1987; Nicholson, 1990; Sunstein, 1990). In other words, the argument is that the fundamental premises of science and law are not neutral with respect to gender or with respect to cultural ethnicity. It has been difficult to see these biases because they are hidden in taken-for-granted ways of conceptualization, often nearly invisible.

One task, along with making visible and depathologizing femaleness in science and law, is to make visible and denormalize maleness. Unfortunately, criminology and criminal law have not yet been subjected to this level of critique, although recent efforts have been made (Daly and Chesney-Lind, 1988; Smart, 1989). As was true 20 years ago, criminology is implicitly about men, unless it is feminist—in which case it is only about women! And much of the latter is restricted to querying which traditional (masculinist) theories may pertain to women's behaviors!

An example of how criminology might conduct this critique of criminology as fundamentally gendered would be to use the problem of women not being taken seriously as victims and witnesses. Alongside the challenges to common negative images of women victims/witnesses (untrustworthy, provocative, complicit), we would analyze for its gendered content the normal or idealized positive image of the victim/witness (uninvolved with the victimizer, randomly chosen, harmed in public). One question would be, Is this an implicitly male victim/witness?

Another undone task is to constitute a feminist epistemology and methodology, and there has been much debate over what these might look like, if grounded in women's experiences. There has been little development of an explicitly feminist criminological methodology, although some recent studies of women offenders and victims attempt to involve them as subjects rather than examine them as objects. There is only a glimmer of understanding of exactly how women are made the objects of knowledge and power, of the unconscious male identification of the omniscient gaze of experts in criminology (see Benhabib and Cornell, 1987; Diamond and Quinby, 1988). To see the nexus of policing and correctional power, one must first transgress the traditional framework of criminology (Cain, 1989).

For those attempting to reorient their gaze from that of the controller to the standpoint of the dominated, the question changes from What should the discipline do with these people? to How can certain groups of people use the discipline?

One aspect of this shift must be the denormalizing and stepping outside of the dominant ethnic perspective. Race, unlike gender, has never been ignored in criminology, but this is not to say that mainstream criminology has sensitively or accurately addressed the deep and complex associations between criminalization and racism, or between violence and inequality.[5]

Critical criminology, from the days of "Etiology" onward, certainly has perceived the enormous effects of race and class on criminal justice. A basic premise has been that correctionalism serves to shape and control the lives of the lower classes and people of color, incorporating different strategies: sometimes universalizing standards of the affluent, other times applying differential standards for the poor.

Nonetheless, there has been little development of these issues within either the critical or feminist paradigms during the past 20 years. There has been scant in-depth examination of criminal justice in minority communities. Among feminists, there has been infrequent intellectual exchange between those concerned with criminalized women offenders, who emphasize the repressive and racist character of criminal justice, and those supporting victims of violence, who emphasize the protective and potentially reconciliatory aspects (Klein, 1988). Yet feminist criminology has the greatest potential of any discipline to make these connections (Bertrand, Daly, and Klein, 1992). Women in minority communities often directly perceive criminal justice as neither simple protector nor mere oppressor but as the hydra-headed hybrid it is (Gordon, 1988; Klein, 1990). Feminist criminology would benefit from a reexamination of criminal justice from these women's viewpoint, thus addressing "human needs, rather than those of the state."

3. A third issue that feminist criminology must tackle is that of the definition of crime. As an applied field, criminology has tended to take its scope of study from government and policy rather than chart its own course. But to say merely that crime is anything that breaks the law, while self-evident, is tautological. Crime certainly has no natural or universal status. In fact, formerly criminalized activities are continually being legalized, such as abortion or (in Nevada) prostitution; and new crimes are continually being politically constructed, as in the case of recent laws on domestic violence (Klein, 1981). To take for granted the official definition of crime is to forgo both an analysis of the roots of law and the penal system and the possibility of developing alternative visions of justice.

Early radical criminologists of the 1970s, while not always explicitly challenging the official definition of crime in every discussion such as "Etiology," rarely accepted it as given, arguing that it is steeped in racial and class and gender domination. Which activities are legal and which illegal and which laws are enforced are connected to the relative degrees of power of those involved. Many of us were very much aware of the necessity for disaggregating and transforming the suspect category crime (Schwendinger and Schwendinger, 1970). Yet even now this enterprise remains in the formative stages.

The feminist critique has the specific potential to contribute to what could be called the deconstruction of the taken-for-granted concept we call crime, through the prism of gender. Both law and order, on the one hand, and its opposite, criminality, on the other, are very much linked to complex constructions of power, including masculinity. But these possible connections are concealed by layers of rarely debated official morality.

In more practical terms, feminists have wrestled with whether to advocate the enhancement or the abolition of the criminal justice "apparatus of control." An example of the dilemma is the feminist debate over criminalizing violent or harmful pornography. Recently there have emerged tentative discussions about what feminist justice might look like (Gilligan, 1982; Daly, 1989; Sunstein, 1990; Bertrand, Daly, and Klein, 1992). Despite many disagreements over the potential role of criminal justice, there is consensus that it should not resemble the existing cycles of partial punishment that characterize contemporary U.S. criminal justice, "partial" referring to the deeply rooted systemic biases (Rafter, 1985).

In conclusion, the current feminist debates relevant to criminology are those concerning defining crime and justice for women and men, gender and racial bias in science, and the validity of fundamental scientific concepts based on nature and dualism. Few of these debates have been concluded, few dilemmas resolved. Yet they have advanced our understanding to the point that today a proposed article titled "Etiology of Female Crime" would probably be challenged. One would very likely be informed that the scientific concept of etiology is suspect, that the term "female" must be deconstructed, and that the definition of crime itself should be reexamined.

NOTES

1. One important thing to note in assessing our accomplishments and limits is that most of us were European-American (as distinct from African-, Asian-, or Latino-American), although we did focus on racism as a fundamental issue for feminist criminology.
2. I was inspired to do this by the work then being engaged in by one of my professors, Herman Schwendinger (Schwendinger and Schwendinger, 1974).
3. Ironically, biologism is more influential in feminist theory than in contemporary criminology. Within the movement to end violence against

women, influential works have drawn upon implicit assumptions about male biology (e.g., physical strength, sexual aggression) as explaining rape and other victimizations (Brownmiller, 1975; MacKinnon, 1989). Furthermore, feminist legal defenses for accused women have evolved around such controversial conceptualizations as the premenstrual syndrome.

4. Within mainstream criminology, and its ongoing search for the causes of crime, there has been little interest in this search for the roots of patriarchy. Unfortunately, gender issues have largely remained ignored, as in the days of "Etiology."

5. Instead, criminologists debate the accuracy and meaning of African-American, Latino, and Anglo/European rates of criminality in an exercise even longer and less productive than the debate over women's and men's rates.

REFERENCES

Benhabib, Seyla, and Drucilla Cornell (eds.). 1987. *Feminism as Critique: On the Politics of Gender.* Minneapolis: University of Minnesota.

Bertrand, Marie-Andreé. "Advances in Feminist Epistemology of the Social Control of Women," presented at the American Society of Criminology, San Francisco, November 1991.

Bertrand, Marie-Andreé, Kathleen Daly, and Dorie Klein (eds.). *Proceedings of the International Feminist Conference on Women, Law and Social Control.* Vancouver: International Centre for the Reform of Criminal Law and Criminal Justice Policy, 1992.

Brownmiller, Susan. *Against Our Will: Men, Women and Rape.* New York: Simon and Schuster, 1975.

Cain, Maureen (ed.). *Growing Up Good: Policing the Behaviour of Girls in Europe.* Newbury Park, Calif.: Sage, 1989.

Daly, Kathleen. "New Feminist Definitions of Justice." *Proceedings of the First Annual Women's Policy Research Conference.* Washington, D.C.: Institute for Women's Policy Research, 1989.

Daly, Kathleen, and Meda Chesney-Lind. "Feminism and Criminology." *Justice Quarterly,* 5: 4, 1988.

Diamond, Irene, and Lee Quinby (eds). *Feminism and Foucault: Reflections on Resistance.* Boston: Northeastern University Press, 1988.

Gilligan, Carol. *In a Different Voice: Psychological Theory and Women's Development.* Cambridge, Mass.: Harvard University Press, 1982.

Gordon, Linda. *Heroes of Their Own Lives: The Politics and History of Family Violence.* New York: Viking, 1988.

Issues in Criminology, 8: 2, Fall 1973.

Klein, Dorie. "Violence against Women: Some Considerations Regarding Its Causes and Its Elimination." *Crime and Delinquency,* 27: 1, 1981.

Klein, Dorie. "Women and Criminal Justice in the Reagan Era," presented at the Academy of Criminal Justice Sciences, San Francisco, April 1988.

Klein, Dorie. "Losing (the War on) the War on Crime." *Critical Criminologist,* 2: 4, 1990.

MacKinnon, Catherine. *Towards a Feminist Theory of the State.* Cambridge, Mass.: Harvard University Press, 1989.

Nicholson, Linda (ed.). *Feminism/Postmodernism.* New York: Routledge, 1990.

Rafter, Nicole. *Partial Justice: Women in State Prisons, 1800–1935.* Boston: Northeastern University Press, 1985.

Schwendinger, Herman, and Julia Schwendinger. "Defenders of Order or Guardians of Human Rights?" *Issues in Criminology,* 5: 2, 1970.

Schwendinger, Herman, and Julia Schwendinger. *The Sociologists of the Chair.* New York: Basic Books, 1974.

Smart, Carol. *Feminism and the Power of Law.* New York: Routledge, 1989.

Sunstein, Cass (ed.). *Feminism and Political Theory.* Chicago: University of Chicago Press, 1990.

CHAPTER 3

THEORETICAL CRIMINOLOGY AND GENDER

EILEEN LEONARD

ABSTRACT

In this chapter Leonard reviews the major sociological theories of crime espoused in the mid-twentieth-century United States that are still widely popular today. She does this in order to evaluate the ability of these theories to explain the crime patterns of women. She asks if such theories as anomie (Merton), labeling (Becker), differential association (Sutherland), subculture (Cloward and Ohlin), and Marxism (Quinney) can be applied to female offenders today. As the reader, can you explain how she does that for each theoretical perspective?

She concludes that the traditional theories do not work and, as a result, are basically flawed. Leonard, like Sokoloff and Price (Chapter 1) and Klein (Chapter 2), makes the case that new theoretical efforts are needed to understand women's crime, efforts that take into account not only gender but also race, class, and culture. The results of this important work could substantially strengthen criminology and its ability to inform the understanding of crime generally. Compare Leonard's analysis here with that of Chapter 4, where Chesney-Lind describes the inadequacy of traditional delinquency theories in explaining girls' offending. What similarities or differences do you find in Leonard's evaluation of sociological theories of crime for adult women and Chesney-Lind's evaluation for juvenile girls? Can you suggest how feminist thinking might be useful in explaining both female and male crime? both adult and juvenile?

Although Americans are deeply concerned about crime, one blunt fact that often gets ignored in public (and academic) discussions of crime is its remarkable variation in terms of gender: women have lower rates of crime in *all nations, in all communities* within nations, for *all age groups,* for *all periods of recorded history,* and for practically *all crimes* (Sutherland and Cressey, 1960: 111; Daly and Chesney-Lind, 1988). One would expect criminologists to have seriously explored the implications of gender in terms of crime, but until recently this was basically ignored (see Klein, Chapter 2 in this volume).

Criminology offers an incisive group of theories that try to explain crime. Each theory should explain not only why certain people are criminal but, by implication, why others are not. This chapter examines several sociological theories of crime and contends that they cannot explain female patterns of crime and therefore are theoretically flawed. Although they claim to be *general* explanations of criminal behavior, at best they are explanations of *male* patterns of behavior. Moreover, the omission of a serious consideration of gender is not easily remedied: a profound reconstruction of criminology will be needed to make it more inclusive. The chapter ends by noting recent efforts at that reconstruction.

WOMEN AND CRIME

FBI crime statistics consistently document the fact that many more men are arrested than women. Although women's arrests for *property* offenses have risen, women's involvement in *violent* crime has fluctuated very little. Indeed, *larceny theft* is the only serious crime with significant female involvement,

This article was written expressly for inclusion in this text.

and women are still *less than one-third* of those arrested for that crime. In terms of less serious offenses, women's arrests approach those of men for three crimes: forgery and counterfeiting, fraud, and embezzlement. The only crime categories where arrests of women actually *exceed* those of men are prostitution and runaway violations. Throughout the 1980s women's crime generally increased, but by 1989 they still accounted for only 18.1 percent of *all* arrests, although women are more than half the population (FBI, 1990: 189).

The "new female criminal," much heralded by the media, is more myth than reality. The most puzzling and unexplained social fact remains the comparative *absence* of criminality among women. Let us analyze various theories of crime to determine if they can explain the low involvement of women in crime as well as current increases in property offenses.

ANOMIE THEORY

Robert Merton's influential analysis of crime, anomie theory, is rooted in the work of sociologist Emile Durkheim and aims to provide a comprehensive explanation of crime and deviance. Dismissing biological explanations of crime, Merton contends that *social structures* pressure certain individuals to engage in nonconformist behavior. He argues that American society overemphasizes its *cultural goals* (aspirations that are socially learned) without sufficient attention to *institutionalized means* (the available opportunities to achieve these goals in acceptable ways). Merton specifically refers to the overwhelming desire for financial success and material goods in American society and the willingness to use *any* means to attain these goals. Deviant behavior results when people want to attain the socially accepted goals (financial success) but do not have the legitimate means to do so (a lucrative job).

Merton diagrams the possible results that can occur when goals have been internalized but cannot be achieved through legitimate means. His approach is thoroughly sociological, since it focuses on one's position in the social structure, not biological or psychological conditions. The following table summarizes these adaptations (Merton, 1938: 676). The symbol (+) refers to acceptance, (–) refers to elimination, and (±) is "rejection and substitution of new goals."

		Cultural goals	Institutionalized means
I	Conformity	+	+
II	Innovation	+	–
III	Ritualism	–	+
IV	Retreatism	–	–
V	Rebellion	±	±

Merton claims that conformity, accepting both goals and legitimate means, is most common in American society; retreatism is least common. Retreatists, "in the society but not *of* it," include psychotics, vagrants, tramps, drug addicts, and chronic alcoholics (Merton, 1938: 677). These desperate people accept the goals and means but do not have access to legitimate opportunities and thus give up on both. The ritualist has lost hope of attaining the goals but nonetheless conforms rigorously to the accepted means. The rebel wants to bring about a new social order.

Merton is concerned primarily with the innovator: the person who uses illegitimate but effective means to attain the cultural goals. (One who achieves financial success by robbing a bank is, for example, an innovator.) Merton explains that social structures actually push some people in the direction of innovation by encouraging them to accept cultural goals while simultaneously denying them the legitimate opportunities to succeed. Merton claims that the problem is not simply a lack of opportunity:

It is only when the system of cultural values extols, virtually above all else, certain *common* symbols of success *for the population at large* while its social structure rigorously restricts or completely eliminates access to approved modes of acquiring these symbols *for a considerable part of the same population,* that anti-social behavior ensues on a considerable scale (Merton, 1938: 680).

He implies that the problem of crime would be alleviated if more people had access to legitimate opportunities, or if those with less opportunity had lower expectations. But he contends that in American society *everyone* is expected to achieve, and those who are denied the structural opportunities to do so are in a position of enormous strain. Merton (1938: 680) notes that the American emphasis on financial success for everyone encourages "exaggerated anxieties, hostilities, neuroses, and anti-social behavior."

In later revisions and elaborations of anomie theory, Merton (1957) acknowledged that wealth is not the only success symbol in American society, but he continued to emphasize its centrality. He recognized that upper-class people can experience pressure to "innovate," since there is no stopping point in the American dream (one can *never* have enough money), but he continued to insist that lower classes are subjected to the greatest amounts of strain and thus exhibit the most crime. Merton (1957) also expanded his thoughts on ritualism, which he claims is most often found in the lower middle class, where children are socialized to obey rules and limited in terms of their opportunities for success. He (1966) acknowledged that people in power exercise a crucial role in determining what particular behavior violates social standards and that punishment may be differentially imposed in terms of class, race, or age.

Anomie and Women

Anomie theory is an outstanding attempt to comprehensively explain crime and deviance by delineating the relationship between one's social position, the strain that accompanies it, and the resulting deviant or nondeviant adaptations. Merton, however, made no attempt to apply this scheme to women, and initially his theory seems inapplicable to them. Women, after all, represent more than half of the lower-class population—the group supposedly subjected to the most anomic strain—and yet they are far from equally represented in terms of "innovation." Why? Merton is silent on this. He argues that the dominant goal in American society is monetary success, and yet this too is questionable regarding women. Ruth Morris (1964) contends that women and girls aim for successful relationships with others rather than the traditional financial goals of men. More specifically, women are socialized to seek marriage and children more than a lucrative career. Today more women may aspire to careers, but marriage and family is at least an equally important goal.

Merton claimed that various goals could be considered within his framework, although he neglected to mention the possibility that half our population may not strive primarily for financial success. If, however, marriage and family is substituted as a goal for women, can anomie theory explain their relatively low involvement in crime? Most white women marry and have children, perhaps avoiding the anomic pressure men experience when unable to achieve social goals. Merton may also illuminate increases in crime among women: if women's goals shift toward male success goals, for example, their crime may increase, since their access to such goals is limited in our unequally structured society.

This application of anomie theory seems plausible, yet following Merton's problematic assumptions we have posited a common goal for all women, ignoring any consideration of subcultural differences. His theory utilizes a middle-class perspective and does not consider different norms and patterns of socialization (see, for example, Anderson and Collins, 1992; Ladner, 1972). Thus, anomie theory directs one's thinking toward *common* goals, not class, race, or ethnic variations. Moreover, when it comes to analyzing the crime that does occur among women, anomie theory becomes unworkable. Regarding innovation, Merton's prime concern, it is exceedingly difficult to think of illegal means to the goal of marriage and the family. Larceny, theft, and prostitution are not alternative means to marriage. In addition, many women arrested for crime have followed normatively accepted patterns and are married with children. Finally, a ritualistic adaptation is not more likely among lower-middle-class women, since they are not particularly restricted from the accepted goals for women.

Thus anomie theory fails to explain why women deviate the way they do or what type of strain leads to each outcome. The theory applies largely to men and mainly to the goal of financial success. Anomie theory ignores social variations in terms of gender, race, or ethnicity, and when a group as significant as women is examined, it is not a matter of making minor revisions; the theory fails in important respects. Thus, Merton's "common" symbols of success may not be so common after all.

LABELING THEORY

Robert Merton's perspective on crime assumes that deviant behavior occurs in a world that is basically stable and culturally homogeneous. This view has been challenged by a relatively new perspective, labeling theory, which claims that the social world is diverse and conflict-laden and that attempts to control deviance may in fact increase it. Labeling theory gained popularity through the 1960s and now assumes a position of major importance in criminology. Previously, theoretical criminology sought to explain why certain people or groups of people engage in crime, but labeling theory assumes that *most* people perform deviant acts and examines instead why society officially brands some people, and not others, criminal. For example, many citizens steal, but lower-class males who steal cars are more likely to be officially labeled than business executives who embezzle funds. Labeling shifts the focus to the audience—to those who label and the effects of this. Labeling theorists argue that deviance is "created" by those with the power to make and enforce rules.

Some of the details of labeling theory are evident in the work of sociologist Howard Becker. In *Outsiders*, Becker notes that we often ignore the fact that deviance is created by society not just in the sense that social conditions elicit deviance, but rather in the sense *"that social groups create deviance by making the rules whose infraction constitutes deviance."* Becker continues, "deviance is *not* a quality of the act the person commits, but rather a consequence of the application by others of rules and sanctions to an 'offender'" (Becker, 1963: 9). Becker is less concerned with the characteristics of deviants than with the common process they experience. He argues that power differentials in terms of race, class, age, and gender determine whose rules are operating and social reaction. Thus labeling theory reemphasizes the fact that crime and deviance are socially defined and that certain groups are more likely than others to be officially stigmatized as deviant.

Labeling and Women

In certain respects labeling theory may help explain the limited involvement of women in crime. The theory recognizes that certain groups (usually middle- and upper-class people) are not associated with criminal behavior and thus are less likely to be officially labeled and to suffer the pernicious effects of such labeling. Certain preconceptions about women (as passive, dependent, nonassertive) may allow them to avoid arrest and punishment. By avoiding official labeling, women may in turn maintain low levels of criminal involvement and return more easily to nondeviant lives. Assuming that traditional stereotypes of women have protected them from official labeling, changes in how women are perceived may result in declining protection, and this may lurk behind the current (though limited) increases in their arrest rates. The result, according to labeling theory, is an increased likelihood that criminal involvement will become deeper and more intractable.

There are, however, obvious difficulties in attempting a systematic application of this theory to women, and these difficulties highlight the limitations of labeling theory itself. Perhaps women have low crime rates because they are unlikely to be officially labeled, but it is equally plausible that their crime rates simply reflect less involvement in crime. If this is so, labeling theory cannot explain why, since it focuses on official reaction, *not* the initial causes of criminal behavior. Similarly, rising arrest rates may indicate more female involvement in crime, not just attitudinal changes toward women. Given differences in socialization, social control, and financial status, it seems reasonable to assume that white middle-class women (for example) may be less likely to be involved in certain types of criminal behavior as compared with young, black, lower-class males. Structural explanations for this must be combined with an analysis of social reactions.

Social stereotypes that protect women from official labeling must also be reconsidered in terms of race and class differentials. It is unlikely that a lower-class minority woman would reap the benefits of lenient treatment, and yet her crime rate is still comparatively low, although higher than that for a white middle-class woman.

Labeling theory comes dangerously close to implying that initial behavior is meaningless; it also ignores the possibility that official sanctions may deter future crime rather than increase it. Two types of deviance in which women are overrepresented highlight these problems. A career in prostitution may be explained in terms of labeling theory by arguing that prostitution violates the rules of society, powerless women are arrested for it, and they are subjected to the negative effects of official sanctioning. This encourages them to view themselves as prostitutes, thus pushing them further into crime. How does this compare with shoplifting? Here we find evidence that official reprimands often *deter* women from further involvement. Labeling is unable to explain these discrepancies in terms of official reaction. Perhaps the initial reasons why women engage in these activities are as important as official reaction in terms of understanding future behavior. Labeling disregards this and thus fails to explain *not only* initial deviance but its subsequent development as well.

Finally, labeling theory argues that the powerless are not necessarily more criminal; rather, they suffer the detrimental effects of biased laws and differential law enforcement. This, however, ignores patterns of female crime and why, although women are certainly powerless, their criminal involvement is so different from that of (lower-class) men. Women are infrequently labeled criminal, and when they are labeled, the results may be less pernicious. Why? Labeling theory fails to explain the phenomenon of women and crime because it lacks an analysis of why people do or do not engage in crime in the first place, an examination of the impact of (positive and negative) labeling, and a thorough

analysis of structures of power as they impinge on women.

Labeling theory offers insights in terms of understanding female patterns of crime. It encourages a deeper analysis of lawmaking, it emphasizes the impact of social reaction on the development of the self, and it advises that official reaction can (often) push a person further into crime. But this is incomplete. Labeling lacks structural explanations, a clear discussion of the impact of labeling, and a full treatment of power in society.

DIFFERENTIAL ASSOCIATION

Edwin Sutherland contributed substantially to the development of criminology with his theory of differential association, which he believed explains *all* criminal behavior (Sutherland and Cressey, 1960: 77–79). Sutherland regards crime as similar to any other learned behavior: individuals learn to rob a bank in much the same way they learn to fix a car—someone teaches them. His approach diverges sharply from theories that assume crime is rooted in biological or psychological disorders. If criminal activity is learned in a "normal" fashion, individual abnormality is not necessarily a factor. Sutherland, like the labeling theorists, stresses the social processes by which an individual becomes criminal. He maintains that criminal patterns are transmitted through social groups that support the violation of laws.

According to Sutherland, most criminal behavior is learned within intimate personal groups. Individuals learn techniques of crime as well as ways to explain and rationalize it. Basically, a person becomes criminal because of a predominance of contact with criminal rather than law-abiding patterns. The essence of differential association is that crime is learned through interaction with others who define law violation as acceptable. Although mainly concerned with the processes that lead individuals to become criminal, Sutherland began to discuss "differential social organization" in order to explain varying *rates* of crime. In other words, it is necessary to explain why one person rather than another becomes criminal (John as opposed to Mary), but it is also imperative to understand why one group is more criminal than another (males as opposed to females). Unfortunately, Sutherland did not systematically elaborate this aspect of his work.

Differential Association and Women

Sutherland (Cohen, Lindesmith, and Schuessler, 1956: 19) specifically mentions that differential association seems to explain "why males are more delinquent than females." He did not, however, pursue the matter. His assertion that criminal behavior is simply learned behavior is intriguing, since female crime has frequently been associated with biological or psychological abnormality (see Klein, Chapter 2 in this volume). Sutherland proposes that a person becomes delinquent because of excessive contact with criminal as opposed to noncriminal patterns. If the crucial primary group for most females is a relatively restrictive family, they may simply be less likely than males to learn criminal behavior. Females also lack the opportunity for contact with adolescent gangs, or groups that generate white-collar crime, and this further limits the possibility of learning criminal behavior. Even within the same groups as males (like the family), their social position is unequal, and they are frequently taught dissimilar attitudes.

The differential treatment of males and females may culminate, then, with women exposed to an excessive number of definitions of behavior *un*favorable to violating the law. Sutherland (Sutherland and Cressey, 1960: 115) indicates this in a discussion of the sex ratio in crime when he states: "Probably

the most important difference is that girls are supervised more carefully and behave in accordance with anti-criminal behavior patterns taught to them with greater care and consistency than in the case of boys." Females encounter more anticriminal patterns (within the family, where they are more isolated and controlled) over a longer period of time (owing to external supervision) than males. Sutherland suggests these differences might have originated because females become pregnant and, hence, require more supervision. Thus, differential association interprets the low crime rate among women in terms of their associations, which tend to ensure that they will learn patterns of behavior favoring adherence to the law. Recent research has, however, alerted us to the fact that women may actually learn criminal behavior within the family (Miller, 1986) and that the home is often a site of violence against women (Dobash and Dobash, 1979; Stanko, 1985).

Cressey (1964: 55) notes that the sex ratio is decreasing—that changes have occurred over time. He contends that as the social position of women begins to approach that of men, the male-female differential will decline. Increasing employment and education for women has brought them into contact with more groups. Likewise, weakening restrictions on females, combined with the growing number of broken families and increasing urbanization, may play a role in increasing female crime.

Problematic Aspects of Differential Association and Women

Differential association offers a reasonable if incomplete explanation for the limited involvement of females in crime. Sutherland argues that it is unnecessary to explain *why* people have the associations they do. I disagree. Perhaps one theory cannot explain everything, but if structural issues are not addressed, the phenomenon of women and crime is unresolved. Why do males and females have such different associations and, given the *same* associations, such different definitions of the legal code? Sutherland admits that men and women share the same neighborhoods, the same homes, and the same parents, but he claims that they are subject to different degrees of care and supervision. His ultimate explanation, that women get pregnant, is an inadequate analysis of the different social conditions of women and men. Differential association offers a valuable interpretation of the process of learning criminal and noncriminal behavior. It fails, however, to explain not only how certain behavior is transmitted but why such patterns exist in the first place and why they vary so much from one group to another. It de-emphasizes (at the very least) wider historical and structural changes and the responses of women to these changes.

Differential association is helpful in emphasizing that criminal behavior is learned, not biologically or psychologically determined, and that association with criminal or noncriminal patterns is essential and varies from one group to another. It reminds us that women are not permitted the same associations as men and that even within the same groups they are treated unequally. Thus, their crime rate may be expected to vary from that of men. This theory, however, leaves us with the same puzzling questions regarding women and crime. It clarifies that women have different associations but does not explain why. It asserts that they are more controlled and differentially socialized but offers a flimsy explanation for this. Thus we learn (and this is important) that associations are critical in the emergence of criminal behavior and that women are forbidden certain associations and treated differently within others, but we never learn why. As with labeling theory, structural as well as processual explanations are needed.

Thus, Sutherland offers a framework to explain crime in general, but this framework must be expanded to include structural considerations and refined to explore the implications of gender and the active role individuals may play in shaping their destinies, as opposed to merely reacting to a given situation.

SUBCULTURAL THEORY

An analysis of criminal subcultures has played a central role in theoretical explanations of crime. Rooted to a large extent in anomie theory, these approaches concentrate on the criminal behavior of lower-class, adolescent boys in gangs. Contributors to the study of subcultures include Albert Cohen, Walter B. Miller, Richard Cloward, and Lloyd Ohlin.

Albert Cohen concentrated on the content of the delinquent subculture, why it exists, and why it is found in some communities and not others. His explanation is class related: gang delinquency is a group solution to the frustrations of lower-class boys who are denied status in middle-class terms and thus seek it in a delinquent group. Cohen portrays this subculture as nonutilitarian, malicious, and negativistic; it embodies a repudiation the middle-class values. He (1955: 59) considers how delinquent subcultures arise and argues that "the crucial condition for the emergence of new cultural forms is the existence, *in effective interaction with one another, of a number of actors with similar problems of adjustment.*" Cohen contends that men and women achieve status in different ways: for women, status depends on marriage to a successful male; men, however, must be occupationally successful.

Albert Cohen's work on delinquent gangs has been criticized on a number of grounds. His view of the delinquent subculture as an inversion of middle-class values is questionable. Lower-class youths often do not reject middle-class values (Gibbons, 1976: 138) but offer rationalizations for their actions in order to engage in delinquent behavior (Sykes and Matza, 1957). In addition, the activities of delinquents are far more serious (Kitsuse and Dietrick, 1959) and far more diverse (Gibbons, 1976) than Cohen initially realized.

Walter B. Miller (1958) developed subcultural theory in part through a critique of Cohen's work. He argues that gang delinquency is *not* a reaction to middle-class values but a positive attempt to achieve status in lower-class terms. He claims that lower-class life is characterized by certain "focal concerns," including trouble, toughness, smartness, excitement, an emphasis on fate, and autonomy. Lower-class life, in general, and the delinquent gang, in particular, have distinct traditions of their own and cannot be regarded as inversions of middle-class culture. Miller also contends that the one-sex peer group is a significant aspect of the lower class and is probably related to the widespread female-based household. He (1970: 277) argues, "It is the *one-sex peer unit* rather than the two-parent family unit which represents the most significant relational unit for both sexes in lower-class communities." Miller's work has been challenged for positing a much deeper rift between middle- and lower-class values than probably exists. His analysis is also criticized for being static and ignoring the origins of "focal concerns" (Taylor, 1971) and for ignoring the diversity of delinquent subcultures (Cloward and Ohlin, 1960).

Richard Cloward (1959) combines anomie theory and differential association in his attempt to explain delinquent subcultures. He states that *both* legitimate means (as recognized by Merton) and illegitimate means (as noted by Sutherland) are, first, limited and, second, differentially available depending on one's location in the social structure. In this way he explores the concept of "differential opportunity structures." This work was extended and deepened in Cloward and Ohlin's book *Delinquency and Opportunity* (1960). The originality of this work lies in its discussion of different forms of delinquent subcultures: criminal, conflict, and retreatist. All are found predominantly in lower-class areas of large urban centers, especially among adolescent boys. The criminal subculture of adolescent boys involves activities like stealing and extortion in order to gain prestige and success. This subculture arises when illegitimate opportunities are available and adults are the role models. The conflict subculture uses violence to gain status and focuses on the courage and bravery of its members. It develops when both legitimate and illegitimate opportunities are unavailable. The retreatist subculture involves the search for ecstatic experiences and the use of drugs. It develops not only when legitimate opportunity is restricted but when illegitimate opportunity (including violence) is restricted because of internal constraints or lack of success in the illegitimate world. Cloward and Ohlin explain the class differences in delinquency in terms of blocked legitimate opportunity, but they ignore gender differences—they simply note that this would be a "potentially fruitful" line of inquiry (1960: 33). It has been observed that the work of Cloward and Ohlin is not always empirically accurate. Some neighborhoods, for example, have several types of subcultures (Taylor, 1971). Moreover, gangs themselves engage in a variety of delinquent activities, thus making distinctive subcultures hard to find (Campbell, 1984; Gibbons, 1976).

Subcultural theory is primarily concerned with (urban, working-class) male delinquency. Cohen discusses female delinquency briefly; Cloward and Ohlin say they focus on males but never explain why; Miller simply speaks of lower-class culture and never acknowledges that his analysis excludes females. A more complete theory would explain this specificity and confront the problematic aspects of discussing the criminality of one group in view of the relative noncriminality of another group that shares so many of the same conditions.

Cohen asserts that males and females have different problems that require different solutions. He argues that boys are mainly concerned about their achievements compared with those of other males; girls are concerned about their relationship with males. Although Cohen does not regard this as "natural," he believes that girls are mainly fulfilled through their relationships with the opposite sex. In light of this Cohen concludes that the problems of adjustment that lead to delinquent gangs are fundamentally male problems and that the delinquent subculture is completely inappropriate for female role problems: "It is inappropriate because it is, at best, irrelevant to the vindication of the girl's status as a girl, and at worst, because it positively threatens her in that status in consequence of its strongly masculine symbolic function" (Cohen, 1955: 143–144).

Cohen does not elaborate; he simply proposes that a female's "peace of mind" depends on her assurance of sexual attractiveness and that sexual delinquency is one response to the central problems of females: establishing satisfying relationships with men. Cohen ignores class and ethnic differences as well as any consideration of how women interpret their behavior. It is also unclear how female sexual delinquency provides a solution to establishing satisfactory relationships with males. Since female delinquency rates are low, are we to assume that most girls have satisfactory relationships with boys? Cohen does not explain the lack of criminality among women who have not married successful males or whose personal relationships are less than satisfactory. In fact, his work does not offer any insights beyond what we were able to glean from Merton's anomie theory.

Walter B. Miller makes no attempt to consider criminal activity among women, and his thesis fails when applied to them. Miller's focal concerns supposedly characterize lower-class life in general, but if this were so, male and female delinquency rates would be similar. In fact, a focus on trouble, toughness, smartness, excitement, fate, and autonomy is probably not as relevant to women. Miller recognizes cultural differences in terms of class; a similar awareness is needed regarding gender.

The theory of differential opportunity is more amenable to a consideration of gender because it addresses the unavailability of *both* legitimate and illegitimate opportunities. The lower participation of women in crime may be explained by their limited access to illegitimate opportunities (Harris, 1977). Cloward (1959: 173) acknowledged that women are frequently excluded from criminal activities, although he believed class differences are more important regarding access to illegitimate opportunity than gender differences. Other researchers have observed that girls are less likely to have subcultural supports for delinquency and in fact are faced with much stricter disapproval of delinquent behavior when compared with boys (Morris, 1965: 265. See also Campbell, 1984; Chesney-Lind, 1989; Figueira-McDonough, 1984; McCormack et al., 1986). Thus Cloward and Ohlin's theory is enhanced by their consideration of the availability of illegitimate opportunity. They still fail, however, to overcome the problems associated with anomie theory, which underlies their framework. They emphasize common (not diverse) cultural goals, they ignore societal reactions, and they fail to explain crime among women who have achieved social goals. They do not question (let alone explain) why such profound structural differences exist in the behavior and expectations of males and females.

When we turn to the three delinquent subcultures described by Cloward and Ohlin, their unrelievedly male orientation and its inapplicability to females become increasingly apparent. Each of these subcultures is viewed primarily in terms of male success goals. Increasing crime among women is also difficult to explain in terms of Cloward and Ohlin's analysis. Rita Simon (1975) suggests that rises in female crime may result from increased female participation in the labor force, which gives women more opportunity to commit crime. This is problematic, however, since these women by definition have legitimate opportunities and should not be driven toward criminal behavior. Moreover, it is ironic to consider labor force participation as illegitimate opportunity.

Thus an application of subcultural theories to women is difficult at best mainly because these theories are aimed implicitly or explicitly at males (Campbell, 1984; Chesney-Lind, 1989). Moreover, our limited information on female subcultures makes a comparable analysis difficult. The criminal patterns of different social classes must be explored, although subcultural theories too often leave the mistaken impression that crime is entirely the domain of the poor.

MARXIST APPROACHES

In the 1970s a unique perspective emerged from attempts to analyze structural causes of crime while dealing adequately with the issue of power. Grounded in the work of Karl Marx, this "new criminology" (also known as radical or critical criminology) focuses on rule making as well as rule breaking. Exploring connections between law, crime, and society, it challenges major assumptions in American criminology. The new criminology regards law as intimately connected to the interests of the lawmakers and as fundamentally serving the interests of the ruling class. Since the law is so biased,

Marxists tend to reject a simple analysis of *why* someone breaks the law. Rather, their focus shifts toward analyzing the law itself. Crime is generally viewed as resulting from the contradictions inherent in capitalism, and thus its solution lies not in the treatment or punishment of criminals but in the creation of an alternative society (Balkan, Berger, and Schmidt, 1980; Messerschmidt, 1986, 1988; Rafter and Natalizia, 1982; Schwendinger and Schwendinger, 1983).

Karl Marx wrote relatively little on crime, but the new criminology looks to his general sociological analysis for guidance and inspiration. A group of British theorists—Ian Taylor, Paul Walton, and Jock Young—have been central in the development of a new criminology. Their well-known book, *The New Criminology* (1973), critiques existing criminology theory and is an initial step in the construction of a critical criminology. Their edited book, *Critical Criminology* (1975), further explicates the new criminology and the part they have played in shaping it. According to Taylor, Walton, and Young, strikingly different assumptions have characterized the theoretical frameworks within criminology. Liberal theory, for example, is prescriptive, suggesting institutional reforms to improve human life, but it basically accepts existing social arrangements. Most contemporary criminology is based on such liberal understandings. Radical theory, however, is quite different. Human beings are seen as having unlimited potential under certain social conditions, determined by the arrangements of production. Human life can be self-directed, egalitarian, and richly diverse, but radical change is needed to make this a reality. Whether discussing social change or crime, Taylor, Walton, and Young emphasize the role of the political economy. They claim (1975: 20) that it is the basic determinant of the social framework and that "the processes involved in crime-creation are bound up in the final analysis with the *material* basis of contemporary capitalism and its structures of law."

Taylor, Walton, and Young believe that radical social science must encourage change through research that highlights the activities of the powerful which *could* be defined as illegal but often are not, or if so defined remain unprosecuted or unpunished. Such research challenges the myth of a crime-free ruling class. Radical criminology also examines the stratified nature of crime and law in capitalist society. The criminal justice system, for example, is criticized for its ideology of equality coupled with the reality of differential law enforcement. Radical criminology aims to abolish the present distribution of power and wealth and to create a just society. The method of historical materialism is used to analyze crime in light of the given mode of production. One's position in society (class) must be studied and historical dimensions kept clearly in focus. This implies that any explanation of crime is meant to be valid not for all societies but only for a given society, at a given historical time. In a materialist criminology, law must also be examined in historical terms. Legal relations do not crudely reflect economic conditions, but material conditions shape social relations and therefore law.

Another prolific writer who has shaped critical criminology is Richard Quinney. He (1972) explicitly criticizes the consensus image of law in capitalist society and claims that society is in fact diverse and constantly changing. Rather than protecting all citizens, law essentially protects the interests of a select group by controlling any behavior that threatens the established order. Thus Quinney insists that crime control is, in reality, class control. The root of crime, as he sees it, is found not in individualistic explanations of deviance but in an exploration of the political nature of crime-defining procedures. Anthony Platt (1975) sounds another theme in critical criminology by calling for a new definition of crime. He asserts that present legal definitions implicitly incorporate the myth of an unbiased law. He claims that the subject matter of criminology must be reconsidered and based on a class and materialist perspective.

The new criminology is neither unified nor fully elaborated. It does, however, emphasize some common themes. Among these is an explicit commitment to a fundamentally *new* criminology that departs from liberal understandings in significant ways. Critical criminologists suggest new definitions of crime founded, for example, on notions of social injury rather than strictly legalistic conceptions (Schwendinger and Schwendinger, 1970). They agree that the crime problem will only be solved through widespread change: crime is intimately connected with capitalism, which must be fundamentally altered or crime as we know it will continue. These criminologists also call for political involvement in the struggle against oppression.

Criticisms of Marxist Theory and Application to Women

The new criminology has been criticized for its oversimplified model of stratification, which implies a stark dichotomy between the poor and the powerful (Sykes, 1974). It is also criticized for ignoring the subtleties and impact of power (Lemert, 1974). Although this perspective developed to overcome the problems of labeling theory, it is criticized in the same terms: for its inadequate sense of the complexity of law (which constrains lawmakers as well as lawbreakers) and for viewing law as fundamentally manipulative (Gibbons, 1977). The new criminologists have yet to describe carefully the processes of lawmaking and the exercise of power (Gibbons, 1977), and they have not specified the connections between capitalist exploitation and various forms of deviance (Gibbons and Jones, 1975).

The new criminology has not been fully elaborated or empirically tested. Unlike most other perspectives, it is directly interested not in crime but in the law, new definitions of crime, and the methods and purposes of social control. Although radical criminology is still unfolding, current work can be assessed regarding its consideration of gender. We find that although the new criminology contains themes and ideas that are applicable to women, it does not consider gender any more systematically than traditional theoretical criminology. Thus there are indications that it may fall prey to the same defects as its liberal and conservative predecessors.

The new criminology contends that material conditions are the basis of crime as well as law and recommends using the framework of historical materialism to explore this. Since a class system within capitalism shapes both the opportunities for crime and differential enforcement policies, it might be an excellent place to begin exploring how gender differences interact with class in terms of crime. This, however, has yet to be done—or even recognized as worthwhile. A Marxian analysis of social relations under capitalism involves an analysis of law as a means of social control and as a tool of the ruling class. Assuming that the law enables the powerful to maintain their standards, protect their property, and control anyone who threatens the status quo, it is intriguing to consider how this may vary in terms of gender. Women are apparently controlled with significantly less criminalization than men.

A thoroughly radical analysis of law and crime also entails redefining crime, and this, too, presents an opportunity to explore issues of particular concern regarding women. Treating prostitution, abortion, and the sexual behavior of young women as criminal has enabled society to maintain stricter control over women. Exploring the sensationalized image of the female offender may be particularly enlightening, since this may reflect the interests of the ruling class and efforts to control women.

Thus the new criminology offers an opportunity to rethink fundamental sociological issues through its discussion of law, new definitions of crime, social change, and so forth. Currently, however, this analysis is underdeveloped, and women's criminality is rarely discussed except in explicitly feminist texts (see Daly and Chesney-Lind, 1988; Messerschmidt, 1986; Rafter and Natalizia, 1982). To the extent that this perspective relies strictly on a class analysis, it is unable to explain why female patterns of crime vary as they do. This may be corrected as the new criminology advances; otherwise, the problems of the "old" criminology will be duplicated. Unfortunately, Taylor, Walton, and Young's massive criticism of criminology (1973) does not contain *one word* about women; Quinney is all but blind to considerations of gender. The inadequacies that hamper traditional criminology may well be repeated within a radical framework.

TOWARD A FEMINIST UNDERSTANDING OF CRIME

Traditional theoretical criminology basically applies to the activities, interests, and values of men—ignoring a comparable, let alone inclusive, analysis of women. Existing theories simply cannot explain female patterns of crime. The ultimate goal, however, is not a "criminology of women," which is given one chapter in each criminology text and one lecture in each criminology course, but a major reconsideration of our understanding of criminal behavior. The task that confronts criminology is a fundamental reconstruction of that field. Preparatory to this, much empirical research is needed.

In the last 25 years, an intriguing literature on women, gender, and crime has begun to develop. Overviews of this literature are available elsewhere (Chesney-Lind, 1986; Daly and Chesney-Lind, 1988; Simpson, 1989); this chapter simply highlights some new directions that are being taken, their profound value, and the challenge feminist analyses present to traditional assumptions in criminology.

ETHNOGRAPHY, WHITE-COLLAR CRIME, AND INTERSECTIONS OF CLASS, RACE, AND GENDER

Until recently, virtually all ethnographic information within criminology was male-centered; now a rich and compelling literature on women and girls is emerging. This work explores, for example, the lives of girls in gangs, prostitutes, and women in prison (Campbell, 1984; Carlen, 1985; Miller, 1986). Ethnographic research is enormously useful in refining and developing our theoretical understanding of gender and crime. It informs us about the lives of female offenders and helps us account for gender differences in the development of crime and delinquency. This includes the possibility of a link between physical or sexual abuse and female criminality. Increasing evidence indicates that girls "are running away from profound sexual victimization at home, and once on the streets are forced further into crime in order to survive" (Chesney-Lind, 1989: 22; Silbert and Pines, 1981; McCormack, Janus, and Burgess, 1986). Current theories of delinquency, focused on males, are totally inadequate to deal with this type of information.

A recent feminist analysis of white-collar crime (Daly, 1989) challenges assumptions that increasing female arrests for embezzlement, fraud, and forgery indicate that women are entering positions of importance in employment and that their offenses are similar to those of men. Kathleen Daly's (1989: 790) research indicates that women's white-collar crimes are virtually all petty, that higher proportions of these women are black and *not* in the paid labor force, and that fewer of them have college degrees. Crimes like fraud and embezzlement can be committed by women in "pink-collar" jobs—bank tellers or cashiers. Indeed, a welfare mother can be arrested for forging a check. Economic marginality seems more at issue in these crimes than greater economic opportunity. Thus, women's white-collar crime must be examined in its own terms and not burdened with assumptions based on our knowledge of the white-collar offenses of men.

Another area of feminist analysis that has dramatic implications for criminological theory entails a careful consideration of the links between race, class, and gender. Sally S. Simpson (1991) observes that "underclass" black females have higher rates of homicide and aggravated assault than white females but relatively lower rates than black males. Indeed, for some personal crime victimizations, the offense rates of black females are closer to those of white *males* than white *females*. Thus, gender alone does not explain differences in violent behavior; its interaction with race needs analysis and clarification.

Similarly, Roland Chilton and Susan Datesman (1987) have discovered that nonwhite women and white men now have similar arrest rates for larceny. Recent increases in women's arrests for larceny are mainly the result of the arrests of nonwhite women. The combined effects of race and gender are seldom explored in attempts to understand crime, but such analysis is obviously necessary. Chilton and Datesman contend that increases in larceny arrests are probably best explained by the deteriorating economic situation of black women, not by their presumed emancipation or expanding opportunities.

The research of Gary Hill and Elizabeth Crawford (1990) also suggests the need to consider differences among women in order to explain female patterns of crime. Using National Longitudinal Survey data, they analyzed the capacity of different theoretical frameworks when operationalized to explain the self-reported criminality of white and nonwhite young women. Their results suggest differences in the causes of crime among young women in different social circumstances. The criminality of young white women appears connected to social-psychological variables, whereas the criminality of young black women is more closely associated with structural forces. They (p. 622) call for more research but conclude that "the criminality of black and white women may be tied to very different experiences and/or to different ways of responding to similar experiences."

In conclusion, feminist criminology presents an impressive challenge to traditional criminology and enriches our understanding of factors that impinge on the social construction of crime. It has much to offer in terms of its increasing attention to race, class, and cultural differences—and how these interact with gender. Although much work remains, we can be confident that future research will be both vital and engaging and hopeful that it will dramatically advance the field of criminology.

REFERENCES

Anderson, Margaret L., and Patricia Hill Collins (eds.). *Race, Class, and Gender: An Anthology.* Belmont, Calif.: Wadsworth, Inc., 1992.

Balkan, Sheila, Ronald J. Berger, and Janet Schmidt. *Crime and Deviance in America: A Critical Approach.* Belmont, Calif.: Wadsworth Publishing Co., 1980.

Becker, Howard S. (ed.) *Outsiders: Studies in the Sociology of Deviance.* New York: The Free Press, 1963.

Campbell, Anne. *The Girls in the Gang.* New York: Basil Blackwell, 1984.

Carlen, Pat. *Criminal Women.* Cambridge: Polity Press, 1985.

———. *Women's Imprisonment: A Study in Social Control.* London: Routledge and Kegan Paul, 1983.

Chesney-Lind, Meda. "Girls' Crime and Woman's Place: Toward a Feminist Model of Female Delinquency." *Crime and Delinquency* (January 1989) 35: 5–29.

———. "Women and Crime: The Female Offender." *Signs* (1986) 12: 78–96.

Chilton, Roland, and Susan K. Datesman. "Gender, Race, and Crime: An Analysis of Urban Arrest Trends, 1960–1980." *Gender and Society* (June 1987) 1: 152–171.

Cloward, Richard A. "Illegitimate Means, Anomie, and Deviant Behavior." *American Sociological Review* (April 1959) 24: 164–176.

——— and Lloyd Ohlin. *Delinquency and Opportunity: A Theory of Delinquent Gangs.* New York: The Free Press, 1960.

Cohen, Albert K. *Delinquent Boys: The Culture of the Gang.* New York: The Free Press, 1955.

———, Alfred Lindesmith, and Karl Schuessler (eds.). *The Sutherland Papers.* Bloomington: Indiana University Press, 1956.

Cressey, Donald. *Delinquency, Crime and Differential Association.* The Hague: Martinus Nijhoff, 1964.

Currie, Elliott. "Beyond Criminology." *Issues in Criminology* (Spring 1974) 9: 133–142.

Daly, Kathleen. "Gender and Varieties of White-Collar Crime." *Criminology* (1989) 27: 769–793.

——— and Meda Chesney-Lind. "Feminism and Criminology." *Justice Quarterly* (1988) 5: 497–538.

Dobash, R. Emerson, and Russell Dobash. *Violence against Wives: A Case against the Patriarchy.* New York: The Free Press, 1979.

Federal Bureau of Investigation. *Uniform Crime Reports.* Washington, D.C.: U.S. Government Printing Office, 1990.

Figueira-McDonough, J. "Feminism and Delinquency: In Search of an Elusive Link." *British Journal of Criminology* (October 1984) 24: 325–342.

Gibbons, Don C. *Delinquent Behavior,* 2d ed. Englewood Cliffs, N.J.: Prentice-Hall, 1976.

————. *Society, Crime, and Criminal Careers: An Introduction to Criminology*, 3d ed. Englewood Cliffs, N.J.: Prentice-Hall, 1977.

———— and Joseph Jones. *The Study of Deviance: Perspectives and Problems*. Englewood Cliffs, N.J.: Prentice-Hall, 1975.

Harris, Anthony. "Sex and Theories of Deviance: Toward a Functional Theory of Deviant Type-Scripts." *American Sociological Review* (February 1977) 42: 3–16.

Hill, Gary D., and Elizabeth M. Crawford. "Women, Race, and Crime." *Criminology* (1990) 28: 601–623.

Kitsuse, John I. "Societal Reaction to Deviant Behavior: Problems of Theory and Method." *Social Problems* (Winter 1962) 9: 247–256.

———— and David Dietrick. "Delinquent Boys: A Critique." *American Sociological Review* (April 1959) 24: 208–215.

Klein, Dorie. "The Etiology of Female Crime: A Review of the Literature." *Issues in Criminology* (Fall 1973) 8: 3–29.

Ladner, Joyce. *Tomorrow's Tomorrow: The Black Woman*. New York: Doubleday, 1972.

Lemert, Edwin M. "Beyond Mead: The Societal Reaction to Deviance." *Social Problems* (April 1974) 21: 457–468.

McCormack, Arlene, Mark-David Janus, and Ann Wolbert Burgess. "Runaway Youths and Sexual Victimization: Gender Differences in an Adolescent Runaway Population." *Child Abuse and Neglect* (1986) 10: 387–395.

Merton, Robert K. "Social Problems and Sociological Theory." In R. K. Merton and R. Nisbet (eds.). *Contemporary Social Problems*. New York: Harcourt Brace Jovanovich, 1966, pp. 775–823.

————. "Social Structure and Anomie." *American Sociological Review* (October 1938) 3: 672–682.

————. *Social Theory and Social Structure*. New York: The Free Press, 1957.

Messerschmidt, James. *Capitalism, Patriarchy, and Crime: Toward a Socialist Feminist Criminology*. Totowa, N.J.: Rowman and Littlefield, 1986.

————. "From Marx to Bonger: Socialist Writings on Women, Gender and Crime." *Sociological Inquiry* (Fall 1988) 58: 378–392.

Miller, Eleanor M. *Street Women*. Philadelphia: Temple University Press, 1986.

Miller, Walter B. "Lower Class Culture as a Generating Milieu of Gang Delinquency." *Journal of Social Issues* (1958) 14: 5–19. In H. Vass (ed.). *Society, Delinquency and Delinquent Behavior*. Boston: Little, Brown, 1970, pp. 270–281.

Morris, Ruth. "Attitudes toward Delinquency by Delinquents, Non-Delinquents and Their Friends." *British Journal of Criminology* (July 1965) 5: 249–265.

————. "Female Delinquency and Relational Problems." *Social Forces* (October 1964) 43: 82–88.

Platt, Anthony. "Prospects for a Radical Criminology in the U.S." In Ian Taylor et al. (eds.). *Critical Criminology*. London: Routledge and Kegan Paul, 1975, pp. 95–112.

Quinney, Richard. "The Ideology of Law: Notes for a Radical Alternative to Repression." *Issues in Criminology* (Winter 1972) 7: 1–35.

Rafter, Nicole Hahn, and Elena M. Natalizia. "Marxist Feminism: Implications for Criminal Justice." In Barbara Raffel Price and Natalie J. Sokoloff (eds.). *The Criminal Justice System and Women: Women Offenders, Victims, Workers*. New York: Clark Boardman, 1982, pp. 465–483.

Schwendinger, Herman, and Julia Schwendinger. "Defenders of Order or Guardians of Human Rights?" *Issues in Criminology* (Summer 1970) 5: 123–157.

———— and ————. *Rape and Inequality*. Beverly Hills, Calif.: Sage, 1983.

Silbert, Mimi, and Ayala M. Pines. "Sexual Child Abuse as an Antecedent to Prostitution." *Child Abuse and Neglect* (1981) 5: 407–411.

Simon, Rita. *Women and Crime*. Lexington, Mass.: D.C. Heath, 1975.

———— and Jean Landis. *The Crimes Women Commit. The Punishments They Receive*. Lexington, Mass.: Lexington Books, 1991.

Simpson, Sally S. "Caste, Class, and Violent Crime: Explaining Difference in Female Offending." *Criminology* (1991) 29: 115–135.

————. "Feminist Theory, Crime, and Justice." *Criminology* (1989) 27: 605–631.

Stanko, Elizabeth. *Intimate Intrusions: Women's Experience of Male Violence*. London: Routledge and Kegan Paul, 1985.

Sumner, Colin. "Marxism and Deviancy Theory." In Paul Wiles (ed.). *The Sociology of Crime and Delinquency: The New Criminologies*. New York: Barnes and Noble, 1976, pp. 159–174.

Sutherland, Edwin, and Donald Cressey. *Principles of Criminology.* Philadelphia: Lippincott, 1960.

Sykes, Gresham. "The Rise of Critical Criminology." *The Journal of Criminal Law and Criminology* (June 1974) 65: 206–213.

———— and David Matza. "Techniques of Neutralization: A Theory of Delinquency." *American Sociological Review* (December 1957) pp. 664–670.

Taylor, Ian, Paul Walton, and Jock Young. *The New Criminology: For a Social Theory of Deviance.* New York: Harper and Row, 1973.

————, ————, and ———— (eds.). *Critical Criminology.* London: Routledge and Kegan Paul, 1975.

Taylor, Laurie. *Deviance and Society.* London: Michael Joseph, 1971.

CHAPTER 4

GIRLS, DELINQUENCY, AND JUVENILE JUSTICE: TOWARD A FEMINIST THEORY OF YOUNG WOMEN'S CRIME

MEDA CHESNEY-LIND

ABSTRACT

This chapter points out that existing delinquency theories are fundamentally inadequate to the task of explaining female delinquency and official reactions to girls' deviance. Chesney-Lind reviews the degree of androcentric (male-oriented) bias in theories of delinquency. Next she explores the need for a feminist model of female delinquency by reviewing the available evidence on girls' offending within a patriarchal context. Her review shows that the focus on disadvantaged-male delinquency in public settings has meant that girls' sexual and physical victimization in the private arena of the home and the relationship between that experience and girls' crime has been systematically ignored.

The role of status offenses for the society is explored in this chapter. As a product of the court's history of extralegal paternalism, status offenses have involved the system in the maintenance of traditional family norms, which require a more restrictive role of greater obedience and chastity from females than from males. More than one-third of all girls' cases in juvenile courts are for status offenses. The enforcement of status offenses has created a de facto double standard of juvenile justice. The system punishes girls whose behavior threatens parental authority and boys whose behavior is beyond that which can be excused as "boys will be boys."

Despite the move to deinstitutionalize status offenders in the 1970s, Chesney-Lind reports, especially for girls, both (1) an increase in the use of status offenses beginning in the politically more conservative 1980s and (2) a trend toward transinstitutionalization, particularly for middle-class white girls: adolescent admission to private mental hospitals for "troublesome" youth—especially girls with "acting out" problems and a range of less serious, noncriminal behaviors.

The role played by the juvenile justice system in the sexualization of female delinquency and the criminalization of girls' survival strategies has also been ignored. Chesney-Lind suggests that the official actions of the juvenile justice system should be seen as a major force in women's oppression. The system has historically served to reinforce the obedience of all young women to the demands of patriarchal authority, no matter how abusive and arbitrary. We will return to a particular example of this in Chapter 8, when Arnold describes the experience of a group of young black women in this context.

I ran away so many times. I tried anything man, and they wouldn't believe me. . . .
As far as they are concerned they think I'm the problem. You know, runaway, bad label.
—16-YEAR-OLD GIRL. *After having been physically and sexually assaulted, started running away from home. Was arrested as a "runaway" in Hawaii.*

You know, one of these days I'm going to have to kill myself before you guys are gonna listen to me. I can't stay at home.
—16-YEAR-OLD TUCSON RUNAWAY *with a long history of physical abuse.*

The academic study of delinquent behavior has, for all intents, been the study of male delinquency. "The delinquent is a rogue male" declared Albert Cohen (1955:140) in his influential book on gang delinquency. More than a decade later, Travis Hirschi (1969), in his equally important *Causes of Delinquency*, relegated women to a footnote which suggested, somewhat apologetically, that in the analysis, the "non-Negro" becomes "white," and the girls disappear.

This pattern of neglect is not unusual. All areas of social inquiry have been notoriously gender blind. What is perhaps less well understood is that theories developed to describe the misbehavior of working or lower class male youth fail to capture the full nature of delinquency in America; and they are woefully inadequate to explain female misbehavior and official reactions to girls' deviance.

To be specific, delinquent behavior involves a range of activities far broader than those committed by the stereotypical street gang. Moreover, many more young people than the small numbers of visible "troublemakers" commit juvenile offenses and many of these youth have brushes with the law. One study revealed, for example, that 33 percent of the boys and 14 percent of the girls born in 1958 had at least one contact with the police before reaching the age of 18 (Tracy, Wolfgang, and Figlio, 1985). Indeed, some forms of serious delinquent behavior, such as drug and alcohol abuse, are far more frequent than the stereotypical delinquent behavior of gang fighting and vandalism and appear to cut across class and gender lines.

Studies that ask youth themselves about their delinquent behavior consistently confirm that many adolescents engage in at least some form of misbehavior which could result in arrest. Thus, it is largely trivial misconduct, rather than serious crime that shapes the actual nature of juvenile delinquency. One national study of youth aged 15–21 in 1986, for example, noted that only a small number reported involvement in a serious assault (5 percent) or a gang fight (1 percent). In contrast, many admit to having used alcohol (90 percent), marihuana (37 percent), and having been publicly drunk (44 percent). In a 1980

The author would like to acknowledge this chapter's origins in "Girls' Crime and Woman's Place," *Crime and Delinquency* 35:1 (January 1989): 5–29. This chapter is expanded, updated, and completely revised expressly for inclusion in this text. Used by permission of Sage Publications, Inc.

version of the same survey, teenagers admit to having skipped classes (truancy, 42 percent), had sexual intercourse (44 percent), and stealing from the family (15 percent) (Flanagan and Maguire, 1990). Clearly, not all these activities are equally serious. But young people can be arrested for all these behaviors.

Indeed, one of the most important points to understand about delinquency, particularly female delinquency, is that youth can be taken into custody for both criminal acts and "status offenses." These offenses, unlike criminal violations, are violations of parental authority: "running away from home," being a "person in need of supervision," being "incorrigible," truant, in need of "care and protection," and so on. Juvenile delinquents,

then, are youths arrested for either criminal offenses or non-criminal status offenses; and, as we will see, the role played by status offenses is by no means insignificant, particularly in female delinquency.

Examining the types of offenses for which youth are actually arrested again shows that most are arrested for less serious criminal acts and status offenses. Of the over 1.5 million youth arrested in 1990 for example, only 5 percent were arrested for such serious violent offenses as murder, rape, robbery, or aggravated assault (FBI, 1991). In contrast, 20 percent were arrested for a single offense (larceny theft) much of which, particularly for girls, is shoplifting (Shelden and Horvath, 1986).

Table 1 shows that while trivial offenses dominate both male and female delinquency,

TABLE 1

Rank Order of Adolescent Male and Female Arrests for Specific Offenses, 1981 and 1990

Male				Female			
1981	% of total arrests	1990	% of total arrests	1981	% of total arrests	1990	% of total arrests
1. Larceny-theft	21.0	1. Larceny-theft	20.4	1. Larceny-theft	22.3	1. Larceny-theft	27.2
2. Other offenses	12.9	2. Other offenses	13.7	2. Runaway	18.8	2. Runaway	19.6
3. Burglary	13.2	3. Burglary	8.0	3. Other offenses	13.0	3. Other offenses	12.6
4. Drug abuse violations	5.4	4. Vandalism	7.1	4. Liquor laws	8.2	4. Liquor laws	8.4
5. Vandalism	6.7	5. Drug abuse	4.0	5. Curfew and loitering violations	3.7	5. Curfew and loitering violations	4.5

	1981	1990		1977	1986
Arrests for serious violent offenses*	4.5	5.6	Arrests for serious violent offenses	2.0	2.48
Arrests for all violent offenses[†]	8.6	12.4	Arrests for all violent offenses	6.2	9.4
Arrests for status offenses[‡]	6.6	8.0	Arrests for status offenses	22.7	24.1

*Arrests for murder and nonnegligent manslaughter, robbery, forcible rape, and aggravated assault.
[†]Also includes arrests for other assaults.
[‡]Arrests for curfew and loitering law violation and runaway.
Source: Compiled from Federal Bureau of Investigation (1991, p. 179).

trivial offenses, particularly status offenses, are more significant in the case of girls' arrests: the five offenses listed in the table accounted for nearly three-quarters of female offenses during the two periods reviewed and only slightly more than half of male offenses.

More to the point, though neglected in most delinquency research, status offenses play a significant role in girls' official delinquency. They accounted for 24.1 percent of all girls' arrests in 1990 (compared to 22.5 percent in 1981) but only about 8 percent of boys' arrests (compared to 6.6 percent in 1981). These figures are surprising since dramatic declines in arrests of youth for these offenses might have been expected owing to the passage of the Juvenile Justice and Delinquency Prevention Act (JJDPA) in 1974 which encouraged jurisdictions to divert and de-institutionalize youth charged with non-criminal offenses. While the number of youth arrested for status offenses did drop considerably in the 1970s (by 24 percent for girls, and by 66 percent for boys) (FBI, 1980), this trend was reversed in the 1980s. Between 1981 and 1990, for example, girls' arrests for running away increased 18.5 percent and for curfew violations increased a striking 36.6 percent (FBI, 1991).

In 1985 status offenses accounted for 35 percent of all girls' cases in U.S. juvenile courts, but only 9.9 percent of boys' cases (Snyder et al., 1989). Another way to look at this is to note that males were 85 percent of those charged with criminal offenses, while girls were 43 percent of those charged with status offenses (Snyder et al., 1989). One status offense, runaway, is 63 percent female. (See similar earlier figures in Black and Smith, 1981.) Fifteen years earlier, about half of girls and 20 percent of boys were referred to court for these offenses (Children's Bureau, 1965). These data do seem to signal a drop in female status offense referrals, though not as dramatic a decline as might have been expected.

For many years statistics showing large numbers of girls arrested and referred for status offenses were taken to indicate differences between male and female delinquency. However, self-report studies of male and female delinquency do not reflect the dramatic differences in misbehavior found in official statistics. It seems that girls charged with these non-criminal status offenses have been and continue to be significantly over-represented in court populations.

Teilmann and Landry (1981) compared girls' contribution to arrests for runaways and incorrigibles with girls' self-reports of these two activities, and found a 10.4 percent over-representation of girls among those arrested for runaway and a 30.9 percent over-representation in arrests for incorrigibility. Likewise, Figueira-McDonough (1985:277) analyzed the delinquent self-report conduct of 2,000 youths and found "no evidence of greater involvement of females in status offenses." And Canter (1982) found in the National Youth Survey that there was no evidence of greater female involvement, compared to males, in any category of delinquent behavior. Indeed, in this sample, males were significantly more likely than females to report status offenses.

Comparing Canter's national data on the extensiveness of girls' self-reported delinquency to data on official arrests of girls (see Table 2) reveals that girls are under-represented in every arrest category except for status offenses and larceny theft. These figures strongly suggest that official practices exaggerate the role played by status offenses in girls' delinquency.

Delinquency theory, because it has virtually ignored female delinquency, failed to pursue anomalies such as these in the few early studies examining gender differences in delinquent behavior. Indeed, most delinquency theories have ignored status offenses. Thus, there is considerable question as to

TABLE 2
**Comparison of Sex Differences in Self-Reported
and Official Delinquency for Selected Offenses**

	Self-report* M/F ratios, 1976	Official statistics[†] M/F arrest ratio	
		1976	1990
Theft	3.5:1 (felony theft) 3.4:1 (minor theft)	2.5:1	2.5:1
Drug violation	1:1 (hard drug use)	5.1:1	7.4:1 (drug abuse violations)
Vandalism	5.1:1	12.3:1	10.9:1
Disorderly conduct	2.8:1	4.5:1	3.8:1
Serious assault	3.5:1 (felony assault)	5.6:1	5.7:1 (aggravated assault)
Minor assault	3.4:1	3.8:1	3.3:1 (other assaults)
Status offenses	1.6:1	1.3:1	1.1:1 (runaway, curfew)

*Extracted from Rachelle Canter (1982, p. 383).
[†]Compiled from Federal Bureau of Investigation (1980, p. 173; 1991, p. 179).

whether existing theories which were admittedly developed to explain male delinquency can adequately explain female delinquency. Will the "add women and stir approach" be sufficient? Are these really theories of delinquent behavior as some (Simons, Miller, and Aigner, 1980) have argued?

This chapter will suggest that they are not. The extensive focus on male delinquency and the inattention to the role played by patriarchal arrangements in the generation of adolescent delinquency and conformity have rendered the major delinquency theories fundamentally inadequate to explain female behavior. There is, in short, an urgent need to re-think current models in light of girls' situation in patriarchal society.

To understand why such work must occur, it is first necessary to briefly explore the dimensions of the androcentric bias found in

the dominant and influential delinquency theories. Then the need for a feminist model of female delinquency will be explored by reviewing the available evidence on girls' offending. We will also see that the proposed overhaul of delinquency theory is not, as some might think, solely an academic exercise: it is incorrect to assume that because girls are charged with less serious offenses, they actually have few problems and are treated gently when drawn into the juvenile justice system. Indeed, the predominant focus on disadvantaged males has meant that girls' victimization and its relation to girls' crime has been systematically ignored. Also missed has been the central role played by the juvenile justice system in the sexualization of girls' delinquency and the criminalization of girls' survival strategies. Finally, it will be suggested that the juvenile justice system's official actions should be seen as major forces in girls' oppression as they have historically served to reinforce the obedience of all young women to demands of patriarchal authority no matter how abusive and arbitrary.

THE ROMANCE OF THE GANG OR THE WEST SIDE STORY SYNDROME

From the start, delinquency research focused on visible lower class, male delinquency often justifying the neglect of girls in the most cavalier of terms. Take, for example, the extremely important and influential work of Clifford Shaw and Henry McKay who, beginning in 1929, took an ecological approach to the study of juvenile delinquency. Their impressive work, particularly *Juvenile Delinquency in Urban Areas* (1942) and intensive biographical case studies such as Shaw's *Brothers in Crime* (1938), set the stage for much of the subcultural research on gang delinquency. Despite their almost exclusive focus on boys, in none of these works is any justification given for the equation of male delinquency with delinquency.

Early field work on delinquent gangs in Chicago set the stage for another style of delinquency research. Yet, here too researchers were only interested in talking to and following the boys. Thrasher (1927) studied over 1,000 juvenile gangs in Chicago during roughly the same period as Shaw and McKay. He spends only one page out of 600 on the five or six female gangs he encountered in his field work.

Another major theoretical approach to delinquency focuses on the subculture of lower class communities as a generating milieu for delinquent behavior. Here again, noted delinquency researchers concentrated either exclusively or nearly exclusively on male lower class culture. Cohen's famous work on the subculture of delinquent gangs, written nearly 20 years after Thrasher's,

deliberately considers only boys' delinquency. He justifies the exclusion of girls on the basis of their femininity!

Cohen (1955:140) argues that the delinquent response "however it may be condemned by others on moral grounds, has at least one virtue: it incontestably confirms . . . his essential masculinity." Much the same line of argument appears in Miller's (1958) influential paper on the "focal concerns" of lower class life with its emphasis on the importance of trouble, toughness, excitement, etc. These, the author concludes, predispose poor, particularly male, youth to criminal misconduct.

Emphasis on blocked opportunities (also called "strain" or anomie theories) emerged out of the work of Robert Merton (1938), which influenced delinquency research largely through the efforts of Cloward and Ohlin, who discussed access to "legitimate" and "illegitimate" opportunities for male youth. No mention of female delinquency can be found in their *Delinquency and Opportunity* but women are blamed for male delinquency: boys, "engulfed by a feminine world and uncertain of their own identification . . . tend to 'protest' against femininity" (Cloward and Ohlin, 1960:49). In an attempt to test Cloward and Ohlin's blocked opportunity thesis for girls, Ruth Morris (1964) was unable to find a clear relationship between blocked "female" goals and delinquency.

The work of Edwin Sutherland (1978) emphasized the fact that criminal behavior was learned in intimate personal groups. His work, particularly the notion of differential association, which also influenced Cloward and Ohlin's work, was similarly male-oriented as much of his work was affected by case studies of male criminals. Finally, the work of Travis Hirschi (1969) on the social bonds which control delinquency ("social control theory") was, as stated earlier, derived out of research on male delinquents (though he, at least, studied delinquent behavior as reported by youth themselves rather than studying only those who were arrested).

Such a persistent focus on (lower) social class and such an absence of interest in gender in delinquency is ironic for two reasons. As even the work of Hirschi demonstrated, and as later studies would validate, a clear relation between social class position and delinquency is problematic, while it is crystal clear that gender has a dramatic and consistent effect on delinquency causation (Hagan, Gillis, and Simpson, 1985). The second irony, now as then, is the fact that while scholars had little interest in female delinquents, the same could not be said for the juvenile justice system. Indeed, work on the early history of a separate system for youth reveals that concerns about girls' immoral conduct was really at the center of what some have called the "childsaving movement" (Platt, 1969) which set up the juvenile justice system.

"THE BEST PLACE TO CONQUER GIRLS"

The establishment of separate institutions for youthful offenders was part of the Progressive movement, which was keenly concerned about prostitution and other "social evils" (e.g., white slavery) (Schlossman and Wallach, 1978; Rafter, 1990). Childsaving was also a celebration of women's domesticity, though ironically women were influential in the movement (Platt, 1969; Rafter, 1990). Ultimately, many of the early childsavers' activities revolved around the monitoring of young girls', particularly immigrant girls', behavior to prevent their straying from the path (Feinman, 1980; Freedman, 1981).

Girls were often the clear losers in this reform effort. Studies of early family courts reveal that virtually all the girls who appeared in these courts were charged for waywardness or immorality (which usually

meant evidence of sexual intercourse) (Schlossman and Wallach, 1978; Shelden, 1981). Typically, gynecological examinations were routinely ordered for the girls (Chesney-Lind, 1971). More to the point, the sanctions for such misbehavior were extremely severe. For example, in Chicago (where family court was founded), half of the girl delinquents, but only one-fifth of the boy delinquents, were sent to reformatories between 1899–1909. In Milwaukee, twice as many girls as boys were committed to training schools (Schlossman and Wallach, 1978); equally disproportionate figures have been published for Memphis (Shelden, 1981) and Honolulu (Chesney-Lind, 1971). Indeed, girls were half of those committed to training schools in Honolulu well into the 1950s (Chesney-Lind, 1973).

Not surprisingly, large numbers of girls' reformatories and training schools were established during this period as well as places of "rescue and reform." For example, Schlossman and Wallach (1978) note that 23 facilities for girls were opened during 1910–1920 (between 1850 and 1910, the average was only five per decade), and these institutions did much to set the tone of official response to female delinquency. Obsessed with precocious female sexuality, they sought to hold the girls until marriageable age, isolating them from all contact with males and occupying them in domestic pursuits during their sometimes long incarceration.

The links between these attitudes and those of juvenile courts some decades later are, of course, arguable; but an examination of the record of the court does not inspire confidence. A few examples of the persistence of what might be called a double standard of juvenile justice will suffice here.

A study conducted in the early 1970s in a New Jersey training school revealed large numbers of girls incarcerated "for their own protection." Explaining this pattern, one judge said, "Most of the girls I commit are for status offenses. I figure if a girl is about to get pregnant, we'll keep her until she's sixteen and then ADC (Aid to Dependent Children) will pick her up" (Rogers, 1972). For more evidence of official concern with adolescent sexual misconduct, consider Linda Hancock's (1981) content analysis of police referrals in Australia. She noted that 40 percent of the referrals of girls to court (but only 5 percent of the boys) made specific mention of sexual and moral conduct. Such results suggest that all youthful female misbehavior has traditionally been subject to surveillance for evidence of sexual misconduct. This sexualization of female deviance is highly significant and explains why criminal activities by girls (particularly in past years) were overlooked so long as they did not appear to signal defiance of parental control (see Smith, 1978).

Juvenile justice workers rarely reflected on the broader nature of female misbehavior or on the sources of this misbehavior. It was enough for them that girls' parents reported them out of control. Indeed, court personnel tended to "sexualize" virtually all female defiance that lent itself to that construction and ignore other misbehavior (Chesney-Lind, 1973; Smith, 1978). For their part, academic students of delinquency were so entranced with the notion of the delinquent as a romantic rogue male that they spent little time on middle-class delinquency, trivial offenses, or status offenses—which make up the vast bulk of delinquent behavior.

Some have argued that such an imbalance in theoretical work is appropriate as minor misconducts, while troublesome, do not threaten the safety and well-being of the community. This argument might be persuasive if two additional points could be established: that some small number of youth "specialize" in serious criminal behavior while the rest commit only minor acts, and that the juvenile court rapidly releases those youth that come into its purview for these minor offenses thus reserving resources for the most serious youthful offenders.

The evidence is mixed on both of these points. Despite determined efforts, researchers have failed to locate a group of offenders who specialize only in serious violent offenses. For example, analysis of national self-report data by Elliot, Huizinga, and Morse (1987) noted that serious violent offending appears imbedded in a more general involvement in a wide range of serious and non-serious offenses.

More to the point, police and court personnel are far more interested in youth they charge with trivial or status offenses than anyone imagined. Efforts to deinstitutionalize "status offenders," for example, ran afoul of juvenile justice personnel who were reluctant to release youth guilty of non-criminal offenses (Chesney-Lind, 1988). As has been established, much of this is due to the system's history, which encouraged court officers to involve themselves in the non-criminal behavior of youth to "save" them from a variety of social ills.[1]

The most influential delinquency theories, however, have largely ducked the issue of status and trivial offenses and thus have neglected the role played by the agencies of official control (police, probation officers, juvenile court judges, detention home workers, and training school personnel) in the shaping of the "delinquency problem." The less than distinct picture that emerges from the actual distribution of delinquent behavior, however, seems to show that agents of social control have considerable discretion in labelling or choosing not to label particular behavior as "delinquent." This symbiotic relation between delinquent behavior and the official response to that behavior is particularly critical when the question of female delinquency is considered.

DEINSTITUTIONALIZATION AND GENDER BIAS

Court officials always have been extremely critical of deinstitutionalization (see Schwartz, 1989). Not surprisingly, then, while there were great hopes when the JJDPA was passed, a 1978 General Accounting Office (GAO) report concluded that the Law Enforcement Assistance Administration (LEAA, the agency which implemented the legislation) was less than enthusiastic about the deinstitutionalization provisions of the act. Reviewing LEAA's efforts to remove status offenders from secure facilities, it was concluded that during certain administrations LEAA had actually "downplayed its importance and to some extent discouraged states from carrying out the Federal requirement" (GAO, 1978:10).

The GAO report found that monitoring systems to assess states' compliance with the law were lax or non-existent, definitions of detention and correctional facilities were confused (e.g., children in jail were often not counted), and LEAA was apparently reluctant to take action against states that had taken federal monies while failing to implement the deinstitutionalization of status offenders.

The anti-deinstitutionalization sentiment among juvenile justice officials ran very deep. Ultimately, judges narrowed the definition of a status offender in the amended act so that any child who had violated a "valid court order" would no longer be covered under the deinstitutionalization provisions (U.S. Statutes, 1981). This change, which was never publicly debated in Congress, effectively gutted the act. It meant that a young woman who ran away from a court ordered placement (a halfway house, foster home, etc.) could be re-labelled a delinquent and locked up.

Previous to this change, judges apparently engaged in other, less public, efforts to "circumvent" the deinstitutionalization compo-

nent of the act. These included converting status offenders into delinquents by issuing criminal contempt citations which turned them into law violators, referring or committing status offenders to secure mental health facilities, and developing "semi-secure" facilities (Costello and Worthington, 1981–1982).

One recent Florida study (Bishop and Frazier, 1990) found these contempt proceedings to clearly disadvantage female status offenders. This study, which reviewed 162,012 cases referred to juvenile justice intake units during 1985–1987, found only a weak pattern of discrimination against female as compared to male status offenders. However, the impact of contempt citations showed a different pattern. Female offenders referred for contempt were more likely than females referred for other criminal offenses to be petitioned to court. (They were more likely to be petitioned to court than males referred for contempt, and far more likely than boys to be sentenced to detention.) The typical female offender in the study had a probability of incarceration of 4.3 percent, which increased to 29.9 percent if she was held in contempt. (This pattern was not observed among the males.) The authors conclude, "Clearly neither the cultural changes associated with the feminist movement nor the legal changes illustrated in the JJDP Act's mandate to deinstitutionalize status offenders have brought about equality under the law for young men and women" (p. 22).

Sadly, powerful opponents to efforts to deinstitutionalize status offenders continue to appear. Having said this, it would be remiss not to note that the deinstitutionalization movement has reduced the number of girls in detention centers and training schools. Indeed, this may explain the fact that recent studies fail to find such dramatic evidence of discrimination against girls charged with status offenses (see Carrington, 1990; Johnson and Scheuble, 1991). These studies, though, miss the more subtle forms of bias (such as bootstrapping and abuse of the contempt process) and, in the process, underestimate the robust nature of patriarchal commitment to the sexual control of young women. Perhaps the starkest example of the durability of official concern for girls' obedience, though, can be found in the rising numbers of girls being institutionalized by their parents in private mental hospitals when the detention centers and training schools are denied them—a trend to be discussed in the next section.

DEINSTITUTIONALIZATION OR TRANSINSTITUTIONALIZATION? GIRLS AND THE MENTAL HEALTH SYSTEM

Despite considerable resistance, it is clear that incarceration of young women in public training schools and detention centers fell dramatically after the passage of the JJDPA. Before the act was passed, nearly three-quarters (71 percent) of the girls and 23 percent of the boys in the nation's training schools were incarcerated for status offenses (Schwartz, Steketee, and Schneider, 1990). Between 1974 and 1979 the number of girls admitted to public detention facilities and training schools dropped by 40 percent. Since then, however, the trend has slowed in some areas of the country, particularly at the detention level. Between 1979 and 1989, for example, the number of girls held in these same public facilities increased by 10 percent (Jamieson and Flanagan, 1987; Allen-Hagen, 1991).

In addition, the placement of girls in private facilities has increased. This is not necessarily an improvement. Some (Schwartz, Jackson-Beeck, and Anderson, 1984) have, in fact, called this a system of "hidden" private juvenile corrections where incarceration can occur without any legal procedure and without the consent of the youths (since they are underage).

The clearest problems with private institutions arise in the case of private psychiatric hospitals. As a study by Weithorn (1988) reports, adolescent admissions to psychiatric units of private hospitals have jumped dramatically, increasing four-fold between 1980 and 1984. There has also been a marked shift in the pattern of juvenile mental health incarceration. Juvenile admissions to private hospitals went from 37 percent of all juvenile admissions in 1971 to 61 percent by 1980. Finally, it is estimated that fewer than one-third of juveniles admitted for inpatient mental health treatment were diagnosed as having severe or acute mental disorders in contrast to between half and two-thirds of adults so admitted. A closer look at youth in such institutions in Virginia suggests that 36 to 70 percent of the state's hospital population "suffer from no more than 'acting out' problems and a range of less serious difficulties" (p. 789). Nonetheless, Weithorn continues, juvenile psychiatric patients remain in the hospital about twice as long as adults.

These patterns have very clear implications for the treatment of girls, though data on gender of admissions are sketchy. The chief concern is that admissions procedures to such private facilities have never been formalized. In addition, the U.S. Supreme Court has rejected an attempt to guarantee procedural protections that have been extended to adults in Parham v. J.R. [442 U.S. 584 (1979)].

Perhaps as a result of both the Supreme Court's decision and the partial success of deinstitutionalization within the juvenile justice system, many private hospitals, whose profits are enhanced by filling beds, advise institutional care for "troublesome" youth. Some of the criteria generated by these institutions are of specific concern to those worried about the overuse of institutionalization. For example, Weithorn stresses (p. 786) one set of criteria suggests that "sexual promiscuity" is an example of a "self-defeating" or "self destructive behavior" necessitating "immediate acute-care hospitalization [as] the only reasonable intervention." Another cause of incarceration is "inability to function" in family life, vocational pursuits, and "choice of community resources" (which is defined very broadly and includes choice of recreation and choice of friends)" (p. 786).

Given this sort of vague language and the problems that public systems of control have had with sexist interpretations of status offense labels, it is no surprise that a number of the examples of egregious abuse of institutionalization cited by Weithorn are of girls. Some of these cases make a direct link between status offenses and incarceration. Take, for example, the case of a 12 year old girl who was hospitalized in a state psychiatric facility after spending a week in a juvenile detention center because she was said to be a "Child in Need of Supervision." Weithorn cites another case (p. 790), a 16 year old girl, who was admitted into a private psychiatric hospital because she "'seduced' older men, drank vodka, skipped school, ran way from home, and disobeyed her divorced mother."

In essence, though the data are far from complete, the evidence seems to point to the incarceration of girls, in this case particularly middle class white girls, in private hospitals for much the same behavior that, in previous decades, placed them in public institutions. Given the lack of procedural safeguards in these settings, some might even argue that there is greater potential for sexist practices to flourish in these closed and private settings.

TOWARD A FEMINIST THEORY OF DELINQUENCY

To completely sketch out a feminist theory of delinquency is beyond the scope of this chapter. It may be sufficient to simply identify a few of the most obvious problems with attempts to adapt male oriented theory to explain female conformity and deviance. Most significant of these is the fact that all existing theories were developed with no concern about gender stratification.

Note that this is not simply an observation about the power of gender roles (though this power is undeniable). It is increasingly clear that gender stratification in patriarchal society is as powerful a system as class. A feminist approach to delinquency would construct explanations of female behavior that are sensitive to its patriarchal context and would also examine ways in which agencies of social control—the police, the courts, and the prisons—act to reinforce women's place in male society (Chesney-Lind, 1986). Efforts to construct a feminist model of delinquency must first and foremost be sensitive to the situations of girls. Failure to consider the existing empirical evidence on girls' lives and behavior can quickly lead to stereotypical thinking and theoretical dead ends.

An example of this sort of flawed theory building was the early fascination with the notion (now mostly discredited) that the women's movement was causing an increase in women's crime (Steffensmeier, 1980; Gora, 1982). A more recent example can be found in work on the "power-control" model of delinquency (Hagan, Simpson, and Gillis, 1987). Here, the authors speculate that girls commit less delinquency in part because their behavior is more closely controlled by the patriarchal family. The authors' promising beginning quickly gets bogged down in a very limited definition of patriarchal control (focusing on parental supervision and intrafamily variations in power). Ultimately, this leads them to argue that mothers' work force participation leads to increases in daughters' delinquency since these girls find themselves in more "egalitarian families."

This is essentially a variation on the earlier "liberation" hypothesis. Now, mother's liberation causes daughter's crime! Not only are there many methodological problems with the study (e.g., the authors assume that most adolescents live in families with both parents) but there is a more fundamental problem: no evidence exists to suggest that as women's labor force participation has increased, girls' delinquency has increased. Indeed, during the last decade, as women's labor force participation accelerated and the number of female headed households soared, aggregate female delinquency measured both by self-report and official statistics either declined or remained stable (Ageton, 1983; Chilton and Datesman, 1987; OJJDP, 1992).

By contrast, a feminist model of delinquency would focus more extensively on the little that is known about girls' actual lives and the role played by girls' problems, including those caused by racism and poverty, in their delinquency behavior. Fortunately, a considerable literature is now developing on girls' lives and much of it bears directly on girls' crime.

CRIMINALIZING GIRLS' SURVIVAL

It has long been understood that a major reason for girls' presence in juvenile courts was their parents' insistence on their arrest. In the early years, conflicts with parents were by far the most significant referral source; in Honolulu 44 percent of the girls who appeared in court in 1929–30 were referred by parents.

Recent national data, while slightly less explicit, also show that girls are more likely to be referred to court by "sources other than law enforcement agencies" (e.g., parents). In 1985, only 22 percent of youth referred for delinquency offenses, but 60 percent of youth referred for status offenses were referred to court by such sources. The pattern among youth referred for those status offenses for which girls are over-represented is also clear. Over three-quarters of the youth referred for running away from home (55 percent of whom were girls) and 88 percent of the youth charged with ungovernability (over half of whom were girls) were referred by non–law enforcement sources compared to only 9 percent of youth charged with liquor offenses (which was 72 percent male) (Snyder et al., 1989; see also Pope and Feyerherm, 1982).

The fact that parents are often committed to two standards of adolescent behavior is one explanation for such a disparity and should not be discounted as a major source of tension even in modern families. Despite expectations to the contrary, gender specific socialization patterns—especially parents' relations with their daughters—have not changed very much (Katz, 1979; Ianni, 1989). Clearly, parental attempts to adhere to and enforce these traditional notions will continue to cause conflict between girls and their elders. Another important explanation for girls' problems with their parents that only recently has received attention is physical and sexual abuse. It is increasingly clear that childhood sexual abuse is a particular problem for girls.

Girls are, for example, much more likely to be the victims of child sexual abuse than are boys. Finkelhor estimates from a review of community studies that roughly 70 percent of the victims of sexual abuse are female (Finkelhor and Baron, 1986). Girls' sexual abuse also tends to start earlier than boys' (Finkelhor and Baron, 1986), they are more likely than boys to be assaulted by a family member (often a stepfather) (DeJong, Hervada, and Emmett, 1983; Russell, 1986), and thus their abuse tends to last longer than male sexual abuse (DeJong, Hervada, and Emmett, 1983). All these factors are associated with more severe trauma—causing dramatic short and long term effects in victims (Adams-Tucker, 1982). The effects noted by researchers in this area range from "fear, anxiety, depression, anger and hostility, and inappropriate sexual behavior" (Browne and

Finkelhor, 1986:69) to behaviors better known to criminologists: e.g., running away from home, difficulties in school, truancy, and early marriage (Browne and Finkelhor, 1986; Herman, 1981).

Recent national research shows clearly the role played by physical and sexual abuse in girls' delinquency. According to a study of girls in juvenile correctional settings (ACA, 1990), a very large proportion had experienced physical abuse (61.2 percent) with nearly half saying that they had experienced this 11 or more times. Many had reported the abuse, but the results of this reporting were sobering: most said that either nothing changed (29.9 percent) or the reporting just made things worse (25.3 percent). Nearly as many (54.3 percent) had experienced sexual abuse and for most this was not an isolated incident; a third reported that it happened 3–10 times and 27.4 percent reported that it happened 11 times or more. Most were 9 years of age or younger when the abuse began. Again, while most reported the abuse (68.1 percent), it tended to result in no change or in making things worse.

Given this history, it should be no surprise that the vast majority had run away from home (80.7 percent), and of those that had run, 39 percent had run 10 or more times. Over half (53.8 percent) said they had attempted suicide and when asked why they said it was because they "felt no one cared." What might be called a survival or coping strategy has been criminalized: girls in correctional establishments reported that their first arrests were typically for running away from home (20.5 percent) or for larceny theft (25 percent). The offenses for which they are currently incarcerated were more varied, but the most significant were probation/parole violation (14.6 percent), aggravated assault (9.5 percent), larceny theft (9 percent), and runaway (6.5 percent). The large number of girls incarcerated for probation/parole violation may be a measure of

new efforts to "bootstrap" status offenders into delinquents by incarcerating them for these offenses (ACA, 1991).

Many young women, then, are running away from profound sexual victimization at home, and once on the streets they are forced further into crime to survive. Interviews with girls who have run away from home clearly show that they are not very attached to their delinquent activities. In fact, they are angry about being labeled as delinquent, yet all engaged in illegal acts (Koroki and Chesney-Lind, 1985). A Wisconsin study found that half (54 percent) of the girls who ran away found it necessary to steal money, food, or clothing to survive, and a few exchanged sexual contact for money, food, and/or shelter (Phelps et al., 1982). In a study of runaway youth, McCormack, Janus, and Burgess (1986) found that sexually abused female runaways were significantly more likely than their non-abused counterparts to engage in delinquent or criminal activities such as substance abuse, petty theft, and prostitution. No such pattern was found among male runaways.

Research by Chesney-Lind and Rodriguez (1983) on the backgrounds of adult women in prison underscores the important links between women's childhood victimizations and later criminal careers. The interviews revealed that virtually all the women in this sample were victims of physical and/or sexual abuse as youngsters; over 60 percent had been sexually abused; and about half had been raped as young women. This situation prompted these women to run away from home (three-quarters had been arrested for status offenses) where once on the streets they began engaging in prostitution and petty property crime. They also begin what becomes a lifetime problem with drugs. As adults, the women continue in these activities since they have little education and virtually no marketable occupational skills (see also Miller, 1986; Arnold, Chapter 8 in this volume).

Confirmation of the consequences of child-hood sexual and physical abuse for adult female criminal behavior also has come recently from a large quantitative study of 908 women with histories of victimization. Widom (1988) found that abused or neglected females were twice as likely as a matched group of controls to have an adult record (16 percent v. 7.5 percent). (Among men, the difference exists but was not so dramatic—42 percent v. 33 percent.) In addition, when women with abuse backgrounds became involved with the criminal justice system, their arrests tended to involve property and order offenses (e.g., disorderly conduct, curfew and loitering violations). In contrast, men with abuse backgrounds were more likely to contribute to the "cycle of violence" with more arrests for violent offenses as adult offenders than the control group.

Given this information, a brief example of how a feminist perspective on the causes of female delinquency might look seems appropriate. First, like young men, girls are often victims of violence and sexual abuse. But girls' victimization and their responses to it are specifically shaped by their status as young women. Perhaps because of the gender and sexual scripts found in patriarchal families, girls are much more likely than boys to be the victim of family related sexual abuse. Men, particularly men with traditional attitudes towards women, are likely to define their daughters or stepdaughters as their sexual property (Finkelhor, 1982). In a society that idealizes inequality in male/female relationships and venerates youth in women, girls are easily defined as sexually attractive by older men (Bell, 1984). Girls' vulnerability to physical and sexual abuse is heightened by norms requiring that they stay at home where their victimizers have access to them.

Moreover, their victimizers (usually males) have the ability to invoke official agencies of social control to keep young women at home and vulnerable. That is, abusers have been able to use the juvenile justice system's uncritical commitment to parental authority to force girls to obey them. Girls' complaints about abuse were, until recently, routinely ignored. Thus, legal statutes that were originally written to "protect" young people have, in the case of girls' delinquency, criminalized their survival strategies. As girls run away from abusive homes, parents have been able to employ agencies to enforce their return. If the girls persisted in refusing to stay in that home, however intolerable, they were incarcerated.

Young women, many of whom are on the run from homes characterized by sexual abuse and parental neglect, are forced by the very statutes designed to protect them into lives of escaped convicts. Unable to enroll in school or take a job to support themselves because they fear detection, young female runaways are forced into the streets. Here they engage in panhandling, petty theft, and occasional prostitution to survive.

In addition, the fact that young girls (but not necessarily young boys) are defined as sexually desirable and, in fact, more desirable than their older sisters due to the double standard of aging means that their lives on the streets (and their survival strategies) take on unique contours—once again shaped by patriarchal values. It is no accident that girls on the run from abusive homes, or on the streets because of profound poverty, get involved in criminal activities that exploit their sexual object status. American society has defined as desirable youthful, physically perfect women. This means that girls on the streets, who have little else of value to trade, are encouraged to utilize this "resource" (Campagna and Poffenberger, 1988). It also means that the criminal subculture views them from this perspective (Miller, 1986).

FEMALE DELINQUENCY, PATRIARCHAL AUTHORITY, AND FAMILY COURTS

The early insights into male delinquency were largely gleaned by intensive field observation of delinquent boys. Very little of this work has been done on girls' delinquency, though it is vital to an understanding of girls' definitions of their own situations, choices, and behavior (for exceptions, see Arnold, Chapter 8 in this volume; Campbell, 1984; Chesney-Lind and Shelden, 1992; Miller, 1986). Time must be spent listening to girls. Fuller research on the settings, such as families and schools, that girls find themselves in and the impact of variations in those settings should also be undertaken (Figueira-McDonough, 1986). A more complete understanding of how poverty and racism shape girls' lives is also vital (see Messerschmidt, 1986; Arnold, Chapter 8 in this volume). Finally, qualitative research on official agency reaction to girls' delinquency must be conducted. This latter task, admittedly more difficult, is particularly critical to the development of delinquency theory that is as sensitive to gender as it is to class and race.

It is clear that throughout most of the court's history, virtually all female delinquency has been seen in the context of the girls' sexual behavior. One explanation for this pattern is that familial control over girls' sexual capital has been central to the maintenance of patriarchy (Lerner, 1986). The fact that young women have relatively more of this capital has been one reason for the excessive concern that both families and official agencies of social control have expressed about youthful female defiance (otherwise much of the behavior of criminal justice personnel makes virtually no sense). Only if one considers the role of women's control over their sexuality at the point in their lives that their value to patriarchal society is so pronounced, does the historic pattern of jailing of huge numbers of girls guilty of minor misconduct make sense.

This framework may also explain some of the enormous resistance that the movement to curb the juvenile justice system's authority over status offenders encountered. Supporters of the change were not prepared for the political significance of giving youth, particularly girls, the freedom to run. Horror stories told by the opponents of deinstitutionalization about victimized youth, and youthful prostitution and involvement in pornography (OJJDP, 1985), all neglect the unpleasant reality that most of these behaviors were in direct response to earlier victimization—often by parents—that officials had, for years, routinely ignored. What may be at stake in efforts to roll back deinstitutionalization efforts is not so much "protection" of youth as it is curbing young women's right to defy patriarchy.

In sum, research on both the dynamics of girls' delinquency and official reactions to that behavior is essential to the development of theories of delinquency that are sensitive to its patriarchal as well as class and racial context.

NOTE

1. Recently, the notion that juvenile courts were extensively involved in the sexual regulation of girls' behavior has been challenged by Carrington (1990) who suggests that this "reading" of female delinquency fails to note that boys are also quite likely to be charged with status offenses. She, however, neglects to explain the fact that the types of status offenses that boys and girls are charged with are quite different (with girls being more likely to be charged with offenses that are "buffer charges" for sexual misconduct like running away from home), and she fails to account for the fact that status offenses comprise a far larger portion of girls' than boys' total delinquencies. Her suggestion

is that feminist scholars should stop "essential-izir.g" female delinquency and instead focus on the "masculinity of criminality." While she cloaks this plea in feminist rhetoric, such a call is ironic given the intense fascination traditional criminology has always given boys' delin-quency.

REFERENCES

Adams-Tucker, C. 1982. "Proximate Effects of Sexual Abuse in Childhood." *American Journal of Psychiatry* 193:1252–1256.

Ageton, S. 1983. "The Dynamics of Female Delin-quency, 1976–1980." *Criminology* 21:555–584.

Allen-Hagen, B. 1991. *Children in Custody 1989.* Washington, D.C.: U.S. Department of Justice.

American Correctional Association (ACA). 1990. *The Female Offender: What Does the Future Hold?* Washington, D.C.: St. Mary's.

Bell, I. Powell. 1984. "The Double Standard: Age," in J. Freeman (ed.). *Women: A Feminist Perspec-tive.* Palo Alto: Mayfield.

Bishop, D., and C. Frazier. 1990. "Gender Bias in the Juvenile Justice System: Implications of the JJDP Act." Paper presented at the annual meet-ing of the Academy of Criminal Justice Sciences.

Black, T. E., and C. Smith. 1981. *A Preliminary National Assessment of the Number and Characteris-tics of Juveniles Processed in the Juvenile Justice Sys-tem.* Washington, D.C.: Department of Justice, U.S. Government Printing Office.

Browne, A., and D. Finkelhor. 1986. "Impact of Child Sexual Abuse: A Review of Research." *Psychological Bulletin* 99:66–77.

Campagna, D., and D. Poffenberger. 1988. *The Sex-ual Trafficking in Children.* Dover: Auburn House.

Campbell, A. 1984. *The Girls in the Gang.* Oxford: Basil Blackwell.

Canter, R. 1982. "Sex Differences in Self-Report Delinquency." *Criminology* 20:373–393.

Carrington, Kerry. 1990. "Feminist Readings of Female Delinquency." *Feminism, Law and Society* 8(20):5–31.

Chesney-Lind, M. 1971. *Female Juvenile Delinquency in Hawaii.* Master's thesis. University of Hawaii at Manoa.

———. 1973. "Judicial Enforcement of the Female Sex Role." *Issues in Criminology* 8:51–71.

———. 1986. "Women and Crime: The Female Offender." *Signs* 12:78–96.

———. 1988. "Girls and Deinstitutionalization: Is Juvenile Justice Still Sexist?" *Journal of Criminal Justice Abstracts* 20:144–165.

——— and N. Rodriguez. 1983. "Women under Lock and Key." *Prison Journal* 63:47–65.

——— and R. G. Shelden. 1992. *Girls, Delinquency, and the Juvenile Justice System.* Pacific Grove: Brooks/Cole.

Children's Bureau, Department of Health, Educa-tion and Welfare. 1965. *1964 Statistics on Public Institutions for Delinquent Children.* Washington, D.C.: U.S. Government Printing Office.

Chilton, R., and S. Datesman. 1987. "Gender, Race and Crime: An Analysis of Urban Arrest Trends, 1960–1980." *Gender and Society* 1:152–171.

Cloward, R., and L. Ohlin. 1960. *Delinquency and Opportunity.* New York: Free Press.

Cohen, A. 1955. *Delinquency in Boys: The Culture of the Gang.* New York: Free Press.

Costello, J. C., and N. L. Worthington. 1981–1982. "Incarcerating Status Offenders: Attempts to Cir-cumvent the Juvenile Justice and Delinquency Prevention Act." *Harvard Civil Rights–Civil Liber-ties Law Review* 16:41–81.

DeJong, A., A. Hervada, and G. Emmett. 1983. "Epidemiologic Variations in Childhood Sexual Abuse." *Child Abuse and Neglect* 7:155–162.

Elliott, D., D. Huizinga, and B. Morse. 1987. "A Career Analysis of Serious Violent Offenders," in I. Schwartz (ed.). *Violent Juvenile Crime: What Can We Do about It?* Minneapolis: Hubert Humphrey Institute.

Federal Bureau of Investigation (FBI). 1980. *Crime in America 1979: Uniform Crime Reports.* Washing-ton, D.C.: U.S. Department of Justice.

———. 1991. *Crime in America 1990: Uniform Crime Reports.* Washington, D.C.: U.S. Department of Justice.

Feinman, C. 1980. *Women in the Criminal Justice System.* New York: Praeger.

Figueira-McDonough, J. 1985. "Are Girls Differ-ent? Gender Discrepancies between Delinquent Behavior and Control." *Child Welfare* 64:273–289.

———. 1986. "School Context, Gender, and Delin-quency." *Journal of Youth and Adolescence* 15:79–98.

Finkelhor, D. 1982. "Sexual Abuse: A Sociological Perspective. *Child Abuse and Neglect* 6:95–102.

———— and L. Baron. 1986. "Risk Factors for Child Sexual Abuse." *Journal of Interpersonal Violence* 1:43–71.

Flanagan, T., and K. Maguire (eds.). 1990. *Sourcebook of Criminal Justice Statistics—1989.* Washington, D.C.: U.S. Department of Justice, Bureau of Justice Statistics.

Freedman, E. 1981. *Their Sisters' Keepers.* Ann Arbor: University of Michigan.

General Accounting Office (GAO). 1978. *Removing Status Offenders from Secure Facilities: Federal Leadership and Guidance Are Needed.* Washington, D.C.: GAO.

Gora, J. 1982. *The New Female Criminal: Empirical Reality or Social Myth?* New York: Praeger.

Hagan, J., A. R. Gillis, and J. Simpson. 1985. "The Class Structure of Gender and Delinquency: Toward a Power-Control Theory of Common Delinquent Behavior." *American Journal of Sociology* 90:1151–1178.

————, J. Simpson, and A. R. Gillis. 1987. "Class in the Household: A Power-Control Theory of Gender and Delinquency." *American Journal of Sociology* 92:788–816.

Hancock, L. 1981. "The Myth that Females Are Treated More Leniently than Males in the Juvenile Justice System." *Australian and New Zealand Journal of Sociology* 16:4–14.

Herman, J. 1981. *Father-Daughter Incest.* Cambridge, Mass.: Harvard University.

Hirschi, T. 1969. *Causes of Delinquency.* Berkeley: University of California.

Ianni, F. 1989. *The Search for Structure: A Report on American Youth Today.* New York: Free Press.

Jamieson, K. M., and T. Flanagan (eds.). 1987. *Sourcebook of Criminal Justice Statistics—1986.* Washington, D.C.: U.S. Department of Justice, Bureau of Justice Statistics.

———— and ———— (eds.). 1989. *Sourcebook of Criminal Justice Statistics—1988.* Washington, D.C.: U.S. Department of Justice, Bureau of Justice Statistics.

Johnson, David R., and Laurie K. Scheuble. 1991. "Gender Bias in the Disposition of Juvenile Court Referrals: The Effects of Time and Location." *Criminology* 29(4):677–699.

Katz, P. 1979. "The Development of Female Identity," in C. B. Kopp (ed.). *Becoming Female: Perspectives on Development.* New York: Plenum.

Koroki, J., and M. Chesney-Lind. 1985. *Everything Just Going Down the Drain.* Report 319. Hawaii: Youth Development and Research Center.

Lerner, G. 1986. *The Creation of Patriarchy.* New York: Oxford.

McCormack, A., M-D. Janus, and A. Wolbert Burgess. 1986. "Runaway Youths and Sexual Victimization: Gender Differences in an Adolescent Runaway Population." *Child Abuse and Neglect* 10:387–395.

Merton, R. K. 1938. "Social Structure and Anomie." *American Sociological Review* (October) 3:672–682.

Messerschmidt, J. 1986. *Capitalism, Patriarchy, and Crime: Toward a Socialist Feminist Criminology.* Totowa, N.J.: Rowman and Littlefield.

Miller, E. 1986. *Street Woman.* Philadelphia: Temple University.

Miller, W. B. 1958. "Lower Class Culture as a Generating Milieu of Gang Delinquency." *Journal of Social Issues* 14:5–19.

Morris, R. 1964. "Female Delinquency and Relational Problems." *Social Forces* 43:82–89.

Office of Juvenile Justice and Delinquency Prevention (OJJDP). 1985. *Runaway Children and the Juvenile Justice and Delinquency Prevention Act: What Is the Impact?* Washington, D.C.: U.S. Government Printing Office.

————. 1992. *Arrests of Youth 1990.* Washington D.C.: OJJDP Update on Statistics.

Phelps, R. J., et al. 1982. *Wisconsin Female Juvenile Offender Study Project Summary Report.* Wisconsin: Youth Policy and Law Center, Wisconsin Council on Juvenile Justice.

Platt, A. 1969. *The Childsavers.* Chicago: University of Chicago.

Pope, C., and W. Feyerherm. 1982. "Gender Bias in Juvenile Court Dispositions." *Social Service Research* 6:1–17.

Rafter, N. Hahn. 1990. *Partial Justice: Women, Prisons and Social Control.* New Brunswick, N.J.: Transaction.

Rogers, K. 1972. "'For Her Own Protection . . .': Conditions of Incarceration for Female Juvenile Offenders in . . . Connecticut." *Law and Society Review* (Winter): 223–246.

Russell, D. E. H. 1986. *The Secret Trauma: Incest in the Lives of Girls and Women.* New York: Basic Books.

Schlossman, S., and S. Wallach. 1978. "The Crime of Precocious Sexuality: Female Juvenile Delinquency in the Progressive Era." *Harvard Educational Review* 48:65–94.

Schwartz, I. M. 1989. *(In) Justice for Juveniles: Rethinking the Best Interests of the Child.* Lexington, Mass.: Lexington.

———, M. Jackson-Beeck, and R. Anderson. 1984. "The 'Hidden' System of Juvenile Control." *Crime and Delinquency* 30:371–385.

———, M. Steketee, and V. Schneider. 1990. "Federal Juvenile Justice Policy and the Incarceration of Girls." *Crime and Delinquency* 36:503–520.

Shaw, C. 1938. *Brothers in Crime.* Chicago: University of Chicago.

——— and H. D. McKay. 1942. *Juvenile Delinquency in Urban Areas.* Chicago: University of Chicago.

Shelden, R. 1981. "Sex Discrimination in the Juvenile Justice System: Memphis, Tennessee, 1900–1971," in M. Q. Warren (ed.). *Comparing Male and Female Offenders.* Beverly Hills: Sage.

——— and J. Horvath. 1986. "Processing Offenders in a Juvenile Court: A Comparison of Males and Females." Paper presented at the annual meeting of the Western Society of Criminology, Newport Beach, Calif.

Simons, R., M. Miller, and S. Aigner. 1980. "Contemporary Theories of Deviance and Female Delinquency: An Empirical Test." *Journal of Research in Crime and Delinquency* 17:42–57.

Smith, L. Shacklady. 1978. "Sexist Assumptions and Female Delinquency," in C. Smart and B. Smart (eds.). *Women, Sexuality and Social Control.* London: Routledge and Kegan Paul.

Snyder, H., et al. 1989. *Juvenile Court Statistics 1985.* Pittsburgh, Pa.: National Center for Juvenile Justice.

Steffensmeier, D. J. 1980. "Sex Differences in Patterns of Adult Crime, 1965–1977." *Social Forces* 58:1080–1109.

Sutherland, E. 1978. "Differential Association," in B. Krisberg and J. Austin (eds.). *Children of Israel: Critical Perspectives on Juvenile Justice.* Palo Alto: Mayfield.

Teilmann, K., and P. Landry, Jr. 1981. "Gender Bias in Juvenile Justice." *Journal of Research in Crime and Delinquency* 18:47–80.

Thrasher, F. 1927. *The Gang.* Chicago: University of Chicago.

Tracy, P., M. Wolfgang, and R. Figlio. 1985. *Delinquency in Two Birth Cohorts: Executive Summary.* Washington, D.C.: U.S. Department of Justice.

U.S. House of Representatives, Subcommittee on Human Resources of the Committee on Education and Labor. 1980. *Juvenile Justice Amendments of 1980.* Washington, D.C.: U.S. Government Printing Office.

U.S. Statutes at Large. Ninety-sixth Congress, 2d Sess. 1981. *Public Law 96-509—December 1981.* Washington, D.C.: U.S. Government Printing Office.

Weithorn, L. A. 1988. "Mental Hospitalization of Troublesome Youth: An Analysis of Skyrocketing Admission Rates." *Stanford Law Review* 40:773–838.

Widom, C. Spatz. 1988. "Child Abuse, Neglect, and Violent Criminal Behavior." Unpublished manuscript.

CHAPTER 5

TRENDS IN FEMALE CRIME: IT'S STILL A MAN'S WORLD

DARRELL STEFFENSMEIER

ABSTRACT

When the first edition of this book was published, a key question in the public's mind was whether the women's movement and greater equality for women had led to increasing similarity for women and men in their crime patterns. More recently the focus of concern has shifted to whether women are becoming more like men in committing violent crimes. In both cases, according to this chapter, the answer is emphatically "no."

Steffensmeier analyzes national arrest data from the Federal Uniform Crime Reports (UCR) for a 30-year period, 1960 to 1990. He concludes that a careful analysis of the data does not indicate that female crime is becoming similar to male crime in either amount or type. While some increases in female crime have emerged, Steffensmeier warns that these should not be given undue attention, because female arrest rates historically started very low in comparison with men's rates. And an increase in rates over time has occurred for both genders, particularly for larceny, fraud, liquor as well as drug violations, and assault. However, relative to that for men, the arrest profile for women has not changed: women's involvement is relatively high in minor property crimes (larceny, fraud, forgery) and low in "masculine" or serious violent and property crime.

The chapter pays particular attention to these most serious, violent crimes—homicide, aggravated assault, robbery, and burglary. Very little change is found in female arrest rates over the 30 years. In fact, when larceny (particularly shoplifting and minor theft) is treated as a nonserious crime instead of a serious offense (as it is currently by the UCR), sensational claims about dramatic changes in crimes by women are easily invalidated. Given this analysis of crime data, the reader should ask why the press and others claim that a new, dangerous female criminal has arrived on the scene. Finally, given the profound effect of racism in our society, how might an analysis by race *and* gender impact on the findings? This topic will be addressed in large part in Chapter 7.

For generations, men were considered the primary perpetrators of most criminal activities. Now, according to some commentators, this male dominance is changing. The role of women in crime is responding to changes in gender roles and the emancipation of women. Women are fast becoming both feared and revered participants in the criminal world. The past quarter-century witnessed a marked change in patterns and levels of crime among American women. Or did it?

Most frequently, claims regarding the changing character of female crime are linked to the arrest statistics of the *Uniform Crime Reports* (UCR). Published by the FBI, these statistics are the only continuous national data available that indicate whether the arrestee is male or female. My purpose in this article is to examine the arrest statistics of the *Uniform Crime Reports* (UCR) as they relate to patterns of female offending in the United States. Other sources of evidence are used to supplement the UCR data, however.

The conclusions derived from analysis of the FBI data are contrary to the view often depicted in the mass media and embraced by some social scientists. These data do not show that the criminal activities of females are approaching similarity with those of males in either kind or degree. Rather, substantial arrest gains of females are limited largely to the minor property crime categories, particularly larceny and fraud, and the gains in these two categories appear due to more females being arrested for traditional types of female offenses such as shoplifting and "bad check" passing (e.g., insufficient funds). American women are not catching up with males in the commission of violent, masculine, serious, or white-collar crimes.

This article was written expressly for inclusion in this text.

Table 1 displays male and female arrest rates/100,000 for the years 1960, 1975, and 1990, for all the offense categories in the *Uniform Crime Reports* except forcible rape (a male crime) and runaways/curfew (juvenile offenses). Since few crimes are committed either by those under age 10 or by those over the age of 65, the rates are calculated on persons aged 10 through 64—that is, on the population at risk. Table 1 also displays the female percentage of arrests and the profiles of male and female offenders, as we discuss later. For both males and females, the size of the rates increased in some categories, decreased in others, and did not change in still others. Overall, the pattern of change was similar for both sexes, with large increases occurring only for the offenses of larceny, fraud, driving under the influence, drug violations, and assault, and with decreases in arrest rates actually occurring in the categories of public drunkenness, sex offenses, vagrancy, suspicion, and gambling. This suggests that the rates of both sexes are influenced by similar social and legal forces, independent of any condition unique to women.

SOME CAUTIONS IN USING UCR ARREST STATISTICS FOR TREND COMPARISONS

Three major problems are associated with using UCR data to assess trends in female crime. First, the rate of arrests, like any other official measure of crime, is a function of behavior defined as criminal and the control measures established to deal with it. Because of changes in reporting practices and policing, the ability of law enforcement agencies to gather and record arrest statistics has improved greatly over time—especially since 1960. However, gauging the effect of these changes on the reporting of female crime is

TABLE 1

Male and Female Arrest Rates/100,000, Female Percentage of Arrests, and Male and Female Arrest Profiles

Offenses	Male rates			Female rates			Female percentage (of arrests)			Profiles, %			
										Males		Females	
	1960 (1)	1975 (2)	1990 (3)	1960 (4)	1975 (5)	1990 (6)	1960 (7)	1975 (8)	1990 (9)	1960 (10)	1990 (11)	1960 (12)	1990 (13)
Against persons													
Homicide	9	16	16	2	3	2	17	14	12	0.1	0.2	0.2	0.1
Aggravated assault	101	200	317	16	28	50	14	13	13	1	3	2	2
Weapons	69	137	165	4	11	14	4	8	7	1	2	0.5	0.7
Simple assault	265	354	662	29	54	129	10	13	15	4	6	4	5
Major property													
Robbery	65	131	124	4	10	12	5	7	8	1	1	0.5	0.5
Burglary	274	477	319	9	27	32	3	5	8	4	4	1	2
Stolen property	21	103	121	2	12	17	8	10	11	0.3	1	0.2	0.5
Minor property													
Larceny-theft	391	749	859	74	321	402	17	30	30	6	10	9	20
Fraud	70	114	157	12	59	133	15	34	43	1	2	2	7
Forgery	44	46	51	8	18	28	16	28	34	0.5	0.5	1	1
Embezzlement	—	7	8	—	3	5	—	28	37	—	0.2	—	0.1
Malicious mischief													
Auto theft	121	128	158	5	9	18	4	7	9	2	1	1	1
Vandalism	—	187	224	—	16	28	—	8	10	—	2	—	1
Arson	—	15	13	—	2	2	—	11	14	—	0.3	—	0.1
Drinking/ drugs													
Public drunkenness	2573	1201	624	212	87	71	8	7	9	36	8	25	4
DUI	344	971	1193	21	81	176	6	5	11	5	15	3	9
Liquor laws	183	276	428	28	43	102	13	14	17	3	5	4	5
Drug abuse	49	523	815	8	79	166	15	13	14	1	7	1	6
Sex/sex-related													
Prostitution	15	18	30	37	45	62	73	73	65	0.2	0.4	4	3
Sex offenses	81	55	78	17	5	7	17	8	8	1	1	2	0.3
Disorderly conduct	749	597	499	115	116	119	13	17	18	11	5	14	6
Vagrancy	265	45	26	23	7	4	8	14	12	4	0.3	3	0.2
Suspicion	222	31	13	28	5	3	11	13	15	3	0.1	3	0.1
Miscellaneous													
Against family	90	57	51	8	7	12	8	10	16	1	0.5	1	0.5
Gambling	202	60	14	19	6	2	8	9	15	3	0.2	2	0.2
Other except traffic	871	1139	2109	150	197	430	15	15	15	13	23	19	20
Total	7070	7850	9211	831	1383	2122	11	15	19				

difficult. It is generally recognized that comparing sex differences in arrest rates over a given period of time (between-sex comparison or the female percentage of arrests) is safer than using the rates either as a measure of the incidence of female crime for a specific year or to assess changes in the levels of female crime over time, e.g., to compare arrest rates of females today with those of a decade or so ago (within-sex comparison).

A glance at Table 1, which compares female arrest rates in 1960 with rates in 1990, certifies the considerable reliability problem that exists in within-sex comparisons. Note, for example, that female arrest rates are smaller today for offenses like public drunkenness (female rate/100,000 dropped from 212 in 1960 to 71 in 1990) and gambling (female rate/100,000 dropped from 19 to 2). Should we conclude from these rates that substantially *less* drinking and gambling is occurring among women today?

The changes from category to category may reflect shifts over time in public attitudes and police practices, more than actual behaviors of arrested persons, either male or female. In 1960 public drunkenness ranked #1 in arrests among all UCR offense categories, constituting more than one-third of all male arrests and one-fourth of all female arrests (versus 8 percent and 4 percent in 1990, respectively). In contrast, increasing public concern over alcohol- or drug-impaired operation of motor vehicles has caused arrest rates to rise sharply in the offense category of "driving under the influence" (DUI), which now ranks as the #1 arrest statistic. Observed arrest patterns such as these help explain why we (and most researchers) focus on *sex differences* in arrest rates. Nonetheless, using the UCR arrest data to make between-sex comparisons over time has some risks, which are described later.

A second problem with the UCR data is that the offense categories are *broad* and are derived from a heterogeneous collection of criminal acts. For example, the offense category of larceny-theft includes shoplifting a $10 item, theft of a radio from a parked auto, theft of merchandise by an employee, and cargo theft amounting to thousands of dollars. The broad offense category of fraud includes passing "bad" checks of small amounts and stock frauds involving large sums of money. Burglary includes "unlawful entry" into a neighbor's apartment to steal a television and safecracking. Arrests are not distinguished in terms of whether the suspect is the sole or major perpetrator, an accomplice, or a bystander. In sum, offenses representing dissimilar events and covering a range of seriousness are included in the same category. The UCR arrest data do not permit an assessment of variation *within* offense categories. We will be returning to this crucial point frequently throughout our discussion.

A third problem concerns the label "serious crime" that is used in the UCR to refer to the Index (or Type I) offenses—homicide, forcible rape, aggravated assault, robbery, burglary, larceny-theft, auto theft, and arson. It sometimes is claimed that the proportion of women arrested for serious crimes has been increasing dramatically and that the increase has been greater among females than males. On closer inspection, however, we find that the increased arrests of women for serious, or Index, crimes are almost entirely due to more women being arrested for larceny, especially for shoplifting. However, neither law enforcement nor the citizenry view larceny as a comparably serious crime.

TRENDS IN INDIVIDUAL OFFENSES

In any discussion of changing gender roles and their relation to female criminality, the central issue is whether sex differences in crime patterns diminish as men and women move toward greater equality in their rights and privileges. A major difficulty, however, in making comparisons over time between the sexes is the dramatic differences in initial arrest levels, since female arrest rates are partly a statistical artifact of low female starting points and rising rates for both sexes. (This chapter does not discuss changes in absolute differences in male/female arrest rates. For most offenses, however, absolute differences in arrest rates have become greater since 1960—that is, females have lost ground to males). As Table 1 shows, nonetheless, arrest rates of males continue to be considerably larger than those of females in all offense categories, except prostitution and possibly fraud.

Also shown in Table 1 (in the middle columns—7, 8, and 9) is the female percentage (or share) of all arrests for a particular offense for the years 1960, 1975, and 1990, calculated as

$$\frac{\text{Female rate}}{\text{Male rate} + \text{Female rate}} \times 100$$

The third set of columns (10–13) provides profiles of male and female arrest patterns by showing the percentage of male and female arrests represented by each crime category. Those percentages are given for the two end years of 1960 and 1990. The homicide figures of .2 for males in 1990 and .1 for females mean, respectively, that only two-tenths of 1 percent of all male arrests were for homicide, and only one-tenth of 1 percent of all female arrests were for homicide.

There are considerable similarities between the male and the female profiles and in their arrest trends. For both males and females, the three most common arrest categories in 1990 are DUI, larceny-theft, and "other except traffic"—a residual category that includes mostly criminal mischief, public disorder, local ordinance violations, and other minor types of crime. Together, these three offenses account for 48 percent of all male arrests and 49 per-

cent of all female arrests. Similarly, arrests for murder, arson, and embezzlement are relatively rare for males and females alike, while arrests for offenses such as liquor law violations (mostly underage drinking), simple assault, and disorderly conduct represent "middling ranks" for both sexes.

The most important gender differences in arrest profiles are in the proportionately greater involvement of women in minor property crimes (about 28 percent of all female arrests versus 12 percent of male arrests) and in prostitution-type offenses, and the relatively greater involvement of males in crimes against persons and major property crimes (17 percent of all male arrests versus 11 percent of all female arrests). The relatively high involvement of females in minor property crimes (larceny, fraud, forgery), coupled with their low involvement in the more "masculine" or serious kinds of violent and property crime (homicide, aggravated assault, robbery, burglary), is a pattern that shows in most comparisons of gender differences in crime.

Our major concern is with the female percentage of arrests (Columns 7–9) and with male/female arrest trends (Columns 1–6). Is the female percentage increasing or decreasing? Are sex differences in offending narrowing or widening? Several patterns are noteworthy.

First, when total arrests across all offenses are considered, the female percentage rose substantially—from 11 percent in 1960 to 15 percent in 1975 and to 19 percent in 1990. The bulk of that rise, as we show below, is due to the sharp increase in the numbers of women arrested for minor property crimes.

Second, for the majority of offenses the female percentage has tended to rise somewhat (about 1 to 2 percent each period), including arrests for DUI, receiving stolen property, burglary, and simple assault.

Third, for a number of offenses, the female percentage has held steady or declined slightly, including arrests for public drunkenness, drug law violations, aggravated assault, and homicide. The female share of homicide arrests is now about 10 percent, while it was about 17 percent in 1960.

The final and most significant pattern in male/female arrest trends is that the female percentage of arrests has narrowed considerably for minor property offenses—from an average of 16 percent in the early 1960s to 29 percent in the mid-1970s to 35 percent in 1990. The female share of all larceny arrests increased from 17 percent in 1960 to about 30 percent in 1990, while the female share of fraud and forgery arrests increased from about 15 percent to 43 percent and 34 percent, respectively. The female share of all embezzlement arrests has also been rising (from about 28 percent in 1975 to 37 percent in 1990), but very few females or males are arrested for embezzling, and therefore, arrest rates for embezzlement are of little significance in terms of overall male/female arrest trends.

Thus far, we have seen that females have made arrest gains in many UCR offense categories but that the changes in arrest profiles of females parallel those of males. To further determine whether new and different patterns of criminality are occurring within the female population, the 27 offense categories of the UCR by the size of the arrest rates for the years 1960 and 1990 were rank-ordered for both males and females and then examined as to whether the ordering had shifted more for females than males.

Among both males and females, there have been shifts in nine offense categories: drug law violations, DUI, fraud, and stolen property rose in order, while the categories of public drunkenness, gambling, suspicion, vagrancy, and sex offenses declined in rank order. This means that of all persons arrested in 1990 versus 1960, a larger share of *both* male and female arrests were for drug law

violations, DUI, and so on, whereas a smaller share were for public drunkenness, etc. Two conclusions can be drawn from this rank-ordering of arrest rates. First, the distribution of offenses for which both males and females are arrested has remained fairly stable. Second, and most crucial, the shifts occurring in arrests of females are not greater than the shifts occurring among males. Relative to that of males, the profile of the female offender has not changed.

TRENDS IN MALE/FEMALE ARRESTS BY TYPE OF CRIME

So far, we have examined arrest rates for each individual offense category, but a more parsimonious approach in portraying trends is to group the offenses by types and then sum up or aggregate the arrest rates for each type. We focus on four types: violent, masculine, Index ("serious"), and minor property.

These were chosen so we can evaluate popular and scientific claims that women are increasingly engaging in crimes that have traditionally been the province of men. The relationship between greater gender equality and what is perceived as a new trend in female criminality hinges on the notion that as women become increasingly involved in activities similar to those of men and as they attempt to emulate the male role, they will become more like men in terms of participation in crime. Female crime, therefore, represents a masculinization of female behavior.

Masculine and Violent Crimes

Masculine crimes are defined as offenses involving physical strength, elements of coercion and confrontation with the victim, and/or specialized skills. The eight offenses we categorized as masculine are listed at the bottom of Table 2, which shows that the summed arrest rates for masculine-type

TABLE 2

Male and Female Aggregated Arrest Rates/100,000 for Serious Violent, Masculine, Index, Index without Larceny, and Minor Property Crimes, 1960, 1975, and 1990

Types of crime	Male rate* (1)	Female rate* (2)	Female percentage[†] (3)	Absolute difference[‡] (4)	Percentage of all male arrests (5)	Percentage of all female arrests (6)
Serious violent[a]						
1960	176	22	11.1	154	3	3
1975	347	41	10.6	306	4	3
1990	457	64	12.1	393	5	3
Masculine[b]						
1960	784	63	7.5	721	11	8
1975	1518	150	9.0	1368	19	11
1990	1841	269	12.5	1572	20	13
Index[c]						
1960	962	108	10.1	854	14	13
1975	1702	397	18.9	1305	22	29
1990	1793	517	22.4	1276	20	25
Index w/o larceny						
1960	570	35	5.5	535	8	4
1975	953	77	7.5	876	12	5
1990	935	112	10.5	823	10	5
Minor property[d]						
1960	505	94	15.7	411	7	11
1975	917	400	30.4	517	12	30
1990	1075	568	34.6	507	12	27

*Rates are averaged across three-year periods: 1960–1962, 1974–1976, and 1988–1990.

[†] $\dfrac{\text{Female rate}}{\text{Female rate} + \text{Male rate}} \times 100$

[‡] Male rate – Female rate

[a] Serious violent crimes are murder, aggravated assault, and robbery.

[b] Masculine crimes are murder, aggravated assault, minor assaults, weapons, robbery, burglary, vandalism, and arson.

[c] Index crimes are murder, robbery, aggravated assault, burglary, larceny-theft, and auto theft.

[d] Minor property crimes are larceny-theft, fraud, forgery, and embezzlement.

crimes increased substantially from 1960 to 1990 for both males and females and that the female share of arrests also inched upward— 7.5 percent in 1960, compared with 12.5 percent in 1990. The bulk of the female gain in arrests for masculine crimes is due *(a)* to greater numbers of females being arrested for minor assaults and *(b)* to sharp declines since the mid-seventies in the number of males arrested for burglary (and to a lesser extent for robbery), as compared with small increases in female rates. The reasons for these trends are obscure, but some evidence indicates that the male drop in robbery and burglary arrests reflects an increasing drift of would-be male offenders toward drug trafficking as a more open route for illegal monetary gains. Finally, it is worth noting that being arrested for one of these masculine crimes does not necessarily connote "masculine" involvement; it is widely recognized, for example, that many females arrested for robbery or burglary acted as accomplices to male offenders and that many females arrested for homicide or assault acted in response to considerable victim provocation.

Table 2 also provides a comparison of the percentages that arrests for masculine-type offenses constituted of all male arrests and all female arrests. For all male arrests, the percentage of arrests that were for masculine crimes increased 9 percent (20 percent minus 11 percent) from 1960 to 1990, while for all female arrests, the increase was 5 percent (13 percent minus 8 percent). In sum, the increase in arrests for masculine-type crimes was greater for males than females.

If we separate from the masculine crimes those offenses which can be classified as serious violent offenses—homicide, aggravated assault, and robbery—we find parallel changes between the sexes. Of all the UCR categories, criminologists and law enforcement officials agree that these offenses best fit the definition of "serious crime." The female share of violent offending has not changed (11 percent in 1960, 12 percent in 1990), and out of all arrests the percentage that were for violent crimes increased slightly among males and was stable among females. The percentage of arrests that were for violent crimes was 3 percent in both 1960 and 1990 for all female arrests, while for all male arrests, it was 3 percent in 1960 and 5 percent in 1990.

For masculine and serious violent crimes, then, females have made small gains in arrests for masculine crimes (mainly in arrests for minor assaults) but have not gained ground on males in arrests for serious violent crimes like murder, aggravated assault, and robbery. Nor has there been a shift in arrest profiles toward greater commission of these offenses on the part of females.

Female Increases in Index Crimes

The eight Index (or Type I) offenses of the UCR are homicide, forcible rape, aggravated assault, robbery, burglary, larceny-theft, auto theft, and arson. For a mix of historical reasons, these offenses are categorized as "serious crime" by the FBI. It is frequently claimed that the proportion of women arrested for serious, or Index, crimes has been increasing dramatically and that the increase has been greater among females than males. It will be seen, however, that while these claims have some validity, they are misleading and deceptive. The increase in arrests of women for Index crimes is due mainly to more women being arrested for larceny and, more specifically, to greater numbers of women being arrested for shoplifting. A sharp drop in male burglary rates since the mid-seventies, along with female burglary rates holding more steady, has contributed to gains in the female percentage of arrests for Index crimes.

The data in Table 2 show that females indeed have gained ground compared with males in arrests for Index crimes. The female percentage of arrests has increased substantially, going from 10 percent in 1960 to 22 percent in 1990. Also, the increase in the percentage of all arrests that were for serious crimes was greater for females than males. In 1990, a hefty 25 percent of all female arrests were for Index crimes, compared with 13 percent in 1960. For males, arrests for Index crimes increased more modestly, going from 14 percent in 1960 to 20 percent in 1990.

To define larceny as a serious crime and include it with other Index offenses such as murder and robbery, however, is to use the term "serious" in a rather shortsighted and nondiscriminating fashion. Most arrests for larceny involve minor thefts such as shoplifting items of small monetary value; these thefts, therefore, are nonserious compared with other Index offenses and are not regarded as very serious in the opinion of the general public.

The available research indicates that the majority of arrests of females for larceny are for shoplifting, that most arrests for shoplifting are for petty theft, and that the increase in arrests of females for larceny is due largely to greater numbers of females being arrested for shoplifting.

When larceny is, in fact, treated as a nonserious offense, the data in Table 2 reveal a different picture of trends in Index crimes. Now, the female share of Index arrests shows a modest increase (from 5.5 to 10.5 percent), and from 1960 to 1990, the percentage of all female arrests that were for Index crimes (without larceny) is unchanged. Without larceny, therefore, the data on serious crimes contradict the sensational claims about dramatic changes in the kinds of crimes committed by females.

Minor Property Crimes

In addition to larceny, females have made arrest gains in the offense categories of fraud and forgery, and to a lesser extent in embezzlement. Contrary to the view of some analysts of female crime who refer to these as white-collar or occupational crimes, these offenses are more accurately classified as minor theft or property crimes and can be viewed as traditionally "female" crimes. Larceny also can be classified as a minor property crime.

These four offenses represent extensions of female domestic and consumer role activities, rather than new role patterns. None of these offenses requires particularly masculine attributes, such as the use of force or confrontation with the victim. Each of these crimes, with the exception of embezzlement, fits well into the everyday round of activities in which women engage, especially their role of buying most family necessities and paying family bills.

The available research indicates that most arrests of women for larceny, fraud, and forgery are for shoplifting, passing bad checks, credit card fraud, fraudulent theft of services, welfare fraud, and small con games. Women are not being arrested for frauds which are occupationally related or which tend to be real white-collar or corporate crimes such as false advertising, product defects, or insider trading. The frauds and forgeries committed by female offenders are consistent with female gender roles and fit into the everyday round of activities in which women engage, especially since the skills and techniques required to forge checks or credit cards are learned in the normal process of growing up. It is the case that those arrested for fraud or forgery tend to be amateurs, or "naive forgers."

Contrary to widespread assumptions, the person arrested for embezzlement is usually more a petty thief than a serious white-collar offender. Most arrestees for embezzlement (or employee theft) are not persons of high social standing and responsibility who, in the course of their occupation, commit a crime that involves large sums of money. Rather, the typical embezzler is the trusted clerk, cashier, or secretary who takes his or her employer's money, and the amount taken is usually small. Also, a very small proportion of all female arrests (only one-tenth of 1 percent in 1990) is for embezzlement, and so embezzlement is relatively insignificant in terms of overall female arrest trends. (The same is virtually true for males at two-tenths of 1 percent.)

Since as far back as Clarence Darrow (roughly the 1920s), some criminologists have believed that more women in the paid workplace would lead to more female employee theft and white-collar crime, which in turn would be reflected in greater numbers of women arrested for larceny and fraud. Employee theft and white-collar crime involving women are (probably) greater today than a decade or two ago. It is reasonable to assume that at least some proportion of the increasing number of working women have capitalized on their opportunities for work-related thefts and frauds. In this regard, the similarity is considerable between the current situation and that of the late nineteenth century, when female involvement in domestic theft (also an occupational crime) was unusually high owing to the kinds of work roles then available to women.

But it is wrong to conclude that recent trends in female employment have had much of an impact on female arrest trends. That view overlooks the fact that the crime categories of larceny and fraud are poor indicators of white-collar offenses. The available evidence shows that the *typical arrestee* in these offense categories committed a *nonoccupational* crime such as shoplifting or passing bad checks. One recent analysis of 1981 police files in an SMSA county in Pennsylvania found that less than 2 percent of all arrests for larceny, fraud, and forgery were for an occupational crime.[1] Moreover, while the embezzler is usually a trusted employee (an exception is the club treasurer who embezzles), so few persons are arrested for embezzlement (fewer than for any other crime) that the crime is relatively insignificant in terms of overall crime patterns. Thus, while in fact there may be more employee theft by women today than a decade or two ago (e.g., because there are more women in the paid labor force), that cannot be extrapolated or determined by the UCR arrest statistics.

Age × sex trends in female arrests (i.e., comparing the female percentage across age groups) for the minor property crimes provide further confirmation. The trends in female employment, and in women's status more generally, should have more of an impact on the arrest patterns of young adult and middle-aged women than on arrest

levels of adolescent and elderly women. Younger women have been most affected by changing gender role attitudes and employment trends. However, changes in the female share of arrests are comparable across age groups whether the entire period (1960 to 1990) is considered or the individual decades (e.g., 1960 to 1970) are examined.[2] For instance, the change in the female percentage of arrests for larceny is as large among juvenile females and older females (aged 50 and over), who for the most part are not in the labor force or have been affected only minimally by the employment trends.

Largest Female Gains Are for Larceny and Fraud (Forgery)

It is the offense categories of larceny and fraud, in particular, that are most responsible for change in patterns of female arrests. The female percentage of arrests has grown considerably since 1960, going from 17 percent to 30 percent for larceny, from 15 percent to 43 percent for fraud, and from 16 percent to 34 percent for forgery (see Table 1). In addition, a sizable portion of female arrest gains are due to the rise in arrest rates for larceny and fraud, more so than for males. Larceny accounted for 9 percent of all female arrests in 1960 versus a hefty 20 percent in 1990, while the percentage of fraud arrests rose from 2 percent in 1960 to 7 percent in 1990. These arrest gains of females notwithstanding, petty thefts and frauds are the kinds of crimes that women have always committed. Therefore, even though women are making gains in comparison with men, they are not committing new types of crimes. More women are being arrested for traditional types of female crimes.

Larceny-Theft The female percentage of arrests for larceny-theft almost doubled between 1960 and 1975 (increasing from 17 percent to 30 percent) but held steady after that time. This pattern reflects a combination of factors, some of which are offsetting. First, it reflects increased opportunities for shoplifting—a female-type crime—across the three decades but especially in the 1960s, which saw a rapid growth in shopping malls, self-service marketing, and small, portable products that outraced protection-against-theft measures. Particularly in the 1960s, moreover, there were major improvements in store surveillance methods and a greater willingness by store officials to prosecute apprehended shoplifters. This would tend to increase female more than male arrests for larceny, since males are more likely to commit larcenies other than shoplifting. Second, that trend has been countered somewhat by increased opportunities for male-type crimes, such as bicycle theft and theft from parked automobiles, across the three decades but especially in the 1980s, when the availability of bicycles and motor vehicles expanded rapidly. At the same time, recent changes in store security policies toward less formal handling of shoplifters has enabled male arrests for larceny to keep pace with female arrests in the 1980s.

Fraud The female percentage of fraud arrests has risen continuously over the years, from about 15 percent in the early 1960s to about 43 percent today. This increase can be attributed to several factors, including the growing numbers of poor women and the increased efficiency in detecting fraud offenders (e.g., "welfare cheats" and "bad check" recidivists), as well as the growth in a credit-based currency in American society that has contributed to greater opportunities for check and/or other kinds of credit-related frauds. A cross-national comparison helps to show the significance of this factor.[3] The female percentage of arrests for fraud and forgery is much higher in the United States (roughly 40 percent) than in the European nations (about

15 percent), even though the percentage of women working in those countries is as high as or higher than the percentage in the United States. The apparent reason for this difference is that the European nations lag behind the United States in a monetary system that is credit-based and thus provide fewer opportunities for bad checks, credit card fraud, and so forth. Note, also, that many of the European countries are moving toward a monetary system that is credit-driven, and so we would expect the percentage of female arrests for fraud or forgery to rise during the 1990s in the European nations.

Explaining Female Arrest Patterns

So far, we have seen that recent decades have witnessed an increase in the female share of offending for some kinds of crime, especially property crime. Criminologists have offered a number of explanations of these trends, including:

- *More formal/less biased policing.* Changes in female arrest trends are due not so much to changes in levels of female offending *per se* as to less biased or more effective official responses to female criminality.

- *Liberation or greater female employment.* The improved status of women (especially their advances in the paid workforce) is the social trend most relevant to the increase in female criminality.

- *Economic adversity or feminization of poverty.* Higher levels of poverty and economic insecurity faced by large subgroups of women in American society is the social trend most relevant to female crime trends.

- *Expanded opportunities for female-type crimes.* Shifts in dimensions of crime favoring female involvement is the social trend most relevant to female crime trends (e.g., technological, monetary, governmental, and market consumption trends since World

War II have expanded the opportunities for "female-type" crimes more rapidly than for "male-type" crimes).

• *Drug use/dependency trends.* Drug addiction amplifies income-generating crime for both sexes, but more so for females than for males.

It appears that female-to-male arrest trends reflect a convergence of a number of social and legal trends. For example, the increase in arrests of females for larceny and fraud is due to market consumption trends and the worsening economic position of many females in the United States. The opportunities for minor thefts and frauds have increased as a result of greater reliance on self-service marketing; the production of small, lightweight goods; and a credit-based currency. In addition, a number of economic and demographic factors have pushed more women into handling family finances and marketplace activities. The economic adversities facing many women have worsened in recent years because of increases in illegitimacy, in divorce, and in female-headed households. Over the past three decades, poverty has become more and more a female problem.

Changing gender roles and the Women's Movement of the late 1960s and early 1970s have been linked to changing patterns of female crime. To investigate further the effects of the Women's Movement on female crime, we examined male/female arrest rates throughout the 1960–1990 period, in particular the rates for the pre- versus post-1975 periods, since it is generally assumed that the Women's Movement began in the late 1960s; therefore, its effects on female crime would be most obvious after 1975. Our analysis revealed that whatever changes were occurring began prior to the spread of the Women's Movement. Specifically, changes in the female share of arrests were generally similar before,

during, and after the rise of the Women's Movement. The movement appears to have had a greater impact on changing the image of the female offender than on changing the level or types of criminal behavior that she is likely to commit. Note also that studies of the characteristics of female offenders document that they typically bear little resemblance to the liberated "female crook" described by some commentators. Instead, they are unemployed women or women working at low-paying occupations, or they are minority women drawn from backgrounds of profound poverty; also, a sizable portion of female offenders have histories of drug dependency and have been victims of physical or sexual abuse.

The trends in arrest rates of women in the United States are consistent with traditional gender role expectations, behaviors, and opportunities. Indeed, it would be surprising if substantial changes have been occurring in the illegitimate activities of women. Attitudes have shifted toward greater acceptance of women working and combining career and family, but there has been little change in other areas of gender roles: in gender-typing in children's play activities and play groups, in gender differences in conversational styles, in the kinds of personality characteristics that both men and women associate with each gender, in the expectation that women will be the gatekeepers of male sexuality, in the importance placed on physical attractiveness of women and their pressures to conform to an ideal of beauty and/or "femininity," and in female responsibilities for child-rearing and nurturing activities (e.g., caring for the sick and the elderly). Although female roles have become more flexible and the gender role system favors more individual latitude, women's lives continue to center on two traditional focal concerns: virtue/beauty expectations and nurturing obligations. The female's status continues to be defined in terms of relationships with men, and the traditional gender roles of wife-mother and sex object have remained remarkably stable. Also, male roles have changed little, if at all, and so gender role standards and patterns by and large have not undergone much change.[4]

Statistics on the current economic status of American women show that changes have occurred in some areas but not in others and that the economic situation is better today for some women but worse for others.[5] More women are in the labor force full-time, more have completed college and obtained professional degrees, and more hold managerial and professional positions. At the same time, however, a larger segment of the female population faces poverty and economic insecurity today than 30 years ago. Recent labor force statistics reveal that women continue to be concentrated in "pink-collar" jobs—teaching, clerical work, and retail sales work. Women are virtually excluded from top management positions and those industrial and service occupations requiring the highest levels of technical and mechanical skills. Most crucially, women are not increasing their participation in occupations such as truck driver, warehouse worker, delivery person, dockworker, carpenter, mechanic, and so on, that would provide opportunities for theft, drug dealing, fencing, and other "racketeering" activities or that would provide the specialized tools, skills (e.g., mechanical), and contacts conducive to criminal activities. Thus, the barriers are not coming down in (many) legitimate occupational categories that would provide opportunities for criminal activities and thereby would lead to increased crime among females.

Most important, perhaps, relative to women in the past, women today are just as limited by male constrictions on their roles and male leadership in the illegal marketplace as they are in the legal one. Autobio-

graphical and case history studies of professional and street criminals indicate that women continue to have limited access to criminal subcultures and the criminal underworld. In fact, traditional gender role attitudes and the structure of sexism appear to be more pervasive within the arena of crime than "above ground."[6]

Lastly, trends in drug usage and addiction may help account for female crime trends. It is commonly observed that drug addiction amplifies income-generating crime for both sexes, but more so for females than for males. Females face greater constraints against crime and thus need a greater motivational "push." Female involvement in burglary and robbery, in particular, typically occurs after addiction and is likely to be abandoned when drug use ceases. Drug use is also more likely to initiate females into the underworld and criminal subcultures, especially by connecting them to drug-dependent males who utilize them as crime accomplices or exploit them as "old ladies" who support the man's addiction. In these ways, although female drug arrests have not outraced male arrests since 1960, the rise in drug dependency among both males and females would impact more strongly on female criminality.

FUTURE PROSPECTS

The findings from the FBI's *Uniform Crime Reports*, when examined carefully, do not support widespread beliefs about increases or changes in female crime. Evidence from other sources on crime trends also shows more stability than change in female crime relative to male crime over the past several decades. Data from the National Crime Survey on the victim's perception of the offender's sex show that from 1973 to 1990 sex differences held stable for robbery (female share was 7 percent in 1973 and in 1990) and for assault (about 14 percent in both years). The

National Youth Survey, generally recognized as the best of the self-report delinquency studies, also provides information on delinquency trends for male and female adolescents from the late 1960s to the early 1980s. The survey indicates increases in certain delinquent behaviors (for example, alcohol and drug use) among both male and female adolescents and decreases in other delinquent behaviors (for example, theft and assault), but stable gender differences in delinquency. After reviewing the data, Delbert Elliott and associates conclude that during this time frame, the self-report data "show no significant decline in the [male-to-female] sex ratios on eight specific offenses."[7]

The evidence also shows that female gang activity is neither much different nor more violent now in comparison with such activity in the past. Gang expert Walter Miller specifically observes that "despite claims by some that criminality of females, either in general or in connection with gang activity, is both more prevalent and violent than in the past, what data were available did not provide much support to such claims."[8] Elsewhere he adds that "stories told about the nature of female participation in gang activities (weapons carriers, decoys for ambush killings, participants in individual or gang fighting) do not differ significantly from those told in the past . . . the part played by females did not represent a particularly serious aspect of current gang problems."

Statistics on males and females incarcerated in state and federal prisons provide additional information on female crime trends. From roughly the mid-1920s to the present, the female percentage of the total prison population has held between 3 and 5 percent. The female percentage was about 5 percent in the 1920s and about 3 percent in the 1960s, and it is about 6 percent today. Like male incarceration rates, female rates rose very sharply—more than doubled—during the 1980s. Most women in prison today are there for homicide or assault (usually against spouse, lover, or child), for property crimes such as larceny-theft and fraud, and for drug-related offenses.[9] During the 1980s, a larger percentage of female new court commitments than of male new court commitments entered prison each year for drug offenses. Also, a higher percentage of female prison inmates than of male inmates were under the influence of drugs or alcohol at the time of their current offense.

Finally, female involvement in professional and organized crime has not been rising and continues to lag far behind male involvement. Women continue to be hugely underrepresented in traditionally male-dominated associations that involve safecracking, fencing operations, gambling operations, and racketeering. In 1991 the state of Pennsylvania released its *1990 Report,* which surveyed organized crime and racketeering activities in the state during the 1980–1990 period. That report identified only a handful of women who were major players in large-scale gambling and racketeering activities, and their involvement was a direct spin-off of association with a male figure (i.e., the woman was a daughter, spouse, or sister). The *1990 Report* also noted that the extent and character of women's involvement in the 1980s was comparable to their involvement during the 1970s.[10]

These sources strongly document that crime—especially in its more serious and lucrative forms—remains a man's world. Indeed, contrary to some current rhetoric, the effects of "women's liberation" are not necessarily in a one-sided, criminogenic direction. Rather than increasing their propensities to commit crimes, more women in the paid workplace, especially in well-paying jobs, may in fact show the opposite effect. Not only may work lessen temptations toward crime by assuring a steady income, but also for many women their working is indicative of upward mobility, and upwardly mobile persons tend to be more conforming. Also, the new work roles have not freed women from traditional domestic ones, and so they have little time and energy for criminal enterprise.

Female economic participation per se does not lead necessarily to greater female criminality (just as improved economic opportunities do not lead necessarily to greater male criminality). This does not mean that changes in the family and economy have had no impact on female patterns of offending. As noted earlier, recent changes in the household economy and family have resulted in greater participation of women in economic production and the public sphere. This greater participation has led to more opportunities for certain kinds of crime and to fewer familial or "private" social controls on women in some aspects of their lives (but they are more subject to legal controls, including "arrest" and official sanctioning). The female arrest gains, for example, in minor property crime and driving under the influence reflect those trends. But female arrest trends also reflect the interplay of other factors outlined earlier, including the greater economic insecurity of women in modern times and the increased opportunities for "female-type" property crimes.

What about the future? Whether the female share of offending will rise or fall during the next decade or two depends on a variety of would-be societal trends. For example, in recent years an increase has occurred in special white-collar units in many police departments. That trend may push up the rate of arrests for occupation-related thefts and frauds within the relevant UCR categories, particularly for women. Second, the increasing numbers of women who drive and more stringent law enforcement directed at DUI offenders will sustain the upward trend in the female share of persons arrested for DUI. Third, trends in female poverty and drug

dependency, especially within minority populations, will shape female crime trends during the 1990s. If the trends of the past two decades persist (toward greater female drug use and greater female economic adversity), we can expect small increases in the female percentage of arrests for property crime, including burglary and robbery. Finally, changes in technology, in marketing and money exchange, in governmental programs, and so forth, will shape female arrest trends. Indeed, female-to-male arrest trends are likely to be influenced more by the nature of crime opportunities characterizing American society than by changes in female motivations or in the social and economic position of women.

On the whole, however, we should expect to see in the foreseeable future little change in the nature and extent of female criminality. At least in the illegitimate sphere, the aspirations, expectations, and experiences of women are not apt to move beyond traditional roles.

NOTES

1. Darrell Steffensmeier (1987). "Update on Male/Female Arrest Patterns." Paper presented at annual meeting of the American Society of Criminology. Montreal.
2. Darrell Steffensmeier and Cathy Streifel (1991). "The Distribution of Crime by Age and Gender across Three Historical Periods—1935, 1960, and 1985." *Social Forces* 69:869–894.
3. See Darrell Steffensmeier, Emile Allan, and Cathy Streifel (1989). "Modernization and Female Crime: A Cross-National Test of Alternative Explanations." *Social Forces* 68:262–283.
4. For a review of the relevant research on the issue of whether gender roles are becoming less traditional, see Darrell Steffensmeier and Cathy Streifel (1992). "Time-Series Analysis of Female-to-Male Arrests for Property Crimes, 1960–85: A Test of Alternative Explanations." *Justice Quarterly* 9:78–103. And see Deborah Tannen (1991). *You Just Don't Understand:*

Women and Men in Conversations. New York: Morrow.

5. For example, see Sarah Fenstermaker Berk, ed. (1990). *Women and Household Labor.* Beverly Hills: Sage. See also Martha Ozawa, ed. (1989). *Women's Life Cycle and Economic Insecurity.* New York: Greenwood.

6. See Darrell Steffensmeier and Robert Terry (1986). "Institutional Sexism in the Underworld: A View from the Inside." *Sociological Inquiry* 56:304–323. See also Darrell Steffensmeier (1986). *The Fence: In the Shadow of Two Worlds.* Totowa, N.J.: Rowman & Littlefield.

7. Delbert Elliott, Suzanne Ageton, and David Huizinga (1987). "Social Correlates of Delinquent Behavior." Unpublished paper.

8. Walter Miller (1975). *Violence by Youth Gangs and Youth Groups as a Crime Problem in Major American Cities.* U.S. Department of Justice, pp. 23–24. Also, see Martin Sanchez Jankowski (1991). *Islands in the Street: Gangs and American Urban Society.* Berkeley: University of California Press.

9. Lawrence Greenfeld and Stephanie Minor-Harper (1991). "Women in Prison." Bureau of Justice Statistics, Special Report. Washington, D.C.: U.S. Department of Justice.

10. *Organized Crime in Pennsylvania—A Decade of Change: The 1990 Report.* Pennsylvania Crime Commission, Conshohocken, Pa. (Darrell Steffensmeier, Project Director and Principal Writer.)

CHAPTER 6

RETHINKING WOMEN'S IMPRISONMENT: A CRITICAL EXAMINATION OF TRENDS IN FEMALE INCARCERATION

MEDA CHESNEY-LIND

ABSTRACT

In this chapter we learn of the extraordinary growth that has recently come about in the number of women imprisoned: from 12,300 in 1980 to 43,800 in 1990. Chesney-Lind considers possible causes for this large increase: greater amount of crime by women; tougher, more dangerous women offenders; a change in the criminal justice system's response to women offenders. In this chapter we also learn about the historical legacy of racism as exhibited in the disproportionate punishment of African-American women that persists today.

To further an understanding of the rapid growth in women's imprisonment, a profile is presented of women who are in prison. The profile does not suggest a new type of violent offender. As one might anticipate from Steffensmeier's arrest data in Chapter 5, women are first imprisoned for larceny-theft and drug offenses; the percentage of women incarcerated for violent offenses declined during the 1980s from 49 to 41 in prisons and from 21 to 13 in jails. Rather, argues Chesney-Lind, the data indicate that (1) the system is imprisoning more women than in the past, especially for drug offenses; (2) mandatory sentencing laws have reduced the amount of discretion previously available to judges, thereby increasing the numbers and lengths of sentences for *both* men and women; and (3) rather than being affected by a crackdown on women's crime specifically, women are caught up in a societal move to "get tough on crime"—driven by images of violent criminals (almost always men) "getting away with murder."

Chesney-Lind proposes a political agenda that includes a halt to prison construction, the decarceration of women, and the alternative funding of such chronically underfunded programs as shelters for victims of domestic violence. What is the underlying reasoning for her proposals? Who benefits from prison construction and women's imprisonment? What has made our society so punishment-prone? What alternatives might you suggest to realistically limit or reduce the number of imprisoned women?

Since 1980, the number of women imprisoned in the United States has tripled. Now, on any given day, over 80,000 women are locked up in American jails and prisons.[1] Increases in the rates of women incarcerated surpassed male rate increases every year in the last decade, and an unprecedented number of expensive prison cells are being built for women (Bureau of Justice Statistics, 1991a:2; Bureau of Justice Statistics, 1991b:4).

It is now clear that while the notion that the women's movement produced a flood of female crime, which received extensive publicity in the 1970s, has been largely discredited (see Chesney-Lind, 1986, for a review of this debate), another trend—that of skyrocketing increases in the numbers of women in prison—is an incontrovertible fact, and yet this situation has met with far less media attention.

This chapter will attempt to make sense of this dramatic shift in the pattern of women's imprisonment. In particular, this is an effort to determine whether the increase in women's imprisonment is a product of a change in women's crime or a shift in the criminal justice system's response to women offenders.

Discussing the situation of women offenders, including women in prison, has historically attracted far less interest in both mainstream and feminist criminology than considerations of women as victims. As a consequence, there has been little effort made by feminist as well as traditional scholars to interpret this unprecedented interest in the imprisoning of women. Such has not been true of the correctional establishment, whose primary response to overcrowding in women's prisons has been a rush to build more prison space, often at an enormous cost. Such a willingness to spend millions of dollars—per state—incarcerating women stands, of course, in stark contrast to the paucity of resources made available to other women's programs.

Given these patterns, this chapter contends that the feminist movement and feminist scholars must make the decarceration of women a part of their political agendas. Since, as this chapter attempts to show, there are clear indications that the extraordinary increases in women's imprisonment have been a product of criminal justice policy shifts rather than significant changes in women's criminal behavior, equally dramatic reductions in women's prison populations ought to be within reach. Indeed, this paper contends that the decarceration of women is a viable political strategy and might well be a model for reducing our reliance on imprisoning men as well.

IMPRISONING WOMEN

Stark increases in the number of women held in state and federal prisons marked each year of the last decade. In 1980, there were 12,331 women in our nation's prisons. By 1990, that number had grown to 43,845, an increase of 256 percent. In 1980, there were 303,643 males in prison. This number grew to 727,398 in 1990, an increase of 139.6 percent (Bureau of Justice Statistics, 1991b:1). Clearly, while the numbers of incarcerated men far exceed the numbers of incarcerated women (women are 5.5 percent of the state prison population, 7.5 percent of the federal prison population, and 9.5 percent of the jail population) (Bureau of Justice Statistics, 1991a:2; Bureau of Justice

The author would like to acknowledge this chapter's origins in two earlier works: "Women's Prisons: Overcrowded and Overused," by Russ Immarigeon and Meda Chesney-Lind, published by the National Council on Crime and Delinquency, and "Prisons, Patriarchy and Jails," published by *The Prison Journal*. Continued discussions with Russ Immarigeon, Nicole Hahn Rafter, and Kathleen Daly on this topic have all informed the perspective and conclusions in this paper. The errors, of course, remain the author's own.

This article was written expressly for inclusion in this text.

Statistics, 1991b:4), the increase in the number of incarcerated women is alarming and deserves our attention. In fact, the United States now imprisons more people than at any other time in its history. According to a recent study by the Sentencing Project (LaFranier, 1991:A-3), the United States has the highest rate of incarceration in the world.

These trends have triggered two types of responses. First, among those in the correctional bureaucracies across the United States there has been a "boom" in the creation of new women's institutions. Second, among many in the media, and some in academia, there has again been speculation that these numbers signal the emergence of a new, tougher female criminal whose appearance has necessitated increased reliance on imprisonment. It is to these matters, and their implications, that this discussion now turns.

BUILDING CELLS FOR WOMEN

The United States has gone on a building binge where women's prisons are concerned. Prison historian Nicole Hahn Rafter observes that between 1930 and 1950, roughly two or three prisons were built or created[2] for women each decade. In the 1960s, the pace of prison construction picked up slightly, with seven units opening, largely in southern and western states. During the 1970s, seventeen prisons opened, including units in states such as Rhode Island and Vermont that once relied on transferring women prisoners out of state. In the 1980s, thirty-four women's units or prisons were established; this figure is ten times larger than the figures for earlier decades (Rafter, 1990:181–182). (See Figure 1.)

Moreover, this growth in prison facilities for women during the 1980s occurred with little thought or planning; rather, it appeared to be a piecemeal and somewhat chaotic response to the soaring number of women committed to prison during the last decade.

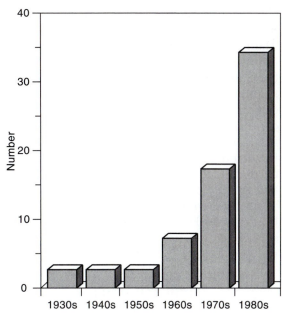

FIGURE 1
Creation of State Prison Facilities for Women, 1930–1990 (*Source:* Nicole Hahn Rafter. *Partial Justice.* New Brunswick, N.J.: Transaction Books, 1990, pp. 181–182.)

Commitments to women's prisons have more than tripled in the last decade, and few states were prepared for this. Instead of carefully reviewing which women required secure confinement and which could safely be housed in the community, authorities placed women almost anywhere—in abandoned hotels, motels, mental hospitals, nurses' dormitories, and youth training schools. This experience has been repeated across the country in, for example, Hawaii, Oklahoma, New Mexico, and West Virginia (DeConstanzo and Scholes, 1988:104–108; Immarigeon and Chesney-Lind, 1992).

The conditions in these makeshift and/or overcrowded women's prisons often were deplorable (Chesney-Lind, 1987:6–7; Rafter, 1990:182–184). California, Michigan, Minnesota, and Wyoming were among the states that built new prisons for women (Immarigeon and Chesney-Lind, 1992). In some cases, we know the costs of such expansion. For example, New York doubled its capacity to imprison women in the space of three years (1988 to 1991) at a cost of $300 million. As a result, Tracy Huling of the Correctional Association of New York estimated that in 1991, on any given day, nearly 6,000 women were incarcerated in New York's prisons and jails—roughly one-tenth of the women incarcerated in the United States (Huling, 1991a and 1991b).

Are the women currently doing time in U.S. prisons there because their offenses were so serious that no choice but imprisonment was possible?

NEW, TOUGHER WOMEN CRIMINALS?

Increases in women's imprisonment surpassed increases experienced by men every year between 1981 and 1989—a pattern that was finally broken in 1990 when the male rate of increase edged slightly ahead of the women's rate (8.3 percent compared with 7.9 percent). This pattern was not found in the commitments to federal prisons, however; here women's incarceration jumped 36.8 percent between 1989 and 1990, compared with only 13 percent for men. It must be recalled, however, that the male rate of incarceration is still substantially higher than that of women. In 1990, for example, the male incarceration rate was 566 per 100,000, compared with 31 per 100,000 for women (Bureau of Justice Statistics, 1991b:4).[3]

Some may suggest that the dramatic percentage increases in women's incarceration are simply an artifact of the smaller base numbers involved in women's imprisonment. For this reason, the increases in the jailing of women should be placed in historical context. Women made up 4 percent of the nation's

imprisoned population shortly after the turn of the century. By 1970 the figure had dropped to 3 percent. By 1990, however, more than 5.7 percent of those incarcerated were women. In addition, the rate of women's imprisonment grew from 6 per 100,000 in 1925 to 31 per 100,000 in 1990 (Cahalan, 1986; Bureau of Justice Statistics, 1991b). Finally, the base numbers involved in women's imprisonment are no longer small, and large increases continue. In 1990, for example, the relatively "small" increase in the number of women incarcerated in federal and state prisons meant that the number of women behind bars climbed from 40,566 to 43,855.

By contrast, total arrests of women (which might be seen as a measure of women's criminal activity) increased by 60 percent between 1981 and 1990. The FBI reports that Part 1 arrests (including arrests for murder, rape, aggravated assault, robbery, burglary, larceny-theft, motor vehicle theft, and arson) of women increased by about 46 percent during the same time period, while Part 1 arrests of men increased by about 26 percent (Federal Bureau of Investigation, 1991:178). While these trends in women's crime may appear to be serious, it should be noted that most of the increase in women's arrests is accounted for by more arrests of women for nonviolent property offenses such as shoplifting, check forgery, and welfare fraud, as well as for substance abuse offenses such as driving under the influence of alcohol and drug offenses.

Figures 2 and 3 show the disproportionate increase in both male and female jail and prison populations compared with the number of arrests during the same period. In one five-year period (1986–1990) arrests of women increased by about 29.3 percent, while arrests of men increased by 19.5 percent. Arrests of women for Part 1, or crime index, offenses showed a slightly smaller increase (21.2 percent), while male arrests for these offenses

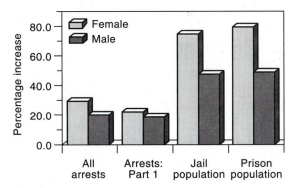

FIGURE 2
Percentage Increase, Male and Female, 1986–1990

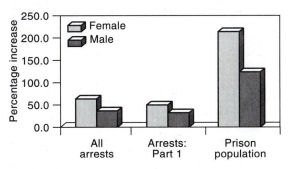

FIGURE 3
Percentage Increase, Male and Female, 1981–1990

increased by 17.4 percent (Federal Bureau of Investigation, 1991:181). Jail populations for both men and women grew significantly during the same time—the women's jail population increased by 73 percent, while the men's grew by 45.6 percent (Bureau of Justice Statistics, 1991a:2). The prison population grew by 76.9 percent for women and a lesser 46.2 percent for men (Bureau of Justice Statistics, 1991b:4). These figures suggest that increases in women's imprisonment cannot be explained by increases in women's crime, at least as measured by the number of arrests; the figures also show that the increases in women's imprisonment far outstrip those seen in the imprisonment of males.

PROFILES OF WOMEN IN PRISON

A look at national data on the characteristics of women in state prisons confirms that women are not being imprisoned because of a jump in the seriousness of their offenses. In fact, the proportion of women imprisoned for violent offenses actually dropped during the 1980s; in 1979, nearly half (48.9 percent) of the women in prison were incarcerated for a violent offense, but by 1986, this figure had fallen to 40.7 percent. By contrast, the number of women incarcerated for property offenses increased from 36.8 percent of women's commitments in 1979 to 41.2 percent in 1986, with most of the increase accounted for by a jump in the number of women committed for larceny-theft. Increases were also noted in the percentage of women imprisoned for public order offenses (e.g., gambling, carrying weapons, and prostitution). Women were also slightly more likely to be incarcerated for drug offenses, but the Bureau of Justice Statistics reports that the increase was explained by a jump in the number of women incarcerated for possession of drugs rather than drug trafficking. Finally, while these same statistics also show that the majority of women in prison for drug offenses are sentenced for "trafficking" (7.3 percent compared with 4.0 percent in 1986) (Bureau of Justice Statistics, 1988), other research notes that women tend to cluster near the bottom of the drug distribution network, since, in the words of one researcher, "the serious business of trafficking, i.e. smuggling and bulk sales, is controlled and conducted by men" (Simpson, 1992; see also Steffensmeier, 1983).

Perhaps the clearest evidence that the United States is not seeing a shift in the character of women's crime comes from a recent national study on the backgrounds of women under lock and key. This research both challenges the image of a new, "tougher" woman inmate and begins to hint at the real causes of women's crime.

The American Correctional Association (ACA) recently conducted a national survey of imprisoned women in the United States and found that overwhelmingly they were young, economically marginalized women of color (57 percent) and mothers of children (75 percent), although only a third were married at the time of the survey (American Correctional Association, 1990). This portrait is remarkably similar to the profile found by Glick and Neto (1977) in their national study of women inmates nearly a decade and a half earlier. They found that the typical woman inmate was young, poor, nonwhite, and unmarried and was also a high school dropout and a mother.

The backgrounds of the women in the ACA study, as well as their current status, clearly show the price they have paid for being poor. About half of them ran away from home as youths, about a quarter of them had attempted suicide, and a sizable number had serious drug problems. One-half of the women used cocaine; about a quarter of them used it daily. One-fifth said they used heroin daily. Indeed, about a quarter of the adult female offenders said they committed the crime for which they were incarcerated to pay for drugs.

The ACA survey found that over half of the women surveyed were victims of physical abuse, and 36 percent had been sexually abused. Another study of women in prison in Massachusetts suggests that if anything, these figures are conservative. Mary Gilfus (1988) found that when childhood physical abuse, childhood sexual abuse, and adult rape and battering were combined, fully 88 percent of her sample had experienced at least one major form of violent victimization. About one-third of the women in the ACA study never completed high school; of those, 34 percent failed to graduate because they were pregnant.

Twenty-two percent had been unemployed in the three years before they went to prison. Just 29 percent had only one employer in that period. Generally, they had worked in traditional women's service, clerical, and sales jobs. Two-thirds had never earned more than $6.50 an hour for their labor.

Most of these women were first imprisoned for larceny-theft or drug offenses. At the time of the survey, they were serving time for drug offenses, murder, larceny-theft, and robbery. While these latter offenses sound serious, like all other crimes they are heavily gendered. Research indicates, for example, that of women convicted of murder or manslaughter, many had killed husbands or boyfriends who repeatedly and violently abused them (Browne, 1987; Ewing, 1987). One early national investigation into homicide in the United States, for example, concluded that homicides committed by women were seven times as likely as male homicides to be in self-defense ("Causes of Violence," 1969, cited in Browne, 1987).[4] Other studies confirm the importance of this. A 1977 study (Lindsey, 1978) of women in prison in Chicago found that 40 percent of those serving time for murder or manslaughter had killed lovers or husbands who had repeatedly attacked them. In New York, of the women committed to the state's prisons for homicide in 1986, 49 percent had been the victims of abuse at some point in their lives, and 59 percent of the women who killed someone close to them were being abused at the time of the offense. For half of the women committed for homicide, it was their first and only offense (Huling, 1991b). Earlier studies of women charged with robbery often show that they were less active participants and noninitiators of these crimes (Fenster, 1977; Ward et al., 1968). One recent study takes some issue with this image of women's passivity and instead stresses the role that drug addiction and prior history of prostitution play in women's robberies (Sommers and Baskin, 1991).

Other recent figures from several states suggest more strongly that the "war on drugs" has translated into a war on women. A study done by the Rhode Island Justice Alliance noted that in their state (which has seen the number of women imprisoned there jump from 25 to 250 in the last five years), 33 percent of the women imprisoned were incarcerated for a drug crime (Rhode Island Justice Alliance, 1990). Finally, nearly half (47 percent) of women held as state-sentenced offenders in Massachusetts prisons are there for drug offenses (LeClair, 1990).

Huling reports that in New York's prisons, only 23.3 percent of women inmates were incarcerated for drug offenses between 1980 and 1986. By February 1991, that proportion had risen to 62 percent (Huling, 1991b). In Hawaii, 24 percent of the sentenced felons in 1987 and 1988 were doing time for a drug-related offense, according to the official records; interviews with women in prison in Hawaii, however, put the figure far higher (Nowak, 1990). Finally, a study comparing Connecticut women awaiting trial or sentenced in 1983 with those in 1986 (Daly, 1987:3) found that, in three years, the proportion of women incarcerated for drug sale or possession had increased from 13 percent to 22 percent.

Another criminal offense, that of driving under the influence (DUI), has recently been the subject of much debate, and the penalties have escalated. Coles reviewed arrest trends in California, a state that now has the largest incarcerated female population in the world. She notes that California has seen a shift in women's arrests for DUI. Previously, women were rarely arrested for this offense unless the DUI involved a traffic accident or they physically or verbally abused an officer. But that pattern appears to be eroding. Coles found

that while female misdemeanor DUI arrests have decreased, the felony arrest rate for this offense has increased; she also notes that women's share of these arrests appears to be increasing, at least in California (Coles, 1991). Coles's findings suggest that women's traditional insulation from certain forms of arrest has been eroded in the wave of get-tough legislation in the last 10 years.

Profiles of women offenders from smaller states suggest even more strongly that women's incarceration is not being fired by the appearance of a new, serious woman offender. In Hawaii, only 15.7 percent of incarcerated women were doing time for a violent crime during 1987 and 1988. Forty-one percent were serving time for a property crime, and, as was noted above, a substantial percentage (24 percent) were incarcerated on a drug-related offense.

A study done in Rhode Island found that only 10 percent of the imprisoned women were serving time for violent offenses, one-third of the women were incarcerated for prostitution or loitering, and another one-third were confined for some form of drug offense. Two-thirds of the women were serving sentences of 18 months or less (Rhode Island Justice Alliance, 1990). In Connecticut, the proportion of women incarcerated for any sort of violent activity declined from 37 percent to 32 percent in the space of three years (1983 to 1986), while the proportion incarcerated for any sort of drug offense increased from 13 percent to 22 percent. In 1987, 26 percent of the women in the Connecticut Correctional Institution at Niantic were convicted of drug violations (Daly, 1987:3).

In Massachusetts, in 1990, only 22 percent of the women under the supervision of the Department of Corrections were incarcerated for violent offenses (the comparable figure for males was 48 percent). As noted earlier, a large percentage of the women (47 percent) were incarcerated for drug offenses, compared with 19 percent of the men, and about a quarter of the women (26 percent) were doing time for property offenses. For state-sentenced offenders, the proportion of women incarcerated for violent offenses increased, but 35 percent is still lower than the 49 percent of men held for such offenses. Finally, nearly half (47 percent) of the women held in Massachusetts prisons were there for drug offenses (LeClair, 1990).

Even in large states such as California, the same pattern is seen. In a comparison of the institutional populations of women and men for the years 1984 and 1989, the data show that the proportion of women incarcerated for violent offenses fell from 32.7 percent to 23.9 percent in that five-year period. By contrast, the number of women incarcerated for drug offenses climbed from 17.9 percent to 37.9 percent. Looking more closely at these numbers reveals that over a third (37 percent) of these women in California prisons were simply there for possession of drugs or for marijuana offenses. If the offense category "possession for sale" is included, the figure jumps to 64.1 percent (*California Prisoners and Parolees*, 1990:122). Again, these figures do not indicate large numbers of women in prison for high-level drug trafficking.

The war on drugs, coupled with the development of new technologies for determining drug use (e.g., urinalysis), plays another, less obvious role in increasing women's imprisonment. In Hawaii, a recent study of women felons revealed that fully half were in prison because they had been returned there for violating the conditions of their parole by failing to pass random drug tests (Kassebaum and Chandler, 1992). In California, 40,460 parole violators were returned to prison in 1991. This figure clearly helped that state earn the dubious distinction of having over 100,000 people in prison, or the highest incarceration rate in the world (Garnett and Schiraldi, 1991:2).

Many of these returns, especially those of women inmates, were the result of failed urinalysis (Garnett, 1991).

The profiles of women under lock and key suggest that crime among women has not gotten more serious. Rather, it appears—especially in small states—that what has happened is that incarceration is being used where other forms of nonincarcerative responses previously were utilized.

GETTING TOUGH ON WOMEN'S CRIME

Data on the characteristics of women in prison suggest that factors other than a shift in the nature of women's crime are involved in the dramatic increases in women's imprisonment. Simply put, it appears that the criminal justice system now seems more willing to incarcerate women. Other evidence on the sentences women receive also support this interpretation. A recent California study found that the proportion of females who received prison sentences for the commission of felonies increased from 54 percent to 79 percent between 1978 and 1987 (California Department of Justice, 1988).

What exactly has happened in the last decade? While explanations are necessarily speculative, some reasonable suggestions can be advanced. First, it appears that mandatory sentencing for particular offenses at both the state and federal levels has affected women's incarceration, particularly in the area of drug offenses. Sentencing "reform," especially the development of sentencing guidelines, also has been a problem for women. As noted earlier, in California this has resulted in increasing the number of prison sentences for women (Blumstein et al., 1983). Sentencing reform has created problems in part because the reforms address issues that have developed in the handling of male offenders and are now being applied to women offenders.[5]

Daly's (1991) review of this problem notes, for example, that federal sentencing guidelines ordinarily do not permit a defendant's employment or family ties/familial responsibilities to be used as a factor in sentencing. She notes that these guidelines probably were intended to reduce class and race disparities in sentencing, but their impact on women's sentencing was not considered.

Finally, the criminal justice system has simply become tougher at every level of decision making. Langan notes that the chances of a prison sentence following arrest have risen for all types of offenses (not simply those typically targeted by mandatory sentencing programs) (Langan, 1991:1569). Such a pattern is specifically relevant to women, since mandatory sentencing laws (with the exception of those regarding prostitution and drug offenses) typically have targeted predominantly male offenses such as sexual assault, murder, and weapons offenses. In essence, Langan's research confirms that the whole system is now "tougher" on all offenses, including those that women traditionally have committed.

A careful review of the evidence on the current surge in women's incarceration suggests that this explosion may have little to do with a major change in women's behavior. This stands in stark contrast to the earlier growth in women's imprisonment, particularly to the other great growth of women's incarceration at the turn of the twentieth century.

Perhaps the best way to place the current wave of women's imprisonment in perspective is to recall earlier approaches to women's incarceration. Historically, women prisoners were few in number and were, it seemed, an afterthought in a system devoted to the imprisonment of men. In fact, early women's facilities were often an outgrowth of men's prisons. In those early days, women inmates were seen as "more depraved" than their male counterparts because they were acting in contradiction to their whole "moral organization" (Rafter, 1990:13).

The first large-scale and organized imprisonment of women occurred in the United States between 1870 and 1900, when many women's reformatories were established. Women's imprisonment then was justified not because the women posed a public safety risk but rather because women were seen to be in need of moral revision and protection. It is important to note, however, that the reformatory movement that resulted in the incarceration of large numbers of white working-class girls and women for largely noncriminal or deportment offenses did not extend to women of color. Instead, as Rafter has carefully documented, African-American women, particularly in the southern states, continued to be incarcerated in prisons, where they were treated much like the male inmates. They not infrequently ended up on chain gangs and were not shielded from beatings if they did not keep up with the work (Rafter, 1990:150–151). This racist legacy, the exclusion of black women from the "chivalry" accorded white women, should be kept in mind when the current explosion of women's prison populations is considered.

Indeed, the current trend in adult women's imprisonment seems to signal a return to the older approaches to women offenders: women are once again an afterthought in a correctional process that is punitive rather than corrective. Women also are no longer being accorded the benefits, however dubious, of the chivalry that characterized earlier periods. Rather, they are increasingly likely to be incarcerated not because the society has decided to crack down on women's crime specifically but because women are being swept up in a societal move to "get tough on crime" that is driven by images of violent criminals (almost always male) "getting away with murder."

This public mood, coupled with a legal system that now espouses "equality" for women with a vengeance when it comes to the punishment of crime and rationality in sentencing, has resulted in a much greater use of imprisonment in response to women's crime. There also seems to be a return to the imagery of depraved women from earlier periods—women whose crimes put them outside of the ranks of "true womanhood." As evidence of this, consider the new hostility signaled by the bringing of child-abuse charges against women who use drugs, even before the birth of their children (Noble, 1988; Chavkin, 1990:483–487). The fact that many of the women currently doing time in U.S. prisons are women of color further distances them from images of womanhood in which women are seen as requiring protection from prison life. All of this noted, it still seems that the escalation in women's imprisonment is largely the indirect and unanticipated consequence of the mood of a society bent on punishment.

DISCUSSION AND CONCLUSION

We must begin to take seriously a moratorium on construction of women's prisons and consider the need to decarcerate women, while we provide more and better options for women. The standard correctional response to an influx of new female inmates has been to crowd women into existing facilities and then to propose building out of the trouble caused by overcrowding. Ironically, the construction response often follows being sued or threatened with litigation (by prisoners and feminists) regarding the inadequacy of existing facilities. For this reason, those concerned about the situation of women inmates must be somewhat cautious about litigation as a sole response to the problem of conditions in women's prisons, since their work can ulti-

mately fuel the development of new, larger women's prisons (see Chesney-Lind, 1991).

Unfortunately, legislators propose spending enormous sums of money to build prison beds for women (e.g., $200,000/bed for 96 beds in my own state of Hawaii) at the same time that they cut hundreds of thousands of dollars out of services to women—especially funds for shelters and domestic violence programs. This trade-off has surfaced in many states. In California, prison construction, funded by $6.2 billion in bond issues passed during the 1980s, has continued despite drastic budget cuts in other departments. The University of California and California State University systems face, for example, possible campus closures and budget cuts of $255 million, and welfare aid to families with dependent children in the same state was cut by $225 million in fiscal year 1991. New York State has just spent $180,000 per bed to add 1,394 new prison spaces for women. Yet 12,433 women and children were denied needed shelter in 1990, and nearly three-quarters of these denials were because of lack of space (Huling, 1991b:6).

Such skewed priorities are particularly tragic, since the availability of welfare assistance and shelters is clearly related to women's crime. For example, an analysis of partner homicide from 1976 to 1984 in the United States revealed a "sharp decline" of 25 percent in the numbers of women killing male partners during that period—a decline linked by researchers to the passage of domestic violence legislation and the growth of legal resources for abused women (Browne, 1990). Every dollar that is spent locking women up could be spent far better on services which would prevent women from becoming so desperate that they resort to some form of criminal activity, sometimes to outright violence.

Besides examining priorities that appear to be misplaced, we must also question who benefits from the incarceration of women. This requires a shift in focus from simply studying the offender to studying the system that locks up women. What role, for example, do political contributions play in the enthusiasm with which lawmakers embrace the building of prisons? In Hawaii, many of the companies and individuals who build prisons are also heavy contributors to political campaigns (Lind, 1991). Every year, the engineering firms and the architectural firms (who may get these "jobs" without even bidding) give the governor and others in the state thousands of dollars. As the prison construction industry becomes a major component of many local economies, we must document its structure and politics. We must also challenge the politics of prison location, where legislators see the establishment of a prison in their jurisdiction, particularly if it has been hard-hit economically, as pork barrel politics for their constituents (e.g., Immarigeon, 1992).

This willingness to spend millions of dollars—per state—incarcerating women stands, of course, in stark contrast to the paucity of resources made available to other needed community-based programs to assist women in their everyday lives. Given these patterns, it seems essential that the feminist movement and feminist scholars make the decarceration of women a part of their political agendas. Since the extraordinary increases in women's imprisonment have been a product of criminal justice policy shifts rather than significant changes in women's criminal behavior, equally dramatic reductions in women's prison populations ought to be within reach. Indeed, the decarceration of women, and the investment of the dollars saved in opportunities and services for people on the economic margins of our society, might well serve as a model for challenging America's "ideology of incarceration" (Immarigeon, 1991).

NOTES

1. During 1990, 43,845 women were imprisoned, and on a typical day, 37,198 women were in U.S. jails.
2. It is important to note here that women's prisons are not always "constructed"; instead, they are created in a variety of ways. It is not uncommon, as this chapter demonstrates, for facilities designed for other purposes to be converted into a women's prison.
3. Again, the rates in 1980 were only 274 per 100,000 for men and 11 per 100,000 for women—meaning that while the male rate of incarceration doubled, the women's rate tripled (Bureau of Justice Statistics, 1991b:4; Jamieson and Flanagan, 1989:612).
4. Clearly, some of this research is having an impact. Recently, outgoing Governor Richard Celeste of Ohio granted clemency to 25 women who had been convicted of killing or assaulting abusive husbands or boyfriends after reviewing "records of more than 100 women" (Wilkerson, 1990).
5. Blumstein and his associates note that California's Uniform Determinate Sentencing Law "used the averaging approach, one consequence of which was to markedly increase the sentences of women—especially for violent offenses" (Blumstein et al., 1983:114).

REFERENCES

American Correctional Association. 1990. *The Female Offender: What Does the Future Hold?* Washington, D.C.: St. Mary's Press.

Austin, Jim, and Aaron McVey. 1989. "The NCCD Prison Population Forecast: The Impact of the War on Drugs." *NCCD Focus.* San Francisco: National Council on Crime and Delinquency.

Blumstein, Alfred, Jacqueline Cohen, Susan E. Martin, and Michael H. Tonry (eds.). 1983. *Research on Sentencing: The Search for Reform.* Vols. 1 and 2. Washington, D.C.: National Academy Press.

Browne, Angela. 1987. *When Battered Women Kill.* New York: The Free Press.

———. 1990. "Assaults between Intimate Partners

in the United States." (December 11, 1990.) Washington, D.C.: Testimony before the United States Senate, Committee on the Judiciary.

Bureau of Justice Statistics. 1988. *Profile of State Prison Inmates, 1986*. Washington, D.C.: U.S. Department of Justice.

———. 1991a. *Jail Inmates 1990*. Washington, D.C.: U.S. Department of Justice.

———. 1991b. *Prisoners in 1990*. Washington, D.C.: U.S. Department of Justice.

Cahalan, M. W. 1986. *Historical Corrections Statistics in the United States 1950–1984*. Washington, D.C.: U.S. Department of Justice.

California Department of Justice. 1988. "Women in Crime: The Sentencing of Female Defendants." Sacramento: Bureau of Criminal Statistics.

California Prisoners and Parolees. 1990. Sacramento, Calif.

"Causes of Violence." 1969. A staff report to the National Commission on the Causes and Prevention of Violence. Washington, D.C.: U.S. Government Printing Office.

Chavkin, Wendy. 1990. "Drug Addiction and Pregnancy: Policy Crossroads." *American Journal of Public Health*. Vol. 80: 4 (April): 483–487.

Chesney-Lind, Meda. 1986. "Women and Crime: The Female Offender." *Signs* 12 (Autumn): 78–96.

———. 1987. "Women's Prison Reform in Hawaii: Trouble in Paradise." *Jericho* 43 (Spring): 6–7.

———. 1991. "Patriarchy, Prisons, and Jails: A Critical Look at Trends in Women's Incarceration." *The Prison Journal* LXXI (Spring–Summer): 51–67.

Coles, Frances S. 1991. "Women, Alcohol and Automobiles: A Deadly Cocktail." Paper presented at the Western Society of Criminology Meetings, Berkeley, Calif., February.

Crites, Laura (ed.). 1975. *The Female Offender*. Lexington, Mass.: Lexington Books.

Daly, Kathleen. 1987. "Survey Results of the Niantic Interviews, December 1983 and May 1986." Mimeographed, January.

———. 1991. "Gender and Race in the Penal Process: Statistical Research, Interpretive Gaps, and the Multiple Meanings of Justice." Mimeographed, April.

DeConstanzo, Elaine J., and Helen Scholes. 1988. "Women behind Bars: Their Numbers Increase." *Corrections Today*. Vol. 50 (June) 3:104–108.

Ewing, C. 1987. *Battered Women Who Kill*. Lexington, Mass.: Lexington Books.

Federal Bureau of Investigation. 1991. *Uniform Crime Reports 1990*. Washington, D.C.: U.S. Department of Justice.

Fenster, C. 1977. "Differential Dispositions: A Preliminary Study of Male-Female Partners in Crime." Unpublished paper presented to the annual meeting of the American Society of Criminology.

Garnett, Rick. 1991. Personal communication with the author.

——— and Vincent Schiraldi. 1991. "Concrete and Crowds: 100,000 Prisoners of the State." San Francisco: The Center on Juvenile and Criminal Justice.

Gilfus, Mary. 1988. "Seasoned by Violence/Tempered by Law: A Qualitative Study of Women and Crime." A dissertation presented to the faculty of the Florence Heller School for Advanced Studies in Social Welfare at Brandeis University, Waltham, Mass.

Glick, Ruth, and Virginia Neto. 1977. *National Study of Women's Correctional Programs*. Washington, D.C.: U.S. Department of Justice.

Huling, Tracy. 1991a. "New York Groups Call on State Lawmakers to Release Women in Prison." Correctional Association of New York. Press release, March 4.

———. 1991b. "Breaking the Silence." Correctional Association of New York. Mimeographed, March 4.

Immarigeon, Russ. 1991. "Instead of Prisons: Observations from Elsewhere." Paper presented at the annual meeting of the Movement for Alternatives to Prison, Auckland, New Zealand.

———. 1992. Personal communication with the author.

——— and Meda Chesney-Lind. 1992. "Women's Prisons: Overcrowded and Overused." San Francisco: National Council on Crime and Delinquency.

Jamieson, Katherine M., and Timothy Flanagan (eds.). 1989. *Sourcebook of Criminal Justice Statistics—1988*. Washington, D.C.: U.S. Department of Justice, Bureau of Justice Statistics.

Kassebaum, Gene, and Susan Chandler. 1992. "Polydrug Use and Self-Control among Men and Women in Prison." Paper presented at the

Hawaii Sociological Association Meetings, Honolulu.

LaFranier, Susan. 1991. "U.S. Has Most Prisoners Per Capita in the World." *Washington Post.* (Jan. 5): A-3.

Langan, Patrick A. 1991. "America's Soaring Prison Population." *Science.* Vol. 251 (Mar. 29): 1569.

LeClair, Daniel. 1990. "The Incarcerated Female Offender: Victim or Villain?" Research Division, Massachusetts Department of Correction, October.

Lind, Ian. 1991. "Campaign Finance Practices Create Industry Outlaws." *Building Industry Magazine* (December). Honolulu: Honolulu Trade Publishing Co.

Lindsey, Karen. 1978. "When Battered Women Strike Back: Murder or Self Defense?" *Viva* (September): 58–59, 66, 74.

Mauer, M. 1992. *Americans behind Bars: One Year Later.* Washington, D.C.: The Sentencing Project.

Noble, Amanda. 1988. "Criminalize or Medicalize: Social and Political Definitions of the Problem of Substance Use during Pregnancy." Report prepared for the Maternal and Child Health Branch of the Department of Health Services, University of California, Davis.

Nowak, Carol. 1990. "A Psychological Investigation of Women's Decisions to Participate in Criminal Activities." Dissertation submitted to Saybrook Institute, San Francisco.

Rafter, Nicole Hahn. 1990. *Partial Justice: Women, Prisons and Social Control.* New Brunswick, N.J.: Transaction Books.

Rhode Island Justice Alliance. 1990. "Female Offender Survey, Rhode Island Adult Correctional Institution, Women's Division." Mimeographed.

Simpson, Sally S. 1992. "Distinguishing Drug Involvement by Gender." Paper presented at the annual meeting of the American Society of Criminology, San Francisco, November.

Sommers, I., and D. R. Baskin. 1991. "The Situational Context of Violent Female Offending." Paper presented at the American Society of Criminology Meetings, San Francisco.

Steffensmeier, Darrell. 1983. "Organizational Properties and Sex-Segregation in the Underworld." *Social Forces,* 61:1010–1032.

Ward, David, et al. 1968. "Crimes of Violence by Women," in Donald J. Mulvihil et al. (eds.). *Crimes of Violence.* Vol. 13. Staff report to the National Commission on the Causes and Prevention of Violence. Washington, D.C.: U.S. Government Printing Office.

Wilkerson, Isabel. 1990. "Clemency Granted to 25 Women Convicted for Assault or Murder." *New York Times* (Sat., Dec. 22): 1, 11.

CHAPTER 7

WOMEN OF COLOR AND THE CRIMINAL JUSTICE SYSTEM

CORAMAE RICHEY MANN

ABSTRACT

In this chapter the author explains how the criminal justice system has widened the net for women of color, particularly African-American and Latina (Hispanic) women. First, Mann provides an overview of women's crimes most frequently studied—prostitution, drug offenses, and homicide. In the next two sections, she explores the arrest data on women of color in three states—California, Florida, and New York. These states alone incarcerate almost one-third of all the women in the United States who are in prison. She finds that public order crimes (alcohol and drug offenses), as distinct from violent and property crimes, are more likely to lead to the arrests of white women; drug violations and prostitution are the most frequent causes of arrests for African-American women. The pattern for Latina women shows that public order crimes slightly exceed property crime, followed by violent crime.*

The fourth section of the chapter describes the criminal justice system's processing (pretrial treatment and sentencing) of women of color, with a focus on the harsher treatment meted out to these women. Mann clearly documents disproportionality in prison sentences by comparing arrest rates with sentencing rates in the three states under consideration. The fifth section of this chapter describes the incarceration of women of color. Most striking are the data documenting the rapid increase in jail incarceration rates for women of color while at the same time rates for white women decreased slightly. And federal and state prison data show disproportionate numbers of women of color imprisoned, while white women are underrepresented in relation to their numbers in the general popula-

---

*It is important to note that data on Latinas is classified differently by the three states; in fact, one state collapses the classification of Latinas/os into whites.

tion. The chapter concludes with observations on some of the unique problems of incarcerated women of color and the need for major changes within both the criminal justice system and the larger society.

Review the recommendations that Mann proposes as solutions to her fundamental finding of pervasive racism at every stage of the criminal justice system. To which would you give highest priority? How might you go about making that recommendation a reality? What else needs to be done? How would these recommendations vary for different groups of women of color and white women? Most important, what larger structural changes outside the criminal justice system need to occur in order for real change within the system to come about? Keep in mind that Mann's analysis sets the stage for many of the ideas Arnold will introduce in Chapter 8.

This chapter addresses the status of historically disadvantaged women offenders of color (African-American, Hispanic, Native American, and Asian-American) from arrest and incarceration to the death rows of our nation. It synthesizes the scattered information on minority women, who face double discrimination because of their gender and race/ethnicity. When class level is included, these women often face triple jeopardy. Since the paucity of studies on the processing of women at each level of the criminal justice system is exacerbated in the instance of women of color, the major focus throughout this chapter is on African-American women, the most frequently studied female minority group.

THE CRIMES OF
WOMEN OF COLOR

For years the infrequent studies of women's deviance available were limited to prostitution and other kinds of sexual deviance thought to be "typical" female offenses. It soon became apparent that not all women offenders fit this stereotype and that women were involved in a wide variety of criminal activities. In addition to prostitution, drug offenses and homicide are the most frequently examined offenses involving women and will be described more fully.

Prostitution

Historically, Chinese and African-American women met the high demand for prostitutes when, between 1880 and 1920, the sexual demands of white men doubled the volume of prostitution in Chinatowns and trebled prostitution in black ghettos (Mann, 1993). More recently, in 1986, the last year that the *Uniform Crime Reports* (UCR) included Hispanic arrests, African-Americans and Hispanics were the only persons of color arrested for prostitution and commercialized vice in proportions higher than their population percentages (38.8 percent and 10.1 percent, respectively). One possible explanation for this unbalanced number of prostitution arrests is that many women of color are forced onto the streets to work. "Streetwalking" not only increases the possibility of contact with law enforcement personnel but also introduces potential police harassment and racial bias.

This article was written expressly for inclusion in this text.

Drugs

Much of the recent growth in women's arrest rates and incarceration has been attributed to women's increased drug use and related crime (possession, selling, and petty theft) in an era of much harsher drug laws. Though a greater proportion of whites than African-Americans—both men and women—consistently admit to using drugs, including heroin and cocaine, the media continue to report vast drug use, and therefore incarceration, among women of color (Hutchinson, 1990; Lusane, 1991; Isikoff, 1991). Thus, the criminal justice system has been widening its net where women of color are concerned. For example, studies of drug use by arrestees repeatedly show a higher percentage of female than male arrestees who test positive, particularly for multidrug use (DeWitt, 1990; Harlow, 1991).

Pettiway (1987:746) reports female heroin and other opiate users to be ethnically split: African-Americans were 35 percent; whites, 33.8 percent; and Hispanics, 31.2 percent (Puerto Rican, 16.4 percent; Cuban, 14.8 percent). Further, a comparison study of Anglo (white) and Chicana (Hispanic) narcotics addicts, reported by Anglin and Hser (1987), found extensive criminal involvement and multidrug use. Chicana women were found to have committed crimes as much as and sometimes more than Chicano men. According to these authors (p. 394), some of the major differences between Anglo and Chicana women addicts were that Chicanas had a "more deviant life style," including more "gang membership, problems in school, poor family histories, and low socioeconomic status."

In a study of drugs and violence among a sample of 133 female drug users or distributors, African-American women were overrepresented as "big cocaine users" (78 percent of the African-American women sampled). "Big users" reported slightly more robberies and con game convictions than "small users,"

who reported more prostitution and shoplifting (Goldstein et al., 1991). While more than half (59 percent) of the women in the sample reported some participation in violent events, women cocaine users were as likely to be victims as offenders. One study of females convicted of homicide showed twice as many Hispanic killers in the substance abuse (alcohol and narcotics) group as in the nonusing group (Mann, 1990a).

Homicide

For a number of years studies have repeatedly found African-American women second to African-American men in the frequency of arrests for homicide (Wolfgang, 1958; Pokorny, 1965), with conviction rates reportedly 14 times greater than those for white female murderers (Sutherland and Cressey, 1978:30). African-American men, in 1986, had the highest homicide rates (52.3 per 100,000), followed by African-American women (12.3), then white men (7.9) and white women (2.9) (Whitaker, 1990). The most recent comprehensive study of female homicide offenders found such offenders in six U.S. cities to be predominantly African-American (77.7 percent) and typically single, 31 years old, and unemployed, and a mother with less than a high school education (Mann, forthcoming). Hawkins (1986) interprets the higher African-American homicide rates for both men and women as evidence of historical-structural experiences and current economic factors that lead to high levels of stress, rage, and powerlessness in African-American lives, particularly among the most disenfranchised.

THE ARRESTS OF WOMEN OF COLOR

People of color believe that police have a readiness to arrest them, a belief that has some basis in reality for women. Kratcoski and Scheuerman (1974) found that incarcerated African-American women were more likely than white women to perceive police officers as excessively brutal, harassing, and unwilling to give them a break through nonarrest. The researchers concluded that white women were treated more liberally than African-American women when police discretionary power not to arrest was involved. Moyer and White (1981) suggest, on the basis of police officers' perceptions, that characteristics seen by some whites as "typical" of African-Americans—"loud, boisterous, aggressive, vulgar, and disrespectful"— might influence police decisions. And Visher (1983:22–23), on the basis of observations of police on patrol, explains the fact that African-American women were almost three times as often arrested as white women (21.8 percent versus 7.8 percent) in the following way: "female suspects who violate typical middle-class standards of traditional female characteristics and behaviors (i.e., white, older, and submissive) are not afforded chivalrous treatment during arrest decisions."

Since the UCR compiled by the FBI report arrests by gender but not by gender and race/ethnicity, data for this chapter were collected on gender and race/ethnicity from the three states that incarcerate the highest proportions of minority women—California, Florida, and New York.[1] Although these states are not necessarily representative of the entire nation, their prisons hold almost one-third (31.7 percent) of all women incarcerated in the United States. They additionally offer a microcosm of the nation owing to their locations.

The percentages of 1990 adult female arrests by race/ethnicity in the three states examined are shown in Table 1 (UCR, 1991:188). In all three states, women of color, particularly African-Americans, were disproportionately arrested. The table also compares the rankings of the top 10 female arrests by race/ethnicity in the three states under examination with the UCR's 10 highest rankings for 1990.

The rank ordering of arrests for four Crime Index (most serious) crimes—larceny/theft, aggravated assault, burglary, and robbery— can be seen in Table 1. These data clearly suggest that arrests for Index crimes have a greater rank order among women of color, especially African-American women.

As seen in Table 1, an analysis of 1990 UCR data shows that the three most frequent Index (serious) crimes for all women arrested in 1990 were larceny-theft, aggravated assault, and burglary,[2] a trend that has existed for the past dozen or more years. Arrests for Index property crimes (larceny-theft and burglary) are rather consistent in the UCR as well as across the three states for white women and most women of color, whereas the rankings for violent Index crimes (aggravated assault and robbery) vary by race/ethnicity, with women of color more frequently arrested for such offenses.

According to the UCR, the 10 most frequent adult female arrests in 1990 (excluding the category "all other offenses"[3]) were for larceny-theft (17.5 percent), driving under the influence (10.5 percent), drug violations (8.2 percent), fraud (7.3 percent), other assaults (6.1 percent), disorderly conduct (5.4 percent), drunkenness (4.2 percent), liquor law violations (4.1 percent), prostitution (3.5 percent), and aggravated assault (2.5 percent). With minor exceptions these offenses are rarely studied among female populations.

In the past, women appeared to be arrested primarily for offending the public morality or for "unladylike" behavior, and this situation persists today. In other words, women are most likely to be arrested for vice, or public order, crimes, which indicate deviance from the proper female role: offenses that allegedly offend public morals. "Crimes" related to alcohol (DUI, disorderly conduct, drunken-

TABLE 1 Rank Order of the Top 10 Adult Female Arrest Offenses by Race/Ethnicity: California, Florida, New York State, 1990

Arrest offense	All adult females	White			African-American			Hispanic*		Native American*	Asian-American†	Other		
	UCR	CA	FL	NY	CA	FL	NY	CA	NY	CA	CA	CA	FL	NY
Percentage	80.7	44.1	53.9	22.8	31.5	45.8	52.8	20.4	23.2	0.5	0.7	2.7	0.3	1.2
Larceny-theft‡	1	7	1	1	7	1	1	7	2	7	3	5	1	1
Driving under the influence (DUI)	2	1	2	2 (incl. other traffic)	10			2		3	2	2	2	2
Drug violations	3	9	3 (poss.) 9 (sale)		2	2 (poss.) 5 (sale)		4		10	9		7 (poss.)	
Fraud	4	8	8	3		10								9
Other assaults	5	8	6		9	6		9		5	6	6	4	
Disorderly conduct	6													
Drunkenness	7	3			5			5		1	7	10		
Liquor law violations	8		4			8								
Prostitution	9	6	5	7	3	4	5	10	5	8	3	7	3	3
Aggravated assault‡	10	10	7	6	6	3	3	8	4	6	4	9	6	6
Other thefts		2		8			7	1	6	2	1	1		8
Other drugs		4			4			3		4	10	4		
Dangerous drugs		5		5			2		1					4
Forgery				10			9				8			10
Intimidation			10			7							8	
Burglary‡				9	8	9	6	6	7	9	5	8		5
Public order				4			4		3					
Robbery‡							8		9					
Escape							10							7
Gambling									8					
Firearms									10					
Destruction and vandalism													9	
Embezzlement/ stolen property/ weapons													10	

*Florida only categorizes by white, black, and other; New York only includes white, black, Hispanic, and other.
†Includes Chinese, Japanese, Filipino, and Pacific Islander.   ‡A Crime Index offense.
Source: Compiled from data received from the California Department of Justice, the Florida Department of Law Enforcement, and the New York State Division of Criminal Justice Services.

ness, liquor law violations) or drug use, "offenses against the public order" (New York State), gambling, and prostitution account for 43.5 percent of women's arrests (10 of 23). The seven property crimes (larceny-theft, fraud, other thefts, forgery, burglary, destruction and vandalism, embezzlement) constitute 30.4 percent of the total, while the six violent crimes (other assaults, aggravated assault, intimidation, robbery, escape, and firearms) make up the final 26.1 percent.

RACE/ETHNICITY ARREST COMPARISONS

Once again, let us examine Table 1 for certain crime patterns based on race/ethnicity. Women of color show higher rank orders for aggravated assault (an Index crime) and other assaults than do white women. White and African-American women show higher rank orders for larceny-theft (an Index crime) than do other women of color, and white women show higher rank orders for fraud, whereas women of color show higher rank orders for other thefts, burglary (an Index crime), and forgery. White women tend to exceed women of color, except for Native American women, in the rank ordering of alcohol-related offenses—DUI, drunkenness, and liquor law violations.

The following sections provide more detail on the arrests of women of color in the three states examined.

African-American Women

In contrast to the alcohol-related public order crimes leading to the arrests of whites, drug violations and prostitution are the distinguishing arrest offenses within the public order offense category for African-Americans (see Table 1). Drug offenses are the second most frequent cause of arrests for African-American women in all three states.

On average, property crimes rank slightly lower among arrests of African-American women than they do among arrests of white women. But there is variation within the classification: the "white-collar crime" of fraud ranks higher among white women, whereas the more serious Index crime of burglary characterizes property crime committed by African-American women.

Arrests for violent crimes even more clearly distinguish the white and African-American groups. For both subgroups, rankings for arrests for other (or less serious) assaults are similar, but African-American women are clearly differentiated by the higher arrest frequencies for the Index crime of aggravated assault. Further, robbery and escape are ranked eighth and tenth, respectively, among African-American women in New York State but are not among the top 10 frequent arrest offenses of white women in any of the three states.

Hispanic Women

Although Hispanic female arrest rankings are only reported from California and New York State,[4] it is important to note that both of these states have large Latina populations—primarily Mexican-American in California and Puerto Rican in New York. Table 1 shows that the same patterning of public order, property, and violent crimes found for white and African-American women also holds for Latinas: that is, arrests for public order crimes are the most frequent, followed by arrests for property offenses and arrests for violent crimes. Drug offenses predominate among Hispanic public order arrests. In New York, for example, arrests for dangerous drugs are the most frequent arrest category for Latinas. While alcohol and drug-related offenses are ranked about the same for California Latinas, New York Latinas are apparently also involved in a variety of vice crimes and are the only subgroup studied who have gambling ranked as one of the top 10 arrest offenses. With the exception of arrests for aggravated assault and weapons violations in New York State, Hispanic arrests for violent crimes show lower rankings than those for white or African-American women.

Native American Women

As with the arrest rankings for other subgroups, public order offenses dominate Native American arrests. Drunkenness is the primary offense for which Native American women in California are arrested, and driving under the influence of alcohol (DUI) is ranked third. Also, as with arrests of African-American and Hispanic women, drug offenses are influential in the arrests of California Native Americans. In the property crime category, other (or minor) thefts are the second most frequent arrest offense of this subgroup; yet burglary and larceny-theft, both Index crimes, are notable.

Although limited to only two offenses (aggravated assault and other assaults), the arrests of Native American women for violent crimes appear to mirror the arrest frequencies for other women of color. Native American women were more likely to be arrested for other assaults than white, African-American, Hispanic, or Asian-American women. Studies of Native American males suggest a strong relationship between alcohol abuse and violent crime that may be applicable to their female counterparts (see Mann, 1993).

Asian-American Women

California was the only state that reported arrest statistics on Asian-Americans. There are more Asian-Americans in California than in any other state in the nation; therefore, the frequency rankings may offer a fairly accurate depiction of the crimes of Asian-American women. Although four public order offenses

are among the top 10 arrest rankings for Asian-American women, only arrests for driving under the influence are of conspicuous frequency (rank = 2). In contrast to the offense rankings for the other subgroups, however, Table 1 reveals that property crimes are the most frequent arrest offenses for Asian-American women: other thefts and larceny-theft (an Index crime) are ranked 1 and 3, respectively. Forgery (rank = 8) and burglary (rank = 5) are additional property offenses in the top 10 arrest rankings for Asian-American women in California. Arrests for violent crimes ranked fairly high among Asian-American women, owing to the contributions of aggravated assault (rank = 4) and other assaults (rank = 6).

THE CRIMINAL JUSTICE PROCESSING OF WOMEN OF COLOR

Minority communities commonly believe that like the police, the white and male-dominated judicial system treats racial/ethnic minorities more stringently than whites (Deming, 1977). The few studies of the criminal justice processing of women appear to substantiate this belief by suggesting differential treatment of women of color, typically African-Americans, at every stage of the process.

The "black-shift phenomenon" was first described in a Washington, D.C., study when McArthur (1974) observed that African-Americans were 73 percent of those first booked into detention but 83 percent of those returned to jail from the initial court hearing. African-Americans were 92 percent of the women who received sentences of 30 days or more and 97 percent of those sentenced for three months or more. In contrast, the proportions of the District's white females decreased at each step of the process: they were 37 percent of the adult female population, 27 percent of first detention bookings, 17 percent of women returned to jail, 8 percent of women who received sentences of 30 days or longer, and only 3 percent of the women sentenced to three months or longer (Adams, 1975:185). In his reanalysis of these data, Adams (1975: 193) did not find that the type of offense adequately explained the racial differences: "As compared with whites, African American women seem underdefended and oversentenced. . . . [T]hey may have been overarrested and overindicted as well."

Pretrial Experiences

An analysis of samples of grand larceny and felonious assault cases from all 50 states identified a pattern of discriminatory treatment of African-American women at virtually every stage of the criminal justice process, including a greater likelihood of being jailed before and after conviction than for white women (Nagel and Weitzman, 1971).

Detention   Other early studies reported that minority women were often unable to make bail and were held in jail until their court hearing or were disproportionately held in detention relative to the types of offenses committed (e.g., Barrus and Slavin, 1971). An estimated 53 percent of arrested prostitutes are African-American women, and since many judges deny bail or insist upon increasingly higher bail for each prostitution arrest, the impact on these women of color is manifest (DeCrow, 1974).

More recently, it has been reported that the detention status of women offenders may not be related to race/ethnicity in some U.S. jurisdictions. For example, in the Fulton County (Georgia) criminal courts "no overall relationship was found between race and whether a defendant was held in detention before the court hearing, since 66.7 percent of the African American women and 63.6 percent of the white women were in jail at the time of their court hearing" (Mann, 1984a:168). How-

ever, not one African-American female in that study was released on her own recognizance. There was also a tendency for African-American women to have higher bails set.

In a comparison of Seattle and New York City courts, Daly (1987a) found lower detention rates for African-American and Hispanic women than for white women in both jurisdictions. Apparently, being married mitigates more strongly against detention for African-American women than for Hispanic women in New York City. Elsewhere, Daly (1987b:286) suggests that "familial paternalism" may account for the "in-out" decision, since it reflects the "court's interest in protecting family life and those dependent on the defendant."

An observational study of women's processing in the Fulton County (Georgia) criminal courts lends support to Daly's position: "leniency because the defendant was identified as a mother occurred almost 30 percent of the time among black women, and only once among white women" (Mann and Berg, 1986:206). However, it was also observed that some judges admitted their reluctance to put an additional financial burden on the state by having to maintain a mother in prison as well as her children at home.

Prosecution   Criminal court prosecutors have almost unlimited discretion such that minorities have an increased likelihood of being "charged, overcharged, and indicted" (Mann, 1993). Noting that researchers tend to focus on sentencing and conviction decisions rather than prosecutorial decisions related to issues of race and gender, Spohn, Gruhl, and Welch (1987) studied the prosecutor's rejection or dismissal of charges in racial/ethnic minority felony cases in Los Angeles. They suggest that "a significant amount of racial bias could exist at these and other less formal and visible pre- and posttrial stages [which] may not require decision makers to follow equally strict procedures" (p. 176). They examined the prosecutor's initial decision whether to prosecute and the decision to dismiss (after a formal charge had been filed). In the first instance, Anglos (whites), regardless of gender, had higher rejection rates than any other group. Spohn et al. found that Anglo females had strikingly lower prosecution rates (19 percent) than any other subgroup. Both African-American (30 percent) and Hispanic females (31 percent) were prosecuted more often than Anglo males but less often than their racial/ethnic male counterparts.

Sentencing

A recent review of the literature addressing differential sentencing of American women and men notes the "dearth of research on the possible interactive effects of gender and ethnicity" and the inconclusiveness of the available information on the influence of race/ethnicity on criminal justice dispositions (Odubekun, 1992:344). Those few studies that do report "race-specific gender differences" indicate more punitive treatment of women of color. Like arrest figures, however, sentencing statistics may reflect sexism, racism, or both, that occurred in earlier decision-making steps of the criminal justice process.

Foley and Rasche (1979) found that African-American women received longer sentences (55.1 months) than white women (52.5 months) in their study of one Missouri institution over a 16-year period. African-Americans' sentences were longer for property crimes (32.8 months) than such sentences for whites (29.9 months), and African-Americans served longer prison terms. For personal crimes, despite white women's much longer sentences than those for African-American women (182.3 versus 98.5 months), African-American women served more actual time (26.7 versus 23 months). Even when the same offense was committed, Foley and Rasche

found differences based on race. For example, white women imprisoned for murder served one-third less time than African-American women incarcerated for the same offense. While the two groups showed no significant difference in mean sentence length for drug offenses, African-American women served much more time in prison for these crimes than did white women (20.4 versus 13.2 months).

In a study of sentencing outcomes for 1,034 female defendants processed in a northern California county between 1972 and 1976, Kruttschnitt (1980–1981:256) reports that in three of the five offense categories studied, a defendant's race or income affected her sentence. "Specifically, African American women convicted of either disturbing the peace or drug law violations are sentenced more severely than their white counterparts; lower-income women convicted of forgery receive the more severe sentences. . . . [T]he status of welfare is generally given the greatest weight and appears to have a more consistent impact than either race or income alone on the sentences accorded these women."

Kruttschnitt undertook to determine if the relatively harsh sentences were due to race, low income, or welfare status and found that most of the effect of race on sentencing was direct: "the impact of race on sentencing appears to have little to do with the fact that African Americans are more likely to be welfare recipients than whites" (p. 258).

According to Mann (1989), in 1979, 32 percent of the women arrested and sentenced to prison in California were African-American, 14.9 percent were Mexican-American, 0.8 percent were Native American, and 52.4 percent were white. By 1990, felony prosecutions of women of color in California, shown in Table 2, had increased to 34.4 percent for African-Americans, 19 percent for Hispanics, and 2.5 percent for other women of color; prosecutions of white female felons had

TABLE 2
Dispositions of Women Felony Cases by Race/Ethnicity: California and New York State, 1990

	California						New York				
	Total	White	African-American	Hispanic-American	Other	Unknown	Total	White	African-American	Hispanic-American	Other
Total felony prosecutions											
Number	12,772	5,598	4,395	2,431	319	29	6,013	1,038	3,193	1,737	45
%	100.0	43.8	34.4	19.0	2.5	0.2	100.0	17.3	53.1	28.9	0.7
Total convictions											
Number	12,142	5,289	4,204	2,320	303	26	5,505	930	2,921	1,619	35
%	100.0	43.6	34.6	19.1	2.5	0.2	100.0	16.9	53.1	29.4	0.6
(% Prosecuted/ convicted)	(95.1)	(94.5)	(95.7)	(95.4)	(95.0)	(89.7)	(91.6)	(89.6)	(91.5)	(93.2)	(77.8)
Total prison sentences											
Number	2,370	943	803	579	45	—	1,898	146	1,007	739	6
%	100.0	39.8	33.9	24.4	1.9	—	100.0	7.7	53.1	38.9	0.3
(% Convicted/ prison)	(19.5)	(16.9)	(19.1)	(25.0)	(14.9)	—	(34.5)	(15.7)	(34.5)	(45.7)	(17.1)
(% Prosecuted/ prison)	(18.6)	(16.8)	(18.3)	(23.8)	(14.1)	—	(31.6)	(14.0)	(31.5)	(42.6)	(13.3)

Source: Compiled from data received from the California Department of Justice and the New York State Division of Criminal Justice Services.

decreased to 43.8 percent. California female convictions in 1990 were fairly consistent across racial/ethnic subgroups. After conviction, Hispanic females, however, were the most harshly treated. They were only 19.1 percent of convicted women but almost one-fourth (24.4 percent) of the women who received prison sentences. African-American and other women of color were slightly less likely to receive prison sentences after conviction. White women were treated even more leniently in this regard. Looked at another way, 23.8 percent of Latinas arrested for felonies were sentenced to prison compared with 18.3 percent of African-American women, 16.8 percent of white women, and 14.1 percent of other women of color in California.

A comparison of arrest figures with figures on women's imprisonment [data not shown] for the major felonies leading to women's imprisonment (drug violations, theft, burglary, and robbery) in the three states examined in 1990 (California, Florida, and New York) shows that women of color who are arrested for these crimes end up sentenced to prison more often than white women with similar arrests. A few examples of this pattern are discussed below.

California incarcerates more women than any other state in the nation and has the "largest incarcerated female population in the world" (Welling, 1990: Sec. 7, p. 3). Together only a few offenses represent the crimes of 78.4 percent of California female inmates in the following proportions: drug violations, 37.6 percent; theft, 26.0 percent; burglary, 10.2 percent; and robbery, 4.6 percent. [Data not shown.] While white women felons in California were those most often arrested for three of the primary imprisonment offenses (drugs, theft, and burglary), they were less likely to be incarcerated for drug violations or theft than African- or Hispanic-American women. And whereas white women were

nearly half of the women arrested for drug violations (48.5 percent), only 38.3 percent were sent to prison. African-American female drug law violators were 30.5 percent of those arrested but 34.1 percent of those imprisoned. For Hispanic women the figures are even more disparate: they were only 18.7 percent of arrestees for drug violations but 26.1 percent of those incarcerated. The same pattern is found for theft and robbery but not for burglary, for which the statistics seem more equitable.

The processing of Hispanic female felons in New York State (see Table 2) reflects even more disproportionate figures. Although Latinas were 28.9 percent of the women prosecuted in 1990, they were 38.9 percent of those sentenced to prison in New York. Only 7.7 percent of the women sentenced to prison for felony convictions were white; more than half (53.1 percent) were African-American. Thus, we find a Latina rate that is over five times that for whites and an African-American rate that is almost seven times the white rate.

The primary felony offenses leading to women's incarceration in New York State were an astounding 78.9 percent for drug violations, which together with robbery (7.1 percent), theft (4.3 percent), and burglary (1.6 percent) totaled 91.9 percent [data not shown]. New York Hispanic women were the most harshly treated subgroup for drug violations. They were only 28.8 percent of the women arrested for this offense but 41.2 percent of those sentenced to prison. Similarly, Hispanic women in New York were just 13.7 percent of the women arrested for burglary but were almost twice as likely to go to prison for that offense (26.8 percent). In contrast, white women were 35.8 percent of those arrested but only 24.4 percent of those imprisoned for burglary.

How can these discrepancies be explained? A partial answer is found in the last two rows of data in Table 2—i.e., the percentage of those prosecuted who were sentenced to prison and the percentage of those convicted who were sentenced to prison. In New York, African-American and Hispanic-American women were far more likely than their white counterparts to be prosecuted, convicted, and sentenced to prison in 1990. Hispanic-American women in California experienced similar treatment. The differential treatment of these racial/ethnic subgroups suggests discrimination at the sentencing level, since, as we have seen, all subgroups were convicted at about the same rate (see Table 2).

Unfortunately, no data were available on the previous records of these women felons, but it would take a real stretch of imagination to assume that the influence of prior arrests would so drastically affect three separate racial/ethnic groups, in three different states, in the manner we have seen. An examination of the offenses leading to women's imprisonment in the three states[5] suggests that women of color are treated more punitively by the courts than their white counterparts. However, as previously noted, disparate treatment of women of color could also have occurred at prior stages in the criminal justice process (e.g., when decisions were made regarding arrest, prosecution, and indictment).

THE INCARCERATION OF WOMEN OF COLOR

Jail

The 37,253 women in local jails in 1989 were 9.5 percent of jailed inmates (Snell, 1992). The number had increased by 138.0 percent between 1983 and 1989—almost twice the increase of jailed male inmates. Over this same period, the proportion of white female inmates decreased from 41.8 percent to 37.8 percent; that of nonwhite female inmates increased from 58.2 to 62.2 percent. The major contribution to this minority increase came from Hispanic women, who went from 12.7 to 16.3 percent.

In 1989 one of every three women in jail (33.6 percent) was there for drug offenses. The next most frequent incarceration offenses were property crime (31.9 percent), other public order violations (19.0 percent), violent crimes (13.2 percent), and all other offenses (2.2 percent). Among the convicted female inmates, white and African-American women were almost equally convicted and jailed for drug offenses (African-American, 33.8 percent; white, 32.2 percent) but differed in the type of offense. African-American women were more frequently convicted for drug possession and white women for drug trafficking.

Jailed African-American women were convicted almost twice as often for violent offenses as white women (12.6 percent versus 6.4 percent), particularly for robbery and assault, and twice as often for homicide (1.7 percent versus 0.8 percent). Conversely, more than one in four white women in jail (27.9 percent) were convicted of a public order offense, compared with one in eight African-American women (11.9 percent). Finally, among women convicted of property crimes, both white and African-American women were incarcerated primarily for larceny-theft and fraud, but African-American women were more likely to be jailed (38.8 percent versus 31.8 percent).

Prison[6]

Women of color were 61.4 percent of all incarcerated females in state institutions and 64.5 percent of women in federal prisons as of June 30, 1991 (ACA, 1992). As seen in Table 3, African- and Hispanic-American women make up a disproportionately large proportion of the inmate population. The imprisonment percentage for African-American women is almost four times their population proportion, and Hispanic-American women

TABLE 3

Proportions of Incarcerated Women in Federal and State Prisons, as of 6/30/91, Compared with the General Female Population, by Race/Ethnicity

	Percentage in state prison	Percentage in federal prison	Total percentage	Percentage in female population*
White women	38.6 (14,820)	35.5 (1,651)	38.3 (16,471)	75.4 (96,143,708)
African-American women	48.5 (18,601)	38.6 (1,794)	47.4 (20,395)	12.3 (15,733,972)
Hispanic-American women	10.5 (4,018)	23.7 (1,103)	11.9 (5,121)	8.6 (10,965,936)
All others	2.4 (923)	2.2 (1,017)	2.4 (1,024)	3.7 (4,626,909)
Totals	100.0 (38,362)	100.0 (4,649)	100.0 (43,011)	100.0 (127,470,525)

*Adjusted by percentage Hispanic.
Sources: American Correctional Association, 1992; data received from Population Administration, U.S. Census; and estimations from U.S. Census, 1992, Tape File 1C.

are overrepresented by about 30 percent. In federal institutions, both African-American and Latina inmates are overrepresented by about three times their proportions in the general female population. In contrast, white females are substantially underrepresented as an incarcerated group.

Table 4, which reflects the American Correctional Association (1992) numbers and percentages for the three states as of June 30, 1991, shows the extreme disproportion of imprisoned women of color in the three states we have been scrutinizing throughout this chapter: California (64.2 percent), Florida (62.4 percent), and New York (85.6 percent).

Unique Problems of Imprisoned Women of Color

In an atmosphere that is already tense and oppressive, women of color face additional problems related to the rural locations of women's prisons. Most staff members are whites recruited from the rural areas surrounding the prisons, whereas the majority of the inmates are racial/ethnic minorities from inner-city areas; this is a mixture that tends to augment existing discord.

A majority of both white and nonwhite (African-American and Native American) female inmates in a study of the Minnesota Correctional Institution for Women (MCIW), where 93 percent of the staff and administration were white, felt that racial/ethnic status influenced the way correctional officers treated female inmates. Racial discrimination was perceived by over two-thirds of the women of color, and 29.4 percent felt that job assignments in the institution were influenced by race. Women of color, who constituted 42 percent of the MCIW prison population, cited "race relations" as the most frequent cause of intra-inmate assaults (Kruttschnitt, 1983).

In the criminal justice system, parole is a privilege and not a right. Parole from prison

TABLE 4
Adult Female Inmate State Prison Populations, as of 6/30/91:
California, Florida, and New York State by Race/Ethnicity

	California	Florida	New York	Totals	As percentage of all female state inmates
White women					
No.	2,380	983	417	3,780	(14,820)
%	35.8	37.6	14.4	31.1	38.6
African-American women					
No.	2,372	1,571	1,424	5,367	(18,601)
%	35.6	60.1	49.2	44.1	48.5
Hispanic-American women					
No.	1,515	59*	1,038	2,612	(4,018)
%	22.8	2.3	35.9	21.5	10.5
All others					
No.	389	0[†]	14	403	(923)
%	5.8	0.0	0.5	3.3	2.4
Totals					
No.	6,656	2,613	2,893	12,162	(38,362)
%	100.0	100.0	100.0	100.0	100.0
As percentage of all female state inmates	17.4	6.8	7.5		31.7

*Considering the large Hispanic population in Florida, this figure is questionably low.
†This figure is debatable because there are large numbers of Native Americans in Florida.
Source: American Correctional Association, 1992.

is earned by demonstrating the ability to function in society in an "acceptable way." Parole boards use vague standards in their decision making that include both institutional and noninstitutional criteria. They often expect women to meet higher standards of proper conduct than are required of men. Since women of color, particularly unwed mothers, are seen by society as more sexually carefree and as having looser morals, the influence of such stereotypes on parole board members can be detrimental to the potential freedom of minority women.

The existence of prior offense records is often included in the release decision. Women convicted of property crimes, drug offenses, or alcohol-related offenses—the specific crimes that usually result in the incarceration of women of color—are those with less successful parole outcomes (Simon, 1975). There is evidence that release from prison differs significantly because of race/ethnicity. Foley and Rasche (1979) found that in Missouri white women were more likely to receive parole than African-American women (41.3 percent versus 33.3 percent). As a result, African-Americans served significantly more actual time (19.4 months) than whites (14.9 months).

African-American women are disproportionately represented on the death rows of this country relative to their proportion in the general female population. In January 1993, 13 of the 34 female death row inmates were

African-American (38 percent), and 3 were Hispanic-American (9.0 percent): a total of 47.0 percent women of color on death row in 14 states (Streib, 1993).

In a preliminary inventory of confirmed lawful executions of female offenders from 1625 to 1984, Victor Streib (1988) reports that among the 346 female offenders for whom race is known, 229 (66 percent) were African-American and 108 (31 percent) were white. These proportions have apparently reversed in recent years,[7] since of the 37 women "legally" executed since 1900, 32 percent were African-American and 68 percent were white (Gillispie and Lopez, 1986). Nonetheless, these statistics are also disproportionate relative to the general female population.

Since the reinstitution of the death penalty in 1976, 35.7 percent of the 168 persons executed as of the spring of 1992 were minority defendants with white victims (NAACP LDF, 1992). The race of the victim has recently been found to possibly influence the sentencing of women homicide offenders as well. In a study of female homicide offenders in six U.S. cities for 1979 and 1983, Mann (1990b) found moderate support for a devaluation hypothesis:[8] 40 percent of African-American women who killed other African-Americans but 66.7 percent of those who killed whites were sentenced to prison. In contrast, if both victim and offender were white, 45.3 percent of the female offenders were imprisoned. Shields (1987) examined female homicide in Alabama from 1930 to 1986 and reported that in the smattering of cases crossing racial lines, the offenders, all African-American, received severe sentences, the majority of which were for life.

SOME SOLUTIONS

In the 1970s, but more so in the 1980s and 1990s, criminological research shifted to include the study of women offenders. Unfor-

tunately, though studies of women offenders have consistently documented disparate treatment of women of color because of their race/ethnicity, insufficient empirical attention has been focused on such offenders. Discrimination and a lack of consideration for the concerns and needs of nonwhite women and the needs of their families are found at every level of the system—arrest, pretrial treatment, courts, and corrections. To provide a factual basis for desperately needed policy changes to alleviate many of the problems in the U.S. criminal justice system's treatment of women of color, a comprehensive national study and survey of all female offenders should be undertaken to chronicle these injustices.

Certain measures can be instituted while we await the study results. We have seen that a lack of understanding of peoples of color and their cultures often results in unwarranted arrests because of cultural unfamiliarity and insensitivity on the part of law enforcement personnel. To improve police interaction with minority women, intensive police training in gender, race, and minority community relations should be immediately included in police academy training at local, state, and federal levels. Since many poor, minority women are single heads of household, women of color who are arrested for less serious offenses should be released on their own recognizance or should have low bail assigned to minimize disruption in their families. Current prostitution laws and their enforcement discriminate against poorer, minority women while ignoring their white, more affluent customers. Such laws should be more equitably applied, abolished altogether, or, at the very least, decriminalized. Substance abuse is one of the major causes of the arrest and incarceration of women of color. Drug and alcohol use should be viewed as a medical, not a criminal, problem, and appropriate and effective therapy should be available for women addicts. To ensure equal justice at the court level, more women and minority judges should be installed at every level of the judicial system. Finally, dramatic changes in the correctional system must be enacted. Efforts should be made to strengthen the family ties of imprisoned women of color through home furloughs, conjugal visits, and family life and child-care education. If new women's facilities must be built, they should be located in the inner cities, where most women of color who are caught in the criminal justice web reside. Such institutional locations would facilitate family visits as well as expand potential educational, training, employment, and placement opportunities. Since Justice is depicted as a blindfolded woman, obviously, she should also be color-blind.

NOTES

1. My sincere thanks are extended to the following persons who generously and expeditiously supplied the requested state data: Tricia Clark, State of California, Department of Justice, Bureau of Criminal Statistics and Special Services; Linda Booz, Florida Department of Law Enforcement, Division of Criminal Justice Information Systems; and Mark L. Cimring, State of New York, Division of Criminal Justice Services.

2. With the exception of motor vehicle theft (ranked fourth), the numbers for the remaining Crime Index offenses (murder and nonnegligent manslaughter, forcible rape, and arson) were not included because the numbers were too small to classify among the 10 arrest offenses for the three states (see Table 1).

3. "All other offenses" are arrests for violations of city ordinances and most traffic violations. Because these crimes are of little consequence, they were excluded from the analyses.

4. Florida also has a substantial proportion of Hispanics in its population, primarily Cubans and Latin Americans. Since it does not report Hispanics separately, no information is available on this subgroup. In fact, characterizing the extent of Hispanic-American crime is inordinately

problematic. The *Uniform Crime Reports* prior to 1987 at least provided a Hispanic/non-Hispanic category, but now it has been eliminated.

5. Although prosecution data were not available from Florida, that state is included for comparative purposes. For the most part, the Florida and the New York figures are for 1990 incarceration offenses and in some cases reflect dispositions on women sentenced in 1989 and 1990. It is possible that even earlier arrests are involved and the offenders were imprisoned in this time frame. Since the state of California undoubtedly maintains the best criminal justice statistics, the California data more closely represent the actual processing and imprisonment of the same individuals.

6. As of 1991, there were 67 state prison institutions for adult women in 42 states, 33 state coed facilities, 7 federal women's prisons, and 5 federal coed facilities (American Correctional Association, 1992). The states without women's prisons—Alabama, Kansas, Maine, North Dakota, South Dakota, Washington, and West Virginia—have coed prisons.

7. These figures do not include the lynchings of untold numbers of African-American females in the early years of this nation.

8. The idea here is that the criminal justice system values white lives and devalues African-American and other minority lives; one result is the imposition of harsher sentences if the victim is white.

REFERENCES

Adams, Stuart N. 1975. "The 'Black-Shift' Phenomenon in Criminal Justice." *Justice System Journal:* 185–194.

American Correctional Association (ACA). 1992. *Juvenile & Adult Correctional Departments, Institutions, Agencies, and Paroling Authorities.* Laurel, Md.: ACA.

Anglin, M. Douglas, and Yihing Hser. 1987. "Addicted Women and Crime." *Criminology* 25 (2) : 359–397.

Barrus, C., and A. Slavin. 1971. *Movement and Characteristics of Women's Detention Center Admissions, 1969.* Washington, D.C.: D.C. Department of Corrections.

Daly, Kathleen. 1987a. "Discrimination in the Criminal Courts: Family, Gender, and the Problem of Equal Treatment." *Social Forces* 66 (1): 152–175.

———. 1987b. "Structure and Practice of Familial-Based Justice in a Criminal Court." *Law & Society Review* 21 (2): 267–290.

DeCrow, Karen. 1974. *Sexist Justice.* New York: Vintage.

Deming, Richard. 1977. *Women: The New Criminals.* New York: Thomas Nelson.

DeWitt, Charles B. 1990. *DUF—Drug Use Forecasting.* Washington, D.C.: U.S. Government Printing Office.

Foley, Linda A., and Christine E. Rasche. 1979. "The Effect of Race on Sentence, Actual Time Served and Final Disposition of Female Offenders." In John A. Conley (ed.), *Theory and Research in Criminal Justice.* Cincinnati: Anderson.

Gillispie, L. Kay, and Barbara Lopez. 1986. "What Must a Woman Do to Be Executed?" Paper presented at annual meetings of the American Society of Criminology.

Goldstein, Paul J., Patricia A. Bellucci, Barry J. Spunt, and Thomas Miller. 1991. "Volume of Cocaine Use and Violence: A Comparison between Men and Women." *The Journal of Drug Issues* 21 (2): 345–367.

Harlow, Caroline Wolf. 1991. *Drugs and Jail Inmates, 1989.* Washington, D.C.: U.S. Government Printing Office.

Hawkins, Darnell F. 1986. "Black and White Homicide Differentials: Alternatives to an Inadequate Theory." In D. F. Hawkins (ed.), *Homicide among Black Americans.* New York: New York University.

Hutchinson, Earl Ofari. 1990. *The Mugging of Black America.* Chicago: African American Images.

Isikoff, Michael. 1991. "Study: White Students More Likely to Use Drugs." *Washington Post,* Feb. 25: A4.

Kratcoski, Peter C., and Kirk Scheuerman. 1974. "Incarcerated Male and Female Offenders' Perceptions of Their Experiences in the Criminal Justice System." *Journal of Criminal Justice* 2: 73–78.

Kruttschnitt, Candace. 1980–1981. "Social Status and Sentences of Female Offenders." *Law and Society Review* 15 (2): 247–265.

———. 1983. "Race Relations and the Female Inmate." *Crime and Delinquency* (October): 577–591.

Lusane, Clarence. 1991. *Pipe Dream Blues: Racism and the War on Drugs.* Boston: South End.

Mann, Coramae Richey. 1984a. "Race and Sentencing of Female Felons: A Field Study." *International Journal of Women's Studies* 7 (2): 160–172.

———. 1984b. *Female Crime and Delinquency.* Tuscaloosa: University of Alabama.

———. 1989. "Minority and Female: A Criminal Justice Double Bind." *Social Justice* 16 (3): 95–114.

———. 1990a. "Female Homicide and Substance Use: Is There a Connection?" *Women and Criminal Justice* 1 (2): 87–109.

———. 1990b. "Black Female Homicide in the United States." *Journal of Interpersonal Violence* 5 (2): 176–210.

———. 1993. *Unequal Justice: A Question of Color.* Bloomington: Indiana University.

———. (Forthcoming.) *Women Murderers: Deadliest of the Species?* Albany, N.Y.: SUNY.

——— and Bruce L. Berg. 1986. "The Use of Systematic Observation in Criminal Court Research." *Journal of Social and Behavioral Sciences* 32 (4) : 99–217.

McArthur, Virginia A. 1974. "From Convict to Citizen: Programs for the Woman Offender." Mimeographed.

Moyer, Imogene L., and Garland F. White. 1981. "Police Processing of Female Offenders." In L. Bowker (ed.), *Crime in America.* New York: Macmillan.

NAACP Legal Defense Fund (NAACP LDF). 1992. *Death Row, U.S.A.* New York: NAACP.

Nagel, Stuart, and Lenore Weitzman. 1971. "Women as Litigants." *Hastings Law Journal.* 23 (1): 171–198.

Odubekun, Lola. 1992. "A Structural Approach to Differential Gender Sentencing." *Criminal Justice Abstracts* 24 (2): 343–360.

Pettiway, Leon E. 1987. "Participation in Crime Partnerships by Female Drug Users: The Effects of Domestic Arrangements, Drug Use, and Criminal Involvement." *Criminology* 25 (3): 741–765.

Pokorny, Alex D. 1965. "A Comparison of Homicide in Two Cities." *Journal of Criminal Law, Criminology and Police Science* 56 (4): 479–487.

Shields, Alan J. 1987. "Female Homicide: Alabama 1930–1986." Paper presented at the annual meetings of the American Society of Criminology.

Simon, Rita. 1975. *The Contemporary Woman and Crime.* Washington, D.C.: U.S. Government Printing Office.

Snell, Tracy L. 1992. *Women in Jail 1989.* Washington, D.C.: U.S. Department of Justice.

Spohn, Cassia, John Gruhl, and Susan Welch. 1987. "The Impact of the Ethnicity and Gender of Defendants on the Decision to Reject or Dismiss Felony Charges." *Criminology* 25 (1): 175–191.

Streib, Victor L. 1988. "American Executions of Female Offenders: A Preliminary Inventory of Names, Dates, and Other Information (3rd Edition)." Xeroxed.

———. 1993. "Capital Punishment for Female Offenders: Present Death Row Inmates and Death Sentences and Executions of Female Offenders, Jan. 1, 1973, to Dec. 31, 1992." Photocopied.

Sutherland, Edwin H., and Donald R. Cressey. 1978. *Criminology.* Philadelphia: J. B. Lippincott.

Uniform Crime Reports (UCR). 1991. *Crime in the United States 1990.* Washington, D.C.: U.S. Government Printing Office.

Visher, Christy A. 1983. "Gender, Police Arrest Decisions, and Notions of Chivalry." *Criminology* 21 (1): 5–28.

Welling, Bobbie L. 1990. "Achieving Equal Justice for Women and Men in the Courts." (Draft.) San Francisco: The Judicial Council of California, Administrative Office of the Courts.

Whitaker, Catherine J. 1990. *Black Victims.* Washington, D.C.: U.S. Department of Justice.

Wolfgang, Marvin E. 1958. *Patterns in Criminal Homicide.* Philadelphia: University of Pennsylvania.

Young, Vernetta D. 1986. "Gender Expectations and Their Impact on Black Female Offenders and Victims." *Justice Quarterly* 3 (3): 305–327

CHAPTER 8

PROCESSES OF VICTIMIZATION AND CRIMINALIZATION OF BLACK WOMEN

REGINA A. ARNOLD

ABSTRACT

In Chapter 4, Chesney-Lind suggested that a feminist analysis of crime causation among young women requires an understanding of the connection between their victimization—through physical and sexual abuse at home—and their criminalization. Moreover, she recommended that this process be investigated in different racial/ethnic communities to learn how the structural components of race and class play themselves out in a patriarchal society for different groups of women. Arnold does exactly this by interviewing 60 black women serving time in a city jail or state prison. Intensive interviewing provides a useful contrast with studies that use other methods of collecting data, and it provides valuable insights in studies of women's lives.

In discussing the close relationship between victimization and criminalization for young black women, Arnold introduces the concept of "structural dislocation." By this she means the removal of an individual from the primary socializing units of family, education, and employment. Arnold explains how institutional race, class, and gender discrimination impact on young black women's inability to remain in their families and at school, leading to noncriminal behavior (status offenses such as running away or incorrigibility) and later criminal behavior.

The interrelated processes of victimization and criminalization are described in this chapter as ones that begin with abuse—physical and/or sexual, economic, or racial. The young women resist by either running away, leaving home, or stealing. By refusing to accept or participate in their own victimization, the black women in this study, as young girls, are labeled and processed as deviants, and later as criminals. In the process of resistance the victim engages in status offenses or low-level crime and also becomes structurally dislocated. Once on the street, lacking support or resources, she may turn to crime and, in many cases, to drugs.

In depicting the lives of young, poor, minority women, the author forces the reader to consider a number of serious social problems with which our society is confronted. Readers should ask why so few government resources have been devoted to solutions to these problems (the front end) while resources are available for jail construction and imprisonment (the back end).

In this article, I examine the dual process of victimization and criminalization for young Black women who end up in prison. Dimensions of victimization include patriarchy, family violence, economic marginality, racism, and mis-education. Dimensions of criminalization include structural dislocation, association with deviant and criminal others (including drug addicts), processing and labeling as a status offender, and re-creation of familial relationships within the criminal world.

I argue that for young Black girls from lower socioeconomic classes, involvement in "precriminal" behavior may be viewed as active resistance to victimization: these behaviors include running away from home, stealing, and leaving school. Typically, young Black girls who engage in these behaviors will pay a tremendous price for resisting. Such a price will be exacted upon them by the criminal justice system, sometimes in conjunction with parents or legal guardians. They may be labeled as status offenders, institutionalized in girls homes, or imprisoned for vagrancy and other nonviolent crimes. Once this process of criminalization is set in motion, sustained criminal involvement becomes the norm as well as a rational coping strategy. Even imprisonment becomes normalized among criminals, in the sense of providing a family, community, an opportunity for employment, and as a means of obtaining

food, lodging, and rest from life on the streets.

This article is informed by scholarship on female crime and delinquency (Chesney-Lind, 1989; Miller, 1986; Mann, 1984; Price and Sokoloff, 1982; Davidson, 1982; Rosenbaum, 1981; Chapman and Gates, 1978); child abuse and family violence (Russell, 1986; Gutierres and Reich, 1981; Rhoades and Parker, 1981; Smith, Berkman, and Fraser, 1980); and girls and women in prison (Chesney-Lind, 1988; Chesney-Lind and Rodriguez, 1983; Arnold, 1979; Shakur, 1978). A prevalent theme in the work of Chesney-Lind (1988) and Chesney-Lind and Rodriguez (1983) suggests the existence of a systematic process of criminalization unique to women that magnifies the relationship between ongoing societal victimization and eventual entrapment in the criminal justice system. The findings presented here enlarge and enhance our understanding of this emerging issue in the study of women and crime: the relationship between the experience of having been victimized and subsequent offending.

Using data from participant-observation, interviews, and questionnaires administered to 50 Black female prisoners serving sentences in a city jail (Arnold, 1979) and 10 women in a state prison (Arnold, 1986), I discuss how females, as young girls, are labeled and processed as deviants—and subsequently as criminals—for refusing to accept or participate in their own victimization. Second, I show how this refusal results in struc-

Reprinted by permission from *Social Justice.*

tural dislocation from three primary socializing institutions (the family, education, and occupation), and leads to entry into the criminal life. Third, I reveal how crime becomes a rational choice in the face of dislocation from family, education, and finally work in the paid labor force, and how drugs are used to dull the pain of the reality of their lives.

PATRIARCHY AND FAMILY VIOLENCE

In recent years, hidden violence in the lives of women and children at home, at school, and in the social sphere has been increasingly made public. Although violence against women and children has been declared unacceptable, it endures pervasively. For example, in research on incest in the lives of girls and women, Russell (1986) warns that millions of American girls are being socialized into victim roles that lead to future self-destructive behavior. Some female prisoners talked about the gender oppression and sexual violence perpetrated against them by their fathers, stepfathers, or father substitutes in the home.

Alicia R. was reared by her father after her mother died in childbirth. Of this event, Alicia says, "I must have been born for all bad luck to fall on me." At the age of 11 she was raped by her father, his way of punishing her for being "too attracted to girls" at the Catholic girls school she attended. At age 12, she ran away from home and has been on her own ever since.

Barbara G., serving time in a state prison for a felony offense, talks about being "sexually molested" by her stepfather when she was 13. "My stepfather molested me twice. My mother didn't believe it. I was angry, I was hurt, I was afraid. I was going through a lot of things then."

Barbara confided in her mother, whose response was to send her to live with her aunts. Although they were sympathetic, they eventually sent her back home to work out her problems with her mother. Barbara's response to being sexually victimized was to leave the situation. She ran away from home, only to be brought back by the very man who had molested her.

> Eventually I ran away from home. I met a man, a much older man. I was almost 14. He used to lock me up in his apartment, so I was like a runaway prisoner. My stepfather found me and brought me back home.

Once at home, while her mother worked the night shift as a nurse, Barbara's stepfather tried to molest her again. This time she hit him over the head with one of her school sports trophies, leaving a huge gash. When she told her mother, her stepfather's explanation was that he had been "working under the hood of his car when the hood fell on his head." He explained that Barbara was just a chronic liar. Barbara says, "Before my 15th birthday, I ran away again, and I've been on my own ever since."

Violence in the family and being victimized as a young girl was evident in the situation of Harriette D., who also was serving time in a state prison for a felony offense. As an infant, Harriette was placed in foster care by her mother. She was sexually abused by her foster father, and ran away from home. She says:

> I was with this foster lady who was very cruel. She was abusive. And I was no more than a maid as a child . . . that was my purpose. She received welfare for foster kids . . . that was her purpose. I stayed there till I was 13, then ran away. I was tired of the physical abuse. I ran to my mother's. The man she lived with sexually abused me and I ran away again.

A system of male dominance and control was operative in the lives of these young girls; a set of social relations of power in which the male gender was dominating their sexuality. When they were young girls, many interviewees acted against their oppressors by fleeing—running away—rather than physically defending themselves. This was consistent with both their age and gender role socialization. Indeed, the combination of size, age, and gender made fleeing the more rational response, fighting the least feasible. Unlike so many young girls similarly situated, these girls were unwilling to passively accept domination and abuse.

Research has suggested a connection between child abuse and delinquent behaviors (Cavaiola and Schiff, 1988; Garbarino and Plantz, 1986; Geller and Ford-Somma, 1984; Bolton and Reich, 1977) and between childhood sexual abuse and delinquency (Cavaiola and Schiff, 1988; Runtz and Briere, 1986; Gutierres and Reich, 1981; Rhoades and Parker, 1981). Some of this literature cites the tendency for abused children to be more involved in escape behaviors such as running away. This is most frequent with victims of sexual abuse. As Gutierres and Reich (1981) point out, running away may be a coping mechanism in response to child abuse, rather than a delinquent behavior.

ECONOMIC MARGINALITY

Besides gender oppression, class oppression also figured significantly in the victimization of young girls whose lives were jeopardized by the very socioeconomic situation into which they were born.

The typical woman in prison is poor, as are most of the women discussed in this article. Both the National Study (Glick and Neto, 1977) and the San Francisco jail study (Lewis and Bresler, 1981) indicated that as children, Black women came from a more impoverished socioeconomic background than did white women, and that they were more than twice as likely to have been on welfare when arrested.

To be young, Black, poor, and female is to be in a high-risk category for victimization and stigmatization on many levels. Class oppression was alluded to in the women's comments about growing up poor and turning to deviant behavior as a way of helping themselves and their families. Mable P. discusses the economic situation of her family and its impact upon her:

> There were eight children in the family. My father had a mover's job, but we also got welfare. We moved from hotel to hotel and ended up in the projects. I needed things, so I had no choice but to steal. I've been stealing since I was 10.

Similarly, Clara R. comments on how the socioeconomic situation of her family and hardships endured by her mother affected her behavioral choices as a young girl. She says that what frustrated her most was:

> The living situation my family was in. My father beat my mother and neglected his children. He could have taken care of us, but he left. We were on welfare. I began stealing when I was 12. I hustled to help feed and clothe the other [12] kids and help pay the rent.

In both of the above cases, Mable and Clara took it upon themselves to fulfill adult role responsibilities, but they did this through deviant means. Considering their youth, inexperience, and lack of skills, the deviant route became the choice for assisting other family members, and for helping themselves. They chose an assertive, nontraditional course of action, out of step with the cultural mandates for young girls in the society. As Ladner (1972) revealed in her research on young Black girls, when few options are available for meeting basic human needs for food and clothing, thus forcing one to steal, this becomes the necessary proof that the social system can and should be violated.

Often, economic need interfered with a young Black girl's ability to continue her education, or to concentrate on school work. Responding to open-ended questions about school and teachers, some women commented as follows on the connection between their socioeconomic circumstances and their schooling: "[My teachers] tried talking to me, but talk didn't buy my clothes"; "I was a good student, but other things were on my mind, like cash money"; "I dropped out of school to work."

Although school was a refuge for many women, it was not a sufficient counterbalancing force for the significant damage to personhood and self-esteem that occurred within an impoverished environment, and within the institution of the family. Without the support of the family, which requires a solid economic base, one's life chances are severely stunted, and such was the case for these women.

RACISM AND MIS-EDUCATION

Many of the women were victimized as children by an educational system that was alienating and oppressive. They spoke of going to school every day and still not learning anything, of teachers who had their education but who didn't see to it that they got theirs, of teachers who were just there to pick up a paycheck. Jan D. commented in the following manner: "It was hard for me to get along with the teachers. Some were prejudiced, and one had the nerve to tell the whole class he didn't like black people."

If racial oppression in the schools is offset by parents who take an activist role in their children's education, children are more likely to remain in school, coping as best they can (Higginbotham, 1985). However, for the women discussed here, such parental or other support was not available, and so most took it upon themselves to leave alienating school environments and teachers who denigrated them as Black girls.

CRIMINALIZATION OF YOUNG BLACK WOMEN

When young Black girls become structurally dislocated from two of the primary socializing institutions, the home and the school, others in similar situations become their socializing agents. Deviant and criminal behavior was learned in association with criminal-others on the streets. As Sutherland argued, deviant behavior is learned in association with others in intimate social relations (Sutherland and Cressey, 1970). An excess of definitions favorable to violation of the law and conventional norms over definitions unfavorable to violation of the law and conventional norms, states Sutherland, is critical in the criminalization of the individual. In the case of these girls, definitions favorable to criminal behavior played an increasing role in their lives after they were structurally dislocated from the home and the school.

Structural dislocation is defined as removal, by choice, force, or some combination of circumstances, from a social institution—with little chance of reassociation due to the nature of the rift between the individual and the institution. This factor of structural dislocation has been discussed in the context of homeless women for whom displacement often occurs as a consequence of domestic violence, abuse, or the breakup of extended family households (Hope and Young, 1986). In the face of structural dislocation, and the absence of a strong family substitute, deviance and criminality became the modus operandi very early in life for these young Black girls. The family is subsequently recreated with other deviants and criminals, with whom they are in close association over a long period of time.

Lemert (1967) argues that if a reduction in economic opportunities and conventional social relationships increases the probability of involvement in deviance, being publicly labeled a deviant should increase the probability of further deviance. Girls easily acquire labels as status offenders for behaviors that would not be the focus of attention if they were adults (truancy, sexual promiscuity, incorrigibility). An examination of the lives of Black female prisoners as young girls reveals the processes of defining deviance and labeling deviants through a complex of reinforcements involving societal reaction to gender, class, and race.

STRUCTURAL DISLOCATION, LABELING, AND ASSOCIATIONS WITH DEVIANT/CRIMINAL OTHERS

The trajectory from gender victimization to imprisonment is an increasingly common path of female criminalization. Barbara G. discusses her experience. After being twice sexually molested by her stepfather, and running away from home before her 15th birthday, she was picked up by the police for vagrancy and running away and was processed and labeled a status offender. When discussing dislocating herself from the institution of the family, Barbara states:

> I felt like my only alternatives were either to stay at home and deal with this man or leave and deal with the world the best way [I] knew how. And dealing with the world at that time seemed a lot better than to stay there dealing with this [reference to the sexual abuse].

Although Barbara continued her education for a short time thereafter (she had been a good student), once her ties to the family were severed, the mechanics of getting to school became increasingly impossible. This is not unlike the situation of women who experience homelessness, trying to hold on, for as long as possible, to their conventional roles in society. As Barbara states:

> I slept in hallways for about a week, and I was going to school. I washed my clothes out in the

bus station and I'd still go to school, rough-dry, but clean. The truant officer had to notify my parents for something I did, fighting or whatever, and my mother admitted I didn't live there [i.e., at home]. So the school called the authorities, and the authorities had me arrested for vagrancy.

Again, this trajectory can be observed in the case of Harriette D. Harriette was sexually abused by her foster father. She subsequently ran away from home and dropped out of school. In the interview, Harriette talks about being processed as a deviant. She says:

> I was in the street. I got arrested for shoplifting. I was picked up for vagrancy when I was almost 15. The judge gave my mother an option to take me home or he would have no other choice but to send me away. She says, send her away, I don't want her. So they sent me away. I went to a state home for girls.

Many of the interviewees who were abused runaways were also homeless prior to being institutionalized in girls homes. Victimization, resistance to victimization, and structural dislocation preceded early institutionalization.

The connection between physical abuse of young girls and their subsequent entry into the juvenile justice system has been well documented (Chesney-Lind, 1989; Chesney-Lind and Rodriguez, 1983; Davidson, 1982; Smith, Berkman, and Fraser, 1980). In a 1980 report of the National Juvenile Justice Assessment Center, Smith and his colleagues concluded that although most abused and neglected children are referred to the juvenile court because they are victims, they leave the system being defined as offenders. For status offenses, or such noncriminal acts as truancy, ungovernability, incorrigibility, sexual activity or promiscuity, and running away from home, girls specifically are referred to family court as persons in need of supervision (Chesney-Lind, 1982). The very children who are abused are often referred to court by the abusive parent.

Female prisoners discussing their family backgrounds, and what it was like for them to grow up as young Black girls, were often clear about the connection between running away from home, living on the streets, and associations with criminal others. Fending for herself at the age of 15, with no institutional support, Harriette states:

> I was in the street and I couldn't work. I had no skills. I was a kid with a record, so I started stealing, and I would steal for my food. I would go in restaurants and order food and not pay for it, and things like that. A lady introduced me to another way of making money. All I had to do was what had been done [reference to being sexually abused], have sex. At 16, I was arrested for prostitution.

In a study of 200 street prostitutes in San Francisco, Silbert and Pines (1981) found that about two-thirds of the women had run away to escape sexual or other brutality in their homes.

CRIMINAL BEHAVIOR AND THE RE-CREATION OF FAMILY

For many female prisoners who were in and out of prison frequently, other criminals became their family. Other researchers (Romenesko and Miller, 1989; Miller, 1986; Campbell, 1984) have discussed the delinquent group as a family unit, or the "pseudo-family." Interviewees in this sample spoke of drug addicts as their family who used drugs as a way of blotting out what they had to do to survive on the streets, and crime as a way of supporting the drug habit. As Harriette states:

> I started using drugs—heroin, cocaine. Not only was I selling my body to support the habit, I was doing robberies, burglaries, whatever I had to do. Within a six-month period, I was back in

jail, and it didn't faze me because I was secure there. I had a home, had a roof over my head, had three hot meals. I had clean clothing. I didn't have to sell my body for a chicken dinner.

Harriette's sustained criminal involvement was supported by a "family" of other drug addicts and criminals. She gives us an idea of what her life was like:

> There was really nowhere for me to go. So, I went up on the corner, hung out, and reverted back to selling myself and doing stickups or robberies, or burglaries, whatever I needed to do. I ended up living in a shooting gallery—where dope fiends go to get high, sleeping on a chair. And I'm sitting in there, and I sleep in there, and I eat in there, and I get high in there. I wasn't changing my clothes. I had long hair—I wasn't combing it. All I wanted to do was stay high. Drug addicts accept you. This was your family, you know. And I don't care what time of night it was, if you needed one of 'em, they were there. And in my mind, I always had a place to go.

Alicia was raped by her father at the age of 11. Subsequently, she was shunted between institutions and foster homes as a young girl, began using drugs to blot out the pain of the past, and became an addict. She, too, became involved in criminal activity to support an increasing habit, and is now in prison more than she is out of prison. Her friends and newly constituted family are fellow criminals and prisoners.

Repeat offenders are usually drug addicts who engage in illegal activities to obtain monetary rewards that can be used to sustain their lifestyle. In the larger cities, over 50% of the female jail population are convicted prostitutes (Mann, 1984), and research on females involved in prostitution and drug-sale offenses shows that the stated motivations for such crimes are economic (Silbert and Pines, 1981; James, 1976). In addition, as Chapman's (1980) work shows, crimes such as drug abuse are associated directly with economic need and therefore relate directly to economic crime. Rosenbaum (1981) and Chesney-Lind and Rodriguez (1983) have also documented the connection between female addicts and female criminals. Being "in the life" or involved in the drug world is, as Rosenbaum and others have revealed, especially attractive to poor women who are jobless and unable to reap many of the advantages the society has to offer.

Josey, Edna, and Ann are three young women for whom drug addiction and crime have become a persistent reality. Josey B., who is 26, has been addicted to heroin since age 19. Initially, she would get high between jobs, but in less than one year after she began using, she was arrested and charged with petty larceny and forgery. The cycle of addiction and crime persists for Josey. Like Josey, Edna P., who is 27, worked in the paid labor market until she became addicted to drugs (in her case, heroin). Edna thinks her life took a turn for the worse when she reunited with her husband and started using drugs. Since then, she has been arrested often for a variety of crimes, including forgery, burglary, larceny, possession of stolen property, and prostitution. Similarly, Ann T., who says she was introduced to heroin by her husband at age 24, became involved in prostitution as a way of earning money for "the bare necessities." For each of these women, crime was the alternative available once they were removed from normative social networks and, at the same time, addicted to drugs.

The women talked about their criminal behavior both in terms of not being prepared to do anything else, and in racial terms. Responses to the open-ended statement, "Crime is," included: "[Crime is] a trade to one that knows nothing else"; "[Crime is] black people's support, if they're not working for a living—and that's bad"; "[Crime is] the ultimate source of survival in the world of

those who are black." Another Black woman speaks of her criminal involvement in racial terms. She states boldly:

> I don't mess with black women. And the reason for that is because I'm black myself, okay. I look at it like this—I know we struggle. We're struggling for whatever we get, we earned it. So, you know, leave them alone. But the white people; like, they've always had. That's the way I've always looked at it. Taking these white people's money made me feel good inside.

Although the majority of women arrested and imprisoned are first offenders, a large number are repeat offenders, or recidivists—women for whom the cycle of crime-arrest-imprisonment has become a way of life. These recidivists are disproportionately poor and Black, and structurally dislocated from the major socializing institutions of the society. They are women who have rarely worked in the paid labor force, who are essentially unskilled, undereducated, and marginal. They are part of the underclass.

Women with little education, few skills, and, for some, periodic employment in the labor force as waitresses, cashiers, maids, factory workers, or filing clerks commented briefly on the relationship between lack of employment and their criminal behavior. Mary W. said:

> I'm not proud of what I'm doing. It's just that I need these things. I had a job at one time and was doing good. It kept me out of trouble. I'd take any kind of job as long as I got some way to get some money. Now it's hard to get a job.

In the words of three other women: "I know crime is not something to get involved in, but I get nervous when I don't have money"; "Prior to coming to jail I supported myself by prostitution and stealing"; "Crime nowadays seems to be a necessity."

Female recidivists suffer from chronic disabilities (alcoholism, drug use), from personal crises (physical/sexual abuse), and from economic difficulties (unemployment/poverty). People who are homeless have been similarly described by Hope and Young (1986). Before becoming involved in crime, a sexually abused girl may run away from home, drop out of school, abuse drugs, and occupy a marginal role in the paid labor force. Similarly, a young girl may begin stealing to augment the family welfare check, become addicted to drugs, and, having learned no other skill or trade, persist in this behavior as an adult woman.

WOMEN IN PRISON

The typical contemporary woman in prison is young, poor, a member of a minority group, a high-school dropout, unmarried, and the mother of two or more children for whom she is the sole support (Mann, 1984). Economic pressures, particularly on the poor, and the spread of drugs throughout the population are playing a major role in increasing the number of imprisoned women. Despite the growing percentage of women incarcerated for participating in violent activities, the majority of women in prison have been charged with economic nonviolent crimes. Within the last decade, the rate of increase for property crimes, forgery, counterfeiting, fraud, embezzlement, stolen property, prostitution, and drug-related activities among women has been greater than the rate of increase for violent crimes without economic motives. When not in prison, these women can be counted among the hard-core unemployed, the homeless, the drug addicted, and the sexually abused.

SUMMARY

By examining early childhood, adolescent, and adult experiences of Black women incarcerated in jail and prison, this article reveals the process of victimization, labeling, and subsequent criminalization. Of particular importance is the concept of structural disloca-

tion as a salient factor in the understanding of sustained criminal behavior by women. There is a real need for institutional connections in the lives of the women discussed here. If society is not willing to address the multiple layers of victimization and structural dislocation of young girls, then we will continue to witness the attachment of young girls and women to criminal families and total institutions, such as the prison.

The findings support a socioeconomic analysis of female criminality in conjunction with attention to issues of patriarchy and racism. The women discussed in this article were victims of triple jeopardy; they were victims of class, gender, and race oppression who were structurally dislocated from the major social institutions for women in the society: the family, the school, and work. The findings are thus consistent with research on female criminality that suggests a process of criminalization unique to women that involves victimization.

If we are to witness a drop in the numbers of imprisoned women, legislators and policymakers need to reevaluate what happens to young girls who are victimized by gender, class, and race, and stop blaming the victim by processing and labeling her as deviant and/or criminal.

REFERENCES

Applebome, Peter. 1987. "Women in U.S. Prisons: Fast-Rising Population." *New York Times* (June 16): A16.

Arnold, Regina. 1986. Unpublished focused oral history interviews with women in a state prison, New York.

———. 1979. "Socio-Structural Determinants of Self-Esteem and the Relationship between Self-Esteem and Criminal Behavioral Patterns of Imprisoned Women." Unpublished Dissertation, Bryn Mawr College.

Balkan, Sheila, Ronald Berger, and Janet Schmidt. 1980. *Crime and Deviance in America: A Critical Approach.* Belmont, Cal.: Wadsworth, Inc.

Bolton, F. G., and J. W. Reich. "Delinquency Patterns in Maltreated Children and Siblings." *Victimology* 2,2: 349–357.

Campbell, Ann. 1984. *The Girls in the Gang.* Oxford: Basil Blackwell.

Cavaiola, A. A., and M. Schiff. 1988. "Behavioral Sequelae of Physical and/or Sexual Abuse in Adolescents." *Child Abuse and Neglect* 12:181–188.

Chapman, Jane Roberts. 1980. *Economic Realities and the Female Offender.* Lexington, Mass.: Lexington Books.

———— and Margaret Gates. 1978. *The Victimization of Women.* Beverly Hills, Cal.: Sage Publications.

Chesney-Lind, Meda. 1989. "Girls' Crime and Woman's Place: Toward a Feminist Model of Female Delinquency." *Crime and Delinquency* 35,1 (January): 5–29.

————. 1988. "Girls in Jail." *Crime and Delinquency* 34,2 (April): 150–168.

————. 1982. "Introduction," and "From Benign Neglect to Malign Attention: A Critical Review of Research on Female Delinquency." Sue Davidson (ed.), *Justice for Young Women.* Arizona: New Directions for Young Women: 51–71.

————. 1978. "Chivalry Reexamined: Women and the Criminal Justice System." Lee Bowker (ed.), *Women, Crime, and the Criminal Justice System.* Lexington, Mass.: D.C. Heath.

———— and Noelie Rodriguez. 1983. "Under Lock and Key: A View from the Inside." *The Prison Journal* 63,2: 47–65.

Davidson, Sue. 1982. *Justice for Young Women.* Arizona: New Directions for Young Women.

Garbarino, J., and M. C. Plantz. "Child Abuse and Juvenile Delinquency: What Are the Links?" J. Garbarino (ed.), *Troubled Youth, Troubled Families.* New York: Aldine-DeGruyter: 27–39.

Geller, M., and L. Ford-Somma. *Violent Homes, Violent Children: A Study of Violence in the Families of Juvenile Offenders.* New Jersey: Department of Corrections, Division of Juvenile Services.

Glick, Ruth, and Virginia Neto. 1977. *National Study of Women's Correctional Programs.* Washington, D.C.: Government Printing Office.

Gutierres, Sara E., and John W. Reich. 1981. "A Developmental Perspective on Runaway Behavior: Its Relationship to Child Abuse." *Child Welfare* 60,2: 89–94.

Higginbotham, Elizabeth. 1985. "Race and Class Barriers to Black Women's College Attendance." *Journal of Ethnic Studies* 13,1 (Spring): 89–107.

Hope, Marjorie, and James Young. 1986. *The Faces of Homelessness.* Lexington, Mass.: Lexington Books.

James, Jennifer. 1976. "Motivation for Entrance into Prostitution." Laura Crites (ed.), *The Female Offender.* Lexington, Mass.: D.C. Heath: 125–139.

Ladner, Joyce. 1972. *Tomorrow's Tomorrow: The Black Woman.* New York: Doubleday, Anchor.

Lemert, Edwin M. 1967. *Human Deviance, Social Problems and Social Control.* Englewood Cliffs, N.J.: Prentice-Hall.

Leonard, Eileen. 1982. *Women, Crime and Society: A Critique of Criminology Theory.* New York: Longman.

Lewis and Bresler. 1981. "Is There a Way Out? A Community Study of Women in San Francisco County Jail." San Francisco: Unitarian-Universalist Service Committee.

Mann, Cora R. 1984. *Female Crime and Delinquency.* Montgomery: University of Alabama Press.

Miller, Eleanor M. 1986. *Street Woman.* Philadelphia: Temple University Press.

Miller, Brenda A., William R. Downs, and Dawn M. Gondoli. 1989. "Delinquency, Childhood Violence, and the Development of Alcoholism in Women." *Crime and Delinquency* 35,1 (January): 94–108.

Price, Barbara R., and Natalie J. Sokoloff. 1982. *The Criminal Justice System and Women.* New York: Clark Boardman.

Rafter, Nicole Hahn. 1986. "Left Out by the Left: Crime and Crime Control." *Socialist Review* 89,16: 7–23.

Rhoades, Philip W., and Sharon L. Parker. 1981. *The Connections between Youth Problems and Violence in the Home: Preliminary Report of New Research.* Portland, Oregon: Oregon Coalition against Domestic and Sexual Violence.

Romenesko, Kim, and Eleanor M. Miller. 1989. "The Second Step in Double Jeopardy: Appropriating the Labor of Female Street Hustlers." *Crime and Delinquency* 35,1 (January): 109–135.

Rosenbaum, Marsha. 1982. "Work and the Addicted Prostitute." N. Rafter and E. Stanko (eds.), *Judge, Lawyer, Victim, Thief: Women, Gender Roles and Criminal Justice.* Boston, Mass.: Northeastern University Press: 131–150.

————. 1981. *Women on Heroin*. New Brunswick, N.J.: Rutgers University Press.

Rosenberg, Debby, and Carol Zimmerman. 1982. "Listen to Me." Sue Davidson (ed.), *Justice for Young Women*. Arizona: New Directions for Young Women.

Runtz, M., and J. Briere. 1986. "Adolescent 'Acting Out' and Childhood History of Sexual Abuse." *Journal of Interpersonal Violence* 1,3: 326–334.

Russell, Diana E. H. 1986. *The Secret Trauma: Incest in the Lives of Girls and Women*. New York: Basic Books.

Sarri, R. 1976. "Juvenile Law: How It Penalizes Females." Laura Crites (ed.), *The Female Offender*. Lexington, Mass.: D.C. Heath.

Shakur, Assata/Joanne Chesimard. 1978. "Women in Prison: How We Are." *The Black Scholar* 9 (April): 8–15.

Silbert, Mimi, and Ayola Pines. 1981. NIMH Study of 200 Female Street Prostitutes in San Francisco.

Smith, C. P., O. J. Berkman, and W. M. Fraser. 1980. Reports of the National Juvenile Justice Assessment Center. Washington, D.C.: American Justice Institute.

Sutherland, Edwin, and Donald Cressey. 1970. *Principles of Criminology*. New York: Lippincott.

CHAPTER 9

IN SEARCH OF THE FEMALE URBAN "GANGSTA": CHANGE, CULTURE, AND CRACK COCAINE

LISA MAHER / RICHARD CURTIS

ABSTRACT

In Chapter 5, Steffensmeier examined national arrest data in order to challenge the claim that a new violent female offender has burst upon the scene. In Chapter 6, Chesney-Lind found that while women have greatly increased their rate of incarceration for drug offenses in the United States, their rates of violent crime have declined. For example, as reported in this chapter, even though incarceration for drug offenses in New York State increased between 1980 and 1990, on the average from 22 to 73 percent, incarceration for violent offenses dropped off sharply, from 50 to 17 percent. Thus, Maher and Curtis go further in challenging the overly simplistic connection between drugs and violent crime. They do so by shifting the focus of analysis from the individual woman to the changing social and economic context of drugs and violence in a neighborhood in social and economic decline.

Using participant observation and in-depth interview techniques, the authors bring the reader directly into the lives of drug-using, street-level sex workers (prostitutes) in two New York City neighborhoods. However, rather than blaming violence on women "crazy on drugs," the authors look to the violent social, economic, and cultural contexts within which the women live and work.

Maher and Curtis do report greater drug-related violence, but they attribute it to the advent of crack, which intensified larger social processes already in operation that facilitate violence: in particular, the collapse of structures of formal and informal social control in communities already in decline. This includes, most importantly, the depletion of capital and human resources necessary to sustain a formal economy. When jobs are lost, educational systems are sacrificed, and housing is abandoned in a community, the result is increased participation in the informal drug economy in that community. Since street-level prostitution is highly dependent on changes in the economic and drug markets, the women experience greater violence as drug markets dry up and become more concentrated; competition increases, the conditions of street-level sex work deteriorate, and prostitution becomes less profitable.

Much of the chapter is devoted to the exact words of women describing the violent incidents in which they became involved. This chapter is important because the reader is asked to consider the sources of violence that these women participate in and experience. Maher and Curtis's research shows that while women on the street do engage in violent acts, they are most often the targets rather than the initiators of violence. Once again, the reader needs to consider the reasons for the disparity between the reality and the myth of the violent female urban "gangsta."

> *There are more girls in gangs, more girls in the drug trade, more girls carrying guns*
> *and knives, more girls in trouble. . . . They are more violent, they get angry*
> *quicker, they are trying to prove they are just as tough as the boys, . . . I'm noting*
> *more girls on the corner with the drug trade than a year ago. They are more physical*
> *than girls used to be."*
> —*New York Times,* Nov. 25, 1991

Evidence seems to suggest that if these statements are credible, then they will be especially true with respect to women who live in inner cities. We are repeatedly told by the media that we are witnessing the rise of a new and violent type of "criminal woman"— the female urban "gangsta." Although official statistics indicate that nationwide, the proportion of women incarcerated in state correctional facilities for "violent" offenses actually decreased from 48.9 percent in 1979 to 40.7 percent in 1986 (Bureau of Justice Statistics, 1991),[1] a growing number of women are being arrested and imprisoned in the wake of the "war on drugs" (e.g., see Chesney-Lind, Chapter 6 in this volume). During the 1980s, female arrest rates for drug law violations increased at approximately twice the rate for men. Between 1980 and 1989, there was a 307 percent increase in the number of women arrested for drug crimes as opposed to a 147 percent increase in the number of men arrested for drug violations (Bureau of Justice Statistics, 1991).

On face value statistics such as these tell us little. While they appear to lend support to the thesis that drug-related lawbreaking by women has increased, it does not necessarily follow that women have become more violent. Most research has concluded that the violent female offender is something of a cultural anomaly (see Harris, 1977; Weiner and Wolfgang, 1985). Moreover, the bulk of violent acts committed by women are directed toward intimates.[2] There is also a growing body of qualitative research, particularly urban ethnography, which presents the possibility of an alternate interpretation: one which locates the source of violence not within individuals but, rather, within the contexts in which they live. In this view, women are not intrinsically more violent today than they

---

This article was written expressly for inclusion in this text.

were ten, twenty, or a hundred years ago. The contexts in which they live, however, have changed dramatically, and within them are found explanations for much of the violence that is increasingly blamed on women "crazy on drugs." It is these contexts and the women who live within them that form the subject of this paper.

The main purpose of this chapter is to expose the reader to a contextual examination of women's violence—one that is rooted in an immediate, local, and very specific context. To do this, we use data generated through ethnographic research conducted in Brooklyn, New York, from 1988 to 1992 among a group of 62 crack-using women, most of whom were also street-level sex workers. Contrary to some research (e.g., Sommers and Baskin, 1991) and much public opinion (e.g., *New York Times,* 11/25/91), the women who participated in this study were not found to have become more violent over time, even as their reliance upon commercial sex work as a sole means of income increased and their addictions to crack—and often heroin, too—became more pronounced. Many were involved in violent events, but usually as victims rather than perpetrators. The violent acts committed by these women were more often in response to intimated or actual harms perpetrated against them, the antecedents of which, for the most part, can be located in changing social and economic relations at the local level. These women's experiences of violence lead us away from explanations that focus on individual psychology; they suggest that larger social forces are at work. An examination of the social context of these women's lives will begin to demystify the sources of violence that are all too easily explained away as the result of drug-induced behavior.

Concern in relation to "rising tides" of female criminality is not new and in fact has been around at least since 1849 (see Worsley, 1849, cited in Morris, 1987:36–37). However,

the idea that women are becoming more violent and that this is due, in large part, to their involvement with crack signals the resurgence of the "emancipation thesis," which gained currency with the publication of Adler's (1975) *Sisters in Crime: The Rise of the New Female Criminal.* The thesis suggested in this book posits the existence of a causal nexus between changes in the social roles of women (attributed to the "feminist" or "women's liberation movement") and shifts in patterns and rates of women's lawbreaking. The argument is that as women are "liberated" and begin to assume "male" social roles (e.g., as wage earners and breadwinners), they will be "masculinized"/adopt "masculine" behaviors, i.e., become aggressive, violent, and "criminal."[3]

Numerous critiques have been made of this "emancipation thesis," (see Smart, 1976; Crites, 1976; Chapman, 1980; Chesney-Lind, 1986; Messerschmidt, 1986; Naffine, 1987), including several that utilize empirical data (see Smart, 1979; Steffensmeier, 1980, 1983; Box and Hale, 1983; Morris, 1987; Daly, 1989; Maher and Waring, 1990) and, more recently, qualitative studies that are concerned about interrogating the material conditions of women's lives (see Cook, 1987; Carlen, 1988; Maher and Curtis, 1992). The bulk of this research indicates that neither the status of women lawbreakers nor patterns of female offending have changed in the wake of women's "liberation."

However, recent data on drug-related arrests and imprisonment appear to suggest that long-standing patterns of female offending may be changing. On a local level, between 1980 and 1986, an average of 22.3 percent of women incarcerated in New York State were imprisoned for drug offenses (New York State Department of Correctional Services, 1988). In 1987, however, this proportion had increased to 42.4 percent, or 340 women, and by the end of 1989, 66.4 percent, or 1,059 women, were incarcerated for drug offenses in New York State (New York State Department of Correctional Services, 1990a). More recent reports suggest that in 1990, approximately 73 percent of the female commitment population in New York State were incarcerated for nonviolent drug offenses—possession and/or sale (*Correctional Association Reporter*, 1991).[4]

A closer examination of these data confirms that women drug users do not represent Adler's hypothesized "new violent female criminal." Despite recent increases in the rates of incarceration for women, the percentage of women committed to state prison for violent felonies declined from 50 percent of total admissions for women in the early 1980s to only 17 percent of admissions in 1990 (*Correctional Association Reporter*, 1991). Increases in women's imprisonment in New York State can clearly be attributed to state and local responses to drug-related crime in the wake of the "war on drugs."[5]

Rather than argue the merits or inadequacies of statistical models that purport to measure "violent female criminality," the research presented in this paper examines the issues of violence, drug use, crime, and women in a specific context over a particular period of time, using ethnographic methods and techniques. While statistical analyses often tend to simplify complex social realities and encourage deterministic explanations based upon a few crucial variables, ethnographic approaches, on the other hand, often demand that researchers resist the temptation to strip down explanations to bare essentials, demanding instead that researchers account for a multitude of complex and interrelated factors in explaining specific behaviors.

RESEARCH METHODS

Ethnography is the use of direct observation and extended fieldwork to provide a "thick description" of groups or cultures (Weppner, 1977). Ethnographic research techniques permit researchers to enter a particular cultural setting and to observe and participate within it. In interpreting and describing this process, ethnographers attempt to preserve the integrity and properties of the phenomena observed by utilizing the symbols, categories, definitions, and "worldviews" used by subjects, rather than seek to impose external cultural definitions (Geertz, 1973).

The ethnographic research discussed in this paper was conducted in two adjacent neighborhoods in Brooklyn, New York, between 1988 and 1992. During this period, hundreds of crack-smoking women were encountered in the course of conducting fieldwork. In this paper, we draw on data generated among a group of 62 crack-using women, most of whom were also street-level sex workers. The reason why a sample primarily composed of sex workers was chosen was that more than any other group of women, sex workers are more likely to be involved in a substantial number of violent events (Silbert and Pines, 1984). If women are indeed becoming more violent, then we would expect to see that tendency reflected in this subgroup of women.

Detailed fieldnotes that describe daily events in the lives of these women and other participants in the cocaine/crack economy were collected. This rich, descriptive repository of fieldnotes allows us to take note of rapid shifts in local social and economic conditions that often accompany neighborhoods where crack and/or heroin markets have taken hold and thus place the lives of the women in their proper context. In addition to daily fieldnotes, we collected over 150 in-depth interviews with crack users in both neighborhoods, 97 of which were with women.[6]

As it is not possible to select a random sample from these populations (because their parameters are unknown), a sample was selected by employing several techniques: self-identification, "snowballing" (Weppner, 1977; Biernacki and Waldorf, 1981), "chains of referral" (McCall, 1978), and "theoretical sampling" (Glaser and Strauss, 1970). While ethnographic interviews were checked for internal consistency against field observations, the technique of triangulation (Denzin, 1970; Spradley, 1979) was used in order to ensure the validity of all the data. This meant that the accuracy of field observations and the veracity of ethnographic interviews were often confirmed from at least three different sources. As most of the interview respondents knew each other—often as members of common networks, e.g., crack-smoking networks—they were often able to confirm or refute claims made by a third party. In the case of field observations, triangulation was assisted by the use of two ethnographers (male and female) observing the same phenomenon and/or people over a period of time.

THE WIDER SOCIAL CONTEXT OF POVERTY IN NEW YORK CITY

To understand the relationship between women, drugs, crime, and violence, it is necessary to know something about the wider social context in which the women described in this paper live, especially their economic circumstances. Like many other large urban centers in the United States, New York City—and Brooklyn in particular—has been moving from a unionized manufacturing economy to a more competitive, less unionized service economy.[7] As the "primary sector" of good jobs shrinks, the "secondary sector" of less desirable employment grows (Harrison, 1974). Hourly earnings and skill requirements are dropping, while educational achievement requirements are rising (Braverman, 1974).

These changes in regional economies have had a disproportionate effect upon minorities (Wilson, 1987). For example, while the annual earnings of young men between the ages of 25 and 29 declined by 20 percent between 1973 and 1986, the decline among blacks was 28 percent, and 36 percent among those without a high school diploma (Sum, Fogg, and Taggart, 1988). While most research on the impact of these shifts in the economy has focused on the declining fortunes of young men in the labor market, we suggest that in some neighborhoods, poor minority women have been even more profoundly affected by these changes. Many of the women in our sample experience debilitating economic oppression by virtue of the interrelationships between gender, ethnicity, and class in determining economic activity (see Malveaux, 1990; Simms and Malveaux, 1989; McLanahan et al., 1989; Amott and Matthaei, 1991).

While some authors have argued that the relative economic position of women has improved during the last few decades, women still work in predominantly "female" occupations and continue to receive less pay than men (Acker, 1988).[8] Moreover, for single-parent, female-headed households and poor minority women the situation is much worse (see Goldberg and Kremen, 1987; McLanahan et al., 1989). These women were seldom participants in the primary sector of stable, unionized jobs during the previous era, and they remain in that position today. As the primary sector shrinks and men are systematically displaced from the primary sector to the more competitive secondary sector, within some neighborhoods, they are displacing even more marginal labor, such as minorities, women, and undocumented aliens, further down the economic job ladder. Thus, for many populations, even secondary-sector employment is becoming difficult to locate. It is within this context that the growing participation of these groups in the "informal" or "illegal" economy may be understood.

The informal economy, like the formal economy, is stratified, with less competitive groups—particularly women—nearly always bottlenecked at the closed end of the opportunity structure. Men often have a wide variety of options for making money within the informal economy, while women have traditionally occupied a select and/or specialized niche within this sector. Most occupations within the informal sector are dominated by men. Street-level drug distribution, for example, is almost exclusively a male occupation (Maher and Curtis, 1992).

DRUGS AND VIOLENCE

As Lindesmith (1967) and Schur (1969) have suggested, the drugs-crime relationship is largely a social construction—the result of the illegality of certain types of drugs. The links between illicit drugs and crime are not so much the product of either specific pharmacologies or individual pathologies but, rather, the legacies of history and politics. As Musto's (1973) historical research illustrates, moral panics surrounding the use of certain types of drugs by certain types of people led to the creation of new categories of "crime" and a whole new class of "criminals" in the United States. In particular, racist beliefs in relation to cocaine use by black men were among the factors that prompted the Harrison Narcotics Act of 1914, which sought to regulate and control narcotics traffic. As Goode (1984:221) has noted, this piece of legislation was responsible for

> . . . the dramatic emergence of a criminal class of addicts—a criminal class that had not existed previously. The link between addiction and crime—the view that the addict was by definition a criminal—was forged.

Similarly, it seems reasonable to suggest that illegality will account for a proportion of the correlation between drugs and violence.

Our previous research indicates that drug use and violence covary but are not related in a deterministic way. Rather, this relationship is mediated by the complexities of users' social and economic worlds (Maher and Curtis, 1992). Many of these mediating factors or intervening variables can be elaborated by an examination of social and occupational relations as they exist within the local informal economy. As Hamid (1991) has argued, populations of drug users are perhaps best viewed as a "type of laboring population whose income generation enables it to perform vital (but variable) functions for the overall community" (Hamid, 1991:833).

However, many of the social problems experienced in U.S. cities—especially inner cities—are increasingly blamed on the scourge of drugs: homelessness, unemployment, increasing infant mortality rates, increasing violence, the decline in educational achievement levels among youth, etc. Drugs have become a lightning rod onto which all other problems can be collapsed, as if solving the "drug problem" will somehow magically put the city back on the road to a healthy social and economic environment. As Lapham (1989:45) has commented,

> The war on drugs thus becomes the perfect war for people who would rather not fight a war, a war in which politicians who stand so fearlessly on the side of the good, the true, and the beautiful need do nothing else but strike noble poses as protectors of the people and defenders of the public trust.

While the popular image portrayed by politicians and the media is one that blames many of our social ills on drugs, when social problems are examined in more detail, researchers have discovered that drugs are more often the consequence of these problems—like homelessness—rather than their cause (see Burt, 1991; Wallace, 1985; Wallace and Wallace, 1986).

The crack epidemic of the 1980s in New York City made the words "drugs" and "violence" synonymous for many people. Local tabloids sold millions of newspapers with headlines about babies being tossed out of windows by crack-crazed parents and helpless grandmothers being strangled for their welfare checks by addicted grandchildren. The relationship between women's use of crack cocaine and violent crime—in particular, child abuse—has been the focus of considerable media attention and speculation (see *New York Times*, 3/17/90, 12/3/90, 1/15/91; *New York Newsday*, 4/15/91). While such headlines painted an indelible image in the public's mind, scientific investigation about the link between drug use and violence is seriously lacking.

To elaborate this link, an influential article by Goldstein (1985) posits three types of drug-related violence: psychopharmacological, economic-compulsive, and systemic.[9] This tripartite model of drug-related violence provides a good starting point from which to consider the relationship between drugs and violence. While psychopharmacological violence commands headlines, the majority of violence associated with drugs is related to the other two types, economic-compulsive and systemic. However, when the model is used to analyze the experiences of the women who form the subject of this paper, it appears less useful.

While it is possible to search our data and find clear examples of women initiating each type of violence described by Goldstein, to "shoehorn" the data into this theoretical orientation would be misleading.[10] The accounts of violent incidents related by the majority of our respondents indicate that they are usually the victims of violence rather than the perpetrators and that these incidents are not so easily pigeonholed into Goldstein's ideal types. Our data appear to contradict the conclusions reached by Sterk and Elifson (1990), when

they state that "more violent episodes on the prostitution market are related to the prostitutes' drug-using behaviors and increased involvement in the drug trade" (Sterk and Elifson, 1990:218). Our research suggests that most commercial sex workers are marginally involved in drug distribution and that both drug use on behalf of their "dates" and the deteriorating conditions of street-level sex work are the source of a much larger share of the violent episodes taking place in the street-level sex markets or "strolls" where the women work (see below).

WOMEN, DRUGS, AND VIOLENCE

Inciardi (1972) was among the earliest drug researchers to suggest that "drugs" created a new violent breed of criminal whose criminality was "situational," random, and wanton. In a study of heroin-using commercial sex workers, Goldstein (1979) noted a link between withdrawal and violent crime. In his study, commercial sex workers experiencing withdrawal told him that they would sometimes rob clients (see also Goldstein, 1990). Rosenbaum (1981) also found that the women in her sample reported ripping off their "tricks" when they were "sick" and "desperate for a fix" (Rosenbaum, 1981:76).

Perhaps the strongest advocacy of a purported link between drug use and violent criminal behavior in women can be found in Inciardi (1986). Among his sample of women drug users there was a "small core" of women who committed a wide variety of offenses. Although he does not provide data illustrating offenses by gender (leaving no idea of how many are in this "small core" and the types and frequencies of the crimes they commit), Inciardi assures us that Adler's "new female criminal" has indeed arrived. These women, he asserts, have "gone beyond the traditional limits of prostitution and shoplifting into major-league drug trafficking, extortion, auto-theft, loan sharking and hijacking" (Inciardi, 1986:137). Inciardi's later research with a sample of drug-using commercial sex workers in Miami and New York also led him to conclude that not only were opiate-using prostitutes "more criminally involved [than non-opiate-using commercial sex workers], but they were also considerably more violent as well" (1986:168).

More recent research conducted by Goldstein et al. (1991a, 1991b) on both female and male cocaine users with respect to the relationship between violence and the frequency and volume of cocaine use suggests quite the contrary. This research indicates that whereas regular cocaine use by men was strongly associated with the perpetration of violence, regular use by women was most strongly associated with violent victimization and accompanied by increased involvement in commercial sex work (Goldstein et al., 1991a). In another analysis utilizing these same data, Goldstein et al. (1991b) found that for men, increased volume of cocaine use was associated with a greater likelihood of being a perpetrator of violence, whereas for women, volume of cocaine use predicted that involvement in violence was more likely to be as a victim than as a perpetrator. Similarly, Spunt et al. (1990) also found significant racial/ethnic and gender differences in relation to the number of violent events manifesting drug-related dimensions of violence.

Despite the competing and often contradictory nature of research claims concerning the relationship(s) between patterns of [female] drug consumption and patterns of [female] lawbreaking and violence, the nature of the relationship(s) has only begun to be explored for women crack users. Attempts to explicate the relationship(s) will need to bear in mind that in many inner-city neighborhoods, the advent of crack cocaine has intensified the *social processes* that facilitate violence. Recent ethnographic research suggests that increases in crack-related violence in urban areas can be attributed to the collapse of formal and informal social controls, the depletion of capital and human resources necessary to sustain a formal economy, and the resultant increased participation in the drug economy (see Hamid, 1990).

THE LOCAL SETTING: WILLIAMSBURG AND BUSHWICK

The neighborhoods chosen for this research have long histories of widespread drug distribution and use. Within the Southside of Williamsburg and the northern tier of Bushwick in Brooklyn—the research sites for this paper—are found highly structured drug distribution organizations. Although the Southside is home to a sizable enclave of Hasidic Jews, ethnically it is dominated by Latinos. A major trucking route that runs through the area has been the site of "strolls" for more than 50 years. Housing stock in the area has experienced a gradual decline in recent years, and there are large tracts of abandoned and boarded-up buildings. Crack distribution is modeled on the heroin markets that have been an entrenched feature of life on the Southside since the 1950s. Everyone who sells crack on the Southside is selling it for someone else. It is a highly structured and to some degree regimented marketplace of street-level distributors and consumers.[11]

The Southside has undergone a number of changes since October 1989, when it was the subject of a "cleanup" campaign by New York City's Tactical Narcotics Team (TNT), a specialized policing unit entrusted with enforcing the "war on drugs" against street-level drug trafficking. TNT interventions often serve as a catalyst for a broader citywide process of shrinkage and consolidation of drug markets (Curtis, forthcoming). By 1988, the phase of street-level distribution and consumption of crack had clearly peaked. With a decline in the overall number of users and the failure of crack to attract new initiates, many previously flourishing drug markets began to experience a sizable contraction (Curtis, forthcoming; Hamid, forthcoming). Since 1989, this shrinkage has led many hard-core distributors and users to concentrate themselves in pools that take on the appearance of a vortex: everyone is funneled into small geographic areas where drug activity is heightened (Curtis, forthcoming). Bushwick is an example of such a vortex.

Historically a working-class Italian neighborhood, Bushwick is no newcomer to the drug trade. Since the late 1960s, the area has gradually come to be dominated by low-income Latino populations, predominantly Puerto Ricans and, more recently, Dominicans and Mexicans. The housing stock is primarily multiple-family dwellings, although the drug market area itself consists of run-down apartment buildings set amongst a mix of light manufacturing and industry. The current highly active drug markets have evolved rapidly over the past two years, and there are frequent confrontations over "turf" as drug-dealing organizations compete to establish hegemony over respective markets.[12]

RESEARCH FINDINGS

Although some commentators have argued that there has been an increase in female participation in drug dealing within recent years, women's entry into this male-dominated field has seldom penetrated up to the managerial level. In four years of ethnographic fieldwork spanning four Brooklyn neighborhoods, we encountered only one female manager (in Bushwick) and no business "owners." Women are almost always used as temporary workers when males have been arrested or when it is particularly "hot" with police and regular workers (men) refuse

to work, or they are used as couriers, lookouts, touts, or stash-house sitters.[13] For example, Hope,[14] a 35-year-old African-American woman from Bedford-Stuyvesant who currently works the "stroll" in Bushwick, spoke about her short-lived and tangential involvement with the heroin business.

> I moved up to Harlem, and hooked up with this guy selling heroin. We used to get the quarter bags, and cut it. The shit used to be good, so I used to tap the bags. I didn't know I had a chippie [mild habit] till about three years later. All that time he trusted me. I was handling the money and everything; everything was right there with me. But as soon as he found out that I was messing with it, it was like I was cut off.

While the experience of most of the women we interviewed was often as the "girlfriend" of a distributor, a few were directly involved in the business. Migdalia, a 25-year-old Puerto Rican crack seller in Bushwick, was typical of those women who managed from time to time to secure low-level selling positions working for street distributors. She spoke about her unstable position within the organization.

> I'm currently working for White Top [crack]. They have a five bundle limit. It might take me an hour or two to sell that, or sometimes as quick as half an hour. I got to ask if I can work—they say yes or no.

More often than not, the managers said no. Unlike many of the male street-level sellers who worked on a regular basis for this organization, Migdalia was forced to work off-hours (e.g., daylight hours), which were often riskier and less financially rewarding. Regular distributors worked in "shifts" (usually lasting eight hours); temporary workers were often given a "bundle limit" (one bundle = 24 vials), thereby ensuring that they would work for shorter periods of time.

The position of women within the informal sector in these neighborhoods, as within the formal sector, remains marginal at best, even within the realm of drug distribution. The exception is street-level sex work. Sex work often provides the only opportunity for women in this system of constricted choices. For example, Patricia, a 32-year-old African-American commercial sex worker from Bedford-Stuyvesant who worked the "stroll" in Bushwick, spoke about women's limited choices:

> [Do you think that it's harder for a guy to make money out here than a girl?] No, cause if they so bad, go and stick somebody up. [What, a woman couldn't do that?] I wouldn't. I may go in somebody pocket, but I wouldn't just cold-blooded stick somebody up. [What other kinds of opportunities do women have to make money besides work on the stroll?] I don't know. The "avenue" [stroll] is the only opportunity that comes to my mind.

Lorraine, a 27-year-old Puerto Rican woman who worked the "stroll" in Williamsburg, spoke about the lack of opportunity for women in the area:

> I don't think that most of the girls out here could do anything else except sell themselves. I think once you're here, you're stuck, it's a rut. I don't think you can get out until you do something. If you're drug addicted, you have to do something about that. That's the only way you're ever going to get out. But the girls are luckier than the guys. Guys have a hard time, they're limited. Girls got something that everybody wants. That's all they can do, but that's all they have to do.

Like many of the other women interviewed, Lorraine was reluctant to embrace the view that commercial sex workers occupied the lowest rung on the economic ladder. While many agreed that their options were limited, they felt that women were fortunate to have steady work—"something that everybody wants"—whereas some men, though their employment options may have seemed greater, were often unable to find employment, legal or illegal. Lorraine also hints at another truth: though women may not participate in the drug economy as distributors, their participation as consumers has become substantial in recent years. Despite considerable efforts, we were unable to find a single commercial sex worker working in these neighborhoods who did not use drugs in one form or another.

While the greatest economic opportunity for women working within the informal sector was in commercial sex work, even that occupation has traditionally been stratified. The most lucrative strolls are located in Manhattan. In Brooklyn, prior to the crack era, strolls were spread throughout a wide geographic area, and there was a clear hierarchy among them. The better strolls—where working conditions were better and income potential was higher—were located near major transportation arteries, such as Williamsburg's Southside. The worst strolls were located in interior or isolated neighborhoods, such as Bedford-Stuyvesant and Bushwick.

The evolution of street-level commercial sex markets in these neighborhoods has been directly tied to the fate of local drug markets, to which they function as an adjunct. As drug markets have shrunk and become concentrated into vortices of activity, so too have strolls. As the drug trade in Williamsburg withered, the number of women on the stroll dwindled. When drug trafficking became concentrated in Bushwick, the local stroll began to draw women from many surrounding strolls (some better, some worse) which were becoming less viable as moneymaking locations. Most women noted that the conditions of work and wages in Bushwick were a real step down for them, while few said that working conditions and wages were about the same as or better than where they had come from.

One woman, Candy, is a 42-year-old Italian-Irish woman who had been steadily working the "stroll" in Bushwick since 1988. She has been involved in sex work and drug use on and off for almost 30 years and is currently homeless. Candy recalled that at first, the business was not too bad:

> Many moons ago, when I started off [in Bushwick] there was three girls—Jo, Ellen and myself. Blow jobs had been five dollars and ten dollars. Everything goes up but the meat rack business. It's still the same. That was about, maybe, twelve, thirteen, fourteen, fifteen years ago when it was more discreet. We had to do all the talkin, you know: "it'll cost you a few dollars," "you can give us a present if you want," "you can give us money for a meal," you know. It was so much different and more fun back then too. Those were friends. Now these girls out here are just for the drug and themselves. There's no friendship. Everyone's out to cut everyone's throat. . . . These people don't know how to be ho's [prostitutes].

Although Candy had a heavy heroin habit for many years, it was the only drug she did until the early 1980s, when cocaine and crack became popular.

> I was shooting heroin for sixteen years and never even thought to do it with speed. I never started the speed—doing coke—till about 6 or 7 years ago. I have three abscesses going at one time. My legs full of abscesses. Look at my breasts. I never had fuckin' abscesses in my life. All the years doing dope, and here I go starting shooting [coke] .

The introduction of cocaine into her repertoire of drugs was extremely damaging to Candy's health and paralleled the development of the crack epidemic in New York City. Around the same time that she started using cocaine regularly (both injecting and smoking it), many of her drug-use and personal habits changed, and she developed her first case of syphilis, which went undetected for six months. Candy also developed a heart condition (mitral valve prolapse), and her asthma worsened, occasionally requiring hospitalization. During this period she continued to work the strolls on the Southside and, increasingly, in Bushwick.

The advent of crack in these neighborhoods led not only to increased competition on the strolls but also to fundamental shifts in the nature of sex work (e.g., from vaginal intercourse to blow jobs, indoor to outdoor locations) and drastically deflated the going rates for sexual exchanges (Maher and Curtis, 1992). Below, two women who work the stroll in Bushwick talk about competition and the increasing difficulty in making money:

> Normally you try to ask for $15 for a blow job. These girls do it for five—less. That's self-degradation. You can't even blame the men because, of course, if you can get a blow job for five instead of ten or fifteen, you're going to take it. (Tina)

> We got a girl we call "Two Dollar Mindy." Mindy will stay with a date forty-five minutes and come back an' she wanna get down on a crack [share the cost]. . . . I've never seen a girl stay that long in a car and come back an' she wants to get down. On a good date, she got four—she come back and she need a dollar (to cop a $5 vial). Why would you pick up a girl for ten when you can get one for two. . . . (Patricia)

Many women who had worked the stroll in Bushwick before it became flooded with refugees from adjacent strolls were particularly hard-hit by these changes. For example, many of Candy's "dates" were steady customers, some of whom she had had relationships with for years. Candy's relationships with these men were cordial but very businesslike. As she puts it,

> . . . if I'm going out with a client for a couple of months and he comes to me and says, "I'm a little short this week. Can I pay you next time?" Or, "I'll give you a few dollars now." I'll go for it. It's like having a grocery store and you give credit. If they don't pay you, they don't get no credit no more.

Recent changes in the conditions on the stroll, however, have undermined many of those relationships, forcing Candy, and other women like her, to work longer hours for less money (Maher and Curtis, 1992).

> A lot of my steadies pass me up. They say, "I'm not going out today." Meanwhile, twenty minutes later, you see them passing by with another bitch in the car. Now you're starting to think, "what's going on here?" A lot of Johns are afraid today because of the diseases going around.

Even though Candy accepts that, as part of the business, a "steady" might opt for another woman on any particular night, she nevertheless perceives such behavior as a breach of their relationship. In retaliation, she might not give him credit on their next "date," or she might decide to demand more money than their usual price. If truly angered, she might decide to "vic"[15] him by robbing him when he's in a vulnerable position. For example, she told us about one occasion when a local man whom she had known for some time offered her two dollars for a blow job. Candy said that she was insulted and ordinarily would have turned him down, but given that it was 5 a.m. and she was suffering from withdrawal, she had little choice but to take the offer. In the middle of being aroused, the man decided that he wanted to have "straight sex" rather than just oral sex, and he proceeded to take his pants off. Still seething from his stingy offer, Candy noticed that he had a considerable amount of money in his pocket. She snatched his pants and ran off with them, leaving him standing in an empty lot in his underwear. Candy laughed, wondering how the man was going to explain this to his wife. Later she explained:

> I don't want to rip anybody off. I don't make it a habit. But that guy got me so pissed off. Sunday morning, I was hungry, I was stressing like

a son of a bitch. And here comes this sucker offering me two bucks, and he got a pocketful of money. shit! That's a guy that's insulting you and I don't like that. I mean, you going to get off on me? I'm going to get off on you!

While the price deflation of sexual services has undermined many long-lasting relationships between women and their "steadies," it has also, in turn, spawned a self-selection process of cheaper, "rougher" dates that has made the stroll itself "rougher." Below, Bay, an African-American crack user, spoke about how tough the stroll in Bushwick had become in recent years.

> The dates are rougher and nastier too. You're always gonna run into an asshole out there, but there's more assholes now. With the girls, it's let's see who can beat each other. The majority of the women try to challenge each other. It's pathetic . . . it's just fucked up, they just want that hit so bad. They're not pathetic, they're sick.

In this atmosphere of intense competition and drastically deflated prices, the stroll in Bushwick has also become the site of considerable violence—and women were usually the victims rather than the perpetrators. The women we interviewed had all been robbed and/or sexually assaulted/raped in the recent past. For example, Candy had been raped by a Polish date several months prior to the interview cited above. At the time of this interview, she was six months pregnant, having been unable to go through with an abortion. She told us that this interview was the first time that she was able to relate the full impact of that incident to anyone:

> I saw his face and I saw my father at the same time. We were right by the waterfront. I was in the shower [when] my father raped me. I've done everything: I lay, blowjobs, that and the other thing. I was still feeling dirty [after being raped]. It's a different feeling. It's different to

me. It just don't feel right . . . no matter what I am.

While the deterioration of the stroll in Bushwick has led to an increase in violent incidents committed by strangers, it has also undermined many long-standing relationships. For example, Patricia, whose physically abusive "boyfriend" regularly beat her on the street, talked about how easily the two of them were set against each other:

> Me and a guy had a beef because he wanted to pay me two dollars to get him off on the sidewalk—c'mon, I'm not that stupid. And I tells D [her "boyfriend"] about the beef. Little do I know that dude gave D a hit of crack and D told him, "fuck the bitch, just don't tell her that I said so. . . ."

Though women were often the victims of violent crime, there were occasions when some of them got violent with others. Most of them, however, did not carry weapons.[16] Occasionally, one might carry a folding knife or box cutter, but these were infrequently used. The story related below by Suzy Q. when she cut a date's face with a broken bottle was perhaps typical of the kind of violence engaged in by these women. Suzy Q. is a 32-year-old Jewish woman from Mill Basin (Brooklyn). She had worked the stroll in Bushwick for about two years before this incident occurred. Suzy Q. is about 5′1″ and weighs about 80 lb. On this particular occasion, she picked up a date who promised to give her $20, in return for which she agreed to purchase crack for him and accompany him to a nearby motel for a blow job.

> Like yesterday, I had a pretty bad experience with a guy. He took up most of my night. I tell them whatever you want to do, lay the cards out on the table. Either I'll say yes, or I'll say no. . . . Later on, everything he wanted was different. He was talking about fucking me in the ass, and this and that. . . . In the beginning I took care of him like he wanted. But all this time is going by and he is not giving me more money. . . . Anyway, he had me copping for him, and after the third time I said, "You know, you said you would take care of me." He said that he had to go over to his house to get more money. In the middle of the highway he wanted to throw me out. . . . I didn't know where the hell I was, how to get back, plus I didn't have any money at this point, and he is being a real scum-bag. I could have been making money. I could have been doing anything. . . . Yeah, he actually threw me out of the car. So the bottle of soda that I had, I broke it and I cut him with it. I didn't stab him with it, I cut him with it. But, I don't get mad easy. For me to get mad it really takes a lot. This guy really hurt me. . . . You know, it was fucked up with him. I don't go around cutting people. That was fucked up.

This account by Suzy Q. is important for several reasons. It suggests that many incidents where women appear to be the initiators of violence—our work suggests that the police are called in many such incidents—may, in fact, be the culmination of a lengthy string of events that are necessary to understand before the actual violence can be properly interpreted. It also suggests that the tripartite model of drug-related violence proposed by Goldstein (1985) may not allow us to consider all, or even some, of the most important factors that contribute to an incident. Clearly, the account related to us by Suzy Q. had something to do with drugs. However, are we able to describe Suzy Q's use of the broken bottle to cut her "date's" face as an example of any of the three types of violence outlined by Goldstein? Our reading of this event tells us that incidents such as this are not easily explained by reference to a single variable or categorized as a single type of violence. Without knowing the recent history of the "stroll" in this neighborhood and without appreciating the background of this particular incident, categorizing it as a particular type of violence—on the part of either party—is, at best, misleading.

CONCLUSION

The growing debate surrounding the question of an increase in female violence has tended to obscure more important questions that concern the sources of violence in American society as a whole. By imbuing individuals and/or groups with explanatory power, simplistic explanations are encouraged and more important and complex issues are pushed to the background. This paper has attempted to steer away from explanations that focus on individuals and/or psychology. By employing ethnographic methods and techniques, the research presented here focused on describing and interpreting the violence experienced by a group of women within a specific time and context. By locating these women within a specific economic, social, and cultural context it became possible to explain the violence they experienced in terms of the confluence of broader social forces and economic relations rather than individual pathologies.

We contend that any explanatory framework which seeks to understand violence—male or female—must begin with an understanding of the contexts in which people live. While a full delineation of this context is not possible in a chapter of this size, an outline was provided. The structure of economic opportunity for women in New York City in general and the study neighborhoods in particular has gotten progressively worse, especially within the last 10 years. Within these neighborhoods, women are increasingly relegated to marginal forms of employment, often within the informal economy, and even those employment opportunities are becoming scarce. Likewise, "criminal" moneymaking opportunities have also decreased with the worsening economic condition of the neighborhoods. Crimes like "mugging" or chain-snatching that may have presented opportunities for young men and women several years ago are no longer viable simply because most people in these neighborhoods have long since pawned their gold chains to pay rent or put food on the table (Maher and Curtis, 1992).

While some commentators claim that there has been an increase in females participating in drug distribution, our research suggests that most women remain on the fringe of drug distribution circles and perform menial or entry-level tasks that provide little opportunity for advancement. Prostitution remains the only consistent source of income for many women, and even that has become less financially rewarding owing to changes in local conditions. Our research suggests that drug markets and street-level sex markets often develop in tandem. As street-level drug markets in Brooklyn in the late 1980s began to dry up and contract into smaller pools of concentrated activity, so, too, did commercial sex "strolls." The result of this concentration was a heightening of competition among street-level sex workers and the emergence of much "rougher" and "cheaper" strolls. Within the context of these worsening conditions, violence has indeed increased; however, our research indicates that women are overwhelmingly the targets of violence rather than its initiators. Conditions on the street have become so bad that it is unsafe for any woman to walk alone. While most street-level sex workers reported having had trouble with bands of local male youths who chase and beat them for sport (see *New York Times*, 7/23/90), several women who were not commercial sex workers also reported having been chased and beaten.

Violence is indeed a serious and worsening problem in American society, but it is also one whose antecedents are poorly understood because of our penchant for simplistic, monocausal explanations that focus too much attention on individuals and their pathologies. While many people cite the "breakdown" of families as one of the main culprits contributing to this problem, such explanations tend to devolve into fingerpointing at individuals (often the mother). Our research suggests that the debate about whether women are becoming more violent is often an abstract and/or rhetorical exercise that contributes little to our understanding of the problem. What is needed are examinations of the problem, which begin by locating individuals within specific social, cultural, and economic contexts.

As this chapter has suggested, there are few caricature female gangstas, of which the mass media are so fond, to be found in the study sites discussed here. What we have attempted to do is to highlight the fact that both the nature and the frequency of the violence that these women have experienced—both as victims and as perpetrators—have changed in recent years. These changes are in response to shifting social and economic conditions as they manifest themselves at the local level (Maher and Curtis, 1992). Moreover, it is the everyday contexts in which these women live and work that provide a high propensity for violence, not the women themselves. Our research suggests that these women's experiences of violence are, for the most part, attributable to neither the pharmacology of crack cocaine nor individual pathologies. Rather, we have sought to illustrate the need for a grounding of individual experiences within a local political and social economy. By examining the ways in which crack has impacted on specific and local processes and relations, we have tried to draw attention to the kinds of sociocultural processes that facilitate violence, as opposed

to the view that certain kinds of individuals are propelled toward violent and criminal behavior.

NOTES

1. Similarly, while the number of women imprisoned in local jails more than doubled from 1983 to 1989, the percentage of women incarcerated for violent offenses decreased from 21.3 percent in 1983 to 13.2 percent in 1989. During this period, the number of women being held accused or convicted of drug violations increased almost threefold—from 13.1 percent in 1983 to 33.6 percent in 1989 (Bureau of Justice Statistics, 1992).

2. Recent data indicate that approximately 37 percent of women serving time in state correctional facilities for a violent crime had victimized a relative or intimate. More than 25 percent of these women were convicted of the homicide of a relative or intimate as opposed to less than 6 percent of males (Bureau of Justice Statistics, 1991; see also Mann, 1987).

3. It is interesting to note that this paradigm is not confined to criminology. It has recently emerged in street drug studies as a construct for "explaining" women's participation in the crack culture. For example, Bourgois (1990), drawing on ethnographic fieldwork conducted in New York's Spanish Harlem, cites the "fact" that women "comprise a large share of the crack addict population and are the fastest growing segment being arrested for street crimes" as "proof" of the *emancipated status of women on inner city streets*" (Bourgois, 1990:643–44; emphasis added).

4. While the five counties that constitute New York City account for approximately 80 percent of yearly drug admission populations, a greater proportion (60 to 72 percent) of offenders from upstate New York were committed for serious drug offenses, compared with their New York City counterparts (33 to 50 percent). This may be reflected in sentencing decisions, with average minimum sentences being lowest in the New York City area and highest in

upstate counties (New York State Department of Correctional Services, 1990a). However, data such as these may also reflect the fact that authorities in upstate counties may be less willing to negotiate pleas.

5. Many of these women are sentenced as felony offenders under the 1973 Rockefeller Laws, which mandate felony prison sentences for repeat offenders, regardless of the nature of the offense or the background and motivation of the offender. Exacerbated by rigorous enforcement practices in the wake of the "war on drugs," the effect of this statute has been the mandatory imprisonment of thousands of low-level, nonviolent drug sellers and users—most of them minorities and many of them women (*Correctional Association Reporter*, 1991).

6. For a full elaboration of these women's lives, see L. Maher, "Women and Crack Cocaine," Ph.D. dissertation, Rutgers University, School of Criminal Justice (forthcoming).

7. This process is characterized by a new international division of labor and the globalization of financial markets. On a local level the economy is characterized by a decline in manufacturing and a corresponding decline in the demand for semi- and unskilled workers. Simultaneously, however, there has been a marked expansion of the service sector and the proliferation of the new "information technologies," which have increased the demand for service and white-collar workers (see Hall, 1989; for a description of the impact of this shift at the neighborhood level, see Curtis and Maher, 1991).

8. For example, Blau and Ferber (1985) suggest that despite substantial increases in women's participation, especially that of white women, female labor force commitment "is still often less than complete" (1985:24). Rising participation rates have extended the female work life expectancy (based on a 20-year-old woman) from approximately 12 years in 1940 to 26 years in 1972. This figure of 26 years, however, still represents only 71 percent of the male work life expectancy of 37 years (Blau and Ferber, 1985:27). Moreover, any increase in women's access to the labor market has not been accompanied by marked changes in the occupational distribution of women. Despite evi-

dence of a recent decrease (e.g., Beller, 1984), occupational segregation remains widespread and continues to be primarily determined by gender (see Treiman and Hartman, 1981; Reskin and Hartman, 1986). As Dex (1987) has noted, women tend to be concentrated in a narrow range of occupations, usually encompassing clerical work, semiskilled factory work, and semiskilled domestic work. Finally, it is clear that as a sex, women earn less than men, with the earnings differential currently indicating that for every dollar earned by men, women earn only 64 cents (Hartmann et al., 1985). The reasons advanced for the persistence of this differential are varied and complex; however, the three dominant explanations that emerge from the literature are (1) labor market discrimination, (2) sex differences in qualifications (Blau and Ferber, 1985), and (3) the role of familial and household responsibilities in influencing women's employment (O'Neill, 1985:51).

9. Psychopharmacological violence is attributed to the effects of drugs on behavior—effects that are thought to include paranoia, irrationality, and an inability to control anger and violent impulses. Economic-compulsive violence refers to crimes committed in order to attain money and/or other resources to purchase drugs. Systemic violence is the use of violence as a form of regulation intrinsic to the drug trade and/or drug-using lifestyles.

10. This is precisely what some researchers have attempted to do. For example, Sterk and Elifson (1990) use the tripartite model to describe violence among street-level commercial sex workers in New York and Atlanta. They state that "over 69 percent . . . mentioned that they had robbed a customer at least once and used the money to buy drugs" (p. 217). While this might indeed be true—and certainly we can find similar examples in our own data—is this type of behavior representative of their everyday behavior or representative of the type of violent incidents in which they are involved? Our data suggest that it is not.

11. See Curtis and Maher (1991) for a detailed history and analysis of the Southside's drug markets.

12. This is reflected in an increase in reported homicides in the neighborhood. In 1988, 58 homicides were reported in Bushwick. By 1990, this figure had increased to 77—a jump of more than 35 percent in a two-year period (*New York Newsday*, 4/21/91).

13. A stash-house sitter is someone who sits in a house or an apartment and is responsible for safeguarding large quantities of drugs.

14. Pseudonyms are used throughout to protect the anonymity of the women.

15. The act of "viccing" usually involves taking money and/or resources from a "victim of circumstance" (usually male) to purchase drugs. It is typically characterized by a prior relationship (the circumstance) between the "vic" and the victimizer and may or may not involve the use of physical force. For a full elaboration of the term and its origins, see Maher and Curtis, 1992.

16. This finding is supported by a recent report on self-identified inmate substance abusers, which indicates that of 2,546 female substance abusers, only 1 percent, or 19 women, were committed to prison for weapons charges (New York State Department of Correctional Services, 1990b). Similarly, national surveys of inmates in state correctional facilities indicate that less than 1 percent of women are imprisoned for weapons offenses (Bureau of Justice Statistics, 1991).

REFERENCES

Acker, J. (1988). "Class, Gender, and the Relations of Distribution." *Signs: Journal of Women in Culture and Society.* 13:473–497.

Adler, F. (1975). *Sisters in Crime: The Rise of the New Female Criminal.* New York: McGraw-Hill.

Amott, T. L., and J. A. Matthaei (1991). *Race, Gender and Work: A Multicultural Economic History of Women in the United States.* Boston: South End Press.

Beller, A. (1984). "Trends in Occupational Segregation by Sex and Race, 1960–1981." In B. F. Reskin (ed). *Sex Segregation in the Workplace.* Washington: National Academy Press.

Biernacki, P., and D. Waldorf (1981). "Snowball Sampling: Problems and Techniques of Chain Referral Sampling." *Sociological Methods and Research.* 10(2):141–161.

Blau, F. D., and M. A. Ferber (1985). "Women in the Labor Market: The Last Twenty Years." In L. Larwood, A. H. Stromberg, and B. A. Gutek. *Women and Work: An Annual Review.* Vol. 1 (pp. 19–49). Beverly Hills: Sage.

Bourgois, P. (1990). "In Search of Horatio Alger." *Contemporary Drug Problems.* 16(4):619–649.

Box, S., and C. Hale (1983). "Liberation and Female Criminality in England and Wales." *British Journal of Criminology.* 23(1):35–49.

Braverman, H. (1974). *Labor and Monopoly Capital: The Degradation of Work in the 20th Century.* New York: Monthly Review Press.

Bureau of Justice Statistics (1991). *Special Report: Women in Prison.* Washington, D.C.: U.S. Department of Justice, March.

——— (1992). *National Update.* Washington, D.C.: U.S. Department of Justice, April.

Burt, M. (1991). *Over the Edge: The Growth of Homelessness in the 1980's.* Washington, D.C.: The Urban Institute.

Carlen, P. (1988). *Women, Crime and Poverty.* Milton Keynes: Open University Press.

Chapman, J. R. (1980). *Economic Realities and the Female Offender.* Lexington, Mass.: Lexington Books.

Chesney-Lind, M. (1986). "Women and Crime: The Female Offender." *Signs: Journal of Women in Culture and Society.* 12(1):78–96.

Cook, D. (1987). "Women on Welfare: In Crime or Injustice." In P. Carlen and A. Worrall (eds.). *Gender, Crime and Justice.* Milton Keynes: Open University Press.

Correctional Association Reporter (1991). New York, April: Correctional Association of New York.

Crites, L. (ed.) (1976). *The Female Offender.* Lexington, Mass.: Lexington Books.

Curtis, R. (forthcoming). "An Ethnographic Study of the Effects of the Tactical Narcotics Team on Street Level Drug Markets in Three Police Precincts in Brooklyn, New York." Ph.D. dissertation, Columbia University, Teachers College, Department of Applied Anthropology and Education.

——— and L. Maher (1991). "Highly Structured Crack Markets in the Southside of Williamsburg,

Brooklyn." Paper prepared for publication, under contract with the Social Science Research Council/Guggenheim Foundation Working Group on the Ecology of Crime and Drugs Nationwide.

Daly, K. (1989). "Gender and Varieties of White Collar Crime." *Criminology.* 27:769–794.

Denzin, N. (1970). *The Research Act.* Chicago: Aldine.

Dex, S. (1989). *Women's Occupational Mobility: A Lifetime Perspective.* London: Macmillan.

Geertz, C. (1973). *The Interpretation of Cultures.* New York: Basic Books.

Glaser, B., and A. Strauss (1970). *The Discovery of Grounded Theory.* Chicago: Aldine.

Goldberg, G. S., and E. Kremen (1987). "The Feminization of Poverty: Only in America?" *Social Policy.* 17:3–14.

Goldstein, P. J. (1979). *Prostitution and Drugs.* Lexington, Mass.: Lexington Books.

——— (1985). "The Drugs/Violence Nexus: A Tripartite Conceptual Framework." *Journal of Drug Issues.* 15:493–506.

——— (1990). "Female Substance Abusers and Violence." In B. Forster and J. Colman Salloway (eds.). *The Socio-Cultural Matrix of Alcohol and Drug Use: A Sourcebook of Patterns and Factors.* Lewiston, N.Y.: Edwin Meller Press.

———, B. Spunt, P. Belluci, and T. Miller (1991a). "Frequency of Cocaine Use and Violence: A Comparison between Men and Women." In S. Schuber and C. Schade (eds.). *The Epidemiology of Cocaine Use and Abuse.* NIDA Research Monograph 110, pp. 113–138. Rockville, Md.: National Institute on Drug Abuse.

———, ———, ———, and ——— (1991b). "Volume of Cocaine Use and Violence: A Comparison between Men and Women." *Journal of Drug Issues.* 21(2):345–367.

Goode, E. (1984). *Deviant Behavior.* Englewood Cliffs, N.J.: Prentice-Hall.

Hall, S. (1989). "The Meaning of New Times." In S. Hall and J. Martin (eds.). *New Times: The Changing Face of Politics in the 1990's.* London: Lawrence and Wishart.

Hamid, A. (1990). "The Political Economy of Crack-Related Violence." *Contemporary Drug Problems.* 17(1):31–78.

——— (1991). "Crack: New Directions in Drug Research." *International Journal of the Addictions.* 26(8):835–849.

——— (forthcoming). *Beaming Up: Contexts for Smoking Cocaine.*

Harris, A. R. (1977). "Sex and Theories of Deviance." *American Sociological Review.* 42:3–16.

Harrison, B. (1974). *Urban Economic Development.* Washington, D.C.: Urban Institute.

Hartmann, H. I., P. A. Roos, and D. J. Treiman (1985). "An Agenda for Basic Research on Comparable Worth." In H. I. Hartmann (ed.). *Comparable Worth: New Directions for Research.* Washington, D.C.: National Academy Press.

Inciardi, J. A. (1972). "The Poly-Drug Abuser: A New Situational Offender." In F. Adler and G. O. W. Mueller (eds.). *Politics, Crime, and the International Scene: An Inter-American Focus*, pp. 60–68. San Juan, Puerto Rico: North-South Center for Technical and Cultural Exchange.

——— (1986). *The War on Drugs: Heroin, Cocaine, and Public Policy.* Palo Alto, Calif.: Mayfield.

Lapham, L. H. (1989). "A Political Opiate: The War on Drugs Is a Folly and a Menace." *Harpers,* December.

Lee, F. R. (1991). "For Gold Earrings and Protection, More Girls Take Road to Violence." *New York Times,* 11/25/91 at A1.

Lindesmith, A. R. (1967). *The Addict and the Law.* Bloomington: Indiana University Press.

Maher, L. (forthcoming). "Women and Crack Cocaine." Ph.D. dissertation, Rutgers University, School of Criminal Justice.

——— and R. Curtis (1992). "Women on the Edge of Crime: Crack Cocaine and the Changing Contexts of Street-Level Sex Work in New York City." *Crime, Law and Social Change.* 18:221–258.

——— and E. J. Waring (1990). "Beyond Simple Differences: White Collar Crime, Gender and Workforce Position." *Phoebe: An Interdisciplinary Journal of Feminist Scholarship, Theory, and Esthetics.* 2(1):44–54.

Malveaux, J. (1990). "Gender Difference and Beyond: An Economic Perspective on Diversity and Commonality among Women." In D. L. Rhode (ed.). *Theoretical Perspectives on Sexual Difference.* New Haven: Yale University Press.

Mann, C. R. (1987). "Black Female Homicide in the United States." Paper presented at the Conference on Black Homicide and Public Health.

McCall, G. J. (1978). *Observing the Law: Field Methods in the Study of Crime and the Criminal Justice System*. New York: Free Press.

McLanahan, S., et al. (1989). "Sex Differences in Poverty 1950–1980," *Signs: Journal of Women in Culture and Society*. 15(1):102–122.

Messerschmidt, J. W. (1986). *Capitalism, Patriarchy and Crime*. Totowa, N.J.: Rowan and Littlefield.

Morris, A. (1987). *Women, Crime and Criminal Justice*. Oxford: Basil Blackwell.

Musto, D. F. (1973). *The American Disease: Origins of Narcotic Control*. New Haven: Yale University Press.

Naffine, N. (1987). *Female Crime: The Construction of Women in Criminology*. Sydney: Allen and Unwin.

New York Newsday, 4/15/91.

———, 4/21/91.

New York State Department of Correctional Services (1988). *Female New Court Commitments 1976–1987*. Albany, N.Y.: Division of Program Planning, Research and Evaluation.

——— (1990a). *Female Drug Commitment Population 1987–1989*. Albany, N.Y.: Division of Program Planning, Research and Evaluation.

——— (1990b). *Identified Substance Abusers*. Albany, N.Y.: Division of Program Planning, Research and Evaluation.

New York Times, 3/17/90.

———, 7/23/90.

———, 12/3/90.

———, 1/15/91.

———, 11/25/91.

O'Neill, J. (1985). "Role Differentiation and the Gender Gap in Wage Rates." In L. Larwood, A. H. Stromberg, and B. A. Gutek. *Women and Work: An Annual Review*. Vol. 1 (pp. 50–75). Beverly Hills: Sage.

Reskin, B., and H. Hartman (1986). *Women's Work, Men's Work*. Washington, D.C.: National Academy Press.

Rosenbaum, M. (1981). *Women on Heroin*. New Brunswick, N.J.: Rutgers University Press.

Schur, E. (1969). *Our Criminal Society: The Social and Legal Sources of Crime*. Englewood Cliffs, N.J.: Prentice-Hall.

Silbert, M. H., and A. M. Pines (1984). "Occupational Hazards of Street Prostitutes." *Criminal Justice and Behavior*. 8(4):395–399.

Simms, M. C., and J. Malveaux (eds.) (1989). *Slipping through the Cracks: The Status of Black Women*. New Brunswick, N.J.: Transaction.

Smart, C. (1976). *Women, Crime and Criminology: A Feminist Critique*. London: Routledge and Kegan Paul.

——— (1979). "The New Female Criminal: Reality or Myth?" *British Journal of Criminology*. 19:50–59.

Sommers, I., and D. Baskin (1991). "The Situational Context of Violent Female Offending." Paper presented at the Annual Meetings, American Society of Criminology, San Francisco, November.

Spradley, J. P. (1979). *The Ethnographic Interview*. New York: Holt, Rinehart and Winston.

Spunt, B., P. J. Goldstein, P. Belluci, and T. Miller (1990). "Race, Ethnicity and Gender Differences in the Drugs-Violence Relationship." *Journal of Psychoactive Drugs*. 22(3):293–313.

Steffensmeier, D. (1980). "Sex Differences in Patterns of Adult Crime 1965–1977: A Review and Assessment." *Social Forces*. 58:1080–1108.

——— (1983). "Organization Properties and Sex Segregation in the Underworld: Building a Sociological Theory of Sex Differences in Crime." *Social Forces*. 61(4):1010–1032.

———, R. H. Steffensmeier, and A. L. Rosenthal (1979). "Trends in Female Violence 1970–1977." *Sociological Focus*. 12(3):217–227.

Sterk, C. E., and K. W. Elifson (1990). "Drug-Related Violence and Street Prostitution." In M. de La Rosa, E. Y. Lambert, and B. Gropper (eds.). *Drugs and Violence: Causes, Correlates, and Consequences*. NIDA Research Monograph 103. Rockville, Md.: National Institute on Drug Abuse.

Sum, A., N. Fogg, and R. Taggart (1988). "Withered Dreams: The Decline in the Economic Fortunes of Young, Non-College Educated Male Adults and Their Families." Paper prepared for the William T. Grant Foundation Commission on Family, Work, and Citizenship.

Treiman, D., and H. Hartman (1981). *Women, Work and Wages*. Washington, D.C.: National Academy Press.

Wallace, R. (1985). *Shock Waves of Community Disintegration in New York: Public Policy and the Burning of the Bronx*. New York: PISCS Inc.

——— and D. Wallace (1986). *Origins of Public Health Collapse in New York City: The Dynamics of*

Planned Shrinkage, Contagious Urban Decay, and Social Disintegration. New York: PISCS Inc.

Weiner, N. A., and M. E. Wolfgang (1985). "The Extent and Character of Violent Crime in America." In L. A. Curtis (ed.). *American Violence and Public Policy.* New Haven: Yale University Press.

Weppner, R. S. (ed.) (1977). *Street Ethnography: Selected Studies of Crime and Drug Use in Natural Settings.* Beverly Hills: Sage.

Wilson, W. J. (1987). *The Truly Disadvantaged: The Inner City, the Underclass and Public Policy.* Chicago: University of Chicago Press.

CHAPTER 10

MOTHERS AND CHILDREN, DRUGS AND CRACK: REACTIONS TO MATERNAL DRUG DEPENDENCY

DREW HUMPHRIES / JOHN DAWSON / VALERIE CRONIN /
PHYLLIS KEATING / CHRIS WISNIEWSKI / JENNINE EICHFELD

ABSTRACT

In Chapter 9, Maher and Curtis suggested that the "war against drugs" is blamed for many of today's urban ills—homelessness, unemployment, and high infant mortality rates—rather than considered a consequence of these social problems. Unfortunately, all too often, the war against drugs has become a "war against women." This is readily apparent in attempts across the country to criminalize individual women's behavior, most recently drug use during pregnancy.

In several highly publicized cases prosecutors charged pregnant women who use drugs with drug trafficking or child abuse. The rationale for such prosecutions is the asserted state interest in the health of the fetus. Yet, feminists have argued, criminalizing such behavior is likely to harm a fetus by discouraging drug-using pregnant women from entering drug treatment programs or seeking proper prenatal care.*

The American Bar Association and the American Civil Liberties Union, among others, have raised serious questions about the prosecutorial ethics of these cases. However, turning pregnant women into criminals appears to be an extension of the national trend toward intensive prosecution and punishment by imprisonment of female drug offenders. Given that such legislation would disproportionately affect poor and minority women, we must consider the racial and class biases of this patriarchal control of women. Moreover, the fact that most drug treatment programs refuse to accept pregnant women only highlights the cruel double bind of these women.

---

*See Lynn Paltrow, "When Becoming Pregnant Is a Crime," *Criminal Justice Ethics*, vol. 9 (Winter/Spring), 1990, pp. 41–47.

By 1992, 167 women in 24 states had been charged with abusing an unborn child—almost all through illegal drug use during pregnancy. Yet of the 17 appeals made in these cases so far, all resulted in the dismissal of charges.* It is possible that this particular form of state intrusion will be struck down by the courts and disappear as an issue. However, we ask the reader to consider the persistence of the underlying patriarchal relations that foster government control over women's bodies. Abortion is a good example of rights won, eroded, reestablished, and yet seriously challenged by some at the time of this writing. Indeed, it is not impossible that abortion could become criminalized at some time in the future.

This chapter reports that health care providers who must report suspected drug-using pregnant women tend to bring these women to the attention of family courts rather than prosecutors. In family courts mothers are not prosecuted but are likely to have to give up their babies to institutional or foster care when they are born. The chapter goes on to discuss the severe lack of drug treatment for women.

As you read this chapter, you might ask: Is state intrusion justified? Should the state have control over women's behavior as it pertains to their pregnancies? If your answer is affirmative, under what conditions? Why is the father not prosecuted—even when he is a drug addict and/or batters the pregnant woman and harms the fetus? Discuss the strengths and weaknesses of criminalization and/or mandatory reporting of suspected drug use during pregnancy as a "quick fix" for reducing the number of drug-addicted newborns. Consider, alternatively, the need for long-term solutions involving societywide changes such as readily available health care, rehabilitation, drug treatment, education, housing, and decent employment.

---

*Kirk Johnson, "Child Abuse Is Ruled Out in Birth Case," *New York Times,* Aug. 18, 1992, pp. B1, B4.

Fear that prosecutors are making pregnancy a crime rests on a handful of highly publicized cases. Brenda Vaughan, an African-American woman, was charged with and convicted of second-degree theft for check forgery in Washington, D.C. Although probation is the normal sentence for first-time offenders like Vaughan, the judge decided to imprison the pregnant woman after she tested positive for cocaine. "I'm going to keep her locked up until the baby's born," said Judge Peter Wolf at the time of sentencing (Churchville, 1988:A1). No drug charges were brought against Vaughan nor did the prosecution seek a trial on possession or use of illegal drugs. Vaughan's attorney worked to amend the sentence (Churchville, 1988).

Drew Humphries et al., "Mothers and Children, Drugs and Crack: Reactions to Maternal Drug Dependency," *Women and Criminal Justice,* vol. 3, no. 2, 1992, pp. 81–99, The Haworth Press, Inc., 10 Alice Street, Binghamton, NY 13904-1580.

When she was charged with and convicted of two counts of delivering drugs to a minor, the prosecution alleged that Jennifer Johnson, an African-American woman, had passed cocaine to her newborn child through the umbilical cord after the baby was delivered, but before the cord was cut (Curriden, 1990). Prosecutor Jeff Deen defended the move: "We needed to make sure this woman does not give birth to another cocaine baby. The message is that this community cannot afford to have two or three cocaine babies from the same person" (Curriden, 1990:51). The Florida court gave Johnson fifteen to twenty-four years probation, mandatory drug rehabilitation, drug and alcohol prohibitions, and required her to report subsequent pregnancies to her probation officer and to enter a court-approved prenatal care program (Curriden, 1990; Sherman, 1989). The American Civil Liberties Union and fourteen other public interest and public health groups appealed the drug trafficking conviction in the Florida District Court of Appeals (Sherman, 1989).

In Rockford, Illinois, Melanie Green, African-American, became the first woman to be charged with manslaughter for the death of her two-day old infant due allegedly to her cocaine use during pregnancy. Apparently, doctors at the hospital where Green gave birth reported that the child had tested positive for cocaine (Curriden, 1990; Sherman, 1989). When an Illinois grand jury refused to indict Green, the charges were dropped.

Pamela Rae Stewart, a white woman, was arrested under a California child support statute when she delivered a brain-damaged baby that died soon after birth. She had failed to "follow her doctor's advice to stay off her feet, to refrain from sexual intercourse, to refrain from taking street drugs, and to seek immediate medical attention if she experienced difficulties with the pregnancy" (Paltrow, Fox, Goetz, 1990:1). The San Diego Municipal Court dismissed the charges,

declaring that "California's criminal child support statute was not intended to apply to the actions of a pregnant woman and does not create a legal duty of care owed by a pregnant woman to her fetus" (Paltrow, Fox, Goetz, 1990:1).

In other words, pregnancy combined with drug use, especially cocaine use, has been made grounds for punitive sentencing and novel application of criminal and child protection statutes. These developments give meaning to the phrase criminalizing pregnancy. This paper reviews practices which make pregnancy a crime. Because the prosecutions are a response, we begin with the perceived problem, drug-dependent mothers. We then return to reactions, both legal and medical, before discussing treatment and policy issues.

MATERNAL DRUG USE AND COCAINE-EXPOSED CHILDREN

The perceived problem consists of (1) the presumably large number of infants born to drug-using mothers, (2) the damaging effects of drug use on fetal and infant development, and (3) the fear that the long-term needs of these infants will overwhelm social, health, and educational systems.

Maternal Drug Use

The widely publicized claim that 375,000 babies are born annually to mothers who use drugs[1] is the basis of fears about crack and crack-addicted babies. The 375,000 figure, reported by Chasnoff,[2] a leading researcher in the field of perinatal drug exposure, represents about eleven percent of births in the United States. It has been extrapolated from case studies of urban hospitals where one might expect that drug use, especially the use of illicit drugs, might be relatively high (Chasnoff, 1988, 1987). A Los Angeles study cited by Chasnoff reported that nine percent of the births surveyed involved neonatal withdrawal due to maternal drug use (Chasnoff, 1988). Another case study conducted at Harlem Hospital in New York City showed that ten percent of the newborns (3,300) tested positive for cocaine in their urine (Chasnoff, 1987). By 1988, trends suggested that maternal drug use was on the increase. In New York City, it increased from eight percent in 1980 to 30 percent in 1988, affecting from 20 to 25 percent of all women giving birth (Drucker, 1989).

Cocaine use is of special concern. Not only have estimates of cocaine use spawned a moral panic; the awareness that women, including pregnant women, use cocaine and crack contributes to the medical and legal reactions. The National Drug Control Strategy Report, the key source for President Bush's war on drugs, singled out pregnant cocaine users estimating that 100,000 cocaine babies[3] are born each year (Kusserow, 1990). This figure is consistent with the results of an eight-city survey conducted by the U.S. Department of Health and Human Services (Kusserow, 1990). The eight-city survey found that 9,000 babies had been born addicted to crack in 1989.

Effects of Exposure

There is ample evidence that maternal cocaine use adds avoidable risks to pregnancy (Chasnoff, 1986). Cocaine increases maternal blood pressure and the risk of stroke. When used by a pregnant woman, the drug crosses the placenta, exposing the fetus which cannot excrete the foreign substance quickly enough. Cocaine stimulates fetal movement, increasing the risk of miscarriage during the first trimester and risking premature labor during the last trimester. Cocaine has been associated with an abstinence syndrome (Chasnoff, 1987). If the mother abruptly stops taking the drug, the fetus experiences withdrawal-like symptoms. Shortly after birth, the cocaine-exposed infant experiences withdrawal symptoms which can persist for two to three weeks (Chasnoff, 1988). Symptoms include wakefulness, irritability, trembling, body temperature variations, rapid breathing, hyperactivity, exaggeration of reflexes, and increased muscle stiffness. Neonates suffer diarrhea, sweating, respiratory distress, runny nose, apneic attacks (failure to breathe), and failure to gain weight. The babies have a high-pitched persistent cry, are painfully sensitive to sound, cannot suck properly, and are very difficult to comfort (State of Oregon, 1985).

In addition to withdrawal symptoms, infants delivered to mothers who used cocaine during pregnancy are smaller in size, tend to be shorter, and have lower birth weights. Their smaller than normal head size, indicative of growth retardation, is thought to result from cocaine-induced constriction of the blood supply to the uterus. Babies born addicted to cocaine can develop convulsions and strokes. They are also at significantly higher risk for Sudden Infant Death Syndrome (Chasnoff, 1988).

While no one would dispute the toll maternal cocaine use may take, two points require attention. First, the studies reviewed for this paper point out that the women in question are polydrug users, using among other drugs, heroin, methadone, marijuana, tobacco, alcohol, and over-the-counter medications. Polydrug use makes it difficult to trace all but a few newborn symptoms to cocaine, these being irritability and the risk of premature delivery (Chasnoff, 1986, 1987). Other effects, like low birth weights or growth reductions, may have social roots in the lack of prenatal and health care, or can be traced to other illicit or licit drugs.

Second, Koren et al. recently reported what they call "the bias against the null hypothesis" in the literature on cocaine effects. In other words, studies that fail to show that cocaine has adverse effects on pregnancy tend to be ignored (Koren et al., 1989). Of 58 abstracts on fetal outcomes following exposure to cocaine that were submitted for presentation at the Society of Pediatric Research conference, nine reported no effects and 28 reported adverse effects. Only one of the abstracts reporting no effects was accepted for presentation, despite the fact that these studies verified cocaine use and used control cases more often than the other studies. Reviewers, however, accepted over half of the abstracts reporting adverse effects. Findings led researchers to conclude that there may be a "distorted estimation of the teratogenic risk of cocaine" (Koren et al., 1989:1440).

Long-Term Needs

Predictions about the long-term needs of cocaine-exposed infants are dire. According to a 1989 survey by the U.S. Department of Health and Human Services, the cost of caring for 9,000 crack-addicted children from infancy through age five would be 500 million dollars (Kusserow, 1990). To mitigate this cost, the U.S. Department of Health and Human Services recommends that state and local governments provide prenatal care for pregnant women at risk for addiction. It further recommends revising laws on child custody to make it easier to place "boarder babies" in foster care and adoptive homes. The report also estimates that the additional cost of preparing the 9,000 crack babies for school could exceed one and a half billion dollars. With confirmation of the national estimate of 100,000 crack babies a year, the annual cost could come to ten billion dollars.

It may be difficult to reconcile spending such sums on children thought to have suffered permanent, irreversible damage, including emotional detachment, inability to relate to others, and neurological impairment. The

results of long-term studies are not yet in. But whatever their outcome, one thing is clear: investments that improve a child's environment pay off in minimizing drug-related damage. Environment, not drugs, has the larger influence on development. A two-year study of three groups of newborns (opiate addicted, nonopiate addicted, and a control group) showed a downward trend in mean developmental scores, a phenomenon not uncommon in infants from low socio-economic circumstances (Chasnoff, 1986). A study of methadone-exposed infants from birth to four years of age produced similar findings (Kaltenbach and Finnegan, 1984). The strongest correlates of developmental status were again social factors. Biological risk, researchers concluded, is either attenuated or potentiated by the child's social environment. The point is, biological risk including drug related ones can be minimized.

CRIMINALIZATION, DRUG TRAFFICKING AND CHILD ABUSE

State and federal prosecutors have argued that pregnant women who use drugs are engaging in illegal activity, and that they ought to be arrested, prosecuted, and convicted. The purpose, they claim, is to stop maternal drug use by incarcerating the women or by forcing them into drug treatment. Patricia Toth[4] of the National Center for the Prosecution of Child Abuse says, "Prosecutors seem to agree that the ultimate solution is not criminal prosecutions, but prevention and treatment" (Curriden, 1990:53). Lynn Paltrow of the American Civil Liberties Union's Reproductive Freedom Project argues, however, that these prosecutions, in effect, "criminalize" pregnancy. She asserts that "none of these women have been arrested for the crime of illegal drug use or possession. Instead, they are being arrested for a new and independent crime, becoming pregnant while addicted to drugs" (Paltrow, 1990:41–42).

Clearly, the debate over how to handle the problem of maternal drug abuse has aroused passionate feelings on both sides of the issue. Those who favor prosecution state that women must be held accountable for prenatal conduct that may injure the fetus. Those who oppose it feel that the creation of a "prenatal police force" would only succeed in driving the problem underground, preventing many women from obtaining the help that they desperately need (Paltrow, 1990). In examining this issue, it is important to outline the theories behind the prosecutions and explore the consequences of prosecuting pregnant addicts.

Of the more than forty cases reported around the country in the past three years, over half are based on the mother's alleged violation of drug trafficking laws (Paltrow, Fox, and Goetz, 1990). In the case of Jennifer Johnson, the state of Florida succeeded in convicting her of passing cocaine to her newborn through the umbilical cord (Curriden, 1990). Prosecutors have argued in similar cases that delivery of the controlled substance occurs during the sixty to ninety seconds after birth, before the cord is severed (Kolbert et al., 1990). A drug trafficking conviction can carry with it a prison sentence of up to ten to fifteen years. Only three women have been successfully prosecuted on these grounds and all three cases have been appealed at the state level.

Other methods of prosecution center on the issues of child abuse or infant neglect. This is the instance in nearly every case cited in the American Civil Liberties Union's summary of criminal proceedings involving pregnant women (Paltrow, Fox, and Goetz, 1990). Prosecutors allege that maternal drug use during pregnancy imposes serious health risks on the developing fetus or can result in postnatal trauma including narcotic withdrawal and physical and mental defects (Chasnoff, 1987). This type of prosecution is more likely to result in a conviction, although these decisions are also later appealed since most states do not have child abuse statutes that pertain to prenatal conduct.

Civil and women's rights advocates have denounced these proceedings and offer many reasons why they may be considered unethical, unproductive, and in some ways, unconstitutional. First and foremost, there are the problems of legislative intent and due process of law. Specifically, it is argued that prosecutions based on drug trafficking go beyond the expressed intention of the law. In other words, these laws are designed to apply to the sale or exchange of controlled substances between "born persons." Arbitrarily using them to convict pregnant women violates due process since there has been no notice that these laws are applicable to this situation (Paltrow, 1990). Using existing child abuse statutes also falls under this criticism. Since the fetus is not legally defined as a child, these types of prosecutions violate due process rights of the mother. While evidence concerning the negative effects of drug use during pregnancy exists, prosecutors are not always able to prove that the mother's drug use is the cause of specific postnatal defects, if indeed such defects occur at all.[5]

The child abuse issue leads us into the area of "fetal rights." In her article, "Fetal Rights: A New Assault on Feminism," Katha Pollit discusses the problems created by placing the interests of the unborn above those of the mother. Not only does this kind of action violate the constitutionally guaranteed right to privacy, she argues, it also places an undue burden, a "duty of care" on the pregnant women (Pollit, 1990). Prosecutors, like University of Texas law professor John Robertson, insist that "if the pregnant woman decides to go to term, she takes on additional responsibilities so the child will be born healthy" (Curriden, 1990:52). But Pollit (1990) insists that the emphasis on the woman's responsibility is merely a convenient way of dismissing the multitude of factors which affect pregnancy but which are beyond the ability of the woman to control.[6] If prosecutors succeed in establishing fetal rights, she argues, women will come to be seen as "incubators," unable to control pregnancies or maintain bodily integrity.

Prosecuting drug-addicted pregnant women leads inevitably down a "slippery slope." Lynn Paltrow suggests that "prosecutions . . . cannot rationally be limited to illegal conduct because many legal behaviors cause damage to developing babies. Women who are diabetic or obese, women with cancer or epilepsy who need drugs that could harm the fetus, and women who are too poor to eat adequately or to get prenatal care could all be categorized as fetal abusers" (Paltrow, 1990:7). She also points out that the more than 900,000 women who suffer still births and miscarriages each year could be subject to these same types of criminal proceedings (Kolbert et al., 1990).

The overwhelming majority of prosecutions involve poor women of color. The criminal justice system may accentuate the class-racial bias, but it originates in the requirement that medical providers report drug use among pregnant women. Cases normally come to the prosecutor's office from the police, but few maternal drug-use cases come to prosecutors this way. This is what makes Brenda Vaughan's case unusual. She entered the system through conventional channels: she was arrested for and charged with forgery; her pregnancy and drug use were discovered in the course of criminal processing. In contrast, most of the women against whom prosecutors have pressed charges enter the system through hospitals and clinics.

MEDICALIZATION: REPORTING CHILD ABUSE

The wave of prosecutions described in the introduction began not with drug arrests, but as doctors or other health workers started to report the positive results of drug tests for women who, like Melanie Green and Pamela Rae Stewart, had just delivered babies. Such practices reflected medical providers' belief that without law enforcement assistance, they could do little to halt the increasing numbers of drug-exposed infants (Goetz, Fox, and Bates, 1990). They supported the "reporting laws" which by the mid-eighties had already imposed a legal and ethical duty on medical providers to report infants born addicted to drugs (Angel, 1988). The purpose of such laws, according to Catherine Tracy of Los Angeles County Children's Services, was to prevent child abuse, child neglect, or health endangering situations (Angel, 1988). But in creating a "duty," reporting guidelines, even in states without applicable child abuse statutes, turned health care providers into medical police officers (McNulty, 1988).

The procedures developed to implement child abuse statutes require medical providers to report evidence of abuse or neglect to social service agencies with the authority to remove the infant from the mother's custody. Evidence of neglect consists of the mother's admission of drug use, positive drug screens for the mother, and positive drug screens for the newborn (Chasnoff, 1990).

When the mother admits to drug use, the medical provider has a duty to report. The admission, which is in other circumstances a condition for getting help, jeopardizes the mother's custody of the newborn and, depending on local prosecutors, places her at risk for criminal prosecution. The focus of reporting is unrelated to maternal health or illness. If it were, the U.S. Supreme Court's definition of drug addiction as an illness would bar prosecution (Chavkin, 1989). Instead, the duty to report arises from the newborn's exposure to drugs. So in addition to the mother's admitted use of drugs, courts accept the positive results of drug tests on mothers or newborns as evidence of abuse.

Drug testing, however, has limited value in identifying the drug-exposed newborns protected by the abuse laws. It is important to understand what drug tests can and cannot tell us (see Chasnoff, 1990). What drug tests can tell is that a drug was ingested by the mother within the last twenty-four to seventy-two hours (Moss and Crockett, 1990). They do not indicate the quantity of drug nor do they reveal the prevalence of its use (Chasnoff, 1990). They cannot discriminate between the habitual and the occasional user. They cannot determine whether miscarriage, neonatal death, or early childhood illness or injury are due to maternal or paternal drug use (American Public Health Association, n.d.). Finally drug tests do not always tell exactly what drug was used. In one case, a woman tested positive for an illegal substance which was actually an antihistamine (Moss and Crockett, 1990). Laboratory technicians are not infallible, and false positives can occur.

Nonetheless, drug testing takes place. In public hospitals drug testing is periodic or routine (Chavkin, 1989; Moss and Crockett, 1990), but many private hospitals test only when drug use is suspected (Angel, 1988). Guidelines like those established in South Carolina (Goetz, Fox, and Bates, 1990) reveal the circumstances that justify testing: no prenatal care, late prenatal care, incomplete prenatal care, abruptio placentae, intrauterine fetal death, preterm labor, intrauterine growth retardation, previously known drug or alcohol abuse, or unexplained congenital abnormalities. Some criteria pertain to medical emergencies where maternal and infant health depend on the physician knowing

what drugs, if any, a woman may have taken. But other criteria like the deviations from the monthly and weekly visits to the obstetrician, are rooted in the way the poor use the health care system. Poor women tend to delay prenatal care which risks the pregnancy and turns them into candidates for drug testing.

To evaluate bias in drug testing and reporting, a Florida study identified the drug using pregnant women in the community and then compared them to the group of women selected by public and private hospitals for drug testing (Chasnoff, 1990). The study first collected urine samples from black and white women receiving obstetrical care in private and public hospitals. It found no significant difference in the prevalence of positive results between private and public patients or between black and white women. It did, however, identify a significant difference between socio-economic status and race. Middle-income, white women tested positive for marijuana, while low-income black women tested positive for cocaine. The second phase of the study reviewed the characteristics of pregnant women that medical providers tested under the Florida child abuse statute. The women actually tested by medical providers came from poorer socio-economic backgrounds than the middle- and low-income women whose urine samples had tested positive for drugs. But the strongest bias revealed by the study was racial. The rate of reporting was ten times higher among black women than among white women. The racial discrepancy held true for black women receiving care in both public and private hospitals. The research team suggested that discrimination reflects (1) the reluctance of private physicians to risk alienating affluent patients, and (2) stereotypes about minority drug use held by doctors practicing in large urban hospitals.

Despite technical deficiencies and discrimination, drug tests are the vehicle by which medical providers refer drug-exposed infants to social service agencies. Under Florida's Child Abuse Statute, medical providers must report exposed infants to the Department of Health and Rehabilitative Services (Chasnoff, 1990). Community health nurses are then required by the Florida statute to determine the suitability of the home and whether the agency should continue supervision or recommend to family court that the child be placed in foster care. The foster care solution is well documented in New York City (Chavkin, 1989) where a positive drug screen, evidence of maternal drug use, and child neglect must be reported to Special Services for Children. The agency investigates, files charges in Family Court, and places neglected children in foster care. The number of children, shortage of foster homes, and delays in investigating have created the so-called boarder baby crisis, the approximately 300 babies under the age of two that are to be found on any given day boarding in New York City hospitals.

TREATMENT: FROM LIMITED OPTIONS TO ONE-STOP SHOPS

Both the child abuse and drug trafficking approaches rest on the assumption that current drug programs can accommodate the pregnant women referred for drug treatment by family or criminal courts. There is, however, widespread recognition that the assumption is false. Congressman George Miller, Chairman of the Select Committee on Children, Youth and Families, reports that "two-thirds of the hospitals have no place to refer substance-abusing pregnant women" (Kolbert et al., 1990:5). The need for drug treatment programs that include prenatal care is urgent.

Existing treatment programs discriminate against pregnant women. In a recent survey of 78 drug treatment programs in New York City, Dr. Wendy Chavkin found that 54 percent refused to treat pregnant women: 67 percent refused to treat pregnant women on Medicaid, and 87 percent had no services available for Medicaid patients who were both pregnant and addicted to crack (Chavkin, 1989). The bias against admitting pregnant women reflects the perception that obstetrical care adds unacceptable risks to drug rehabilitation (McNulty, 1988; Moss, 1990).[7]

In Michigan where the situation is similar only nine of the thirteen residential treatment programs available to women will "consider" pregnant women (McNulty, 1988). Long waiting lists, delayed examinations, and admission policies restricting treatment to women who are less than three months pregnant deter pregnant women attempting to get help. A Detroit study found that the average lag time for an initial prenatal appointment at Detroit hospitals was 4.2 weeks (Potti, 1990). The initial appointment does not ordinarily include an obstetrical examination which is scheduled about two weeks later, making the total waiting time, from first contact to initial examination anywhere from three to thirteen weeks (Potti, 1990).

Limited treatment facilities and restricted admissions cast doubt on official responses to the problem. Katha Pollit mentions that Jennifer Johnson had sought admission to a drug abuse clinic but was turned away, presumably because she was pregnant (Pollit, 1990). Punishing women who are not likely to get the treatment they seek, Paltrow argues, "raises serious questions about prosecutorial ethics" (Paltrow, 1990:11). Similarly, the lack of programs that admit pregnant women creates untenable choices. If a woman has a drug problem and a family to care for, she must choose between helping herself or caring for her family (McNulty, 1988). Typically, there is no choice. When women coming before the criminal or family court are ordered into drug rehabilitation, their children are placed in foster care.

Despite inadequate facilities, our survey of available literature has identified programs combining prenatal care and drug treatment. Born Free, associated with the San Diego Medical Center, is the country's first residential treatment program for pregnant addicts. It now has several homes for women and their children. The women are required to undergo detoxification either in the program or under another auspice before entering residential treatment (Abraham, 1988). Harlem Hospital Center, one of the first in the country to care exclusively for pregnant addicts, has had some success (French, 1989). In Detroit, the Hutzel Hospital takes virtually all high-risk pregnancies in the city, including pregnant addicts, and provides prenatal, delivery, and post-partum care. It encourages women to enter day or residential treatment in the Hutzel Recovery Center. Patients enter treatment on a voluntary basis, but patients facing court dates chose treatment in order to retain custody of their older children (Teltsch, 1990). Also, the Neil J. Houston House in the Roxbury section of Boston cares for pregnant addicts who have been convicted of crimes and who would have normally served at least five months in state prison. The program requires detoxification, covers delivery of the baby, and then requires participation in a one-year follow-up program (*New York Times*, 1989). Finally, the Family Center at Thomas Jefferson Medical College of Thomas Jefferson University, like Hutzel Hospital, has a self-referred, high-risk obstetrical clinic (Reagan, 1987). Other programs, including MABON, Hale House, and CARE, rely on court referrals for patients.

The programs for which we hold out the most hope are voluntary, involve family-centered treatment, and offer a variety of social services in addition to prenatal care and drug therapy. Pregnant drug users voluntarily seeking help with the pregnancy and for the drug problem have the greatest chance of recovery. Short of self-admissions, court referrals that offer women a choice between entering treatment or serving custodial sentences represent more difficult trade-offs. The element of coercion introduced by court orders reduces the likelihood of recovery, but the terms of the choice are important. Entering a treatment program that keeps the mother, her newborn, and older children together is better than remanding the mother to prison and forcing her to surrender the children to foster care. But little is gained if the treatment option looks like boot camp or participation entails loss of her children. Such punitive choices serve to drive women away from prenatal care and drug treatment almost as much as prison. On the other hand, the chance for maternal or family recovery disappears entirely when women have no control over what happens to them or their children.

Social therapies that keep families together fare better than those that treat family members in isolation. High on our list are the residential treatment and follow-up programs that admit the mother, the newborn, and older siblings. Such programs attend to the needs of the whole family, although the focus on the mother unfortunately overlooks the effect of the adult male drug user on the family. Nonetheless, the principle keeps children out of the already overburdened and frequently dangerous foster care system.

And finally, programs that recognize that drug abuse is a medical problem with deeper social roots stand to contribute more than others. Most programs offer classes in prenatal and infant care, parenting, nutrition, and general health care as well as drug, alcohol, and AIDS education. Others add coping skills, day care, and job training. And still others combine all these services in "one-stop shopping centers." By most accounts, community-based one-stop shops are the vehicle for delivering the range of services required by a particular community (Abraham, 1988; French, 1989; Teltsch, 1990; *New York Times*, 1989; Reagan et al., 1987).

CONCLUSION

Two ill-conceived national policies have greatly exacerbated maternal drug use. Aimed at eliminating cocaine production in South America, the national drug policy directs less money to drug treatment facilities which are needed to accommodate all who seek rehabilitation, including pregnant women. Rehabilitation ranks third after domestic enforcement and international drug control efforts according to priorities set by President Bush. The health care system's financial difficulties, precipitated by a reduction of federal funds, makes health care the province of the insured. Hospitals and clinics which continue to serve the poor risk bankruptcy. Being poor and pregnant may still get you prenatal care, that being a public health priority; but being poor, pregnant, and drug-dependent puts you in jail, your children in foster care. Humane alternatives have neither been created nor defended in the decade-long attack on social services.

It is easy to oppose the prosecution of drug-using pregnant women. Medical and public health organizations condemn the prosecutions as discriminatory. Women's groups have cited violation of fundamental reproductive rights. Such prosecutions, some medical and health care professionals argue, are detrimental to the health and safety of women and their children. They undermine the trust in the confidentiality of the physician-patient relationship. They drive women at high risk of complications during pregnancy away from the health care system,

creating a situation that is potentially harmful to women and their children.

While the prosecutions have received more attention, it is fair to say that the reporting laws have done more harm. Defining drug use as child abuse and requiring medical providers to report drug use admittedly allows more room for debate. There is something compelling in the fact that these laws are designed to protect newborns. But consider the following. Defining the use of controlled drugs as child abuse does not, as some think, solve the problem. It only shifts the burden from the criminal courts to the family court, breaks up families, and produces boarder babies, half of whom go into congregate or foster care. The boarder baby crisis makes a mockery of claims that the statutes protect children.

The drug use as child abuse formula ought to be opposed for several other reasons. Although this paper focused on controlled drugs, some states have included alcohol use in the definition of child abuse, raising the possibility that a range of otherwise legal conduct may fall within the meaning of child abuse. Additionally, reporting procedures under the child abuse statutes are discriminatory, they undermine patients' confidence in physicians and drive the women in need of help away from care facilities. Finally, drug testing is an unwarranted invasion of women's right to privacy. The decision to test rests on subjective standards, its application is discriminatory, and evaluations of results are plagued with technical problems.

The most telling criticism that can be made against the drug trafficking and child abuse approaches, however, is the lack of treatment programs for pregnant drug users. Without treatment, prosecutions are simply punitive stop gaps, and reporting laws force minority and poor women to surrender their children. Health care, drug treatment, and social services must be, as we have already argued, among the first priorities if the goal is to help these women and protect their children.

NOTES

1. Health providers determine drug use in three ways. The mother may tell the health provider she has used or is currently using drugs. The health provider may, in addition, screen the mother's urine or that of the newborn for drugs. Among the estimated 375,000 babies exposed to drugs (both licit and illicit drugs), some suffer withdrawal symptoms at birth.

2. Dr. Ira Chasnoff, head of the Perinatal Center for Chemical Dependency at Northwestern University Medical School, is founder of the National Association for Perinatal Addiction Research and Education, a group which advocates mandatory testing of pregnant women for drug use.

3. Of the 375,000 drug-exposed newborns, 100,000 are thought to have been exposed to cocaine. The U.S. Department of Health and Human Services uses the term addicted to refer to these infants, presumably on the basis of tremors produced when the umbilical cord is cut and the drug supply stops.

4. The prosecution of drug-using pregnant women has produced unlikely alliances. While Patricia Toth might be expected to take the prosecutors' side, she prefers treatment provided the pregnant drug user takes advantage of it. Otherwise, Toth argues that pregnant women do not have a license to use drugs nor immunity against prosecution as child abusers.

5. See Chasnoff. Studies have not conclusively established the extent of the harm posed by prenatal drug use. Ill effects are not always exhibited by the infant and the effects of poor nutrition and lack of obstetrical care are not emphasized by prosecutors.

6. Pollit discusses the lack of adequate medical care for poor minority women, substandard living conditions, spousal abuse, and poor diet as factors that have significant impact on pregnancy but which legislatures have refused to address.

7. According to a 1985 study on prenatal care in Orlando, Florida, "it's safer for a baby to be born to a drug abusing, anemic or diabetic mother who visits the doctor throughout her pregnancy than to be born to a normal mother who does not" (Paltrow, 1990:8).

REFERENCES

Abraham, Lauris. 1988. "They Cure Their Habits to Save Their Babies: Unique Program Helps Women Stay Off Drugs." *American Medical News* January 8, p. 2, 50–51.

American Public Health Association, n.d. "Legal Brief to *People of the State of Michigan v. Kimberly Hardy.*"

Angel, Carol. 1988. "Addicted Babies: Legal System's Response Unclear." *Los Angeles Daily Journal* February 29, p. 1, 24.

Chasnoff, Ira J. 1990. "The Prevalence of Illicit-Drug or Alcohol Use during Pregnancy and Discrepancies in Mandatory Reporting in Pinellas County, Florida." *New England Journal of Medicine* April: 1202–8.

Chasnoff, Ira J. 1988. "Newborn Infants with Drug Withdrawal Symptom." *Pediatrics in Review* March (9): 273–277.

Chasnoff, Ira J. 1987. "Perinatal Effects of Cocaine." *Contemporary OB/GYN* May: 163–176.

Chasnoff, Ira J., Kayreen Burns, William J. Burns, and Sidney H. Schnoll. 1986. "Prenatal Drug Exposure: Effects on Neonatal and Infant Growth and Development." *Neurobehavioral Toxicology and Teratology* 8:357–362.

Chavkin, Wendy. 1989. Testimony before the House Select Committee on Children, Youth, and Families. U.S. House of Representatives, April 27.

Churchville, Victoria. 1988. "D.C. Judge Jails Women as Protection for Fetus." *Washington Post* July 23, pp. A1, A8.

Curriden, Mark. 1990. "Holding Mom Accountable." *American Bar Association Journal* March: 50–53.

Drucker, Ernest. 1989. "Notes from the Drug Wars." *The International Journal on Drug Policy* 1(4): 10–12.

French, Howard W. 1989. "For Pregnant Addicts: A Clinic of Hope." *New York Times* September 29, p. B1.

Goetz, Ellen, Hilary Fox, and Steve Bates. 1990. "Poor and Pregnant? Don't Go to South Carolina. . . ." ACLU Memorandum: Initial Report on RFP's (Reproductive Freedom Project) Carolina Investigation, February 1.

Kaltenbach, Karol, and Loretta P. Finnegan. 1984. "Developmental Outcome of Children Born to Methadone Maintained Women: A Review of Longitudinal Studies." *Neurobehavioral Toxicology and Teratology* 6: 271–75.

Kolbert, Kathryn, Lynn Paltrow, Ellen Goetz, and Kary Moss. 1990. "Discriminatory Punishment of Pregnant Women." ACLU Memorandum, February 15.

Koren, Gideon, Karen Graham, Heather Shear, and Tom Einarson. 1989. "Bias against the Null Hypothesis: The Reproductive Hazards of Cocaine." *The Lancet* December: 1440–42.

Kusserow, Richard P. 1990. "Crack Babies." U.S. Department of Health and Human Services, Office of the Inspector General, OEI-03-89-01540, June.

McNulty, Mollie. 1988. "Pregnancy Police: The Health Policy and Legal Implications Punishing Pregnant Women for Harm to Their Fetuses." *New York University Review of Law and Social Change* 16: 277–319.

Moss, Kary, and Judy Crockett. 1990. Testimony on Children of Substance Abusers before the U.S. Senate Subcommittee on Children, Family, Drugs and Alcoholism, February 22.

New York Times. 1989. "Trying to Free Children from Shackles of Crime." August 30, p. A9.

Paltrow, Lynn. 1990. "When Becoming Pregnant Is a Crime." *Criminal Justice Ethics* 9 (Winter/ Spring): 41–47.

Paltrow, Lynn, Hilary Fox, and Ellen Goetz. 1990. "State by State Case Summary of Criminal Prosecutions against Pregnant Women." ACLU Memorandum, April 20.

Pollit, Katha. 1990. "Fetal Rights: A New Assault on Feminism." *The Nation* March 16: 409–18.

Potti, Lisa. 1990. Testimony before the House Select Committee on Children, Youth, and Families. U.S. House of Representatives, April 23.

Reagan, D. D., S. M. Ehrlich, and Loretta P. Finnegan. 1987. "Infants of Drug Addiction: At Risk for Abuse Neglect and Placement in Foster Care." *Neurotoxicology and Teratology* 9: 315–377.

Sherman, Rorie. 1989. "Keeping Babies Free from Drugs." *The National Law Journal* October: 1, 28.

State of Oregon. 1985. "Women, Drugs, and Babies." Unpublished survey conducted by the Division of Youth and Family Services.

Teltsch, Kathleen. 1990. "A Drug Recovery Center that Welcomes the Pregnant Addict." *New York Times* March 20, p. A4.

PART TWO

WOMEN VICTIMS OF CRIME

Introduction by A N D R E W   K A R M E N

Acts of male-on-female aggression—especially rapes and batterings, but also sexual molestations of girls, the sexual harassment of women on the street and in the workplace, stalkings, and certain murders—are outgrowths of gender-based conflict. Offenses in which boys and men harm girls and women reflect the antagonisms that arise out of gender-role differences and symbolize the social costs of male domination and female subordination. The plight of victimized girls and women was overlooked for centuries because of institutionalized sexism within the legal system. The way the criminal justice system routinely fails to meet the needs of female crime victims is finally being systematically examined (Rafter and Stanko, 1982; Russell, 1984; Frug, 1992; Muraskin and Alleman, 1993).

However, academic researchers, government policymakers, practitioners in the helping professions, victim advocates, political activists, police administrators, prosecutors, defense attorneys, judges, jurors, students of criminal justice, and members of the public bitterly disagree about the specific causes of and cures for the violence men direct at women. Therefore, the primary contribution of this introduction to the section on the victimization of women will be to provide a framework for classifying the ideological interpretations of the problem (what is wrong) and its possible solutions (what must change).

COMPETING FRAMEWORKS:
(1) VICTIM BLAMING VS.
(2) VICTIM DEFENDING/OFFENDER BLAMING VS.
(3) VICTIM DEFENDING/INSTITUTION BLAMING

Whenever offenders harm victims, whether through property crimes like burglary or auto theft, or in interpersonal acts of violence such as assaults, this question always arises: Who—or what—is to blame? Determining responsibility is an important matter because isolating a "cause" can lead to a "cure." In gender-based crimes, particularly battering and rape (but also sexual harassment, incest, stalking, and murder), three distinct responses can usually be discerned (see Karmen, 1990). The first (and oldest) perspective is *victim blaming*, which faults the injured woman and holds her accountable to a greater or lesser degree for what happened. The second outlook is *victim defending coupled with offender blaming*. It rejects unfounded accusations that it was her fault and insists that the offender alone is fully culpable for the violation of the law. The third (and most complex) approach is *victim defending followed by institution blaming*. It, too, dismisses notions of victim responsibility but then asserts the fundamental sociological insight: that people—offenders as well as their victims—are largely products of their environments, with attitudes and behaviors profoundly shaped by social conditions not of their choosing and beyond their individual abilities to escape or control. This perspective interprets criminal behavior as an outgrowth of basic social institutions (organized ways of accomplishing goals) such as the family, schooling, the job market, and government. The root causes of crime are believed to be the inequities and irrationalities embedded in the prevailing social arrangements: how economic resources are controlled and squandered by the corporate elite and their governmental partners; the way decision-making authority is concentrated; the gender roles and scripts people are pressured to follow; and the norms of contemporary culture that define the limits of acceptable conduct.

The stakes are very high in this three-sided debate, since diagnosing the reasons why men victimize women is a prerequisite for developing effective crime prevention and control strategies. If victim blaming is accepted, then the burden of responsibility falls squarely on women: as vulnerable targets, they must change their ways and take precautions to avoid being harmed by the physically and sexually aggressive men they are sure to encounter. Girls must be taught to watch what they say, how they dress, with whom they associate, and how they act; women must limit their exposure to risky situations and potentially dangerous men.

If the victim-defending/offender-blaming approach is adopted, however, then the injured parties are not at fault. Only the perpetrators—deviant men—are said to be responsible for the male-on-female crime problem. Consequently, this view stresses the importance of asserting formal, legal control over the behavior of known offenders. Rapists, batterers, child molesters, stalkers, and lesbian-bashers must be arrested, prosecuted, convicted, and imprisoned. The solution to the problem is a vigilant and efficient criminal justice system.

But what if key institutions churn out generation after generation of exploiters and abusers? Then the roots of the problem lie much deeper in the very structure of society. The offender-blaming strategy of relying on the machinery of criminal justice to incapacitate and rehabilitate dangerous "deviants" one case at a time seems too little too late. Furthermore, to count on the largely male leadership (of legislatures, the police, prosecutors' offices, the judiciary, and prisons) to protect women from men is a strategy doomed to failure. The victim-blaming strategy of pressuring women to take precautions to thwart the intentions of predatory men also appears to be a mere stopgap measure. If institution blaming makes sense, it follows that sweeping changes are necessary: genuine equality that permits individual autonomy must replace traditional mechanisms of patriarchal control; blatant and subtle mechanisms of discrimination against those of the "wrong" races and social classes must be overcome; and women and men must help raise boys and girls to think about and act toward one another in entirely new ways. The feminist dictum that "the personal is political" sums up this outlook: the particular troubles and traumas individual women experience in their everyday lives are concrete manifestations of more abstract and general social problems afflicting millions of women; hence, the victimization of women can be alleviated only by a social movement struggling on many fronts to overhaul contemporary society's basic institutions.

Blaming Victims for Their Plight

As a mode of thought, victim blaming proceeds by scrutinizing the victim's actions right before and during the incident. Often it becomes "obvious"—in hindsight—what she should have said and ought to have done to avoid being sexually harassed, stalked, battered, raped, even murdered. Victim blaming rests on a doctrine of individual responsibility that holds everyone—victims as well as offenders—personally accountable for their actions.

Charges about the degree to which victims share responsibility with offenders for crimes can vary, from mere facilitation (making the offender's tasks easier to accomplish), through precipitation (singling out one-self for trouble through reckless or careless actions), to outright provocation (inciting or instigating male violence).

Condemning Rape Victims Victim-blaming viewpoints assume that there are "certain kinds" of women who go around "asking for trouble" and ultimately "get themselves raped." Such harsh condemnations rest on two premises: that the offender was overwhelmed by sexual desire and lost his self-control, and that the victim facilitated (perhaps through drugs or alcohol), precipitated (by setting up a temptation-opportunity situation), or even provoked (by suggestive and seductive words or deeds) the man's forceful response (Gibbs, 1991). Victim blaming chastises women who suffer sexual assaults for acts of omission (not being cautious) as well as acts of commission (like hitchhiking) (Amir, 1971). Sometimes the woman's mental health is questioned, with accusations that she secretly harbored fantasies of being taken against her will (MacDonald, 1971). The victim-blaming interpretation of date rape characterizes the incident as a "terrible misunderstanding" in "he said–she said" terms: he says she wanted to, while she says he forced her. Miscommunication results when a woman fails to protest vehemently enough about unwanted sexual advances, a common problem during this period of rapid change in courtship rituals, sexual mores, and the rules of the "dating game" (Warshaw, 1988; Muelenhard et al., 1992).

The victim-blaming approach places the burden of rape prevention squarely on the backs of potential victims; they must take precautions to reduce the risks they face by imposing strict limits upon themselves in terms of those with whom they interact, how they dress, what they say, and where and when they travel. They must continue to observe the old-fashioned "dos and don'ts" restrictions of defensive dating (Brownmiller, 1975).

Castigating Battered Women Victim-blaming arguments proceed from the assumption that a battered woman must have done something to infuriate her lover and provoke his wrath. Perhaps she arouses his anger by her assertive actions, or she invites abuse by her submissiveness. Maybe she knowingly starts fights, or she unconsciously enjoys suffering. Some criticize her if she "breaks up" the family by "deserting" him, while others disapprove if she doesn't leave him (Walker, 1984; Pagelow, 1984; Frieze and Browne, 1989).

If the cycle of violence spirals upward and a battered woman kills her mate, victim-blaming accusations escalate as well. The victim is condemned for turning the tables, reversing roles, and transforming into a vigilante, appointing herself as judge, jury, and executioner. She is denounced for not exhausting all other options (having him arrested, getting an order of protection from the courts, fleeing their home to escape his clutches) before resorting to deadly force. Her violence cannot be excused and must be punished (Jones, 1980; Saunders, 1986; Walker, 1989).

Defending Victims from Charges that They Are Partly to Blame

Victim defending regards victim blaming as a pernicious ideology that adds insult to injury: it is a validation of the offender's point of view because it shifts the burden of responsibility from the perpetrator to the target. Victim defending seeks to expose the falseness and unfairness of accusations of victim facilitation, cooperation, precipitation, escalation, or provocation. Whatever happened was not the victim's fault in any legal or moral sense. [After this, victim defending evolves into either offender blaming (not discussed here) or institution blaming (summarized below).]

Clearing the Reputation of Rape Victims   The victim-defending perspective developed in the early 1970s as antirape activists challenged the widely held traditional view that sexual assaults were outpourings of uncontrollable lust stimulated knowingly or unwittingly by the victim's behavior. Sexual assaults were reinterpreted as outbursts of aggression, hatred, and contempt, motivated by a desire to dominate, subjugate, and humiliate. Nothing "suggestive" or "erotic" that the victim did, said, or wore could provoke or justify such hostile and degrading reactions from a complete stranger or an acquaintance (Russell, 1975; Clark and Lewis, 1978; Griffin, 1979).

As for date rapes, victim defending asserts that whenever forced intercourse occurs, a "real rape" has been committed and not a "seduction" as the culmination of a "romantic" courtship ritual. The boy or man has used coercion to "take" from her what he wanted and planned to "get" all along, violating her personhood in the process (Estrich, 1986; La Free, 1989). Further, any silence or a lack of physical resistance on her part was not a sign of apparent acquiescence, because that interpretation overlooks the paralyzing effects of the aggressor's overwhelming physical strength, his possible use of force at the outset, his tactics that caught the victim by surprise, or the implied threat of a weapon (Estrich, 1986; La Free, 1989; Caringella-MacDonald and Humphries, 1991).

Understanding Battered Women   Victim defending assumes that a husband's violence is really not triggered by his wife's shortcomings or instigations. His attempts to pin responsibility on her "provocations" are just rationalizations designed to justify and excuse his behavior. Her apparent resignation to his repeated assaults, irrational as it might seem, makes sense when the "battered woman's syndrome" is understood as a type of learned helplessness leading to post-traumatic stress disorder (Walker, 1984). This syndrome is only now becoming allowed in some court proceedings (Sargeant, 1991).

Victim defending provides a number of reasons why battered women stay with their abusive mates: they still love their partners and cling to the belief that their men can and will change, as they often promise to do; they feel trapped (economically dependent and socially isolated); they worry about their children's welfare (emotional damage, loss of support, loss of custody); they are burdened by guilt and shame because of cultural and religious exhortations against "abandoning a husband" in a "failed marriage"; and they are intimidated by men with a jealously possessive "you belong to me" mentality who threaten severe reprisals if they dare to try to escape. They often do not call the police during a beating because they have been raised to believe that their troubles are a personal matter and that the police would not want to be bothered. When officers are called to the scene, they might side with the man, arrest both parties, pressure the woman to leave, or insist that she seek professional help and marital counseling (Frieze and Browne, 1989; Barnett and LaViolette, 1993; Browne, Chapter 13 in this volume).

In those rare instances in which a battered woman kills her abusive mate, the victim-defending perspective identifies with the survivor and charges that the dead husband brought about his own demise. She had turned to the criminal justice system, but either it was unresponsive or its services (arrest, prosecution, conviction, punishment, compulsory treatment, order of protection) failed to stem the spiraling violence. She tried to escape, but he tracked her down and became even angrier with her. She lived in constant fear, even when she was not under immediate attack, and eventually committed a justifiable homicide in self-defense (Jones, 1980; Browne, 1987; Walker, 1989; Bannister, 1992).

The Institutional Roots of Crimes by Males against Females

From the institution-blaming standpoint, both victim blaming and victim defending/offender blaming are nearsighted approaches that focus too closely on the two leading actors in the drama, and in so doing, overlook the broader social context that influences their interactions, and countless others like them. Freedom of action, individual responsibility, and personal accountability do exist but are constrained by larger political, economic, and sociocultural forces. Although the "facts" surrounding each crime are important, and it is worthwhile to try to reconstruct the motives and responses of both parties, such a limited interactionist approach fails to grasp the influences of key social institutions. Instead of putting either the criminal or the victim specifically "on trial," institution blaming indicts the "system," particularly as it relates to male dominance and control in a racist capitalist patriarchy: inequities in the distribution of power and wealth; intense competition over scarce resources and desirable jobs; inequities between men and women in all spheres of life; the institution of marriage and the social isolation of nuclear families; harmful child-rearing practices; discriminatory mechanisms based on class, race, and gender; oppressive cultural traditions; and outmoded religious teachings. This analytical framework condemns existing inequalities and injustices, "what exists," and points to "what ought to be."

Underpinnings of Woman Battering The institution-blaming perspective rejects attempts to pathologize violence within romantic relationships (as a problem for a small number of emotionally unstable couples who need marriage counseling) or to normalize it (as an inevitable expression of conflict that arises in nearly all families under stress). The problem is often traced back to the traditional prescribed roles of "husband" and "wife," which place the two parties on a collision course. The unjust division of domestic labor into dominant and submissive roles, with its male prerogatives and wifely duties, sows the seeds of potential conflict. The patriarchal "head of the household" may resort to physical force as a means of maintaining "order" and control when his "subordinate" challenges his "rightful authority." In fact, the "rule of thumb" allowed a husband to beat his wife so long as he did not use a stick wider than his thumb. Although the law no longer grants a husband his former privilege of "domestic chastisement" ("disciplining his wife as he sees fit"—within "reasonable" limits, of course), a cultural legacy remains that encourages men to think of a marriage license as a hitting license. That ideology is best summed up by the well-known marriage vow, sanctioned by religion and the state, that a wife should love, honor, and obey her husband (Dobash and Dobash, 1977; Straus, Gelles, and Steinmetz, 1980). The ideology of patriarchy bestows upon the "protector" and "provider" a small compensation-domination over his wife and children—as a substitute for real autonomy or economic and political clout (Schechter, 1982). Women serve as convenient scapegoats and targets for displaced male anger (Klein, 1981).

The cycle of violence that mars so many intimate relations persists from generation to generation for two main reasons: socialization (boys and girls are raised to expect and accept male aggression and female passivity) and economic dependency (limited job opportunities and lower incomes force wives to rely on husbands to support them and their children) (Rhode, 1989).

Cultural Supports for Rape An institutional analysis of the root causes of rape proceeds from the realization that in a market economy, sexual satisfaction has been transformed into a commodity to be bought, sold, bargained over, and sometimes stolen or taken (Clark and Lewis, 1978). Furthermore, in contemporary American culture, the intertwining of sex and violence has become eroticized, not only in hard-core pornography but also in other forms of entertainment, advertising, and popular music (Lederer, 1980).

Recognizing that acquaintance rape is much more common than stranger rape (although it is reported far less often to the authorities), the institution-blaming approach rejects psychopathological explanations that view forced sex as a rare transgression perpetrated only by mentally disturbed men. The social roots of date rape lie in the unequal power relationships and differing expectations that men and women bring to courtship. Young men expect a "return on their investment" of time and money, and young women, by accepting the terms of the date, implicitly accept that "bargain." Her reneging at the end can provoke his wrath (Gibbs, 1991). On college campuses, fraternities and athletic teams promote a notion of brotherhood that extols a narrow, macho definition of masculinity which demeans and mocks "femininity." Young women are viewed as sex objects, prey, or pawns in a game or contest (Martin and Hummer, 1989).

Institution blaming goes beyond a social learning or socialization explanation: boys are taught that to be "masculine" means to be sexually aggressive and exploitive; girls are brought up to be passively receptive, expecting and accepting abuse, and blaming themselves when it happens. These are stubbornly entrenched cultural traditions that still dichotomize all young women as either virtuous "good girls" who deserve chivalrous treatment or promiscuous "bad girls" who are fair game for manipulation, exploitation, and even violation. This stereotypic imagery with its crude labels "virgin" and "whore" is used to justify a lingering double standard in the way rape victims are treated, long after the so-called sexual revolution of the 1960s (Russell, 1975; Benedict, 1992).

An institution-based analysis concludes with the observation that the threat of being forced to submit to a sexual assault serves to deter females from being fully active in all aspects of daily life. The message is: "Don't step out of line! Accept your lot in life!" The future of patriarchal control is assured as long as women are compelled to seek the protection of "trustworthy" men to safeguard them from other, more threatening men (Klein, 1981; Muelenhard et al., 1992). The incidence of sexual assaults will diminish only when men reject traditional patriarchal norms and no longer believe they benefit from oppressing the females in their lives; men are no longer provided greater material conditions of power, wealth, and dominance; children are no longer subjected to rigid sex role socialization; people grow intolerant of misogynist themes in popular culture; and males (especially in fraternities, organized sports, the military, and other bastions of "masculinity") are educated to accept "No!" as an answer (Sorenson and White, 1992; Buchwald, Fletcher, and Roth, 1993).

REFORMING THE CRIMINAL JUSTICE SYSTEM

Victim blaming advocates risk reduction measures women must take to avoid dangerous situations. *Institution blaming* emphasizes the need for collective political action to eradicate the social, cultural, and economic conditions that breed male-on-female crime and produce generation after generation of abusers and exploiters. *Victim defending/offender blaming* stresses the importance of swift and sure criminal justice responses to outbreaks of male violence. From this perspective, men found guilty of offenses against women must be imprisoned to prevent them from striking again (incapacitation); to make an example of them to serve as a warning to other would-be perpetrators contemplating similar crimes (general deterrence); to teach them a lesson so they stifle any urges to harm females again (specific deterrence); and to compel these husbands, boyfriends, brothers, fathers, and would-be lovers to undergo treatment until they no longer pose a threat to the girls and women in their lives (rehabilitation).

Turning to the police, courts, and prisons for redress may be necessary, but it is not a sufficient response, according to the *institution-blaming* perspective. Historically, the criminal justice system itself has been part of the problem rather than part of the solution. Most perpetrators of crimes against women are never arrested or prosecuted, and certainly not convicted. Case processing is routinely infected by discriminatory tendencies against minorities and the poor and by built-in biases against female victims. Relying on state intervention is a particularly ineffective and unreliable strategy of protection and prevention for poor women of color. Attempts to "get tough" with rapists or wife beaters are more likely to lead to punitive crackdowns against poor men, immigrant groups, and minority communities; efforts to treat victims better are prone to favor "respectable" affluent white women. Equal protection under the law remains an elusive goal (Klein, 1981; Caringella-MacDonald and Humphries, 1991; Wyatt, 1992; also see chapters in this volume, especially Chapter 14, by Rasche, and Chapter 12, by Matthews.)

Over the centuries, the men at the helm of state legislatures, police departments, prosecutors' offices, defense attorneys' associations, the judiciary, and correctional agencies have not assigned a high priority to the well-being of women when they crafted laws, implemented policies, and evaluated their operations (Rafter, 1990). Even though it is vital to understand the need for sweeping institutional changes in the long run, a strategy of empowerment can help victims in the short run. To improve the chances that the needs and wants of female victims might be better addressed, antirape and antibattering activists are pursuing a strategy of empowerment to enable victims to act in defense of what they perceive to be their own best interests. Empowerment facilitates the transformation from victims to survivors (people who have put the worst behind them and are ready to move forward into the next phase of their lives). Empowerment within criminal justice means having a say or voice in crucial decisions concerning arrest and prosecution, all the way to restitution and parole.

Treating Battering as a Crime

In the not-too-distant past, the criminal justice system was clearly part of the problem rather than part of the solution because of its failure to intervene in behalf of battered women. Long-standing legal traditions about the sanctity of family life held that "lovers' quarrels" and "domestic disturbances" were not "real crimes" and therefore not the law's business (Yllo and Bograd, 1988; Dobash and Dobash, 1977; Buzawa and Buzawa, 1992).

But when a battered-women's movement arose, police departments and district attorneys were criticized (and sued) for failing to protect victims of repeated beatings who wound up in hospitals—or even morgues. Judges were condemned for routinely handing down lenient sentences to batterers and for issuing orders of protection that were not seriously enforced (Hilton, 1993; Ferraro, Chapter 15 in this volume). During the late 1980s, proarrest policies were adopted in a number of jurisdictions after a widely publicized policing experiment (Sherman and Berk, 1984) suggested that punishment seemed to have a specific deterrent effect (i.e., the men learned a lesson). But the conventional wisdom of routinely arresting batterers was questioned in the early 1990s when other studies failed to replicate the reported lower recidivism rate and even indicated that unemployed and unmarried men were more likely to get violent again with their partners if they were arrested (Sherman and Smith, 1992). Clearly, the institutions of the economy and the family are generating problems that criminal justice responses alone cannot satisfactorily resolve.

To enable women caught in abusive situations to exercise additional options so they wouldn't feel so helpless or trapped, the battered-women's support movement started to set up shelters in the early 1970s. These "safe houses" provide peer support groups, counseling, opportunities to improve educational credentials, job training, housing assistance, and legal advice (around such issues as divorce, child custody, and child support) (Schechter, 1982).

Toward Justice for Rape Victims

Although rape has been recognized as a serious crime for hundreds of years, the victims' plight was largely ignored until the antirape movement focused on their suffering in the early 1970s. Historically, rapes were seen as threats to male interests—of fathers who wanted to safeguard the market value of their virgin daughters against those who would "defile" and "devalue" them; of husbands who wanted to protect the honor of their wives, who would be stigmatized as "fallen" women if they were "despoiled," as well as to preserve the clarity of patrilineal arrangements for inheritance; and of whole groups of powerful men who wanted to keep "their women" off-limits to outsiders and subordinates (Brownmiller, 1975).

Antirape activists have tried to eliminate the double standard and to ensure that all rapes are taken seriously: not only attacks by strangers on girls and married women—or, worse yet, just violations of white women by black men (Wyatt, 1992)—but all kinds of sexual assaults, including by husbands against their wives (Finkelhor and Yllo, 1985).

Historically, victims who dared to invoke the machinery of justice ostensibly set up to serve them found that the legal system put them on trial and demanded that they prove their innocence. Victims were deterred from pressing charges by the initial skepticism of detectives that their complaints were "unfounded"; by the reluctance of prosecutors to hold trials; by the high acquittal rates reflecting jurors' prejudices; by the relatively low conviction rates compared with such rates for other violent crimes; and by the low incarceration rates, short sentences, and early releases from confinement, mirroring the disparaging attitudes of judges and parole boards.

To make the system more accountable, activists have organized rape crisis centers that dispatch advocates to accompany victims through the criminal justice process; self-help groups of survivors who offer support; watchdog projects that track the outcomes of cases and monitor how victims are handled; clearinghouses on date rape and marital rape that raise public awareness about the depth of these problems; outreach groups that carry out educational campaigns like "Take Back the Night" marches and date rape prevention programs on college campuses; and political coalitions to lobby for better police training and legal reforms.

The laws prohibiting rape and governing the handling of accusations have been rewritten in most states since the 1970s. New statutes are supposed to remove unfair requirements of corroboration of the complainant's charge and proof of her vehement resistance; to guarantee the confidentiality of personal information victims share with their counselors; to shield complainants from degrading cross-examinations about their past sexual experiences by defense attorneys during trials (unless such testimony is deemed relevant by the judge); and to end the automatic immunity from prosecution previously extended to husbands. Criminologists and victimologists who have evaluated the impact of new state laws intended to improve the way the system handles rape cases have found mixed results. There are some indications that reporting, arrest, prosecution, and conviction rates have gone up. However, most rapes still go unreported and unsolved, charges are still substantially reduced during plea negotiations, conviction rates remain low, and sentences continue to be light. The credibility of complainants is still routinely challenged, and the same questions surrounding corroboration, resistance, and the admissibility of testimony about past sexual relationships continue to undermine the victims' search for justice (Polk, 1985; Caringella-MacDonald and Humphries, 1991).

OVERVIEW OF THE ARTICLES IN PART TWO

The articles in this section examine the many ways that males can victimize females: men sexually harassing women at work and lesbians on the streets, fathers sexually abusing their daughters, husbands and boyfriends beating up the women they profess to love, rapists forcing themselves on girls and women whom they regard as mere objects, and men killing women primarily because they are members of the despised "opposite sex."

All the articles present arguments that can be identified as victim-blaming, victim-defending, or institution-blaming. Scully (Chapter 11) points out numerous limitations of victim blaming as well as offender blaming concerning cases of rape. She argues in favor of a sociocultural and structural analysis of the causes of rape. As for victim defending, Browne (Chapter 13) examines in depth why some battered women are driven to kill their tormentors. Her explanations focus on the level of threat and violence posed by the men rather than on the mental states of the women themselves. Gordon (Chapter 17) casts doubt on the accusation that generations ago some daughters passively acquiesced to their fathers' sexual demands. Rather, as Arnold (Chapter 8 in this volume) argued, the victimization of young (in Arnold's case, black) girls is rooted in the social inequality that arises from socially structured distinctions based on race, class, and gender. MacKinnon (Chapter 18) defends sexual harassment victims from charges that they either imagined or encouraged unwanted advances.

As for institution blaming, the cultural and structural underpinnings that encourage male sexual violence are exposed by Scully (Chapter 11) in her analysis of rape, as well as by Caputi and Russell (Chapter 16), who view hate-motivated attacks on women by men as "sexual terrorism" and murder as "femicide." Gordon (Chapter 17) traces the roots of incestuous exploitation back to the patriarchal family. Robson (Chapter 20) argues that attacks on lesbians result from an oppressive social control system of legally enforced, male-defined heterosexuality. And Ferraro (Chapter 15) concludes that the criminal justice system has a limited effect on curbing woman battering because spouse abuse is rooted in the social order and its systems of inequality; the criminal justice system actually reinforces the patriarchal order by merely punishing the most egregious offenders. Finally, racist as well as sexist structures of control impinge on women from different racial/ethnic backgrounds in a number of ways. Matthews (Chapter 12) traces the impact of discrimination on victims of rape, Rasche (Chapter 14) on battered women, and MacKinnon (Chapter 18, see abstract) on women who endure sexual harassment.

Several articles emphasize the need to continue reforming the criminal justice system as part of a larger project for social change. Ferraro (Chapter 15) exposes the limitations in the ways the police and prosecutors respond to calls for help by battered women. Robson (Chapter 20) notes that even though unprovoked "gay-bashing" attacks are "hate crimes" that are supposed to carry extra penalties in some jurisdictions, lesbian complainants receive second-class treatment. Focusing on the persistence of racial discrimination, Rasche (Chapter 14) highlights the special problems faced by battered women from minority groups, while Matthews (Chapter 12) describes the special solutions devised by African-American rape victims.

The upcoming articles emphasize the need for victims and their allies to organize and work together to change the social conditions that breed violence against women. Empowering victims within and beyond the criminal justice system, so that they can pursue their own best interests while reforming key social institutions, is a strategy endorsed by all the authors, especially Matthews (Chapter 12), Gordon (Chapter 17), and Robson (Chapter 20). The authors in this section also understand that immediate reforms, while absolutely necessary, are not sufficient. Sweeping changes that touch the lives of *all* women—poor, minority, and lesbian, as well as affluent, majority, and heterosexual—require a fundamental transformation in class, race, and gender relationships throughout the major institutional pillars of society.

REFERENCES

Amir, M. 1971. *Patterns in Forcible Rape.* Chicago: University of Chicago.

Bannister, S. 1992. "Battered Women Who Kill Their Abusers: Their Courtroom Battles." In R. Muraskin and T. Alleman (eds.), *It's a Crime: Women and Justice.* Englewood Cliffs, N.J.: Regents/Prentice-Hall, pp. 316–333.

Barnett, O., and A. LaViolette. 1993. *It Could Happen to Anyone: Why Battered Women Stay.* Newbury Park, Calif.: Sage.

Benedict, H. 1992. *Virgin or Vamp: How the Press Covers Sex Crimes.* New York: Oxford University.

Browne, A. 1987. *When Battered Women Kill.* New York: Free Press.

Brownmiller, S. 1975. *Against Our Will: Men, Women, and Rape.* New York: Simon and Schuster.

Buchwald, E., P. Fletcher, and M. Roth. 1993. *Transforming a Rape Culture.* Minneapolis: Milkwood Editions.

Buzawa, E., and C. Buzawa. 1992. *Domestic Violence: The Changing Criminal Justice Response.* Westport, Conn.: Greenwood.

Caringella-MacDonald, S. 1988. "Parallels and Pitfalls: The Aftermath of Legal Reform for Sexual Assault, Marital Rape, and Domestic Violence Victims." *Journal of Interpersonal Violence* 3, 2: 174–189.

———— and D. Humphries. 1991. "Sexual Assault, Women, and the Community: Organizing to Prevent Sexual Violence." In H. Pepinsky and R.

Quinney (eds.), *Criminology as Peacemaking.* Indianapolis: Indiana University, pp. 98–113.

Chappell, D., R. Geis, and G. Geis (eds.). 1977. *Forcible Rape—The Crime, the Victim, and the Offender.* New York: Columbia University.

Clark, L., and D. Lewis. 1978. *Rape: The Price of Coercive Sexuality.* Toronto: The Woman's Press.

Dobash, R. E., and R. P. Dobash. 1977. "Love, Honor, and Obey: Institutional Ideologies and the Struggle for Battered Women." *Contemporary Crises* 1 (June–July): 403–415.

Dobash, R. P., and R. E. Dobash. 1979. *Violence against Wives: The Case against Patriarchy.* New York: Free Press.

Elias, R. 1986. *The Politics of Victimization: Victims, Victimology and Human Rights.* New York: Oxford University.

Estrich, S. 1986. *Real Rape.* Cambridge, Mass.: Harvard University.

Finkelhor, D., and K. Yllo. 1985. *License to Rape: Sexual Abuse of Wives.* New York: Holt, Rinehart and Winston.

Frieze, I., and A. Browne. 1989. "Violence in Marriage." In L. Ohlin and M. Tonry (eds.), *Crime and Justice: An Annual Review of Research,* vol. 10, pp. 163–218. Chicago: University of Chicago.

Frug, M. 1992. *Women and the Law.* Westbury, N.Y.: Foundation.

Gibbs, N. 1991. "When Is It Rape?" *Time Magazine* (June 3): 48–55.

Gillespie, C. 1989. *Battered Women, Self-Defense, and the Law.* Columbus: Ohio State University.

Goldberg-Ambrose, C. 1992. "Unfinished Business in Rape Law Reform." *Journal of Social Issues* 48, 1: 173–185.

Griffin, S. 1979. *Rape: The Power of Consciousness.* New York: Harper and Row.

Hilton, N. 1993. *Legal Responses to Wife Assault.* Newbury Park, Calif.: Sage.

Humphries, D., and S. Caringella-MacDonald. "Murdered Mothers, Missing Wives: Reconsidering Female Victimization." *Social Justice* 17, 2: 71–89.

Jones, A. 1980. *Women Who Kill.* New York: Holt, Rinehart and Winston.

Karmen, A. 1990. *Crime Victims: An Introduction to Victimology,* 2d ed. Pacific Grove, Calif.: Brooks/Cole.

Klein, D. 1981. "Violence against Women: Some Considerations Regarding Its Causes and Elimination." *Crime and Delinquency* 27, 1: 64–79.

La Free, G. 1989. *Rape and Criminal Justice.* Santa Fe: University of New Mexico.

Largen, M. 1981. "Grassroots Centers and National Task Forces: A Herstory of the Anti-rape Movement." *Aegis* 32 (Autumn): 46–52.

———. 1987. "A Decade of Change in the Rape Reform Movement." *Response* 10, 2: 4–9.

Lederer, L. 1980. *Take Back the Night.* New York: Morrow.

LeGrande, C. 1973. "Rape and Rape Laws: Sexism in Society and the Law." *California Law Review* 61: 919–941.

MacDonald, J. 1971. *Rape: Offenders and Victims.* Springfield, Ill.: Charles C. Thomas.

Marsh, J., A. Geist, and N. Caplan. 1982. *Rape and the Limits of Law Reform.* Boston: Auburn House.

Martin, D. 1976. *Battered Wives.* San Francisco: Glide.

Martin, P., and R. Hummer. 1989. "Fraternities and Rape on Campus." *Gender and Society* 3 (December): 457–473.

Muelenhard, C., I. Powch, J. Phelps, and L. Giusti. 1992. "Definitions of Rape: Scientific and Political Implications." *Journal of Social Issues* 48, 1: 23–44.

Muraskin, R., and T. Alleman (eds.). 1993. *It's a Crime: Women and Justice.* Englewood Cliffs, N.J.: Prentice-Hall.

Pagelow, M. 1984. *Women-Battering: Victims and Their Experiences.* Beverly Hills: Sage.

Polk, K. 1985. "Rape Reform and Criminal Justice Processing." *Crime and Delinquency* 31: 191–205.

Rafter, N. 1990. "The Social Construction of Crime and Crime Control." *Journal of Research in Crime and Delinquency* 27, 4: 376–389.

——— and E. Stanko (eds.). 1982. *Judge, Lawyer, Victim, and Thief: Women, Gender Roles, and Criminal Justice.* Boston: Northeastern University.

Rhode, D. 1989. *Justice and Gender: Sex Discrimination and the Law.* Cambridge, Mass.: Harvard University.

Russell, D. 1975. *The Politics of Rape: The Victim's Perspective.* New York: Stein and Day.

———. 1982. *Rape in Marriage.* New York: Macmillan.

———. 1984. *Sexual Exploitation: Rape, Child Molestation, and Workplace Harassment.* Newbury Park, Calif.: Sage.

Sargeant, G. 1991. "Battered Woman Syndrome Gaining Legal Recognition." *Trial* 27, 4: 17–20.

Saunders, D. 1986. "When Battered Women Use Violence: Husband Abuse or Self-defense?" *Victims and Violence* 1, 1: 47–60.

Schechter, S. 1982. *Women and Male Violence.* Boston: South End.

Schwendinger, H., and J. Schwendinger. 1983. *Rape and Inequality.* Beverly Hills: Sage.

Sherman, L., and R. Berk. 1984. "The Specific Deterrent Effects of Arrest for Domestic Assault." *American Sociological Review* 49 (April): 261–272.

——— and D. Smith. 1992. "Crime, Punishment, and Stake in Conformity: Legal and Informal Control of Domestic Violence." *American Sociological Review* 57 (October): 680–690.

Sorenson, S., and J. White. 1992. "Adult Sexual Assault: Overview of Research." *Journal of Social Issues* 48, 1: 1–8.

Straus, M., R. Gelles, and S. Steinmetz. 1980. *Behind Closed Doors: Violence in the American Family.* New York: Doubleday.

Walker, L. 1984. *The Battered Woman Syndrome.* New York: Springer.

————. 1989. *Terrifying Love: Why Battered Women Kill and How Society Responds*. New York: Harper and Row.

Warshaw, R. 1988. *I Never Called It Rape*. New York: Harper and Row.

Wyatt, G. 1992. "The Sociocultural Context of African American and White American Women's Rape." *Journal of Social Issues* 48, 1: 77–91.

Yllo, K., and M. Bograd. (eds.). 1988. *Feminist Perspectives on Wife Abuse*. Newbury Park, Calif.: Sage.

CHAPTER 11

RAPE IS THE PROBLEM

DIANA SCULLY

ABSTRACT

Rape is a brutal act of violence against women whereby men use sex to intimidate, dominate, and control women. Historically, rape has been understood as a crime of one man against another man's property—his woman. In the past, the fact that a human being, a woman, was brutally victimized was not the issue before the law. But today, the women's movement and feminist consciousness have invalidated that legal perspective and led to our understanding rape as a multifaceted crime that occurs not only between strangers but also between acquaintances, dates, and marital partners.

Despite these changes in consciousness, the frightening frequency of sexual violence in the United States (the FBI estimates that a woman is raped every minute of every day) leads Scully to examine in this chapter several different commonly held explanations of rape: men's irresistible impulse, male disease or psychopathology, and victim precipitation by women. She contrasts these with developing feminist theory.

Scully maintains that the medical model, viewing rape as a disease involving mental illness and/or uncontrollable sexual impulse, is an inadequate theory not supported by research findings. Another theory, that of victim precipitation, holds that women consciously or unconsciously cause their own rape to occur either through acts of commission (e.g., agreeing to drink or to ride with a stranger) or through acts of omission (e.g., failing to react "strongly enough" to sexual suggestions). Scully identifies several problems with this perspective and claims that sexual crimes are the only ones in which the victims are seriously accused of causing the crimes committed against them.

Scully argues that impulse, disease, and victim precipitation theories provide a rationalization for male sexual aggression, absolve the offender of his behavior, shift the responsibility of rape onto the victim, cast sexually violent men as outside the realm of "normal" male behavior, and look for the causes of complex social problems within the individual—ignoring cultural and structural contexts within which rape occurs.

In contrast to these commonly held explanations, Scully describes feminist theory that explains sexual aggression, including rape (an extreme form of sexual abuse), as linked to cultural and structural conditions in society. These conditions include unequal power relationships between men and women, women's disadvantaged social and economic status relative to that of men, and the overall level of violence in society. Feminist theory holds that rape, as socially learned behavior, is an *extension* of normal male behavior and, therefore, is not "pathological." Various legal, religious, and social definitions of women as inferior and men as superior and normally sexually aggressive combine to create a culture in which violence is used to preserve male dominance.

Discuss the relative strengths and weaknesses of the different theoretical explanations of rape presented by Scully. How would acceptance of any one of these theories guide the development of preventive strategies? What implications would these strategies have for both rape victims and rapists? Which theory helps you most to understand and eliminate rape in our society?

Sunny afternoon
chase away my blues
start me thinking
of the times
I spent with you
Summer days
the midnight waves . . .
I'M GOING TO RAPE YOU
going to ripe [sic] off you dress
make your life a mess
I'M GOING TO RAPE YOU
In the ally [sic] by the store
I'll be waiting at the door
I'M GOING TO RAPE YOU
turn you into a little whore
when I'm done you'll beg for more
I'M GOING TO . . .
I'M GOING TO RAPE YOUR BODY . . . YOUR MIND . . .
YOUR SOUL
No one will claim they knew ya
even your husband
I'M GOING TO RAPE YOU
—Anonymous, *found pasted on a storefront*

RAPE AS WOMEN'S PROBLEM

Sparked by the efforts of concerned women, during the decade of the 1970s, rape was "discovered." This period witnessed heightened media attention to the victimization of women as well as a growing body of rape literature in both the popular and the scholarly press. Women's groups mobilized to educate the public and to assist the victims of rape. A number of states yielded to the pressure of the women's movement and revised rape statutes that had been insensitive to the rights of rape victims. In Washington, D.C., a national center, established and funded by Congress, was mandated to direct efforts toward the prevention and control of rape. Indeed, a serious social problem, no stranger to women, had been identified. Yet, despite this enlightenment and the passing of two decades, rape remains firmly embedded in the public regard as a "women's problem."

Rape, of course, is a serious problem for women. Johnson (1980) employed life-table analysis to calculate the lifetime risk of rape to females aged 12 and over.[1] Excluding sexual abuse in marriage and assuming all women are equally at risk,[2] if rape rates remain unchanged, Johnson conservatively estimates that 20 to 30 percent of girls now 12 years old will suffer a violent sexual attack during the remainder of their lives. Although Johnson's estimate has been criticized as too high (Gollin 1980), another recent prediction, based on an independent data source, suggests his estimate may be accurate. Again, assuming no future change in rape rates, Russell and Howell (1983) estimate that there is at least a 26 percent probability that a woman living in San Francisco will become the victim of a completed rape at some time in her life

(see also Russell 1982). Additionally, they estimate there is a 46 percent probability that she will be victimized by a completed rape or attempted rape during her lifetime.[3]

These estimates, which demonstrate the frightening frequency of sexual violence in the United States, suggest that a critical examination of popular explanations for rape is in order. Johnson (1980) makes a similar observation as he questions how responsibility for such a common occurrence can rest solely with a "small lunatic fringe of psychopathic men." Instead, he argues, "the numbers reiterate a reality that American women have lived with for years: sexual violence against women is part of the everyday fabric of American life" (p. 146).

The research reported here also challenges the assumption that individual psychopathology is the predisposing factor that best explains the majority of sexual violence against women. Instead, the position taken here is that psychopathology, or the "disease" model, is too limited an explanation, which, by focusing on "sickness," ignores ample evidence that links sexual aggression to cultural factors and suggests that rape, like all behavior, is learned and, from the actors' perspective, serves a purpose. This is important because the disease model has retarded efforts to arrive at a general explanation for sexual violence and, ultimately, has narrowed our perception of rape to that of a "women's problem" to avoid rather than a "men's problem" to end.

THE MEDICALIZATION OF RAPE

Rape is only one of several social problems (like alcoholism, drug use, and gambling) that has been medicalized over the past several decades (for example, see Conrad and Schneider 1980). Indeed, in the case of rape, psychiatry dominated the literature for 50 years. Because members of the medical profession

Diana Scully, "Rape Is the Problem," *Understanding Sexual Violence*, Routledge, New York, 1990, pp. 33–61.

are widely regarded as experts, they have been relatively free to define problems, like rape, from their own perspective. As behaviors like rape came to be viewed as caused by disease—that is, as having origins in biogenic factors—medicine increasingly came to be viewed as the legitimate agent of social control. Thus, the medical profession acquired the power to designate appropriate treatments and interventions that also depended on medicine for implementation. The rise of sexual psychopathy legislation is a good example of the general trend toward the medicalization of deviant behavior.

By 1965, under the influence of psychiatry, 30 states and the District of Columbia had sexual psychopath laws, which generally define a rapist in sexual terms as "a person unable to control his sexual impulse or having to commit sex crimes" (Bowman and Engle 1965). As the expert on sexual psychopathy, psychiatry became an integral part of the legal process. However, critics argue that the sexual psychopath designation "subsumes a long, broadly descriptive list of personality traits and is not a specific diagnostic label based on scientific data" (Bowman and Engle 1965, 766). They point out that legal definitions mixed with psychiatric terms have proven to be administratively ineffective. Research has demonstrated, for example, that individuals who would be defined as having more serious emotional disturbances quite often commit minor offenses, and vice versa (Ellis and Brancale 1956). Other research points to the observation that psychiatrists frequently disagree with each other's expert testimony and suggests that diagnostic findings often depend upon which side of a case has engaged the expert (for a review, see Simon and Zusman 1983). Some psychiatrists also are critical of the idea of a sexual psychopath and, in 1977, the Group for the Advancement of Psychiatry, with a membership of some 300 psychiatrists, called for the repeal of sexual psychopath legislation. After an extensive study and evaluation, the group's Committee on Psychiatry and Law (1977) concluded that sexual psychopath statutes are approaches that have failed, that the categorization process projected by these statutes lacks clinical validity, and that predictions about "sexual dangerousness" are unreliable.

Despite these criticisms, psychiatry moved from an advisory position to one in which the profession exercised control over the labeling and, consequently, the sentencing and release of sex offenders. To accomplish this, psychiatry claimed a professional monopoly over a body of expert knowledge. Once the idea of sexual psychopathology had been established, the profession also could claim that medicine held the solution. Over the past 50 years, to varying degrees, medicine has experimented with castration, psychosurgery, electric shock, and hormonal and mind-control drug therapy, as well as psychotherapy, all in the name of rape prevention and control.[4] And although men who rape are not confined to one social class, the object of these "therapies" generally has been lower-status men who lack the means to protect themselves from the more intrusive forms of treatment. But while the debate over medicine's role and effectiveness in law continues, psychiatry remains firmly entrenched in the legal process.

IS RAPE A DISEASE?

The psychopathological perspective is one of a number of ways in which human behavior, including sexual violence, can be conceptualized. However, in the case of sexual violence, until recently, the assumptions of psychopathology have been at the core of most research on rapists and the elements emphasized in the disease model became the popularly accepted explanations for why men rape.

At the core of the disease model are essentially two assumptions: that rape is the result of a mental illness, and that it often includes an uncontrollable sexual impulse.[5] The assertion is that men who rape lack the ability to control themselves and that they are "sick," disordered individuals. Especially in the early psychoanalytic literature, rapists were often described as suffering from a disease that weakened their self-control and created an "irresistible impulse" to commit a sexual act. Thus, rape was viewed as the "explosive expression of a pent up impulse" (Guttmacher and Weinhofen 1952, 116). Clearly, since men who rape could not control their behavior, they were not responsible for it either.

Despite historically widespread usage in psychiatric literature, impulse theory lacks empirical support. No one has been able to demonstrate that men who rape are more or less prone to impulsive behavior than other known groups of men. In fact, if anything, research has demonstrated the opposite of impulse theory. For example, Amir (1971) analyzed the police records of 646 rapes and found that 71 percent were premeditated, not sudden, impulsive acts. Hypothetically, impulse theory could be used to explain any behavior, and if the courts extended the logic of irresistible impulse to its limits, no one would be responsible for anything. It has, however, been used primarily to explain rape and other forms of sexual violence. Certainly the idea of an uncontrollable male sex urge fits the traditional image of a naturally boundless and untamable male sex drive, in contrast to the natural passivity of women (see Scully and Bart 1973; also, Scully 1980).

Irresistible impulse does not necessarily imply a character disorder, but when rape is viewed as a disease, it does suggest a sex act perpetrated by a perverted and sick individual. For example, Littner (1973, 7) states, "The single most important item we need to know about the sex offender is how sick he is emotionally. This is far more important than the

nature of the crime he has committed." Likewise, Karpman (1951, 1990) has argued that "sexual psychopaths are, of course, a social menace, but they are not conscious agents deliberately and viciously perpetrating these acts, rather they are the victims of a disease from which many suffer more than their victims." Given the presumption of illness, many psychiatrists concluded that rape is merely symptomatic of the real disease or underlying disorder. And frequently in the older literature, the psychiatric shibboleths of homosexuality and hostility toward a mother figure . . . were conjured up to explain the hidden motive. . . .

Some men who rape, like some people who steal, undeniably are mentally ill. In the case of rape, however, empirical studies indicate that only as few as 5 percent of men are psychotic at the time of their crimes (Abel et al. 1980), fairly strong evidence that psychopathology does not explain the vast amount of sexually violent behavior. The problem is with absolute statements such as the claim, made by one psychiatrist, that "I have never studied a rapist where there was not present, together with many other problems, a rather severe sexual disorder" (quoted in Albin 1977, 31). The presumption of psychopathology is also evident in the often-cited work of Groth (1979), a prison psychologist. While Groth emphasizes the nonsexual nature of rape—power, anger, and sadism— he also concludes, "Rape is always a symptom of some psychological dysfunction, either temporary and transient or chronic and repetitive" (p. 5). Before considering the implications of these explanations, there is one other major theme—victim precipitated rape—that deserves attention.

BLAMING THE VICTIM

Traditionally, support for the allegation that women precipitate rape came from victimology, a subfield of criminology, in which the victim's contribution to the genesis of crime was the subject of study. Recently, victimology has also focused on crime from the victim's perspective.

Criminologist Hans von Hentig was one of the first to articulate the victimologists' position. In a work published in 1940, he states that "the human victim in many instances seems to lead the evildoer actively into temptation. The predator is—by varying means—prevailed to advance against the prey" (p. 303). If there are born criminals, he argues, there are born victims, who are self-harming and self-destructive. Central to his thesis is the question of why a specific victim is chosen. In the case of incest and rape, according to von Hentig, seduction plays a prominent role, leading him to question whether rape may not be considered a case of "the oversexed on the oversexed" (p. 209).

The work of sociologist Menachem Amir is a more contemporary example of the application of victimology to rape. Amir (1972) makes a distinction between victim-precipitating behaviors through acts of *commission* and through acts of *omission.* Commissive behavior includes "last moment retreating from sexual advancement" or "agreeing voluntarily to drink or ride with a stranger" (p. 155). Acts of omission include failure to take preventive measures, such as failing to react strongly enough to sexual suggestions, or "when her outside appearance arouses the offender's advances which are not staved off" (p. 155). Amir states that, under these circumstances, "the victim becomes functionally responsible for the offense by entering upon and following a course that will provoke some males to commit crimes" (p. 155). Thus Amir argues that attention should be focused upon the victim-offender relationship, the moral character of the victim, and the "victim's personality makeup which may orient her toward the offender and the offense" (p.

132). While the field of victimology can be accused of overidentifying with offenders, in the case of rape, psychoanalytic theory provided the theoretical basis that could be used to discredit victims.

In psychoanalytic terms, the core female personality consists of three characteristics: narcissism, masochism, and passivity. The masochistic element accounts for women's alleged unconscious desire to be raped. In her summary of the psychoanalytic view of the female personality, Horney (1973, 24) states:

> The specific satisfactions sought and found in female sex life and motherhood are of a masochistic nature. The content of the early sexual wishes and fantasies concerning the father is the desire to be mutilated, that is castrated by him. Menstruation has the hidden connotation of a masochistic experience. What the woman secretly desires in intercourse is rape and violence, or in the mental sphere, humiliation. . . . This swinging in the direction of masochism is part of the woman's anatomical destiny.

While the psychoanalytic view of women has been widely criticized for its obvious bias (for example, see Chesler 1972), with the exception of Albin (1977), no one has noted how easily it can be translated into a rationalization for male sexual aggressive behavior.

In the psychoanalytic literature, victims of sexual violence have frequently been sorted into categories on the basis of personal or circumstantial characteristics. Littner (1973, 23), for example, distinguishes between "true victims," those who do not consciously or unconsciously wish to be raped, and "professional victims," those who have an inner masochistic need to be raped. According to Littner, "professional victims" have an inner need to be sexually molested or attacked even though consciously they are totally unaware of their motivation. Because of these unconscious desires, they "unwittingly cooperate with the rapist in terms of covertly making themselves available to the rapist" (p. 28). It is perhaps unnecessary to point out that the victims of other types of crimes are rarely alleged to have an inner need to be victimized, nor are they routinely accused of causing the crimes committed against them.

In some psychoanalytic literature, not only victims and mothers, but also the wives of rapists have been held responsible for their husbands' sexual violence. Abrahamsen (1960, 163), in his discussion of eight wives who had been subjected to sexual aggression by their rapist husbands, states, "The offender needs an outlet for his sexual aggression and finds a submissive partner who unconsciously invites sexual abuse and whose masochistic needs are being fulfilled." The fact that these women had divorced their rapist-husbands did not alter Abrahamsen's belief in the psychoanalytic model. Instead, he argues that the wives were also latently aggressive and competitive. In Abrahamsen's scheme, the rapist-husband was the innocent victim of his wife, his mother, and the woman he raped. . . .

Perhaps even more perplexing than the treatment of women is what has been said about girls who are the victims of rape and/or incest. Girls have been alleged to have the same subconscious motives as their adult counterparts. For example, Abrahamsen presents the thesis that sexual trauma is often unconsciously desired by the child and that it represents a form of infantile sexual activity. . . .

"Research" that incorporated this perspective typically blamed children for the behavior of their adult molesters. For example, a frequently quoted study of girls who were the victims of adult sex offenders distinguished between "accidental" victims and "participating" victims, "those who took part in the initiating and maintaining of the relationship" (Weiss et al. 1955). Half, or 23 out of 44, of the victims labeled as "participating" were under age 10, and some were as young as 4 or 5 years old. Furthermore, "participation" was

determined on the basis of psychiatric evaluations of the victims' personalities rather than on the objective facts of the cases. Weiss et al. conclude that the girls had severe emotional problems that motivated their initiation and participation in their own victimization. These psychiatrists apparently never even considered the possibility that the girls' problems might be the result, not the cause, of the rape or incest. Elsewhere in the literature, girl victims have been described as very attractive, charming, appealing, submissive, and seductive, even though some were as young as 4 years old (see Bender 1965).

Boys as well as girls are sexually victimized. However, discussions of male victimization traditionally have lacked the suggestion that victim precipitation is the root of the problem. For example, Halleck (1965) states, "Most girl victims are familiar with the offender and many are willing or passive participants in the sexual act." About males, he states, "A significant number of male victims may be considered truly 'accidental' in the sense that they did not know the attacker and did not willingly participate in the act" (p. 680).

WHY ISN'T RAPE MEN'S PROBLEM?

The studies that have been discussed above span four decades—the 1940s through the 1970s—and have been influential in shaping our thinking about rape in very important ways. Each of the explanations—irresistible impulse, disease, and victim precipitation—embraces a view of rape that has several implications. First, each explanation absolves the offender of responsibility for his behavior. When rape is viewed as a disease, it casts the offender in the sick role. Behavior attributed to an incapacity beyond the individual's control carries an obligation to admit illness and seek medical help. The idea that women consciously or subconsciously precipitate their own victimization has a similar consequence.

Attention is focused on the behavior and motives of the victim rather than on the offender. Thus, responsibility is also shifted to the victim. The assumptions that underscore allegations of victim-precipitated rape are also a clear example of the way ideology shapes theory and thus research, despite claims of objectivity. There is little doubt whose interests are served by these supposedly scientifically neutral formulations. And the influence of this ideology extends well beyond scholarly journals. As numerous observers have noted, in court, it is often the rape victim who is on trial.

Second, psychopathological explanations make the assumption that male aggressive sexual behavior is unusual or strange. Thus, sexual violence is removed from the realm of the everyday or "normal" world and placed in the category of "special" behavior. As a result, sexually violent men are cast as outsiders, and any connection or threat to "normal" men is eliminated.

Third, and perhaps most salient, the psychopathological model views rape as no more than a collection of individualistic, idiosyncratic problems. This creates the tendency to look for the cause of and solution to a complex social problem within the individual and to ignore the cultural and structural context in which it occurs. The net effect of individualistic explanations is to create an approach to the problem that never reaches beyond the individual offender. When sexually violent behavior is presumed to be confined to a few "sick" men, the solution becomes to use drugs, surgery, shock therapy, or psychotherapy to "cure" those few individuals who are causing the problem. Women can help to prevent "their problem" by avoiding contact with this "lunatic fringe." Thus the psychopathological model of rape removes the necessity of investigating or changing those elements within a society that may precipitate sexual violence against women. The conse-

quence of defining responsibility this way is that men never have to confront rape as their problem. After all, either men who rape are defective or the real culprits are women. In a society where status and power belong to men, such an ideology is not unexpected.

The psychopathological model, developed by a profession dominated by men, is a prime example of reductionist thinking in which androcentric blinders diminish a complex social problem to a singular simplistic cause. At worst, the model blames the victim; at best, it leaves the vast majority of sexual violence unexplained. Additionally, the psychopathological model does not explain why women in some societies are the targets of so much uniquely male "disease." To do it justice, the parameters of the problem must be broadened to incorporate new perspectives and behavioral theories. The competing feminist model embraces culture and social structure as dynamic and contributing factors and takes an alternative multifaceted view of sexual violence and its origins.

CULTURE'S CONTRIBUTION

Anthropological data provide insight (albeit limited) into the cultural antecedents of rape in preindustrial tribal societies. In one study, using Murdock and White's Standard Cross-Cultural Sample, researchers determined that of the 34 groups for which frequency could be established, rape was absent in 8, rare in 12, and common in 14 societies (Broude and Greene 1976). Sanday (1979), using an altered coding scheme and additional sources, found a larger number of societies in which rape appears to be absent or rare—44 out of 95 tribal groups. Despite these discrepant numbers, ethnographic data do establish the existence of rape-free preindustrial societies.[6] The absence of rape in some societies provides support for the proposition that while human behavior, including sexual behavior, may have biological or physiological components, it is always patterned and expressed in cultural terms.

Taking her analysis a step further, Sanday examined differences between "rape-free" and "rape-prone" societies. She argues that male dominance and the forcible control of women evolve as societies become more dependent on male destructive capacities than on female fertility. Thus, Sanday relates sexual violence to contempt for female qualities and suggests that rape is part of a culture of violence and expression of male dominance.

In contrast, Blumberg (1979) proposes a structural approach to the examination of women's oppression within and among different cultures. The key to her elaborate paradigm is women's degree of control over the means of production and generated surplus relative to men of the same group. Blumberg argues that women are more likely to lack important life options and to be oppressed physically and politically where they do not have any appreciable economic power. Using a pilot sample of 61 preindustrial societies from the Human Relations Area Files, Blumberg found preliminary support for her hypothesis. The higher women's relative economic power, the less likely they are to be beaten by the men in their lives. Thus, it appears that in preindustrial societies economic power enables women to win immunity from males' use of force against them. Schwendinger and Schwendinger (1983) make a similar point, arguing that rape is related to sexual inequality, women's participation in social production, and the degree to which violence is institutionalized in other aspects of the culture. To summarize, anthropological research suggests that sexual violence is related to cultural attitudes, the power relationship between women and men, the social and economic status of women relative to the men of their group, and the amount of other forms of violence in the society.

While there may be no example of a rape-free modern culture, the frequency of rape varies dramatically among societies, and the United States is among the most rape-prone of all. . . .

THE ALL-AMERICAN CRIME

In feminist theory rape is viewed as a singularly male form of sexual coercion—an act of violence and social control that functions to "keep women in their place." The justification for forced sexual access is buttressed by legal, social, and religious definitions of women as inferior male property and sex as an exchange of goods (for example, see Brownmiller 1975; Clark and Lewis 1977; Griffin 1979; Russell 1975). MacKinnon (1987) asserts that legal definitions of rape are based on what men, not women, think violates women. From women's point of view, MacKinnon (1983) argues, rape is not prohibited, it is regulated. Bart (1979) refers to rape as a paradigm of sexism. She notes that definitions, notably legal definitions, reflect the belief system of the dominant group. Therefore, she argues, it is not by accident that the *de facto* and *de jure* definitions of rape embody sexist beliefs; for example, intercourse forced on a wife by her husband is not rape. Indeed, a number of feminists have observed that rape laws and the corresponding penalties are not intended to protect women as much as they are intended to protect men's property, which, having been damaged, loses market value (for example, see LeGrand 1973; MacKinnon 1987).

In feminist theory rape is related to the power relationship between men and women, which, Lipman-Blumen (1984) argues, is at the very core of our social fabric and forms the blueprint for all other power relationships. Hanmer and Maynard (1987) conclude that recent feminist research reveals the existence of a complex social structure where power, inequality, and oppression function along socially constructed gender lines and, in this system, violence is used to control women. In this sense, feminist theorists have pointed out that, because it preserves male dominance, sexual violence benefits all men, not just those who actually rape. Systematic gender-based stratification is sustained through legal, economic, political, and social institutional supports. Women don't revolt, Lipman-Blumen asserts, because both genders have been taught through "control myths" to believe that female/male differences are innate. In her view, two "control myths" in particular are important—that men are more capable and knowledgeable than women and that men have women's best interests at heart (colonialism revisited). These "control myths" not only prevent women from gaining access to institutional resources—which, as Blumberg (1979) points out, is critical to gaining immunity from male sexual violence—but they also contribute to a social climate in which women often are not believed when they say they have been raped.

Feminist theorists view rape as an extension of normative male behavior, the result of conformity to the values and prerogatives that define the male role in patriarchal societies. Crucial are the "control myths" that teach the innate superiority of men and the corresponding inferiority of women. Equally important are socialization practices that teach men to have expectations about their level of sexual needs and corresponding female accessibility, which functions to justify forcing sexual access. Weis and Borges (1973) point out that socialization prepares women to be "legitimate" victims and men to be potential offenders. Herman (1984) concludes that the United States is a rape culture because both genders are taught to regard male aggression as a natural and normal part of sexual relations.

THE BOY NEXT DOOR

Early feminist literature, Anne Edwards (1987) points out, tended to approach various types of male violence as discrete behavioral categories. With theoretical maturity, however, sexual aggression/violence is now conceptualized as a continuum or series of behaviors ranging from verbal street harassment and harassment in the workplace to wife battering, incest, and rape—connected by the common underlying function of the systematic control of women (for example, see Kelly 1987). Likewise, men can be thought of as varying along a continuum of sexual aggression, with some men more likely than others to commit aggressive acts against women. Striking evidence for this proposition is found in a growing body of research that indicates that many men in this society are capable of sexual aggression.

Koss and Leonard (1984) adopted the continuum approach to measure the amount of "hidden" rape in a normal population. Their measurement varies the degree to which aggression has been used on a female partner to accomplish intercourse and distinguishes among four categories: (1) sexually assaultive—admits to obtaining vaginal, oral, or anal intercourse through the threat or use of force (legally rape in most states); (2) sexually abusive—admits to some degree of force or use of force but intercourse did not take place (attempted rape in most states); (3) sexually coercive—admits to obtaining intercourse with an unwilling woman by threatening to end the relationship, by lying about feelings (false statements of love and so on), or after continual arguments; (4) sexually nonaggressive—admits to none of the categories. In their sample of 1,846 college males, 4.3 percent reported sexually assaultive behavior; 4.9 percent, sexually abusive behavior; 22.4 percent, sexually coercive behavior; and 59.0 percent reported no sexually aggressive behavior but did report mutually desired sexual experiences. Finally, 9.4 percent of the males reported no sexual experience of any kind. Extending this research to a national sample of 6,159 male and female students enrolled in 32 colleges and universities across the United States, Koss et al. (1987) found that 53.7 percent of women respondents indicated some form of sexual victimization since age 14, including the following: sexual contact, 14.4 percent; sexual coercion, 11.9 percent; attempted rape, 12.1 percent; and rape, 15.4 percent (categorized by most serious event). Among male students, 25.1 percent revealed involvement in some form of sexual aggression, including the following: sexual contact, 10.2 percent; sexual coercion, 7.2 percent; attempted rape, 3.3 percent; and rape, 4.4 percent (categorized by most serious act). These findings are consistent with research reported by Kirkpatrick and Kanin (1957) conducted during the mid-1950s on college women (see also Kanin 1957, 1965, 1967, 1969, 1970). In their sample of 291 women, they found 56 percent reported offensive experiences at some level of erotic intimacy, including 21 percent who had been offended by "forceful attempts at sexual intercourse" and 6 percent who had experienced "aggressively forceful attempts at sexual intercourse in the course of which menacing threats or coercive infliction of physical pain were employed." The authors conclude that sexual aggression is commonplace in dating relationships.

Equally disturbing are the findings of research designed to gauge sexual aggression in a normal population by asking men to rate their own likelihood of raping if they are assured they would not be caught. Replicating earlier research by Malamuth, Haber, and Feshbach (1980), Briere and Malamuth (1983) found that out of 356 college men, 28 percent indicated some likelihood of both raping and using force, 6 percent some likelihood of rape but not force, 30 percent some likelihood of

force but not rape, and 40 percent no likelihood of either rape or force. A second purpose of their research was to gather data on the two competing theories of rape: that rape is a form of sexual psychopathy committed by men who cannot control their sexual impulses versus the sociocultural explanation, that rape is the logical extension of a male dominant–female submissive gender role stereotyped culture. They found that self-reported potential willingness to be sexually aggressive was unrelated to a variety of sexual variables. However, in support of the sociocultural explanation, they found that rape-supportive attitudes and beliefs did predict likelihood to rape or to use sexual aggression.

In similar but unrelated research, Tieger (1981) obtained results highly compatible with those of Briere and Malamuth. In Tieger's sample of 172 college males, 37 percent indicated some likelihood of raping if assured of not being caught; 20 percent indicated a likelihood greater than or equal to the midpoint of the rating scale ("somewhat") that they themselves would rape (labeled HLR). Compared to non-HLR males, analysis of the HLR group revealed a greater degree of belief that rape victims act seductively and enjoy being raped, and that other males are also likely to rape. The HLR males were also more likely than non-HLR males to view rape as a less serious crime, and they held a more sympathetic view toward rapists.

Quite clearly, self-reports of college males and victim reports reveal that sexual aggression is commonplace in college dating relationships. An even larger number of college males express willingness to rape or sexually aggress against women given the absence of a penalty. Indeed, in their research, Martin and Hummer (1989) found that college fraternities, in particular, create an environment in which the use of coercion in sexual relationships with women is regarded as normal. If such patterns are found in college populations, there is every reason to believe the situation is similar in non-college-educated populations. Finally, callous attitudes toward women and belief in rape myths are the most consistent predictors of male sexual aggression.

In light of these findings, it is important to comment, at least briefly, on typical campus rape prevention strategies. Precautions such as increased lighting and escort services are premised on the assumption that the greatest threat to women is a psychotic stranger. The media, it should be pointed out, contribute to this image by focusing so much print and air-time on spectacular and unusual criminals when, in fact, those offenders are responsible for only a small proportion of crime. Indeed, contrary to popular wisdom, a long history of data clearly indicate that college women are at greater risk of being raped or aggressed against by the men they know and date than they are by lunatics in the bushes, yet little is done to prevent the more common occurrence. As I argue here, theories of causation are important because they beget strategies for prevention.

PORNOGRAPHY AND THE NORMALIZATION OF RAPE

Considerable evidence supports the observation that sexual violence has been so trivialized in the United States that rape has come to be regarded as normal and acceptable under certain conditions. The widely publicized 1983 rape of a woman who went to Big Dan's Bar in New Bedford, Massachusetts, to buy a pack of cigarettes is but one example. In this ordeal, which lasted more than two hours, several Portuguese men raped a young Portuguese woman on a pool table while other men prevented the bartender from calling the police and cheered the attackers on. While the closely knit Portuguese community initially reacted with shock and sympathy for the victim, within a brief span of time the situation changed to one of hostility toward the victim and sympathy for the rapists, whose

actions were justified as appropriate under the circumstances. Both men and women in the community, in part to counter the anti-Portuguese sentiment provoked by the notoriety of the case, attempted to neutralize the crime by blaming the victim for being in the bar at night alone while her children were left unattended at home (for a full analysis, see Chancer 1987). Said one woman, "They did nothing to her. Her rights are to be home with her two kids and to be a good mother. A Portuguese woman should be home with her kids and that's it" (quoted in Chancer 1987, 251) and 16,000 people signed petitions asking for leniency for the rapists (p. 251).

Many feminists and others point to the growing accessibility of violent and degrading pornography as one (but certainly not the only) of the more potent nourishers of a cultural climate that accepts sexual violence.[7] A critical issue is the nature and direction of the relationship between violent, degrading pornography and sexual aggression. In this chapter, the research on pornography's role in the trivialization of rape will be explored; in a separate chapter in Scully (1990), the effect of violent pornography on male aggression is examined.

Advocates of pornography typically refer to several sources of data as evidence that pornography has no antisocial effect and may even be beneficial. Often quoted are the Denmark studies (see Ben-Veniste 1971; Kutchinsky 1971), which seem to indicate a relationship between a reduction in sexually related crimes and the lifting of legal restrictions on pornography. Based in part on the Danish data, the 1970 U.S. Commission on Obscenity and Pornography issued what became a highly controversial conclusion—that no relationship, positive or negative, exists between pornography and sexual offenses. Others, however, challenged the 1970 commission's conclusion (see Bart and Jozsa 1980).

Court (1984), in an extensive review of the studies considered by the 1970 commission, points to a number of problems. He argues that the use of sex crimes as an index of effect is open to confusing and conflicting interpretations. Not only are there problems with underreporting of these crimes, but, Court observes, one must distinguish between *major* and *minor* sexual offenses, since the trends for these do not correlate well. His and others' data indicate that reports of minor sexual offenses (e.g., carnal knowledge, voyeurism) have generally declined in Denmark and elsewhere over the past decade, whereas reports of more serious offenses, such as rape, have increased. He points out, "Since the minor offenses are cumulatively greater in number than the major offenses, it follows that a reduction in the former will result in the aggregated total giving false reassurance about trends by masking an increase in serious offenses" (p. 148). Therefore, he insists, if anything is to be concluded about the effect of violent pornography from crime trends, it is minimally necessary to distinguish between sex crimes that include elements of violence, like rape and attempted rape, and sex offenses, like peeping and exhibitionism, that are nonviolent. The latter offenses are not relevant to the pornography debate.

The debate over pornography was reopened on the federal level when, in 1985, Attorney General William French Smith established the 1985 Attorney General's Commission on Pornography. . . .[8] The findings of the 1985 commission differed markedly from those of the earlier commission, and, while hailed by many, the 1985 commission's report also has been criticized by some as too sweeping in its conclusions about the harmfulness of various types of pornography. . . .[9] Also important, the 1985 commission included violent and degrading pornography, including child pornography, in its investigation, while the 1970 commission excluded these materials. Finally, feminists had a voice in the 1985 commission deliberations, whereas in 1970 the second wave of feminism was at an early stage of reemergence.

Of concern to many feminists (for example, see Dworkin 1980) is not sexual explicitness, but rather the profusion of degrading images of women as well as the increasing amount and degree of violence that has appeared in pornography since the 1970s (see Malamuth and Spinner 1980; Slade 1984). Not only is sex increasingly fused with violence, but, equally alarming, contemporary depictions often suggest that sexual violence has a positive outcome. For example, Smith (1976) content analyzed 428 "adults only" paperbacks and found that a major theme was the use of force on a woman who initially resists. However, in the end, regardless of the type or amount of force used, the victim is depicted as eventually becoming aroused and, to her humiliation, responding physically.

Such depictions of women and rape convey several dangerous messages. First, the use of force and violence is presented as part of normal male-female sexual relations, thus trivializing and normalizing rape. Another message suggests that women desire and enjoy rape—that, in fact, sexual violence has positive consequences. This image has more potential for damage than the violence per se and is the characteristic that distinguishes rape from other types of violent fictional depictions. Victims are never portrayed as enjoying murder, bombings, robberies, or other crimes. Such displays seem to be reserved for the pornographic depiction of women being raped.

Evidence from research, conducted primarily on male college students, supports the premise that exposure to sexually violent pornography increases antagonistic attitudes toward women and intensifies belief in rape myths, particularly that victims are responsible for rape and that women are aroused by sexual violence. For example, in one in a varied series of laboratory experiments, Malamuth and Check (1985) exposed male college students to one of eight pornographic audiotapes in which the content—a woman's consent, her pain, and the outcome (her arousal versus disgust)—were systematically manipulated. Later, the men listened to a second passage depicting either consenting or nonconsenting sex. Afterwards, a series of questions and scales were used to measure the men's perceptions of the second passage and their belief in rape myths. The researchers state that their findings from this series of experiments support the hypothesis that media depictions suggesting that rape results in the victim's arousal can contribute to men's belief in a similar rape myth. Further, they found that it is men with relatively higher inclinations to aggress against women (as measured by a pretest likelihood of raping scale) who are particularly likely to be affected by media depictions of rape myths.

Malamuth and Check (1981) obtained similar results in a field experiment not vulnerable to the artificiality of a laboratory setting. In this study, 271 male and female students agreed to participate in research ostensibly focused on movie ratings. Students viewed two movies, either *Swept Away* and *The Getaway* (films that portray sexual aggression and suggest positive outcome) or two neutral films. All films were viewed in a theater on campus with regular audience members who were not part of the experiment. Several days later, in class, students completed a sexual attitude survey embedded with scales measuring acceptance of interpersonal violence toward women and rape myth acceptance. Students were not aware of any connection between the survey and the films. Results indicated that exposure to the films portraying aggressive sexuality with positive consequences significantly increased male, but not female, subjects' acceptance of interpersonal violence toward women and tended to increase males' acceptance of rape myths.

Even more alarming, Linz et al. (1984) have demonstrated that the more prolonged the exposure to filmed violence, the lower the sensitivity to victims of violence in other contexts (see also Malamuth 1981a; Zillman and Bryant 1982). In their experiment, male college students were exposed to five films depicting sexuality and violence toward women—one per day, for five consecutive days. All the films had been commercially released and some had been shown on campus or on cable television and included *Texas Chainsaw Massacre, Maniac, I Spit on Your Grave, Vice Squad*, and *Toolbox Murders*. Over the course of the five days, the men who viewed these films came to have fewer negative emotional reactions to the films, to perceive them as significantly less violent, and to consider them considerably less degrading to women. Additionally, viewing these films affected their judgment of women in other contexts. In response to a videotaped reenactment of a complete rape trial, the men who viewed these films judged the victim to be significantly less injured and evaluated her as generally less worthy than did men in a control group who had not seen the films. It should be noted that in all these experiments, subjects were debriefed in an effort to erase the effects of the research on individual participants.

The results of these experiments are important because research also indicates that belief in rape myths is related to a variety of other phenomena. A number of studies have shown that strong belief in rape stereotypes results in restricted definitions of rape, not guilty verdicts in mock jury rape trials, denial or reduction of perceived injury to rape victims, and blaming rape victims for their victimization, and is a predictor of self-reported likelihood of raping (see Burt and Albin 1981; Borgida and White 1979; Calhoun et al. 1976; Jones and Aronson 1973). Further, my research demonstrates that men convicted of rape both believe these myths and use them to justify their own sexually violent behavior (Scully, 1990).

In addition to published research, the 1985 commission listened to expert testimony at a series of six thematic public hearings held at different locations around the United States. Because of the research I was conducting on convicted rapists, I was invited to testify at the Houston, Texas, hearing, where differing opinions on the relationship between pornography and human behavior were expressed by a roster of social and behavioral scientists.[10] Essentially, I argued that research is ongoing and perhaps one day would discover a method capable of establishing whether a *causal* relationship exists between pornography and actual sexual violence against women. To do so, it will be minimally necessary to move beyond the experimental laboratory and into a broader social context. In the meantime, even in the absence of causal data, there is reason to be concerned. At the very least, we can posit an indirect relationship. That is, the more cultural support, in forms like violent and degrading pornography, that exists in a society for hostile and aggressive acts toward women, the more likely it is that such acts will occur in that society. There is ample reason to believe that these cultural supports provide the justification, if not the motivation, necessary for some men to commit sexually violent acts. Indeed, as women are only too painfully aware, the widespread availability of violent pornography in the United States has not resulted in a decrease in violent crimes against women.

RAPE AS LEARNED AND REWARDING BEHAVIOR

In this investigation I apply a feminist sociocultural framework, predicated on a presumption of normality rather than pathology, to actual men who have been convicted of rape. There is another way in which this research departs from the psychopathological tradition of men. My questions are generated

from experience that women, not men, have of rape. As Harding (1987), among others, has pointed out, this is a critical distinction.

In applying a feminist sociocultural perspective to rape, I have made a number of assumptions. Starting with the observation that cultures can and do generate predispositions to behaviors that are, at the same time, defined as conditionally deviant (that is, normal deviance), I assume that rape, for the most part, is socially learned behavior. The fundamental premise is that all behavior is learned in the same way—socially through direct association with others as well as indirectly through cultural contact. Learning includes not only behavioral techniques but also a host of values and beliefs, like rape myths, that are compatible with sexual aggression against women.

Viewed this way, my approach to the men described in my research is considerably different from the bulk of previous research, which has attempted to understand why men rape by looking for evidence of pathology through an examination of individual case histories. Instead, for me, the men represent a group who have reached the apex of the sexual violence continuum, a continuum that rewards men and victimizes women. They are interesting not because of their personal histories, but because, as men who rape, they are excellent informants on our sexually violent society. Rather than assuming that rape is dysfunctional behavior, I use these informants to understand what men who rape gain from their sexually violent behavior. This approach leads to new questions about the goals men learn to achieve through sexually violent means.

But it is important to ask not only *why* but also *how* sexual violence is made possible in a society, such as ours, so prone to rape. To answer that question, it is necessary to explore the motives and rationalizations of men who rape, and their beliefs about men, women, and sexual violence in general, as well as their own victims and crimes in particular.

NOTES

1. Johnson's (1980) estimate is based on the incidence rate for completed rapes found in the 1972 crime panel survey involving 10,000 households in 26 U.S. cities (250,000 people over age 11). The study was conducted by the Law Enforcement Assistance Administration in conjunction with the U.S. Census Bureau.
2. There are age, class, and race differences in reported rapes that suggest that all women are not equally at risk.
3. Russell and Howell (1983) applied life-table analysis to the age-specific rape rates that Russell found in a randomly selected sample of 930 adult women living in San Francisco.
4. For a full discussion of various treatments, see Rada (1978).
5. For a full discussion of the psychiatric perspective, see Scully and Marolla (1985).
6. A number of factors limit the quantity and quality of cross-cultural data on rape. It was not customary in traditional ethnography to collect data on sexual attitudes and behavior. Further, where data do exist, they are often sketchy and vague and of questionable reliability. For these reasons, the research of Broude and Greene (1976) and Sanday (1979) do not include a number of societies found in Murdock and White's Standard Cross-Cultural Sample.
7. The issue of censorship will not be debated here. However, research linking pornography and sexual aggression is relevant to the arguments presented here (see Scully, 1990).
8. The formation of the Attorney General's Commission on Pornography was announced and the eleven members named on May 20, 1985, by Edwin Meese III, who replaced William French Smith as attorney general of the United States.
9. It is not my intent here to summarize the 1,960-page report of the commission. See Attorney General's Commission on Pornography (1986).
10. The following people testified at the Houston hearing devoted to the relationship between pornography and human behavior:

    - Gene Abel, professor of psychiatry, Emory University
    - Larry Baron, lecturer in sociology, Yale University
    - Jennings Bryant, professor and chair of radio and television, University of Houston
    - Don Byrne, professor and chair of psychology, SUNY—Albany
    - Mary Calderone, cofounder, Sex Information and Education Council of the U.S.
    - Victor Cline, professor of psychology, University of Utah
    - John Court, psychologist, director of Spectrum Psychological Counseling Center
    - Edward Donnerstein, professor of communication arts, University of Wisconsin—Madison
    - Richard Green, professor of psychiatry, SUNY—Stony Brook
    - Kathryn Kelley, associate professor of psychology, SUNY—Albany
    - Neil Malamuth, professor and chair of communications, UCLA
    - William Marshall, professor of psychology, Queens University, Ontario, Canada
    - John Money, professor of medical psychology and pediatrics, Johns Hopkins University
    - Donald Mosher, professor of psychology, University of Connecticut
    - Diana Russell, professor of sociology, Mills College
    - Diana Scully, associate professor of sociology, Virginia Commonwealth University
    - Wendy Stock, sex therapist and assistant professor, Texas A&M University
    - C. A. Tripp, psychotherapist, New York
    - Ann Welbourne-Moglia, executive director, Sex Information and Education Council of the U.S.

BIBLIOGRAPHY

Abel, G. G., J. V. Becker, and L. J. Skinner (1980). "Aggressive Behavior and Sex." *Psychiatric Clinics of North America,* 3, 133–51.

Abrahamsen, David (1960). *The Psychology of Crime.* New York: John Wiley.

Albin, Rochelle (1977). "Psychological Studies of Rape." *Signs,* 3, 23–35.

Amir, Menachem (1971). *Patterns in Forcible Rape.* Chicago: University of Chicago Press.

——— (1972). "The Role of the Victim in Sex Offenses." In H. Resnik and M. Wolfgang, eds., *Sexual Behavior: Social, Clinical, and Legal Aspects.* Boston: Little, Brown.

Attorney General's Commission on Pornography (July, 1986). *Final Report,* 2 vols. Washington, DC: Government Printing Office.

Bart, Pauline B. (1979). "Rape as a Paradigm of Sexism in Society—Victimization and Its Discontents." *Women's Studies International Quarterly,* 2, 347–57.

——— and M. Jozsa (1980). "Dirty Books, Dirty Films and Dirty Data." In L. Lederer, ed., *Take Back the Night: Women on Pornography.* New York: William Morrow.

——— and Patricia H. O'Brien (1984). "Stopping Rape: Effective Avoidance Strategies." *Signs,* 10, 83–101.

——— (1985). *Stopping Rape: Successful Survival Strategies.* New York: Pergamon.

Bender, L. (1965). "Offended and Offender Children." In R. Slovenko, ed., *Sexual Behavior and the Law.* Springfield, IL: Charles C Thomas.

Ben-Veniste, R. (1971). "Pornography and Sex Crime: The Danish Experience." In *Technical Reports of the Commission on Obscenity and Pornography,* Vol. 8. Washington, DC: Government Printing Office.

Blumberg, Rae Lesser (1979). "A Paradigm for Predicting the Position of Women: Policy Implications and Problems." In Jean Lipman-Blumen and Jessie Bernard, eds., *Sex Roles and Social Policy.* London: Sage.

Borgida, E., and P. White (1979). "Judgmental Bias and Legal Reform." Unpublished manuscript, University of Minnesota.

Bowman, K., and B. Engle (1965). "Sexual Psychopath Laws." In R. Slovenko, ed., *Sexual Behavior and the Law.* Springfield, IL: Charles C Thomas.

Briere, John, and Neil Malamuth (1983). "Self-Reported Likelihood of Sexually Aggressive Behavior: Attitudinal versus Sexual Explanations." *Journal of Research in Personality,* 17, 315–23.

Broude, Gwen, and Sarah Greene (1976). "Cross-Cultural Codes on Twenty Sexual Attitudes and Practices." *Ethnology,* 15, 409–28.

Brownmiller, Susan (1975). *Against Our Will: Men, Women and Rape.* New York: Simon & Schuster.

Burt, Martha, and Rochelle Albin (1981). "Rape Myths, Rape Definitions, and Probability of Conviction." *Journal of Applied Social Psychology,* 11, 212–30.

Calhoun, L. (1978). "The Effect of Victim Physical Attractiveness and Sex of Respondent on Social Reaction to Victims of Rape." *British Journal of Clinical Psychology,* 17, 191–92.

———, J. Selby, and L. Warring (1976). "Social Perception of the Victim's Causal Role in Rape: An Exploratory Examination of Four Factors." *Human Relations,* 29, 517–26.

Chancer, Lynn S. (1987). "New Bedford, Massachusetts, March 6, 1983–March 22, 1984: The 'Before and After' of a Group Rape." *Gender and Society,* 1, 239–60.

Chesler, Phyllis (1972). *Women and Madness.* Garden City, NY: Doubleday.

——— (1978). *About Men.* New York: Simon & Schuster.

Cicone, M., and D. Ruble (1978). "Beliefs about Males." *Journal of Social Issues,* 34, 5–16.

Clark, Lorenne, and Debra Lewis (1977). *Rape: The Price of Coercive Sexuality.* Toronto: Women's Press.

Committee on Psychiatry and Law (1977). *Psychiatry and Sex Psychopath Legislation: The 30s to the 80s.* (Publication No. 98.) New York: Group for the Advancement of Psychiatry.

Conrad, Peter, and Joseph W. Schneider, eds. (1980). *Deviance and Medicalization: From Badness to Sickness.* St. Louis: C. V. Mosby.

Court, John H. (1984). "Sex and Violence: A Ripple Effect." In Neil M. Malamuth and Edward Donnerstein, eds., *Pornography and Sexual Aggression.* New York: Academic Press.

Dworkin, Andrea (1980). "The Prophet of Perversion." *Mother Jones,* April 24.

Edwards, Anne (1987). "Male Violence in Feminist Theory: An Analysis of the Changing Conceptions of Sex/Gender Violence and Male Domination." In Jalna Hanmer and Mary Maynard, eds.,

Women, Violence and Social Control. Atlantic Highlands, NJ: Humanities Press International.

Ellis, A., and R. Brancale (1956). *The Psychology of Sex Offenders.* Springfield, IL: Charles C Thomas.

Gollin, Albert E. (1980). "Comment on Johnson's 'On the Prevalence of Rape in the United States.'" *Signs,* 6, 346–49.

Griffin, Susan (1971). "Rape: The All American Crime." *Ramparts,* September 10, 26–35.

——— (1979). *Rape: The Power of Consciousness.* New York: Harper & Row.

Groth, A. Nicholas (1979). *Men Who Rape: The Psychology of the Offender.* New York: Plenum.

Guttmacher, M., and H. Weinhofen (1952). *Psychiatry and the Law.* New York: W. W. Norton.

Halleck, S. (1965). "Emotional Effects of Victimization." In R. Slovenko, ed., *Sexual Behavior and the Law.* Springfield, IL: Charles C Thomas.

Hanmer, Jalna, and Mary Maynard (1987). "Introduction: Violence and Gender Stratification." In Jalna Hanmer and Mary Maynard, eds., *Women, Violence and Social Control.* Atlantic Highlands, NJ: Humanities Press International.

Harding, Sandra (1986). *The Science Question in Feminism.* Ithaca, NY: Cornell University Press.

——— (1987). "The Method Question." *Hypatia,* 2, 19–36.

——— and Jean F. O'Barr, eds. (1987). *Sex and Scientific Inquiry.* Chicago: University of Chicago Press.

Herman, Dianne (1984). "The Rape Culture." In Jo Freeman, ed., *Women: A Feminist Perspective.* Palo Alto, CA: Mayfield.

Horney, Karen (1973). "The Problem of Feminine Machochism." In J. Miller, ed., *Psychoanalysis and Women.* New York: Brunner/Mazel.

Johnson, Allen Griswold (1980). "On the Prevalence of Rape in the United States." *Signs,* 6, 136–46.

Jones, C., and E. Aronson (1973). "Attribution of Fault to a Rape Victim as a Function of Responsibility of the Victim." *Journal of Personality and Social Psychology,* 26, 415–19.

Kanin, E. (1957). "Male Aggression in Dating-Courtship Relations." *American Journal of Sociology,* 63, 197–204.

——— (1965). "Male Sex Aggression and Three Psychiatric Hypotheses." *Journal of Sex Research,* 1, 227–29.

——— (1967). "Reference Groups and Sex Conduct Norm Violation." *Sociological Quarterly,* 8, 495–504.

——— (1969). "Selected Dyadic Aspects of Male Sex Aggression." *Journal of Sex Research,* 5, 12–28.

——— (1970). "Sex Aggression by College Men." *Medical Aspects of Human Sexuality,* September, 28ff.

Karpman, B. (1951). "The Sexual Psychopath." *Journal of Criminal Law and Criminology,* 42, 184–98.

Kelly, Liz (1987). "The Continuum of Sexual Violence." In Jalna Hanmer and Mary Maynard, eds., *Women, Violence, and Social Control.* Atlantic Highlands, N.J.: Humanities Press International.

Kirkpatrick, C., and E. Kanin (1957). "Male Sex Aggression on a University Campus." *American Sociological Review,* 22, 52–58.

Koss, Mary P., Christine A. Gidycz, and Nadine Wisniewski (1987). "The Scope of Rape: Incidence and Prevalence of Sexual Aggression and Victimization in a National Sample of Students in Higher Education." *Journal of Consulting and Clinical Psychology,* 55, 162–70.

——— and Kenneth E. Leonard (1984). "Sexually Aggressive Men: Empirical Findings and Theoretical Implications." In Neil Malamuth and Edward Donnerstein, eds., *Pornography and Sexual Aggression.* New York: Academic Press.

Kutchinsky, B. (1971). "Toward an Exploration of the Decrease in Registered Sex Crimes in Copenhagen." In *Technical Reports of the Commission on Obscenity and Pornography,* Vol. 7. Washington, DC: Government Printing Office.

LeGrand, Camille (1973). "Rape and Rape Laws: Sexism in Society and Law." *California Law Review,* 61, 919–43.

Linz, Daniel, Edward Donnerstein, and Steven Penrod (1984). "The Effects of Multiple Exposure to Filmed Violence against Women." *Journal of Communication,* Summer, 130–47.

Lipman-Blumen, Jean (1984). *Gender Roles and Power.* Englewood Cliffs, NJ: Prentice-Hall.

Littner, Ner (1973). "Psychology of the Sex Offender: Causes, Treatment, Prognosis." *Police Law Quarterly,* 3, 5–31.

MacKinnon, Catharine A. (1983). "Feminism, Marxism, Method, and the State: Toward Feminist Jurisprudence." *Signs,* 8, 635–59.

——— (1987). *Feminism Unmodified: Discourses on Life and Law.* Cambridge, MA: Harvard University Press.

Malamuth, Neil M. (1981a). "Aggression against Women: Cultural and Individual Causes." In Neil M. Malamuth and Edward Donnerstein, eds., *Pornography and Sexual Aggression,* New York: Academic Press.

——— (1981b). "Rape Fantasies as a Function of Exposure to Violent Sexual Stimuli." *Archives of Sexual Behavior,* 10, 33–47.

——— and James V. P. Check (1981). "The Effect of Mass Media Exposure on Acceptance of Violence against Women: A Field Experiment." *Journal of Research in Personality,* 15, 435–46.

——— and ——— (1985). "The Effects of Aggressive Pornography on Beliefs in Rape Myths: Individual Differences." *Journal of Research in Personality,* 19, 299–320.

———, Scott Haber, and Seymour Feshbach (1980). "Testing Hypotheses Regarding Rape: Exposure to Sexual Violence, Sex Difference, and the 'Normality' of Rapists." *Journal of Research in Personality,* 14, 121–37.

——— and Barry Spinner (1980). "A Longitudinal Content Analysis of Sexual Violence in the Best-Selling Erotic Magazines." *Journal of Sex Research,* 16, 226–37.

Martin, Patricia Yaney, and Robert A. Hummer (1989). "Fraternities and Rape on Campus." *Gender and Society,* 3, 457–73.

Rada, Richard, ed. (1978). *Clinical Aspects of the Rapist.* New York: Grune & Stratton.

Russell, Diana E. H. (1975). *The Politics of Rape.* New York: Stein & Day.

——— (1982). "The Prevalence and Incidence of Forcible Rape and Attempted Rape of Females." *Victimology: An International Journal,* 7, 81–93.

——— and Nancy Howell (1983). "The Prevalence of Rape in the United States Revisited." *Signs,* 8, 688–95.

Sagarin, E. (1976). "Prison Homosexuality and Its Effects on Post-Prison Sexual Behavior." *Psychiatry,* 39, 245–57.

Sanday, Peggy Reeves (1979). *The Socio-Cultural Context of Rape.* Washington, DC: U.S. Department of Commerce, National Technical Information Services.

Schwendinger, Julia A., and Herman Schwendinger (1983). *Rape and Inequality.* Beverly Hills, CA: Sage.

Scully, Diana (1980). *Men Who Control Women's Health.* Boston: Houghton Mifflin.

——— (1988). "Convicted Rapists' Perceptions of Self and Victim: Role Taking and Emotions." *Gender and Society,* 2, 200–13.

——— (1990). *Understanding Sexual Violence: A Study of Convicted Rapists.* Boston: Unwin Hyman.

——— and Pauline Bart (1973). "A Funny Thing Happened on the Way to the Orifice: Women in Gynecology Texts." *American Journal of Sociology,* 78, 1045–51.

——— and Joseph Marolla (1984). "Convicted Rapists' Vocabulary of Motive: Excuses and Justifications." *Social Problems,* 31, 530–44.

——— (1985). "Rape and Psychiatric Vocabularies of Motive: Alternative Perspectives." In Ann Wolbert Burgess, ed., *Rape and Sexual Assault: A Research Handbook.* New York: Garland.

Simon, Jesse, and Jack Zusman (1983). "The Effect of Contextual Factors on Psychiatrists' Perception of Illness: A Case Study." *Journal of Health and Social Behavior,* 24, 186–98.

Slade, Joseph W. (1984). "Violence in the Hard-Core Pornographic Film: A Historical Survey." *Journal of Communication,* Summer, 148–63.

Smith, Don D. (1976). "The Social Construction of Pornography." *Journal of Communication,* Winter, 16–24.

Tieger, Todd (1981). "Self-Rated Likelihood of Raping and Social Perception of Rape." *Journal of Research in Personality,* 15, 147–58.

von Hentig, Hans (1940). "Remarks on the Interaction of Perpetrator and Victim." *Journal of Criminal Law and Criminology,* 31, 303–9.

Weis, Kurt, and Sandra Borges (1973). "Victimology and Rape: The Case of the Legitimate Victim." *Issues in Criminology,* 8, 71–115.

Weiss, J., E. Rogers, M. Darwin, and C. Dutton (1955). "A Study of Girl Sex Offenders." *Psychiatric Quarterly,* 29, 1–29.

Zillman, Dolf, and Jennings Bryant (1982). "Pornography, Sexual Callousness, and the Trivialization of Rape." *Journal of Communication,* Autumn, 10–21.

CHAPTER 12

SURMOUNTING A LEGACY: THE EXPANSION OF RACIAL DIVERSITY IN A LOCAL ANTI-RAPE MOVEMENT

NANCY A. MATTHEWS

ABSTRACT

In Chapter 11 Scully described several theoretical models that have been used to conceptualize rape. In this chapter Matthews argues that historical dynamics of feminism, race, and rape discouraged extensive early black involvement in anti-rape work in the United States. These dynamics included both the prevalence of lynching which focused black women's activism against violence in the United States, and the lack of racial/ethnic and class diversity in early phases of the contemporary women's movement.

Matthews reports on the experiences of two rape crisis centers in black communities in Los Angeles in the mid-1980s. She points out several important contradictions that ironically have led to the success of these centers. First, in Los Angeles, concern among women of color in the antirape movement and government initiatives to fund underserved areas converged to produce these two new black rape crisis centers. Thus, racial and ethnic diversity in Los Angeles's antirape movement was facilitated by the traditionally conservative vehicle of state funding.

Second, unlike earlier antirape organizations connected to the wider feminist movement through a grassroots process, these two new centers were begun as part of existing bureaucratic organizations in the black community. Both were respected social service agencies that did not have strong links to contemporary feminism.

Third, these racially homogeneous organizations contributed more to diversifying the movement than efforts to racially integrate within individual organizations. This was in large part due to the specific needs and concerns of rape victims, especially in poor black communities. There, poverty, homelessness, unemployment, the difficulties of feeding one's children, violence in the community, fear of the police, and racism were the primary concerns of black women who had been raped. Only after these other problems were addressed did rape victims begin to talk about their own rapes. In short, the rape crisis center had to meet other needs of women in the black community before problems of rape could even be acknowledged.

Finally, despite conflict between primarily white women from earlier feminist groups and women from the new community-oriented black centers, Matthews finds that these different groups of women are working successfully together in coalitions for prevention. What new perspectives (other than the more individualistic medical, psychopathological, or victim-precipitative) or new ways (modifying, changing, or superseding more white-middle-class-oriented feminist perspectives) would you expect racially and ethnically mixed coalitions to adopt as rape prevention strategies?

The anti-rape movement in Los Angeles originated from collectivist feminism and feminist social work networks. Between 1973 and 1980, five grassroots-led rape crisis organizations were started, including the Los Angeles Commission on Assaults Against Women (LACAAW), the Pasadena YWCA Rape Crisis Center and Hotline, the East Los Angeles Rape Hotline (ELA), the Center for the Pacific-Asian Family, and the San Fernando Valley Rape Crisis Service. While the bilingual, Latina-run East Los Angeles hotline and the multilingual Pacific-Asian hotline brought some women of color into the movement, very few Black women were involved, and the predominantly Black areas of the county (South Central Los Angeles) were virtually unserved. Since 1980, when the California Office of Criminal Justice Planning began

funding rape crisis services, the state has promoted a relatively conservative, social service approach to this work. Yet ironically, during these years, state money also furthered one of the more progressive goals of the American anti-rape movement, to become multiracial and multicultural and to expand services to all women.

This chapter examines the problem of racial and ethnic diversity in the Los Angeles anti-rape movement, shows how racial diversity in the local movement was facilitated by the state's involvement in establishing two new Black rape crisis centers in the mid-1980s, and explores the consequences for race relations in the anti-rape movement in the United States.

FEMINISM, RACE, AND RAPE

The predominance of whites, problematic for the American feminist movement as a whole, also affected the anti-rape movement. Despite collectivist feminist roots in the civil rights movement and the new left of the 1960s, the women's liberation movement in the United States remained dominated by white and middle-class women (Ferree and Hess 1985). Evans (1979) attributes this narrowness to the

Author's note: This article originated as a presentation at the 1988 annual meeting of the American Sociological Association. I want to thank William G. Roy, Karen Brodkin Sacks, Sondra Hale, Lise Vogel, and Gail Dubrow for their comments at various stages in its development. I also appreciate the helpful suggestions of the reviewers, Pauline Bart and Elizabeth Stanko.

Reprinted with permission from *Gender & Society.* vol. 3, no. 4, December 1989, pp. 518–532. © 1989 Sociologists for Women in Society.

historic conjunction of the birth of feminism within the new left just when the Black movement was becoming separatist.

Many Black women who were interested in feminism in the early 1970s agreed with Black Panther Kathleen Cleaver that Black and white women would have to work in separate organizations, coming together in coalitions, because the problems each group of women faced were different enough that they could not be solved in the same organizations (Giddings 1984, p. 311). Thus the early anti-rape movement in the United States arose in a context of the distrust Black women felt of white feminism and the beginnings of Black feminism. This legacy, combined with the general level of racism in American society, has made multiracial organizing, feminist or otherwise, difficult.

Long before the anti-rape movement, the issues of race and rape were linked in the United States. From the 1880s through the 1950s, lynchings of Black men were justified on the basis of their threat to white women's virtue. Although Ida B. Wells investigated over 700 lynchings and found that accusations of rape had been made in less than one-third, the myth of Black men's proclivity for rape became ingrained in our culture (Davis 1981; Giddings 1984; Hooks 1981) and was manipulated to keep both Black men and white women in their places. Lynching, rather than rape, became the focus of Black women's activism against violence.

Incidents that linked race and rape caused further disjuncture between white feminists and Blacks in the current feminist movement in the United States. First, as the nationalist phase of the Black movement crested, several male leaders, most notably Eldridge Cleaver in *Soul on Ice* (1968), called for the raping of white women as a political act. Second, Susan Brownmiller, in her eagerness to prove the seriousness of rape, echoed the racist justification of lynching in her path-breaking book

Against Our Will (1975), perpetuating the "myth of the Black rapist" (Davis 1981). Rather than confront the issue of rape, even when Black women were raped by Black men, a special issue of *Ebony* magazine on Black-on-Black crime omitted rape (Bart and O'Brien 1985, p. 90).

In 1973, Roz Pulitzer, a Black member of the Manhattan (New York) Women's Political Caucus, which was lobbying on rape issues, said she did not expect Black women to get very involved in the issue. Like Kathleen Cleaver, she felt that "the splits between the concerns of white women and our concerns was so great that strategically we had to have a black organization to give the women's movement credibility in our own communities. Every group must go through its period of self-identity" (New York Radical Feminists 1974, p. 243). However, Pulitzer, who had been instrumental in forming a Mayor's Task Force on Rape in New York City in 1973, hoped that Black women would take what white women had learned and use it to set up rape counseling and public education in the Black community.

In Los Angeles, it took more than 10 years to happen, and when it did, the impetus came not from grassroots Black feminist groups, but Black community organizations responding to the state's call for proposals. This study of the expansion of racial diversity in the Los Angeles anti-rape movement is based primarily on oral-history interviews with participants since its beginning in the early 1970s through 1988 and with officials in the California Office of Criminal Justice Planning (OCJP). I conducted 35 interviews between 1987 and 1989 with women who were known as leaders, formal and informal. The interviews took from one to three hours and covered the participant's experience in rape crisis work, her account and perceptions of historical events, and explanations of how the organizations worked. Movement documents, in particular the monthly minutes of the Southern California Rape Hotline Alliance from 1979 to 1988, supplemented the oral accounts.

WOMEN OF COLOR AND THE LOS ANGELES ANTI-RAPE MOVEMENT

The early 1980s were a period of increasing awareness of racial and ethnic issues in the U.S. anti-rape movement. Although there were relatively few women of color in the movement in California, the formation of the Southern California Rape Hotline Alliance and the statewide Coalition of Rape Crisis Centers brought them together and provided the forum in which to raise issues about doing rape crisis work among Black, Latina and Chicana, Asian, and Native American women. The Coalition's Women of Color Caucus brought together women of color in southern California.

The East Los Angeles Rape Hotline, founded in 1976, was the earliest, and one of the few anti-rape organizations that was not predominantly white. It was founded by Latina women concerned about providing bilingual and culturally appropriate services in the largely Latino, Chicano, and Mexicano area of east Los Angeles county. As one of the few bilingual hotlines of any kind, it was kept busy with all kinds of community services, not just rape crisis work. Its connection to the other local anti-rape organizations waxed and waned over the years until 1979, when the Alliance grew and the statewide Coalition provided a forum for meeting other women of color in the movement.

Another ethnically based rape hotline also existed by the late 1970s, although it was less connected to the Los Angeles anti-rape movement. In 1978, Nilda Rimonte started a project to provide rape crisis services to Pacific and Asian immigrant women in Los Angeles. Although Rimonte participated in the Alliance regularly, the Center for the Pacific-Asian Family, as the hotline she founded was called, was not a grassroots organization to the same extent as other hotlines. Because it was set up to serve many language groups (Vietnamese, Korean, Laotian, Cambodian, Filipino, and others), counselors were generally staff members. They also ran a battered women's shelter, so the rape hotline was only one project of the organization. Nevertheless, Rimonte was a central figure in raising ethnic and racial issues in the California anti-rape movement.

By 1982, racism had become a central issue in the movement and in groups' disputes with the state funding agency. Santa Cruz Women Against Rape was defunded (Mackle, Pernell, Shirchild, Baratta, and Groves 1982) and later that year, the East Los Angeles Rape Hotline was audited by the OCJP. Although the organization was told that the OCJP planned "to very carefully scrutinize all rape crisis centers receiving funds" (Alliance Minutes, June 12, 1982), the fact that it was singled out seemed to carry racist overtones. Hotlines had also begun to treat racism as a serious topic in counselor training and the Women of Color Caucus had begun meeting regularly.

The National Coalition Against Sexual Assault (NCASA) had also begun to pay attention to racial diversity. Beverly Smith, a nationally known Black feminist, was a keynote speaker at its 1984 conference and tried to transform the historic connection between race and rape into a positive one by comparing the two crimes rather than setting them in opposition to each other. She made the analogy that "lynching is to racism as rape is to sexism," suggesting that the cultural context makes such acts possible (Roth and Baslow 1984, p. 56).

By 1983, the Women of Color Caucus had made a connection between OCJP funding criteria and problems of rape crisis centers serving Third World people. According to Alliance minutes of January 15, 1983, Emilia Bellone and Teresa Contreras noted that state allocations were based primarily on the number of victims served by particular programs. In addition, the state allocated funds for "new and innovative" programs, encouraging new grant proposals, while money was most needed for basic services, community education, and outreach. An Alliance committee prepared a position paper asking the OCJP to revise its funding allocation criteria. Their central criticism was that using the number of victims served as the key criterion caused "inequities in the distribution of funds, which especially handicaps ethnic minority rape crisis centers":

> One concern stems from the fact that in order to provide rape crisis services in ethnic minority communities, a great deal of time and effort has to go into doing strong outreach and community education. Although in recent years there has been a marked increase in awareness and information about sexual assault for the general public, much of this has not permeated ethnic minority communities. Many factors affect this—language barriers, racism, distrust of educators and the media, etc. (Position Paper 1983, p. 1)

The paper goes on to point out several related problems: traditional coping strategies among some cultures that discourage going outside the family for help, the need for materials to be translated to reach nonassimilated people, and the extra hours of work required both for outreach in ethnic communities and to provide adequate services to individual survivors. They linked class issues with those of race and ethnicity:

> Typically, more time must be spent with a survivor who has fewer personal resources. These survivors tend to be ethnic minority women. Often, a non-assimilated ethnic minority survivor requires translating and interpreting, transportation, overnight shelter for herself and possibly children, and counseling to significant others in addition to the usual counseling and advocacy services. So, if a rape crisis center serves a predominantly ethnic minority population, the "average" number of hours of service provided to each survivor is much higher than for a center that serves a predominantly white population. (Position Paper 1983, p. 2)

Grant proposals for "innovative" programs had been the only strategy centers had to increase funding for special outreach. A major issue for the East Los Angeles Rape Hotline was how to include families, especially the men, in their services, which was essential in order to gain legitimacy in the Latino community. In 1983, through a grant for innovative projects from the OCJP, they produced a *fotonovela* about a family in which a teenage girl has been sexually assaulted by her uncle. The story line upholds the cultural value placed on the family, but modifies it so that the young girl's integrity is not sacrificed. They also had an innovative theater program for education in rape prevention. These programs were successful for reaching their community, but were costly to the organization in the time spent creating new programs, and did not solve the problem of more money for basic services.

Although the Alliance committee that wrote the position paper did not get a direct response, Marilyn Peterson, the Branch Manager of the Sexual Assault Program at the OCJP, began pursuing avenues of additional money for "high crime" and "minority" areas. The OCJP studied the rates of rape reported by police agencies and rape crisis centers in communities across the state, assuming that the rate of underreporting was consistent. They then surveyed the availability of services in the community by district attorneys' offices, law enforcement, hospitals, family service agencies, and so on. In addition to a high crime rate, the poverty rate was factored in, because areas with few resources tend to have fewer social services. According to Peterson, the survey was a necessary formality—a bureaucratic justification for what she already knew was needed. The target money was awarded to some of the existing rape crisis centers in Los Angeles, but its most significant effect in the county was the establishment of two new programs located in predominantly Black areas, South Central Los Angeles and Compton. Women in these areas could theoretically use one of the existing hotlines, but geographical distance made providing in-person services such as hospital accompaniment more difficult. The primarily white hotlines did sparse outreach to the Black community. Furthermore, women of color in the anti-rape movement were developing a theory of service provision that recognized that women in crisis were most likely to feel comfortable and use services if they were provided by someone like themselves (Dubrow et al. 1986; Kanuha 1987; Lum 1988; Rimonte 1985). This notion reflects the influence of the peer-counseling roots of rape crisis work as well as increasing awareness of cultural issues. For outreach to succeed, it was important for services like rape crisis to be *of* the community, which the white hotlines were not. Thus homogeneous organizations of different ethnic groups were more effective.

CONSEQUENCES OF FUNDING: A DIFFERENT APPROACH

The first of the new hotlines, the Rosa Parks Sexual Assault Crisis Center, began in late 1984, in anticipation of the target funding. Avis Ridley-Thomas, who was instrumental in its founding, was at the nexus of several networks that led to the founding of Rosa Parks. She had been working for the new Victim Witness Assistance Program out of the city attorney's office since 1980. Because of her work there, she had been recommended by Assembly-woman Maxine Waters to be on

the State Sexual Assault Services Advisory Committee (SAC), which advised the OCJP on funding for rape crisis services, training for prosecutors, and funding for research. Ridley-Thomas became chair of the committee, which at first had very little money to give out. Hers was another voice, in addition to those of the Alliance members, raising the issue of underfunding of minority areas. It was clear from her knowledge of South Central Los Angeles that this area had the highest rate of reported sexual assault in the state and no community-provided services.

A longtime activist in the Black community, she tried to organize women's groups to take on rape crisis services as a project, but none that she approached felt they could do that in addition to their other work. She and her husband, Mark Ridley-Thomas, who was the director of the local branch of the Southern Christian Leadership Conference (SCLC), applied for and received an OCJP grant to start a rape crisis service. Thus Avis Ridley-Thomas's position in the funding agency, her involvement in service provision to victims, and her relationship to SCLC converged to create a place for the new service.

The Compton YWCA was the second new organization to start a rape crisis program in a predominantly Black community. When the OCJP called for proposals for target funding, the city's police chief encouraged the YWCA director, Elaine Harris, to apply for it. Compton, one of the small cities that compose Los Angeles county, is located south of South Central Los Angeles. Although the rate of home ownership is high, so are the poverty and crime rates. As in many of the economically abandoned areas of the county, gangs are an important source of social identity for young people, which, combined with their involvement in drug dealing, has created a violent environment. The Compton YWCA has struggled to be a community resource in this context. In addition to traditional programs ranging from fitness to music, it offers a minority women's employment program, a job board, a support group for single parents, a food program for needy families, drug diversion counseling, and a support group for families of incarcerated people. With crime and violence a major social and political issue in the community, the organization had a cooperative relationship with the police, which led to the application for target funding. The YWCA had numerous resources, including experience with grant proposal writing, that could be enlisted in starting the Sexual Assault Crisis Program.

How these two new rape crisis programs were started differed markedly from the existing anti-rape organizations, which had consequences for the nature of the movement and relationships between the new organizations and the older ones in the Alliance and the Coalition. All of the older organizations had been founded out of some kind of grassroots process and with some connection to the wider feminist movement of the 1970s. The stands on feminism differed among the older organizations, but because they were founded in the midst of vibrant feminist activism, they associated what they were doing with the women's movement at some level. The Rosa Parks and Compton programs, by contrast, were founded with substantial state funding and without strong links to contemporary feminism.

Their parent organizations were not simply social service agencies. Both SCLC and the YWCA were progressive organizations with grassroots origins, but had long since become established and "becalmed" (Zald and Ash 1966), with hierarchical leadership and bureaucratic structures. The women who were hired to direct the sexual assault programs were social service administrators, not activists. Nevertheless, many of the women who worked in the new organizations were drawn by the opportunity to work with Black women. As Joan Crear, a staff member at Rosa Parks, said:

> Personally, I got involved because I was very much interested in women's issues, in particular Black women, and I didn't feel that there was a forum in my community for them. I know there was resistance to the whole notion of violence, women's issues, feminism, and I wanted to work in an environment that advocated on behalf of Black women. As for the Rosa Parks Center, it seemed like a good place to start, and I envisioned the center as a place where eventually, while we're funded to deal with sexual assault, that it's very difficult to separate sexual assault from just what it means to be a woman in the universe, so it gave me an avenue to do that kind of work.

Similarly, Monica Williams, director of the Compton YWCA program, said:

> I had a genuine concern for women's issues and rights and moreover, I think I had a real concern for living, since I live in this community [Compton] now, a real concern for Black women. I think our image has always been of strong and persevering and you can take it all, and it doesn't make a difference, and I started to notice that most of the women who were assaulted, that it wasn't a priority for them, that they couldn't see that they were hurting, too. And that usually their first concern was their children, or their home or their husband, or how'm I going to make ends meet, so for me it's just, it's a challenge.

Drawn by their interest in combining working with Black women and working for the Black community, and influenced by the articulated feminism of the women they met through the Alliance, these women began to see themselves as feminists, but the primary interpretive framework in their organizations was community service.

The community action framework, very much a part of the mission of both parent organizations, provided a rationale within which to fit rape crisis services, which replaced the feminist impetus of the older groups. SCLC linked the rape crisis service with their philosophy of nonviolence. The YWCA had a long history of programs to help women and girls in crisis, and many Ys around the country sponsored rape crisis services. Additionally, the emphasis of the target grants on racial and ethnic inequity in service and funding resonated with the national YWCA imperative adopted in 1970 and used in much of their literature: "to thrust our collective power as a women's movement toward the elimination of racism wherever it exists and by any means necessary."

Despite these ideological frames, the new centers were more influenced by the OCJP's definition of rape crisis work than the older anti-rape organizations. Founded with OCJP grants, they had not gone through the grassroots stage of scraping together precious resources from their communities and therefore did not have independent community roots. As a consequence of their dependence on the OCJP, they were more bureaucratized from the beginning and less suspicious of the OCJP, in contrast to the contentious history that members of the Alliance had with the agency, but similar to the feelings of many less radical rape crisis people around the state. (See Rodriguez [1988] and Schecter [1982] for accounts of similar splits in the battered women's shelter movement between those who resisted conventional bureaucratic organization and those who accepted it.)

Nevertheless, the community context in which the new services were provided posed contradictions with the state's bureaucratic concerns and practices. The special grants that led to the founding of Rosa Parks and Compton were intended to adjust for problems in the delivery of services, such as "hazardous working conditions, an absence of complementary service providers or agencies, high cost of providing services, lack of alternative funding sources, geographical and/or

economic conditions; and unmet need for culturally and/or ethnically appropriate services" (OCJP *Guidelines* 1987, p. 33). These new organizations were therefore encouraged to design programs that met the basic guidelines *and* the specific needs of their communities. The sponsoring organizations, the YWCA and SCLC, were both practiced at responding to their communities and developed rape crisis programs with emphases that differed from other anti-rape programs. For example, the Rosa Parks staff set up support groups to deal with the intertwined problems of incest and alcoholism.

The ways the Compton women served their community despite standardized guidelines was an even sharper contrast. There, rape crisis workers confronted the reality of gangs on a daily basis as part of the context of the community they served. For example, to avoid confrontations among participants, they had to monitor what colors the young women wore to educational and support group meetings. Some of the women they counseled were survivors of gang-related rapes. Because basic survival was often the presenting problem of the women served, they evolved a broader approach to support and counseling. As the director said:

> A woman may come in or call in for various reasons. She has no place to go, she has no job, she has no support, she has no money, she has no food, she's been beaten, and after you finish meeting all those needs, or try to meet all those needs, then she may say, by the way, during all this, I was being raped. So the immediate needs have to be met. So that makes our community different than other communities. A person wants their basic needs first. It's a lot easier to discuss things when you're full. So that we see people who, when they come in with their children, and their children are running around and the person is on edge, we may find out that she just hasn't eaten in a few days. And we may have to pool together money and give her everybody's lunch, or take them to lunch, and

days later, maybe months later, the person will say, by the way, I did come in because I was raped, but since you brought up . . . the other things, I do need a place to stay, and I do need a job, and I can't go to the police. So . . . needs are different.

Approaching rape crisis work in such a holistic way did not conform to the requirements of the bureaucracy that provided the funding. In spite of this director's positive view of the OCJP, she also expressed frustration that very labor-intensive work was often not counted toward funding:

> A lot of what we do cannot be documented. That there's no place on that form for this woman called and she's standing outside with three kids and she don't have no place to go. [Because the form asks about] rape! So you know you just, it's almost like you end up having this group that's so concerned that it's very difficult for us when a woman calls and says she's battered, not to tell her to come here for counseling, even though that's not what we're supposed to do. When she says, but I'm right up the street, I don't want to go to the shelter, I just want to talk to somebody, and a staff person like Irma or Roslyn will spend hours with this person and afterwards come in and say, god she's feeling better, and I think this, and I'm going to take her over to the shelter, and . . . it fits no place. It's just something you did. It was an "information and referral."

These "special service delivery problems," as the OCJP *Guidelines* (1987) puts it, are also different from the kind of issues other rape crisis centers face, largely because of this center's location in a relatively impoverished community in which services are scarce.

NEED FOR INNOVATIVE OUTREACH

The challenge of successful outreach to ethnically and racially diverse communities was one of the issues that prompted the Alliance position paper. Getting clients was more than a simple issue of publicity and involved

changing the cultural ethic about seeking help. The ELA and Pacific-Asian rape hotlines had faced this problem for years, and women at the hotlines in the Black communities tackled it anew. Despite the high rates of sexual assault in these communities, there was no mobilized citizens' group demanding services. Once the services were funded, women from both Rosa Parks and Compton had to work on legitimizing the idea of seeking a support group or therapy from the outside, a relatively new idea in the Black community. Joan Crear of Rosa Parks explained:

> In our community confidentiality, whether it's rape or anything else, is really the key; a community where things don't go outside your family; you know, have a history of family taking care, says don't tell. . . . [I]n terms of picking up and using a hotline, when we're doing education, it's not just about rape, it's about . . . you can call us, we won't tell anybody, we'll keep your secrets. Also in a community where you talk about gang violence, you have people that are afraid. It's really difficult when I talk to a teenager and she's been raped by a gang member. I don't want to . . . tell her to tell the police necessarily, 'cause she's scared for her brother, you know, and she's scared for her family.

Ethnographic studies of Black communities have illuminated the extent of informal networks among members of even the poorest communities that provide both material and emotional support (e.g., Liebow 1967; Stack 1974), but the pursuit of more formal support through counseling is new. Avis Ridley-Thomas, founder of Rosa Parks, talked about the pressure to "strain up"—be tough and take the hard knocks—which militates against seeking outside help with emotional or psychological problems. Williams elaborated:

> I think we work on empowerment a lot more because of the community we serve. That it's difficult for a person to sit in a group and talk about their rape and the rapist and go through all of the psychological changes without first understanding that they have some other prob-

lems too. So that what's been helpful is for Black women to see other Black women to say I understand what it's like, to have to worry about the kids and him. . . . [T]he former sources of support are gone. That now you see more of us putting children in childcare and daycare, whereas before we had mothers and sister and aunts, and you know, the extended family. So that now, we're kind of [little rueful laugh] socialized a little more, so that we're running into the same things that other people are running into. We say we're stressed. Before we just said life was tough.

The emergence of an ethic to protect victims' rights was a bridge by which rape crisis services came to Black communities. Competition between the Sexual Assault and Victim-Witness Programs within OCJP led Marilyn Peterson to look for creative ways to increase rape crisis funding, and the target grants were one such strategy that succeeded. Despite this internal competition, victims' rights was a significant factor in Black communities' receptivity to rape crisis services.

The movement for victims' rights helped legitimize the culture of therapy. Because people of color are more likely to be victims of violent crime in the United States, much of the outreach by the newly established victim-witness programs in the early 1980s was to Blacks, according to Avis Ridley-Thomas. Seeking help for emotional traumas became more acceptable, not only in state supported services, but also in grassroots victims' groups. While these groups are only loosely connected to the rape crisis organizations, they contributed to a climate in which reaching and helping sexual assault victims was less alien than it might have been earlier.

RACISM, HOMOPHOBIA, AND FEMINISM

The dynamics of interpersonal racism in the Los Angeles anti-rape movement are intertwined in a complex way with differences of political perspective and homophobia.

Although the anti-rape movement had become more diverse, the dominant subculture within the local movement is (white) feminism, strongly influenced by a lesbian perspective. The combination of feminist jargon and political viewpoints and the high number of lesbians in leadership positions create an alienating environment for many of the Black women in the anti-rape movement. Although white activists are ideologically predisposed to accept women of color because they believe it is right, their theory about what women of color should be—that is, they should be radical because they are oppressed—does not always fit with reality. Black women hired to work in rape crisis centers have tended to identify with the social service orientation, thus the more conservative side of the movement, which creates tension with the more politically radical women who have dominated the Alliance.

Racial and political differences are compounded by homophobia. Homosexuality is even more hidden in the American Black community than in the general society. Blacks are not alone in the anti-rape movement in their discomfort with the openly lesbian presence; dissension has also surfaced in the statewide Coalition, often between centers outside the major urban areas, which tend to be more conservative, and those from Los Angeles and the Bay Area. However, locally, because a substantial number of the white women are lesbians and most of the Black women are heterosexual, the overlap of racial and sexuality differences exaggerates the schism. Both sides feel they have a moral cause for offense when someone from the other side is inadvertently racist or homophobic.

Despite the fact that all of the centers include these topics in their volunteer and staff training, these tensions affect both interpersonal interactions and organizational processes. Differences in life-style lead to divergent concerns. For example, several

Black women mentioned that they wished there were support in the Alliance for dealing with husbands and families while working in rape crisis. This concern for intimate others was shared by heterosexual white women, but not by lesbians, because their partners were less likely to be threatened by their work with survivors of male violence. Lesbians, expecting Black women to be homophobic, sometimes have challenged and tested their sexuality. Even differences of style separated women: for example, the convention of dressing up in the Black community and of dressing down in white feminist circles.

Black women, like some Chicana women earlier, have also felt marginalized by being outside the shared reference system of white feminists. As Teresa Contreras of ELA put it:

> I'm fairly sure that some of us felt threatened by the jargon, the politics, the feminist politics, and the real assertiveness of the women involved in the rape crisis movement, and their confrontational style was totally contrary to the Chicano style.

In interviews, some Black women noted that they did not really understand what "feminism" was and yet felt expected to know and support its precepts. Being thrown into the Alliance and the Coalition where this was the political vocabulary could be intimidating and alienating. Over time, however, some have come to put the name "feminist" to their own positions. Joan Crear, for example, was tentatively identifying herself as a feminist at the time I interviewed her, after working in the anti-rape movement for over two years. She said:

> It has become important for me to say "I'm a feminist" to other women in my community, but I work on a definition where it doesn't sound like it's such a big thing, because I believe that most women, or a lot of women are under . . . some of the things that feminism

encompasses. . . . [F]or me it means to want to be or to demand to share power in relationships, so I don't know if that's an appropriate term, because when I think about sharing power within relationships I have to look at that in terms of sharing power with my children, my boss, whether male or female, and so it means . . . I take responsibility for things that happen in my life. . . . I see myself as an adult woman, as an adult.

Not all women of color live in South Central or East Los Angeles, so the existence of the ethnically based rape crisis centers is only one step toward serving all women and having a multiracial movement. The predominantly white hotlines in Los Angeles are still concerned about recruiting women of color, but face a dilemma when that goal conflicts with maintaining their integrity on feminism and homophobia. But according to Rochelle Coffey, director of the Pasadena hotline, the existence of the Black hotlines has helped give the predominantly white hotlines credibility with women of color in other parts of the county.

CONCLUSION

Whether states co-opt or facilitate social movements is historically contingent on particular political forces (Tilly 1978), and in the historical period described here, both processes occurred. Without state funding, the new Black anti-rape organizations might not exist. But their founding also resulted in the further infusion of a bureaucratic orientation into the anti-rape movement, because the new organizations bear the stamp of their origins. However, there is also a new source of resistance, in addition to the feminists, to the state's demands. The commitment of Rosa Parks and Compton to "serve their community" means that they make demands back to the state to shift its policies so that service is possible.

Despite conflicts, women in the Alliance, Black and white, lesbian and heterosexual, work together. The prediction from the early 1970s that women of color would need to establish their own organizations in order to become active in feminist causes seems to be borne out. Racially and ethnically homogeneous organizations have contributed more to diversifying the movement than integration within organizations. They successfully work together in mixed coalitions when they have powerful common interests, but independent bases.

REFERENCES

Bart, Pauline, and Patricia H. O'Brien. 1985. *Stopping Rape: Successful Survival Strategies.* New York: Pergamon.

Brownmiller, Susan. 1975. *Against Our Will: Men, Women, and Rape.* New York: Bantam.

Cleaver, Eldridge. 1968. *Soul on Ice.* New York: Dell.

Davis, Angela. 1981. *Women, Race, and Class.* New York: Random House.

Dubrow, Gail, et al. 1986. "Planning to End Violence against Women: Notes from a Feminist Conference at UCLA." *Women and Environments* 8:4–27.

Evans, Sara. 1979. *Personal Politics.* New York: Vintage Books.

Ferree, Myra Marx, and Beth B. Hess. 1985. *Controversy and Coalition: The New Feminist Movement.* Boston: Twayne.

Giddings, Paula. 1984. *When and Where I Enter: The Impact of Black Women on Race and Sex in America.* New York: Bantam.

Hooks, Bell. 1981. *Ain't I a Woman: Black Women and Feminism.* Boston: South End Press.

Kanuha, Valli. 1987. "Sexual Assault in Southeast Asian Communities: Issues in Intervention." *Response* 10:4–6.

Liebow, Elliot. 1967. *Tally's Corner.* Boston: Little, Brown.

Lum, Joan. 1988. "Battered Asian Women." *Rice* (March):50–52.

Mackle, Nancy, Deanne Pernell, Jan Shirchild, Consuelo Baratta, and Gail Groves. 1982. "Dear Aegis: Letter from Santa Cruz Women against Rape." *Aegis: Magazine on Ending Violence against Women* 35:28–30.

New York Radical Feminists. 1974. *Rape: The First Sourcebook for Women,* edited by Noreen Connell and Cassandra Wilson. New York: New American Library.

Office of Criminal Justice Planning. 1987. *California Sexual Assault Victim Services and Prevention Program Guidelines.* Sacramento: State of California.

Rimonte, Nilda. 1985. Protocol for the Treatment of Rape and Other Sexual Assault. Los Angeles County Commission for Women.

Rodriguez, Noelie Maria. 1988. "Transcending Bureaucracy: Feminist Politics at a Shelter for Battered Women." *Gender & Society* 2:214–27.

Roth, Stephanie, and Robin Baslow. 1984. "Compromising Positions at Anti-Rape Conference." *Aegis: Magazine on Ending Violence against Women* 38:56–58.

Schecter, Susan. 1982. *Women and Male Violence: The Visions and Struggles of the Battered Women's Movement.* Boston: South End Press.

Southern California Rape Hotline Alliance. 1982. Minutes.

———. 1983. "Position Paper." Drafted by Emilia Bellone and Nilda Rimonte for the Committee to Develop OCJP Position Paper.

Stack, Carol. 1974. *All Our Kin: Strategies for Survival in a Black Community.* New York: Harper & Row.

Tilly, Charles. 1978. *From Mobilization to Revolution.* Reading, MA: Addison-Wesley.

Zald, Mayer N., and Roberta Ash. 1966. "Social Movement Organizations: Growth, Decay and Change." *Social Forces* 44:327–41.

CHAPTER 13

FEAR AND THE PERCEPTION OF ALTERNATIVES: ASKING "WHY BATTERED WOMEN DON'T LEAVE" IS THE WRONG QUESTION

ANGELA BROWNE

ABSTRACT

All too often people ask battered women, "Why don't you just leave him?" In this chapter Browne explains how this is the wrong question. She also points out that, in fact, many women do leave. However, leaving does not necessarily end the violence. For many, it simply escalates it. More battered women are killed in the process of leaving than at any other time.*

In this chapter, Browne describes the psychological and practical barriers women encounter in leaving a battering partner. The practical barriers include such issues as finding a place to live, fear of losing one's children, and inability to receive public assistance because the woman is still married or does not have an address. The fear of retaliation is equally as powerful. Not only have many of the women been beaten in earlier attempts to leave, but almost all the women report death threats if they were to leave. Most important, leaving does not guarantee safety for the women or their children.

Browne likens women's victimization to the experiences of abuse suffered by prisoners of war. Some battered women eventually kill their abuser. She is interested in discovering what leads those battered women to kill. Her study suggests that the explanation is to be found not in the women who murder but in the men: the murdered men were more assaultive, raped more frequently, made more threats to kill, used alcohol and drugs more often, and had higher rates of child abuse than batterers who were not killed. As Browne concludes, "the women's behavior seemed to be primarily in reaction to the level of threat and violence

---

*Jane E. Brody, "Personal Health: When Love Turns Violent: The Roots of Abuse," *The New York Times*, Mar. 18, 1992, p. C12.

coming in." The violence became "outside the 'normal' range of violent behavior"!

In the recent past, some women who react with violence to their being seriously battered have used in a defense of their behavior the "battered woman's syndrome" (prolonged abuse convinces the victim that violence is the only way out). As one might expect, prosecutors are divided as to whether it is "a valid defense or an exaggerated claim by someone groping for a way out of a murder conviction."* Since women who kill their batterers strongly believe they were in a kill-or-be-killed situation, why isn't the women's behavior seen as self-defense?

Elsewhere, Evan Stark[†] argued that homicide is part of a larger pattern of interpersonal violence grounded in unequal gender relations in the family, which is embedded in the broader systems of unequal economic, social, and sexual control. How might you use Stark's argument to understand Browne's findings?

---

*Jane Gross, "Abused Women Who Kill Now Seek Way Out of Cells," *The New York Times,* Sept. 15, 1992, p. A16.

[†]Evan Stark, "Rethinking Homicide: Violence, Race, and the Politics of Gender," *International Journal of Health Services,* 1990, 20:1, 3–26.

Probably the most frequently asked question about women who are being abused by their partners is, "Why don't they just leave?" Especially when the abuse is severe, it is hard to understand why a woman would stay around for the next attack. Actually, many women do leave; they are among our friends and neighbors, and possibly our families. The majority of them, however, are never identified as abused women. Typically, they do not realize how many other women have shared the same experiences; being afraid that other people would not understand or would think less of them if they knew, they do not discuss the abuse they suffered in the past. They may still blame themselves for having become involved with an abusive man in the first place, or for the failure of their interactions with him, and so carry their memories and the lingering confusion alone. In the comparison group, over half (53 percent) of the women had left their battering relationships by the time they were interviewed; many had never talked about them before. Even in the homicide group, women left or attempted to leave their violent partners. Some had been separated or divorced for up to two years prior to the lethal incident.*

The question, "Why don't battered women leave?" is based on the assumption that leaving will end the violence. While this may be

---

**Editors' note:* In this study Browne compares battered women who have killed their abusers (the homicide group) with battered women who have not killed their batterers (the comparison group). The *homicide group* consists of 42 women from 15 states charged with murder or attempted murder of their mates. Their average age was 36 years; 66 percent were white, 22 percent were black, and 12 percent were Spanish-American or Chicano. Half were from working-class backgrounds; one-quarter each were from the middle and lower classes; 2 women (5 percent) were raised in upper-class homes. The *comparison group* of 205 women in abusive relationships were from six states. More than half (55 percent) were working-class, 41 percent were lower-class, and 4 percent were middle-class. Despite the self-identified class differences, there were no differences in educational levels between the homicide and comparison groups.

true for some women who leave after the first or second incident (these women are rarely identified as battered, and still less often studied), even the smoothness of those separations depends on the abuser's sense of desperation or abandonment and his willingness or tendency to do harm when faced with an outcome he does not want or cannot control. The longer the relationship continues, and the more investment in it by both partners, the more difficult it becomes for a woman to leave an abusive mate safely. Some estimates suggest that at least 50 percent of women who leave their abusers are followed and harassed or further attacked by them.[1] To separate from an individual who has threatened to harm you if you go increases—at least in the short run—the very risk from which you are trying to escape.

Additionally, getting away is not as simple as it sounds. After a crime such as a rape or robbery committed by a stranger, victims often change apartments or even houses to avoid another offense by the attacker. But it is difficult for an abused woman to just "disappear" from her partner or husband. Even if it were possible to sever an intimate relationship so cleanly, couples often hold property in common, have children in common, know one another's daily routines, families, and places of employment, and have mutual friends. It is extremely difficult for an abused woman to go into long-term hiding. Another way to look at this issue is to ask, "Why should the *woman* leave?" Why should the victim and, possibly, her children, hit the road like fugitives, leaving the assailant the home and belongings, when he is the one who broke the law?

Women initially remain with these men out of love and commitment. They may hope for a favorable change and make attempts toward understanding and resolution, especially in the early days of a relationship when the violence is less frequent and less severe.

Often, they are ashamed to let others know what is occurring in their relationships, and lose time attributing the problems to themselves and attempting to make adaptions that will eliminate further assaults. They also worry about the impact a separation might have on the children, and may stay for their sake, if the man is not abusive to them. Yet, as the severity and frequency of abuse increases, three additional factors have a major impact on the women's decision to stay with violent partners: (1) practical problems in effecting a separation, (2) the fear of retaliation if they do leave, and (3) the shock reactions of victims to abuse.

PRACTICAL PROBLEMS IN LEAVING

The point at which many outsiders suggest a woman should decide to leave a violent relationship—immediately after an abusive incident—is precisely when she is least able to plan such a move. Frightened, in shock, and often physically injured, all she wants to do is survive. Shelters that house abused women are now established in many cities (although in rural areas, these facilities are often lacking or are located many miles from the women's home).[2] Yet they are often full. Even when a shelter has room for a woman, the maximum stay is usually less than six weeks, so the woman still must find alternative housing, provide for her children if she has any with her, obtain whatever legal help may be necessary, and plan for her continued safety from further abuse. During this time, the woman will also be trying to decide whether to file for a divorce, and where to find money to pay for fees and services—decisions most people find difficult to make, even under the best of circumstances.

If the woman leaves her children behind, the man may refuse to let her have them and may charge her with desertion. If she takes the children with her, however, she disrupts their daily lives and runs the risk that any retaliatory violence may involve them as well. If she initiates divorce proceedings against the children's father, he will usually be granted some kind of visitation rights, and the woman may be enjoined against moving out of state, even after the divorce is final. In many cases, the abuser fights the woman for custody of the children, and sometimes wins.[3] In litigation concerning custody, a man's violence against his wife is not the issue before the court, especially if there is no evidence that he has physically abused the children. In addition, if he seems established and has a job, while the woman appears in transition and unstable, he may be considered better able to care for the children, regardless of his wife's accusations of violence.

A move into hiding is particularly difficult to manage. If the woman is working, she must try to keep the transition from interfering with her job, since that job will now be crucial to her survival. Yet, if she has reason to fear retaliation by her partner, she must weigh the necessity of going to work against the danger that he will follow her there and cause her further harm. If she has school-age children, she must choose between keeping them out of school and her concern for their education, or be faced with the danger that their father may remove them from the school grounds if she lets them attend. She must also find a place to live where the man cannot find and harm her: she must weigh the benefits of leaving town for her own safety against the disruptive impact it would have on her work situation and her children's lives, as well as the complications such a move could produce in following through on litigation. If the woman does move, she might not be able to go to her family, because the man would be apt to find her there and could endanger her family as well as herself. Obviously, if an abused woman is forced to relocate to a new city or state, away from her source of income

and from family and friends—especially if she is moving children with her—the alternatives become more and more difficult to accomplish.

In one instance, the woman had lived with the man for a year before the first incident of threatened violence. After two more physically assaultive incidents during the next two years, the last one endangering the couple's infant son, she decided to leave her mate and file for divorce. Although she loved him, she knew his verbal abuse was uncalled for and was unwilling to risk further physical assaults. She wrote a letter explaining why she was leaving and, taking their child, went into hiding with relatives. She called a few nights later to let him know she and the baby were safe. She also consulted an attorney to file protection orders and help her obtain a divorce.

At the same time, the husband went to court to obtain custody of his son. He claimed that his wife had been depressed and emotionally unstable in recent months, and cited her "unexplained disappearance" from their home as evidence of her unpredictable mental state. He expressed strong concern for the safety of his child, and requested that she be found and the child removed from her care. Based on his allegations, when the woman appeared in court to obtain an order of protection, her son was taken from her and custody was awarded to the state until a temporary hearing could be arranged. The state placed the child with the abuser's family, since their place of residence was considered the most stable. The woman was allowed to have her baby one weekend every other week until temporary orders were established.

Even this visitation right was soon canceled, after further charges were made against her by the husband and his family. At this point, she was allowed only brief supervised visits each week; this supervision was provided by her husband's relatives, and her husband was frequently present. Formally, the husband was now charging her with neglect, although the charges were unfounded and she had performed all the childcare duties while they were together. Privately, he was pleading with her to come back and warning that she would never have her son again if she did not. Each court date was postponed by the husband's attorneys, as she was urged by family members to "come home." At the time of this writing, the case is still pending. The woman has been separated from her small child for nearly a year, and forced to remain in almost constant contact with her husband. Welfare is now recommending that custody of the child be awarded to the husband's relatives, with whom the baby has been staying. As one state worker told me, the fact that their stories are so contradictory makes both parents seem unreliable.

This woman's story provides one answer to the question, "Why don't battered women leave?" The woman acted independently and rationally: She left the situation when she began to realize that it would not improve; she refused to tolerate victimization; she sought legal remedies. She escaped her abuser before the violence became serious. She may also have lost her child.

FEAR OF REPRISAL

In the homicide group, many of the women stayed because they had tried to escape and been beaten for it, or because they believed their partner would retaliate against an attempt to leave him with further violence. Almost all of the women in both the homicide and the comparison groups—98 percent and 90 percent, respectively—thought the abuser could or would kill them; and many, especially in the homicide group, were convinced that they could not escape this danger by leaving. Susan Jefferson's case is an example. After Don's death, Susan said:

We were separating, but I don't think that would have solved anything. Don always said he would come back around—that I belonged to him. Just that day he had gotten an apartment, but it was only right down the street. I knew he would come after me if he saw someone he didn't know come to the house. I was scared. It seemed like the more I tried to get away, the worse things got, He was never going to quit.

The women's fears of retaliation were supported by their past experiences with the men's violence, as well as by threats of further violence if they attempted to leave. As noted earlier, 83 percent of men in the homicide group had made threats to kill, and the women took these threats quite seriously. In the case of Karen and Hal Simon, Hal wrote in his journal:

Every time, Karen would have ugly bruises on her face and neck. She would cry and beg me for a divorce, and I would tell her, "I am sorry. I won't do it again. But as for the divorce, absolutely not. If I can't have you for my wife, you will die. No one else will have you if you ever try to leave me."

Abused women's primary fear—that their abusers will find them and retaliate against their leaving—is justified. Some women who have left an abusive partner have been followed and harassed for months or even years; some have been killed.[4] The evidence suggests that, in many cases, the man's violence continues to escalate after a separation.[5] In a 1980 report to the Wisconsin Council on Criminal Justice, investigators noted: "Simply leaving the relationship does not provide adequate protection for some women. . . ." Thirty percent of the assaulted women in that study were separated from their partners when the attack occurred. Many had called the police for help, and still the assaults continued. As one woman, charged with the death of her husband, reported:

I knew if I ran he would find me. He tracked down his first wife with only her social-security number. Can you imagine what it would be like to go through life knowing that a man who intends to kill you may be just around the corner?

Violent men do search desperately for their partners once the woman leaves.[6] Often, they spend their days and nights calling her family and mutual acquaintances; phoning her place of employment or showing up there; driving around the streets looking for her; haunting school grounds, playgrounds, and grocery stores. If they believe the woman has left town, they frequently attempt to follow her, traveling to all locations they think she might be found. She is theirs. She *cannot* leave and refuse to talk to them. They may nearly kill their mates, but they do not want to lose them. Some of the women in the homicide group had been separated or divorced for up to two years before the final incident, yet were still experiencing life-threatening harassment and abuse from men unwilling to relinquish their connection.

For many battered women, leaving their mates and living in constant fear of reprisal or death seems more intolerable than remaining, despite their fears of further harm. Women in hiding relate how they are afraid to go into their apartment when they get home; to go to work in the morning or to leave at night; to approach their car in a parking lot; to visit friends. They know if their estranged partner finds them, he may simply retaliate and not wait to talk. And if he does begin a conversation and they do not agree to go home, they know it may trigger an attack. Every sound in the night, every step in the hall, every pair of headlights pulling up behind them might be him. Accomplishing daily tasks against this wall of fear becomes exhausting. Added to the other difficulties these women are facing, and the life-changing decisions that must be made, it is often too much and the women

return home. Shelter personnel who work with battered women struggle against their frustration when women return to their abusers; yet in many cases, the women are simply overwhelmed.

ESCAPE ATTEMPTS

The point of, or even the discussion of, separation is one of the most dangerous times for partners in a violent relationship. Abusive men threatened with the loss of their mates may be severely depressed, angry, agitated, homicidal, or suicidal.[7] Even attempts to discuss a separation can set off a violent attack.

> Susan couldn't take it anymore. She had been living with Don for six months, and the violence kept getting worse. Something happened nearly every week; Don would say he was sorry, but it never got any better. She decided that the only solution was to leave. When Don came home, Susan sat down to talk with him about it. She told him that she couldn't stand the fights, couldn't understand what was happening, couldn't take the things he said to her. She wanted him to understand. She wanted their parting to be amicable.
>
> Don began acting very strangely—running around and pulling furniture in front of the door; acting as though he was angry, but laughing and joking at the same time. Susan had never seen him behave like this and was suddenly very frightened. It seemed crazy to her. Don kept saying, "You're not going anywhere! You're my prisoner here. I'm going to put bars on the doors and windows, and keep you here. . . . You're my prisoner." He would laugh like he was kidding with her, then suddenly act furious and throw her across the room or onto the floor. He would smash things in the room with his fists or his foot, and throw things against the wall. He

made her sit in a corner like a child, saying, "Sit here. Face the wall. Hold still now. You just sit there and listen to me. Look at me now. . . . Don't look at me like that. . . ." He had a stick, and he'd hit her with it if she tried to move or speak to him. Susan was wearing a cotton shirt and he reached down and tore it off, slapping her across the back and face with it. He'd laugh; then suddenly grab and choke her, shaking her by the neck, panting with anger and exertion. Susan kept thinking, "I may never leave this house alive."

Finally, Don said, "OK. You go ahead and leave." Susan thought about not having anything on above the waist, but decided that was unimportant. She made it as far as the door when Don grabbed her and pulled her back inside, laughing, then saying angrily, "No . . . you're not going anywhere like that. You're my prisoner here. I'll never let you go now. I'm going to keep you here forever." He resumed hitting her with the stick and his hands and made her sit on the floor again. Finally, he said again that she could go and Susan ran outside and to the corner, but Don was right behind her. He started yelling at her on the street about "deserting" him. Then he suddenly became quiet and passive, took her hand, and walked her home. Susan remembers the feeling of the sun on her back and her hand in his. She knew any further move on her part would only anger him. They cleaned up the house together and threw out the broken things. Then Don made her take a nap with him, although he left the heavy furniture stacked in front of the door.

Irene Miller's experience also illustrates how dangerous it can be for an abused woman to talk with her mate about separation. The threat of abandonment is so devastating to some men that they would rather kill the woman than see her go.[8] Irene's case is typical of many women in the homicide group, in that repeated attempts at separation and escape always failed.

Irene gradually came to from a beating the night before, frightened, exhausted, and throwing up. Mark came into the bedroom to check on her, and Irene told him she thought they should get a divorce; she couldn't stand any more beatings, just please let her go. She reminded him of how much worse the violence was getting. This time, she wasn't sure if she'd been sleeping or unconscious. She confessed she was afraid he would kill her someday, and tried to persuade him that being apart would be the best thing for both of them.

Mark's mood changed suddenly. He denied that he beat her and held her down on the bed, shouting, "You'll *never* leave me. I'll fucking kill you if you ever try to do that!" He grabbed her ankle and was bending her foot back, like he was going to break it, then came for her face. Irene turned on her stomach to protect herself and Mark grabbed a heavy vase from the dresser and hit her on the back of the head, splitting the skin open. Then he began hitting her repeatedly with the vase, yelling, "I'll kill you. I'll fucking kill you." Irene screamed to her son to get help, and Mark left the room to pursue him.

Irene was still struggling to get up when Mark came back. He tilted her head up toward him, she thought to see how badly she was hurt, but instead jammed his forefinger into her eye. Irene cried out and reached up reflexively, and Mark bit her hand so deeply that it required stitches. A neighbor pounded on the door, yelling at Mark to let him in, but Mark ignored him. He began to choke Irene, but then seemed to notice the blood running down her head for the first time. He seemed worried about that and quit being violent, saying to her, "Honey, what happened? What did you do here?" He was still trying to curtail the bleeding when the police arrived. Mark fought with them, and it took three men to subdue him. He was taken to jail, and an ambulance transported Irene to the hospital, where she had stitches and surgery on her eye.

After she was released from the hospital, Irene left Mark. She pressed assault charges against him and she and the children stayed with various relatives. But when Mark got out of jail he began calling everyone they knew, begging to talk to her, begging them to help him find her. She obtained a restraining order and filed for divorce, but after Mark was awarded weekly visitation rights to the children, she found it impossible to keep their whereabouts a secret.

Irene got an apartment, and she and the kids moved in. Mark would come to visit the children while she was at work and then refuse to leave. The children were too afraid not to let him in and, if Irene locked the door, he broke in. Irene tried to have the restraining order enforced, but the police said it had already been violated when she let him visit the children at home. Arresting Mark always meant a fight; Irene thought they just didn't want to get involved.

In desperation, she took the children and left the state. It took Mark several months, but he quit his job and found them. Irene and the children moved again. Again he found them. After this, Irene just gave up. She thought, "What's the use? I can't get away from him. All I'm doing is moving my kids around the country like gypsies." Both children were nearly a year behind in school, and both were doing poorly. She took them back to the schools they were used to, and as soon as she set-

tled in, Mark moved in too. They were "reconciled" in March 1982. Mark died in January the following year.

Many times, women attempted escape when they could sense that an attack was imminent, or during a break in an assaultive episode.

It was Saturday morning, and Karen and Hal Simon were sitting at the kitchen table. Hal was already drinking when Karen said they were spending too much money on beer. Hal always warned Karen not to tell him what to do. He reached over and, holding her wrist, put his cigarette out in the palm of her hand. Karen ran to the sink to run cold water over it and, to calm him down, said she was sorry. But Hal followed and slammed her into the counter, yelling at her about never leaving him alone. He hit her several times and then said he was going to get the gun. Karen knew what that meant and just stood there; they had been through this before. She never knew if someday he would really use it, but she knew she didn't have time to get away. She had terrible nightmares about him shooting her in the back as she ran across the yard, so she never tried.

Hal came back with the rifle. He pressed it against her temple and clicked the hammer, then began ramming it into her stomach, yelling, "I'll kill you, goddamn it! I'll kill you this time!" Finally, he laid the gun down and went outside. Karen could see him pacing around and knew he was still angry. He'd talk to himself about all the things she had done wrong and really attack her later.

When Hal left to get more beer, Karen fled, taking her small dog with her. Hal had nearly killed the dog several times when he was angry. She couldn't bear to leave it at home, knowing what would happen to it. Hal never allowed her to have keys to the car, so Karen walked all the way to the nearest town and asked for directions to the police department, hoping they would help her. She told them she had to get away from Hal before he killed her. The police advised her to swear out a warrant for his arrest, but Karen was so afraid of what Hal would do that she hesitated. Finally, she called a friend for advice, but the friend called Hal and he showed up at the police station a short while later. Hal was furious. He said she was not going to swear out a warrant against anyone; she was his wife, and he was taking her home. He took her elbow and walked her out the door, and nobody intervened.

All the way home, Hal was saying, "You goddamn bitch! You think you're going to leave me? When I get home we'll show you about leaving!" He snatched her over close to him, holding her clothes so she couldn't jump out. Karen was so terrified she couldn't focus on anything. She just sheltered the dog in her arms and prayed. When they got to the house, Hal came around and jerked her door open. He yanked her out of the seat and onto the ground, then began kicking her in the ribs. Each blow knocked Karen farther across the driveway. She knew she was sliding on her face, but there wasn't time to change positions. Finally, he stood over her, daring her to get up. Karen was afraid to move. The dog was still hiding in the truck; Hal carried it to the house and threw it against the concrete of the patio until he apparently thought he'd killed it. Then he made Karen go inside.

Several days later, a friend helped Karen get to the emergency room of a local hospital. Karen had been in so much pain she could hardly breathe, and walking was difficult. They found that several ribs were broken, and there seemed to be damage to

her spleen. The doctor was sympathetic and tried to get her to report it, but she told him, "That is how I got hurt so badly in the first place . . . trying to report it." She finally agreed to go to a local shelter and to receive outpatient care, but when they called to make arrangements they learned that the shelter wouldn't take dogs. Karen went home. The animal had survived, but it was badly hurt, and Karen felt responsible. She wanted to be there to take care of it; she knew Hal would kill it in retaliation if she left. After this, Karen was afraid to seek any more help. Instead, she began thinking about dying. She had always feared it, but now she thought it might not be so bad; like passing out, only you never got beaten again.

It is important to remember that, had these women been able to leave their abusers, this still would not have guaranteed their safety from further assault. The case of Sharon and Roy Bikson provides an example of repeated attempts at self-protection, and the continuation of harassment and assault after separation and divorce.

Sharon had been separated from Roy for over two years and was divorcing him, yet he continued to harass her. He broke into her home, destroyed her furniture, poured acid in the motor of her car, and slit the seats with a knife. He cut power and phone lines to the house, set small fires, and bragged to others about how he was going to kill her. He attacked and severely injured her at work, and she finally took a leave of absence from her job. She had unlisted phone numbers, but he always got them. She repeatedly called the police for protection, but they came only after Roy had already broken in.

Sharon left home and moved to different apartments to try to escape Roy, and sent her two small children to live with a babysitter. Roy found the children, threatened to kill the babysitter, and kidnapped her infant son. When Sharon appealed for help to the judge involved in the divorce proceedings, she was advised that she couldn't leave the area with the children until the divorce action was complete and the court had ruled on custody. She obtained a restraining order and several warrants, but they were never enforced. Most of her requests were simply not processed at all.

After Roy's death, the district attorney's office admitted that "her complaints were not taken seriously down here." The head deputy said that he didn't send some of the warrants on for evaluation because he "only sent those" he thought were "really important." And the hearing officer, who approves warrants for delivery, said he hadn't approved some of Sharon's because he "wasn't a marriage counselor"; they "sort of felt sorry for the guy, he seemed so upset"; and "some of these things just work themselves out, anyway." Sharon's desperate requests for help were being winnowed out at every step of the process.

Women are often blamed, or at least severely questioned, if they don't leave an abusive man, and they are too often ignored if they do. Occasionally—as demonstrated by the reaction of the hearing officer in Sharon's case—the situation gets completely turned around, and a woman's *leaving* is blamed for the subsequent violence of her partner.

In June 1983, the Denver *Rocky Mountain News* carried an article entitled, "Work term given in wife-killing: Judge says woman's departure provoked murder." It described the killing of Patricia Burns, an elementary school teacher, who attempted to escape her husband of 15 years after an abusive incident in August 1982. There was a documented his-

tory of prior abuse; she sought legal assistance immediately after leaving; she was reportedly terrified. An excerpt from the news article read as follows:

> A woman who was murdered by her estranged husband "provoked" her death by secretly leaving him without warning, according to a Denver judge who sentenced the man Wednesday to two years of work-release in the Denver County Jail.
>
> Partly because of the "highly provoking acts" of Patricia Burns, Denver District Judge Alvin Lichtenstein ruled out a stiffer prison sentence for Clarance Burns, who shot his wife five times in the face at close range last Aug. 15.
>
> Lichtenstein said that Mrs. Burns had deceived her husband by being "extremely loving and caring" up to the morning that she left the family home to proceed with a divorce.

Such incidents lend credence to the fears of abused women that leaving their abusers could cost them their lives, and demonstrate a blatant lack of understanding for their plight. The prosecutor in the Burns case commented, "I hope battered women hear about this. They're damned if they do, and damned if they don't."

BATTERED WOMEN AND OTHER VICTIMS

Even given the practical problems in leaving and the risks that may accompany separation from a violent man, battered women's apparent passivity in the face of danger is still a troubling factor in their reactions to the abuse they experience. Leaving the abuser in *spite* of the difficulties and risks seems the best option. The apparent helplessness of abused women who stay for years in a situation in which they are repeatedly brutalized—especially those who never attempt to escape—leads us to search for explanations for their apparent lack of ability to cope.[9] Why didn't they just walk out one day when their abuser was away? Why don't they get in the car and drive in one direction, and figure it out when they get there? Anything seems better than living with repeated brutalization and threat.

Yet it is interesting to note that the reactions of abused women to the violence they experience correspond quite closely with the reactions of other types of victims to catastrophe or threat.[10] In contrast to theories that would interpret their behavior as indicative of a personality disorder, their response to the violence is what we would expect from any individual confronted with a life-threatening situation. This consistency in victim reaction applies whether the victims are male or female and whether they are the victims of crime, war, natural disaster, or some other trauma.[11] (For purposes of comparing the literature on victims, the term "trauma" is used here to denote an event that inflicts pain or injury, whether this event is caused by accident or by deliberate action. The term "victim" applies to one who is threatened by, or suffers from, such an event.)

For instance, research on both disaster and war victims indicates that, during the "impact phase," when the threat of danger becomes a reality, an individual's primary focus is on self-protection and survival. Like battered women, the victims experience reactions of shock, denial, disbelief, and fear, as well as withdrawal and confusion.[12] They often deny the threat, which leads to a delay in defining the situation accurately, and respond with dazed or apathetic behavior.[13] After the initial impact, disaster victims may be extremely suggestible or dependent and, during the period that follows, may minimize the damage or personal loss. This is often followed by a "euphoric" stage, marked by unrealistic expectations about recovery.[14] The victims convince themselves that they can "rebuild"; that somehow everything will be alright; that they will wake up and find it was all a horrible dream. For individuals in war situations,

initial reactions also include responses of shock, disbelief, and apparent passivity. As the level of danger becomes overwhelming, individuals often respond by withdrawing and fail to employ appropriate escape behaviors, even when those are possible.[15]

In a closer parallel to the victimization of battered women, emotional reactions of victims of assault include fear, anger, guilt, shame; a feeling of powerlessness or helplessness such as is experienced in early childhood; a sense of failure, and a sense of being contaminated or unworthy.[16] Experiences of personal attack and intrusion, such as rape, often lead to acute perceptions of vulnerability, loss of control, and self-blame.[17] During a personal assault, the victim may offer little or no resistance, in an attempt to minimize the threat of injury or death. Again, the emphasis is on survival.

Long-term reactions of trauma victims are also quite similar to the responses of battered women. Victims report reactions of fear and confusion, and acute sensations of powerlessness and helplessness. They may become dependent and suggestible, and find themselves unable to make decisions or to function alone. Some victims remain relatively withdrawn and passive, and exhibit long-term symptoms of depression and listlessness.[18] Bard and Sangrey, writing about the responses of crime victims, note that even "normal" recoveries can take months, and are characterized by lapses into helplessness and fear.[19] (Remember that the majority of these reactions were based on a single occurrence of a traumatic event, whereas most abused women are reacting to continuing threat and assault.) Chronic fatigue and tension, intense startle reactions, disturbances of sleeping and eating patterns, and nightmares are often noted in assault victims.[20] With all types of trauma, whether related to a natural disaster, war, or a more personal offense, the fear is of a force that has been out of control. Victims become aware of their inability to manage their environment or to assure their own safety, and either attempt to adapt to a powerful aggressor or reassure themselves that the traumatic event will never occur again.

Captives and Captors

Probably the type of victimization that most closely approximates the experiences of battered women is abuse in captivity, such as that experienced by prisoners of war. In these situations, the assailant or captor has a major influence on how the victim evaluates the situation and the alternatives available to him or her. Studies show that victims select coping strategies in light of their evaluation of the alternatives and their appraisal of whether a particular method of coping will further endanger them, and to what degree.[21] A crucial factor in this decision is the perceived balance of power between the captor and the victim: The coping strategy selected is weighed against the aggressor's perceived ability to control or to harm.

For example, in situations of extreme helplessness, such as in concentration camps, surprisingly little anger is shown toward the captors; this may be a measure of the captors' power to retaliate. "Fight or flight" responses are inhibited by a perception of the aggressor's power to inflict damage or death, and depression often results, based on the perceived hopelessness of the situation. The victims' perceptions of their alternatives become increasingly limited the longer they remain in the situation, and those alternatives that do exist often seem to pose too great a threat to survival.[22]

Because of the perceived power differential, victims in hostage situations may even come to view the captor as their protector, and become ingratiating and appeasing in an effort to save themselves.[23] In writing about the dynamics of captivity, Biderman discusses

"antagonistic cooperation," a situation in which the dimension of conflict actually dominates the relationship, but where there is also a degree of mutual dependence. The relationship is then developed by the weaker partner in order to facilitate survival and obtain leniency. Biderman also suggests that a normal human being might be incapable of sustaining a totally hostile or antagonistic interaction over an extended period, and that periods of acquiescence might be necessary for physiological and emotional survival.[24]

Parallels also exist between the principles of brainwashing used on prisoners of war and the experiences of some women in battering relationships. Key ingredients of brainwashing include isolation of the victim from outside contacts and sources of help, and humiliation and degradation by the captor; followed by acts of kindness coupled with the threat of a return to the degraded state if some type of compliance is not obtained.[25] Over time, the victims of such treatment become apathetic, sometimes react with despair, and may finally totally submit.[26]

SURVIVAL VERSUS ESCAPE

The responses of battered women fit in well with this model of victim reactions. The women in the present study perceived themselves as being trapped in a dangerous situation, and as having little or no control over the abusers' violent behavior. Their perception of their partners' ability to inflict harm was reinforced by each successive assaultive incident, and by threats to kill or perpetrate further violence against them. The women in these situations often attempted to appease the aggressor by compliance, and to work through the relationship to obtain leniency and safety. Their primary concern during assaultive incidents was to survive. Their main concern after abusive incidents was to avoid angering the partner again.

Like other victims, battered women's affective, cognitive, and behavioral responses are likely to become distorted by their intense focus on survival.[27] They may have developed a whole range of responses such as controlling their breathing or not crying out when in pain, in an effort to mitigate the severity of abuse during violent episodes, but not have developed any plans for escaping the abusive situation. Women in the homicide group showed a marked tendency to withdraw from outside contacts immediately after an abusive incident, rather than attempting to escape or to take action against the abuser. They experienced feelings of helplessness and fear, and found it extremely difficult to make decisions or plan ahead. They also tended to underestimate the "damage"—as shown by their tendency to under-report the severity of abusive acts and resultant injuries—and, at least early in their relationships, entertained unrealistic hopes for improvement of the abuser's behavior or of the relationship in the future.

As the violence escalated in frequency and severity, the women's perceptions of alternatives for escape became increasingly limited, and taking action on any of those alternatives seemed too dangerous to pursue. Although frequently in terror, the women felt constrained in the situation by the men's threats of harm or death if they left or attempted to leave. They were further persuaded of the dangers of this alternative if they had tried to leave and been beaten for it, or had sought outside intervention and found the intervention inadequate or that the violence only worsened after these efforts. The abusers' power to constrain and punish was supported by a lack of societal awareness of the plight of abused women, and by the difficulties in obtaining effective legal protection when your assaulter is your mate.[28]

A lack of adequate provision for safe shelter, relocation, or protection from further attack contributed to their sense of entrapment; most women in the homicide group concluded that their only alternative was to survive within the relationship. As Thibaut and Kelley noted in their theory of nonvoluntary interactions, when the probability of escape appears to be extremely low, "the least costly adjustment" for a victim may involve a "complex of adaptions," including a "drastic shortening of one's time perspective" to a "moment-by-moment or day-to-day focus."[29] Trapped in an increasingly dangerous situation, women in the homicide group narrowed their focus to efforts to deal with the immediate threat of violence, and to gathering or maintaining their strength between attacks.

Still, the question remains: Why did these women *kill?* Women in the comparison group had also experienced assaults from a violent partner; they also would have had the perception of the abuser's power to inflict harm, and have experienced some victim responses to assault. Yet they did not kill their abusers, and many managed to leave them. What was different about women in the homicide group, that they were unable to escape and eventually took lethal action against their partners?

Differences between Women in the Homicide and Comparison Groups

Few differences can be found in characteristics of the women in the homicide and comparison groups; the differences exist primarily in the behaviors of the men. Men in the homicide group used alcohol and drugs more often than did those in the comparison group, and were generally more violent to others. The incidence of child abuse, for instance, was much higher among them than among men in the comparison group. They also assaulted their partners more frequently, and the women's injuries were more severe. In addition, men in the homicide group more frequently raped or otherwise sexually assaulted their partners, and many more of them had made threats to kill. Over time, physical abuse tended to become more severe in both the homicide and the nonhomicide groups, but such increases were much more common in the homicide group, while the decline in contrition was more precipitous.

In a test of which variables most clearly distinguished women who had killed their abusive mates from women who were abused but took no lethal action, seven key dynamics were identified: the frequency with which abusive incidents occurred; the severity of the women's injuries; the frequency of forced or threatened sexual acts by the man; the man's drug use; the frequency of his intoxication; the man's threats to kill; and the woman's threats to commit suicide.[30]

Thus, the women's behavior seemed to be primarily in reaction to the level of threat and violence coming in. Women in the homicide group reported that they had felt hopelessly trapped in a desperate situation, in which staying meant the possibility of being killed, but attempting to leave also carried with it the threat of reprisal or death. Their sense of helplessness and desperation escalated along with the assaultive behavior of their partners. In her book on marital rape, Dianna Russell suggests that: "The statistics on the murder of husbands, along with the statistics on the murder of wives, are both indicators of the desperate plight of some women, not a sign that in this one area, males and females are equally violent."[31]

THE TURNING POINT

Given the extreme level of abuse and injury to which they were subjected, how did women in the homicide group go from a seemingly passive response of helplessness and adaption to the highly active one of homicide? Although individuals have the legal right to defend themselves against the threat of imminent serious bodily harm or death, the process by which a woman makes the transition to this mode of reacting is still largely unknown.

One way to understand the shift from victim to perpetrator is suggested by the principles of social judgment theory.[32] For example, Sherif and Hovland's model of social judgment involves the concept of a continuum on which incoming stimuli—or experiences—are ordered. The "latitude of acceptance" is that range of possibilities an individual is willing to agree with or adapt to; stimuli that fall outside that range are either in the latitude of rejection or the latitude of noncommitment (neither acceptable or unacceptable).[33] These latitudes are defined by endpoints, or anchors, that determine the extremes of the scale. Internal anchors are those originating within the individual, while external anchors are provided by outside factors or social consensus. Past learning experiences also affect how acceptable or unacceptable a person will find a particular stimulus. In the absence of outside factors, a person's internal anchors play a major role in how he or she evaluates a situation. According to social judgment theory, if an event falls at the end of the continuum, or even slightly above the endpoint, it will produce a shift of the range toward that anchor—or *assimilation*. However, if the stimulus is too far beyond the others, a *contrast* effect will ensue, and the stimulus will be perceived as being even more extreme than it really is.

If one views the escalation of violent acts by the abuser as ordered along a continuum, then the latitude of acceptance for a battered woman would be that range of activities to which she can adapt. This latitude would be affected by the degree to which she had been socialized to adjust to or accept a partner's behavior, by prior experiences with similar stimuli—such as violence in her childhood home—and by the degree to which she perceives herself as trapped within the violent situation and as having to incorporate the abuse of her partner. Because society's standards on violence against wives are ambiguous, and because abused women rarely discuss their victimization with others, most battered women are quite dependent on such "internal" anchors to determine the latitude of behaviors they will accept.

As abusive acts continue to fall near the endpoints of the range, a battered woman's latitude of acceptance shifts in order to incorporate them. As demonstrated by the findings on victims of various kinds of trauma, human beings in extreme environments are able to alter their behavior quite dramatically if it seems necessary to survive. Thus, when the behaviors of the abuser are extreme, a woman may adapt far beyond normal limits, in order to coexist peacefully with him. A certain level of abuse and tension becomes the status quo: Women progress from being horrified by each successive incident to being thankful they survived the last one. Survival becomes the criterion. The latitude of acceptance is what these women think they can live through. By the end of their relationships, women in the homicide group were experiencing attacks they would not have thought endurable at an earlier stage. They were involved in a constant process of assimilation and readjustment.

According to the principles of social judgment theory, a contrast phenomenon should come into effect when an act occurs that the woman perceives as significantly outside the "normal" range of violent behavior. In recounting the events that immediately preceded the lethal incident, women frequently said, "He had never done *that* before." Often there was a sudden change in the pattern of violence, which indicated to them that their death was imminent. One attack would be so much more brutal or degrading than all the

rest that, even with their highly developed survival skills, the women believed it would be impossible to survive the next one. Or an act would suddenly be beyond the range of what the women were willing to assimilate. Frequently, this involved the physical abuse of a child or the discovery that the man had forced sexual activity on a teenage daughter. The women would say, "He had never threatened the baby before," or "It was one thing when he was beating me, but then he hurt my daughter."

Contrast theory would predict that, once the woman had defined an act as significantly outside the latitude of what she could accept, she would then perceive that act as being more extreme than it actually was. However, given the amount of minimalization and assimilation engaged in by all types of victims, and the tendency of abused women to understate the levels of violence in their relationships, it is more probable that women in the homicide group were at last simply making a realistic appraisal of the danger. Their final hope had been removed. They did not believe they could escape the abusive situation and survive, and now they could no longer survive within it either.

The current study focused on the perceptions of women victims, and their reactions to abuse by their partners. These perceptions are crucial, both from a legal and a psychological standpoint, if we are to understand the dynamics that lead an abused woman to take lethal action against her mate. Lack of effective response by the legal system to assaults in which the victim is a wife, along with a lack of adequate and established alternatives to assure the woman's protection from further aggression, allows the violence in abusive relationships to escalate, leaving a battered woman in a potentially deadly situation from which she sees no practical avenue of escape. As is typical of victims, women who are being attacked by their partners react with responses of fear and adaption, weighing their alternatives in accordance with their perceptions of the threat and attempting to choose options which will mitigate the danger and facilitate their survival.

Yet, in some cases, the violence escalates beyond the level a victim can assimilate. By the end of their relationships, women in the homicide group were subjected to frequent and injurious attacks from partners who were likely to be drinking heavily, using drugs, sexually assaulting them, and threatening murder. Most of these women had no history of violent behavior; yet, in these relationships, the women's attempts to adapt to an increasingly violent and unpredictable mate eventually resulted in an act of violence on their part as well.

NOTES

1. Moore, 1979.
2. See Schechter (1982) for an excellent history of the development of shelters, and the battered women's movement, in the United States.
3. See, for example, report by the National Center on Women and Family Law, July 1982; Walker & Edwall (1987).
4. See Jones' (1980) chapter, "Totaling Women," pages 298–299; see also Lindsey, 1978; Martin, 1976; Pagelow, 1980, 1981.
5. Fields, 1978; Fiora-Gormally, 1978; Lewin, 1979; Pagelow, 1980, 1981.
6. See, for example, Ewing, Lindsey & Pomerantz, 1984.
7. E.g., Barnett, Pittman, Ragan, & Salus, 1980; Ewing et al., 1984; Pagelow, 1981, 1984; Tanay, 1976.
8. See Tanay's (1976) chapter, "Until Death Do Us Part."
9. E.g., Lenore Walker's (1979, 1984) theory of learned helplessness in battered women; Donald Dutton and Susan Painter's (1981) application of theories on traumatic bonding.
10. See the works of Alexandra Symonds, 1979, and Martin Symonds, 1978, for discussions of psychological effects and aftereffects in female

victims of violence and their parallels to known responses of other victims.
11. Browne, 1980.
12. For example, see the works of Chapman, 1962; and Mileti, Drabek, & Haas, 1975.
13. E.g., Bahnson, 1964; Miller, 1964; Powell, 1954.
14. Mileti, et al., 1975; Powell, 1954.
15. Grinker & Spiegel, 1945; Spiegel, 1955.
16. Bard & Sangrey, 1979.
17. Burgess & Holmstrom, 1974; Notman & Nadelson, 1976.
18. E.g., Chapman, 1962.
19. Bard & Sangrey, 1979.
20. Burgess & Holmstrom, 1974; Nathan, Eitinger & Winick, 1964.
21. E.g., Arnold, 1967; Lazarus, 1967.
22. E.g., Lazarus, 1967.
23. Bettleheim, 1943; M. Symonds, 1978; Stentz, 1979.
24. Biderman, 1967.
25. E.g., A. Symonds, 1979.
26. Meerloo, 1961.
27. Walker & Browne, 1985.
28. Blair, 1979; Field & Field, 1973; U.S. Commission on Civil Rights, 1982.
29. Thibaut & Kelley, 1959, p. 180.
30. Based on a discriminant function analysis (Klecka, 1975 pp. 434–435) using all of the abuse-related variables for which between-group differences reached the .001 significance level. The analysis identified seven of the variables which, in linear combination, best discriminated between women in the homicide and comparison groups. Using these seven variables, we could correctly classify 77 percent of the homicide subjects and 83 percent of the comparison subjects (or 82 percent of all subjects).
31. Russell, 1982, p. 299.
32. This discussion is based on the (1961) model of Sherif and Hovland. Although experimental testing of their theory has produced some contradictory results (Wrightsman, 1972), their concept of a "latitude of acceptance" for stimuli may make a contribution to our understanding of the evolution in a violent relationship toward a homicide committed by a woman.
33. See Browne, 1986.

REFERENCES

Arnold, M. B. (1967). "Stress and emotion." In M. H. Appley & R. Trumbull (Eds.) *Psychology Stress.* New York: Appleton-Century-Crofts.

Bohnson, C. B. (1964). "Emotional reactions to internally and externally derived threats of annihilation." In G. H. Grosser, H. Wechsler, & M. Greenblatt (Eds.) *The Threat of Impending Disaster.* Cambridge, MA: MIT Press.

Bard, M., & D. Sangrey (1979). *The Crime Victim's Book.* New York: Basic Books.

Barnett, E. R., C. B. Pittman, C. K. Ragan, M. K. Salus (1980). "Family violence: Intervention strategies." Department of Health and Human Services, Washington, DC: Government Printing Office. Pub. No. (OHDS) 80-30258.

Bettleheim, B. (1943). "Individual and mass behavior in extreme situations." *Journal of Abnormal and Social Psychology, 38,* 417–452.

Biderman, A. D. (1967). "Captivity lore and behavior in captivity." In G. H. Grosser, H. Wechsler, & M. Greenblatt (Eds.) *The Threat of Impending Disaster.* Cambridge, MA: MIT Press.

Blair, S. (1979). "Making the legal system work for battered women." In D. M. Moore (Ed.) *Battered Women.* Beverly Hills: Sage.

Browne, A. (1980). "Comparison of victim's reactions across traumas." Paper presented at the Rocky Mountain Psychological Association annual meeting. Tucson, Arizona.

Browne, A. (1986). "Assault and homicide at home: When battered women kill." In M. J. Saks & L. Saxe (Eds.), *Advances in Applied Social Psychology, Vol. 3.* Hillsdale, NJ: Lawrence Erlbaum Associates, Inc.

Burgess, A. W., & L. L. Holmstrom (1974). "Rape trauma syndrome." *American Journal of Psychiatry, 131*(9), 981–86.

Chapman, D. W. (1962). "A brief introduction to contemporary disaster research." In G. W. Baker & D. W. Chapman (Eds.) *Man and Society in Disaster.* New York: Basic Books.

Durron, D., & S. L. Painter (1981). "Traumatic bonding: The development of emotional attachments in battered women and other relationships of intermittent abuse." *Victimology, 6,* 139–155.

Ewing, W., M. Lindsey, & J. Pomerantz (1984). *Battering: An AMEND Manual for Helpers.* Denver, CO: Littleton Heights College.

Field, M. H., & H. F. Field (1973). "Marital violence and the criminal process: Neither justice nor peace." *Social Service Review, 47,* 221–240.

Fields, M. D. (1978). "Does this vow include wife-beating?" *Human Rights. 7*(20), 40–45.

Fiora-Gormally, N. (1978). "Battered wives who kill. Double standard out of court, single standard in?" *Law and Human Behavior, 2*(2): 133–65.

Grinker, R. R., & J. P. Spiegel (1945). *Man Under Stress.* New York, NY: Blakiston.

Jones, A. (1980). *Women Who Kill.* New York, NY: Fawcett Columbine Books.

Klecka, W. R. (1975). "Discriminant analysis." In N. H. Nie, C. H. Hull, J. G. Jenkins, K. Steinbrenner, & D. H. Bent (Eds.), *SPSS—Statistical Package for the Social Sciences, 2nd Ed.* New York, NY: McGraw-Hill.

Lazarus, R. S. (1967). "Cognitive and personality factors underlying threat and coping." In M. H. Appley & R. Trumbull (Eds.) *Psychological Stress.* New York, NY: Appleton-Century-Crofts.

Lewin, T. (1979). "When victims kill." *National Law Journal, 2*(7), 2–4, 11.

Lindsey, K. (1978). "When battered women strike back: Murder or self-defense." *Viva* (September) pp. 58–59, 66–74.

Martin, D. (1976). *Battered Wives.* San Francisco, CA: Glide Publications.

Meerloo, J. (1961). *The Rape of the Mind.* New York, NY: Grosset & Dunlop.

Mileti, D. S., T. E. Drabek, & J. E. Haas (1975). *Human Systems in Extreme Environments.* Institute of Behavioral Science, University of Colorado.

Miller, J. G. (1964). "A theoretical review of individual and group psychological reactions to stress." In G. H. Grosser, H. Wechsler, & M. Greenblatt (Eds.) *The Threat of Impending Disaster.* Cambridge, MA: MIT Press.

Moore, D. M. (1979). *Battered Women.* Beverly Hills, CA: Sage.

Nathan, T. S., L. Eitinger, & Z. Winick (1964). "A psychiatric study of survivors of the Nazi holocaust." *Israel Annals of Psychiatry.*

National Center on Women and Family Law (July 1982).

Notman, M., & C. C. Nadelson (1976). "The rape victim: Psychodynamic considerations." *American Journal of Psychiatry, 133*(4), 408–412.

Pagelow, M. D. (1980). "Double victimization of battered women: Victimized by spouses and the legal system." Paper presented at the annual meeting of the American Society of Criminology, San Francisco, CA.

Pagelow, M. D. (1981). *Women-Battering: Victims and Their Experiences.* Beverly Hills, CA: Sage.

Pagelow, M. D. (1984). *Family Violence.* New York, NY: Praeger.

Powell, J. W. (1954). *An Introduction to the Natural History of Disaster (Vol. 2).* Final Contract Report, Disaster Research Project, Psychiatric Institute, University of Maryland.

Russell, D. E. H. (1982). *Rape in Marriage.* New York, NY: Macmillan.

Schechter, S. (1982). *Women and Male Violence.* Boston, MA: South End Press.

Sherif, M., & C. Hovland (1961). *Social Judgment.* New Haven, CT: Yale University Press.

Spiegel, J. P. (1955). "Emotional reactions to catastrophe." In S. Liebman (Ed.) *Stress Situations.* Philadelphia, PA: J. B. Lippincott.

Symonds, A. (1979). "Violence against women: The myth of masochism." *American Journal of Psychotherapy, 33,* 161–173.

Symonds, M. (1978). "The psychodynamics of violence-prone marriages." *American Journal of Psychoanalysis, 38,* 213–222.

Tanay, E. (1976). *The Murderers.* Indianapolis/New York: The Bobbs-Merrill Co., Inc.

Thibault, J. W., & H. H. Kelley (1959). *The Social Psychology in Groups.* New York, NY: Wiley.

United States Commission on Civil Rights. (1982). *Under the Rule of Thumb: Battered Women and the Administration of Justice.* Washington, DC: U.S. Government Printing Office.

Walker, L. E. (1978). "Battered women and learned helplessness." *Victimology, 2(3/4),* 525–34.

Walker, L. E. (1979). *The Battered Woman.* New York, NY: Harper & Row Publishers.

Walker, L. E. (1984). *The Battered Woman Syndrome.* New York, NY: Springer Publishers.

Walker, L. E., & A. Browne (1985). "Gender and victimization by intimates." *Journal of Personality, 53(2),* 179–195.

Walker, L. E., & G. E. Edwall (1987). "Battered women and child custody and visitation determination." In D. J. Sonkin (Ed.) *Domestic Violence on Trial.* New York, NY: Springer.

Wrightsman, L. S. (1972). *Social Psychology in the Seventies.* Belmont, CA: Wadsworth.

CHAPTER 14

MINORITY WOMEN AND DOMESTIC VIOLENCE: THE UNIQUE DILEMMAS OF BATTERED WOMEN OF COLOR

CHRISTINE E. RASCHE

ABSTRACT

There is very little in the growing literature on domestic violence that addresses the special problems that racial, ethnic, or cultural minority women face in dealing with abuse from their partners. In this chapter Rasche synthesizes available information on abuse against women from a variety of minority groups, outlining some of the unique dilemmas faced by abused women of color. In Chapter 12, Matthews pointed out some of the difficulties black women face in trying to make use of traditional rape crisis centers. In this chapter, Rasche argues that while the *experience* of battering may be similar, many battered women of color may not be willing or able to make use of traditional helping agencies in order to escape their victimization. In this way, "women of color face many problems that white battered women generally do not."

For the minority woman, escape from domestic violence may first require recognition that her own culture's tolerance for violence does not mean that she must accept endless battering. However, Rasche reports, social class may have more to do with acceptance of violence than racial/ethnic traditions. Cross-cultural data suggest that social and environmental factors are largely responsible for ethnic variations in violence and its acceptance. Widespread underreporting probably occurs among minority women largely because of cultural prohibitions against seeking outside help, but also because of language difficulties, threats of deportation of immigrant women, and general fear of the police, which is experienced by most minorities.

Rasche reports that police have often minimized the seriousness of domestic disputes, especially when reported by minority women. However, recent research on domestic disputes may help to change police attitudes. As a result of a series of pilot studies conducted in six cities, funded by the National Institute of

Justice (NIJ), police are at least being made more aware of the fact that responding to domestic violence against women is an important police function.* One question asked by the NIJ was: Does arrest by a police officer deter a batterer? The results were inconclusive, in part because of methodological and implementation problems and in part because a white-middle-class male model of offending and deterrence was used.

Rasche identifies another barrier that prevents escape from battering. It is the concerns of minority women with racial/ethnic issues—such as protecting the image of the minority group living in a racist society. Placing loyalty to their minority group over their rights as women may prevent some women from seeking help. This is compounded by the fears minority women often have of maltreatment of minority men by the police. Rasche also highlights the importance of ethnic cultural concerns. For example, second-generation Italian Catholic women's reluctance to seek help, even after the police have been called in, is a consequence of cultural/religious teachings.

This chapter provides the reader with insight into some of the many difficulties facing battered minority women in addition to the abuse itself. In your community, on the basis of *its* racial, ethnic, and class traditions, how might unique problems facing battered women be addressed? Can you suggest issues that have been overlooked in this discussion?

---

*Lawrence Sherman, *Policing Domestic Violence*, Free Press, New York, 1992. Several studies can be found in vol. 57 (1992) of the *American Sociological Review*.

Independent of each other as classes, women, minorities and victims of domestic assault have been "overlooked" by mainstream criminology in the United States. Though there has been a recent increase in research on each of these classes of persons, modern studies are often still prefaced by acknowledgment that previous criminological interest in the subject was sparse and research prior to the 1970's was scanty. Nothing could be scantier, however, than research on persons simultaneously occupying all three categories—racial or ethnic minority women victimized by domestic violence. This paper examines this gap in the research literature, and draws from the available information to outline some of the special problems faced by this forgotten group of victims.

In some ways, the relative lack of interest in the relationship between minority women and domestic violence may not be surprising at all. Until recently, there has been little published literature on minority women in general. Historians were reproached several years ago for having virtually ignored women of color (1) in historical studies (Winkler, 1986). New writings, particularly on black women, have explained this disinterest in several ways which probably apply to most other minority racial/ethnic groups as well.

Source: Journal of Contemporary Criminal Justice, vol. 4, no. 3, 1988, pp. 150–171.

First, as Lynora Williams (1981) has noted, minority women in American society may be viewed as bearing a cross "on each shoulder"—racism and sexism. It is what Epstein (1973) has called the "double whammy." Minority women belong to both a devalued race and a devalued gender, by dominant American values, and are therefore of little intrinsic interest to members of the dominant class. Even when they stand out in some way, such as being disproportionately represented among known female offenders, black women have received little special criminological attention. The criminological literature on women of *other* racial/ethnic backgrounds is virtually nonexistent.

Second, the dual burden of racism and sexism affects not only the interests of the dominant class, but it affects the interests of minority women themselves. Diane Lewis (1977) has observed:

> Black women, due to their membership in two subordinate groups that lack access to authority and resources in society, are in structural opposition with a dominant racial and a dominant sexual group. In each subordinate group they share potential common interests with group members, black men on the one hand and white women on the other. Ironically, each of these is a member of the dominant group: black men as men, white women as whites. Thus, the interests which bind black women together and pull them into opposition against comembers crosscut one another in a manner which often obscures one set of interests over another (p. 343).

Historically, black women have found that "their interests as blacks have taken precedence over their interests as women" (Lewis, 1977: 343). This primacy of concern for racism over sexism may partially account for the fact that there has been little special interest in minority spouse abuse and domestic violence even among minority researchers (Richie, 1985).

The question which arises of course, is whether there is *in fact* a need to treat minority women in some special way when attempting to understand the causes of and appropriate responses to domestic violence. Might it be perhaps wholly appropriate that no special literature has developed simply because the causes of, the dynamics of, the experience of and the response to domestic violence are fundamentally the same for all women? Certainly most of the spouse abuse literature makes a point to assert that domestic violence cuts across all racial, ethnic, and class lines, and this may be a third reason for the minimal exploration of minority domestic violence.

However, to the women involved on the actual firing line of responding to spousal violence—women who are operating refuges, working in victim's assistance programs, or otherwise fighting the problem—the answer to the question above is clearly "no." When the National Coalition Against Domestic Violence (NCADV) was formed in 1978, a Third World Women's Caucus was immediately formed to share insights about non-white women (Zambrano, 1985). The first National Conference of Third World Women Against Violence was held in Washington, D.C., in August of 1908 (Williams, 1981), and it has been followed by a series of similar conferences in the years since. An example is a two-weekend conference entitled "A Movement of New World Women" held in June, 1985, in New York City, sponsored by the Women of Color Caucus of New York Women Against Rape, in cooperation with The Black Women's Development Collective, Inc. The impetus to hold special conferences of this sort is the firm belief on the part of the minority women involved that there *are* special, unique problems faced by minority women victimized by family violence. No empirical evaluation of this belief has ever been undertaken, and most of the concerns remain to date at the grassroots (2) organizing level.

THE EXTENT OF
MINORITY VICTIMIZATION

In explaining how the volunteer staff of a newsletter on domestic violence began to explore the special needs of minority victims, Arnold and Perkins (1984–85) describe how the group of minority women found themselves sharing common concerns as well as peculiar ethnic problems. "As the brainstorming continued, a crucial insight was arrived at by the group: for white women and women of color, the *experience* of battering is quite similar but at the point of seeking help or escape from the abuse, women of color face many problems that white battered women generally do not" (Arnold and Perkins, 1984–85:2).

Perhaps it is precisely because the *experience* of being victimized in one's own home is so similar across racial/ethnic lines that possible *differences* in its causes, frequency, and solutions have not yet emerged as issues. But it seems clear that those differences do exist, at least on the level of obtaining solutions to or escape from the abuse.

It is also quite possible that there are real differences in the frequency of spousal violence in different ethnic groups, though the data on this question are quite inconsistent and contradictory. On the one hand, there seems to be no question that minority peoples in America and elsewhere suffer from higher rates of general victimization than do majority members. The higher risk of minority ethnic peoples to both be arrested and be victimized has been well established for some time. Whether it is native Indians in rural Canada (Chimbos and Montgomery, 1978), Maoris and Polynesians in New Zealand (Sullivan, 1977), Hispanics in the Southwest United States, Puerto Ricans in New York City, or blacks in most major U.S. cities, minority persons have been arrested for crimes in greater numbers than their population would war-

rant, especially for violent crimes. And criminal violence, especially aggravated assault and homicide, is predominantly an *intra*group event (O'Brien, 1987; Wilbanks, 1985; Wilbanks, 1984; Block, 1977; Curtis, 1974; Savitz, 1973). Though white police have been shown to anticipate more physical danger to themselves in minority areas (Holdaway, 1983; Bayley, 1969) and economically motivated crimes such as robbery are more likely to show *inter*racial features (Wilbanks, 1985; Hindelang, 1976), the fact remains that assault and homicide by minority group members are most likely to be directed toward members of the same group. Where rates of violent crime by minority persons are high, the rate of minority victimization tends also to be high.

Especially for blacks, the largest racial minority group in the United States, crime victimization rates have consistently been shown to be higher than those for whites, especially for personal crimes and crimes of violence (Block, 1985a; Hawkins, 1985; Allen, 1980; Hindelang, 1979; Savitz, 1973; Brearley, 1932). Again, most violent crimes among blacks are intraracial; intraracial homicides predominated in both Wolfgang's (1958) and Wilbank's (1984) samples, and Block (1985b) found that homicides committed by blacks were even *more* likely to be intraracial than those committed by whites. An article in the magazine *Ebony* once noted that more blacks were killed by other blacks in the single year of 1977 than were killed altogether during the entire Vietnam War, which spanned a nine-year period! A total of 5,711 blacks died in Vietnam, while 5,734 were killed by other blacks in the United States in 1977 (Kirk, 1982).

Certainly more black males than black females are victimized (males of both races generally have higher offender and victimization rates for most offenses than do females of either race). But for the crime of assault and its companion homicide, the victimization rate for black females has frequently been shown to exceed not only the rate for white females but also for white males (Hawkins, 1985; Allen, 1980; Hindelang, 1976; Wolfgang, 1958). Furthermore, black women are victimized by a higher proportion of "assaults judged to be aggravated" than not only whites but women of Spanish origin (Bowker, 1979). By and large, non-homicide assaults upon black women have been shown to be intraracial but cross-sex (Bowker, 1979), and this is certainly true of fatal assaults upon black women (Rasche, 1988; Wilbanks, 1982; Wolfgang, 1958).

Most victimization data report on violations by reference to the crime categories of the *outcome* (assaults, homicides, etc.) rather than by reference to the situational origins. Until recently there has been little attempt to characterize victimizations by their *interactional context* (economically motivated attacks vs. domestic disputes, etc.), though even early empirical studies on homicide observed the important roles of family murder and spousal murder (Wolfgang, 1958; Von Hentig, 1948). The recent work of Straus, Gelles, and Steinmetz (1979) to measure domestic violence not in a clinical or criminal population but in a representative sample of 2,143 American families, has provided some insights into the nature of violence among minority group members. Rates of spousal violence, and in particular wife abuse, were found to be higher for minority groups than for whites. This was recently confirmed by Shoemaker and Williams (1987). Cazenave and Straus (1979) found that blacks had the highest rates, twice that of other racial minorities and four times higher than whites. These findings are consistent with those of Gelles (1980) and Staples (1976). However, other researchers have found no significant differences in rates of domestic violence between racial groups (Lockhart, 1984; Berk et al., 1983; Parker and

Schumacher, 1979; Walker, 1979; Smith and Snow, 1978), and it must be cautioned that the available data at this point in time is very contradictory.

This may be due, in part, to the fact that even victimization surveys have a very difficult time accurately measuring violence in the home. Probably the vast majority of spousal abuses involve non-fatal assaultive behaviors, acts which would more likely be reported if they were perpetrated between complete strangers. The very fact that such behavior is going on between two persons who have a close, intimate, personal relationship makes for a number of measurement problems. To be sure, police statistics have numerous faults as indicators of crime, not the least of which is their dependence on reporting behavior by victims and observers. In the case of assault, a ". . . simple inspection of existing figures suggests that more victims of spouse abuse do not call the police than do" (Bard, 1980). And while victimization survey data are often used to offset the weaknesses of police data, assault is the one offense which has been acknowledged to have the most measurement problems. Assault victims have the poorest "recall rate" in victimization surveys (e.g., failure to report the victimization to the interviewer even though a known offense occurred). Less than half (47 percent) of National Crime Survey Participants who were known assault victims reported the crime to survey interviewers (Hindelang, 1979). Other nonsampling errors in victimization data abound, leading to the conclusion by the Census Bureau that "assault by relatives is the most underreported of all crimes covered by the NCS" (Gaquin, 1977–78).

The fact that assaultive behavior in the home may be severely underreported leads to the question of whether reporting behavior may vary across ethnic/racial lines. While assault and homicide offense and victimization rates may be higher for some groups (such as blacks) than for others (such as Asian Americans), data on clients using refuges or other services for battered women repeatedly report racial/ethnic breakdowns which are similar to the general population characteristics of that area (Walker, 1983; Kuhl, 1982; Brisson, 1981; LaBell, 1979; Rounsaville, 1978–79; Gelles, 1972). Indeed, victimization surveys specifically focusing on spouse abuse (as opposed to the more general category of assault) similarly show that *rates* for blacks and whites are almost the same (Bureau of Justice Statistics, April 1984; Gaquin, 1977–78; Hindelang, 1976), and one survey in Texas showed that whites, blacks and Mexican-Americans each responded affirmatively to the question of spouse abuse in about 6.0% of the cases (Stachura and Teske, 1979).

It seems clear that when attempting to measure spouse abuse or domestic violence, the measurement which is used may have significant consequences. Objective measures of violence, such as the Conflict Tactic Scales developed by Straus and his associates, may "discover" more violence than do inquiries which require the respondent to decide whether or not she has been abused. It has been suggested by more than one observer that different ethnic or cultural groups may have differing definitions of "abuse."

Indeed, there is evidence that some ethnic groups are much more tolerant of, even approving of, familial violence than are others. Several reports point to the relationship between rigid, patriarchal, male-dominated family relationships and high levels of violence in Mexican-American families (Carrol, 1980; Segovia-Ashley, 1978) and other Latin American families (Skurnik, 1983). This has also been reported for Italian-Americans (Spiegel, 1980) and other rural Mediterranean groups (Loizos, 1978), where "family honor" supercedes all other values. Shoemaker and Williams (1987) found that American Indians in their sample were more tolerant of violence

than the general population or even blacks and Hispanics. Cazenave and Straus (1979) reported that black respondents in their survey were more approving of slapping between partners than were white respondents, and "Black husbands are also more likely to have actually slapped their wives and engaged in severe violence against them within the last year" (p. 285–286). Williams (1981) describes the frustration of trying to get black community leaders to support spouse abuse prevention campaigns when "beating a wife is something that is tolerated. It's just an okay thing to do" (p. 22). For some minority women, therefore, the first problem in escaping battery may be coming to terms with a cultural tolerance level for violence which is higher than that for other groups. Responses to abuse will be quite different in that context than in situations where violent behavior is viewed as somewhat more abnormal.

It is important to note here in passing, that the cross-cultural data which is available provides some interesting contradictions for a biological theory of ethnic variations in violence. An exception to the Hispanic model of hot-blooded interaction may be found in the peaceful Tarahumura Indians of Mexico (West, 1980) and in the fact that *lethal* violence against women by Hispanics has been found to be rare (Zahn and Rickle, 1986; Block, 1985a). Wife abuse in Eastern and Central African cultures varies considerably, from high rates among those societies where hitting wives is viewed as no worse than hitting anyone else, to much lower rates among people such as Ankole, who have strong sanctions against violence towards wives (Mushanga, 1977–78). Data such as this strongly supports the etiological view that social/environmental factors are largely responsible for ethnic variations in the United States in violence toleration. Indeed, some evidence suggests that social class may have more to do with acceptance of violence than ethnic/racial traditions or adaption (Cazenave and Straus, 1979; Lockhart, 1984).

It is easy to see that the situation for women in high-violence cultural groups, where abuse is taken for granted, will be quite different than for women in low-violence groups, where even the accusation of battering may be viewed as extraordinary, even inconceivable. Women in both situations may have a hard time either reporting or escaping the violence, though for vastly different reasons.

UNDERREPORTING AMONG MINORITY WOMEN

While levels of abuse and tolerance of violence may vary considerably among different ethnic or cultural groups, there are other reasons why minority women in abusive domestic situations may be underreported. Specific attributes of ethnic or cultural tradition may be the biggest hurdles faced by abused women in getting help.

For example, the native American Indian woman living on a reservation or in a small rural settlement may find that reservation social service programs are staffed by her own relatives or those of her abuser; similarly, law-enforcement officers (usually county sheriff's department employees but possibly reservation police) may know or be related to her attacker (Feinman, 1985). While this possibility exists in any small town or rural area, the highly interwoven network of Indian society usually makes it much worse. Unfortunately, it is not culturally acceptable to seek help outside of one's own community (American Indian Women Against Domestic Violence, June 1985), and, in any case, there may be no way for the Indian woman to get away from the isolated reservation or rural area when the need for help arises.

In Asian-American communities, presumed to have a fairly low spouse abuse rate,

underreporting in fact may be severe. First, there is a tendency for Asian-Americans to keep to themselves and shun outside assistance or interference, partly in response to a perceived hostile white society (Skurnik, 1983). Asian cultural traditions emphasize respect for and subservience to elders, superiors and persons in authority; talking back or fighting back even against abusive behavior would be viewed as extremely inappropriate. To seek help outside the community means confronting cultural prohibitions against causing any "loss of face" for oneself or one's family. For the traditionally-trained Asian-American woman, even speaking of such things to an outsider (such as reporting attacks to a victimization surveyor) would be unthinkable.

Even if the abuse were so bad that an Asian-American woman *would* seek help outside, this may be virtually impossible for immigrant wives who do not speak English. Calling the police in an extreme emergency may prove to be fruitless:

> So often Asian batterers, many of whom function daily in the English-speaking work world, are able to out talk their wives in front of the police simply because the women cannot communicate effectively (Eng, 1985: 3).

This language barrier exists across a number of ethnic groups, and often the police do not realize that a woman is accusing her spouse of battery simply because they accept the English-speaking husband as translator. Zambrano (1985) warns Latinos:

> Many English speaking husbands take advantage of the fact that their wives don't speak English. They get to say all they want to the police and the women never get to tell what happened in their own words. If at all possible don't use your husband to translate for you (p. 170).

Immigrant women face other obstacles in their efforts to escape from abuse as well.

Women from foreign countries sometimes come to the U.S. for arranged marriages. Immigrant brides-to-be, even if they did speak English, may still find themselves in a vulnerable legal situation if their visas were sponsored by the men who are now their abusers, who may threaten to withdraw their support and cause instant deportation if the women say anything (Skurnik, 1983). Even if they do not like America, going home may result in an impossible loss of face for the bride's entire family, or may be economically devastating. Silence may seem like the only alternative.

For undocumented workers, of course, the escape from abuse may seem to be impossible. Fear not only of the police, but also of the helping agencies such as hospitals, social service organizations, and lawyers, may keep the illegal alien trapped in silence. For example, one study found that while immigrant Mexican women underutilized available maternal health services in San Diego, *undocumented* Mexican women were even less likely to make use of basic health services (Chavez, Cornelius, and Jones, 1986). Furthermore, the woman without proper documentation is probably thousands of miles from her home and family, and, "if this is your situation, you may find that the closest person to you is the one who is beating you, and he is probably well aware of how isolated you are" (Zambrano, 1985:214). Many such women simply do not know that their men do not have the right to beat them up or that, even if they are not citizens, they are entitled to protection under the law while they are in the United States. Those who do know this still fear that any contact with any official agency will result in their deportation. And their fears are not without warrant.

For those immigrant women with work permits, however, the decisions are still tough. Among Latinos, for example, often the wife was the first family member to come here, alone, to work in an illegal sweat shop and earn enough money to send for the rest of the family. By the time the man comes, he finds a radically restructured gender-role situation, in which he is dependent on a (now stronger) wife. He may resort to physical violence to try to regain his power and control. But for the woman to report him places the man in danger of deportation. "On the other hand a batterer can often threaten to turn the wife's whole family (that she has worked so hard to bring to America) over to immigration if she takes any action against him" (Skurnik, 1983: 8). If there is truth to the notion that rates of domestic violence may be higher in Hispanic cultures anyway, the Latina immigrant (especially the illegal alien) may be one of the most abused but underreported battered women in America.

For almost *all* minority women, however, fear of the police may contribute to underreporting. Considerable evidence suggests that a significant proportion of minority group members have a severe distrust of the police and a hesitation to call police in many situations where white majority people would not hesitate to seek help (Carter, 1985; Yates, 1985; Barnett, 1977; Katz, 1973; Bayley and Mendelsohn, 1969). In talking about blacks, Barnett observes that "Based on the historical reputation of the police in the black community, many blacks believe the police function is to support and enforce the political, social and economic interests of the dominant community and only incidentally to enforce the law" (1977: 127). This leads to more "negative expectations" of the police on the part of minority people than is true of dominants, and this in turn leads to "a strong disposition to avoid the police" (Bayley and Mendelsohn, 1969: 120). As White (1985) notes:

> There is no denying that the relationship between the police and the black community has been a problematic one. Historically, the police have been some of the worst offenders in

contributing to or blatantly ignoring the violence in black communities (p. 40).

Minority women, compared to men, may be especially likely to avoid or become frustrated by police involvement, since police are more likely anyway to discriminate against female than male complainants in domestic disputes (Smith and Klein, 1984; Berk and Loseke, 1981). Though arrest upon demand of the complainant is a more likely outcome when the call for assistance is from a high-status area, indicating that police respond differently to disputes depending on their socioeconomic location, arrests are less likely in general when *women* are the complainants and violence is not obvious. Police also tend to minimize "the legal seriousness of nonviolent disputes" involving female complaints (Smith and Klein, 1984: p. 479), and certainly have tended to see domestic disputes as "normal" and unworthy of police action (Edwards, 1986). Only when the situation actually becomes violent do police responses to male and female complainants become the same. The message is clear: if you are a woman, any woman, in a low status area (where minorities often cluster), the police may not be much help unless they actually see you being assaulted physically.

Though Smith and Klein (1984) and others have found that race is *not* a factor which independently influences arrest decisions, there may be subtle ways in which racial/ethnic features operate to influence police behavior. In a guidebook for black women dealing with domestic abuse, White (1985) cautions black women to "make sure the officers see your injuries. You may have to explain to them that bruises on blacks are not always as visible or look as dramatic as they do on white people" (p. 39). Or, in a similar handbook for Latinas, Zambrano (1985) warns Hispanic women that the police may not respond to them properly because "they feel that you don't belong in this country or that you are

not worth helping," especially if the women do not speak English effectively. In any case, whether police are influenced by race or not, the *belief* that they are and they will behave with prejudice and discrimination may in itself deter minority reporting.

Fear of the police may also derive not so much from concern that they won't do anything, but from concern that they will do too much. If police exhibit sexist devaluations of women's complaints, they are also viewed as being overly zealous and racist toward the minority men they do arrest. Garcia (1985) explains that true fear about what will happen to their men in white-controlled institutions such as the jail or the courtroom keep many minority women silent:

> Not only do we fear that *we* will be mistreated by the institutions, but that our men will be also. *We want the violence in our homes to stop but we do not want to contribute in any way to the unjust treatment of our race or ethnic community.* And so colorful women who are battered may hesitate to call the police or pursue arrest, for example, because we fear that our men will be treated more harshly than white batterers (p. 2) (Author's emphasis).

White (1979) notes that in responding to black women, police not only typically respond with "traditional macho attitudes" about domestic violence, but "in our communities they have too frequently treated our husbands, sons, and brothers brutally and with racist contempt" (p. 129). One black activist is quoted by Williams (1981) as saying that "All (abusive) men, regardless of race, should be dealt with, but black men are going to be dealt with more severely." As a result, "There's a lot of guilt involved when you're talking about reporting a man. There's a fear that it's not supporting black and other minority men . . ." (p. 22).

Indeed, this concern for how minority men will be treated by police may be wielded by abusive men as a potent psychological weapon. "Your partner may protest about police brutality against blacks or accuse you of 'betraying' the race by calling them," warns White (1985: 40). Anecdotal evidence indicates men from all ethnic/racial minority backgrounds utilize the same basic argument, and it produces a dreadful conflict for an abused woman with a racial/ethnic conscience. All of the minority feminist literature on domestic abuse, new as it is, addresses this concern, and warns minority women not to be distracted by that ploy. "While it remains critical that black people continue actively struggling against racism and discrimination, it must not be done at the physical and psychological expense of black women," argues Richie-Bush (1983). "We have paid our dues, and black men must be held responsible for every injury they cause" (p. 17–18). Or, as Nkenge Toure of Washington's Rape Crisis Center succinctly put it, "It's a cop-out for brothers to use the issue of racism to make us feel bad" (Williams, 1981: p. 22).

As noted previously, minority women have been more prone to identify with racial/ethnic causes than feminist perspectives, however, and placing their rights as women above their concerns as minorities may not come easily. This is especially true if other components of the minority culture work to keep women in traditional roles. In Latin cultures, for example, women are viewed as being at "the heart" of the family, and the family, in turn, "is the mainstay of Latino culture."

> The Latino culture is a traditional one; in other words, it is a patriarchy with a long-established social system. Although women's roles are critical to the survival of the culture, women are relegated to the less powerful roles of wife and mother, and are often barred from being decision-makers or leaders. . . . The authority and dignity of the family is respected. Individuals often defer to family unity and strength. For the battered woman this often means tolerating abuse for the sake of family pride and preservation (Zambrano, 1985: 226–227).

Chai (1987) found that immigrant Korean women in Hawaii were still expected to carry out traditional roles, but had fewer kin supports, less income, much more work and greater economic dependence on their husbands.

The Catholic religion also plays an extremely important role in Hispanic families, and church teachings will strongly influence individual behavior. Indeed, the parish priest may be the only acceptable non-family authority figure Latinas believe they can consult. The track record for lack of helpfulness by clergy in cases of domestic violence has been documented (Fortune, 1981) and Catholic priests serving Hispanic communities are no exception. Zambrano (1985) notes that the attitudes of clergy at different churches within the same area may be quite different. Zambrano reports that while one church was already mobilizing a support group for battered wives,

> I talked with a group of priests who told me that they had no one in their church who needed "this kind" of help. They told me that women who were beaten could stop it if they really wanted to. They said such women do not honor their husbands and should expect some punishment (Zambrano, 1985: 213).

Little wonder that "Latinas often accept their destiny with resignation, accepting their family life as being the way God wants them to live" (Zambrano, 1985: 227). Reaching such women with the message that they need not submit to continuing abuse may be very difficult; getting them to act on that message may be impossible.

The role of the church, and the importance of keeping the family together, has often had a similar impact in black communities. The image of "strong black womanhood," enduring all in the face of incredible racial oppression, is an ideal often held up to long-suffering women victims by the black community itself (Richie, 1985). Asbury (1987) has noted that "When an abused woman believes that strength and independence are expected of her, she may be more reluctant to call attention to her situation, feeling that she should be able to handle it on her own; she may deny the seriousness of her situation. Thus, she may remain immobile, hampered by her belief in inner resources she may not possess" (p. 101). Unfortunately, the traditions of the black church have tended to encourage acceptance of adversity:

> Throughout our history the church has held a predominant place in black people's lives. It was a deep, abiding faith in a "greater good" and a "Higher Power" that gave slave families their spiritual strength and unity. They endured the wrenching pain of losing loved ones on the auction block because they had a firm belief that their families would be reunited in another life. . . . [Consequently], instead of seeking active change in the "here and now" some people accept their earthly sufferings and look forward to claiming their reward in heaven. This life, they believe, is a burdensome but necessary cross to bear in order to attain life everlasting. Such is the philosophy of many blacks who because of our oppression and the failing of mankind, have simply chosen to put our trust in the Lord (White, 1985: 63).

Such emphasis on endurance may be underscored by the sexist attitudes of some black pastors, who may quote scriptures to complaining women which perpetuate male domination and female subservience. In this regard they are no different than their Hispanic counterparts, or for that matter, than white conservative religious leaders. But the role of the black church in most black communities and the power of the black pastor often far exceeds the effects of the church and its pastor in white communities. Since the church (or temple or synagogue) is often an extremely important institution in minority communities, the role of the religious institu-

tion and its clergy in either addressing or perpetuating the needs of battered women in those communities deserves far more inquiry.

In some cases, church indifference to the plight of battered women may stem not so much from religious tenets as it does from the unwillingness of community leaders to acknowledge the problem for other reasons. Often minority communities place an extremely high value on setting forth a positive racial/ethnic identity and seek to avoid anything which might reinforce stereotypical images. Egley (1982) has documented how this affects the recognition of spouse abuse among deaf people:

> Since the 1960's deaf organizations have made an effort to recount the successes of deaf individuals. The image of competence fights stigma and supports deaf people seeking achievement. . . . Part of the problem for deaf individuals, deaf organizations and deaf communities looking at domestic abuse is whether to seek skills to stop abuse or to avoid stating that such a problem exists (p. 27).

Similarly, among Indians the issue of violence is particularly difficult. Americans have well-established images of the "howling" and "barbaric" Indians who massacred "helpless" and "peaceable" white pioneers. "Because these images are held by most Americans—mostly in their unconscious—writing about violence against Indian women by Indian men is frightening and dangerous to Indian people; it is dangerous to say anything that can be used to perpetuate negative beliefs" (Allen, 1985: p. 1). Even among activists against domestic violence, this concern for protecting the image of the minority group remains strong. In one case, for example, a group of women from a variety of ethnic/racial backgrounds, who were working on a special newsletter issue on battering and minority women, found consensus when ". . . all agreed that the issue should not reinforce the myth that battering is more prevalent in third world homes than in white homes" (Arnold and Perkins, 1984–85: p. 2).

Among black leaders, the strength and well-being of the family is a very sensitive issue. Richie-Bush (1983) notes that some community agencies focus on strengthening the black family as a way of overcoming many of the needs in black communities. One such agency, at which she was employed, seemed particularly successful at helping black families fight exploitation while maintaining cultural and racial identities. However, "After a period of time, I gradually realized that some of these strong, culturally-identified families, which we had been supporting so vehemently, were dangerous places for some women to live." Richie-Bush notes:

> I found myself caught in a trap. . . . It is the trap of silence. Because of the scarcity of agencies such as mine, I hesitated in disclosing my observations. I was immobilized by denial and sadness. Fear of being cast out by the community silenced me in the beginning. Loyalty and devotion are enormous barriers to overcome. . . .
>
> Black women be forewarned. It is a painful unsettling task to call attention to violence in our community. You may find yourselves caught by the trap called loyalty. There is already so much negative information about our families that a need to protect ourselves keeps us quiet (p. 16).

Under these circumstances, recognition and disclosure to the outside world that spouse abuse is a community problem can be, as Richie-Bush describes it, "so easily confused with treason!"

For other minority women, violent stereotypes are not so much the hurdle as is the failure of ethnic leaders to see that a sexist problem within the community may be as important as a racist problem outside of it. Anything which divides the minority community could distract members from the fight for equality which unites them all. As Eng (1985) observes about Asian minorities:

> Battering has not been publicly recognized by the leaders of the Asian communities who are all male. Instead, it has been buried under what are seen as more immediate concerns facing the entire community—low economic status and racial violence (p. 3).

Since individualism is very suppressed in traditional Asian cultures, women who speak up for themselves against abuse are doubly condemned: for placing their own interests ahead of family interests and for dividing the family and the community (her relatives vs. his relatives, female community members against males).

The fears of minority group leaders are understandable even if they are not laudable. Racial and ethnic subcultures in America, especially those of "people of color," are still surrounded by tremendous walls of prejudice, ignorance and deprivation. It hardly matters that spouse abuse is prevalent in white households as well, if spouse abuse in the minority community becomes one more stereotypical expectation added to the burden.

CONCLUSION

This analysis of the available materials on the plight of minority women who are victimized by domestic violence suggests that these women face *three* separate sets of problems.

First, there is the problem of the abuse itself. The available data, admittedly anecdotal, strongly suggest that racial and ethnic minority women experience the battering in much the same way white women do. A punch in the eye or a kick in the stomach is probably the same no matter what color you are or what language is being shouted at the time.

Afterwards, however, minority women find themselves facing problems which may be quite different from those of their white counterparts. A second set of problems for minority women are those which are the product of simple racism. Whether it's fear of police brutality against themselves and their men, or the fear of being viewed as a traitor for disclosing a problem which may tarnish the positive image the minority community has worked so hard to foster, these are problems with which white women simply do not have to contend.

Finally, there are problems typical of or unique to each racial or ethnic group which present special third-level dilemmas to battered women from that group. Some of these problems reflect the traditional cultural heritage or customs of the group, such as the Asian concern about "loss of face." Others reflect the group's particular experience on American soil, such as the destruction of family ties and the cultivation of the image of "strong womanhood" experienced by blacks as slaves. Still others reflect the strong influence of modern institutions which prevail in minority communities, such as the church. Each may work to curtail the recognition among minority women in that cultural group that they do not have to submit to brutalization or that there are ways of escaping their victimization. These cultural attributes may also serve to retard the actual availability of services for battered women within that community. Asbury (1987) neatly sums up the problems by observing that "For a battered woman to be helped, help must be available; she must know that it is available and how to gain access to it; and she must decide to use it" (p. 99).

Minority women are beginning to speak out on their own behalf against domestic violence, and to form special coalitions to explore their own special problems. It seems clear that those who are concerned about extending assistance to battered women must be sensitive to the unique problems of the minority women within their communities, even though these women may not yet have demanded such help. It has been shown here that there are some indications that minority women may be severely underreported in cases of domestic violence, and may be unable or unwilling to make use of traditional helping agencies to escape their victimization.

NOTES

1. The terms "women of color," "minority women" and "third world women" are here used interchangeably when referring to non-white women in the United States as a large class. The reader should note that some persons to whom these terms apply have specific preferences for one or more of these references.

2. The term "grassroots" here refers to organizing done by those who are directly affected by the problem and who are not part of the established political system.

REFERENCES

Allen, N. H. (1980). *Homicide: Perspective on prevention.* New York: Human Sciences Press, Inc.

Allen, P. G. (April 1985). Violence and the American Indian woman. *Working Together.* Center for the Prevention of Sexual and Domestic Violence, 1914 N. 34, Suite 205, Seattle, WA 98103.

American Indian Women against Domestic Violence. (June 1985). Position Paper. In *A Movement of New World Women Conference,* conference packet. (Copies available: Women of Nations, P.O. Box 4637, St. Paul, MN 55704.)

Arnold, M., and S. Perkins (1984–85). Talking about our lives. *Wives Tales: A Newsletter about Ending Violence against Women in the Home.* Fall/Winter, 2.

Asbury, J. (1987). African-American women in violent relationships: An exploration of cultural differences. In R. L. Hampton (ed.), *Violence in the Black Family* (pp. 89–105). Lexington, MA: Lexington Books.

Bard, M. (1980). Function of the police and the justice system in family violence. In M. R. Green (ed.), *Violence and the Family* (pp. 105–120). Boulder, CO: Westview Press.

Barnett, S. (1977). Researching black justice:

Descriptions and implications. In C. Owens and J. Bell (eds.), *Blacks and Criminal Justice* (p. 24–33). Lexington, MA: Lexington Books.

Bayley, D. H., and H. Mendelsohn. (1969). *Minorities and the police*. New York: The Free Press.

Benedek, E. P. (1982). Women and homicide. In B. L. Danto, J. Bruhns, J. and A. H. Kutscher (eds.), *The Human Side of Homicide* (pp. 150–164). New York: Columbia University Press.

Berk, S., and D. Loseke. (1981). Handling family violence: Situational determinants of police arrest in domestic disturbances. *Law and Society Review, 15* (2), 317–344.

Berk, R. A., S. F. Berk, D. R. Loseke, and D. Rauma. (1983). Mutual combat and other family violence myths. In D. Finkelhor, R. J. Gelles, G. T. Hotaling, and M. A. Straus (eds.), *The Dark Side of Families: Current Family Violence Research,* Beverly Hills: Sage Publications.

Block, C. R. (1985a). Race/ethnicity and patterns of Chicago homicide 1965 to 1981. *Crime and Delinquency, 31* (1), 104–116.

Block, C. R. (1985b). *Lethal violence in Chicago over seventeen years: Homicides known to the police, 1965–1981.* Chicago: Illinois Criminal Justice Information Authority.

Block, R. (1977). *Violent crime: Environment interaction and death.* Lexington, MA: Lexington Books.

Bonger, W. A. (1943). *Race and crime.* Translated from the Dutch by M. M. Hordyk. New York: Columbia University Press. Reprinted by Patterson Smith, 1969.

Bowker, L. H. (1979). The criminal victimization of women. *Victimology, 4* (4), 371–384.

Brearley, H. D. (1932). *Homicide in the United States.* Chapel Hill: University of North Carolina Press.

Brisson, N. J. (1981). Battering husbands: A survey of abusive men. *Victimology, 6* (1–4), 338–344.

Bruce, D. D. (1979). *Violence and culture in the antebellum South.* Austin: University of Texas.

Bureau of Justice Statistics. (1984). *Special report: Family violence.* Washington, DC: U.S. Department of Justice.

Carrol, J. (1980). A cultural-consistency theory of family violence in Mexican-American and Jewish ethnic groups. In M. A. Straus and G. T. Hotaling (eds.), *The Social Causes of Husband-Wife Violence* (pp. 68–81). Minneapolis: University of Minnesota Press.

Carter, David L. (1985). Hispanic perception of police performance: An empirical assessment. *Journal of Criminal Justice, 13* (6), 487–500.

Cazenave, N. A., and M. A. Straus. (1979). Race, class, network embeddedness and family violence: A search for potent support systems. *Journal of Comparative Family Studies, 10* (3), 281–300.

Chai, A. Y. (1987). Freed from the elders, but locked into labor: Korean immigrant women in Hawaii. *Women's Studies, 13* (3), 223–234.

Chavez, L. R., W. A. Cornelius, and O. W. Jones. (1986). Utilization of health services by Mexican immigrant women in San Diego. *Women & Health, 11,* 3–20.

Chimbos, P. D., and R. Montgomery. (1978). Violent crimes in a nonmetropolitan area of Ontario. *Crime and Justice, 6* (4), 234–245.

Curtis, L. (1974). *Criminal Violence: National Patterns & Behavior.* Lexington, MA: Lexington Books.

Edwards, S. S. M. (1986). Police attitudes and dispositions in domestic disputes: The London Study. *Police Journal, 59* (3), 230–241.

Egley, L. C. (1982). Domestic abuse and deaf people: One community's approach. *Victimology, 7* (1–4), 24–34.

Eng, P. (1985). Aiding abused Asian women. *Wives Tales: A Newsletter about Ending Violence against Women in the Home, 11* (1), 3.

Eng, P., and S. Messing. (1987). Shelter Asian Women. *New Directions for Women, 16,* 3.

Epstein, C. F. (1973). Black and female: The double whammy. *Psychology Today, 7* (Aug), 57.

Farley, R. (1980). Homicide trends in the United States. *Demography, 17* (2), 177–188.

Feinman, C. (1985). Domestic violence on the Navajo reservation. Paper presented at the annual meeting of the American Society of Criminology, San Diego, CA. Forthcoming in *Victimology.*

Fortune, M. (1981). *Family violence: A workshop manual for clergy and other service providers.* Rockville, MD: The National Clearinghouse on Domestic Violence.

Gaquin, D. A. (1977–78). Spouse abuse: Data from the National Crime Survey. *Victimology, 12* (3–4), 632–643.

Garcia, M. (1985). Double jeopardy: Battered women of color. *Wives Tales: A Newsletter about*

Ending Violence against Women in the Home, 11 (1), 1–2.

Gelles, R. J. (1972). *The Violent Home: A Study of Physical Aggression between Husbands and Wives.* Beverly Hills: Sage.

Gelles, R. J. (1980). Violence in the family: A review of research in the seventies. *Journal of Marriage and the Family, 42,* 873–886.

Hawkins, D. F. (1985). Black homicide: The adequacy of existing research for devising prevention strategies. *Crime and Delinquency, 31* (1), 83–103.

Hindelang, M. (1976). *Criminal Victimization in Eight American Cities: A Descriptive Analysis of Common Theft and Assault.* Cambridge, MA: Ballinger.

Hindelang, M. (1979). Race and involvement in common law personal crimes. *American Sociological Review, 43* (February): 93–109.

Holdaway, S. (1983). *Inside the British Police: A force at work.* Oxford, United Kingdom: Basic Blackwell.

Katz, M. (1973). Family crisis training: Upgrading the police while building a bridge to the minority community. *Journal of Police Science and Administration. 1* (1), 30–35.

Kirk, A. R. (1982). Black homicide. In B. L. Danto, J. Bruhns, and A. H. Kutscher (eds.), *The Human Side of Homicide.* New York: Columbia University Press.

Kuhl, A. (1982). Community responses to battered women. *Victimology, 7* (1–4), 49–59.

LaBell, L. (1979). Wife abuse: A sociological study of battered women and their mates. *Victimology. 4* (2), 258–267.

Lewis, D. K. (1977). A response to inequality: Black women, racism, and sexism. *Signs, 3,* 339–361.

Lockhart, L. L. (1984). A comparative analysis of the nature and extent of spouse abuse (as reflected by several measures) among black and white couples across different social classes. Unpublished dissertation. Florida State University School of Social Work.

Loizos, P. (1978). Violence and the family: Some Mediterranean examples. In J. P. Martin (ed.), *Violence and the Family* (pp. 183–196). New York: Wiley.

Mushanga, T. M. (1977–78). Wife victimization in east and central Africa. *Victimology. 2* (3–4), 479–485.

O'Brien, R. M. (1987). The interracial nature of violent crimes: A reexamination. *American Journal of Sociology, 92* (4), 817–835.

Parker, B., and D. Schumacher. (1979). The battered wife syndrome and violence in the nuclear family of origin: A controlled pilot study. *American Journal of Public Health, 67* (8), 760–763.

Poussaint, A. F. (1972). *Why Blacks Kill Blacks.* New York: Emerson Hall.

Rasche, C. E. (1988). Characteristics of mate-homicides: A comparison to Wolfgang. Paper presented at the annual meeting of the Academy of Criminal Justice Sciences. San Francisco, CA.

Richie-Bush, B. (1983). Facing contradictions: Challenge for black feminists, *Aegis, 37,* 14–20.

Richie, B. (1985). Battered black women a challenge for the black community. *Black Scholar. 16* (March/April), 40–44.

Rounsaville, B. J. (1978–79). Theories in marital violence: Evidence from a study of battered women. *Victimology. 3* (1–2), 11–31.

Savitz, L. (1973). Black crime. In K. Miller and R. M. Dreger (eds.), *Comparative Studies of Blacks and Whites in the United States.* (pp. 467–576). New York: Seminar Press.

Segovia-Ashley, M. (1978). Shelters—Short-term needs. In *Battered Women: Issues of Public Policy.* Washington, DC: U.S. Commission on Civil Rights.

Shoemaker, D. J., and J. S. Williams. (1987). The subculture of violence and ethnicity. *Journal of Criminal Justice. 15* (6), 461–472.

Skurnik, J. (1983). Battering: An issue for women of color. *Off Our Backs, 13* (5), 8.

Smith, D., and J. Klein. (1984). Police control of interpersonal disputes. *Social Problems, 31* (4), 468–481.

Smith, D. L., and R. Snow. (1978). Violent subcultures or subcultures of violence. *Southern Journal of Criminal Justice, 3,* 1–13.

Spiegel, J. P. (1980). Ethnopsychiatric dimensions in family violence. In M. R. Green (ed.), *Violence and the Family* (pp. 79–89). Boulder, CO: Westview Press.

Stachura, J. S., and R. H. D. Teske. (March 1979). *A special report on spouse abuse in Texas,* Survey Research Program, Criminal Justice Center, Sam Houston State University.

Staples, R. (1973). *The black woman in America: Sex, marriage and the family,* Chicago: Nelson-Hall Publishers.

Staples, R. (1976). Race and family violence: The internal colonialism perspective. In G. E. Lawrence and L. P. Brown (eds.), *Crime and Its Impact on the Black Community.* Institute for Urban Affairs and Development Center. Washington, DC: Howard University.

Straus, M. A., R. J. Gelles, and S. K. Steinmetz. (1979). *Violence in the American family.* New York: Anchor/Doubleday.

Sullivan, D. J. (1977). Violence—an active volcano. In M. G. Kerr (ed.), *Violence—The Community and the Administrator* (pp. 70–85). Wellington, New Zealand: New Zealand Institute of Public Administration.

Von Hentig, H. (1948). *The criminal and his victim: Studies in the sociobiology of crime.* Yale University Press, 416–417. Reprinted by Anchor Books, 1967.

Walker, L. E. (1979). *The Battered woman,* New York: Harper and Row.

Walker, L. E. (1983). Victimology and the psychological perspectives of battered women. *Victimology, 8* (1–2), 82–104.

West, L. J. (1980). Discussion: Violence and the family in perspective. In M. R. Green (ed.), *Violence and the Family* (pp. 90–104). Boulder, CO: Westview Press.

White, E. C. (1985). *Chain chain change: For black women dealing with physical and emotional abuse.* Seattle, WA: The Seal Press.

White, J. (1979). Women speak. *Essence, 10* (June), 75+.

Wilbanks, W. (1982). Murdered women and women who murder: A critique of the literature. In N. H. Rafter and E. A. Stanko (eds.), *Judge, Lawyer, Victim, Thief* (pp. 151–180). Northeastern University Press, 1982.

Wilbanks, W. (1984). *Murder in Miami: An analysis of homicide patterns and trends in Dade County (Miami) Florida, 1917–1983.* Lanham, MD: University Press of America.

Wilbanks, W. (1985). Is violent crime intraracial? *Crime and Delinquency, 31* (1), 117–128.

Williams, L. (1981). Violence against women. *Black Scholar, 12* (Jan–Feb), 18–24.

Winkler, K. J. (1986). Scholars reproached for ignoring women of color in U.S. history. *Chronicle of Higher Education, 32* (April 23), 6+.

Wolfgang, M. (1958). *Patterns in criminal homicide.* Montclair, NJ: Patterson Smith Reprint, 1975.

Wolfgang, M. E., and F. Ferracuti. (1967). Subculture of violence—A socio-psychological theory. In M. Wolfgang (ed.), *Studies in Homicide* (pp. 271–280). New York: Harper and Row.

Yates, D. L. (1985). *Correlates of attitudes towards the police: A comparison of black and white citizens in Austin, Texas.* Unpublished dissertation, University of Texas at Austin. Ann Arbor: University Microfilms International.

Zahn, M. A., and W. C. Rickle. (1986). Murder and minorities: The Hispanic case. Paper presented at the Academy of Criminal Justice Sciences, Orlando, FL.

Zambrano, M. M. (1985). *Mejor sola que mal acompanada.* Seattle, WA: The Seal Press. (Includes English translation.)

CHAPTER 15

COPS, COURTS, AND WOMAN BATTERING

KATHLEEN J. FERRARO

ABSTRACT

In this third chapter on woman battering, the focus is on the state's response to this crime. What can the police and the courts do in their roles of crime control, prosecution, and sentencing? Many now believe that we are in a growing epidemic of violence against women; estimates are that at least 4 million American women are beaten by husbands or boyfriends each year.* Tragically, the history of the police response to domestic calls for woman battering consists of largely ineffective practices (for example, telling the victim to go to court and swear out a complaint or, alternatively, taking the batterer out for a walk to "cool off") and unprofessional attitudes (police complain among themselves about having to do a bouncer's job). Despite some experimental research on the efficacy of arrest, the appropriate police response remains unresolved: in some cases, in particular where unemployed males are involved, arrest appears to make the batterer more violent after release from jail. Arrest as a preferred police policy is also complicated by racial/ethnic, class, and sexual orientation attitudes toward victims by the police. Nonetheless, Ferraro provides an excellent overview of the latest perspectives on police intervention in woman battering.

The chapter covers two further areas of governmental responses to this crime: first, prosecution and sentencing of batterers in the criminal courts and, second, the issuing of temporary restraining orders (orders of protection) in the civil courts. In the case of prosecution, victim cooperation is less likely than in criminal assaults where a stranger is involved. Many factors go into women's request to drop charges against a batterer—including economic dependency, fear of the

---

Newsday, May 24, 1993, p. 18.

batterer, and other legal difficulties facing the victim. Lastly, the limited effectiveness of court orders of protection to keep batterers away from their victims is explored.

The chapter concludes by emphasizing a point already made in previous chapters in this book: that the criminal justice system is severely limited in solving a crime embedded in socially structured inequality between men and women that is grounded in a system of class, race, and gender biases and heterosexual privilege. Most important, argues Ferraro, this is a crime that is rooted in the structure of the social order, not the pathological psyche of individual men, and is reinforced by a criminal justice system designed to protect and perpetuate the social order through punishment of individual offenders. What suggestions does Ferraro make to deal with these entrenched problems? What do you see as the pros and cons of these suggested changes?

A feminist perspective on woman battering views male violence as an expression of class, race, gender, and heterosexual privilege. It is a problem rooted primarily in the structure of the social order, rather than the pathological psyches of individual men. The criminal justice system is designed to protect and reinforce the social order through punishment of individual deviants. It is, therefore, fundamentally at odds with a structural, gendered analysis of woman battering.

Prohibitions and sanctions against interpersonal violence have always been imbued with class, race, and gender biases. Violence is condemned most often when it violates existing power and institutional hierarchies. Violence inflicted by dominant groups, such as white, male property owners, against their subordinates, such as slaves, wives, and children, has been accepted as socially necessary and morally just. Historically, the criminal

justice system, including the police, prosecutors, and judges, has not enforced assault and battery laws when the victim-offender relationship reflected prevailing social norms of status hierarchies. Violence by husbands against wives represented a form of social control legitimated by conventional law and morality, and thus beyond the purview of criminal justice agents (Dobash & Dobash, 1979; Martin, 1976).

Battered women and their advocates have often criticized the lack of protection afforded by the criminal justice system (Cobbe, 1878; Gordon, 1988; Stone, 1879). Although statutes prohibiting wife beating have existed in the United States since 1641, their enforcement was almost nonexistent (Pleck, 1987, p. 21). When the battered women's movement of the 1970s began, the criminal justice system became one focus of activism. Since that time, considerable change has occurred in laws, policies, and training regarding intervention in battering (Ferraro, 1989a, 1989b; Dobash & Dobash, 1991). The purpose of this chapter is to describe and assess these changes in three areas: the police, the criminal courts, and the civil courts. The focus for analysis of police is arrest practices; for criminal courts, it is pros-

Author's note: Thank you to M. A. Bertner for commenting on this manuscript.

Source: Violence against Women: The Bloody Footprints, Pauline Bart and Eileen Moran (eds.), 1993, chap. 12, pp. 165–176. Copyright Sage Publications, Inc. Reprinted with permission.

ecution and sentencing; and for the civil courts, it is effectiveness of restraining orders or orders of protection (TROs).

POLICING BATTERING

The traditional response of police to battering was to tell women, "There's nothing we can do; this is a civil matter," or to make one party leave the home (Martin, 1976, pp. 2–3). One early study of police ineffectiveness indicated that in 80 percent of domestic homicides, police had been called to the home at least once. In 50 percent, they had been called more than five times prior to the homicide (Police Foundation, 1977). These data demonstrated that calls to the police had little or no impact on eliminating woman battering. The battered women's movement challenged this response through legislative changes and lawsuits. The 1976 *Bruno v. Codd* (New York) and *Scott v. Hart* (Oakland, California) class action suits charged police departments with failure to protect. Both cases were settled out of court, but they established the responsibility of police to provide protection to battered women. Pressure created by these civil suits and grass-roots activists resulted in state-by-state changes in legislation that shifted the burden of evidence required for officers to make arrests (see Woods, 1986, for a summary of civil cases). Now most states have legislation that expands police power to arrest in "domestic violence" misdemeanor assault cases without witnessing the assault (Lerman & Livingston, 1983).

After 1980, three factors coalesced to pressure police departments to treat "domestic violence" as a crime. These were: (a) federal pressure via the U.S. Attorney General's Office and the National Institute of Justice (NIJ), (b) social science research, and (c) a major civil liability suit (*Thurman v. Torrington*, 1984). The U.S. Attorney General's Task Force on Family Violence published its report

(Hart et al., 1984) recommending that "Family violence should be recognized and responded to as a criminal activity" (p. 10). Second, Lawrence Sherman and Richard Berk (1984) published the findings of their study of the Minneapolis police in the *American Sociological Review,* the most prestigious sociological journal. Sherman and Berk presented their research as an experiment and their findings as scientific evidence that arrest was significantly more effective in deterring future violence in battering situations than either separation or mediation. The original experiment is being replicated in six sites. The National Institute of Justice funded each site with $541,000 to $682,000, investing approximately $3.6 million, or nearly half of the sum allocated by the federal Family Violence Prevention and Services Act to states for direct services. Results from Omaha, Nebraska, have shown no difference in recidivism after one year between cases resulting in arrest, separation, or mediation (Dunford, 1990). Results from the other five sites have not yet been reported.

In 1985, Tracy Thurman won a settlement of $1.9 million from the City of Torrington, Connecticut, police department for its negligence in failing to provide protection to her. Thurman was assaulted and permanently disabled by her husband in the presence of police officers. The large settlement caused insurance companies to request police departments to revamp their arrest policies for domestic violence. The political, academic, and financial pressures to alter police practices led to changes in training, policies, and legislation throughout the country. By the end of 1985, 47 cities with populations over 100,000 had police policies of mandatory or presumptive arrests for "family fights," and 6 states had laws that required arrest under certain circumstances (Crime Control Institute, 1986).

There is general agreement among activists for battered women that a shift from the definition of battering as a "domestic problem" to a criminal activity has taken place, and that this shift is beneficial to battered women. But the implementation of the "get tough" stance has not been without problems and contradictions. Most important, police do not generally share a gendered analysis of battering. Feminists define battering within the context of patriarchy, focusing on male domination within all major social institutions. Criminal justice personnel, including police, view battering in gender-neutral terms as a problem of pathological family interaction. This difference in perspective results in conceptual conflicts in feminist and police definitions of woman battering. Most significant, police standards of harm, responsibility, and victimization exclude an appreciation of women's subordinate status within the family and the economy. Police officers are generally unsympathetic toward women who express ambivalence about their relationships and pressing criminal charges. Although the intent of policies and laws mandating arrest is to reduce the impact of discretionary decision making among police, it is not possible to accomplish this goal entirely through rules imposed on street-level officers by administrators or legislators.

A second major problem with efforts to enhance policing is the historical police repression of people of color, poor people, lesbians and gays, and political activists. Gender is not the only hierarchical theme reinforced by traditional criminal justice policies. Rates of arrest are much higher for low-income and racial and ethnic minority groups, and pressure to increase arrests may exacerbate the use of police force against these groups. Battering in gay and lesbian couples may continue to be ignored due to homophobic police reactions. Research in Duluth, Minnesota, has found a proportionate *decrease* in arrests of minority men, from 32 percent to 8.5 percent of the total, one year after the introduction of

mandatory arrest (Dobash & Dobash, 1991). But these percentages are based on small numbers (22 and 175, respectively), and Duluth is unique in the overall success of its intervention project.

Despite efforts to standardize arrest as the most appropriate response to woman battering, wide variations in police practice persist. The Phoenix, Arizona, police department adopted a presumptive arrest policy in May 1984, after Chief Ruben Ortega returned from serving on the U.S. Attorney General's Task Force. The policy stated that:

> Officers should arrest domestic violence violators even if the victim does not desire prosecution. When probable cause exists, an arrest should be made even if a misdemeanor offense did not occur in the officer's presence. (Ortega, 1984, p. 1)

In a study of the implementation of this presumptive arrest policy, it was found that in 69 cases of family fight calls to police, only 9 (18 percent) resulted in arrests (Ferraro, 1989a, 1989b). This low arrest rate reflects the difficulty of mandating police decision making.

Police move within a complex, ever-changing array of considerations that cannot be simplified or held constant by administrators. Legal considerations may appear straightforward from an outsider's perspective: If you get a family fight call, you make an arrest. In practice, the construction of an arrest involves an evaluation of the presence of probable cause [for arrest] and of fault in which an officer interprets the events observed. Witnesses, injuries, property destruction, and weapons all help an officer determine probable cause, but the interpretation of these factors depends on the officer's beliefs and the particular situation. In the Phoenix study, for example, the researcher observed a case in which smashed doors, plants, knickknacks, and plates and a cut to a woman's face did not establish probable cause for an officer who said, "There's no offense here." Similar facts led to arrests in other cases. This particular officer believed the male abuser held the prerogative to damage "his" property if he wanted to, and viewed the woman's injury as too minor to constitute a crime. If the officer does not perceive probable cause, the call does not fit the policy and does not lead to arrest. The discretion inherent in evaluating probable cause may be limited through more explicit training and instruction, but cannot be eliminated.

At the same time, fault is a negotiable decision. When officers arrive at a "family fight," they decide who is most to blame for the problem. If they view each partner as equally liable, both parties will be arrested (Chaudhuri & Daly, 1992; Dobash & Dobash, 1991). Interviews with 17 women who had called the police for help revealed that 2 of these women were arrested and incarcerated overnight (Ferraro, 1989a). In one case, the arrest facilitated the husband's efforts to obtain an order of protection and move the woman out of the house. The neutrality of legal language provides the context for police to view woman battering as "mutual combat" and the arrest of women as appropriate. The ungendered, "mutual combat" perspective is problematic because when women do use violence against their male partners, it is almost always in self-defense and involves the least severe forms of violence (Saunders, 1988). When police arrest women for defending themselves against battering, the abusers are provided social support for initiating and justifying violence.

Determination of probable cause and fault are influenced by the background assumptions officers hold about women and racial and ethnic groups. Officers tend to view the world as divided into distinct categories of normal citizens and deviants. Those falling into the deviant category are considered voluntary participants in a life-style that includes violence. Officers express the opinion that violence is a way of life for deviants, so that

police intervention in these battering cases is relatively meaningless. Black's research on policing patterns shows that police are more likely to arrest a low-income, minority person for offenses committed against a wealthy white, and are less likely to arrest the same person for an offense committed against a person of the same race and economic status (Black, 1976). Because most battering occurs against women of the same racial and economic categories as their abusers, arrest goes against the typical pattern of policing.

Police also hold stereotypes of battered women that work against an arrest policy. The most common stereotype of battered women is that they will not follow through with prosecution. In our observations of policing, every officer relayed stories about cases in which police had expended extraordinary resources or endangered themselves, only to have the woman recant her story in front of a judge (Ferraro, 1989a). The difficulties of prosecuting batterers will be discussed in the following section. In terms of the police response, however, the prospects of victim cooperation are not a legally relevant consideration for arrest decisions, particularly when presumptive arrest policies are in effect. The police officer's job is to determine probable cause, not to weigh the likelihood of victim cooperation. All the same, police expectations of victims do influence arrest decisions in woman-battering incidents.

The police are the first line of response to battering. Progress has occurred regarding the official policies of policing and the view of battering as a legitimate arena for police intervention. But the problems outlined above continue to limit the effectiveness of the police as a resource for battered women.

PROSECUTION OF BATTERING

There have been few empirical studies of the prosecutorial component of the criminal justice response. This reflects the priority given to the immediate safety function of the police. Also, the proportion of battering cases involved in the criminal justice system diminishes with each step in the process. Research on the prosecution of these cases is difficult because in most jurisdictions, cases are categorized by offense rather than victim-offender relationship.

One assumption about the prosecution of battering that has been shared by activists and academics is that stranger assault is more likely to result in conviction and sentencing than intimate assault or battering. This assumption reflects the knowledge that very few battering cases result in prison sentences. The assumption that woman battering is treated less seriously than stranger assault makes intuitive sense, but there is little published research on this issue.

Ferraro and Boychuk (1992) compared the processing of intimate and nonintimate violent offenses from the filing to the sentencing stage. Most significant, there were few differences between cases involving intimate partners and those involving strangers. In both types of violent offenses, most cases resulted in dismissal. Those that were prosecuted usually resulted in a sentence of probation. Interpersonal violence very rarely led to significant criminal sanctions. Quarm and Schwartz (1984) found similar results for a misdemeanor court in Ohio. Only 4 percent of their sample spent time in jail, and less than 1 percent served at least 3 months.

In prosecutors' records in Maricopa County, Arizona, for 1987 and 1988, the reasons given for not prosecuting violent offenses were very similar for nonintimate and intimate cases (Ferraro & Boychuk, 1992). Cases were most often rejected because they were not considered serious enough to be tried in superior court and were sent to appropriate lower courts to be tried as misdemeanors. Of cases filed for prosecution, a

sample of 104 intimate violent offenses and 100 nonintimate violent offenses was selected (see Ferraro & Boychuk, 1992, for a full discussion). Although all original charges were felony offenses involving serious or permanent injury or the use of lethal weapons, most were bargained to lesser offenses. The nine offenses examined were: murder, kidnap, sexual assault, arson, aggravated assault, resisting arrest, criminal damage, interfering with judicial proceedings, and disorderly conduct. The "intimate" category included victim-offender relationships of current or prior marriage, cohabitation, ongoing sexual relationship, or between immediate family members. Of the intimate victims, 97 individuals (90 percent) were women. Only seven (10 percent) were male intimate partners or family members.

Only 11 percent of defendants in the entire sample received prison sentences, and the relationship between victim and offender was not significantly related to the sentence. The modal category for years in prison was 1.5 years. All but six offenders received 7.5 years or less and almost a third (32 percent) of the cases were dismissed. There was a significant difference between intimate and nonintimate cases on dismissal, with nonintimate cases *more* likely to be dismissed. Of the entire sample, 43 percent received probation sentences from 1 to 70 months. Very few offenders paid restitution to victims (18 percent) or fines (12 percent). In other words, only a small fraction of arrests result in superior court filings, and only a small fraction of filings result in incarceration. The relationship between victim and offender is not a significant variable in predicting prison sentences.

We also examined victims' participation in the prosecution process. Intimate victims were less likely to follow through with prosecution than strangers, but victim cooperation was only one of the factors determining case outcome.

Of all intimate victims, 39 percent wanted charges dropped, whereas only 6 percent of nonintimate victims made this request. But other responses to prosecution diminish differences in cooperation between the two groups: Over one quarter (27 percent) of nonintimate victims were missing at the time of trial, whereas only 7 percent of intimate victims were missing. Another 16 percent of intimate victims cooperated with the prosecution, but specifically stated that they desired help for their abusers rather than prison. This response was entirely absent in the nonintimate group. Of the cases where women victims of intimate assault requested that charges be dropped, 65 percent resulted in guilty pleas. So, even if women do not want to follow through with prosecution, it is likely that there is enough evidence to obtain a plea of guilt if the case is serious enough to warrant felony prosecution. At the same time, 16 percent of cases where victims fully cooperated with and desired prosecution resulted in dismissals. The prevalent belief that prosecuting battering is a waste of time because of victim noncooperation overlooks the importance of other legal and extralegal factors in case dismissal.

There are many factors that influence a woman's request to drop charges against an abuser. Many women are dependent on men's economic contributions for support of children. Imprisonment eliminates current employment and endangers future opportunities. Several months usually pass between the violent incident and court hearings. Most offenders are released from custody during this period and find ways to intimidate and manipulate women into dropping charges against them. Some battered women have other legal problems, such as immigration status or outstanding traffic warrants, which lead them to be wary of involvement with the courts. Women who ask for help for their abusers rather than incarceration may believe that prison will lead to an increase in violence upon the abuser's release.

Most large cities now have victim witness assistance programs to provide advocacy services to victims of crime. Those programs that assist battered women with the prosecution process have had dramatic success in improving victim cooperation. Programs in Santa Barbara, California; Los Angeles; and Philadelphia increased victim cooperation to 80 to 92 percent of all complaints filed (Lerman, 1983). When battered women are provided with information about the legal process and support for testifying, successful prosecution is the norm.

Some jurisdictions have adopted policies of mandating victim witness cooperation by charging women who fail to testify with contempt of court. Women are not given the choice of dropping charges or failing to appear, and may be incarcerated for refusing to testify (Dobash & Dobash, 1991). These policies are an attempt to increase penalties for woman battering, but fail to recognize the diverse needs and experiences of battered women. One study of prosecution found that the only factor that significantly diminishes recidivism among batterers is allowing women to drop charges (Ford & Regolie, 1992). This finding substantiates the feminist principle that women are the best experts on their own lives.

COURT ORDERS OF PROTECTION

A statutory change that accompanied most state laws to enhance police power involved the creation of temporary orders of protection or temporary restraining orders (TROs) designed to protect women from future abuse based on prior experiences. These are court orders that establish the limits of men's access to women and may prohibit a man's presence near a woman, her place of employment, her children, their school, and anyplace else that can be defined as her sphere of activity. Violation of the orders is a civil or criminal offense that can result in immediate arrest. Although these orders were originally limited to married or formerly married people, most states now have provisions for cohabitees and former cohabitees.

The few studies that have examined TROs have found that their effectiveness in controlling male violence depends on the circumstances and history of the men (Chaudhuri & Daly, 1992; Grau, Fagan, & Wexler, 1984). Grau et al. (1984) found that TROs did not reduce verbal and emotional abuse, but did reduce violence in cases where the original violence was not severe. Women who had been severely battered were not effectively protected from future violence by TROs (p. 23).

Chaudhuri and Daly (1992, p. 245) found that TROs generally increased police responsiveness to calls from battered women. But police were *not* more likely to arrest men for violating TROs than for committing battering, unless the men were also involved in other offenses. Future battering was prevented by TROs against employed men with no prior criminal histories, no drug or alcohol abuse, and low levels of initial violence. Men who did not share these characteristics were not deterred by the TROs. Chaudhuri and Daly (1992) note that 1 woman in 10 in their study was beaten *because* she had obtained a TRO (p. 245). In Ferraro's (1989a) police study, 3 of 17 women said that the TRO did not help at all (p. 178). Two women believed that *nothing* could change their husbands.

Yet, TROs may have other positive benefits for women (Chaudhuri & Daly, 1992). The process of obtaining a TRO requires women to talk to attorneys or judges about the battering, and a sympathetic response from these outsiders may help women reinforce the definition of battering as unacceptable (Ferraro & Johnson, 1983). Men responding to petitions for TROs are forced to admit their violence before the court, publicly disclosing what is often privately denied. The majority of abusers, however, do not appear for these hearings or these benefits.

CONCLUSION

The criminal justice approach to woman battering focuses on the control of specific incidents without attention to the complex social and economic problems of women. The isolation of battering from the larger context of women's lives produces absurd contradictions. Women are told that police will arrest, that TROs will keep abusers away, and that judges will send them to prison if the women will only be consistent and cooperative with prosecutors. In the majority of cases, women do not experience these outcomes and continue to be abused, harassed, and threatened. Although frustration accrues from lack of responsiveness to their requests, no assistance with housing, child care, transportation, or employment is available. When battered women "stay with abusers," it is most often a case of their being unable to force the man to leave them alone or to establish an independent economic base.

Defining woman battering as a crime problem radically distorts women's needs and experiences and the larger feminist agenda of the empowerment and emancipation of women. Arrest and incarceration of men who batter women has no direct relationship to enhancing women's economic status, improving and expanding health and reproductive options, softening the rigors of child care and waged labor, or building community. In some cases, the criminal justice system directly opposes these important goals, as when women are incarcerated for hiding their children from sexually abusive fathers (*off our backs*, 1988).

The androcentric, positivistic worldview embodied in legal practices is antithetical to a feminist account of battering. The facts of each case are recorded in legal terms of probable cause, fault, and harm. From this perspective, women become responsible for clearly and consistently demonstrating to police, attorneys and judges that they have been severely injured, have not fought back with greater violence than they received, and do want their abusers arrested and prosecuted. These requirements often exclude women from the system, minimizing their fear and suffering and evoking disdain for the ambivalence and confusion that are a common response to battering.

The data on implementing mandatory arrest suggest that it is difficult to change police responses to woman battering and to eliminate discretion. Data on prosecution of assaults indicates that most interpersonal violence, whether between strangers or intimates, is treated leniently by the courts. The obstacles to increasing protection for women through the criminal justice system are formidable and demand continuous monitoring and involvement from feminists. The projects that have been most successful, such as the Domestic Abuse Intervention Program in Duluth, Minnesota, are located in small communities where a committed group of activists has coordinated the components of the system and insisted on adherence to feminist values (Pence & Shepard, 1988). In large urban centers with entrenched politics, it is much more difficult to hold the criminal justice system accountable to battered women.

This pessimistic overview is not intended as a plea to abandon the criminal justice system as a locus of work against male violence. As stated above, it is often the only option available to women in immediate danger. But it is important to recognize the inherent limitations of the police and courts and the failures of previous efforts. The experience of the past 10 years has demonstrated the case with which feminist concerns are coopted and

transformed by mainstream institutions. It is vital that battering not be viewed only as a crime but also as a manifestation of structured gender inequality.

REFERENCES

Black, D. (1976). *The behavior of law.* New York: Academic Press.

Chaudhuri, M., & K. Daly. (1992). Do restraining orders help? Battered women's experience with male violence and legal process. In E. Buzawa (ed.), *Domestic violence: The changing criminal justice response* (pp. 227–252). Westport, CT: Greenwood.

Cobbe, F. P. (1878, April). Wife torture in England. *Contemporary Review,* pp. 55–87.

Crime Control Institute. (1986). Police domestic violence policy change. *Response, 9*(2), 16.

Dobash, R. E., & R. Dobash. (1979). *Violence against wives.* New York: Free Press.

Dobash, R. E., & R. Dobash. (1991). *Women, violence and social change.* London: Routledge.

Dunford, F. W. (1990). *Long term recidivism in the Omaha domestic violence experiments.* Paper presented at the annual meeting of the American Society of Criminology, Baltimore, MD.

Ferraro, K. J. (1989a). The legal response to battering in the United States. In J. Hanmer, J. Radford, & E. A. Stanko (eds.), *Women, policing, and male violence.* London: Routledge.

Ferraro, K. J. (1989b). Policing woman battering. *Social Problems, 36,* 61–74.

Ferraro, K. J., & T. Boychuk. (1992). The court's response to interpersonal violence: A comparison of intimate and nonintimate assault. In E. Buzawa (ed.), *Domestic violence: The changing criminal justice response* (pp. 209–225). Westport, CT: Greenwood.

Ferraro, K. J., & J. M. Johnson. (1983). How women experience battering. *Social Problems, 30*(3), 325–339.

Ford, D., & M. J. Regolie. (1992). The preventive impacts of policies for prosecuting wife batterers. In E. S. Buzawa & C. G. Buzawa (eds.), *Domestic violence: The changing criminal justices response* (pp. 181–208). Westport, CT: Auburn House.

Gordon, L. (1988). *Heroes of their own lives.* New York: Viking.

Grau, J., J. Fagan, & S. Wexler. (1984). Restraining orders for battered women: Issues of access and efficacy. *Women and Politics, 4,* 13–28.

Hart, W., J. Ashcroft, A. Burgess, N. Flanagan, C. Meese, C. Milton, C. Narramore, R. Ortega, & F. Seward. (1984). *Attorney general's task force on family violence.* Washington, DC: Department of Justice.

Lerman, L. (1983). *The prosecution of spouse abuse.* Washington, DC: Department of Justice.

Lerman, L., & F. Livingston. (1983). State legislation on domestic violence. *Response, 6,* 1–28.

Martin, D. (1976). *Battered wives.* San Francisco, CA: Glide.

off our backs. (1988). Mississippi project to stop child sexual abuse. *off our backs, 18*(8), 12.

Ortega, R. *Operations Digest, 84–85,* 1–2.

Pence, E., & M. Shepard. (1988). Integrating feminist theory and practice. In K. Yllöo & M. Bograd (eds.), *Feminist perspectives on wife abuse* (pp. 282–298). Newbury Park, CA.: Sage.

Pleck, E. (1987). *Domestic tyranny.* New York: Oxford.

Police Foundation. (1977). *Domestic violence and the police.* Washington, DC: Police Foundation.

Quarm, D., & M. Schwartz. (1984). Domestic violence in criminal court: An examination of new legislation in Ohio. *Women and Politics, 4*(3), 29–46.

Saunders, D. G. (1988). Wife abuse, husband abuse, or mutual combat? In K. Yllöo & M. Bograd (eds.), *Feminist perspectives on wife abuse* (pp. 90–113). Newbury Park, CA: Sage.

Scott v. Hart. (1986). C76–2395 WWS National Center for Women & Family Law Resource List: Battered Women, Litigation, Item #24, Laurie Woods.

Sherman, L. W., & R. A. Berk, (1984). The specific deterrent effects of arrest for domestic assault. *American Sociological Review, 49,* 261–272.

Stone, L. (1879, January 11 and 18). [Untitled news article]. *Women's Journal.*

Woods, L. (1986). *Resource list: Battered women: Litigation.* New York: National Center on Women and Family Law.

CHAPTER 16

FEMICIDE: SEXIST TERRORISM AGAINST WOMEN

JANE CAPUTI/DIANA E. H. RUSSELL

ABSTRACT

In 1981, in a pathbreaking approach to understanding socially structured violence against women, Dorie Klein argued that crimes against women are politically defined and depend on the particular historical relationships that exist between men and women.* For example, women condemned as witches were healers of the poor; the violence committed against both witches and midwives (often one and the same person) occurred as men took over legal control and economic monopoly of medicine in the nineteenth century. Today, as a result of feminist theory and activism, age-old violence against women, wife battering, incestuous attacks of young girls by fathers or father substitutes, and rape are beginning to be defined as crimes against women not to be tolerated by society. In short, crimes against women are quintessentially political and are determined by economic, social, and cultural circumstances of a particular period of time.

Caputi and Russell bring the reader up to date in this chapter on the political nature of crimes against women today. They observe that politically motivated violence, such as lynchings and pogroms, was designed to preserve supremacy of one group (whites and gentiles, respectively) over another (blacks and Jews, respectively). In the same way, violence against women—whether conscious or not—is politically motivated and is designed to maintain male supremacy and dominance over women. Caputi and Russell describe the most severe form of violence, the murder of women, which they label femicide. Using the term "femicide" clarifies the gendered nature of "homicide" or "murder": women killed by

---

*Dorie Klein, "Violence against Women: Some Considerations Regarding Its Causes and Its Elimination," *Crime & Delinquency*, January 1981, pp. 64–80. This was reprinted as Chapter 11 in the first edition of our book: *The Criminal Justice System and Women*, Clark Boardman, Ltd., New York, 1982.

men *because* they are women. Femicide is the extreme end of a continuum of antifemale terror that includes, but is not limited to, rape, torture, sexual slavery as in prostitution, incest, genital mutilation, unnecessary gynecological surgery, forced sterilization, and forced heterosexuality. Femicide, they write, is sexist terrorism that is "motivated by hatred, contempt, pleasure, or a sense of ownership of women." And it includes mutilation murder, rape murder, battery murder, immolation of witches in Western Europe and brides and widows in India, and the murder of Latin and Middle Eastern women believed to have lost their virginity prior to marriage. Clearly, femicide has no respect for culture or nationality, nor for race, age, class, or sexuality. Even so, white society's lack of concern about the murders of women of color is all too often ignored.

The authors' thesis is that much of contemporary violence against women is a result of a male backlash to feminism; and with the growth of the feminist perspective since the 1960s, that violence has escalated. The list of lethal and non-lethal assaults against women is so large, the authors argue, that women in the United States can be said to live in a reign of sexist terror comparable to the notorious witch-hunts in Europe from the fourteenth through the seventeenth centuries. The authors urge a widespread boycott of violent and abusive men and their culture in order to bring an end to femicide. Spell out several different ways in which such boycotts could be carried out. What else might individuals, groups, communities, or nations do to eliminate femicide? What effect might the recognition throughout the world that gender-based violence violates women's fundamental human rights have on saving women's lives?* Compare this chapter's radical use of government statistics with that of Steffensmeier in Chapter 5, whose analysis is anchored in traditional criminology which does not question the statistics with which it works.

---

*See Jane Roberts Chapman, "Violence against Women as a Violation of Human Rights," *Social Justice*, vol. 17, Summer 1990, pp. 54–65.

Kill Feminist Bitches

—Graffito, University of Western Ontario, after Marc Lépine's murder of 14 women in Montreal, 1989

Canadian novelist Margaret Atwood once asked a male friend why men feel threatened by women. He replied: "They are afraid women will laugh at them." She then asked a group of women why they felt threatened by men. They answered: "We're afraid of being killed."

However wildly disproportionate, these fears are profoundly linked, as was demonstrated on 6 December 1989 at the University of Montreal. On that day, 25-year-old combat

Adapted by permission of *Ms.* Magazine, © 1990. This version is found in Jill Radford and Diana E. H. Russell (eds.), *Femicide: The Politics of Woman Killing*, Twayne Publishers, New York, 1992.

magazine aficionado Marc Lépine suited up for war and rushed the school of engineering. In one classroom, he separated the women from the men, ordered the men out, and, shouting "You're all fucking feminists," opened fire on the women. During a half-hour rampage, Lépine killed 14 young women, wounded 9 other women and 4 men, then turned his gun on himself. A three-page suicide note blamed all of his failures on women, whom he felt had rejected and scorned him. Also found on his body was a hit-list of 15 prominent Canadian women.

Unable to complete an application to the school of engineering, Lépine felt humiliated ("laughed at") by women he defined as "feminists" because they had entered traditional male territory. His response to the erosion of white male exclusivity and privilege was lethal. It was also eminently political.

In the aftermath of the massacre, media reports regularly denied the political nature of Lépine's crimes, citing comments such as that of Canadian novelist Mordecai Richler, "It was the act of an absolutely demented man [that does not] lend itself to any explanation." Richler ignored Lépine's explanation of his actions. He hated women, particularly feminists. Whether such a killer is "demented" is beside the point. Fixation on the pathology of perpetrators of violence against women only obscures the social control function of these acts. In a racist and sexist society, psychotic as well as supposedly normal men frequently act out the ubiquitous racist, misogynist, and homophobic attitudes with which they are raised and which they repeatedly see legitimized.

Lépine's murders were hate crimes targeting victims by gender, not race, religion, ethnicity, or sexual orientation. In the cases of lynchings and pogroms, no one wastes time wondering about the mental health of the perpetrators or about their previous personal experiences with African-Americans or Jews. Most people today understand that lynchings and pogroms are forms of politically motivated violence, the objectives of which are to preserve white and gentile supremacy. Similarly, the goal of violence against women—whether conscious or not—is to preserve male supremacy.

Early feminist analysts of another form of sexist violence—rape—asserted that it is not, as common mythology insists, a crime of frustrated attraction, victim provocation, or uncontrollable biological urges. Nor is rape perpetrated only by an aberrant fringe. Rather, rape is a direct expression of sexual politics, an act of conformity to masculinist sexual norms (as "humorist" Ogden Nash put it, "Seduction is for sissies. A he-man wants his rape"), and a form of terrorism that serves to preserve the gender status quo.

Like rape, most murders of women by husbands, lovers, fathers, acquaintances, and strangers are not the products of some inexplicable deviance. They are femicides, the most extreme form of sexist terrorism, motivated by hatred, contempt, pleasure, or a sense of ownership of women. Femicide includes mutilation murder, rape murder, battery that escalates into murder, the immolation of witches in Western Europe and of brides and widows in India, and "crimes of honor" in some Latin and Middle Eastern countries, where women believed to have lost their virginity are killed by their male relatives. Calling misogynist killings femicide removes the obscuring veil of nongendered terms such as homicide and murder.

Widespread male identification with killers demonstrates how rooted femicide is in sexist culture. For example, engineering student Celeste Brousseau, who had complained about sexism in the engineering faculty at the University of Alberta, was subjected to chants of "Shoot the bitch!" from hundreds of her "fellow" students when she participated in an engineering society skit-night shortly after the Lépine killings.

Misogyny not only motivates violence against women but distorts the press coverage of such crimes as well. Femicide, rape, and battery are variously ignored or sensationalized in the media, depending on the victim's race, class, and attractiveness (by male standards). The police, media, and public response to crimes against women of color, poor women, lesbians, women prostitutes, and women drug users is particularly abysmal—generally apathy laced with pejorative stereotyping and victim blaming (for example, "All women of color are drug addicts and/or prostitutes who put themselves in danger"). Moreover, public interest is disproportionately focused on cases involving nonwhite assailants and white middle-class victims, such as the uproar in Boston over the 1989 murder of Carol Stuart, a pregnant white woman who, her husband falsely claimed, was shot by an African-American robber. Carol Stuart was not murdered by a Willie-Horton-like phantasm of her husband's concoction, but by her affluent, white husband.

Femicide is on the extreme end of a continuum of antifemale terror that includes a wide variety of verbal and physical abuse, such as rape, torture, sexual slavery (particularly in prostitution), incestuous and extrafamilial child sexual abuse, physical and emotional battery, sexual harassment (on the phone, in the streets, at the office, and in the classroom), genital mutilation (clitoridectomies, excision, infibulations), unnecessary gynecological operations (gratuitous hysterectomies), forced heterosexuality, forced sterilization, forced motherhood (by criminalizing contraception and abortion), psychosurgery, denial of food to women in some cultures, cosmetic surgery, and other mutilations in the name of beautification.

THE MAGNITUDE OF SEXIST TERRORISM IN THE UNITED STATES

Federal statistics do not reveal the scope of violence against women. One feminist researcher, Mary Koss, has described the federal government's efforts to gather national statistics on rape as "a cruel hoax that covers up rather than reveals women's risk of victimization." Surveys by independent researchers indicate shattering rates of female victimization. In Diana Russell's probability sample survey of 930 San Francisco women, for example, 44 percent reported being victimized by rape or attempted rape, 38 percent by incestuous and extrafamilial child sexual abuse and 16 percent by incestuous abuse, and 14 percent by wife rape.

As with rape and child sexual abuse, femicide is most likely to be perpetrated by a male family member, friend, or acquaintance. Ironically, the patriarchy's ideal domestic arrangement (heterosexual coupling) holds the greatest potential for femicide. Although it is not legitimate to assume that a misogynist element is present in all murders of women by men, it is probable that this is the case for most murders of women by their legal or common-law husbands. Table 1 shows that women murdered by their husbands outnumber all other categories of victims where information about the relationship is available. Specifically, in those cases where it is possible to determine the relationship between the murdered women and their murderers, husbands constituted a third of the murderers during the 12-year period analyzed.

Violent crimes against women have escalated in recent decades. Some believe this increase is due to increased reporting. But Russell's research on (largely unreported) rape, for example, establishes a dramatic escalation during the last 50 years. Although it is not yet possible to assess the number of sex

T A B L E   1
Statistics on the Murder of Women Fifteen Years and Older
by Relationship: 1976–1987

Relationship	No. of women murdered	Percentage	Percentage in known relationships*
Husband/common law	11,236	22.81	33.10
Other family	2,937	5.96	8.65
Other intimates[†]	5,318	10.80	15.67
Acquaintances	9,930	20.16	29.26
Strangers	4,521	9.18	13.32
Undetermined	15,320	31.10	
Total	49,262	100.01	100.00

Source: James A. Mercy, "Men, Women, and Murder: Gender-Specific Differences in Rates of Fatal Violence and Victimization," *Journal of Trauma.* Forthcoming.
*$N = 33,942$
[†]Friend, date, cohabiting relationship.

murders in any given year, virtually all experts agree that there has been a substantial rise in such killings since the early 1960s. A surge in serial murder (when one perpetrator kills a number of victims in separate incidents) is recognized by criminologists to have begun in the 1950s and has become a characteristic phenomenon of the late twentieth century in the United States.

We see this escalation of violence against females as part of male backlash against feminism. This doesn't mean it's the *fault* of feminism: patriarchal culture terrorizes women whether we fight back or not. Still, when male supremacy is challenged, that terror is intensified. While many women who stepped out of line in early modern Europe were grotesquely tortured and killed as witches (with estimates ranging from 200,000 to 9 million killed), today such women are regarded as cunts or bitches, deserving whatever happens to them. "Why is it wrong to get rid of some fuckin' cunts?" Kenneth Bianchi, convicted "Hillside Strangler," demanded.

Many law enforcement officials have commented on the growing viciousness in slayings. As Justice Department official Robert Heck said, "We've got people out there now

killing 20 and 30 people and more, and some of them don't just kill. They torture their victims in terrible ways and mutilate them before they kill them." For example:

- Teenager Shirley Ledford screamed for mercy while Roy Norris and Lawrence Bittaker of Los Angeles raped and mutilated her with a pair of locking pliers, hit her with a sledgehammer, and jabbed her ear with an ice pick. The men audiotaped the torture-femicide from beginning to end.
- Sixty-five-year-old Jack King virtually destroyed the face of 16-year-old Cheryl Bess by pouring acid on her head after he tried to rape her. Bess survived the attack, permanently blinded, her hearing severely damaged, and her face totally disfigured.
- One victim of a sexual femicide was found with stab wounds in her vagina and groin and with her throat slashed. Her nipples had been removed and her face severely beaten; her cut-off hair was found hanging from a nearby branch.
- In 1987, police found three half-naked, malnourished African-American women "shackled to a sewer pipe in a basement that doubled as a secret torture chamber"

in the home of Gary Heidnik, a white Philadelphian; "24 pounds of human limbs were discovered stock-piled in a freezer and other body parts were found in an oven and a stew pot."

Such atrocities also are enacted upon women by their male intimates. Joel Steinberg—who murdered his adopted daughter, Lisa, and tortured his companion, Hedda Nussbaum, for years—and Curtis Adams are extreme, but not unique, examples:

• "Steinberg had kicked her [Nussbaum] in the eye, strangled her, beaten her sexual organs, urinated on her, hung her in handcuffs from a chinning bar, lacerated a tear duct by poking his finger in the corner of her eye, broken her nose several times and pulled out clumps of hair while throwing her about their apartment. 'Sometimes he'd take the blowtorch we used for freebasing and move it around me, making me jump [said Nussbaum], . . . I have burn marks all over my body from that. Joel told me he did this to improve my coordination.'"

• In 1989, Curtis Adams was sentenced to 32 years in prison for torturing his wife in a 10-hour attack. After she refused anal sex, Adams handcuffed his wife, repeatedly forced a bottle and then a broomstick into her anus, and hung her naked out the window—taking breaks to make her read Bible passages adjuring women to obey their husbands.

The sex-and-violence culture of the late twentieth century is a breeding ground for such amateur torturers and executioners, who have emerged as the shock troops of male dominance.

A sense of entitlement is another cause of sexual terrorism. Many males believe they have a right to get what they want from females. If girls or women thwart them, some become violent, sometimes to the extent of

committing femicide. Consider the extraordinary hatred exhibited in response to a complaint by female students at the University of Iowa about the loud stereos of male students who lived on the floor above them. A list in graffito, titled "The Top Ten Things to Do to the Bitches Below," was found in the men's bathroom and subsequently published in the university newspaper. The list included exhortations to beat women "into a bloody pulp with a sledgehammer and laugh" and instructions on "how to mutilate female genitalia with an electric trimmer, pliers, and a 'red-hot soldering iron.'" In a similar display of contempt for women, a suggestion was made in the University of Toronto engineering students' newspaper that women "cut off their breasts if they were sick of sexual harassment."

To see where these students get such gruesome ideas, we need only look to pornography and mass media "gorenography" (movies and magazines featuring scenes of sensationalized and eroticized violence). Like many feminists, we believe pornography is a form of antifemale propaganda, peddling a view of women as objects, commodities, "things" to be owned, used, and consumed while also promoting the logical correlates: all women are whores and therefore fair game; sexual violence is normal and acceptable; women deserve and want to be hurt, raped, or even killed. Research indicates that objectifying, degrading, and violent images of women in pornography and gorenography predispose certain males to be turned on by rape and other violence against women and/or undermine their inhibitions against acting out sexualized violence.

An FBI study of 36 sex killers found that pornography was ranked highest in a list of many sexual interests by an astonishing 81 percent. Such notorious killers as Edmund Kemper (the "Coed Killer"), Ted Bundy, David Berkowitz (the "Son of Sam"), and Kenneth Bianchi and Angelo Buono (the

"Hillside Stranglers") were all heavy pornography consumers. Bundy maintains that pornography "had an impact on me that was just so central to the development of the violent behavior that I engaged in." His assessment is consistent with testimony from many other sex offenders, as well as research on the effects of pornography.

Femicidal mayhem is the essential subject matter of slasher films, "splatterpunk" horror novels, or the endless outpouring of sex killer paperback thrillers—all genres that count the vast majority of their fans among men, particularly young men. In contemporary superhero comic books, graphic femicidal visuals abound. For example, a recent issue of "Green Arrow" depicts a near-naked prostitute, tortured and crucified. As a comic book distributor/apologist explained: "The readers are teen-aged boys, so what you have is a lot of repressed anger. . . . They do like to see the characters sliced and diced."

We do not mean to imply that one must go into the side-pockets of culture to encounter femicidal themes. Mainstream filmmaker Brian DePalma once whined, "I'm always attacked for having an erotic, sexist approach—chopping up women, putting women in peril. I'm making suspense movies! What else is going to happen to them?" In *Harlem Nights,* a "comedy," Eddie Murphy first beds, then blows away, Jasmine Guy, the film's object of desire. Misogynist and femicidal themes abound as well in rock and roll. Twenty years ago, Mick Jagger threatened, "Rape, murder, it's just a kiss away." Currently, Guns 'N' Roses croon, "Well I used to love her/but I had to kill her/she bitched so much/she drove me nuts."

Femicidal atrocity is everywhere normalized, explained away as a joke, and rendered into standard fantasy fare. Although the annihilation of women has not been formally institutionalized, our annihilation in media portrayals has been—from comic books through Nobel-prize-winning literature, from box-office smashes through snuff films. "C'mon girls," the refrain goes, "it's just entertainment." Meanwhile the FBI terms sex killings "recreational murder."

Most Americans refuse to recognize the gynocidal period in which we are living—and dying—today. To traverse the streets is often to walk a gauntlet. The nuclear family is a prison for millions of girls and women. Some husbands and fathers act as full-time guards who threaten to kill if defied, a threat all too often carried out.

If all femicides were recognized as such and accurately counted, if the massive incidence of nonlethal sexual assaults against women and girls were taken into account, if incestuous abuse and battery were recognized as torture (frequently prolonged over years), if the patriarchal home were seen as the inescapable prison it so frequently becomes, if pornography and gorenography were recognized as hate literature, then we in the United States might have to acknowledge that we live in the midst of a reign of sexist terror comparable in magnitude, intensity, and intent to the persecution, torture, and annihilation of European women as witches from the fourteenth to the seventeenth centuries.

REMEMORY AND RESISTANCE

Basically, I worshipped him. He was the most wonderful man I had ever met. I believed he had supernatural, godlike powers.
    —Hedda Nussbaum on Joel Steinberg

We do not worship them.
We do not worship what they have made.
We do not trust them.
We do not believe what they say . . .
We do not worship them.
    —Alice Walker, "Each One, Pull One"

It is unspeakably painful for most women to think about men's violence against us, whether individually or collectively. And when we do attempt to think about the unthinkable, speak about the unspeakable, as we must, the violence, disbelief, and contempt we encounter is often so overwhelming that we retreat, denying or repressing our experiences.

In November 1989, 28-year-old Eileen Franklin-Lipsker of Foster City, California, suddenly remembered having witnessed her father sexually abuse her 8-year-old friend, Susan Nason, then bludgeon her to death. Twenty years later, she turned her father in to the police. Such remembrance and denunciation is the work of the entire feminist movement against violence against women: to disobey the fathers' commandments to forget, deny, and maintain silence, and instead to turn in abusive fathers, husbands, brothers, lovers, sons, and friends. The recollection and acknowledgment of the history and experience that has been so profoundly repressed is what Toni Morrison, in her masterpiece *Beloved*, calls *rememory*. *Beloved* concerns the unthinkably painful subject of slavery. In an interview about the book, Morrison noted that there is virtually no remembrance—no lore, songs, or dances—of the African people who died en route to the Americas. "I suspect the reason is that it was not possible to survive on certain levels and dwell on it," Morrison suggested. "People who did dwell on it, it probably killed them, and the people who did not dwell on it probably went forward. . . . There is a necessity for remembering the horror, but . . . in a manner in which the memory is not destructive." Morrison's concept of rememory, though developed to describe the psychic torment inflicted on African-Americans, is crucial for women grappling with a femicidal world. We too must be able to face horror in ways that do not destroy, but save us.

Following the mass femicide carried out by Marc Lépine in Montreal, Quebec prime minister M. Bourassa rejected petitions to close the legislature and universities on the day of the funerals. A day of official mourning was only appropriate, he insisted, "when someone important to the State had died." Some Canadian feminists are working to establish 6 December as a national day of remembrance for the slaughtered women. We encourage women worldwide to join our Canadian sisters in declaring 6 December an international day of mourning and rage, a "Rememory Day" for all women who have been victims of sexual violence. As Ntozake Shange writes, "We shall have streets and monuments named after / these women & children they died for their country."

Still, such commemorations remain palliatives, modes of healing, but not cures. Feminists, collectively and internationally, must take on the urgent task of formulating strategies of resistance to femicide. Progressive people rightly favor an international boycott of South Africa so long as apartheid reigns; why then does no one consider the potential efficacy of boycotting violent and abusive men and their culture? The women in Aristophanes' *Lysistrata* engage in a sexual boycott of men to compel an end to war. In 1590, Iroquois women gathered in Seneca to demand the cessation of war among the nations. We must now demand an end to the global patriarchal war on women.

A femicidal culture is one in which the male is worshipped. This worship is obtained through tyranny, subtle and overt, over our bruised minds, our battered and dead bodies, and our co-optation into supporting even batterers, rapists, and killers. "Basically, I worshipped him," said Hedda Nussbaum. "We do not worship them . . . we do not trust them," writes Alice Walker. In myriad ways, let us refuse nurture, solace, support, and approval. Let us withdraw our worship.

CHAPTER 17

INCEST AND RESISTANCE: PATTERNS OF FATHER-DAUGHTER INCEST, 1880–1930

LINDA GORDON

ABSTRACT

Before the contemporary women's movement, incest was considered a "one-in-a-million" phenomenon. Today, the sexual violation of children by adults, primarily girls by their fathers, is frighteningly acknowledged as a much more common occurrence. Likewise, more traditional ways of understanding incest by many practitioners and researchers have been in terms of sexual violence as part of the family unit and its individual psychology. All too often, these psychological theories end up justifying or excusing the individual abuser (the father), thereby perpetuating the helplessness of the mother and the powerlessness of women and girls in general.

In contrast, more recent feminist theory examines sexual violence in terms of power structures in the family and analyzes the relationship of the family unit to the broader society. Victimization of young girls in the family is due, in large part, to the traditional roles that men and women are supposed to play in society. Thus, according to feminist theory, this form of victimization of women is not an aberration of gender roles but is simply further along the continuum of societally condoned male behavior.

In this chapter, Linda Gordon, a feminist historian, explores father-daughter incest as a form of family violence through case records of three Boston child protection agencies around the turn of the twentieth century. One of the reasons her study is so important is that she uses a feminist analysis to understand two major patterns of incest that emerge from her data. First, she identifies the more common pattern of *domestic incest*. Here family relations made the girl victims into "second wives," taking over many of the roles and functions of mothers, including housework, child care, and sexual relations with their father. This is the family model in which the classic image of the absent or weakened mother is found. The daughter is caught in the sexual double bind: she must be sexually pure and yet submissive and obedient to her father. The parents in these incest families often held strongly conservative views about male supremacy and female subordination in domestic life. The father's attitude of entitlement was key to his committing incest with his daughter and creating an aura of "normality" in the family.

While the "domestic incest" pattern was more common during the period under study than today, Gordon reports that a second pattern of *energetic resistance* simultaneously emerged on the part of many of the girl victims. Thus, she argues, daughters were coerced into incest relations with their fathers, but "they usually fought back." Similarly, Arnold reported (see Chapter 8 herein) that resistance by teenage girls today to sexually abusive fathers and stepfathers often led to both their further victimization and delinquency. When teenage girls ran away from their abusive fathers at home, they often engaged in illegal activities of prostitution or "sexual delinquency" in order to survive.

Can you suggest other similarities between historical and contemporary experiences of incest? What about differences? What else might we learn by comparing what happens to different groups of incest survivors in these two very dissimilar historical periods?

Incest has been traditionally conceived as something rare and alien, a behavior so heinous that it was assumed to produce a powerful natural revulsion. Perpetrators of incest were regarded as pathological, feeble-minded, or unknowing. Until the last decade, many textbooks on deviance and criminology considered incest a one-in-a-million occurrence (Weinberg, 1955). Yet the recent rediscovery of family violence has exposed an incidence of incest between adults and children far too frequent to sustain the view that it is a tabooed behavior. Current surveys have revised estimates of its incidence to one in a hundred (Finkelhor, 1979: tables 4-1, 4-2, 4-3, 6-1, chap. 6; Renvoize, 1982: chap. 3).

The discrepancy between myth and reality about incest derives in part from anxieties about the meanings of this illicit sex, in part from confusion about what incest is and what kind of incest is tabooed. That confusion is being remedied by clinical studies and surveys in the past few decades (Butler, 1978; Herman, 1981), showing that while reproductive mating—the formation of new family units between people defined as kin—has been rather successfully tabooed, nonreproductive sex has had considerably more leeway in practice.

The material presented here was gathered in a study of the history of sexual and family violence supported by the National Institutes of Mental Health, and the paper was written with the support of the John Simon Guggenheim Foundation; I am grateful also to Wini Breines and colleagues at the Bunting Institute for insightful criticisms, and to the staff of the Massachusetts Society for the Prevention of Cruelty to Children and the Boston Children's Service Association for their courtesy in allowing me access to their files. Correspondence to: Department of History, University of Wisconsin, Madison, WI 53706.

The incest problem that is the subject of this paper is sex, not reproduction, and what I mean by sex is genital contact, not necessarily intercourse. Most incestuous sex is probably not discovered. My source material is by no means a representative sample of incestuous experience because its basis is the case records of family violence agencies in Boston between 1880 and 1960. I randomly sampled the case records of three Boston child-welfare agencies—the Massachusetts Society for Prevention of Cruelty to Children, the Boston Children's Service Association, and the Judge Baker Guidance Center. In addition I read approximately 75 other incest cases, although data from these are not included in quantitative statements (see Gordon and O'Keefe, 1984, for a fuller explanation of the research). Of the 502 family violence cases in the sample, 10 percent (50) contained incestuous episodes. In these cases the incest had already been experienced and defined by family members as a serious problem.

The incest in this random sample was virtually always—98 percent—sexual assault by an older male relative, usually the father but also including stepfathers, older brothers, uncles, etc. Furthermore, the incest was predominantly heterosexual: the children involved were almost all girls (93 out of 97), and the four boys involved were victimized together with their sisters. To repeat, this does not mean that other types of incest did not occur. Sibling sexual play frequently leads to actual incest, but this kind of sexual contact is not as frequently or deeply upsetting to the participants or their families. The other incest category—between women and children—is much less frequent, despite the fact that mother-son incest is the most mythologized form. Grown women do not often initiate sexual activity with children (MacFarlane, 1978). Man-child incest is far more frequently experienced by the child as assaultive than sibling or woman-child sex. In other words, incest

when it appears as family violence is essentially a male crime, a form of child sexual abuse.

These facts about incest as family violence—and all references to incest below refer to this type of incest—suggest that studying the problem requires a feminist perspective, that is, one that takes into account the whole system of gender relations in our society; failing that, it seems near certain that critical dynamics in the incestuous situations will be missed. In the long and often rambling case records, the children appear not only as statistical victims but as individual girls and young women facing difficult, certainly unequal, and often contradictory expectations. One cannot evaluate their problems and their chances for escape merely in terms of intrafamily relations, without considering the cultural and societal context.

My goal in this paper is to situate incest socially and historically, in the ordinary conditions of girls' lives. In doing so I cannot *account* for incest—I cannot explain why some girls and not others fell victim to this form of exploitation—because my data provided no control group. I have information only about children who were family violence victims; that is why they appeared in the case records I used. In an uncontrolled qualitative analysis of the incest cases, benefiting also from comparison to nonsexual child abuse cases,[1] it became apparent that one pattern dominated the cases in between 1880 and 1930.[2] In this period, the incestuous relationships grew out of and appeared to participants as part of an overall family pattern of turning girls into second wives. The girls not only became sexual partners to the male heads of household, but also virtual housewives, taking over housework, child care and general family maintenance as well as sexual obligations. I call this pattern "domestic incest."

This historical finding fits with most feminist work on incest, which has emphasized girls' helplessness before fathers who have the combined power of men, parents, and adults (Armstrong, 1978; Butler, 1978; Herman, 1981; Rush, 1980). Many incest victims do not, perhaps cannot, complain about, let alone prevent, their victimization; and even more difficult, they may enjoy and benefit in some measure from these relationships even as they are also humiliated and terrified. However, I also found a second pattern in the incest cases of this period: along with submissive domesticity, these girl victims also displayed energetic resistance and escape tactics which do not match the model of unmitigated victimization. Their resistance often transformed itself, or was transformed by the constriction of their environment, into further victimization. For example, in many cases the girls' attempt to escape from their fathers' homes led them to sexual "delinquency." Nevertheless, the spirit of resistance—as opposed to the resignation and even the deformed gratitude described in many clinical reports—is significant, as I will argue below.

Finding these two patterns, often both in the lives of the same girl at different times, illuminated a contradiction in the dominant standard for daughterly virtue. In the modern version of the sexual double standard, a good girl has been above all sexually pure: a virgin until marriage, innocent of sexual thoughts and experience before that. But she has also been expected to be obedient to and under the protection of her parents. Father-daughter incest creates extreme confusion and double-binds for girls precisely because of their attempts to meet both these criteria of virtue. I do not wish to dwell here on these universal problems of girlhood. Before subjecting the reader to the painfulness of some of the stories that will follow, it seems necessary to emphasize that they are not the norm. Still, the difficulties of these incest victims are reminders of a daily female uneasiness about

virtue, about achieving a feminine balance between modesty and aggression, chastity and vulgarity. On the other hand, in viewing girls' delinquency as a form of escape from victimization by fathers, we see evidence of the girls' willingness to challenge the categories which confined them so tightly in this period. This seems to me cause for optimism, because so much of the damage of sexual abuse for girls is in their blaming themselves.

DOMESTIC INCEST

The common features of the "classic" domestic incest case were an absent or in some way weakened mother; an older daughter who has become the mother and who feels great responsibility towards her whole family, particularly siblings, and is unusually disciplined and self-controlled; and a father committed to and even dependent upon his family yet rigid in his refusal to do the work of family maintenance and in his expectation of being served. An actual story may serve to sharpen this picture. No one case is typical nor can illustrate all the defining features. Real families are quirky, one-of-a-kind, far more complicated than scholarship can be. Still it seems fairer to offer one whole case than to pick features of many cases to support the argument.

In 1910 the Massachusetts Society for the Prevention of Cruelty to Children (hereafter: MSPCC) was asked to help an Italian mother find her deserted husband in order to get him to pay child support for their six children. He was found but refused to pay. The mother successfully resisted the agency's ensuing recommendations that her children be separated among different relatives and that she prosecute her husband. In other words, she did not have the characteristics of a typical incest victim's mother, but displayed unusual strength as a single head of household. Some time during the next eight years her husband returned. In December 1918 she and her eldest daughter died in the influenza epidemic, leaving three daughters and two sons. Her dying request was that the next daughter drop out of school in order to keep the family together, and the daughter sadly complied. In February 1919, just two months later, this daughter telephoned to tell the agency that she had left home, because, she said, of severe beatings by her father; instead she would contribute financially, she said, and went to work at Magee Shirtwaist. A year-and-a-quarter later, in March 1920, the next daughter came to the agency to complain about the father's beatings of the boys and to refuse to continue the housekeeping. The father retaliated by bringing stubborn-child complaints against the younger children whom she was trying to protect; however, these were dismissed by the court. In its investigation of the home the MSPCC complained that there were only two beds. The father responded, "What you think, rich man with so many beds?" The minimal investigation done by the agency uncovered no incest allegation. Yet it hardly seems that the victims were reluctant to talk. For instance, in 1922 a private attorney, a relative of the dead mother, informed the MSPCC that the children had engaged him to prosecute their father for incest with, now, an 11-year-old daughter. At the trial it was revealed that the father had sexually assaulted three daughters, one after another; the youngest now had gonorrhea. The father was sentenced to 8–10 years and the younger children placed with the City of Boston Child Welfare Division (Case #3043).[3]

This case exemplifies how a domestic incest pattern might be imposed even on evidently assertive and self-confident girls. The first daughter had keenly sought education, and gave it up only to honor her mother's wishes. Ironically, this mother's very strength and commitment to her family helped victimize her children. Despite the heavy pressure of a dying mother's wish, the first daughter escaped her victim position within two months. The next daughter, a mere 10 at the time, was too young to resist her father. The older girls turned to the MSPCC to avoid creating a scandal among the relatives; but the youngest girl had to approach relatives, having gotten no help from the agency. It is not surprising that she ended up as the most alienated from the whole family. The older daughters' desire to protect their father despite his behavior re-emerged in 1926 when, in response to his self-pitying letters, they hired another lawyer to get him out of prison. The youngest daughter, far more seriously damaged by him (in 1926 she was again a victim of rape and venereal disease, in other words, a "sex delinquent"), was by contrast unforgiving and afraid of his revenge. Loyalty to this father had divided the sisters, just as in many other cases, loyalty to the father alienated mothers from daughters.

MSPCC workers thought, on the basis of many cases like this, that motherless girls were more vulnerable. The absent mother affected the whole position of the girl in the family, not only her sexual position. In effect, the girl became a mother. Equally important is what did not happen: the father did not become a mother. Widows usually attempted to survive by becoming both mother and father to their children; widowers sought someone else to be mother.

However, similar patterns developed where the mother was alive and present but "weakened" in some way. Against this assertion it could be argued that the normal, conventional family structure in this period gave more power to men. What is unique about the incestuous families was that the mothers were unable to fulfill even the traditional female familial role—that of housekeeper and nurturer of children. In the domestic incest cases, the mothers' inability to function was so thorough-going that daughters were drafted to take over the housekeeping and child-raising, as well as the sexual duties of the wife, even when the mother was living and present. The drudgery these girls experienced was often substantial. They frequently did all the housework for large families, working very long hours, and with little complaint. Many had internalized slavelike images of themselves.

The parents in incest families often held strongly conservative views about male supremacy and gender roles in domestic life.[4] Incestuous fathers often voiced moralistic attacks on loose sexual morals in the community. These fathers were unusually tyrannical; the mothers, when present, self-effacing. It followed, in this family logic, that when mothers could not function, daughters took over their work. Often the mother had helped train and orient the daughter towards becoming, to an unusual degree, the substitute housekeeper/mother/wife. Often there were many younger children who depended on the older sister for care, although aspects of the domestic incest pattern remained when there was only one child, a daughter, whose obligations were exclusively towards her father. But in all cases the victim, or at least the first victim, was the eldest daughter. Frequently, if an older daughter escaped the household a younger daughter would take her place, and protectiveness towards these younger sisters helped keep the older one in her place.

The barb on this domestic hook in the flesh of the girl was that there were often emotional rewards for her, similar to the rewards of motherhood and wifehood. The younger children and the father appeared needy and loving, and were sometimes able to express their appreciation for the nurturance they received.

Mothers sometimes colluded in this domestic incest, although the degree and frequency of their participation has been exaggerated (Breines and Gordon, 1983:490–531). The incestuous situation may have provided relief for the mother from her own exploitation, both as housekeeper and as sexual servant, without her having directly to defy the wishes of the father. However, the high proportion of battered women among the mothers of incest victims suggests that the situation did not often provide freedom from abuse.[5] The most consistent participation of mothers appeared to operate at a deeper level: they promoted within the family a view of the fathers' needs, however brutal, as legitimate and deserving sympathy. Mothers' continuing victimization by beatings only reinforced the message to children that they must submit to male aggression.

Furthermore, mother-daughter relationships were frequently marked by mutually painful hostility and jealousy, sometimes directly stimulated or intensified by the man. Daughters could be treated like classic "other women," their mothers' coldness, cruelty and laziness the topic of repeated complaints to them by their fathers. Sometimes the mother fled, as in one case where a mother explicitly stated that the father and daughter should form the central couple around which the family was constructed (Case #3644). In another case, the father gave all his money to his 14-year-old daughter, deriding his wife and saying to the daughter, "You are my wife, not your mother" (Case #3361).

Contemporary clinical studies of father-daughter incest have reported that daughters are often treated well by their fathers, even rewarded with affection and gifts. This "kind" treatment existed in some of our cases (e.g. #3566A), but in many other cases girls were beaten as well as sexually abused. The fathers were intensely concerned to keep their daughters from telling, and used both rewards and threats to prevent this. In some cases the physical abuse escalated as the sexual abuse stopped, either because the family had discovered it or the girl had become more firm in her refusal (e.g., #3561A). But these beatings must also be interpreted in the context of punishment norms. Beating children was more common and legitimate 50 years ago than it is today and there is no reason to think that incestuous fathers would be less harsh than nonincestuous ones. The fact that the child had become a lover did not exempt her from physical violence, any more than wives were exempt.

However, the power of fathers in the family cannot be measured by or equated with physical violence. Indeed, violence at times indicated the presence of a challenge to the father's power, and the most authoritarian fathers may have been able to impose their wills *without* force. There is a circularity in attempting to measure the father's power, because one index of that power is the result he was able to achieve. The incest itself, which we are trying to explain, is also evidence for the existence of an extremely male-dominant family power structure, which is being considered as a cause. This circularity is, however, part of reality, not a flaw in deductive logic. The victim and other knowing family members colluded in viewing the father as irresistibly powerful in order to rationalize their acquiescence and preserve their self-respect.

The most long-lasting domestic incest cases were characterized by the creation of an alternate psychosocial order within the family. This order, imposed by the father, could be relatively stable despite its contradictory relationship to larger community patterns. Indeed, perhaps the most extraordinary and frightening characteristic of domestic incest is that it could take on the appearance of the ordinary, and could be experienced within the family as normal. This is not to say that victims or other family members believed these incestuous relations to be legitimate. The necessity for secrecy would be enough to make that unlikely, as would the response of any outsiders who sensed the existence of the family secret. However, the assimilation of the sexual relationship with other aspects of the family dynamics and division of labor created an alternative normality, logic, and order. Here it bears repeating that most incestuous relations continued for years. This deviant but quotidian order within the family was more stable when family members were relatively secluded, geographically and/or socially. Isolated, sometimes hardly ever allowed out of the house, the daughters had no access to outside help nor even to outside verification of the possibility of escape. The importance of seclusion is underscored by the prominence of semi-rural cases of domestic incest, even within the highly urbanized locale of this study. The family's deviant order operated as a further centripetal force, encouraging the girl to remain within the domestic scene despite its drudgery. There she felt understood, accepted, and possibly appreciated, while the outside world reminded her of her abnormality and sinfulness, and of the horror and revulsion her story would evoke in others.

The largest single factor in creating the aura of "normality" in these families was the father's attitude of entitlement. No incest assailant in our cases expressed contrition for what he had done nor guilt for having hurt his daughter—only denial, self-justification, and/or shame and humiliation.[6]

In these case records, domestic incest was more common before 1930 than in the last 50 years. Several historical changes might account for this change. Since the 1930s, compulsory education through high school has prevented adolescent girls from being kept at home. New norms of children's rights to leisure and autonomy today make girls who are secluded, or who do many hours of housework every day, strikingly abnormal. The norms for children's household labor have changed not only quantitatively but also qualitatively: it is less common and thus more noticeable today to find girls accepting overall responsibility for tasks such as cooking, shopping, and supervising younger children. And of course the expectation of unquestioning obedience to a father's orders has lessened substantially.[7]

FORMS OF RESISTANCE

If domestic incest once "fit" better into conventional family patterns than it does now, this does not mean that daughters entered these relationships willingly or even with resignation. On the contrary, they were usually coerced, and they usually fought back. The main difference between my historical findings and the reports of recent clinical studies of father-daughter incest is the evidence of substantial resistance on the part of the girl victims in the case records (Butler, 1978; Herman, 1981; Renvoize, 1982; Rush, 1980). There is also evidence of girls' resistance to housework as a form of resistance to the sexual relationship. In one 1930 case an older sister had defied her father by taking a job, paying him $3 per week for board, but refusing to do any housework. She did not wish to move out of the house entirely because she was protecting her two younger sisters from his advances.[8] When her father steadily complained that he needed her housework, she raised her board payment to $4 and then $5 per week but refused to do the work (Case #3556A, 1930).

These girl housewives had the same problems as mother housewives in trying to resist their exploitation: their work involved caring for those they loved, particularly siblings. Leaving the family often appeared to these older sisters as "selfish" and "immoral"—just as it might to a mother contemplating leaving her children to escape an abusive husband. Doing so was called desertion by social workers, courts, and probably by peers. Girls in domestic incest situations were unlikely to have the confidence or skills to find jobs. Already isolated and confident only at housework, they gained a fear of the outside world from their conservative parents.

Thus it should come as no surprise that many incest victims only made their move to get help when their younger sisters were threatened by the father's sexual demands (Cases #3047A, #3556A, #3558A, #3559A, #3840A). In this respect as in others, incest victims behaved like beaten wives, who often tolerated violence until it touched their children. This motherliness was both a strength and a weakness. It encouraged them to tolerate high levels of abuse "for the sake of the children," yet it helped them to draw limits the violation of which they would not tolerate. The limits were hardly stringent ones, but the existence of some area of honor was strengthening and helped preserve sanity.

The relation of many incest victims to their siblings raises questions about labels such as "passive," "acquiescent," and "resistant." Acquiescence, even self-abnegation in relation to a father, might be the mirror image of protective assertiveness towards a younger sister. Indeed, are not these either/or distinctions between passivity and aggressiveness biased against the particular work, familial roles, and strengths of women and children? What would it mean to resist a father with no realistic chance of escaping one's dependence on him? The clients' terrors of the breaking up of families and institutionalizing of children were not illusory or even far-fetched. In developing a strategy aimed at survival, maximum protection of others, and minimum physical and psychological damage to oneself, it is not clear that these incest victims were self-destructive.

Virtuous Resistance

Another case history offers a classic version of the complex bind for the incest victim. This family consisted of an American-born Chinese Christian father who had returned to

China to find a wife. He owned and operated a laundry adjacent to his home and, in 1920 when this case "broke," there were six children in the family, including a newborn. The oldest daughter—"Grace," age 16—worked with her father in the laundry and was extremely overworked as well as beaten and raped by her father. Yet Grace was no simple victim. Her successful resistance to her victimization grew out of her astute understanding of her family and of the changes imposed upon it from without.

The mother was extremely cowed. Also beaten by the father, she was debilitated by a difficult birth when the case opened in 1920. She was aware of the incest, took no action to help her daughter, but said she lay awake nights watching her husband. She could hardly have avoided knowledge of the incest, for, according to Grace's story, the noise must have been substantial—the girl said she put a trunk in front of her door and her father forced it aside. Yet Grace wrote at one point that she was willing to sacrifice herself to save her mother pain; and, when she was taken from her home, she said she felt guilty at leaving her mother. From a contemporary perspective, there appears to be a role reversal here: the daughter felt she ought to be protecting her mother. In fact, in more patriarchal families such an assumption of responsibility by a child was not a reversal at all. In working class and particularly immigrant poor families, it was expected that children should work to spare their mothers; and mothers expected to be able to count on daughters for self-sacrifice. The incestuous pattern, again, is an exaggeration of the patriarchal pattern, not a reversal of it. And the patriarchal pattern defined mother-child as well as father-child relations, particularly in Chinese culture.

In this case, one might have expected the father to justify turning to his daughter for sex by his wife's confinement. He did not in fact say this, but claimed nonresponsibility.

He told a doctor that "he does not know what he does during the night and that he is perfectly surprised in the morning when his wife tells him of the things he has been doing." The doctor appeared to believe him, and so, perhaps, did Grace; but I did not. His behavior towards his daughter was calculating in other ways, and his exploitation of her systematic. For example, he secluded her from outside influences, trying to keep her from going to church or Sunday School (although he too was a Catholic); as soon as allegations against him were made, he redoubled his efforts to marry her off; he successfully forced her to quit school; he opened her mail. Nor did he lose much. He kept his family together except for the one girl. There is no record of agency concern for the safety of the nine-year-old daughter or the mother, and no charges were filed against him.

Grace escaped her domestic incest situation by writing to her Sunday School teacher. While the whole family was Christian, the girl had become intensely religious in a manner resented by her father, suggesting that her religiosity was part of her resistance to his authority. It may not be too far-fetched to suggest that in her religion she was appealing to a higher authority, a strategy often employed by rebellious women. Her letter is worth quoting at some length.

> Dear Miss _____. O, how heartbroken I am because of all these troubles I can't bear. You would not realize, I know, how many troubles I have because I try hard to be cheerful and happy. Now my heart is overflowing with grief. I have brought them to Jesus and I know he will make them right for me. I am telling you so that you may understand why I cannot be with you. I have suffered since childhood my father's abuses. He hates me for what I am. I work for him and obeyed him as much as I can even if they are unjust. After school from two o'clock until seven or eight, I work in his laundry store, rolling collars, doing up bundles, act as book-keeper everything that can be done and yet he

says that I am still a slave to him. I am willing to work if he gives me my freedom to do the right thing. He always did open my letters and if he didn't like them he would burn them. . . . This last month father seemed to like me for he was very kind, but no, it didn't last long. He tried to make *me sin* [emphasis added by MSPCC social worker]. I wouldn't do it so he made me promise not to tell anyone, but the week before last mother found out. I told her all. How many tears were shed, I can't say. Father is very angry and hates me worse than ever. He wants revenge and he torments me in every way. . . . My Church envelopes are burnt and worst of all, he bought a horse-whip Saturday, threaten[s?] to whip me if I dared disobey him. I must, also, speak and talk to him as a daughter ought or I'd get whipped. I haven't spoken to him except [to] answer his questions. Don't you think this is hard? Cruelty cannot seem to rule me, only love can so I disobeyed him last Sunday. I got dressed ready for S.S. [Sunday School], went downstairs and waited for a car in the door-steps. Father ran down, pulled me in, and knocked me about so that my head was in a whirl. My hat was off, my hair was down and o [sic] , I thought my hair was torn by his awful treatment. He told me he would kill me with a knife, I answered and told him I would be very glad to have him. I was ready to die, I couldn't bear it any longer. . . .

The Sunday School teacher brought the case to the MSPCC, who brought in a Chinese-American social worker. Grace expressed reluctance to leave her mother and guilt about creating a family scandal ("We don't want . . . shame to our family"); yet ultimately leaving her home was not only what she wanted, but something she fought for. The social worker thought she ought to stay at home![9] Her father threatened to send agents of a Chinese secret society after her for running away. In fact, if one looks at what Grace did rather than what she said, she was admirably effective at extricating herself from a difficult situation, withdrawing her support from mother and siblings. She never returned

home but went to a seminary. Despite her serious accusations against her father, she protected herself from becoming self-defined as a bad daughter by defending him. "Don't be hard on my father will you?", she wrote, ". . . people talk because they cannot understand . . . I must be thankful for some of parents' kindness so must not bring trouble to them. I cannot be helped if the parents do not love their children. . . . Of course he is sorry for his sin even though he doesn't say it and he doesn't want me to go home to harm me, but he wants me to go home because my family needs me." And, "We cannot hold a sin against a man for life . . . father has sinned, but we all ought to be merciful even as God is merciful. . . ." Yet, underneath this rhetoric of faith, she was rejecting paternal authority and family obligation in a most secular manner. Ironically she used her Catholicism as her road to modernization, Americanization, and escape from patriarchy.

Delinquent Resistance

Grace escaped her father through a relation with a Sunday school teacher, a relation that allowed her a way to remain virtuous, though not daughterly. She was exceptional, for the other daughters in these case records who escape more often did so by being "bad." Their disobedience was likely to begin by staying outside the house as much as possible, even running away or "bunking out," the slang term for children's not coming home to sleep. Their misbehavior might then extend to other levels: at first merely unseemly conduct—using vulgar language, riding in cars, drinking or smoking, walking or dressing immodestly (Schlossman and Wallach, 1978:72). Girls on the streets were extremely vulnerable to sexual victimization—being raped, tricked, pressured or bribed into sexual submission to others, almost always male. However, the coercion used against the girls did not make them appear innocent; their presence on the streets was considered to make them responsible for their sexual victimization. Moreover, child-saving agencies and courts considered their sexual experience as polluting, and innocence a biological category which once taken away was not retrievable, so that these sexual misadventures resulted in girls' being permanently branded as bad.

Some girls who became "sex delinquents" initiated and freely participated in sex, sometimes using it for gain. There were notorious places in Boston where girls would hang out at night, hoping to pick up boys or men, such as the Sullivan Square station, Scollay Square in the old West End, the Charlestown Navy yard, and Revere beach. Girls travelled in groups and covered and solicited for each other. They were truant from school, sought out men in bars (and on ships), and generally engaged in provocative behavior.

Such girls began to appear frequently in the records of child-protection agencies after about 1910, when juvenile delinquency became a major social problem. Indeed, to the child savers of that period, juvenile delinquency was considered *ipso facto* an indicator of parental inadequacy. And in the cases of female sex delinquents, incest victims were disproportionately represented.[10] I examined every female sex delinquent case for the year 1920 and found that 40 percent alleged incest and another 20 percent nonincestuous rape.

Like all victims of abuse, girls in incestuous situations appeared to have had low self-esteem. In contrast to girls abused in other ways, incest victims also had unusually sexualized self-images. This combination could be deadly. The incest victims had learned not only to expect little consideration from those closest to them, but also that sex was their greatest resource, their one means of gaining rewards or even acceptance. In one important way these delinquent girls were worse off

than those who remained compliantly at home with their incestuous fathers: since the delinquents were breaking the law and enraging community moralists, they were punished. Even when allegations of incest were proved or accepted by child-welfare agencies, the girls were likely to be sent to institutions.

Nevertheless, in their flight from home, incest victims may have been successfully preserving an autonomy vital to their survival. The behavior of the sex-delinquent incest victims seems puzzling at first, for they appear to be seeking to repeat that which has made them most miserable. It is no wonder that some observers have branded such girls masochists, suggesting that self-hatred and desire for punishment led them to acquiesce to the incestuous advances in the first place, or that guilt about the incestuous experience led them to seek punishment through further sexual humiliation and cruel treatment. However, it is inadequate to brand such behavior destructive without specifying what the constructive alternatives were. As Lenore Walker (1978) points out in her study of battered women, attempts to assert power may be deformed in situations of powerlessness. Thus women who appear to provoke beating are not necessarily seeking pain for themselves, but may be trying to get an *inevitable* beating to occur at a time and place of their choosing, in a situation which will make it milder.

One aspect of the girls' active participation, even initiative, in these sexual adventures was the fact that in most cases the girls acted in groups. In a tally of all sex assault cases the MSPCC handled in 1910 and 1930, 14 out of 16 and 16 out of 22, respectively, included *groups* of girls. The influence of girls upon other girls—sometimes relatives, sometimes friends—was great. The pattern of these dynamics was often controversial in the case records, because parents usually tried to defend one girl by throwing the blame on another. One girl was often scapegoated, accused of being the ringleader, the corrupter of the others. One 11-year-old in a 1910 case was said to have done more to demoralize young girls in East Boston than any other person (Case #2322A). The girls' attachments to each other were so strong that the male offenders frequently molested them in each other's presence. The group behavior of these sex delinquents increased their power somewhat in negotiations and confrontations with men or boys, and reduced their vulnerability to force. On the other hand the girls were more daring and took more risks in groups than they might have done singly, which increased their chances of getting into trouble. In groups, they went farther from home, stayed out later, and were more willing to defy authorities.

Other evidence of the girls' initiative in their sexual adventures was the frequency with which they became prostitutes.[11] Of the MSPCC sex assault cases for 1910 and 1930, at least 12 out of 16 and 11 out of 22 involved the girls' taking payment. Sexual delinquency in this period, at least until the end of the Depression, led more quickly to prostitution than today. There were several reasons for this. One was that men and boys were more accustomed than they are today to pay for sex. Another, perhaps the main one, was that the girls were so poor. At the low standard of living of many client families, any pittance was of value—a nickel, a piece of food, a bag of coal. Payment, furthermore, was of multiple value to the girls because it also provided them with a contribution to bring back to the family, perhaps enhancing their low status within their family and winning approval from the person they usually felt most rejected by—mother. Many poor children were still expected by their parents to contribute to the family economy. With families no longer working together (as on farms), and wage labor not available or not allowed, chil-

dren were encouraged to contribute through casual bits of paid labor, "gleaning," begging, or stealing. In some cases, as soon as word got out that some man was willing to pay for sexual favors, the number of girls involved would snowball, so eager were they for the coins or treats they might receive. Some parents alleged that they did not know the sources of contributions. Some evidently knew the sources and raised no objections; a few may have participated in the prostitution arrangements.

Among these girl prostitutes one can distinguish between those who accepted rewards, usually the very young, and those who began actively to demand remuneration. Even the passive, for whom the size of the reward was set unilaterally by the man, *expected* payment. There was a process in which girls became more demanding and began to set their own rates. They no longer accepted "tips" and set a piece rate. The rates were not always monetary, nor standardized, but girls engaged in aggressive bargaining. In cases between 1912 and 1920 girls were receiving rates ranging from five cents to five dollars (e.g., Cases #2082A, #3042, #3644).

Prostitution took on special importance when it became part of a plan to leave home permanently, a strategy common among incest victims. Then it was a means of earning a living and becoming economically independent, and as such was more ominous than mere adolescent rebellion. For girls remaining at home, even those contributing earnings from prostitution to the family kitty, the sex adventures might remain pranks, without irrevocable long-term consequences. For those without parents, prostitution was one of a limited number of economic opportunities for girls.

In one way, these girls were becoming more assertive, less victimized, in becoming prostitutes. At least a prostitute was receiving some exchange for the use of her body, as opposed to a girl who was raped or who allowed men and boys to use her sexually with no gain for herself. These girls were not only attempting to get out of their victimizing homes, but they were using their greatest asset—their sexual value to men.[12] The power gained through such a flattened and instrumental view of the self could hardly have brought lasting self-esteem. Nevertheless the very manipulativeness of these girl sex delinquents suggests their refusal to accept victimization. When the police and social workers commented on the insolence, sauciness, aggressive dress and foul language of girls picked up on the streets, they were accurately observing girls' rejection of an obedience that had been self-destructive, and that the girls knew to be self-destructive.

Of course, their rebellion put them only in different situations of victimization. Nevertheless, it is worth questioning whether their legal punishment was worse than other options. Ambivalence pervaded the behavior of incest victims in general, and of sex delinquents in particular. The search for freedom and power was produced as much by deprivation of security as by restraint. The aggressive manipulation of sex stemmed perhaps as much from search for love as from bitterness. This motivation becomes especially plausible given how young many of the "sex delinquents" were. One six-year-old incest victim was accused of what amounts to pimping for her sister, and there were numerous full-fledged fallen women of 10 (e.g., Cases #3543, #3085A).

The case of "Susan," from 1930, illustrates the intricate relations between incest and sex delinquency. At 11-years-old, Susan was already "promiscuous" and blamed for the ruin of a group of other neighborhood girls. She was sleeping with a boarder who was also her mother's lover; indeed Susan's mother had just had a baby by this boarder. Susan's father was at this time in jail for steal-

ing from the school where he was the janitor; and the mother and family were financially dependent on the boarder. Several social workers believed that Susan had also been sexually victimized by her father, who had previously admitted sexual molestation of a niece in their household. Susan's mother was beaten by her husband, but the joint victimization of the women in this family did not bring them together. Instead, their relationship was hostile. Susan told a therapist that her mother had not kissed her for two years, although she frequently hugged and kissed the other children—displaying the jealous hostility typical of the mother of an incest victim. Susan was required to stay home, do housework, look after her younger siblings, and pick up after her older brothers. Susan retaliated by threatening legal charges against her mother.

Whether or not Susan's father molested her, her brothers did, beginning when she was eight. One day one brother told Susan to come over to a store, "and the man in the store took her into the back room and stood her up against the wall and had partial intercourse with her. She thought he was going to give her some money and that was the reason she did it but he only gave her an orange."[13] Soon, Susan began seeking out sex in the neighborhood herself—whether for the adventure or the money is not clear. She frequently told interviewers that she enjoyed her sexual activities. She grew jealous of her friends if any challenged her position as favorite of the men and ringleader. She drew her seven-year-old sister into these activities and this sister's case led agency investigators to a neighborhood child molester known as "Tom the Cat."[14] Susan also pimped for her brothers. Once, she claimed, she brought two neighborhood girls to her house, and her brothers had group sex games that included the sisters, the friends, and a younger brother.

Susan may have enjoyed exaggerating, and her bravado offended and alarmed the social workers. "Money crazy, will do anything for money," her case worker wrote. She was also concerned that Susan smoked, masturbated, and liked to read *True Story*. Professionals treated her as contagious. One psychiatrist wrote that she was "likely to be a great danger to other children." The record contains a detailed description of how she was taught to masturbate by a friend and, in turn, taught her sister. The fear and loathing of Susan displayed in the case notes must have been communicated to her, and she deeply believed in her own badness, saying about herself, "I was always a whore." Surely the outcome of the case confirmed her badness to herself: she and her sister were removed from their family and placed in foster homes, while no action was taken against her father, the boarder, or her brothers (Case #3642).

Several factors made Susan's prognosis unusually bleak: her extreme youth and her location in one of Boston's small and self-contained neighborhoods, where she had little chance of finding any alternative analysis of her situation. Older girls were more able to seek to leave their neighborhoods, thus putting substantial distance between themselves and their family systems which "normalized" incest. One typical kind of case with adolescent girls appeared first as running away. (Indeed it is striking how often runaways were brought home without questioning what they were running away from.) Consider this story of Irish-American teenagers from Cambridge. A mother complained to the MSPCC in 1930 that her husband was "bothering" her 14-year-old daughter Mary; the mother wanted outside intervention because she was afraid of her husband's violence against herself. The agency, ignoring her fear, asked her to bring Mary in for an examination; the mother agreed but, not surprisingly, did not show up. There was no follow-up

until 10 months later when the mother said the problem had ended and that she wanted no interference. We hear of Mary next in 1932 when she had run away with a girlfriend to New York. Hoping for independence, they had instead become hopelessly dependent on the men they picked up to get it. A "fellow they met in a restaurant" in Brooklyn got Mary a job as a waitress where she stayed two months; then the girls did "taxi dancing" in the Strand Ballroom; later they hitchhiked to Los Angeles, hearing that there were more jobs in the West (note that this was the Depression). They complained that "plenty of the men who gave them rides tried to get fresh." In Long Beach they met two waitresses, and the four of them shared a room. Not finding jobs they "went around with various fellows who gave them money towards their room rent and food." During the raid of a party Mary was arrested, found to have gonorrhea, and sent home to Cambridge, as she was still a minor. She was furious, since she understood that home was the source of her problems, not the solution. After five days at home she ran away again to New York. She described her work during this period plainly as prostitution. More and more frightened and unhappy, she returned to Cambridge where she sought out her old girlfriends and lived with some of them in her old Cambridge neighborhood while still trying to avoid her family and looking for work. She was arrested for loitering in the lobby of the Haymarket Hotel (Case #3557A).

CONCLUSION

I do not know what became of Mary, and I suspect the worst—probably reform school for a start. Still, it seems to me that her impulse to run was not a mistake, nor was her attempt to make of her girlfriends some kind of family. Unfortunately, as with many of today's runaways, the mutual help among these girls was not enough to protect them from men operating within a sexual double standard and a depressed economy, and exploiting their low status in the labor market and disastrously low self-esteem.

In this historical study, most of the incest cases had sad endings. The incestuous situation placed most girls in a double bind, caught between injunctions to be virtuous and to be obedient. I have tried to identify here how patterns of acquiescence and resistance were shaped by that double bind. Girls in the typical "domestic incest" situations were being forced to submit not only by the coercion of their assailant, but also by their alienation from their mothers and their entrapment in a family system which "normalized" the incest. Nevertheless, these girls displayed more resistance than did victims of nonsexual child abuse (Gordon and O'Keefe, 1984). When they could not prevent their assault, they often tried to escape their families altogether. In doing so, they often became "sexual delinquents," either through their mere presence on the streets or through their active attempts to gain some power in relations with men. The most "hardened" delinquents, to use the language of the case workers of this period, included those most determined to resist their victimization.

These historical findings contain several implications for contemporary concern with incest victims. First, they suggest that there may be more resistance among these victims, even quite young ones, than has been assumed. Second, they support recent discoveries of high rates of sexual victimization in the earlier lives of today's "sex delinquents." Third, they lend support to contemporary clinical analyses of incest which relate that crime to unusually male-dominant family structures.

Just as incest often occurs in families with exaggerated feminine subordination, so the girls' resistance to incest often assumed, per-

haps had to assume, the form of resistance to the norms of feminine virtue, passivity, and subordination. One odd thing about incest is that despite the revulsion it has provoked, it opens a frightening but vital line of questioning about ordinary family relations. It identifies tensions between family solidarity and individual autonomy, between adult authority and children's rights, between women's status as victims and their responsibility as parents, tensions that one should not expect to resolve easily. It shows that many feminine virtues can support victimization, not only those one might want to reject such as obedience, quietness, or obligingness, but also those one might want to preserve—discipline, responsibility, loyalty. Incest, the most rare and deviant of family scandals, in some ways reveals the ordinary as much as the extraordinary.

NOTES

1. This comparison is summarized fully in Gordon and O'Keefe, 1984.
2. A comparison with the period 1930–1960, showing changes over time, will appear in the incest chapters of my book on the history of family violence and social control (Gordon, Forthcoming).
3. This and all further case numbers cited refer to the coding system used in this study, not the actual agency case number. These case records belong to one of the three agencies; those of the MSPCC and the BCSA from this period are in the University of Massachusetts/Boston Archives, and those of the JBGC are in the Countway Library of Harvard Medical School.
4. A finding corroborated by contemporary clinical incest studies, e.g. Herman (1981).
5. Forty-four percent of the mothers of incest victims in this study were battered, as compared to 34 percent in all the family violence cases.
6. In this period when so many of the agency clients were immigrants from more rural and patriarchal environments, the fact that guilt was notably absent recalls David Riesman's

(1950:24) distinction between shame (tradition-directed) and guilt (inner-directed) cultures. The absence of guilt certainly suggests the absence or at least ineffectiveness of an internalized taboo against father-daughter sex.

7. It would be most useful to have a class and cultural analysis of domestic incest. If this hypothesis about change over time is right, one would expect to find this type of incest less common in groups which were less patriarchal in their expectations of girls. But these more permissive, middle-class and/or "modernized" families were much less likely to become clients of social-work agencies, so we have no records about their family deviance.

8. She had brought first one and then the other to the MSPCC's attention, but their examinations had revealed the girls' "parts" to be normal although there were "suspicious symptoms." These genital examinations were the standard agency practice in cases of alleged sexual abuse. They were often the only response, and fear of such exams discouraged many girls and their mothers from seeking help.

9. It is not clear what the social worker's motives were in this. She may have been responding to the girl's own desire to return home; she may have been fearful of the strong disapproval of the Chinese community for splitting up the family. She offered to get a lock for the girl's room!

10. Indeed I also suspect incest in many sex-delinquency cases where there was no such allegation. See, for example, Breckenridge and Abbott (1916:74, 105); Fernald et al. (1920: chap. XII); Goldberg and Goldberg (1935); Thomas (1923: chap. IV).

11. I use this term to mean any acceptance of money or goods in exchange for sex, although even in this wide definition one must be cautious. Many girls were wrongly labeled as prostitutes. Estimates of the numbers of prostitutes in nineteenth and early twentieth century cities were often inflated, in part because any woman who engaged in casual sex, or was on the street, or looked disrespectable, or lived with men out of wedlock, might be thus labeled (DuBois and Gordon, 1983). Furthermore, there is no clear line between prostitution and other sexual intercourse when women are economically dependent. A variety of exchanges of goods, services, favors, or kindnesses between people in a sexual relationship might be defined alternatively as affection, help, or pay.

12. This view of girls' motives as instrumental rather than sexual was argued persuasively by Thomas (1923).

13. Among the younger sex delinquents a common type of case involved a group of girls involved with a neighborhood "dirty old man." It bears notice how this particular piece of mythology, the "dirty old man," that was dismissed as a prudish "old wives'" fear in the second half of the century, proves to have been accurate. In 1910, 14 out of 16 MSPCC non-incestuous sex assault cases, and in 1930, 20 out of 22, involved such characters. This was also the view of police experts of the time (Williams, 1913). In several of these cases—for example, three in 1930—the problem was defined by the agency exclusively as sex molestation by a stranger even though there was also incest. The accused were often small businessmen, craftsmen, or employees in shops which provided the physical space for secret activities with children—janitors, shopkeepers, cobblers, elevator operators. They were old from the children's point of view, usually over 40 and often over 50. They often appeared as kindly, entertaining children and giving them treats.

14. Such a nickname is among the clues that his activities were known and informally tolerated in the neighborhood.

REFERENCES

Armstrong, Louise. 1978. *Kiss Daddy Goodnight: A Speak-out on Incest.* New York: Hawthorn.

Breckenridge, Sophonisba, and Grace Abbott. 1916. *The Delinquent Child and the Home.* New York: Survey Associates.

Breines, Wini, and Linda Gordon. 1983. "The new scholarship on family violence." *Signs* 8:490–531.

Butler, Sandra. 1978. *Conspiracy of Silence: The Trauma of Incest.* San Francisco: New Glide Publications.

DuBois, Ellen, and Linda Gordon. 1983. "Seeking ecstasy on the battlefield: danger and pleasure in nineteenth-century feminist sexual thought." *Feminist Studies* 9:7–25.

Fernald, Mabel Ruth, Mary Holmes Stevens Hayes, and Almena Dawley. 1920. *A Study of Women Delinquents in New York State.* New York: Century.

Finkelhor, David. 1979. *Sexually Victimized Children.* New York: The Free Press.

Goldberg, Jacob Alter, and Rosamond W. Goldberg. 1935. *Girls on City Streets. A Study of 1400 Cases of Rape.* New York: American Social Hygiene Association.

Gordon, Linda. Forthcoming. *Family Violence and Social Control: Boston, 1880–1960.* New York: Pantheon.

Gordon, Linda, and Paul O'Keefe. 1984. "Incest as a form of family violence: evidence from historical case records." *Journal of Marriage and the Family* 46:27–34.

Herman, Judith. 1981. *Father-Daughter Incest.* Cambridge: Harvard University Press.

MacFarlane, Kee. 1978. "Sexual abuse of children." Pp. 81–110 in Jane R. Chapman and Margaret Gates (eds.), *The Victimization of Women.* Beverly Hills: Sage.

Renvoize, Jean. 1982. *Incest. A Family Pattern.* London: Routledge & Kegan Paul.

Riesman, David. 1950. *The Lonely Crowd.* New Haven: Yale University Press.

Rush, Florence. 1980. *The Best Kept Secret. Sexual Abuse of Children.* Englewood Cliffs, NJ: Prentice-Hall.

Schlossman, Steven, and Stephanie Wallach. 1978. "The crime of precocious sexuality: female juvenile delinquency in the Progressive era." *Harvard Educational Review* 48:65–94.

Thomas, William I. 1923. *The Unadjusted Girl.* Boston: Little, Brown.

Walker, Leonore. 1978. *The Battered Woman.* New York: Harper & Row.

Weinberg, S. K. 1955. *Incest Behavior.* New York: Citadel Press.

Williams, Gurney. 1913. "Rape in children and in young girls." *International Clinics,* 2nd series, 23:151–63.

CHAPTER 18

SEXUAL HARASSMENT: ITS FIRST DECADE IN COURT

CATHARINE A. MacKINNON

ABSTRACT

Study after study has found that women at work experience sexual harassment. Yet it took several high-profile revelations of sexual harassment to bring this form of victimization of women front and center. Most readers will have seen or heard of Law Professor Anita Hill's testimony of sexual harassment by Clarence Thomas, now a Supreme Court judge. And many will also recall the charges by 26 women Navy officers of sexual harassment and violence at a Navy aviators' convention in 1992, known as the "Tailhook incident," which apparently was part of an annual ritual. The problem of sexual harassment makes clear what has *not* changed despite the fact that sexual harassment is an unlawful employment practice under Title VII of the Civil Rights Act of 1964, as amended. Not until the 1980s did the U.S. Supreme Court agree with Equal Employment Opportunity Commission guidelines and court rulings that unwelcome sexual advances that create an offensive or hostile working environment violate Title VII.* While job opportunities have improved and laws have been passed preventing gender discrimination in hiring and promotion, attitudes and behavior surrounding sexual harassment of women appear to have changed little.

Sexual harassment ranges from off-color remarks to humiliating comments to unwanted touching and grabbing to requests or demands for sexual acts and, in extreme cases, to rape and threats of losing one's job for failure to acquiesce to sexual demands. Sexual harassment is coercion; it is unwanted sex under threat; it is sex that is economically enforced; it denies women the exercise of control over their lives. Sexual harassment happens most frequently to those women in

---

*Anna Quindlen, "The Skirt Standard," *The New York Times,* Dec. 6, 1992, p. 19.

subordinate working positions with low pay. However, it is found at virtually all levels and in all occupations, including high-status professions, where women are harassed not only by superiors but also by subordinates, as well as by peers and third parties.

In this chapter Catharine MacKinnon, whose groundbreaking argument is that sexual harassment is sexual discrimination and thus prohibited by federal law, describes the application of the law. Sexual harassment carries serious consequences for the victim, who suffers considerably beyond the discomfort of embarrassment and humiliation. She may experience reduced ability to function at work, have her promotions blocked, lose her job, and have her personal and professional reputation destroyed. Clearly, there is a need for laws prohibiting sexual harassment.

MacKinnon points out that sexual harassment is the first legal wrong to have ever been defined by women. (Past wrongs such as rape were defined in laws written by men.) For this reason, MacKinnon is cautiously optimistic that sexual harassment laws can make some difference in the lives of working women. She warns, however, that in a sexist society, the struggle for empowerment, self-determination, and the right to define the problem must constantly be waged—even after women have been able to shape the law as with sexual harassment.

In other published works,* MacKinnon cites the particular sensitivity that black women have shown to this form of sexual victimization, and she suggests that their vulnerability may be even greater than that of white women. She points out that black women are economically in a more precarious situation than white women and that being black has always meant being a target of sexual abuse in the United States. Further, in a racist as well as sexist society, black women continue to be stereotyped as more sexually accessible than white women.

The purpose of this chapter is to present an assessment of how the law on sexual harassment is working in its first decade of existence. Explore your own college, workplace, or community to evaluate the degree to which sexual harassment against women has changed or remained the same in the past decade. Are there organizational statements and guidelines preventing sexual harassment? Is there an administrative officer to turn to when such problems arise? Is this well known to the members of the community? How does MacKinnon's description and your current study compare with your own personal experiences in this area?

Sexual harassment as a form of exploitation is multifaceted. Explain how it affects women differently than men. Does it affect diverse groups of women of color differently, and does it affect such groups differently than white women? If so, spell out how. Are lesbians harassed in the same way and with the same frequency as heterosexual women? If not, how and why does the harassment differ?

---

*See Catharine A. MacKinnon, *Sexual Harassment of Working Women,* Yale University Press, New Haven, 1979. The section "Sexual Harassment: The Experience" was reprinted as Chapter 19 in the first edition of this book: Barbara Raffel Price and Natalie J. Sokoloff (eds.), *The Criminal Justice System and Women,* Clark Boardman, Ltd., New York, 1982.

Sexual harassment, the event, is not new to women. It is the law of injuries that it is new to. Sexual pressure imposed on someone who is not in an economic position to refuse it became sex discrimination in the midseventies,[1] and in education soon afterward.[2] It became possible to do something legal about sexual harassment because some women took women's experience of violation seriously enough to design a law around it, as if what happens to women matters. This was apparently such a startling way of proceeding that sexual harassment was protested as a feminist invention. Sexual harassment, the event, was not invented by feminists; the perpetrators did that with no help from us. Sexual harassment, the legal claim—the idea that the law should see it the way its victims see it—is definitely a feminist invention. Feminists first took women's experience seriously enough to uncover this problem and conceptualize it and pursue it legally. That legal claim is just beginning to produce more than a handful of reported cases. Ten years later, "[i]t may well be that sex harassment is the hottest present day Title VII issue."[3] It is time for a down-the-road assessment of this departure.

The law against sexual harassment is a practical attempt to stop a form of exploitation. It is also one test of sexual politics as feminist jurisprudence, of possibilities for social change for women through law. The existence of a law against sexual harassment has affected both the context of meaning within which social life is lived and the concrete delivery of rights through the legal system. The sexually harassed have been given a name for their suffering and an analysis that connects it with gender. They have been given a forum, legitimacy to speak, authority to make claims, and an avenue for possible relief. Before, what happened to them was all right. Now it is not.

This matters. Sexual abuse mutes victims socially through the violation itself. Often the abuser enforces secrecy and silence; secrecy and silence may be part of what is so sexy about sexual abuse. When the state also forecloses a validated space for denouncing and rectifying the victimization, it seals this secrecy and reenforces this silence. The harm of this process, a process that utterly precludes speech, then becomes all of a piece. If there is no right place to go to say, this hurt me, then a woman is simply the one who can be treated this way, and no harm, as they say, is done.

In point of fact, I would prefer not to have to spend all this energy getting the law to recognize wrongs to women as wrong. But it seems to be necessary to legitimize our injuries as injuries in order to delegitimize our victimization by them, without which it is difficult to move in more positive ways. The legal claim for sexual harassment made the events of sexual harassment illegitimate socially as well as legally for the first time. Let me know if you figure out a better way to do that.

At this interface between law and society, we need to remember that the legitimacy courts give they can also take. Compared with a possibility of relief where no possibility of relief existed, since women started out with nothing in this area, this worry seems a

---

The original version of this speech was part of a panel on sexual harassment shared with Karen Haney, Pamela Price, and Peggy McGuiness at Stanford University, Stanford, California, Apr. 12, 1983. It thereafter became an address to the Equal Employment Opportunities Section of the American Bar Association, New Orleans, Louisiana, May 3, 1984 and to a workshop for the national conference of the National Organization for Women, Denver, Colorado, June 14, 1986. The ideas developed further when I represented Mechelle Vinson as co-counsel in her U.S. Supreme Court case in the spring of 1986. I owe a great deal to my conversations with Valerie Heller.

Reprinted by permission of the publishers from *Feminism Unmodified* by Catharine MacKinnon, Cambridge, Mass.: Harvard University Press, Copyright © 1987 by the President and Fellows of Harvard College.

bit fancy. Whether the possibility of relief alters the terms of power that gives rise to sexual harassment itself, which makes getting away with it possible, is a different problem. Sexual harassment, the legal claim, is a demand that state authority stand behind women's refusal of sexual access in certain situations that previously were a masculine prerogative. With sexism, there is always a risk that our demand for self-determination will be taken as a demand for paternal protection and will therefore strengthen male power rather than undermine it. This seems a particularly valid concern because the law of sexual harassment began as case law, without legislative guidance or definition.

Institutional support for sexual self-determination is a victory; institutional paternalism reinforces our lack of self-determination. The problem is, the state has never in fact protected women's dignity or bodily integrity. It just says it does. Its protections have been both condescending *and* unreal, in effect strengthening the protector's choice to violate the protected at will, whether the protector is the individual perpetrator or the state. This does not seem to me a reason not to have a law against sexual harassment. It is a reason to demand that the promise of "equal protection of the laws" be *delivered upon* for us, as it is when real people are violated. It is also part of a larger political struggle to value women more than the male pleasure of using us is valued. Ultimately, though, the question of whether the use of the state for women helps or hurts can be answered only in practice, because so little real protection of the laws has ever been delivered.

The legal claim for sexual harassment marks the first time in history, to my knowledge, that women have defined women's injuries in a law. Consider what has happened with rape. We have never defined the injury of rape; men define it. The men who define it, define what they take to be this vio-

lation of women according to, among other things, what they think they don't do. In this way rape becomes an act of a stranger (they mean Black) committed upon a woman (white) whom he has never seen before. Most rapes are intraracial and are committed by men the women know.[4] Ask a woman if she has ever been raped, and often she says, "Well . . . not really." In that silence between the well and the not really, she just measured what happened to her against every rape case she ever heard about and decided she would lose in court. Especially when you are part of a subordinated group, your own definition of your injuries is powerfully shaped by your assessment of whether you could get anyone to do anything about it, including anything official. You are realistic by necessity, and the voice of law is the voice in power. When the design of a legal wrong does not fit the wrong as it happens to you, as is the case with rape, that law can undermine your social and political as well as legal legitimacy in saying that what happened was an injury at all—even to yourself.

It is never too soon to worry about this, but it may be too soon to know whether the law against sexual harassment will be taken away from us or turn into nothing or turn ugly in our hands. The fact is, this law is working surprisingly well for women by any standards, particularly when compared with the rest of sex discrimination law. If the question is whether a law designed from women's standpoint and administered through this legal system can do anything for women—which always seems to me to be a good question—this experience so far gives a qualified and limited yes.

It is hard to unthink what you know, but there was a time when the facts that amount to sexual harassment did not amount to sexual harassment. It is a bit like the injuries of pornography until recently. The facts amounting to the harm did not socially "exist," had no shape, no cognitive coherence; far less did they state a legal claim. It just happened to you. To the women to whom it happened, it wasn't part of anything, much less something big or shared like gender. It fit no known pattern. It was neither a regularity nor an irregularity. Even social scientists didn't study it, and they study anything that moves. When law recognized sexual harassment as a practice of sex discrimination, it moved it from the realm of "and then he . . . and then he . . . ," the primitive language in which sexual abuse lives inside a woman, into an experience with a form, an etiology, a cumulativeness—as well as a club.

The shape, the positioning, and the club—each is equally crucial politically. Once it became possible to do something about sexual harassment, it became possible to know more about it, because it became possible for its victims to speak about it. Now we know, as we did not when it first became illegal, that this problem is commonplace. We know this not just because it has to be true, but as documented fact. Between a quarter and a third of women in the federal workforce report having been sexually harassed, many physically, at least once in the last two years.[5] Projected, that becomes 85 percent of all women at some point in their working lives. This figure is based on asking women "Have you ever been sexually harassed?"—the conclusion—not "has this fact happened? has that fact happened?" which usually produces more. The figures for sexual harassment of students are comparable.[6]

When faced with individual incidents of sexual harassment, the legal system's first question was, is it a personal episode? Legally, this was a way the courts inquired into whether the incidents were based on sex, as they had to be to be sex discrimination. Politically, it was a move to isolate victims by stigmatizing them as deviant. It also seemed odd to me that a relationship was either per-

sonal or gendered, meaning that one is not a woman personally. Statistical frequency alone does not make an event not personal, of course, but the presumption that sexual pressure in contexts of unequal power is an isolated idiosyncrasy to unique individual victims has been undermined both by the numbers and by their division by gender. Overwhelmingly, it is men who sexually harass women, a lot of them. Actually, it is even more accurate to say that men do this than to say that women have this done to them. This is a description of the perpetrators' behavior, not of the statisticians' feminism.

Sexual harassment has also emerged as a creature of hierarchy. It inhabits what I call hierarchies among men: arrangements in which some men are below other men, as in employer/employee and teacher/student. In workplaces, sexual harassment by supervisors of subordinates is common; in education, by administrators of lower-level administrators, by faculty of students. But it also happens among coworkers, from third parties, even by subordinates in the workplace, men who are women's hierarchical inferiors or peers. Basically, it is done by men to women regardless of relative position on the formal hierarchy. I believe that the reason sexual harassment was first established as an injury of the systematic abuse of power in hierarchies among men is that this is power men recognize. They comprehend from personal experience that something is held over your head if you do not comply. The lateral or reverse hierarchical examples[7] suggest something beyond this, something men don't understand from personal experience because they take its advantages for granted: gender is also a hierarchy. The courts do not use this analysis, but some act as though they understand it.[8]

Sex discrimination law had to adjust a bit to accommodate the realities of sexual harassment. Like many other injuries of gender, it wasn't written for this. For something to be based on gender in the legal sense means it happens to a woman as a woman, not as an individual. Membership in a gender is understood as the opposite of, rather than part of, individuality. Clearly, sexual harassment is one of the last situations in which a woman is treated without regard to her sex; it is because of her sex that it happens. But the social meaning attributed to women as a class, in which women are defined as gender female by sexual accessibility to men, is not what courts have considered before when they have determined whether a given incident occurred because of sex.

Sex discrimination law typically conceives that something happens because of sex when it happens to one sex but not the other. The initial procedure is arithmetic: draw a gender line and count how many of each are on each side in the context at issue, or, alternatively, take the line drawn by the practice or policy and see if it also divides the sexes. One by-product of this head-counting method is what I call the bisexual defense.[9] Say a man is accused of sexually harassing a woman. He can argue that the harassment is not sex-based because he harasses both sexes equally, indiscriminately as it were. Originally it was argued that sexual harassment was not a proper gender claim because someone could harass both sexes. We argued that this was an issue of fact to be pleaded and proven, an issue of did he do this, rather than an issue of law, of whether he could have. The courts accepted that, creating this kamikaze defense. To my knowledge, no one has used the bisexual defense since.[10] As this example suggests, head counting can provide a quick topography of the terrain, but it has proved too blunt to distinguish treatment whose meaning is based on gender from treatment that has other social hermeneutics, especially when only two individuals are involved.

Once sexual harassment was established as

bigger than personal, the courts' next legal question was whether it was smaller than biological. To say that sexual harassment was biological seemed to me a very negative thing to say about men, but defendants seemed to think it precluded liability. Plaintiffs argued that sexual harassment is not biological in that men who don't do it have nothing wrong with their testosterone levels. Besides, if murder were found to have biological correlates, it would still be a crime. Thus, although the question purported to be whether the acts were based on sex, the implicit issue seemed to be whether the source of the impetus for doing the acts was relevant to their harmfulness.

Similarly structured was the charge that women who resented sexual harassment were oversensitive. Not that the acts did not occur, but rather that it was unreasonable to experience them as harmful. Such a harm would be based not on sex but on individual hysteria. Again shifting the inquiry away from whether the acts are based on sex in the guise of pursuing it, away from whether they occurred to whether it should matter if they did, the question became whether the acts were properly harmful. Only this time it was not the perpetrator's drives that made him not liable but the target's sensitivity that made the acts not a harm at all. It was pointed out that too many people are victimized by sexual harassment to consider them all hysterics. Besides, in other individual injury law, victims are not blamed; perpetrators are required to take victims as they find them, so long as they are not supposed to be doing what they are doing.

Once these excuses were rejected, then it was said that sexual harassment was not really an employment-related problem. That became hard to maintain when it was her job the woman lost. If it was, in fact, a personal relationship, it apparently did not start and stop there, although this is also a question of proof, leaving the true meaning of the events to trial. The perpetrator may have thought it was all affectionate or friendly or fun, but the victim experienced it as hateful, dangerous, and damaging. Results in such cases have been mixed. Some judges have accepted the perpetrator's view; for instance, one judge held queries by the defendant such as "What am I going to get for this?" and repeated importunings to "go out" to be "susceptible of innocent interpretation."[11] Other judges, on virtually identical facts, for example, "When are you going to do something nice for me?"[12] have held for the plaintiff. For what it's worth, the judge in the first case was a man, in the second a woman.

That sexual harassment is sex-based discrimination seems to be legally established, at least for now.[13] In one of the few recent cases that reported litigating the issue of sex basis, defendants argued that a sex-based claim was not stated when a woman worker complained of terms of abuse directed at her at work such as "slut," "bitch," and "fucking cunt" and "many sexually oriented drawings posted on pillars and at other conspicuous places around the warehouse" with plaintiff's initials on them, presenting her having sex with an animal.[14] The court said: "[T]he sexually offensive conduct and language used would have been almost irrelevant and would have failed entirely in its crude purpose had the plaintiff been a man. I do not hesitate to find that but for her sex, the plaintiff would not have been subjected to the harassment she suffered."[15] "Obvious" or "patently obvious" they often call it.[16] I guess this is what it looks like to have proven a point.

Sexual harassment was first recognized as an injury of gender in what I called incidents of quid pro quo. Sometimes people think that harassment has to be constant. It doesn't; it's a term of art in which once can be enough. Typically, an advance is made, rejected, and a loss follows.[17] For a while it looked as if this three-step occurrence was in danger of going from one form in which sexual harassment can occur into a series of required hurdles. In many situations the woman is forced to submit instead of being able to reject the advance. The problem has become whether, say, being forced into intercourse at work will be seen as a failed quid pro quo or as an instance of sexual harassment in which the forced sex constitutes the injury.

I know of one reported case in employment and one in education in which women who were forced to submit to the sex brought a sexual harassment claim against the perpetrator; so far only the education case has won on the facts.[18] The employment case that lost on the facts was reversed on appeal. The pressures for sex were seen to state a claim without respect to the fact that the woman was not able to avoid complying.[19] It is unclear if the unwanted advances constitute a claim, separate and apart from whether or not they are able to be resisted, which they should; or if the acts of forced sex would also constitute an environmental claim separate from any quid pro quo, as it seems to me they also should. In the education case, the case of Paul Mann, the students were allowed to recover punitive damages for the forced sex.[20] If sexual harassment is not to be defined only as sexual attention imposed upon someone who is not in a position to refuse it, who refuses it, women who are forced to submit to sex must be understood as harmed not less, but as much or more, than those who are able to make their refusals effective.

Getting recoveries for women who have actually been sexually violated by the defendant will probably be a major battle. Women being compensated in money for sex they *had* violates male metaphysics because in that system sex is what a woman is for. As one judge concluded, "[T]here does not seem to be any issue that the plaintiff did not desire to have relations with [the defendant], but it is also altogether apparent that she willingly had sex with him."[21] Now what do you make of that? The woman was not physically forced at the moment of penetration, and since it is sex she must have willed it, is about all you can make of it. The sexual politics of the situation is that men do not see a woman who has had sex as victimized, whatever the conditions. One dimension of this problem involves whether a woman who has been violated through sex has any credibility. Credibility is difficult to separate from the definition of the injury, since an injury in which the victim is not believed to have been injured *because she has been injured* is not a real injury, legally speaking.

The question seems to be whether a woman is valuable enough to hurt, so that what is done to her is a harm. Once a woman has had sex, voluntarily or by force—it doesn't matter—she is regarded as too damaged to be further damageable, or something. Many women who have been raped in the course of sexual harassment have been advised by their lawyers not to mention the rape because it would destroy their credibility! The fact that abuse is long term has suggested to some finders of fact that it must have been tolerated or even wanted, although sexual harassment that becomes a condition of work has also been established as a legal claim in its own right.[22] I once was talking with a judge about a case he was sitting on in which Black teenage girls alleged that some procedures at their school violated their privacy. He told me that with their sexual habits they had no privacy to lose. It seemed he knew what their sexual habits were from evidence in the case, examples of the privacy violations.

The more aggravated an injury becomes, the more it ceases to exist. Why is incomprehensible to me, but how it functions is not. Our most powerful moment is on paper, in complaints we frame, and our worst is in the flesh in court. Although it isn't much, we have the most credibility when we are only the idea of us and our violation in their minds. In our allegations we construct reality to some extent; face to face, their angle of vision frames us irrevocably. In court we have breasts, we are Black, we are (in a word) women. Not that we are ever free of that, but the moment we physically embody our complaint, and they can see us, the pornography of the process starts in earnest.

I have begun to think that a major reason that many women do not bring sexual harassment complaints is that they know this. They cannot bear to have their personal account of sexual abuse reduced to a fantasy they invented, used to define them and to pleasure the finders of fact and the public. I think they have a very real sense that their accounts are enjoyed, that others are getting pleasure from the first-person recounting of their pain, and that is the content of their humiliation at these rituals. When rape victims say they feel raped again on the stand, the victims of sexual harassment say they feel sexually harassed in the adjudication, it is not exactly metaphor. I hear that they—in being publicly sexually humiliated by the legal system, as by the perpetrator—are pornography. The first time it happens, it is called freedom; the second time, it is called justice.

If a woman is sexually defined—meaning all women fundamentally, intensified by previous sexual abuse or identification as lesbian, indelible if a prostitute—her chances of recovery for sexual abuse are correspondingly reduced. I'm still waiting for a woman to win at trial against a man who forced her to comply with the sex. Suppose the male plaintiff in one sexual harassment case who rented the motel room in which the single sexual encounter took place had been a woman, and the perpetrator had been a man. When the relationship later went bad, it was apparently not a credibility problem for *him* at trial that he had rented the motel room. Nor was *his* sexual history apparently an issue. Nor, apparently, was it said when he complained he was fired because the relationship went bad, that he had "asked for" the relationship. That case was reversed on appeal on legal grounds, but he did win at trial.[23] The best one can say about women in such cases is that women who have had sex but not with the accused may have some chance. In one case the judge did not believe the plaintiff's denial of an affair with another coworker, but did believe that she had been sexually harassed by the defendant.[24] In another, the woman plaintiff actually had "linguistic intimacy" with another man at work, yet when she said that what happened to her with the defendant was sexual harassment, she was believed.[25] These are miraculous. A woman's word on these matters is usually indivisible. In another case a woman accused two men of sexual harassment. She had resisted and refused one man to whom she had previously submitted under pressure for a long time. He was in the process of eliminating her from her job when the second man raped her. The first man's defense was that it went on so long, she must have liked it. The second man's defense was that he had heard that she had had sexual relations with the first man, so he felt this was something she was open to.[26] This piggyback defense is premised on the class definition of woman as whore, by which I mean what men mean: one who exists to be sexually done to, to be sexually available on men's terms, that is, a woman. If this definition of women is accepted, it means that if a woman has ever had sex, forced or voluntary, she can't be sexually violated.

A woman can be seen in these terms by being a former rape victim or by the way she uses language. One case holds that the evidence shows "the allegedly harassing conduct was substantially welcomed and encouraged by plaintiff. She actively contributed to the distasteful working environment by her own

profane and sexually suggestive conduct."[27] She swore, apparently, and participated in conversations about sex. This effectively made her harassment-proof. Many women joke about sex to try to defuse men's sexual aggression, to try to be one of the boys in hopes they will be treated like one. This is to discourage sexual advances, not to encourage them. In other cases, judges have understood that "the plaintiffs did not appreciate the remarks and . . . many of the other women did not either."[28]

The extent to which a woman's job is sexualized is also a factor. If a woman's work is not to sell sex, and her employer requires her to wear a sexually suggestive uniform, if she is repeatedly sexually harassed by the clientele, she may have a claim against her employer.[29] Similarly, although "there may well be a limited category of jobs (such as adult entertainment) in which sexual harassment may be a rational consequence of such employment," one court was "simply not prepared to say that a female who goes to work in what is apparently a predominantly male workplace should reasonably expect sexual harassment as part of her job."[30] There may be trouble at some point over what jobs are selling sex, given the sexualization of anything a woman does.

Sexual credibility, that strange amalgam of whether your word counts with whether or how much you were hurt, also comes packaged in a variety of technical rules in the sexual harassment cases: evidence, discovery, and burden of proof. In 1982 the EEOC held that if a victim was sexually harassed without a corroborating witness, proof was inadequate as a matter of law.[31] (Those of you who wonder about the relevance of pornography, get this: if nobody watched, it didn't happen.) A woman's word, even if believed, was legally insufficient, even if the man had nothing to put against it other than his word and the plaintiff's burden of proof. Much like women who have been raped, women who have experienced sexual harassment say, "But I couldn't prove it." They mean they have nothing but their word. Proof is when what you say counts against what someone else says—for which it must first be believed. To say as a matter of law that the woman's word is per se legally insufficient is to assume that, with sexual violations uniquely, the defendant's denial is dispositive, is proof. To say a woman's word is no proof amounts to saying a woman's word is worthless. Usually all the man has is his denial. In 1983 the EEOC found sexual harassment on a woman's word alone. It said it was enough, without distinguishing or overruling the prior case.[32] Perhaps they recognized that women don't choose to be sexually harassed in the presence of witnesses.

The question of prior sexual history is one area in which the issue of sexual credibility is directly posed. Evidence of the defendant's sexual harassment of other women in the same institutional relation or setting is increasingly being considered admissible, and it should be.[33] The other side of the question is whether evidence of a victim's prior sexual history should be discoverable or admissible, and it seems to me it should not be. Perpetrators often seek out victims with common qualities or circumstances or situations—we are fungible to them so long as we are similarly accessible—but victims do not seek out victimization at all, and their nonvictimized sexual behavior is no more relevant to an allegation of sexual force than is the perpetrator's consensual sex life, such as it may be.

So far the leading case, consistent with the direction of rape law,[34] has found that the victim's sexual history with other individuals is not relevant, although consensual history with the individual perpetrator may be. With sexual harassment law, we are having to deinstitutionalize sexual misogyny step by step. Some defendants' counsel have even demanded that plaintiffs submit to an unlimited psychiatric examination,[35] which could have a major practical impact on victims' effective access to relief. How much sexual denigration will victims have to face to secure their right to be free from sexual denigration? A major part of the harm of sexual harassment is the public and private sexualization of a woman against her will. Forcing her to speak about her sexuality is a common part of this process, subjection to which leads women to seek relief through the courts. Victims who choose to complain know they will have to endure repeated verbalizations of the specific sexual abuse they complain about. They undertake this even though most experience it as an exacerbation, however unavoidable, of the original abuse. For others, the necessity to repeat over and over the verbal insults, innuendos, and propositions to which they have been subjected leads them to decide that justice is not worth such indignity.

Most victims of sexual harassment, if the incidence data are correct, never file complaints. Many who are viciously violated are so ashamed to make that violation public that they submit in silence, although it devastates their self-respect and often their health, or they leave the job without complaint, although it threatens their survival and that of their families. If, on top of the cost of making the violation known, which is painful enough, they know that the entire range of their sexual experiences, attitudes, preferences, and practices are to be discoverable, few such actions will be brought, no matter how badly the victims are hurt. Faced with a choice between forced sex in their jobs or schools on the one hand and forced sexual disclosure for the public record on the other, few will choose the latter. This cruel paradox would effectively eliminate much progress in this area.[36]

Put another way, part of the power held by perpetrators of sexual harassment is the threat of making the sexual abuse public knowledge. This functions like blackmail in silencing the victim and allowing the abuse to continue. It is a fact that public knowledge of sexual abuse is often worse for the abused than the abuser, and victims who choose to complain have the courage to take that on. To add to their burden the potential of making public their entire personal life, information that has no relation to the fact or severity of the incidents complained of, is to make the law of this area implicitly complicit in the blackmail that keeps victims from exercising their rights and to enhance the impunity of perpetrators. In effect, it means open season on anyone who does not want her entire intimate life available to public scrutiny. In other contexts such private information has been found intrusive, irrelevant, and more prejudicial than probative.[37] To allow it to be discovered in the sexual harassment area amounts to a requirement that women be further violated in order to be permitted to seek relief for having been violated. I also will never understand why a violation's severity, or even its likelihood of occurrence, is measured according to the character of the violated, rather than by what was done to them.

In most reported sexual harassment cases, especially rulings on law more than on facts, the trend is almost uniformly favorable to the development of this claim. At least, so far. This almost certainly does not represent social reality. It may not even reflect most cases in litigation.[38] And there may be conflicts building, for example, between those who value speech in the abstract more than they value people in the concrete. Much of sexual harassment is words. Women are called "cunt," "pussy," "tits";[39] they are invited to a company party with "bring your own bathing suits (women, either half)";[40] they confront their tormenter in front of their manager with, "You have called me a fucking bitch," only to be answered, "No, I didn't. I called you a

fucking cunt."[41] One court issued an injunction against inquiries such as "Did you get any over the weekend?"[42] One case holds that where "a person in a position to grant or withhold employment opportunities uses that authority to attempt to induce workers and job seekers to submit to sexual advances, prostitution, and pornographic entertainment, and boasts of an ability to intimidate those who displease him," sexual harassment (and intentional infliction of emotional distress) are pleaded.[43] Sexual harassment can also include pictures; visual as well as verbal pornography is commonly used as part of the abuse. Yet one judge found, apparently as a matter of law, that the pervasive presence of pornography in the workplace did not constitute an unreasonable work environment because, "For better or worse, modern America features open displays of written and pictorial erotica. Shopping centers, candy stores and prime time television regularly display naked bodies and erotic real or simulated sex acts. Living in this milieu, the average American should not be legally offended by sexually explicit posters."[44] She did not say she was offended, she said she was discriminated against based on her sex. If the pervasiveness of an abuse makes it nonactionable, no inequality sufficiently institutionalized to merit a law against it would be actionable.

Further examples of this internecine conflict have arisen in education. At the Massachusetts Institute of Technology pornography used to be shown every year during registration.[45] Is this *not* sexual harassment in education, as a group of women complained it was, because attendance is voluntary, both sexes go, it is screened in groups rather than individually, nobody is directly propositioned, and it is pictures and words? Or is it sexual harassment because the status and treatment of women, supposedly secured from sex-differential harm, are damaged, including that of those who do not attend, which harms individuals and undermines sex equality; therefore pictures and words are the media through which the sex discrimination is accomplished?

For feminist jurisprudence, the sexual harassment attempt suggests that if a legal initiative is set up right from the beginning, meaning if it is designed from women's real experience of violation, it can make some difference. To a degree women's experience can be written into law, even in some tension with the current doctrinal framework. Women who want to resist their victimization with legal terms that imagine it is not inevitable can be given some chance, which is more than they had before. Law is not everything in this respect, but it is not nothing either.[46] Perhaps the most important lesson is that the mountain can be moved. When we started, there was absolutely no judicial precedent for allowing a sex discrimination suit for sexual harassment. Sometimes even the law does something for the first time.

NOTES

1. The first case to hold this was Williams v. Saxbe, 413 F. Supp. 654 (D.D.C. 1976), followed by Barnes v. Costle, 561 F.2d 983 (D.C. Cir. 1977).
2. Alexander v. Yale University, 459 F. Supp. 1 (D. Conn. 1977), *aff'd*, 631 F.2d 178 (2d Cir. 1980).
3. Rabidue v. Osceola Refining, 584 F. Supp. 419, 427 n.29 (E.D. Mich. 1984).
4. See data at "Rally against Rape," notes 1–3.
5. U.S. Merit System Protection Board, *Sexual Harassment in the Federal Workplace: Is It a Problem?* (1981).
6. National Advisory Council on Women's Education Programs, Department of Education, *Sexual Harassment: A Report on the Sexual Harassment of Students* (1980); Joseph DiNunzio and Christina Spaulding, Radcliffe Union of Students, *Sexual Harassment Survey (Harvard/Radcliffe)* 20–29 (1984): 32 percent of tenured female faculty, 49 percent of nontenured female faculty, 42 percent of female graduate stu-

dents, and 34 percent of female undergraduate students report some incident of sexual harassment from a person with authority over them; one-fifth of undergraduate women report being forced into unwanted sexual activity at some point in their lives. The Sexual Harassment Survey Committee, *A Survey of Sexual Harassment at UCLA* (185), finds 11 percent of female faculty (N = 86), 7 percent of female staff (N = 650), and 7 percent of female students (N = 933) report being sexually harassed at UCLA.

7. If a superior sexually harasses a subordinate, the company and the supervisor are responsible if the victim can prove it happened. 29 C.F.R. 1604.11(c). With coworkers, if the employer can be shown to have known about it or should have known about it, the employer can be held responsible. 29 C.F.R. 1604.11(d). Sexual harassment by clients or other third parties is decided on the specific facts. *See* 29 C.F.R. 1604.11(e).

8. The EEOC's requirement that the employer must receive notice in coworker cases suggests that they do not understand this point. 29 C.F.R. 1604.11(d). One reasonable rationale for such a rule, however, is that a coworker situation does not become hierarchical, hence actionable as *employment* discrimination, until it is reported to the workplace hierarchy and condoned through adverse action or inaction.

In one inferior-to-superior case, staff was alleged to have sexually harassed a woman manager because of an interracial relationship. Moffett v. Gene B. Glick Co., Inc., 621 F. Supp. 244 (D. Ind. 1985). An example of a third-party case that failed of "positive proof" involved a nurse bringing a sex discrimination claim alleging she was denied a promotion that went to a less qualified female nurse because that other nurse had a sexual relationship with the doctor who promoted her. King v. Palmer, 598 F. Supp. 65, 69 (D.D.C. 1984). The difficulty of proving "an explicit sexual relationship between [plaintiff] and [defendant], each of whom vigorously deny it exists or even occurred," id., is obvious.

9. Catharine A. MacKinnon, *Sexual Harassment of Working Women* 203 (1979).

10. Dissenters from the denial of rehearing en banc in Vinson v. Taylor attempted a revival, however. *Vinson v. Taylor,* 760 F.2d 1330, 1333 n.7 (Circuit Judges Bork, Scalia, and Starr).

11. Scott v. Sears & Roebuck, 605 F. Supp. 1047, 1051, 1055 (N.D. Ill. 1985).

12. Coley v. Consolidated Rail, 561 F. Supp. 647, 648 (1982).

13. Meritor Savings Bank, FSB v. Vinson, 106 S.Ct. 2399 (1986); Horn v. Duke Homes, 755 F.2d 599 (7th Cir. 1985); Crimm v. Missouri Pacific R.R. Co., 750 F.2d 703 (8th Cir. 1984); Simmons v. Lyons, 746 F.2d 265 (5th Cir. 1984); Craig v. Y & Y Snacks, 721 F.2d 77 (3d Cir. 1983); Katz v. Dole, 709 F.2d 251 (4th Cir. 1983); Miller v. Bank of America, 600 F.2d 211 (9th Cir. 1979); Tomkins v. Public Service Electric & Gas Co., 568 F.2d 1044 (3d Cir. 1977); Barnes v. Costle, 561 F.2d 983 (D.C. Cir. 1977); Bundy v. Jackson, 641 F.2d 934 (D.C. Cir. 1981); Henson v. City of Dundee, 682 F.2d 897 (11th Cir. 1982) (sexual harassment, whether quid pro quo or condition of work, is sex discrimination under Title VII). The court in *Rabidue* was particularly explicit on the rootedness of sexual harassment in the text of Title VII. Rabidue v. Osceola Refining, 584 F. Supp. 419, 427–29 (E.D. Mich. 1984). Woerner v. Brzeczek, 519 F. Supp. 517 (E.D. Ill. 1981) exemplifies the same view under the equal protection clause. Gender has also been found to create a class for a 42 U.S.C. § 1985(3) claim if the injury is covered by the Fourteenth Amendment. Scott v. City of Overland Park, 595 F. Supp. 520, 527–529 (D. Kansas 1984). *See also* Skadegaard v. Farrell, 578 F. Supp. 1209 (D.N.J. 1984). An additional question has been whether sexual harassment is intentional discrimination. Courts have been unimpressed with intent-related defenses like, he did it but "it was his way of communicating." French v. Mead Corporation, 333 FEP Cases 635, 638 (1983). Or, I did all of those things, but I am just a touchy person. Professor Sid Peck, in connection with the sexual harassment action brought against him by Ximena Bunster and other women at Clark University, reportedly stated that he exchanged embraces and kisses as greetings and to establish a feeling of safety and equality. *Worcester Magazine,*
Dec. 3, 1980, at 3; *Boston Phoenix,* Feb. 24, 1981, at 6. *But see* Norton v. Vartanian, where Judge Zobel finds, inter alia, that the overtures were never sexually intended, so no sexual harassment occurred. 31 FEP Cases 1260 (D. Mass. 1983). The implicit view, I guess, is that the perpetrator's intent is beside the point of the harm, that so long as the allegations meet other requirements, the perpetrator does not need to intend that the sexual advances be discriminatory or even sex-based for them to constitute sex discrimination. Katz v. Dole holds that a showing of "sustained verbal sexual abuse" is sufficient to prove "the intentional nature of the harassment." 709 F. 2d, 255–56 esp. 256 n.7. As I understand it, this means that so long as the harassment is not credibly inadvertent, acts of this nature are facially discriminatory. Intentionality is inferred from the acts; the acts themselves, repeated after indications of disinclination and nonreceptivity, show the mental animus of bias. In short, the acts may not be intentionally discriminatory, yet still constitute intentional discrimination. The upshot seems to be that sexual harassment allegations are essentially treated as facial discrimination.

14. Zabkowicz v. West Bend Co., 589 F. Supp. 780, 782–83 (E.D. Wisc. 1984).

15. 589 F. Supp., 784.

16. Henson v. City of Dundee, 29 FEP Cases 787, 793 (11th Cir. 1983). In Huebschen v. Dept. of Health, 32 FEP Cases 1582 (7th Cir. 1983), the facts were found not gender-based on a doctrinally dubious rationale. There a man was found to have been sexually harassed by his female superior. This result was reversed on the partial basis that it did not present a valid gender claim. Basically the court said that the case wasn't gender-based because it was individual. I remember this argument: the events were individual, not gender-based, because there was no employment problem until the relationship went sour. In my view, if the defendant is a hierarchical superior and the plaintiff is damaged in employment for reasons of sexual pressure vis à vis that superior, especially if they are a woman and a man, a claim is stated. It is one thing to recognize that men as a gender have more power in sexual

relations in ways that may cross-cut employment hierarchies. This is not what the court said here. This case may have been, on its facts, a personal relationship that went bad, having nothing to do with gender. But these are not the facts as found at trial. The Court of Appeals did suggest that this plaintiff was hurt as an individual, not as a man, because the employment situation was fine so long as the sexual situation was fine—that is, until it wasn't. After which, because of which, the man was fired. Maybe men always stay individuals, even when women retaliate against them through their jobs for sexual refusals. But, doctrinally, I do not understand why this treatment does not state a gender-based claim. Not to, seems to allow employment opportunities to be conditional on the *continuing* existence of an undesired sexual relationship, where those opportunities would never be allowed to be conditioned on such a relationship's *initial* existence. Women have at times been gender female personally: "As Walter Scott acknowledges, he 'was attracted to her as a woman, on a personal basis. Her femaleness was a matter of attraction.'" Estate of Scott v. deLeon, 37 FEP Cases 563, 566 (1985).

17. *Barnes v. Costle* is the classic case. All of the cases in note 13 above are quid pro cases except *Vinson, Katz, Bundy,* and *Henson.* Note that the distinction is actually two poles of a continuum. A constructive discharge, in which a woman leaves the job because of a constant condition of sexual harassment, is an environmental situation that becomes quid pro quo.

18. In Vinson v. Taylor, 23 FEP Cases 37 (D.D.C. 1980), plaintiff accused defendant supervisor of forced sex; the trial court found, "If the plaintiff and Taylor did engage in an intimate or sexual relationship . . . [it] was a voluntary one by plaintiff." At 42. Vinson won a right to a new trial for environmental sexual harassment. Meritor Savings Bank, FSB v. Vinson, 106 S. Ct. 2399 (1986). *See also* Cummings v. Walsh Construction Co., 561 F. Supp. 872 (S.D. Ga. 1983) (victim accused perpetrator of consummated sex); Micari v. Mann, 481 N.Y.S.2d 967 (Sup. Ct. 1984) (students accused professor of

forced sex as part of acting training; won and awarded damages).

19. Vinson v. Taylor, 753 F.2d 141 (D.C. Cir. 1985), *aff'd* 106 S. Ct. 2399 (1983).

20. Micari v. Mann, 481 N.Y.S.2d 967 (Sup. Ct. 1984).

21. Cummings v. Walsh Construction Co., 31 FEP Cases 930, 938 (S. D. Ga. 1983).

22. *Bundy* and *Henson,* note 13 above, establish environmental sexual harassment as a legal claim. Both that claim and the plaintiff's credibility in asserting it, since she was abused for such a long time, were raised in Vinson v. Taylor before the U.S. Supreme Court.

23. Huebschen v. Department of Health, 547 F. Supp. 1168 (W.D. Wisc. 1982).

24. Heelan v. Johns-Manville, 451 F. Supp. 1382 (D. Colo. 1978). *See also* Sensibello v. Globe Security Systems, 34 FEP Cases 1357 (E.D. Pa. 1964).

25. Katz v. Dole, 709 F.2d 251, 254 n.3 (4th Cir. 1983) ("A person's private and consensual sexual activities do not constitute a waiver of his or her legal protections against unwelcome and unsolicited sexual harassment").

26. An attorney discussed this case with me in a confidential conversation.

27. Gan v. Kepro Circuit Systems, 28 FEP Cases 639, 641 (E.D. Mo. 1982). *See also* Reichman v. Bureau of Affirmative Action, 536 F. Supp. 1149, 1177 (M.D. Penn. 1982).

28. Morgan v. Hertz Corp., 542 F. Supp. 123, 128 (W.D. Tenn. 1981).

29. EEOC v. Sage Realty, 507 F. Supp. 599 (S.D.N.Y. 1981).

30. Pryor v. U.S. Gypsum Co., 585 F. Supp. 311, 316 n.3 (W.D. Mo. 1984). The issue here was whether the injuries could be brought under worker's compensation. The suggestion is that women who work in adult entertainment might be covered under that law for sexual harassment on their jobs.

31. EEOC Decision 82–13, 29 FEP Cases 1855 (1982).

32. Commission Decision 83–1, EEOC Decisions (CCH) 6834 (1983).

33. Koster v. Chase Manhattan, 93 F.R.D. 471 (S.D.N.Y. 1982).

34. Priest v. Rotary, 32 FEP Cases 1065 (N.D. Cal. 1983) is consistent with congressional actions in criminal rape, Fed. R. Evid., Rule 412, 124 *Cong. Rec.* H11944–11945 (daily ed. Oct. 10, 1978) and 124 *Cong. Rec.* S18580 (daily ed. Oct. 12, 1978) (evidence of prior consensual sex, unless with defendant, is inadmissible in rape cases) and with developments in civil rape cases. Fults v. Superior Court, 88 Cal. App. 3d 899 (1979).

35. Vinson v. Superior Court, Calif. Sup. SF 24932 (rev. granted, Sept. 1985).

36. A further possibility—more political fantasy than practical—might be to insist that if the plaintiff's entire sexual history is open to inspection, the defendant's should be also: all the rapes, peeping at his sister, patronizing of prostitutes, locker-room jokes, use of pornography, masturbation fantasies, adolescent experimentation with boyfriends, fetishes, and so on.

37. *See, e.g.,* U.S. v. Kasto, 584 F.2d 268, 271–72 (8th Cir. 1978), *cert. denied*, 440 U.S. 930 (1979); State v. Bernier, 491 A.2d 1000, 1004 (R.I. 1985).

38. Another reason women do not bring claims is fear of countersuit. The relationship between sexual harassment and defamation is currently unsettled on many fronts. *See, e.g.,* Walker v. Gibson, 604 F. Supp. 916 (N.D. Ill. 1985) (action for violation of First Amendment will not lie against employer Army for hearing on unwarranted sexual harassment charge); Spisak v. McDole, 472 N.E.2d 347 (Ohio 1984) (defamation claim can be added to sexual harassment claim); Equal Employment Opportunity Commission v. Levi Stráuss & Co., 515 F. Supp. 640 (N.D. Ill. 1981) (defamation action brought allegedly in response to employee allegation of sexual harassment is not necessarily retaliatory, if brought in good faith to vindicate reputation); Arenas v. Ladish Co., 619 F. Supp. 1304 (E.D. Wisc. 1985) (defamation claim may be brought for sexual harassment in the presence of others, not barred by exclusivity provision of worker's compensation law); Ross v. Comsat, 34 FEP Cases 261 (D. Md. 1984) (man sues company for retaliation in discharge following his complaint against woman at company for sexual harassment). Educational institutions have been sued for acting when, after investigation, they find the complaints to be true. Barnes v. Oody, 28 FEP Cases 816 (E.D. Tenn. 1981) (summary judgment granted that arbitrators' holding for women who brought sexual harassment claim collaterally estops defamation action by sexual harassment defendant; immunity applies to statements in official investigation). Although it is much more difficult to prove defamation than to defeat a sexual harassment claim, threats of countersuit have intimidated many victims.

39. Rabidue v. Osceola Refining, 584 F. Supp. 423 (E.D. Mich. 1984).

40. Cobb v. Dufresne-Henry, 603 F. Supp. 1048, 1050 (D. Vt. 1985).

41. McNabb v. Cub Foods, 352 N.W. 2d 378, 381 (Minn. 1984).

42. Morgan v. Hertz Corp., 27 FEP Cases at 994.

43. Seratis v. Lane, 30 FEP 423, 425 (Cal. Super. 1980).

44. Rabidue v. Osceola Refining, 584 F. Supp. 419, 435 (E.D. Mich. 1984). This went to whether the treatment was sex-based. Note that the plaintiff did not say that she was offended but that she was discriminated against.

45. Women students at MIT filed a sexual harassment claim under Title IX, which was dismissed for lack of jurisdiction. Baker v. M.I.T., U.S. Dept. Education Office of Civil Rights #01-85-2013 (Sept. 20, 1985).

46. Particularly given the formative contribution to the women's movement of the struggles against racial and religious stigma, persecution, and violence, it is heartening to find a Jewish man and a Black man recovering for religious and racial harassment, respectively, based on sexual harassment precedents. Weiss v. U.S., 595 F. Supp. 1050 (E.D. Va. 1984) (pattern of anti-Semitic verbal abuse actionable based on *Katz* and *Henson*); Taylor v. Jones, 653 F.2d 1193, 1199 (8th Cir. 1981) (*Bundy* cited as basis for actionability of environmental racial harassment under Title VII).

CHAPTER 19

VIOLENCE AGAINST LESBIANS

RUTHANN ROBSON

ABSTRACT

Radical feminist theory not only recognizes that gendered power relations between men and women dominate in a patriarchal society; it also understands heterosexuality as a system of oppressive social control, not just a private sexual preference. Heterosexuality for all intents and purposes is demanded, enforced, taken for granted, and codified into law in our society. Violence against lesbians (and gay men), which has only been recognized recently by the federal hate crime law of 1990, has existed throughout the history of patriarchal societies.

In this chapter Robson describes violence against lesbians, interweaving throughout the discussion references to the "rule of law." The newly existing hate crimes acts, for the most part, simply authorize the counting and recording of hate or bias crimes. By hate crimes the various state and federal laws mean crimes that are motivated by the perpetrators' prejudice toward or hatred of the victim because of her (or his) race, religion, ethnicity, or sexual orientation. Robson describes the flaws in the federal law. Ironically, the law provides no penalties for such crimes. Its deterrent value is therefore virtually nonexistent. In some jurisdictions there is a sentencing enhancement mandate. This means that when a crime of violence occurs, if the perpetrator has demonstrated hate or prejudice, the judge is empowered to increase the sentence over and above that designated for the crime. However, sentencing enhancement has been successfully challenged in different jurisdictions on the basis that the perpetrators were exercising their rights of "free speech" in expressing their prejudice.

Robson argues that the rule of law, even at its best, manifests its own violence against lesbians. For example, when a lesbian enters the legal system, it is one over which she—as a lesbian—has no control. She must face the antilesbian attitudes and behavior of the court's personnel. If she is "closeted," she may have to reveal her lesbian identity, which is punishable in both legal and nonlegal ways. Moreover, Robson shows how remedies in the law as it exists now are often not available to lesbian victims.

Robson concludes with a call for lesbian self-empowerment. She argues that violence against lesbians will not stop unless lesbians define and develop their own strategies—both inside and outside the law. What do you think of this approach? What might some specific examples of this be? Can you spell out ways in which the larger society and the legal system must be changed to end violence against lesbians?

Most of us do not need statistics to tell us about the violence against lesbians. We have lived our lives as targets for hurled bottles, beery spit, and even bullets; we have been taunted by jeers, incessant threats of rape, and whispers. The violence against us is so pervasive as to be unremarkable. We live in it as the proverbial fish in water.

There has been an increasing awareness, in the last few years, about the violence against lesbians, as well as gay men and bisexuals, and a linking of this violence with the violence perpetrated on the basis of other group identities, such as race, ethnicity, religion, culture, and gender. Much of this awareness is due to the efforts of the Anti-Violence Project of the National Gay & Lesbian Task Force. Along with independent researchers and other antiviolence projects throughout the United States, the Anti-Violence Project has been documenting incidents of violence since the early 1980s.[1] According to their 1990 report, there were 1,588 incidents of anti-gay/lesbian violence in the United States that year. The report does not distinguish between lesbians and gay men, although some other surveys do. The social science wisdom con-

cerning violence against lesbians consists of comparisons with the violence against gay men: we are much less likely to report the violence against us (one survey concludes that 91 percent of lesbians do not report the violence to any community agency); we are more likely than gay men to experience the violence from family members; and we are more likely to be sexually assaulted.

The rule of law has also begun to document the violence against lesbians. Connecticut became the first state, in 1987, to pass a hate crimes statistics act, although this act contained only the vaguest definitions. In 1990, Congress passed the federal Hate Crime Statistics Act, which provides for the compilation of statistics of hate or bias crimes, specifically defined as "crimes that manifest evidence of prejudice based upon race, religion, sexual orientation, or ethnicity." The inclusion of sexual orientation as a category was the result of intense lobbying by lesbian and gay activists amidst much congressional controversy. The compromise necessary in Congress to preserve the sexual orientation category included a statement in the act that "the American family is the foundation of American society; federal policy should encourage the well-being, financial security, and health of the American family; and schools should not de-emphasize the critical value of American family life." Any doubts about the function of this paean to the family operating as

---

Source: Ruthann Robson, *Lesbian (Out)law: Survival under the Rule of Law,* Firebrand Books, Ithaca, NY 14850. © 1992 by Ruthann Robson. Originally published as *The Violence against Us.*

an antidote to the mention of sexual orientation is resolved by the statute's next section: "Nothing in this Act shall be construed, nor shall any funds appropriated to carry out the purpose of the Act be used, to promote or encourage homosexuality." The federal act also includes an antidote to any possible judicial interpretation that a law requiring the collection of statistics about the violence against lesbians might mean that discrimination against lesbians is disfavored: "Nothing in this section creates a right to bring an action, including an action based on discrimination due to sexual orientation."[2]

Perhaps ironically, the very act which seeks to collect statistics about the violence against lesbians is itself a manifestation of that violence. Many legal reformers believe that the repeal of statutes criminalizing lesbian sex and the passage of statutes protecting lesbians from discrimination are necessary steps in the quest to end violence against lesbians, but the act specifically rejects these goals. The signing of the Hate Crime Statistics Act marked the first time openly gay men and lesbians were invited to the White House. Yet under the very rule of law they have been invited to celebrate, lesbians cannot be promoted or encouraged or have any remedies against discrimination. Such ironies do not negate the federal act as an advancement, but do indicate the violence against lesbians that inheres even in rules of law that implicitly disapprove of the violence against lesbians.

The federal act also manifests violence against lesbians through at least three strategies of categorization of our identities. First, the category *sexual orientation* is defined in the act as "consensual homosexuality and heterosexuality." Perhaps "consensual" is meant to modify both homosexuality and heterosexuality, but even assuming such a charitable interpretation, the very inclusion of heterosexuality is problematic. As in discrimination discourse, the category operates to obscure

power differentials between heterosexuals and lesbians or gay men. For example, if a heterosexual man enters a lesbian bar and makes explicit heterosexual advances to the lesbian customers, and the lesbians shove him into the bathroom and lock him in there because they find such flagrant heterosexuality inappropriate and offensive, the lesbians have committed a hate crime, manifesting "evidence of prejudice" based on the sexual orientation of heterosexuality.

Second, the omission of the category *gender* from the federal act artificially isolates lesbianism. If a man rapes a lesbian and says, "What you need is a good fuck, dyke," the word *dyke* may be evidence of a hate crime. However, if the man rapes the same lesbian and neglects to say the word *dyke,* or says other words as well, or there are no other factors indicating his prejudice against lesbians, it might not be a hate crime. Not only is her lesbianism irrelevant, but rape itself is not a crime that "manifests evidence of prejudice" based on any category that the act recognizes.

Third, and most insidiously, the insistence on categorization itself violently atomizes us into separate identities. A rape of a lesbian, to use this example again, is not necessarily separable into discrete identities. As quoted in a recent article: "As I was being raped, I was called a dyke and a cunt. The rapist used those terms as if they were interchangeable. And as I talk to other women who have been raped—straight and gay—I hear similar stories. Was my attack antilesbian? Or was it antiwoman? I think the facts are simple. I was raped because as a woman I'm considered rapeable and, as a lesbian, I'm considered a threat. How can you separate those two things?"[3] Given the federal act, to count as a hate crime, the lesbian must stress her identity as a lesbian over her identity as a woman and hope that the FBI statisticians agree with her. A similar choice of categories occurs if the lesbian has other identities implicated in the crime but not included in the act, such as those based on old age or disability. To be counted, the lesbian must discount these identities if the relevant statute discounts them.

However, even when the lesbian has other identities implicated in the crime, and such identities are included in the act, choices of categories occur. Thus, in state statutes that include gender, the gender/sexuality dichotomy is not dissolved but has different consequences. These consequences are the same for all identities that are categories under a statistics act. For example, if under the federal act the rapist also makes racial slurs, such "evidence of prejudice" should mandate the statistic as a hate crime based on race. But a single incident is supposedly only to be reported once. Does the FBI statistician choose race or sexual orientation? Does the statistician ask the African-American lesbian whether she thinks she was raped because she is African-American or because she is a lesbian? Does the statistician ask the rapist? Any choice does violence to our experiences of the violence against us.

Perhaps paradoxically, however, the absence of categorization in a hate crime statistics act may be a fourth kind of violence. Just as the lack of sexual orientation in a state statute is a violent denial of the violence against lesbians, and the lack of gender in the federal act is a violent denial of our experiences of the violence against lesbians, and the insistence on categorization violently atomizes lesbians into separate identities, the lack of any categories constitutes violence. Many opponents of hate crime bills seek to delete references to specific groups, usually lesbians and gay men. Failing that, another tactic is to seek to delete mention of any group identity. A hate crime act that mandates the collection of statistics of any crime based on bias, bigotry, or hate may appear to be magnanimously broad, but it actually erases the reali-

ties of violence. It also gives government officials wide latitude to determine the contours of bias, bigotry, and hate—allowing for the possibility that violence against lesbians is not biased, bigoted, or hateful—merely natural.

The power of the government official is also exercised in the determination of what counts as a hate crime, regardless of the category. A crime becomes a hate crime when government bureaucrats decide that it should be. The government workers making such determinations include police officers. Police departments are increasingly training officers to make final determinations about whether a suspected bias incident can be confirmed as such. For example, the New York City Police Department's Bias Incident Investigation Unit has issued guidelines stressing the officer's "common sense" in confirming bias incidents. The guidelines list considerations such as motive, display of offensive symbols, suspects' statements, victims' perceptions, and similarity to previous incidents. The guidelines even note that borderline cases should be resolved in favor of confirmation, although they also warn that "mere mention of a bias remark does not necessarily make an incident bias motivated," again stressing the use of common sense judgment. Given the historic hostility of law enforcement officials to lesbians—and the continuing evidence that the perpetrators of violence against us are quite likely to be police officers—it is not only the more cynical among us who find trusting the common sense of police officers to recognize the violence against lesbians a bit ludicrous.

Critiques of the federal act mandating the collection of statistics often operate on the symbolic level because the act itself operates on this level. As a rule of law, the act is neither rule nor law. It provides no rights, no remedies, no penalties. It only requires the Attorney General to "acquire data" from 1990 until 1995 about crimes that manifest evidence of prejudice. Many believe that symbolism is insufficient to deter the violence against lesbians.

The larger question is whether any rule of law can deter this violence. Those who find symbolism and statistics insufficient often advocate enhancement of penalties or more rigorous enforcement of criminal laws. Yet even these rules of law rely upon the formulation of a relatively new term, *hate crime*—its two parts in tension with each other. On the one hand, hate is usually not against any rule of law. On the other hand, a crime is a crime regardless of hate. This tension permeates the responses of the rule of law to the violence against lesbians, resulting in two different perspectives: the special and the neutral.

The special model proposes that some crimes are worse than others and should be accorded special recognition. This is the model that looms behind the federal statistics act, allowing for special treatment in the statistical compilation of crimes evidencing hate. The enhancement of penalties proposal is also within this model. Penalty enhancement can be implemented by a statute that allows a judge to impose longer prison sentences on a finding that the crime was motivated by prejudice. For example, the New Hampshire enhancement statute, allowing judges to impose longer sentences in circumstances including prior convictions, was recently amended to include a hate crime provision: an extended term of imprisonment may be imposed if the defendant "was substantially motivated to commit the crime because of hostility toward the victim's religion, race, creed, sexual orientation, national origin, or sex."[4]

The neutral model suggests that existing criminal laws need to be enforced impartially. This model exhorts the rigorous enforcement of criminal laws and penalties, no matter that the victim is a lesbian. It is a principle advanced by lesbian and gay legal reformers protesting against judges who impose lenient

sentences, or prosecutors who refuse to prosecute crimes committed against lesbians or gay men. A neutral principle is important any time a perpetrator raises a defense based upon the unimportance of the victim. While in practice, most of us recognize that the neutral principle is farcical given power differentials, we may nevertheless believe that if it were reality, the violence against lesbians would be deterred. According to this perspective, what is needed is not special protection but equal treatment. And rigorous law enforcement.

The special approach and neutral approach often conflict in legal theory.[5] However, if we put lesbians at the center—rather than legal theory and its demands for consistency—perhaps this conflict is not troubling. Such a perspective would allow us to avail ourselves of whatever strategies the rules of law offer in order to deter the violence against lesbians. Symbolism, statistics, enhancement, and enforcement—whatever is possible in our particular political situations.

Yet, by putting lesbians at the center, problems other than inconsistencies within legal theory become important. Many of the lesbians at the center experience the rule of law, particularly the criminal justice system, as racist, classist, and elitist. This experience impacts upon any strategies that implicate the criminal justice system, notwithstanding the empirical data that the perpetrators of the violence against us are most likely to be young white men from relatively privileged backgrounds. Even if we can put such considerations aside, or isolate our lesbian identities from all our other identities, the rule of law manifests its own violence against us. This violence makes it difficult to have confidence in the rule of law's interest in our lesbian survival.

The violence of the rule of law may seem to fade when we compare it to the violence against us that we endure daily. This daily violence is magnified and crystalized in the murder of Rebecca Wight and attempted murder of Claudia Brenner. The horror of it has been heard or read by most lesbians; its threatening possibility exists for each of us. The two lovers were camping on the Appalachian Trail in the spring of 1988 when they were assaulted by a barrage of bullets from a man who reportedly lived in a cave and had stalked them on the trail. The man, Stephen Roy Carr, was apprehended and charged with murder. The trial judge rejected his defense that he was provoked to murder them because he witnessed their lesbian lovemaking, and refused to hear evidence about his rejection by women and his mother's lesbianism. The judge convicted him of first degree murder and sentenced him to life imprisonment. Although he appealed, the appellate court agreed with the trial judge: "The sight of naked women engaged in lesbian lovemaking is not adequate provocation to reduce an unlawful killing from murder to voluntary manslaughter."[6] We can claim victory; justice was served.

Yet the jailing of Carr does not breathe life into any lesbian; it is the rule of law that is vindicated and not our lesbian existence. The rule of law punishes Carr, using a neutral approach that the victims did not deserve to be attacked. What remains unaddressed is the defendant's outsider status as an uncivilized "mountain man" that overrides the victims' outsider status as lesbians. What remains unaddressed are the social conditions that produce Carr's violence, although the rule of law encourages us to believe that the underlying violence has been addressed. A less well-known case is that of a New Hampshire man who confessed to the murder of two lesbians, after threatening them many times, because he said he "loathed their life-style." The man was prosecuted unsuccessfully three times and is now free. We cannot claim victory; justice was not served.

Yet one man's freedom does not mean that the lesbians are more dead; it is the rule of law that is implicated, not our lesbian existence. The rights of criminal defendants and the "loopholes" in the law, the trials, the lawyers, the judges, and the juries become the focus.

The rule of law encourages us to believe that it can redress and deter the violence against us, and in believing this, we are domesticated. But even when the perpetrator is quickly apprehended, convicted, and sentenced, the violence against us is not redressed or deterred. We find it almost impossible to think about other methods of redress or deterrence because we have so internalized the methodologies of the rules of law. The criminal justice system operates as therapeutic, and the critiques of therapy that are surfacing within lesbian theory are relevant. The prosecution solution is therapeutic in the sense that it is individualized and based more on our feelings about reality than our realities.

For lesbians who survive violence and enter the labyrinth of the criminal justice system as victims, the therapeutic effect of the rules of law can perpetuate the attack rather than redress it. The lesbian victims become part of a system over which they have no control; the prosecutor's career and the judge's calendar are the paramount considerations. Victims face the antilesbian attitudes of court system personnel. They face the possibility of accusations that they provoked the attack. Lesbians who are closeted face the public revelation of an identity that can be lawfully penalized in a variety of ways. This so-called secondary victimization can be as violent as the initial violence.[7] It domesticates us by absorbing our challenge to the violence against us into its own perpetuation of that violence. Even seemingly nonviolent responses within the rule of law can be domesticating. We are domesticated when we channel our fury at being attacked into a call to the FBI hotline. We are domesticated when we are grateful for an understanding officer from the bias task force unit. We are domesticated whenever we allow our own rage about the violence against us to be funneled into a belief that the rule of law will take care of everything.

For lesbians who survive violence and choose not to enter the labyrinth of the criminal justice system—statistically about 90 percent of us—the rule of law is also domesticating. I have even heard advocates within our own communities insist that each of us has a responsibility to report the violence against us to the police and agitate for prosecutions. For lesbians who do not follow this advice, domestication can take the form of guilt and an assumption of personal responsibility for the violence we have suffered. The (false) promise that the rule of law will remedy the violence against us if only we will let it can domesticate us and prevent us from taking other action.

We are domesticated when our attempts to deter the violence against us without the rule of law are discouraged by the rule of law, as two recent examples from New York illustrate. In one, lesbians collaborated with gay men and others to form a civil patrol group self-named the Pink Panthers. They are being sued for trademark infringement by the entertainment company that has the legal rights to the term *pink panther*. In a second example, lesbians collaborated with other women to attempt yet another "take back the night" march but were denied a parade permit and threatened with arrest for disorderly conduct. A "take back the night" march by "local residents" aimed at eliminating "prostitutes" from the same area was, at almost the same time, unharassed.

Thus, even when we centralize our lesbianism and demand that the legal system address the violence against us, or we attempt

to address the violence apart from the legal system, we cannot be certain we are using the rules of law rather than being used by them. This does not mean that we should abandon all our strategies. In the case of the violence against us—as in most situations—legal reforms have definite positive benefits. The recognition in legal discourse that violence against lesbians counts is not insignificant, even when that counting is done in the context of legal language that manifests its own violence against us. The special approach that distinguishes acts done out of hatred for us condemns the hatred, even as it is perpetuated. The neutral approach that accords victims humanity and rejects blaming the victim is an advancement, even if it is a product of an inhumane and victimizing system.

Yet the ways in which the rule of law domesticates lesbian existence includes our own definitions of the violence against us. There is some evidence that many lesbians do not have feelings of entitlement to survival and safety regardless of what the law says. This lack of entitlement may prevent us from considering threats to our survival anything other than usual and inevitable. Within the rules of law, the very definition of crimes can limit our feelings of entitlement to safety. Lesbians need to continue to challenge the limiting of violence against us to legal crimes. From its inception, the lesbian and gay antiviolence movement, like the women against violence movement, has recognized that a violent act may not necessarily fit the elements of a criminal rule of law. The annual NGLTF Anti-Violence reports are broadly entitled "Anti-Gay/Lesbian Violence, Victimization and Defamation." They include incidents of violence that may not be criminal. Given this gap between violence and crime, proposals for the creation of new crimes such as intimidation and harassment seek to expand the rule of law's recognition and punishment of the violence against us. Another proposal is to create or increase civil liability for such acts, so that the victim could sue the perpetrator for money damages. Because such new crimes or civil causes of action often involve acts of speech, they implicate freedom of speech concerns and have caused rifts within the lesbian legal community in the same way that the pornography debates caused rifts within the lesbian/feminist community.[8]

The creation of hate crimes—as acts to be punished because they demonstrate hate—has occurred mostly in municipalities and on college campuses. Such laws generally provide for sanctions in the case of hateful activity, slurs, or epithets indicating bias. Yet because such crimes are often based upon speech or speech acts, such laws are subject to attack under constitutional free speech doctrine. The law engages in a balancing of governmental interests in preventing hate and individual rights to freedom of speech. Such a balancing act is presently being litigated before the United States Supreme Court. The case involves a challenge to a St. Paul, Minnesota ordinance criminalizing the placing of symbols, objects, or graffiti known to arouse "anger, alarm, or resentment" on the basis of "race, color, creed, religion, or gender." As in many other hate crime provisions, sexuality is omitted. The challenger to the law is a white male juvenile, charged with burning a cross on the lawn of the only African-American family in the neighborhood.[9] Many progressive organizations and advocates are divided on the preferable outcome of the case, as they are divided in many situations involving free speech.

For lesbians, the divisions in our theorizing should not necessarily be based upon First Amendment principles of free speech. The First Amendment is a rule of law with its roots in European liberal individualism and property-based nations. Its value to lesbians must be decided by us, not assumed by us. Our thinking in this area often suffers from the internalization of the propaganda that surrounds free speech. Free speech is a "fundamental value" we like to think is enshrined within the rule of law, just like equality. Yet just as equality is not as fundamental to the rule of law as we might like to think, neither is free speech. When the speech that is supposedly free is lesbian speech, the government routinely suppresses it. Under obscenity laws, the government seizes lesbian books. In prosecutions for obscenity the word *lesbian* often appears in recitations of the titles of the books seized, as if the word alone was proof positive. In the recent National Endowment of the Arts controversy, Congress passed a law forbidding arts grants to be used to "promote, disseminate or produce" art which included depictions of "homoeroticism."[10] That lesbians and others fighting against the repression of lesbian speech often rely on the rule of law's enshrinement of free speech should not necessarily be determinative of issues relating to hate crimes involving speech.

For just as rules of law allowing the repression of speech are used against lesbians, so too are rules of law forbidding the repression of speech. It is not only that lesbians often have no legal remedy for the violent speech directed against them, including speech acts such as burning a symbol, defacing a sign, or writing antilesbian slogans, but also that when lesbians protest such acts they are condemned for their protest on the basis of a denial of free speech. Lesbians have become the quintessential "thought police" who enforce "politically correct" rules—the dominant culture domesticating us against ourselves.

The passage of rules of law that provide criminal penalties for hateful speech is problematic, and like other protections can easily be turned against us. Imagine a prosecution against a lesbian who said hateful things about a certain man's heterosexuality. Yet the presence of "speech" does not make this situation any different from the situation described earlier, in which lesbians shove a heterosexual man into a bathroom. The presence or absence of speech does not fundamentally alter the problems that lesbians face as we try to deal with the violence against us by deciding whether the rule of law can assist us or not. The rule of law that enshrines freedom of speech must be evaluated from a lesbian centered perspective and not taken as sacred in and of itself. This is not to say that we abandon strategies that might protect our lesbian speech, but only that we do not let the rule of law's speech domesticate our lesbian speech.

We must also not let the rule of law define the violence against us—define it as not-speech, as categorized, as not the rule of law itself. In order to stop the violence against us, we must define it for ourselves and then develop our lesbian strategies—both within and without the rule of law.

REFERENCES

Ruthann Robson, "Incendiary Categories: Lesbian/Violence Law," 2 *Texas Journal of Women and the Law* (1992).

ENDNOTES

1. The National Gay & Lesbian Task Force Policy Institute has issued annual reports entitled *Anti-Gay/Lesbian Violence, Victimization and Defamation.* Annual reports can be ordered from NGLTF at 1734 14th Street, N.W., Washington, D.C. 20009–4309, (202) 332-6483. The NGLTF also provides other information concerning proposed and enacted legislation and is a good place to start for any research into the violence against lesbians.

   Kevin T. Berrill, with the Anti-Violence Project of NGLTF, has served as a one-person clearinghouse on the issue. His articles include, "Anti-Gay Violence and Victimization in the United States: An Overview," 5 *Journal of Interpersonal Violence* 274 (1990).

   Another researcher has written a book on the subject, which includes empirical data on victims and perpetrators. Gary David Comstock, *Violence Against Lesbians and Gay Men* (1991).
2. P.L. 101-275, 104 Stat. 140 amending 28 U.S.C. §534.
3. Quoted in Victoria Brownworth, "An Unreported Crisis," *The Advocate* 50, 52 (November 5, 1991).
4. *N.H. Rev. Stat. Ann.* §651:6 (amended by Chapter 68-1990).
5. Feminist legal theory has been especially troubled by this dichotomy, which has been most pronounced in the legal treatment of women's reproductive capacity, especially pregnancy. Are women to be treated absolutely equal to men? Or do their special circumstances, like pregnancy, warrant special treatment? Absolute equality can be discriminatory, as in formulations that allow discrimination against pregnant women because all pregnant "persons" are being treated that way; the nonexistence of pregnant men is irrelevant. Special treatment can also be discriminatory, as in formulations that allow discrimination against pregnant women for their own "protection."
6. Commonwealth v. Carr, 398 Pa. Super. 306, 580 A.2d 1362 (1990).
7. For a discussion of secondary-victimization, see Kevin Berrill, "Primary and Secondary Victimization in Anti-Gay Hate Crimes," 5 *Journal of Interpersonal Violence* 401 (1990).
8. I first heard the observation that the hate crimes acts may be the sex wars of the 1990s expressed by lesbian attorney Mary Dunlap.
9. R.A.V. v. St. Paul, 90-7675 (1991).
10. P.L. 101-121.

WOMEN WORKERS IN THE CRIMINAL JUSTICE SYSTEM

Part Three explores issues surrounding women working in the criminal justice system. The chapters in this section discuss the various subsystems that make up the criminal justice system—the courts, policing, corrections, victim services, and criminal justice education. The focus here is on the functioning of women from diverse racial/ethnic and class backgrounds within the criminal justice system, the occupational settings in which women work, the level of acceptance of women, the numbers of women in traditionally white male occupations, and the promotion of women to policy-making positions.

As women entered the criminal justice system in increased numbers in the 1970s, the common wisdom at that time was that they would eventually be able to influence and change criminal justice policy and practices that adversely affect the disadvantaged—particularly women offenders, women victims of crime, and women who work throughout the criminal justice hierarchy. As we will see, this has not happened to any great extent. For example, many women who work in the criminal justice system accept the dominant ideology and take punitive stances toward women offenders and/or blame women victims. Therefore, one has to be very careful in assuming that merely adding more women workers to any component of the criminal justice field will in and of itself improve conditions for women. Additionally, not all women are alike. Therefore, race, class, and sexual orientation are equally important in assessing the impact of the greater inclusion of women in the criminal justice system.

It is very difficult to discuss workers in the criminal justice system in any singular way. We know, by way of a contrasting example, that many women who are feminists working in a broader social movement have been able to bring about improved conditions for large groups of women. Largely as a result of these efforts there have been some significant changes in the law that affect women offenders, victims, and workers.

How Does Inclusion of Women Workers in the Criminal Justice System Impact on Offenders and Victims?

It is clear that there have been serious practical as well as moral costs to our nation's democratic principles from the past exclusion of women and minorities from the practice of law and related scholarship. To put these costs in the boldest form: when few women were in either law or the criminal justice system, women victims and women offenders frequently did not receive equal treatment under the law. Inequities ranged from sexually discriminatory sentencing practices toward both female juveniles and female adults (see Chesney-Lind, Chapter 4 herein) to the imposition of more severe criteria for women than for men in order to be released on parole (Erez, 1992).

Women undergraduates are now attracted to the fields of law and criminology in growing numbers, perhaps, in part, because of the influence of the women's and civil rights movements and a growing awareness of the need for more women and greater diversity in these fields.* Students soon become tomorrow's professionals pursuing careers in the law, prosecutors' and public defenders' offices, and other local, state, and federal criminal justice agencies. The presence of large numbers of women, many of whom are committed to social change, has been translated into changes in some of the most stubborn discriminatory practices within the legal system. These changes are found, most notably, in federal legislation pertaining to equal employment opportunity, equal access to education, and equal pay. Other changes in the law are specific to women offenders and victims of crime; these include the repeal of the Muncy Act in Pennsylvania and other state laws that required longer sentences for women than

---

*In 1973 women constituted 19 percent of the student body at John Jay College of Criminal Justice, The City University of New York, the only U.S. college devoted entirely to criminal justice and related majors. By 1993 women made up 49 percent of the undergraduate body (as well as 45 percent of master's and one-third of criminal justice doctoral students). This growth suggests that women have come to view careers in criminal justice as a real option, whereas a few decades ago this was not the case. ("Student Data Statistics," John Jay College of Criminal Justice, 1993.)

for men (see Armstrong, 1977) and the changes in rape laws that make it more possible to obtain convictions (see Spohn and Horney, 1991; *Marital Rape Exemption*, 1991). The growing availability of women lawyers interested in litigating—and, indeed, eager to litigate—in court to achieve change cannot be discounted in reviewing legal changes that are more protective of women's rights (see Epstein, 1983, 1993).

Any victory for equal protection under the law is a result of a long chain of events that frequently starts with feminist, class-conscious, and antiracist political efforts to gain economic, social, and political equity. As the women's movement and other movements for social justice grow, they generate interest in understanding socially structured causes and personal consequences of women's criminality and women's victimization. These interests attract women students to criminology and the law, and this development leads to professionals who build new theories of crime to better understand women's offenses, victimization, and empowerment, and who challenge inequitable social policies.

An impact of the presence of many female and some minority criminologists has been that they and their students become forces for change (see Barak, 1991; Young and Sulton, 1991; Koser Wilson and Moyer, Chapter 27 herein). With the emergence of more professionals, we also gain a better understanding of social process as it pertains to crime and victimization and a recognition that legal change does not always result in social change. Constant monitoring, the creation of procedural guidelines, and basic structural changes in society are all essential for meaningful social change. Many professional and paraprofessional women and minorities in the criminal justice system continue to work for fair treatment of women offenders—who are disproportionately poor and minority. Fair treatment, not always accorded all men, is essential for our criminal justice system—the essence of which should be to provide equitable and just treatment for all offenders and their victims. To be sure, the issue of fair treatment is clearly problematic in a system organized to maintain the status quo and the existing social order.

How Does Inclusion of Women Workers Affect Criminal Justice Practitioners?

Women have experienced a great deal of difficulty in the United States in gaining entrance to occupations that traditionally have employed mostly white men. The criminal justice system, with its many and varied positions (police officer, correctional officer, probation officer, parole officer, forensic psychologist, judge, prosecutor, defense attorney), has always had many formidable barriers to equal employment. Even after discrimination in employment in the public sector was outlawed by federal and most state laws,* the underlying institutional and attitudinal changes necessary for abiding by the law in good faith and thereby treating women fairly have only slowly come about. Moreover, in our system of justice, each instance of employment discrimination requires a separate complaint, sometimes on behalf of a class of persons but often involving a single individual. Such actions are always slow and often personally painful.

In the criminal justice system, the judicial branch appears to have made important strides in recent years, yet few women are to be found in such prestigious positions as judgeships. The state appellate courts in 1991 were only 10 percent female, while African-Americans, men and women together, were 5 percent of all judges, and Latinas/os constituted only 1 percent. At the federal level, women make up 12.3 percent of all federal judges, and minorities are 8.4 percent (Schafran and Wikler, 1992). Despite this growth, few women and even fewer minorities have received appointments to clerk under prominent judges, a route frequently followed by white men aspiring to judgeships.[†] Schafran and Wikler (1992:1) conclude after extensive analysis of race and gender in judgeships: "Despite the substantial, albeit fluctuating, increase in the number of women and minority judges appointed or elected to the bench in recent years, state and federal statistics indicate that the judiciary remains overwhelmingly male and white."

There is a serious underrepresentation of minority judges. According to Judge Leon Higginbotham (1992), of 115 appointments to the U.S. Court of Appeals during the 12 years (1980 to 1992) of the Reagan and Bush administrations, only 2 were African-American—neither of whom was a woman. Judge Higginbotham states that "judicial pluralism breeds judicial legitimacy. . . . Judicial homogeneity, by contrast, is . . . a deterrent to, rather than a promoter of, equal justice for all" (p. A21). This is an important point because the courts throughout the country have been found to exercise widespread racial (Gray, 1991; Sullivan, 1992) and gender discrimination (see Woo, 1992; Schafran, Chapter 20 herein). Thus, not only women and minority judges and lawyers but also clients are discriminated against, and this jeopardizes their access to genuine justice.

---

*See Equal Pay Act and Equal Employment Opportunity provisions of the Civil Rights Act of 1964, which is found at 78 Stat. 253, 42 U.S.C. 2000e et seq. (1964).
[†]In the Supreme Court itself, however, women won more clerkships than men for five years in a row, from 1982 to 1987. But as Epstein (1993:24) reminds us, "It remains to be seen whether the proportion of women clerks will continue to be high with the consolidation of conservative members on the high court" and a less expansive economy.

Still, the legal profession itself has been the source of the greatest improvement for women, particularly white women. This is due as much to the changing nature of work and the rationalization of labor in the legal profession as it is to the increase in the number of educated women (Baron, 1983; Spurr, 1990; Hagan et al., 1991). Women continue to enter law school in greater numbers than ever before. In 1967, 4 percent of all law degrees were awarded to women (*Digest of Educational Statistics,* 1979); by 1978, the figure had risen to 26 percent (*Degrees Awarded to Women: An Update,* 1979). At the start of the 1990s, women amazingly progressed to over 40 percent of all law school students (Epstein, 1993). After graduation some women find employment as public prosecutors and public defenders. And while white women have increased dramatically in law schools and law offices, the inadequate representation of members of racial/ethnic minorities substantially continues (Stille, 1985; Weisenhaus, 1988; Hensen, 1990).

As an example of the simultaneous progress of and resistance to women and minorities entering the legal profession and rising to partner, consider the following. By the early 1990s, women constituted about a quarter of all lawyers in the top 251 U.S. law firms and 11.2 percent of all partners (up from 3.5 percent in 1981). Yet of the 23,195 partners in these top law firms, *only* 40—less than 0.2 percent!—were black women. In total, only 1.2 percent ($N = 287$) of all male and female partners were minorities (including African-American, Latina/o, and Asian) (Epstein, 1993). In short, almost 9 out of 10 partners in the largest and most prestigious law firms in the United States in 1990 were white men.* And analysis of recent tenure-track hires at law schools between 1986 and 1991 overwhelmingly shows disfavor toward well-qualified black women lawyers in hiring, initial rank, prestige of law school, and assignments to teach popular courses (Merritt and Reskin, 1993). The point is clearly made: despite the tremendous numerical increase of women, and less so of minorities, to positions of power, the legal profession remains dominated by white men. On the whole, white women and some minorities are allowed into the lowest, least prestigious ranks of the profession.

Chapters 20 to 22 discuss the impact of women on the judicial and legal field and present in detail the points raised so far in this introduction. Schafran (Chapter 20) and Spohn (Chapter 21) describe the discriminatory consequences of racial and gender imbalance in terms of courtroom

---

*For an analysis of racial and gender biases throughout the U.S. professional/technical labor force, despite the many changes experienced because of both political pressure and economic expansion after World War II, see Sokoloff (1992).

treatment of women and minority judges and lawyers and in terms of case outcomes. Still, Schafran (Chapter 20) points out that women lawyers have at least been able to make court bias and discrimination visible issues. Anleu (Chapter 22) continues the discussion of the impact of women lawyers on their profession by examining the question of whether or not "women's voice" is really being heard throughout the legal profession. The chapter makes the case that numbers alone will not lead to change, because gender segmentation in the legal profession restricts the areas in which women participate and the "voice" with which different groups of women may speak. In short, it is necessary to be located within the profession in places where one's voice carries weight and one has the power to effect change. This is as true for racial/ethnic minorities as it is for women, the working class, and the poor.

In policing and corrections, gender integration and the opportunity to impact on public policy have, if anything, been more strongly resisted than in the legal world. Schulz (Chapter 23) provides the historical context. The reader learns that women have transformed their role in policing because of their own determination and struggle. Indeed, the chapter shows that women shaped their police role throughout history by drawing on outside social forces, and in recent times by turning to the law, to support their determination to work as police officers. Acceptance by their male peers has yet to occur. Women receive, at best, a cool reception from male officers and, at worst, a hostile reception (Worden, 1993:229).

In Chapter 24, Susan Martin follows the historical analysis with a national overview of the number of women police working today. There has been a steady growth in the number of women entering police work since the early 1970s; the percentage of women in policing in 1970 was 2, and by 1991 it had risen only to 9 (personal communication, Bureau of Justice Statistics, 1993).

Moreover, law enforcement, as well as corrections, has attracted a disproportionate number of minority women. For example, in 1992, women officers* in the New York City Police Department (NYPD) were 28 percent African-American, 21 percent Latina, and 50 percent white. Nationally, the situation is similar: minority women, approximately 18.4 percent of the U.S. adult female population (*Statistical Abstracts of the US*, 1992), represent as much as 40 percent of all women police officers (*Sourcebook of Criminal Justice Statistics—1991*, 1992). Reasons for this overrepresentation will be discussed below. This is, as you will recall, in stark contrast to the

---

*In 1992, women represented approximately 14 percent of all police in the NYPD.

legal profession, which is about one-quarter female but only about 1 percent black female. It appears that without the educational barriers to becoming lawyers, black women are better represented among all women in the lower-status but well-paying fields of policing and corrections.

Another key point made by Martin in Chapter 24 is that the growth in the number of women police officers has not been reflected in any sizable changes in the number of supervisory and administrative positions held by women. Entry-level positions have not translated into promotions except in some few cases, and so women remain shut out from having a policy-making voice in local and state law enforcement issues. It is not unlikely that limited success in promotion is related to the reluctant acceptance of women by male colleagues, supervisors, and high-level administrators. This leads to the failure of police departments to establish necessary mentoring relationships for women's career advancement. In addition, the fact that the structure of policing—like that of law (see Anleu, Chapter 22 herein)—may be more "male" may strongly affect women's opportunities.

Chapter 25, by Gomez-Preston and Trescott, depicts one outcome of a lack of influence on policy matters and their implementation: a police department's failure to prevent sexual harassment of women officers. Moreover, because the victim was an African-American woman, the dual nature of systemic gender and racial subordination is graphically described. Earlier, MacKinnon (Chapter 18 herein) explained how the law has evolved in recent years so that today sex discrimination suits based on sexual harassment are possible, although, as she notes, the law is not everything. In Chapter 24 Martin also describes the "double whammy" of race and gender: instead of being doubly advantaged, as many believe, black women police officers find themselves doubly disadvantaged because of their race and gender.* Elsewhere, Martin (1993) has written that black women police officers see themselves as forced to compete with both black men and white women for "affirmative action slots." But even as black women gain a little in a predominantly white male occupation like policing, Gomez-Preston's harrowing experience of harassment graphically portrays one example of systemic race/gender discrimination in law enforcement.

The issue of double discrimination is also a central one in corrections. Belknap (Chapter 26) observes that black women are overrepresented in

---

*Remember that this is similar to what happens to black women lawyers in particular (see Merritt and Reskin, 1993; Simpson, 1990), as well as to black women throughout all the professions (see Sokoloff, 1992).

comparison with white women in correctional work just as they are in law enforcement. In fact, this overrepresentation is a phenomenon seen in government employment generally, especially in lower-level jobs. Minority workers are attracted to higher wages and the perceived security and employment protection that government work offers compared with work in the private sector (see E. Higginbotham, 1987; Sokoloff, Price, and Kuleshnyk, 1992; Page, 1993; Martin, Chapter 24 herein). Perhaps this helps explain the disproportionate numbers of minority compared with white women working in policing and corrections.

In the first edition of this book we focused on social structural barriers that keep women from entering positions in the criminal justice system. That issue remains very much alive; but it must be expanded now to include the extent to which women and racial/ethnic minorities are (or are not) promoted into management positions so they can influence the decision-making processes of the criminal justice system. In Chapter 27, Wilson and Moyer help us to step back from the career path and examine how students are prepared through higher education for future practitioner positions in criminal justice. The chapter is concerned with the numbers of women and racial/ethnic minorities serving as faculty to future practitioners. The authors suggest that the changing faculty composition (being more gender- and racially/culturally diverse) can have an impact on the criminology curriculum in terms of liberalizing a politically conservative discipline. Thus, it is possible that a more radical and diverse curriculum could emerge as more women and minorities join criminology and law faculties. Such newly composed faculties have the potential of preparing future practitioners to question more closely current practices in the criminal justice system and the larger society and to be genuine agents of social reform. Despite these potential changes, however, Wilson and Moyer are concerned that affirmative action may be practiced primarily in terms of numbers (i.e., more women and minorities are hired on the faculty); but these new faculty are all too often forced to "fit in" intellectually rather than encouraged to "transform" the existing knowledge base that supports the status quo in the criminal justice system and helps to reproduce conditions of existing social inequality.

The final chapter in this section, "The Politics of Research and Activism," provides an example of the type of multicultural feminist activist research Wilson and Moyer think is possible in higher education, with the potential to transform the criminal justice curriculum and future practitioners and to implement social reform. In Chapter 28, Fine addresses research from the perspective of the practitioner, who can serve as a collaborator to assure that research approaches problems from the lived experience of female survivors of the male violence that has systematically been institutionalized throughout our society. The author cautions us about the potential arrogance of white middle-class feminists' understanding of problems such as battering and rape; their perspective not only may be wrong for different affected individuals but often fails to take into account the firsthand experiences of those who have lived through the victimization, particularly women of different racial/ethnic and class backgrounds than the researchers themselves. Fine makes the case that service providers who work with women victims of crime have important insights into the causes of victimization of women; therefore, they should be encouraged to serve as collaborators in the formulation of research questions to be studied. It is through such research that students learn and social activism becomes possible.

Conclusion

This is a time of renewed (if limited) optimism in the country, as the national agenda has been refocused back toward domestic issues, and particularly toward issues of importance to women, minorities, and gays and lesbians, as a result of changes in the political control of Congress and the administration following the 1992 elections. Most striking are the recent brakes put on laws eroding a woman's right to an abortion, enactment of a new family leave policy allowing fathers as well as mothers to spend time with their newborns without losing their jobs, the movement toward alternatives to incarceration for drug violations, and the Justice Department appointment in 1993 of the first U.S. woman attorney general, Janet Reno. She has signaled her concern for protecting the rights of all citizens, particularly those least protected historically: the poor, women, and people of color.

But, as history teaches us, social change and reform generally proceed unevenly, with forward momentum followed by inevitable setbacks. American women, racial/ethnic minorities, and the poor still have much to achieve in terms of equal employment opportunity in the criminal justice system. Most critical now is the need for women to move beyond entry-level jobs to administrative positions from which previously excluded groups of women and men can refocus policy and practice in ways that assure equality and justice for those who work in the system and for the citizens they serve. The urgency of this need is reinforced on a daily basis, for evidence is far too abundant that racism, sexism, and class bias continue to operate within the criminal justice system, as they do in the larger society.

REFERENCES

Armstrong, Gail. 1977. "Females under the Law—'Protected' but Unequal." *Crime and Delinquency*, April, pp. 109–120.

Barak, Gregg. 1991. "Cultural Literacy and a Multicultural Inquiry into the Study of Crime and Justice." *Journal of Criminal Justice Education* 2 (2):173–192.

Baron, Ava. 1983. "Feminization of the Legal Profession—Progress or Proletarianization?" *ALSA* (American Legal Studies Association) *Forum* 7:330–357.

Degrees Awarded to Women: An Update. 1979. Washington, D.C.: National Center for Education Statistics.

Digest of Educational Statistics. 1979. Washington, D.C.: HEW, National Center for Education Statistics.

Epstein, Cynthia Fuchs. 1983. *Women in Law*. Garden City, N.Y.: Doubleday.

———. 1993. "Women in Law: Lifting the Glass Ceiling?" *Thesis* 7 (Spring):22–27.

Erez, Edna. 1992. "Dangerous Men, Evil Women: Gender and Parole Decision Making." *Justice Quarterly* 9 (1):105–126.

Gray, Jerry. 1991. "Panel Says Courts Are 'Infested with Racism.'" *New York Times*, June 5:B1.

Hagan, John, Marjorie Zatz, Bruce Arnold, and Fiona Kay. 1991. "Cultural Capital, Gender and the Structural Transformation of Legal Practice." *Law and Society Review* 25 (2):239–249.

Hensen, Rita Henley. 1990. "Minorities Didn't Share in Firm Growth." *National Law Journal*, Feb. 19, vol. 12, no. 24. 4 pages.

Higginbotham, Elizabeth. 1987. "Employment for Professional Black Women in the Twentieth Century." In Christine Bose and Glenna Spitze (eds.). *Ingredients for Women's Employment Policy*, pp. 73–91. Albany: SUNY Press.

Higginbotham, Leon A. 1992. "The Case of the Missing Black Judges." *New York Times*, July 29:A21.

Jurik, Nancy C. 1985. "An Officer and a Lady: Organizational Barriers to Women Working as Correctional Officers in Men's Prisons." *Social Problems* 32 (4):375–388.

———. 1988. "Striking a Balance: Female Correctional Officers, Gender Role Stereotypes, and Male Prisons." *Sociological Inquiry* 58 (3):291–304.

Marital Rape Exemption. 1991. New York: National Center on Women and Family Law, Inc.

Martin, Susan E. 1993. "'Double Whammy,' Double Vision: The Impact of Race and Gender on Women Policing." Paper presented at the American Sociological Association Meetings, San Francisco.

Menkel-Meadow, Carrie. 1987. "Excluded Voices: New Voices in the Legal Profession Making New Voices in the Law." *University of Miami Law Review* 42: 29–53.

Merritt, Deborah Jones, and Barbara F. Reskin. 1993. "The Intersection of Sex and Race in Law School Hiring: The Truth about Affirmative Action." Paper presented at the Annual Conference of the Society for the Advancement of Socio-Economics (SASE), New York.

Myers, Ken. 1991. "Hispanic Bar Raps 'Dirty Dozen'—Instituions without Latinos." *National Law Journal*, p. 4.

Page, Paul. 1993. "African-Americans in Executive Branch Agencies." Paper presented at the New York State Political Science Association Meetings, New York City.

Schafran, Lynn Hecht, and Norma J. Wikler. 1992. "Integration of Women and Minority Judges into the American Judiciary." In *The Judges Book*. 1992 ed.

Simpson, Gwyned. 1990. "Black Women in the Legal Professions." Unpublished manuscript, New York City.

Sokoloff, Natalie J. 1992. *Black Women and White Women in the Professions: Occupational Race and Gender Segregation, 1960–1980*. New York: Routledge, Chapman, Hall.

———, Barbara Raffel Price, and Irka Kuleshnyk. 1992. "A Case Study of Black and White Women Police in an Urban Police Department." *Justice Professional* 6 (Winter/Spring): 68–85.

Sourcebook of Criminal Justice Statistics—1991. 1992. U.S. Department of Justice, Bureau of Justice Statistics. Washington, D.C.: U.S. Government Printing Office.

Spohn, Cassia, and Julie Horney. 1991. "The Law's

the Law, but Fair Is Fair: Rape Shield Laws and Officials' Assessments of Sexual History Evidence." *Criminology* 29 (1):137–160.

Spurr, Stephen J. 1990. "Sex Discrimination in the Legal Profession: A Study of Promotion." *Industrial and Labor Relations Review* 43 (April): 406–417.

Statistical Abstracts of the US, 1992. 112th ed. 1992. Washington, D.C.: U.S. Government Printing Office.

Stille, Alexander. 1985. "Little Room at the Top for Blacks, Hispanics." *National Law Journal,* Dec. 23:1, 6–10.

Sullivan, Joseph F. 1992. "Widespread Bias Found in Court System." *New York Times,* Aug. 7:B5.

Weisenhaus, Doreen. 1988. "Still a Long Way to Go for Women, Minorities." *National Law Journal,* Feb. 8:1, 48, 50, 53.

Woo, Junda. 1992. "Widespread Sexual Bias Found in Courts." *Wall Street Journal,* Aug. 20:B1.

Worden, Alissa Pollitz. 1993. "The Attitudes of Women and Men in Policing: Testing Conventional and Contemporary Wisdom." *Criminology* 31 (May):203–242.

Young, Vernetta, and Thomas Sulton. 1991. "Excluded: The Current Status of African-American Scholars in the Field of Criminology and Criminal Justice." *Journal of Research in Crime and Delinquency* 28 (1):101–116.

Zimmer, Lynn. 1987. "How Women Reshape the Prison Guard Role." *Gender & Society* 1 (4): 415–431.

CHAPTER 20

OVERWHELMING EVIDENCE: GENDER BIAS IN THE COURTS

LYNN HECHT SCHAFRAN

ABSTRACT

Sexist jokes in the courtroom, male attorneys demanding sex from women opponents as a price for settling a case, and women being called "honey"—these are just a few examples of how women are sometimes treated in the courtroom. Gender and race bias against lawyers, court employees, litigants, and witnesses has now been documented in court systems throughout the country. Headlines proclaim both "Widespread Sexual Bias Found in Courts"* and "Panel Says Courts Are 'Infested with Racism.'"[†] Within this context, it is important to remember that judges in the United States remain overwhelmingly white and male—with white males representing at least 4 out of 5 state and federal judges today.[‡]

This chapter summarizes the findings of gender (and, to a lesser extent, racial/ethnic) bias resulting from the investigations of court task forces in a number of states. The chapter begins with a review of bias against women litigants in civil and criminal courts. It then turns to gender bias experienced by women who work in the court system—the particular focus of Part Three of this book.

Beginning with the section "Damages," the chapter reveals how sexist attitudes found in society generally invade all aspects of court business (starting with law school curricula) and present obstacles to women lawyers and other workers. Most shocking in this chapter is the admission by one male trial attorney of his purposeful use of sexist comments to throw off a female prosecutor's cross-examination. Equally disturbing is the male lawyer who almost rejected a

---

*Junda Woo, "Widespread Sexual Bias Found in Courts," *Wall Street Journal*, Aug. 20, 1992, p. B1.
[†]Jerry Gray, "Panel Says Courts Are 'Infested with Racism,'" *New York Times*, June 5, 1991, p. B1.
[‡]Lynn Hecht Schafran and Norma J. Wikler, "Integration of Women and Minority Judges into the American Judiciary," in *The Judges Book*, 1992 ed.

case of sexual harassment of a woman because her experience seemed "too awful" to be believed; her cries of despair were initially interpreted as "hysterical" behavior.

The chapter ends with a series of recommendations for the reduction of gender bias in the courts. Are gender biases in case outcome and in court interaction related or separate issues? Elaborate on several of the reforms suggested by Schafran. Which of them might lead to reduction of bias in case outcome and which to court interaction? What parallels exist for men and women of color in terms of the racism that is structured into the daily life of the courts? Considering the unique disadvantages for women of color, double minorities in the court, what practices would you recommend to eliminate race/gender bias in the courts?

When TRIAL published an issue on women and the law in August 1983, the gender bias task force movement was in its infancy. The first of these task forces, the New Jersey Supreme Court Task Force on Women in the Courts, established in 1982, had yet to publish its report. The women's rights attorneys who had been calling attention to gender bias in the courts for more than a decade were still regarded with skepticism or ignored.

Then, in November 1983, the New Jersey task force released its findings at the state's annual judicial college. The *New York Times* carried a front-page article entitled "Panel in Jersey Finds Bias Against Women in the Courts," and women lawyers and judges throughout the country began requesting that their own chief justices initiate similar blue-ribbon investigations. The Conference of Chief Justices featured a program about gender bias in the courts at its 1986 annual meeting and in 1988 adopted a resolution urging every chief justice to establish a task force devoted to the study of gender bias in the courts, and a separate task force on minority concerns.

As of April 1993, 40 states, two federal circuits, Puerto Rico and the District of Columbia had gender bias task forces appointed by the chief justice (or, in a few instances, the state bar association) in some state of formation, collecting data, or implementing reforms. Twenty-five of these task forces (California, Colorado, Connecticut, the District of Columbia, Florida, Georgia, Hawaii, Illinois, Iowa, Kansas, Kentucky, Louisiana, Maryland, Massachusetts, Michigan, Minnesota, Nevada, New Jersey, New Mexico, New York, Rhode Island, Utah, Vermont, Washington State and the Ninth Circuit) had published their findings.[1] Individually and collectively these reports provide overwhelming evidence that gender bias permeates the court system and that women are most often its victims.[2]

The task forces on gender bias in the courts inspired the creation of similar task forces on racial and ethnic bias. As of April 1993 there were 17 such task forces, seven of which (the District of Columbia, Florida, Hawaii, Michigan, New Jersey, New York and Washington State) had published their findings.[3] Like the gender bias task forces, the race/ethnic task forces found that these kinds of biases are widespread in our courts, with negative consequences for both courtroom interactions and case outcome.

TASK FORCE FINDINGS

The Supreme Court task forces on gender bias in the courts are composed of appellate and trial judges, lawyers, bar leaders, law professors, court administrators, judicial educators, legislators, community leaders, and social scientists. The task forces employ a wide range of data-collection methods. These include public hearings with testimony from judges, lawyers, litigants, law professors, experts, and community organizations; regional meetings with judges and lawyers; listening sessions with litigants; reviews of transcripts, written decisions, and relevant existing research; empirical studies; focus groups with practitioners and court employees; and surveys of judges, lawyers, and court personnel.

The twenty-five task forces that have reported investigated gender bias in divorce, in child support, and in domestic violence and the treatment of women as participants in the court system. Several reported on rape, damage awards, juvenile and adult sentencing, and the status of women court employees. Florida examined prostitution. Minnesota inquired into employment discrimination cases.

Although the severity of the problems documented varies in certain instances from state to state, there is an overall uniformity. In the words of the New York Task Force on Women in the Courts, "Gender bias against women litigants, lawyers and court employees is a pervasive problem with grave consequences. Women are often denied equal justice, equal treatment and equal opportunity." Following is an overview of the twenty-five task forces' findings.

Divorce

After divorce, the standard of living of mothers and children plunges, while that of fathers often improves. The courts are directly impli-cated in this trend. Many divorcing women are effectively denied access to the courts because judges disregard the statutory directive to award appropriate interim and final counsel and expert fees to the economically dependent spouse, who in the vast majority of cases is the wife.

The Nevada Supreme Court Gender Bias Task Force described women undergoing divorce in that state as having to "beg [the court], piecemeal, for a few dollars which she must prove is 'needed' to prosecute her action or defense" while "the husband spends freely from community funds for his own legal needs." Experienced family law practitioners are refusing to represent women because of the losses involved in these cases.

Women's unpaid work as homemakers and child-rearers, in family businesses, and on family farms is devalued or ignored in the division of property and the award of alimony. In many states, women receive significantly less than half of the marital assets, but even where courts divide the property evenly, the result is often inequitable. Husbands receive most of the liquid and income-producing property. Half the marital assets cannot compensate for the fact that in most marriages the principal asset is the husband's earning capacity, to which the wife contributed by subordinating her own.

Alimony of any kind, rehabilitative or indefinite, is rarely awarded; when it is awarded, it is poorly enforced. The findings of the Washington State Task Force on Gender and Justice are illustrative. In its examination of 700 dissolution case files from 11 counties, this task force found that alimony was awarded in only 10 percent of cases, and that in 84 percent of those cases the award was of limited duration.

Judges have unrealistic ideas about the employment potential of older homemakers; women with young children; and women who, although they are in the paid work force, have subordinated their careers to those of their husbands and to the needs of the family. Some judges appear to rest their decisions on the impermissible and erroneous assumption that all women remarry after divorce so they will be taken care of by another man.

Child Support

The failure to award and enforce adequate child support is epidemic, even in states whose task forces reported after the federal Child Support Enforcement Amendments of 1984, which required child support guidelines and new enforcement mechanisms. This is an expression of gender bias because when courts protect fathers' income and standards of living it is mothers, who by family agreement are the overwhelming majority of custodial parents, who must shoulder the burden of child support alone. For many women this translates into working multiple jobs, going on welfare, and living on the edge of poverty.

Child support guidelines understate the costs of rearing children. Some judges and hearing officers refuse to use the guidelines or treat them as a ceiling rather than looking at individual family needs. Enforcement is often a nightmare. Judge Charles McClure testified to the Florida Supreme Court Gender Bias Study Commission that when he first became involved in enforcing child support, he saw women in his courtroom who had been to court so many times without success that they had "the look of a prisoner of war."

Many women give up on enforcement because the repeated court appearances necessitated by adjournments granted the obligator jeopardize their employment. In response to task force surveys, judges claim that they are willing to use all available sanctions, including jail, to force nonpaying parents to comply, but they rarely do so.

Custody

With respect to custody, the task forces confirmed that some judges and hearing officers have great difficulty accepting men as primary caretakers, or as able to care for infants, with obvious consequences for decisions about custody and visitation. Nonetheless, fathers are far more successful in custody disputes than is commonly perceived. The Massachusetts Supreme Judicial Court Gender Bias Study reported that fathers who actively seek custody obtain either primary or joint physical custody in more than 70 percent of cases.

The task forces also found that custody awards often punish women who breach the stereotype of the ideal mother, because, for example, they work outside the home or have a sexual relationship outside marriage. There is a growing tendency to award custody to the wealthier parent rather than to award child support. Given women's and men's unequal earning power, this constitutes a paternal preference.

There is also significant indifference to spouse abuse in custody cases. Many judges do not understand why a man who beats his wife but not his child should not be awarded custody, erroneously assuming that husbands' violence against their wives ends with divorce, so requests for supervised visitation can be denied.

Another type of violence that some judges disbelieve or devalue in custody cases is allegations of child sexual abuse, which are usually made by the mother. There is insufficient understanding of why such abuse may only begin or be disclosed at divorce, and some judges find it easier to adhere to the stereotype of hysterical, vindictive wives trying to thwart husbands' rights to visitation than to acknowledge that incest happens in every stratum of society.

Domestic Violence

Domestic violence continues to be an area in which women experience significant bias, despite major statutory reforms to provide them with civil and criminal protections. Courts show little understanding of the circumstances under which battered women survive and the ways in which the cycle of violence, economic dependence, lack of support from family and community, and fear of the batterer combine to keep women in these situations. The Maryland Special Joint Committee on Gender Bias in the Courts cited a judge who said he did not believe a petitioner's story of her husband's holding a gun to her head "because I don't believe that anything like this could happen to me." This statement was confirmed in the court transcript.

Instead of focusing on why men batter and what can be done to stop them, many judges and court personnel ask battered women what they did to provoke the violence, subject them to demeaning and sexist comments, shuttle them from court to court, and issue mutual orders of protection when the respondent has not filed a cross-petition and there is no evidence that the petitioner was violent. These women are then castigated for failing to go forward with their cases. Although initial orders of protection are granted with greater frequency than they were in the past, violators are rarely punished in any meaningful way.

Rape, Juveniles, and Prostitution

As with domestic violence cases, rape cases also are often viewed from the wrong end of the telescope, with the complainant rather than the defendant being put on trial. Her dress, demeanor, conduct, associations, and lifestyle rather than his threats and use of force become the focus. Although evidence suggests that courts are treating stranger-rape cases with greater seriousness and sensitivity than in the past, nonstranger rape, now understood to be the majority of rapes, is still minimized and trivialized. As Justice Rosalie Wahl, chair of the Minnesota Task Force on Gender Fairness in the Courts, stated, "Judicial procedures for handling 'acquaintance rape' promises to be one of the major upcoming issues with which the legal system must learn to deal effectively and with fairness to the victim."

The conflicting stereotypes about women's sexuality evident in rape cases—women are purity incarnate or seductive temptresses—are evident in juvenile justice and prostitution cases as well. Girls, but not boys, are punished for status offenses such as "running away" and "incorrigibility," the subtext being a determination to prevent girls from engaging in sexual activity, which is acceptable for boys.

In prostitution cases, women are jailed while their male clients go free, as if the women alone are responsible for the crime. The Florida task force noted the justice system's major failure to acknowledge that many young women run away and engage in prostitution as the only way to survive because they are running from rape in their own homes.

Damages

Damages cases, like divorce cases, often devalue women's unpaid work as homemakers and mothers. The New Jersey Supreme Court Task Force on Women in the Courts found that the state's model jury charge virtually precluded recognition for work in the home and that some judges were refusing, and some lawyers were failing to make, offers of proof on the economic value of homemaker work. The Rhode Island Supreme Court Committee on the Treatment of Women in the Courts, while in its investigation phase, secured legislation authorizing recovery for the value of unpaid homemaker work in damages cases and recognizing that this value is not limited to moneys expended to replace the homemaker's service.

THE TREATMENT OF WOMEN IN THE COURTS

The gender-biased treatment of women litigants, witnesses, lawyers, and court personnel is a matter of concern everywhere. Even women judges and jurors are not immune. As the Massachusetts task force wrote, "From their entrance into the courthouse and throughout their participation in the business of the courts . . . [women] are faced with unnecessary and unacceptable obstacles that can only be explained in terms of their gender."

Most fundamental is the fact that women's credibility is often devalued on the basis of sex rather than substance. Women are not believed simply because they are women. Women in the courts, particularly women lawyers, are sometimes subjected to demeaning forms of address, comments on their physical appearance and clothing, sexist remarks and "jokes," unwanted touching, and verbal and physical sexual harassment.

Although some judges and court personnel engage in this kind of behavior, male lawyers were repeatedly cited as the worst offenders. Male lawyers were also cited as refusing to take direction from female court employees and as treating them like their personal secretaries.

Female lawyers do not receive their fair share of appointments to challenging and lucrative fee-generating cases. Women seeking judgeships experience biased questioning from bar selection committees and unwarranted low marks from lawyers on these committees and in the community who are hostile to increasing the number of women on the bench.

Women of Color

The New Jersey Supreme Court Task Force on Minority Concerns reported that "Minority litigants, minority witnesses and minority attorneys are subjected to racial and ethnic slights from all levels of court personnel—from the bailiff to the bench. The Committee was very concerned with the deleterious effects caused by bigotry in the halls of justice, especially when it is engaged in, condoned, and tolerated by key judicial personnel."[4] Although neither the race/ethnic nor the gender bias task forces include extended discussions of the particular problems of minority women, it is clear from the many comments in the gender bias task force reports that women of color experience particular disrespect in the courts. As a National Lawyer's Guild representative testified to the New York Task Force on Women in the Courts, "Our members have observed that sexism is often compounded by racism and classism so that poor women and minority women, both litigants and attorneys, are subjected to discrimination even more frequently than white middle class women."[5]

Other task forces received similar testimony about women of color, including court personnel, especially if they are low-income women as well. The Nevada task force noted that poor minority women tend to be treated as if they have less human value, are routinely preempted from juries, and are treated as "untouchables" or "paternalistically." Black women charging domestic violence may be disbelieved because bruises are less visible on black skin. All women of color must deal with the presumption of some judges and court personnel that violence is simply the norm in minority communities.

Black rape victims are particularly devalued based on stereotypes about black women as promiscuous and thus less harmed by forced sex. Those judges and male attorneys who treat white female lawyers as presumptively incompetent are even more denigrating toward female lawyers who are Black, Asian or Latina. With respect to court personnel, minority women, even more than other women, suffer the effects of occupational segregation and are likely to be working for the lowest salaries.

Implications for the Trial Bar

The task forces' focus is the judiciary, but the trial bar is implicated in the groups' findings as well. Gender bias in decision-making often reflects gender bias in advocacy, whether by omission or commission. Both reflect the gender bias in our culture and in our legal education. If trial lawyers are to become truly effective advocates for their female clients, so too continuing legal education must address the way gender bias affects the litigation process, just as judicial education is beginning to explore how gender distorts the decision-making process.

Given that law schools are just beginning to integrate gender bias issues into their curricula, it is not surprising that few lawyers now in practice are attuned to these issues. Because few women were allowed to attend law school until the 1970s, most men practicing today have had little experience with women as professional peers. Consequently, they are uncomfortable with women attorneys and exhibit the demeaning behavior documented in the task force reports.

Biased attitudes toward women are fostered and reinforced in casebooks. A well-known property casebook published in the 1960s advised that "land, like woman, was meant to be possessed." A recent analysis of the fourth edition of a popular contracts casebook demonstrates how it reinforces the view that "men's" work is more important than "women's" work, presents few cases in which women are "characters," and chooses cases in

which women occupy a narrow range of stereotyped life experiences, as someone's relative or in a stereotypically female job.[6]

An analysis of the seven most widely used criminal law texts demonstrates that, in these texts, domestic violence is virtually invisible, rape is considered only from the defense point of view, and the "reasonable" individual is always the average, middle-class, white man.[7]

The consequences of law schools' failure to open students' eyes to the realities of women's and men's lives and the ways in which sex stereotypes can cloud a lawyer's judgment are illustrated by a recent sexual harassment case. In 1988, a Washington, D.C., judge presenting a program about gender bias in torts and damages asked several lawyers whether they had clients who might serve as speakers. One male attorney responded with a letter about a sexual harassment case he almost refused to take because on the telephone the victim sounded "hysterical." When he finally met with her—at his female secretary's urging—he thought her story of outrageous abuse from a distinguished company division head seemed "crazy."

After the woman's psychiatrist and psychologist told this lawyer that they believed her, he went forward with the case. On the eve of trial he learned of two other women sexually harassed by the same man in the same way and that although all three women had complained to their employer's internal Equal Employment Opportunity office, nothing was done. The case settled. The lawyer said he related this story at length because of the importance of the conference's work.[8]

"I do not think I am any less sensitive than most lawyers, but in this case, I was about to reject a meritorious case because it seemed to be too awful to believe. And I was mistaking the client's desperate cries for justice with hysteria."

This lawyer's failure to appreciate the high level of sexual harassment and violence in women's lives and his labeling this woman with the classically sexist epithet "hysterical" is by no means unique. Continuing legal education is essential to bridge the gap in understanding and life experience this case illustrates. Moreover, although women are far more aware than men of gender-biased behavior because they are its object, no one is born understanding the economic consequences of divorce, rape trauma syndrome, or how gender bias in the medical profession leads to delayed diagnosis. The context-free, abstract theorizing that is the hallmark of most legal education fails to provide lawyers with the concrete understanding of the reality of women's lives that is essential to effective advocacy.

And in legal, continuing legal and judicial education, it is essential that gender issues not be relegated to a special seminar once a year, as in what law schools used to call "Ladies' Day," but that these issues be integrated throughout the curriculum. The admission of expert witness testimony on battered women's syndrome should be explored in evidence courses; family law programs should present current data on the economic consequences of divorce; medical malpractice seminars should demonstrate how gender bias in the medical profession results in negligence and delayed diagnosis; sentencing institutes should address rape trauma syndrome and its implications for sentencing rapists who inflict no injury apart from the rape itself.[9]

Codes of Conduct

Even litigators whose substantive law specialties appear to present no issues of gender bias (and there are far fewer of these than one might think) need to understand how gender bias may be affecting their professional interactions with lawyers of the opposite sex, and that they may be disciplined for gender-biased behavior.

It is not uncommon for male lawyers to assert that gender-biased behavior is just another litigation tactic and perfectly acceptable. The hollowness of this argument becomes apparent when we compare it with attitudes toward racial and religious slurs in the courtroom. Although some lawyers engage in this kind of behavior, no one defends it publicly as an acceptable litigation tactic. However, because sex discrimination is in many ways the last publicly acceptable form of discrimination, many lawyers simply do not understand the meaning of what they are doing.

In 1985, I participated in a program about gender bias at the Florida Bar Association annual meeting. One of my co-panelists, a male criminal defense attorney, recounted a case in which he deliberately made a sexist remark to a female prosecutor to break her rhythm during cross-examination. He said it would never occur to him to use a racial slur to distract a minority adversary, but that until he read the background materials for the bar program and listened to the discussion, he had not understood that what he did to the female prosecutor was equally unacceptable.

The 1990 amendments to the American Bar Association Model Code of Judicial Conduct relating to this kind of conduct are of direct concern to all lawyers. A new section in Canon 3 not only requires judges to refrain from biased behavior themselves, but obligates them to eliminate such behavior on the part of those under their direction and control. Lawyers are cited in particular.

When and how judges should intervene in these situations is the subject of increasing discussion in judicial education. Lawyers who persist in biased behavior, both in the courts and at depositions, will find themselves accountable to the judiciary. There is also a trend toward interdicting gender-biased behavior through the codes of professional responsibility.

RECOMMENDATIONS FOR
BAR ASSOCIATIONS

The numerous recommendations for reform in the gender bias task force reports include many addressed directly to the bar. The task forces recommend continuing legal education about every aspect of domestic violence and the economic consequences of divorce and child support. They encourage bar associations to become involved with rape crisis centers and prosecutors in educating the public, as well as the bar, about rape. They ask that bar members be educated about the nature, incidence, and consequences of gender-biased conduct in the courts and the need to demonstrate respect for female court personnel.

Bar associations and judicial nominating commissions are asked to examine the judicial appointments process to eliminate gender bias against female candidates and ensure that possible gender bias against those seeking judgeships is thoroughly explored.

In some of the states whose task forces have reported, the organized bar has already made a strong response. In New York, the State Bar Association, followed by many county and city bar associations, established special committees to implement the task force's recommendations. These committees have drafted reports and legislation, presented educational programs for lawyers and judges, and pursued administrative reforms. The New York State Bar Association Special Committee on Women in the Courts secured amendments to the state's professional responsibility code respecting gender bias in hiring and treatment.

Several New Jersey bar associations presented programs about the economic value of homemaker work in damages cases. According to a former president of the New Jersey Trial Lawyers Association, where the damages are significant, lawyers are now making full offers of proof on this issue.

New Jersey bar associations also took action to improve their own treatment of women in the profession, such as increasing the number of women committee members and chairs. The New Jersey task force counts as one of its signal accomplishments the elimination of the performance by a female stripper at one county bar's annual clambake.

ARE WE MAKING PROGRESS?

With all this activity, we must ask, are we actually making progress? Four years after the first task force issued its report, Professor Norma Wikler (my predecessor as Director of the NOW Legal Defense and Education Fund's National Judicial Education Program) and I evaluated its impact on the New Jersey courts. We examined the status of each recommendation and the extent to which the gender bias documented in case outcome and court interaction had been ameliorated. We found that most of the task force's twenty-three administrative recommendations had been carried out, that there was significant improvement in the area of male judges' and attorneys' behavior toward their female counterparts, and that there were varying levels of improvement in the substantive law areas examined, such as damages and divorce. Perhaps most important, albeit subtle, we found that this first task force had created a climate within the court system in which the nature and consequences of gender bias were both acknowledged to exist and understood to be unacceptable.[10]

Similarly, the chair of the committee charged with implementing the New York task force's recommendations wrote in a report on her committee's second year: "We are pleased to report continuing progress . . . in the more abstract form of a pervasive shift in the attitude of court system participants. We see a legitimization of the problem of gender bias as a matter deserving of our concern."[11]

In December 1992 New Jersey celebrated the tenth year of its task force with an event at which Chief Justice Robert Wilentz observed:

> It may seem strange to believe, but the fact is that when we started, ten short years ago, no one really thought that there *was* a problem for women in the courts. At least no one except women. You let us know. You electrified the Judiciary of this State, and of this country, and perhaps more than just the Judiciary. We'll never be the same.[12]

Although these remarks will strike those who know how much remains to be accomplished as overly optimistic, they capture a kernel of truth that can give us hope for the future.

It took the NOW Legal Defense and Education Fund ten years to establish the National Judicial Education Program to Promote Equality for Women and Men in the Courts (NJEP) because of widespread denial that a need to educate judges about gender bias existed. When NJEP's focus on developing specific data about each state in which it was teaching—in order to minimize this denial—resulted in that first New Jersey task force on gender bias in the courts, we could not know that it was like the proverbial first olive out of the bottle, and that it would lead to a national gender bias task force movement. We did not anticipate amendments to codes of judicial conduct and professional responsibility barring gender-biased behavior, or disciplinary actions against judges and lawyers who transgressed these norms. We did not anticipate the funding of model judicial education programs about spousal support, domestic violence and rape; or the invitation to address the Conference of Chief Justices, noted at the beginning of this article.

Yes, there are states in which attention to gender bias issues stalled after the task force report was released; and there are judges, lawyers and law professors who continue to insist that no problem exists. But the level of activity around this issue in the state and now the federal courts, in bar associations and in law schools continues to grow, giving us hope that with leadership from all segments of the bench and bar, the task force reports can promote the learning and reform that is essential if we are to eliminate gender and racial/ethnic bias in the profession and the courts.

NOTES

1. For information about obtaining these reports, contact the author at 99 Hudson Street, 12th Floor, New York, NY 10013.
2. For a complete review of the history, *see* Schafran, "Gender Bias in the Courts," 21 *Ariz. St. L.J.* 237 (1989).
3. For information about obtaining these reports, contact the National Center for State Courts, 300 Newport Avenue, Williamsburg, VA 23185.
4. New Jersey Supreme Court Task Force on Minority Concerns, Interim Report (1989) at 164.
5. Report of the New York Task Force on Women in the Courts, 15 *Fordham Urban L.J.* 11 (1986–87) at 15.
6. Frug, "Re-Reading Contracts: A Feminist Analysis of a Contracts Casebook," 34 *Am. U. L. Rev.* 1065 (1985).
7. Eirckson, "Sex Bias in the Teaching of Criminal Law." 42 *Rutgers L. Rev.* (1990).
8. For the entire letter, *see* Schafran, "Lawyers' Lives, Clients' Lives: Can Women Liberate the Profession?" 34 *Vill. L. Rev.* 1105 (1989).
9. For additional and detailed suggestions on integrating gender issues into legal education, see Lynn Hecht Schafran, *Promoting Gender Fairness through Judicial Education: A Guide to the Issues and Resources* (1989), available from the Women Judges' Fund for Justice, Washington, D.C. This is a 200-page guide to more than fifty substantive and procedural areas, ranging from judicial writing to law and psychiatry, in which gender bias may be a factor.
10. N. Wikler and L. Schafran, *Learning from the New Jersey Supreme Court Task Force on Women in the Courts: Evaluation, Recommendations and*

Implications for Other States (Women Judges' Fund for Justice, Washington, D.C., 1989).

11. Transmittal letter from Hon. Kathryn A. McDonald to Chief Judge Sol Wachtler, Second Report of the Committee to Implement Recommendations of the New York Task Force on Women in the Courts (1988), first unnumbered page.

12. Celebration of the Tenth Anniversary of the Task Force on Women in the Courts—Opening Remarks by Chief Justice Robert N. Wilentz, Dec. 9, 1992, at 5.

CHAPTER 21

DECISION MAKING IN SEXUAL ASSAULT CASES: DO BLACK AND FEMALE JUDGES MAKE A DIFFERENCE?

CASSIA SPOHN

ABSTRACT

In Chapter 20 we learned of the substantial extent of gender bias in the courts both in case outcome (how women litigants and defendants are treated) and in the interactions between male and female attorneys, judges, and others in the courts (court interaction). One set of remedies includes education programs for members of the bar and heightening awareness of potential gender bias in judicial appointments; another set involves monitoring practices.

A different approach to reform is to increase the presence of women and minorities on the bench. As we learned earlier, women make up only 7 percent of active state judiciaries, while blacks make up 6.6 percent and Latinas/os 4.8 percent (Schafran and Wikler, 1992).* Chapter 21 explores the potential *impact* of women and minorities in terms of case outcome. By comparing the decisions of black and white male and female judges in sexual assault cases, Spohn concludes that decision making was similar for all judges with one exception: black women judges imposed longer prison sentences in sexual assault cases than did all other judges. We can only speculate as to why this occurred. Perhaps black women judges had been exposed to more cases of rape in their personal and professional lives prior to coming on the bench than the other judges. As a result, they may more fully understand the serious damage to rape victims.

Because the numbers in this study are so small and the differences in findings are not great, Spohn concludes that race and gender of a judge is less a factor in judicial sentencing decisions than the nature of the crime—in this case sexual

---

*Lynn Hecht Schafran and Norma Wikler, "Integration of Women and Minority Judges into the American Judiciary," in *The Judges Book*, American Bar Association, Chicago, 1992.

assault. She suggests that the judges in this study are governed more by their legal training and legal socialization than by their socially structured personal experiences when it comes to sentencing for serious crimes. This is similar to one of Elaine Martin's (1990)* conclusions in her study of male and female judges, in which she finds that the different perspective women judges might bring to the bench influences sentencing decisions in only a narrow category of cases.

One interpretation of Spohn's study is that recruiting for gender and racial diversity in the judiciary will not necessarily lead to policy changes regarding gender and race bias. Before this conclusion is drawn, what further types of studies are needed? Race, class, and gender biases may be so pervasive in U.S. society that along with greater diversity of judges and other court personnel, more profound social change may be necessary to bring about meaningful changes in the courts.

Consider the following issue raised by this case study of judicial response to sexual assault cases in one major U.S. city. On the one hand, there are very few women judges in Spohn's study: only 5 black and 4 white—out of a total of 66 judges. One could argue that the study is flawed by the fact that there are "too few" women judges (black and white) to adequately evaluate the meaning of race and gender in judicial decision making.† In one sense this is true. A bigger problem, however, is not "statistical" but rather "social." That is, there simply are too few women judges in such important positions in the court system to begin with—especially women of color. Racist and sexist biases structured into the very fabric of our society appear to cause this problem, not social science sampling procedures. How would you deal with this "social" problem in designing a study to deal with racism and sexism in the courts and their impact on judges' decisions? Finally, do you think the outcome of Spohn's study would have been different if a crime—violent or not—other than sexual assault (rape) were at issue?

---

*Elaine Martin, "Men and Women on the Bench: Vive la Difference?" *Judicature,* vol. 73, December/January, 1990, pp. 204–208.
†Although there are "too few" white women judges in this study, usually, *if* women judges are on the bench, they are far more likely to be white than racial/ethnic minorities.

The vast majority of state and federal judges in the United States have been white males. Robert Morris became the first black judge

© 1990 by the Haworth Press, Inc. This article was originally published in *Women & Criminal Justice,* vol. 2(1), pp. 83–105.

when he was appointed to Boston's Magistrate Court in 1852. The first female judge was Esther Morris, who was appointed a justice of the peace in South Pass Mining Camp, Wyoming, in 1870. Over the next century, progress in recruiting blacks and women to the judiciary was slow. As a result of lobbying during the civil rights and women's movements, increased numbers of blacks and women have been appointed or elected to the bench at both the state and federal levels.

As the proportion of blacks and women on the bench has increased, researchers have begun to analyze their decision making behavior. The study reported here examines the convicting and sentencing behavior of male and female and black and white trial court judges for systematic differences in the treatment of male defendants accused of sexual assault.

PREVIOUS LITERATURE

Assessing the impact of female and black officials on policy outputs is critically important. According to Pitkin (1967) two views exist. Some believe women and racial minorities should hold office in rough proportion to their population simply for reasons of "fair play." Their view is that it is important to have "descriptive" (Pitkin, 1967) representation for blacks and women. That is, as distinct and visible segments of the population, blacks and women are due their fair share of officials at all levels of government, whether or not these officials have distinctive policy preferences. Others contend that black and female officials provide more than symbolic or descriptive representation. Their view is that black and female public officials provide "substantive" (Pitkin, 1967) representation. Blacks and women, in other words, may have slightly different policy preferences and priorities than whites and men; consequently, their election or appointment may bring about important policy changes.

We do not normally think of judges as representatives of a constituency. Unlike legislators, judges are assumed to be neutral, objective and "above politics." This does not mean, however, that judges are not influenced by the attitudes or preferences of those they serve. As Gibson (1980: 347) notes, "judges

are not expected to submit individual cases to some mass 'jury', but more subtle forms of representation are possible." One of the forms of representation he discusses is based on a passive sharing of values. That is, judges and their constituents share a set of values and judges make decisions congruent with these values.

Consistent with this point of view, those who champion the representation of blacks and women on the bench argue that black and female judges could make a difference. They suggest that increasing the proportion of black and female judges might reduce racism and sexism in the legal system. For example, the recruitment of black judges to state trial courts might result in more equitable treatment of black and white defendants. As Uhlman (1978: 885) suggests, within the courtroom the black judge "may act as an educator, reformer, and advocate for social change." Similarly, the recruitment of women trial court judges might result in less paternalistic treatment of female lawyers, victims and defendants. As substantive representatives, in other words, black and female judges would promote the interests of the groups they represent.

Most researchers interested in the relationship between background characteristics and judicial behavior have focused on appellate court judges. Scholars have examined the influence of characteristics such as political party, religion, ethnicity, age, prior judicial experience and prior prosecutorial experience (Gryski and Main, 1986; Goldman, 1966; Nagel, 1961, 1962a, 1962b; Ulmer, 1962). They also have examined appellate judges' attitudes, as reflected by their votes (Pritchett, 1948, 1954; Schubert, 1963, 1965, 1974) or by their opinions (Kort, 1957). These attempts to link background characteristics with appellate court decisions have yielded inconsistent findings. Some models explained a significant proportion of the variance in decision making, while others did not. Some background characteristics, such as political party identification, were strongly and consistently associated with appellate court decision making, while others, such as age, were not.

Researchers have only recently begun to apply these findings to judges at the state trial court level. They have attempted to link judges' background characteristics (Cook, 1979, 1981; Engle, 1971; Frazier and Bock, 1982; Gruhl et al., 1981; Kritzer, 1978; Kritzer and Uhlman, 1977; Myers, 1988; Uhlman, 1978; Walker and Barrow, 1985; Welch et al., 1988) or attitudes and role orientations (Gibson, 1978, 1983) to their sentencing decisions. Here too the results have been inconsistent. Perhaps because of the homogeneity of judges in a particular jurisdiction (see, e.g., Uhlman, 1978), social background characteristics either do not accurately predict criminal sentencing decisions or are much less important than case or defendant characteristics. As Myers (1988: 668) concludes, the effect of judicial background "is subtle and indirect, discernible only after considering social background in conjunction with the offender's attributes and behavior."

Studies focusing on the influence of race or sex on judicial decision making also have reached contradictory conclusions. Several studies used a judge's race as an independent variable. Three of these found few differences in the behavior of black and white judges. Engle (1971) analyzed Philadelphia judges' sentencing decisions and found that although a judge's race was a statistically significant variable in explaining the variance in these decisions, nine other variables were better predictors. Engle concluded that a judge's race exerted a "very minor influence" overall (1971, pp. 226–7). Uhlman (1978) analyzed "Metro City" judges' convicting and sentencing decisions and found that a judge's race was a significant predictor of both decisions, even when the defendant's race was con-

trolled. However, the association between race and these decisions was not strong. Like Engle, Uhlman concluded there were not important differences between black and white judges. Walker and Barrow (1985) compared decisions handed down by federal district court judges appointed by President Carter. They found no significant differences in criminal cases or four other types of cases.

Welch, Combs and Gruhl (1988), on the other hand, found that black judges in "Metro City" were more likely than white judges to send white defendants to prison. Further analysis led them to conclude that this difference reflected black judges' tendency to incarcerate black and white defendants at about the same rate and white judges' tendency to incarcerate black defendants more often than white defendants. They also found, however, that black judges, but not white judges, favored defendants of their own race when determining the length of the prison sentence.

Few studies have used the judge's sex as an independent variable, and those that have yielded mixed results. Cook (1979), Moulds (1980) and Gruhl, Spohn and Welch (1981) produced evidence in support of the contention that male and female public officials behave differently where issues closely related to sex roles are concerned. Cook found that male and female trial judges "decided" simulated court cases dealing with issues related to women's roles somewhat differently. And Moulds showed that the "gentler" treatment accorded women by the criminal justice system may be due in part to the chivalrous or paternalistic attitudes of men judges toward female defendants. This was confirmed by Gruhl et al., who found that men and women judges in one large Northeastern city convicted female defendants at about the same rate, but men judges were much less likely to sentence convicted females to prison. In contrast, Kritzer and Uhlman (1977) concluded that female judges in "Metro City" behaved no differently than their male colleagues.

Given these contradictory findings, it is clear that the issue of behavioral differences among black and white and male and female trial court judges is unresolved. Further studies designed to identify and untangle the effects of a judge's race and gender are needed. This study compares decision making in sexual assault cases by black and white and male and female judges assigned to Detroit Recorder's Court from 1976 to 1985. Since most earlier studies have uncovered few differences in decision making by black and white judges and since there is no reason to expect black and white judges to have significantly different attitudes toward defendants charged with sexual assault, we hypothesized that the judge's race would not affect decision making in sexual assault cases.

On the other hand, there is evidence suggesting that male and female policymakers might behave differently, especially where issues closely related to sex roles or to women's rights are concerned. Studies have shown that women are more likely than men to be interested in and concerned about issues such as abortion and child care (Hershey, 1977; Lee, 1976). Studies also have found that women are more liberal than men on a number of issues, including legalization of marijuana, amnesty for Vietnam deserters, capital punishment, gun control, abortion, family and career responsibilities of women, school busing, nuclear power and foreign policy (Cook, 1979; Diamond, 1977; Erikson and Luttbeg, 1973; Poole and Zeigler, 1985; Soule and McGrath, 1977). More to the point, Cook (1981), using simulated cases, found that female judges were more likely than male judges to approve a woman's request to restore her maiden name.

Although these attitudinal differences might not necessarily translate into behavioral differences, they suggest that male and female judges might respond differently to the crime of sexual assault. As potential victims of a crime directed primarily against women, female judges may view the crime as especially serious and may be more sympathetic toward rape victims than are male judges. Consequently, we hypothesized that female judges would be more likely than male judges to convict, to incarcerate and to impose a severe sentence on defendants charged with sexual assault.

DATA AND METHODS

One problem encountered in designing a study analyzing the effect of race and gender on judicial decision making is the scarcity of black and female trial court judges. To control for such factors as differences in legal definitions of crimes, differences in sentencing guidelines, differences in state appellate court rulings, and differences in local legal norms and practices, one must compare decisions handed down by judges in the *same* jurisdiction. There are very few jurisdictions in the country with more than a handful of black or female judges. Detroit Recorder's Court is an exception; of the 66 judges on the bench from 1976 to 1985 (the period covered by this study), 21 were black and nine were female. Using data from this jurisdiction, we were able to compare decision making by black and white and by male and female judges. Furthermore, since five of the nine female judges were black, we also were able to compare the decisions handed down by black male and female judges. Because of the paucity of cases decided by black female judges in other jurisdictions, no other study has been able to make this type of comparison.

The data for this project were collected as part of a larger study evaluating the impact of rape law reform in six jurisdictions (Horney and Spohn, 1989). As part of that project, we collected data from court records on all of the

3,798 sexual assault cases adjudicated in Detroit from 1976 to 1985. We then eliminated cases in which all charges against the defendant were dismissed or which were settled by a not guilty verdict rendered by a jury. This left 2,472 cases. This included 1,247 cases decided by black male judges, 918 cases decided by white male judges, 151 cases decided by black female judges, and 109 cases decided by white female judges. All of the defendants in these cases were males and over 96 percent of the victims were females.

The data file included information on the type and number of charges against the defendant (all defendants were charged with either first degree, second degree, or third degree criminal sexual conduct[1] but some defendants had collateral charges such as burglary or robbery), on whether the defendant was convicted or not, on the type and number of conviction charges, on whether the case was settled by a guilty plea, a bench trial, or a jury trial, on the type of sentence (probation, jail, or prison), and on the length of sentence imposed. The data file also included information on the race and sex of the judge who tried (for defendants who elected a bench trial) and sentenced (for all convicted defendants) the defendant.

Three dependent variables are examined. The first is a dichotomous variable indicating whether the defendant was convicted or not.[2] For this variable, only cases which were settled by a guilty or not guilty verdict rendered by a judge are included; cases settled by a guilty plea or a jury trial are excluded. The second dependent variable is a dichotomous variable indicating whether or not the convicted defendant was sentenced to prison. The third is a sentence severity scale which measures the length (in months) of the maximum prison sentence. For the two sentencing variables, cases which were settled by a guilty plea, a guilty verdict rendered by a judge or a guilty verdict rendered by a jury are included.

The data on sexual assault cases is examined for significant differences in decision making by black and white and by male and female judges. We first examine the bivariate relationships between race, gender and the dependent variables. Since most (72 percent) defendants are charged with first degree criminal sexual conduct and since combining defendants charged with first, second or third degree criminal sexual conduct in this bivariate analysis would be misleading, at this stage we include only defendants charged with first degree criminal sexual conduct. We also separate the conviction and incarceration decisions into two decisions: the decision to convict or incarcerate the defendant for the most serious charge (first degree criminal sexual conduct) and the decision to convict or incarcerate the defendant for some other charge.

At the second charge of the analysis, we control for the legal and extralegal factors which might affect judges' decisions. For the analysis of judges' convicting decisions, we control for the number and type of charges against the defendant. For the analysis of incarceration and sentence length, we control for the number and type of conviction charges, the type of disposition (guilty plea, bench trial, or jury trial), and whether the number of charges or the severity of the charge was reduced prior to sentencing. All of these variables have been shown to affect judges' decisions.

Unfortunately, we were not able to control for a number of variables that previous research has shown to be associated with case outcomes. The data file used for this study did not include information on the defendant's race, prior criminal record or type of attorney. The multivariate analysis rests on the assumption that there are no systematic differences in the types of defendants assigned to male and female or black and white judges. This assumption is warranted, since the assignment of defendants to judges in Detroit is through a random "blind draw" process. Furthermore, our own analysis of the data showed no substantial differences in the types of cases assigned to male and female or black and white judges.[3] In a sense, then, we have a quasi-experimental design with random assignment of defendants to black and white, male and female judges.[4]

It is possible that characteristics of a judge other than race and gender might affect decision making in rape cases. One might argue that increased time on the bench would harden judges and predispose them to impose severe sentences. Other researchers have found that older judges tend to be more conservative and to impose more severe sentences than younger judges (Kritzer, 1978; Myers, 1988). While time on the bench is not perfectly equivalent to age, the two variables should be related. Similarly, it is possible that judges with prior prosecutorial experience would be more likely to sentence severely than judges without such experience. Consequently, both the length of time a judge has been on the bench and prior prosecutorial experience are used as controls in the analysis. (See Appendix A for a description of the variables used in the analysis.)

The data are analyzed using both ordinary least squares regression and probit analysis. Two different analytic procedures are required because of differences in the nature of the dependent variables. For the sentence severity score, regression can be used. Since many consider OLS regression inappropriate for the analysis of dichotomous variables, the dummy variables measuring whether or not the defendant was convicted or incarcerated are analyzed using probit analysis. Probit analysis yields maximum likelihood estimates (MLE's) which represent the change in the cumulative normal probability resulting from a one-unit change in the independent variable. The MLE's divided by their standard errors are similar to a z distribution, which allows tests for their significance.

FINDINGS

Data comparing the decisions of black and white and male and female judges in first degree criminal sexual conduct (first degree CSC) cases is presented in Table 1. Even without controls for the legal and extralegal factors which might affect these decisions, there are no statistically significant racial differences and very few statistically significant gender differences.

Consistent with our hypothesis, black judges did not decide sexual assault cases differently than white judges. In fact, the similarities for each of the dependent variables are remarkable. Even breaking the dependent variables into two separate variables did not yield significant differences. For example, when asked to decide the guilt or innocence of defendants charged with first degree CSC, black judges convicted 32.9 percent for the original charge and 33.3 percent for some other charge; the comparable figures for white judges were 36 percent and 32.6 percent.

Female judges, on the other hand, did decide these cases somewhat differently than male judges. Although they did not convict or incarcerate defendants at a significantly higher rate, they did impose longer sentences on defendants incarcerated for first degree CSC or for some other charge. These differences in sentence length are striking. The mean prison sentence imposed on defendants convicted of first degree CSC by female judges was nearly four years longer than the mean sentence imposed by male judges.

Table 1 also compares decisions handed down in first degree CSC cases by male and female judges who are white and by male and female judges who are black. Neither white nor black female judges are more likely than

TABLE 1
The Effect of Race and Gender on Judicial Decision Making
in First Degree Criminal Sexual Conduct Cases

	Convicted		Incarcerated		Mean prison sentence	
	Of first degree CSC	Of other charge	For first degree CSC	For other charge	For first degree CSC	For other charge
The effect of race						
White judges	36.0%	32.6%	87.7%	58.9%	249.88	149.63
Black judges	32.9	33.3	89.0	60.3	260.40	147.83
The effect of gender						
Male judges	34.2	33.1	87.8	59.6	250.32	144.49
Female judges	38.7	29.0	93.2	61.3	297.71*	177.55*
The effect of gender						
White judges only:						
Male judges	35.5	33.7	86.8	55.2	249.05	148.28
Female judges	42.1	21.1	97.3*	59.0	263.22	166.50
Black judges only:						
Male judges	32.9	33.0	88.9	59.7	251.89	142.93
Female judges	33.3	41.7	90.2	64.7	321.47*	182.91*

*$P \leq .05$

their male counterparts to convict rape defendants. On the other hand, white females incarcerate defendants convicted of first degree CSC at a higher rate than do white males. And black females impose considerably longer sentences than do black males; the mean prison sentence for defendants convicted of first degree CSC is 321 months for black female judges and 252 months for black male judges, a difference of almost six years.

The data examined thus far suggest that black and white judges decide sexual assault cases similarly, while male and female judges of both races decide these cases somewhat differently. These differences, of course, may be due either to the types of cases assigned to male and female judges or to differences in their background characteristics (length of time on the bench and prior prosecutorial experience). As shown in Table 2, however, the male/female differences do not disappear when these controls are added to the analysis;

female judges continue to impose harsher sentences than do male judges.

Further analysis revealed that the differences in sentence length can be attributed to differences among black judges. Black female judges impose sentences which are significantly longer than those handed down by black male judges. Among white judges, on the other hand, the male/female differences in sentence length are not statistically significant. In fact, the difference in sentence length among male and female judges who are black is the only difference which remains once controls for the other independent variables are added to the analysis. On the whole, then, the decisions made by male and female judges in sexual assault cases are very similar.

We also compared the decisions of white and black female judges. The data presented in Table 1 suggested that white female judges were harsher than black female judges; that is, they were more likely than black female

TABLE 2
The Effect of the Judge's Race and Gender on Convicting and Sentencing Decisions in Sexual Assault Cases—Results of the Multivariate Analyses[a]

	Convict or not		Incarcerate or not		Sentence length		
	MLE	MLE/SE	MLE	MLE/SE	b	beta	t
The effect of race[b]	.07	.78	.11	1.63	−4.17	.01	−.51
The effect of gender	−.05	−.29	−.21	−1.80	−29.76	−.06	−2.23*
The effect of gender:							
White judges only	.00	.00	−.12	−.70	−21.69	−.04	−.96
Black judges only	−.09	−.32	−.26	−1.54	−33.87	−.07	−2.00*

[a]Includes all defendants charged with first degree, second degree or third degree criminal sexual conduct. The judge's gender is coded female = 1, male = 2. The judge's race is coded white = 1, black = 2. See Appendix A for coding of the other variables. See Appendix B for detailed results of the multivariate analyses.
[b]White male judges decided 918 cases, white female judges decided 109, black male judges decided 1247, and black female judges decided 151.
* P ≤ .05

judges to convict or incarcerate. The conviction rate (for first degree CSC) of white female judges was 42.1 percent, compared to only 33.3 percent for black female judges; similarly the incarceration rate was 97.3 percent for white female judges, 90.2 percent for black female judges. The results of the probit and regression analyses, however, revealed that these differences, once controls were added to the models, were not statistically significant.

The multivariate analysis also revealed that neither of the two background characteristics had a statistically significant effect on the convicting or sentencing decisions of black judges. (The results of the multivariate analysis are presented in Appendix B.) However, each of these variables was a significant predictor of decisions handed down by white judges. The relationship between prior prosecutorial experience and the decision to convict or not was in the predicted direction; white judges with prior prosecutorial experience were more likely than those without this experience to convict defendants charged with sexual assault (MLE = .469; MLE/SE = 2.57). The relationship between years on the

bench and the decision to incarcerate or not, on the other hand, was not in the predicted direction. The longer they had served, the less likely white judges were to sentence convicted defendants to prison (MLE = −.026; MLE/SE = −2.06). The reason for this is unclear. We had speculated that time on the bench would harden judges and incline them to impose more severe sentences. Instead, it may be that the longer judges serve, the more they perceive the futility of incarceration.

DISCUSSION

This study compared decision making in sexual assault cases by black and white and by male and female judges assigned to Detroit Recorder's Court. Consistent with our expectations, there were no racial differences. Black judges convicted and incarcerated defendants at about the same rate as did white judges; they also imposed similar sentences.

Our hypothesis concerning male and female judges was not confirmed; female judges were not consistently harsher than male judges. The conviction and incarceration rates for female and male judges were similar.

Female judges did, on the other hand, impose longer prison sentences than their male counterparts, due primarily to the fact that black female judges handed down harsher sentences than black male judges.

The fact that there were no racial differences and very few gender differences in decisions handed down by these judges is congruent with previous research. A number of researchers have concluded that background characteristics are not strongly associated with judicial decision making at the trial court level. This can be attributed in part to the judicial recruitment and socialization process. As Glick and Vines (1973) have shown, judges recruited to state courts share similar background characteristics; most are middle or upper class and were born and attended law school in the state in which they serve. Even black and white judges apparently share similar background characteristics. Studies indicate that "both the black and white benches appear to have been carefully chosen from the establishment center of the legal profession . . . " (Uhlman, 1978: 893).

These similarities are reinforced by the judicial socialization process, which encourages judges to adhere to prevailing norms, practices and precedents. They also are reinforced by the courtroom workgroup, the judges, prosecutors and public defenders who work together day after day to process cases as efficiently as possible. To expedite sentencing, for example, members of the courtroom workgroup may informally establish a range of "normal penalties" for each type of crime and agree to sentence within that range (Sudnow, 1965). Judicial discretion in sentencing, in other words, is limited by these informal agreements among members of the workgroup. While individual judges might deviate from the sentencing norms, there is no reason to expect white judges to deviate more or less than black judges in sentencing defendants convicted of sexual assault. There is no reason

to expect white judges to decide these cases differently than black judges.

On the other hand, there are reasons to expect female judges to decide sexual assault cases differently than male judges. Previous research has demonstrated that male and female elites behave differently where issues closely related to sex roles are concerned. Furthermore, a number of authors have charged that male judges are unduly skeptical of the claims of rape victims and have suggested that female judges would be more sympathetic. According to Schafran (1989), for example, the "life experiences" of women judges are different from those of men judges and will influence their decision making. She cites the example of an Arkansas woman judge who wrote in a concurring opinion affirming a rape conviction:

> The writer of this opinion does not work in her office when the Justice Building is empty because she's unwilling to subject herself to the danger of rape. No male opinion writer is ever faced with this sinister problem. [Schafran (1989: 418) citing *Conley v. State* 590 S.W. 2d 66, 70 (Ark. Ct. App. 1979) (Penix, J. concurring)]

Since the vast majority of rape victims in Detroit are women, it is not unreasonable to expect female judges to empathize with victims and to hand down harsher decisions in sexual assault cases. The fact that there were so few differences among male and female judges is indicative of the powerful influence of socialization on the legal profession and on the judicial role. Even when confronted with an issue of great concern to women, female judges did not deviate dramatically from the norms established by the workgroup.

These results can be interpreted in at least two ways. We might conclude that the similarity between male and female judges is due to the fact that male judges in Detroit are not paternalistic or skeptical of the claims of rape victims; rather, they, like the female judges on the bench there, view sexual assault as a serious crime deserving of harsh punishment. However, it would be just as reasonable to conclude that the women judges are as likely as men judges to question the validity of rape complaints. Since there are no standards against which to judge the decisions of these judges, it is not clear which of these interpretations is the correct one.

We do, however, have evidence to suggest that the correct interpretation is the first one. As part of our larger study of the impact of rape reform legislation, we interviewed 11 of the judges on the bench in 1986. Both male and female judges had very positive and supportive attitudes toward the strong and comprehensive rape law reforms enacted in Michigan. These judges uniformly felt that the changes had resulted in more appropriate treatment of men accused of rape and more humane treatment of the victims of rape. In fact, judges in Detroit were more likely than judges in any of the other five jurisdictions included in the study to believe that evidence of the rape victim's character or past sexual conduct was irrelevant and therefore inadmissible. This suggests that judges in Detroit, males as well as females, view sexual assault as a serious crime and the complaints of rape victims as valid.

This study examined judicial decision making in only one jurisdiction and in only one category of violent crime. We cannot claim that the results can be generalized to other jurisdictions or to other types of crime. In fact, the relatively minor differences uncovered here may reflect the fact that judges' discretion is reduced for serious violent crimes like sexual assault. As Petersilia (1983: 2) has noted, "When the crime is murder, forcible rape, robbery, or aggravated assault, a judge has less latitude in deciding about sentence length, or whether the sentence will be served in jail or prison. . . ." Additional research designed to delineate the effect of the judge's

race and gender in other types of cases clearly is needed.

NOTES

1. In 1975 Michigan redefined rape and other forms of sexual assault by establishing four degrees of gender-neutral criminal sexual conduct based on the seriousness of the offense, the amount of force or coercion used, the degree of injury inflicted, and the age and incapacitation of the victim. First degree criminal sexual conduct is a felony punishable by life or any term of years. Second and third degree criminal sexual conduct are felonies punishable by a maximum of 15 years. Since fourth degree criminal sexual conduct is a misdemeanor it is not included in this study.

2. All defendants are charged with either first, second or third degree criminal sexual conduct. This variable differentiates between those convicted of the original charge or some other charge and those not convicted of any crime.

3. For example, the three types of sexual assault cases appear to be randomly divided among the judges. Overall, black male judges heard 51 percent of the cases in our data file. The percentage of first, second and third degree criminal sexual conduct cases heard by black male judges was 51 percent, 50 percent and 53 percent, respectively. Similarly, the percentage of cases heard by white male judges (who heard 38 percent of all cases) was 38 percent, 39 percent and 35 percent.

4. Obviously, if we were attempting to explain disparity in the sentences imposed on, for example, black and white defendants, it would be mandatory to control for prior criminal record, bail status and type of attorney. Black and white defendants very likely would differ on these factors. However, here all we are assuming is that male and female judges of each race receive a random distribution of defendants with respect to these factors.

REFERENCES

Cook, Beverly B. 1979. "Judicial Attitudes on Women's Rights: Do Women Judges Make a Difference?" Paper presented at the International Political Science Association Roundtable, University of Essex, Essex, England.

———. 1981. "Will Women Judges Make a Difference in Women's Legal Rights? A Prediction from Attitudes and Simulated Behavior." In Margherita Rendel (ed.), *Women, Power and Political Systems*. New York: St. Martin's Press.

Diamond, Irene. 1977. *Sex Roles in the State House.* New Haven, CN: Yale University Press.

Engle, Charles Donald. 1971. *Criminal Justice in the City: A Study of Sentence Severity and Variation in the Philadelphia Court System.* Unpublished PhD dissertation, Temple University.

Erikson, Robert, and Norman Luttbeg. 1973. *American Public Opinion: Its Origins, Content and Impact.* New York: Wiley.

Frazier, Charles E., and E. Wilbur Bock. 1982. "Effects of Court Officials on Sentence Severity: Do Judges Make a Difference?" *Criminology* 20: 257–272.

Gibson, James. 1978. "Judges' Role Orientations, Attitudes, and Decisions: An Interactive Model," *American Political Science Review* 72 (September): 911–924.

———. 1980. "Environmental Constraints on the Behavior of Judges: A Representational Model of Judicial Decision Making," *Law & Society Review* 14 (Winter): 343–370.

———. 1983. "From Simplicity to Complexity: The Development of Theory in the Study of Judicial Behavior." *Political Behavior* 5: 7–50.

Glick, Henry Robert, and Kenneth N. Vines. 1973. *State Court Systems.* Englewood Cliffs, NJ: Prentice-Hall.

Goldman, Sheldon. 1966. "Voting Behavior on the United States Courts of Appeals, 1961–1964," *American Political Science Review* 60 (June): 374–383.

Gruhl, John, Cassia Spohn and Susan Welch. 1981. "Women as Policymakers: The Case of Trial Judges," *American Journal of Political Science* 2 (May): 308–322.

Gryski, Gerard W., and Eleanor C. Main. 1986. "Social Backgrounds and Predictors of Votes on State Courts of Last Resort: The Case of Sex Discrimination," *Western Political Quarterly* 39: 528–537.

Hershey, Marjorie. 1977. "The Politics of Androgyny? Sex Roles and Attitudes Toward Women in Politics," *American Politics Quarterly* 5 (July): 261–288.

Horney, Julie, and Cassia Spohn. 1989. *The Impact of Rape Reform Legislation.* Final report to the National Institute of Justice and the National Science Foundation.

Kort, Fred. 1957. "Predicting Supreme Court Decisions Mathematically: A Quantitative Analysis of the Right to Counsel Cases," *American Political Science Review* 51 (March): 1–12.

Kritzer, Herbert M. 1978. "Political Correlates of the Behavior of Federal District Judges: A 'Best Case' Analysis," *Journal of Politics* 40: 25–58.

Kritzer, Herbert M., and Thomas M. Uhlman. 1977. "Sisterhood in the Courtroom: Sex of Judge and Defendant in Criminal Case Disposition," *Social Science Journal* 14 (April): 77–88.

Lee, Marcia Manning. 1976. "Why Few Women Hold Public Office," *Political Science Quarterly* 91 (Summer): 297–314.

Moulds, Elizabeth F. 1980. "Chivalry and Paternalism: Disparities of Treatment in the Criminal Justice System." In Susan K. Datesman and Frank R. Scarpitti (eds.), *Women, Crime, and Justice.* New York: Oxford University Press.

Myers, Martha. 1988. "Social Background and the Sentencing Behavior of Judges," *Criminology* 26 (No. 4): 649–675.

Nagel, Stuart S. 1961. "Political Party Affiliation and Judges' Decisions," *American Political Science Review* 55 (December): 844–850.

———. 1962a. "Testing Relationships between Judicial Characteristics and Judicial Decision Making." *Western Political Quarterly* 15 (September): 425–437.

———. 1962b. "Ethnic Affiliations and Judicial Propensities," *Journal of Politics* 24 (February): 92–110.

Petersilia, Joan. 1983. *Racial Disparities in the Criminal Justice System.* Santa Monica, CA: Rand Corporation.

Pitkin, Hanna F. 1967. *The Concept of Representation.* Berkeley, CA: The University of California Press.

Poole, Keith T., and L. Harmon Zeigler. 1985. *Women, Public Opinion, and Politics.* New York: Longman.

Pritchett, C. Herman. 1948. *The Roosevelt Court.* New York: Macmillan.

———. 1954. *Civil Liberties and the Vinson Court.* Chicago: University of Chicago Press.

Schafran, Lynn Hecht. 1989. "Gender Bias in the Courts: Time Is Not the Cure," *Creighton Law Review* 22: 413–428.

Schubert, Glendon A. 1963. *Judicial Decision-Making.* New York: Free Press.

———. 1965. *The Judicial Mind.* Evanston, IL: Northwestern University Press.

———. 1974. *The Judicial Mind Revisited.* New York: Oxford University Press.

Soule, John, and Wilma McGrath. 1977. "A Comparative Study of Male-Female Political Attitudes at Citizen and Elite Levels." In Marianne Githens and Jewel Prestage (eds.), *A Portrait of Marginality.* New York: McKay.

Sudnow, David. 1965. "Normal Crimes: Sociological Features of the Penal Codes in a Public Defender Office," *Social Problems* 12: 254.

Uhlman, Thomas M. 1978. "Black Elite Decision Making: The Case of Trial Judges," *American Journal of Political Science* 22 (November): 884–895.

Ulmer, Sidney S. 1962. "The Political Party Variable in the Michigan Supreme Court," *Journal of Public Law* 11: 352–362.

Walker, Thomas G., and Deborah J. Barrow. 1985. "The Diversification of the Federal Bench: Policy and Process Ramifications," *Journal of Politics* 47: 596–616.

Welch, Susan, Michael Combs and John Gruhl. 1988. "Do Black Judges Make a Difference?" *American Journal of Political Science* 32: 126–136.

APPENDIX A
Dependent and Independent Variables Included in the Multivariate Analysis

Variable	Description	Code
Convict or not	Whether or not the defendant was convicted	1 = convicted 0 = not convicted
Incarcerate or not	Whether or not the defendant was incarcerated	1 = incarcerated 0 = not incarcerated
Mean prison sentence	The length (in months) of the maximum sentence	Number of months
Charge	The most serious indictment or conviction charge	Dummy variables
Number of charges	The total number of charges against the defendant	Number of charges
Number of convictions	The total number of charges for which the defendant was convicted	Number of charges or convictions
Type of plea	Plea of guilty or not guilty	1 = guilty plea 0 = not guilty plea
Type of trial	Whether the defendant was tried by a judge or jury	1 = bench trial 0 = jury trial
Reduction in number of charges	Whether the defendant was convicted of fewer crimes than originally charged	1 = reduction 0 = no reduction
Reduction in severity of charges	Whether the defendant was convicted of most serious charge or lesser charge	1 = reduction 0 = no reduction
Race of judge	Whether the judge was white or black	1 = white 2 = black
Gender of judge	Whether the judge was female or male	1 = female 2 = male
Years on bench	Number of years judge on bench at time case decided	Number of years
Prosecutorial experience	Whether or not the judge had prior prosecutorial experience	2 = experience 1 = no experience

APPENDIX B
Results of the Multivariate Analyses

Independent variables	Convict or not		Incarcerate or not		Sentence length		
	MLE	MLE/SE	MLE	MLE/SE	b	beta	t
Judge's race	.07	.78	.11	1.63	−4.17	−.01	−.51
Judge's gender	−.05	−.29	−.21	−1.80	−29.76	−.06	−2.23*
Years on bench	.01	.95	.00	.14	.30	.01	.28
Prosecutor	.19	1.46	.10	1.25	2.82	.01	.28
Number of charges	.12	3.63**					
Charge—1st degree CSC	.16	1.44					
Charge—2nd degree CSC	.33	2.08*					
Number of convictions			.63	7.82**	27.16	.25	9.47**
Convict—1st degree CSC			.95	6.84**	164.45	.52	8.10**
Convict—2nd degree CSC			.16	1.31	56.20	.10	2.79**
Convict—3rd degree CSC			.44	4.90**	75.53	.20	4.80**
Convict—armed robbery			4.56	.77	148.50	.20	6.78**
Convict—robbery			.73	1.81	26.45	.02	.61
Convict—kidnapping			.67	1.14	82.46	.03	1.25
Convict—burglary			.24	.76	38.15	.02	.80
Convict—assault			−.82	−1.95*	29.86	.01	.32
Convict—larceny			−.69	−1.42	−94.15	−.02	−1.01
Convict—other sex offense			−.25	−2.04*	−40.30	−.04	−1.54
Type of plea			−.75	−4.85**	−93.17	−.29	−8.04**
Type of trial			−.62	−3.68**	−84.14	−.23	6.46**
Reduce no. of charges			.19	1.88	21.30	.07	1.39
Reduce severity of charge			−.30	−3.97**	−7.25	−.02	−.84

*P ≤ .05
**P ≤ .01

CHAPTER 22

WOMEN IN LAW: THEORY, RESEARCH, AND PRACTICE

SHARYN L. ROACH ANLEU

ABSTRACT

In Chapter 21 Spohn asked whether women and minority judges spoke in "a different voice" than white male judges. That is, were their socially structured and personal experiences so different that they would decide cases differently than white men? In this chapter, Anleu reviews the debate that exists in the feminist community around the impact of women on the law: some theorists argue that women bring a "different voice" enabling such values as caring, empathy, and mediation to become more central to legal practice (known as the "difference" approach). This position asserts that the increasing number of women lawyers will change the legal profession. Others disagree that the maleness of law can be changed by increasing women's entry or placing more value on so-called female qualities. Instead, they argue, the law—as both ideology and practice—is socially structured to reflect men's experiences and thereby maintains and reproduces male domination (the "domination" approach). This position asserts that women, to the degree they are different from men, will be changed by the legal profession.

What is absent, Anleu argues, is the integration of empirical research and theory; assertions about women and law remain unsubstantiated. This chapter examines the processes whereby men and women lawyers are recruited to inhouse legal departments (usually in large businesses as opposed to law firms) and describes the type of work performed. The central argument is that women's locations within a stratified and segmented legal profession* must be investi-

---

*"Stratification" refers to the establishment or existence of a hierarchy, whereas "segmentation" refers to the compartmentalization of labor.

gated in order to assess the ways in which work settings and organizational differences in recruitment, work, and perceived career opportunities of lawyers constrain or facilitate different approaches to legal work. In short, a lawyer's location in the segmented work setting is key to understanding gender (the "difference" approach) and an entrenched social structure of male domination (the "domination" approach) in assessing the impact of women on the law.

Discuss how the changing nature of the law and a growing awareness of its class, race, and gender biases might affect the relevance of the "difference" and "domination" approaches to our understanding of the influence of women on the law. Given the structural conditions of the legal profession, it is very difficult for women and minorities to resist the negative effects of the segmentation of the legal profession, i.e., finding themselves stuck in low-level, low-status legal jobs. This might lead the reader to question the traditional approach of requiring women to change their attitudes and career goals (i.e., the victim-blaming approach). Instead, the reader might consider an alternative way of understanding women's position in the legal profession by examining the profession's role in channeling women into less valued sectors of the legal profession.

A WOMAN'S VOICE IN LAW?

There have been two divergent responses to the question: 'Whether women will be changed by the legal profession or whether the legal profession will be changed by the increased presence of women?' (Menkel-Meadow, 1986, 899). First, many argue that the entry of women will make a difference as they will adopt a caring rather than competitive, adversarial approach and value empathy and mediation. Women's experiences, orientations, and identities differ from those of men; as the law reflects men's experiences it must re-adjust to incorporate women's experiences. On the contrary, others argue, the law is so imbued with such male values as objectivity, abstract rights and adversarial tactics, and has been so instrumental in perpetrating gender inequality that there is little scope for women to make any difference.

A frequent starting point for proponents of the 'difference' approach is the notion of a 'different voice'. Carol Gilligan's (1982) research on moral development found that men and women have different ways of moral reasoning which cannot be evaluated against each other. Following these findings, Carrie Menkel-Meadow suggests that women's different 'voice' will initiate particular transformative contributions to the practice of law, perhaps resulting in 'an alternative professional culture' (Menkel-Meadow, 1987, 44; 1989a, 313). She suggests that 'not all women will innovate but that a larger, perhaps critical mass of women will have a greater voice in changing the practice of law' (Menkel-Meadow, 1989b, 223). This transformative potential derives from women's experiences of exclusion which create an outsider's critical perception; oppression which engenders greater empathy for subordinated groups;

Source: Excerpt from Sharyn L. Roach Anleu, "Women in Law: Theory, Research and Practice," *Australian and New Zealand Journal of Sociology,* vol. 28, no. 3, November 1992, pp. 391–410, La Trobe University Press, Australia.

and the learned attention to caring and relationships (1989a, 312–313).

Women will be more concerned with substantive justice than with procedural fairness and will be more likely than men to consider contextual factors, not just the legal 'facts' or issues, in understanding and communicating with clients. According to Menkel-Meadow, present legal structures incorporate such male-dominated or male-created values as victory, predictability, objectivity, deductive reasoning, universalism, abstract rights and principles which override so-called 'female values' of mediation, caring, empathy for both parties to a dispute, and preservation of relationships. Increasing numbers of women lawyers might lead to the replacing of confrontational, adversarial processes with alternative, more mediational forms of negotiation and dispute resolution which relate to clients' actual needs (Menkel-Meadow, 1984, 794–801; 1989b, 231–33).

Continuing in this vein, some theorists propose a set of feminist legal methods. They include a distinctive approach to litigation, which emphasises both the centrality of the clients' experiences and women's perspectives, often excluded or silenced by current legal practice and doctrine. Such feminist methods:

> . . . reflect the status of women as 'outsiders', who need ways of challenging and undermining dominant legal conventions and of developing alternative conventions which take better account of women's experiences and needs. . . . Traditional legal methods place a high premium on the predictability, certainty and fixity of rules. In contrast, feminist legal methods, which have emerged from the critique that existing rules overrepresent existing power structures, value rule-flexibility and the ability to identify missing points of view (Bartlett, 1990, 831–32).

Consciousness raising is seen as a central element in empowering the client and moving toward the substantive goal of ending women's disadvantage and inequality by demonstrating to the courts, among other things, how the law affects their lives (Bartlett, 1990, 863–867; Burns, 1990, 196; Cahn, 1990, 4–5; Colker, 1991). According to one proponent, feminist litigation 'is governed by its contribution to the larger feminist enterprise of transforming established social, economic, political and legal power relations that work to the detriment of women' (Burns, 1990, 193). Feminist lawyers also seek to empower their clients through litigation (Cahn, 1991, 20).

This 'difference' viewpoint assigns women considerable agency and ability to change legal practice without examining how the organisation of work constrains the possibilities or the desirability of different approaches.[1] Parallel with cultural feminism more generally, it views so-called female values or orientations as 'natural' or essential characteristics, albeit learned, and as possessed by most women (Alcoff, 1988, 408–414; Olsen 1990). Such values as mediation and negotiation may have more to do with the nature of the work context (in turn affected by market forces and government laws and regulations) than with the gender of the legal practitioners. Indeed, much of lawyers' work does not include adversarial practice or dispute resolution but involves managing uncertainty both for clients and themselves (Flood, 1991; Macaulay, 1979). Ironically, the entry of women into the profession has been accompanied by greater litigiousness which partly reflects the complexity and anonymity of contractual relations and increased government regulation rather than the changed gender composition of the profession.

Alternative dispute resolution procedures emerge in areas of law where human relations skills, for example counselling, are required and where women or children are likely to be victims or complainants, especially in family law and child welfare or protection. It is in these areas that women have made the most inroads and which look most like an extension of women's traditional familial roles thereby reproducing gender segmentation within the profession. Moreover, women and women's groups are adamant about the use of criminal penalties in domestic violence and rape cases, and see little scope for mediation or negotiation because of inequalities in bargaining power between men and women (Bottomley, 1985, 164; Lerman, 1984, 67).

While 'difference' legal theorists see women's gender as having beneficial consequences, the very idea of a difference model ultimately can lead to social inequality. Historically, the assignment to women of particular attributes, especially alleged caring and nurturing skills, has resulted in disadvantage, regardless of whether these attributes are viewed as biological, essential or social (Epstein, 1991, 311, 334–35). Such differences are 'deceptive distinctions' and their emphasis diverts attention from differences among women and the similarities between men and women (Barrett, 1987, 29; Epstein, 1988, 76–83).

For other legal theorists neither increasing women's entry nor placing more value on so-called female qualities will transform legal practice and knowledge. This is because law as ideology and as practice maintains and reproduces male domination (MacKinnon, 1989; Polan, 1982; Rifkin, 1980; Thornton, 1986). From this perspective the law reflects men's experiences and perpetuates gender inequalities. Law's claims to neutrality, objectivity and equal treatment are vacuous because the law is value-laden.

Rejecting the notion of 'different voices' Catharine MacKinnon (1982; 1983; 1987; 1989) suggests that inequality comes first, the most central inequality being gender; differences follow. She argues that focusing on differences serves as ideology which neutralises and rationalises power inequalities. Revalu-

ing empathy, care, mediation, concern for relationships and orientation to others inevitably reproduces gender inequality and reinforces male dominance. Allegedly 'female' attributes are neither 'natural' nor constitute a 'woman's voice' but are by-products of male dominance; their emphasis reproduces that inequality. The qualities attributed to women result from the oppression of male dominance, which is perhaps the most pervasive and tenacious system of power in history, and is 'metaphysically nearly perfect' (MacKinnon, 1983, 638).

Despite this totalising view of law as a conduit of male domination MacKinnon wants her theory to incorporate the possibility of transforming power relations through a feminist method, namely consciousness raising. She suggests that consciousness raising enables women to view the shared reality of their condition from within the perspective of their own experience. This grounding in experience permits a critique of the purported generality, disinterestedness and universality of prior accounts (1982, 536–7). The collective speaking of women's experience uncovers and analyses male dominance (1982, 519). MacKinnon claims that 'the feminist theory of knowledge begins with the theory of the point of view of *all* women on social life' (1987, 50; emphasis added). This suggests that a coherent, holistic women's perspective, transcending ideological distortion, can emerge through consciousness raising and assumes that women's experiences and accounts will complement not conflict.

Taking experience as the level of analysis, however, raises several interpretive questions (Huber, 1973, 280–81). How can accounts or experiences be evaluated? On what basis does a theorist or observer choose one view rather than another? To what extent can structured inequalities be revealed through individuals' accounts and experiences? Some women have access to male power: is their experience less valid than those who do not have access to power? If all accounts are equally as valid, then can the same be said of men's accounts? How does consciousness raising cast off the male point of view which has been imposed? Claims that women will produce an accurate, coherent depiction of reality, either because they are women or because they are oppressed seem problematic (Hawkesworth, 1989, 544).

While MacKinnon views consciousness raising as an important feminist methodology her critique of law is overly deterministic, making it difficult to imagine from where a distinctive women's experience could emerge. How can subjective awareness and individual agency transform the law which reflects and perpetuates male dominance which is 'metaphysically nearly perfect'? If individual intentions and characteristics are constructed totally within and by a male-dominated social reality over which women (and some men) have no control, then it is impossible to account for social change or human action. The problem of agency in MacKinnon's theory is magnified by her conception of women as passive, submissive, dominated, and as victims of rape (1983) sexual harassment (1979) pornography (1986), or more generally of male-defined sexuality. This view of women as victims reinforces a traditional cultural stereotype of women as passive, helpless and irresponsible and does not account for the many historical examples of women's resistance or creativity.

The 'difference' and 'domination' perspectives suffer from opposite limitations. The former assigns women practitioners too much agency; while the latter assigns too little. From the 'difference' approach women's entry into the legal profession will change the nature of accepted legal doctrine and practice. This approach treats gender as an individual characteristic shaping the interests of actors and downplays its role in shaping the macro-

structure of law—as a form of dispute resolution, as an occupation, and as a body of knowledge—within which the action occurs (Wharton, 1991, 374–75). Little attention focuses on the ways in which the structure of the legal profession constrains or enables different approaches to legal work. On the other side, negligible scope for human action exists within the view that law reflects male domination which is hegemonic. Women's location in social life and individual characteristics are completely (over-)determined by male-dominance which their own activities inevitably reproduce and reinforce (cf. Wrong, 1961).

Both approaches offer a one-dimensional view of women as either demonstrating greater sensitivity to clients and adopting a nurturing approach to legal dealings or as passive victims of male dominance. Additionally, they tend to treat the law, both as an occupation and a body of knowledge, as a given; as non-problematic and as unified. This leads to an ahistorical and reified conception of law as an objective fact which women confront. Neither considers the ways in which types of legal practice or employment settings construct gender relations. Some women may exhibit specific qualities held to be evidence of a feminist approach under certain circumstances, for example where clients are relatively powerless and have minimal knowledge of their rights or of the operation of the legal process or where there is little time pressure, thus enabling extended conversations to discover the client's point of view and experiences. Often behaviour deemed to be evidence of gender difference derives from men and women's differential locations within work settings. Kanter's (1977) research on a large industrial corporation demonstrates how women's lack of interest in promotion, low job commitment and concern to develop friendships with co-workers stem from their overwhelming employment as clerical staff in powerless positions with few opportunities for advancement, not from 'natural' female qualities.

The availability and applicability of different approaches to legal work will depend on the structure of the workplace and women's position within it. This requires analysis of the structure and organisation of law and of the ways women and men negotiate for resources which may reproduce or transform legal work and relations with clients. The processes of domination and negotiation may be operating simultaneously. Accordingly we:

> . . . need to explore the various ways women participate in setting up, maintaining, and altering the system of gender relations. . . . Domination explains the ways women are oppressed and either accommodate or resist, while negotiation describes the ways women and men bargain for privileges and resources (Gerson and Peiss, 1985, 322).

Similarly, Alcoff (1988) suggests the concept of *positionality* in order to ground human action and subjectivity in concrete practices and discourses which are subject to continual change. She suggests that:

> . . . the position that women find themselves in can be actively utilized (rather than transcended) as a location for the construction of meaning, a place from where meaning is constructed, rather than simply the place where a meaning can be *discovered* (the meaning of femaleness) (1988, 434; emphasis in original).

Not all women are in the same position nor have the same experience of law. At the same time, many women share experiences of law indicating that they are patterned, not idiosyncratic. While women lawyers have little control over the structure of the legal profession and their position within it, those positions involve opportunities for action as well as constraints. There is scope for agency and change, albeit limited. In order to investigate difference and domination within the legal profession it is essential to examine how women lawyers' positions affect legal practice and knowledge.

STRATIFICATION AND THE LEGAL PROFESSION

Far from being a 'community within a community' (Goode, 1957) the legal profession has always been segmented and stratified (Auerbach, 1976; Heinz and Laumann, 1982; Smigel, 1964). Different kinds of work are differentially evaluated; the division of labour is also a division of status, clientele and visibility (Heinz and Laumann, 1982, 36). The profession has undergone numerous changes, including expansion, increased specialisation, bureaucratisation of employment settings, the growth of large firms, the decline of the solo practitioner, and a relaxation on advertising restrictions (Roach Anleu, 1992). This restructuring coincides with the movement of women into the profession. The profession has become more complex and new dimensions of inequality are emerging; gender cross-cuts other cleavages that stratify legal practice (Hagan, 1990, 848–849).

Recent discussion suggests the existence of dual career structures and 'glass ceilings' which restrict women's opportunities for promotion. In the United States, for example, women who take advantage of flexible working hours, maternity and child care provisions offered by some law firms may be disadvantaged in promotion decisions and relegated to the 'mommy track', many others decide to leave because of incompatibility between motherhood and law (Hochschild, 1989, 110–25; Kingson, 1988). Changes in the structure of the profession seem to benefit men more than women. Aggregate statistics showing women's greater participation in the legal profession obscure gender segmentation within the occupation (Sokoloff, 1988, 37). A simple comparison of men and women according to broad areas of practice and employment glosses over differences in the types of work they perform within organisations.

While large-scale empirical research has been sparse in Australia two studies show that women lawyers have occupational profiles different from those of men (Dixon and Davies, 1985; Hetherton, 1981). Research on Victoria's lawyers in the mid 1970s found that women received just over half the income of men.[2] Nearly 15 per cent of the men were barristers compared to 1.4 per cent of the women and 40 per cent of the former and 18 per cent of the latter were law firm partners. Women were more likely to be employees in private practice whereas men were more likely to be self-employed or employers. Women and men were evenly distributed in corporate or public service employment. This finding indicates that gender segmentation is greater in private law firms than in public organisations and that women were much less likely to become partners and share in firm profits than men. Sixteen per cent of the women worked part-time compared with four per cent of the men. Family law and probate/estate administration accounted for almost twice the proportion of work hours among women than among men. Property law also constituted proportionately more of women's work. In contrast, women spent less time than men in commercial, company and criminal law. These gender differences in income, status and areas of work, the study concludes, seem to be independent of the relative youth of the women and the high proportion of part-time women (Hetherton, 1981, 125–44).

A study of law students and practitioners in Western Australia further documented the tendency for women not to follow the traditional career path of articles then partnership in a private law firm (Dixon and Davies, 1985). Family responsibilities were far more likely to interrupt women's careers and various options to conventional legal practice were more attractive to women. Government employers (public service and law schools) were more accommodating to motherhood, in part due to sex discrimination legislation. Women who worked in private practice were concentrated in smaller firms that paid less than large firms (Dixon and Davies, 1985, 19–25, 73–90).

The different employment locations and work experiences of men and women lawyers are not limited to the legal profession in Australia. A recent Canadian study found women to be under-represented in corporate and commercial work and civil litigation, and over-represented in family law, especially in small to medium firms and in solo practice. The greatest gains for women are in corporate settings, in part due to the expansion of these sectors and specialisations (Hagan, 1990, 842). Men and women lawyers move along gender specific mobility ladders that produce a gender stratified income hierarchy. On average men earn about twice as much as women and the gender gap in income within the legal profession actually may be widening (Hagan, 1990, 838, 849).

In the United States, of the 586 respondents to a questionnaire mailed to women who graduated in 1975 or 1976 from one of 14 eastern-state law schools, 21 per cent were law firm partners; 12 per cent were solo practitioners; 22 per cent worked for public agencies; 14 per cent were corporate counsel; and 14 per cent were associates in law firms (Caplow and Scheindlin, 1990, 404). These lawyers practiced across the range of specialties; 17 per cent specialised in corporate business; 12 per cent in litigation; 10 per cent worked in administrative law. Less than five per cent worked in family law, tax, or trusts and estates. However, about half of the respondents believed that their salary was somewhat or substantially lower than those of comparable male colleagues (Caplow and Scheindlin, 1990, 404–409).

The clear pattern is that women are not competing with men for the same positions or jobs within the legal profession; women earn less, are more likely to experience interrupted careers, specialise in so-called 'female' areas of the law, and are much less likely to make partner. However, little research deals with the processes whereby those outcomes emerge. Do they result from gendered assumptions on the part of law schools or employers? Do they result from women's career choices, albeit made within constraints specific to many women? What kind of work is allocated in accordance with a set of gender norms? Under what conditions are feminist methods employed?

Studies of differential employment outcomes either focus on individual achievements and skills or on the segmentation of the labour market which means that men and women compete for different jobs (Treiman and Terrell, 1975). Neither approach analyses the organisational context in which recruitment or the division of labour occurs. Individual outcomes and the labour market are mediated by the organisation of work as it is within firms that hiring, work and pay decisions are made and in which mobility and stratification occur (Baron and Bielby, 1980, 741). Even when men and women have the same occupation they often work in different kinds of organisations (Bielby and Baron, 1986, 779).

THE STUDY

The present study examines the recruitment of men and women lawyers in one segment of the legal profession, namely in-house legal departments within business corporations. Until recently this was a rapidly expanding area of legal practice, thus enabling examination of new opportunities for equal employment (Spangler, 1986). One dimension of the study focused on recruiters' perceptions and practices regarding the hiring of men and women lawyers. Another compared the location, work, pay, careers, perceived opportunities and aspirations of 34 men and 34 women lawyers in 12 in-house legal departments (Roach, 1986; 1990). Previous studies of women in law have not explicitly examined organisational practices nor investigated inter-organisational differences in the hiring of men and women lawyers (cf. Dixon and Davies, 1985; Epstein, 1983; Hetherton, 1981). Yet it is within organisations that individuals and jobs get matched.

Even though the research was undertaken in the United States its aim to identify general processes contributing to gender segregation in the legal profession is relevant to other societies where the numbers of women lawyers have grown recently.

The research strategy consisted of two stages. The first involved the selection of the legal departments from the *Law and Business Directory of Corporate Counsel*, 1985/86. The departments were categorised as small: ten lawyers and less; medium: between 11 and 25 lawyers; and large: 26 or more lawyers. From each size category two manufacturing and two financial services corporations were studied. The twelve companies, or at least their headquarters, where most of the legal staffs are located, are all in the north-eastern United States. Within each corporation the general counsel (head of the legal department) and/or the legal recruitment officer provided information on recruitment policies and practices during in-depth interviews.

The second stage consisted of semi-structured interviews with men and women in-house counsel. In two of the small departments all the lawyers were interviewed; and in the others, four were interviewed. In the medium-sized departments, six lawyers were interviewed; and in the large departments, eight.

WOMEN LAWYERS IN IN-HOUSE LEGAL DEPARTMENTS

Differences in the employment of men and women lawyers across the twelve in-house legal departments were marked. Nearly one-third of the lawyers (total number of lawyers: 184) in the six financial services companies were women, compared with less than one-fifth in the six manufacturing firms (total number of lawyers: 497). Proportionally more women lawyers worked in the medium-sized legal departments, whereas the large departments employed the least women. Women lawyers were far more likely than men to work in medium-sized departments in financial services companies. Men were more likely to work for manufacturing companies, especially those in electronics, information processing and defense industries—in particular those with small or large legal departments.

The recruitment practices of the different legal departments help explain these differences.

> It's just the way the law schools are composed now . . . half of the students are women, and if you're going to be upset about hiring women, you are going to be in big trouble.

All the recruiters (both general counsel and recruitment officers) offered similar responses to questions regarding the number of women lawyers on their staffs. They explained these gender differences by indicating that recent hiring of men and women were about equal, reflecting the increased number of women entering and graduating from law school. Recruiters observed that older members of the department are predominantly male due

to the composition of law schools when they graduated, whereas the ratio of recent men and women hired is more balanced because of the similar numbers of men and women law school graduates. Even so, this does not account for why some in-house legal departments hired relatively more women than others.

Every general counsel and recruitment officer claimed that they look for and hire the best lawyers—however they do not all define 'best' in the same terms. They hire, or try to hire, the 'best lawyers' from those segments of the labour pool in which they seek recruits. However, women and men are not evenly distributed across the legal labour market. Corporations with large legal departments, opportunities for promotion and career development, and salaries comparable to large law firms can compete with those firms for the same graduates of prestigious law schools.

Manufacturing companies requiring experienced lawyers in specific fields of law recruited from the pool of law firm associates experienced in business and corporate law. Women are also under-represented in this segment of the labour pool. Financial services companies seeking experienced lawyers recruited lawyers with skills in banking, insurance and finance laws, which to some extent are 'female areas' of legal practice. More significantly, though, tertiary sector industries are large employers of women in a variety of jobs and positions. Unlike the manufacturing companies studied the legal departments in the financial services companies are centralised in one location and tend to focus on lawyers with fewer alternative employment opportunities due to immobility, and these lawyers are more likely to be women than men.

The large departments in this study perform most of their companies' legal needs and thereby occupy important positions within those companies. They expect recruits to develop their careers within the host company. The large law departments recruit new law school graduates and compete for the top graduates of the best schools, at which women are under-represented. On the other side, small legal departments tend to recruit associates from the outside law firms, frequently those with whom they have worked previously. This reduces the perception of risk in hiring a completely 'unknown' lawyer and increases the probability of hiring men.

Even if men and women possessed the same law school training and firm experience the recruiters suggested that men were more likely to have contact with corporate clients and responsibility for business cases. This visibility enhanced men's chances of recruitment to an in-house legal department, especially to those in manufacturing companies, because many preferred to hire lawyers with whom they had dealt with previously. The general counsel of a small legal department in a manufacturing company observed that uncertainty in recruitment is minimised by:

> . . . hiring people that we have worked with when they were on the outside. . . . The younger man in the corporate law department worked with us when he was in a large firm downtown, and . . . the litigation counsel was a man we had worked with quite a bit when he was outside. So we got to know them pretty well.

The segment of the labour pool from which this department recruits contains disproportionately few women. Unequal employment of men and women lawyers does not merely reflect conditions in the labour market nor results automatically from employers' intentional discrimination, but corporate recruitment efforts may be insufficient or inadequate to locate certain applicants, in particular women.

Nonetheless, it appears that more opportunities for continuous careers exist for women in in-house legal departments than in private

law firms, or at least the demands of the occupational and domestic spheres are not as incompatible. The most important reason one woman lawyer gave for leaving a large, prestigious law firm was the desire to have children. Another commented that she left a large law firm after five years because of the insecurity, competition, chaotic lifestyle and burnout. She emphasised the corporate lifestyle as one of the main attractions of practicing in-house, especially for women with children for whom 'there are difficulties not only during pregnancy and infancy.' A law school placement officer also observed that generally women lawyers have more interest in corporate employment than men because the level of professional treatment of women is much higher. In corporations there is no 'up or out' promotion policy and women have opportunities to move into management:

> It is not that applicants, especially women, are looking for nine to five jobs with little commitment and responsibility. They are looking for commitment and to work hard, but in places where progress is not impeded by not having the luxury to stay at work until seven on a regular basis. Men look at private firms and corporations as both offering similar kinds of work. They apply to both and see what happens.

From the point of view of the recruiters, more qualified women may be available because of inhospitable work environments within private firms. Regarding the hiring of women one general counsel commented:

> My own personal feeling is that you get a very good buy, you get at least as much experience and so on for the price as you would with a man. I think you get better.

This comment suggests that women have fewer employment options than men. Other employers perceived that hiring 'good' women and making extra efforts to retain them is more efficient than dealing with turnover costs. Many of the women in-house counsel indicated that their current jobs are very 'humane' places to work, and that they had been given 'good deals'. One woman in a small department works a four day week and expressed a strong sense of loyalty to the company. A recruitment officer in a large financial services legal department explained the rationale behind the extra efforts:

> We have a woman who joined our department several years ago who decided to have a family. Well we structured a program . . . she actually structured the program, where she works really on a part-time basis, and [another woman lawyer] works in the afternoon . . . we try to be flexible because we are investing in the future . . . [the two women lawyers] are superb lawyers and you want to keep and encourage people . . . you are looking for the long range, you are looking to develop people from the time they come out of law school, to bring them along in the corporation, and we see the payoff of having people like [the two women].

Within the legal departments significant gender differences existed regarding current position and salary. Women were concentrated in the lower echelons of the legal departments and earned less because they were disproportionately located in financial services companies which pay lower salaries compared with the manufacturing companies. Few differences between the men and women interviewed were found with respect to quality of law school attended, academic performance, previous legal employment, and legal speciality. Men were slightly more likely to be engaged in litigation work but most men and women concentrated on general corporate work. Women spent a little more time on contracts and men more on disputes, trial work and administration.

The division of labour within in-house legal departments appears to be less gendered than in law firms. One in-house lawyer specialising in property law explained that in her previous law firm job she was given home mortgages and personal real estate cases, whereas in the in-house legal department she works on joint ventures, business property acquisitions and commercial real estate involving millions of dollars:

> I would not have been given that kind of work in the private firm, but in a corporation there is none of the personal real estate work to be done.

Another woman lawyer previously employed in a private law firm observed a tendency for some firms to allocate women 'paralegal' tasks, for example, looking up records and examining business correspondence. She indicated that when she was given this kind of work:

> The partner said that even though it was not legal work the client wanted it done, and by assigning the job to a lawyer the firm could bill at a higher rate.

These comments suggest that profit considerations and gender assumptions are more important criteria of work allocation in private legal practice than in corporate legal departments. Because the range of tasks performed in-house is not as great as in private law firms there are fewer different activities to allocate along gender lines. Additionally, as in-house legal departments composed of more than a general counsel are relatively new phenomena, a strict, gendered division of labour has not become institutionalised.

In sum, the kinds of practices women and men end up in is not a direct outcome of the credentials or educational qualifications they possess. Recruitment practices and a firm's ability to compete for certain kinds of lawyers affects the probability of hiring men or women. Men and women do not appear to share the same positions in the legal labour market. At the macro-level gender segmentation is reproduced with men gaining greater (but not exclusive) access to higher paying, more prestigious jobs. However, within certain segments of the profession the difference between men and women in terms of the kinds of law practiced appears minimal. Regarding the assignment of work, gender has more relevance in some settings than in others.

CONCLUSION

The legal profession has undergone numerous changes over the past 20 years which have implications for the entry of women. Admission to law schools and to the profession based on such universalistic criteria as examination performance and new types of legal employment have contributed to the growing number of women lawyers. Nevertheless, research indicates that women and men follow different career paths and have different positions within the labour market. This study of 12 in-house legal departments suggests that some organisational settings are more hospitable to women lawyers than are others. Aggregate data showing increasing numbers of women lawyers are insensitive to organisational differences in the recruitment, work and perceived career opportunities of lawyers.

The central argument of this paper is that discussions about the differences women lawyers might make to the practice of law must be informed by attention to women's actual locations within the legal profession. Rather than viewing women's entry as signalling change for the better, or no change at all it is imperative to examine the women's positions within the occupation and the ways in which they make gender relevant and constrain the nature and content of legal work. Arguments that the mere entry of women must make a difference to the practice of law need to examine the work contexts where different methods might be adopted rather than focusing on the gender of the practitioner.

The idea of feminist methods seems to be applicable only in certain areas of law thereby undermining the assertion that they are potentially transformative. On the other hand, women are not passive victims of the male-dominated legal system but are active participants in it as lawyers, although gender segmentation restricts the areas in which women participate.

NOTES

1. Menkel-Meadow acknowledges occupational segregation within the legal profession but does not theorise the implications of gender stratification for the development of alternative forms of legal practice.
2. This study only dealt with lawyers in practice thus excluding all women law graduates not practicing at the time.

REFERENCES

Abel, R. (1985), 'Comparative Sociology of Legal Professions: An Exploratory Essay', *American Bar Foundation Research Journal*, Winter, 1–80.

Alcoff, L. (1988), 'Cultural Feminism Versus Post-Structuralism: The Identity Crisis in Feminist Theory', *Signs: Journal of Women in Culture and Society*, 13, 3, 405–36.

Anleu, S. L. Roach (1992), 'The Legal Profession in the United States and Australia: Deprofessionalization or Reorganisation?', *Work and Occupations*, 19, 2, 184–204.

Auerbach, J. S. (1976), *Unequal Justice: Lawyers and Social Change in Modern America*, New York, Oxford University Press.

Australian Bureau of Statistics (1947, 1961, 1981, 1986), *Census of the Population*, Canberra, Australian Government Publishing Service.

—— (1991), Labour Force Survey (Unpublished data), Canberra, Australian Bureau of Statistics.

Baron, J. N., and W. T. Bielby (1980), 'Bringing the Firms Back In: Segmentation and the Organisation of Work', *American Sociological Review*, 45, 737–765.

Barrett, M. (1987), 'The Concept of "Difference"', *Feminist Review*, 26, 1, 29–41.

Bartlett, K. T. (1990), 'Feminist Legal Methods', *Harvard Law Review*, 103, 4, 829–88.

Bielby, W. T., and J. Baron (1986), 'Men and Women at Work: Sex Segregation and Statistical Discrimination', *American Journal of Sociology*, 91, 759–799.

Bottomley, A. (1985), 'What is happening to family law? A feminist critique of conciliation', in J. Brophy and C. Smart (eds.), *Women in Law: Explorations in Law, Family and Sexuality*, London, Routledge and Kegan Paul, 162–187.

Burns, S. E. (1990), 'Notes from the Field: A Reply to Professor Colker', *Harvard Women's Law Journal*, 13, 1, 189–206.

Cahn, N. R. (1991), 'Defining Feminist Litigation', *Harvard Women's Law Journal*, 14, 1, 1–20.

Caplow, S., and S. A. Scheindlin (1990), "Portrait of a Lady": The Woman Lawyer in the 1980s', *New York Law School Law Review*, 35, 2, 391–446.

Colker, R. (1990), 'Feminist Litigation: An Oxymoron?—A Study of the Briefs Files in William L. Webster v. Reproductive Health Services, *Harvard Women's Law Journal*, 13, 1, 137–188.

Dixon, M., and M. Davies (1985), *Career Patterns in the Legal Profession and Career Expectations of Male and Female Law Students in W.A.: A Comparative Study*, Perth, University of Western Australia Law School.

Epstein, C. F. (1983), *Women in Law*, Garden City, NY, Anchor Books.

——— (1988), *Deceptive Distinctions: Sex, Gender, and the Social Order*, New Haven and New York, Yale University Press and Russell Sage Foundation.

——— (1991), 'Faulty Framework: Consequences of the Difference Model for Women in the Law', *New York Law School Law Review*, 35, 2, 309–36.

Flood, J. (1991), 'Doing Business: The Management of Uncertainty in Lawyers' Work', *Law and Society Review*, 25, 1, 41–71.

Gerson, J. M., and K. Peiss (1985), 'Boundaries, Negotiation, Consciousness: Reconceptualizing Gender Relations', *Social Problems*, 32, 4, 316–331.

Gilligan, C. (1982), *In a Different Voice: Psychological Theory and Women's Development*, Cambridge, MA, Harvard University Press.

Goode, W. J. (1957), 'Community within a community: The Professions', *American Sociological Review*, 20, 194–200.

Hagan, J. (1990), 'The Gender Stratification of Income Inequality among Lawyers', *Social Forces*, 68, 3, 835–855.

Hawkesworth, M. E. (1989), 'Knowers, Knowing, Known: Feminist Theory and Claims of Truth', *Signs: Journal of Women in Culture and Society*, 14, 3, 533–557.

Heinz, J. P., and E. O. Laumann (1982), *Chicago Lawyers: The Social Structure of the Bar*, New York and Chicago, Russell Sage and American Bar Association.

Hetherton, M. (1981), *Victoria's Lawyers*, Melbourne, Victoria Law Foundation.

Hochschild, A., with A. Machung (1989). *The Second Shift*, New York, Avon Books.

Huber, J. (1973), 'Symbolic Interaction as a Pragmatic Perspective: The Bias of Emergent Theory', *American Sociological Review*, vol. 38, April, 274–84.

Kanter, R. M. (1977), *Men and Women of the Corporation*, New York, Basic Books.

Kingson, J. A. (1988), 'Women in the Law Say Path is Limited by "Mommy Track"', *New York Times*, 9 August, A1.

Law and Business Directory of Corporate Counsel (1985/86), Clifton, New Jersey, Law and Business/Harcourt Brace Jovanovich.

Lerman, L. (1984), 'Mediation of Wife Abuse Cases: The Adverse Impact of Informal Dispute Resolution on Women', *Harvard Women's Law Journal*, 7, 1, 57–113.

Macaulay, S. (1979), 'Lawyers and Consumer Protection Laws', *Law and Society Review*, 14, 1, 115–71.

MacKinnon, C. A. (1979), *Sexual Harassment of Working Women*, New Haven, Yale University Press.

——— (1982), 'Feminism, Marxism, Method, and the State: An Agenda for Theory', *Signs: Journal of Women in Culture and Society*, 7, 515–544.

——— (1983), 'Feminism, Marxism, Method, and the State: Toward Feminist Jurisprudence', *Signs: Journal of Women in Culture and Society*, 8, 635–658.

——— (1986), 'Pornography: Not a Moral Issue', *Women's Studies International Forum*, 9, 1, 63–78.

——— (1987), *Feminism Unmodified: Discourses on Life and Law*, Cambridge, MA, Harvard University Press.

——— (1989), *Toward a Feminist Theory of the State*, Cambridge, MA, Harvard University Press.

Mathews, Judge J. H. (1982), 'The Changing Profile of Women in the Law', *Australian Law Journal*, 56, December, 634–42.

Menkel-Meadow, C. (1984), 'Toward Another View of Legal Negotiation: The Structure of Problem Solving', *UCLA Law Review*, 31, 3, 754–842.

——— (1986), 'The Comparative Sociology of Women Lawyers: The "Feminization" of the Legal Profession', *Osgoode Hall Law Journal*, 24, 4, 897–918.

——— (1987), 'Portia in a Different Voice: Speculating on a Women's Lawyering Process', *Berkeley Women's Law Journal*, 1, 1, 39–63.

——— (1989a), 'Exploring a Research Agenda of the Feminization of the Legal Profession: Theories of Gender and Social Change', *Law and Social Inquiry*, 14, 2, 289–319.

——— (1989b). 'Feminization of the Legal Profession: The Comparative Sociology of Women Lawyers', in R. L. Abel and P. S. C. Lewis (eds.), *Lawyers in Society: Comparative Theories*, Berkeley and Los Angeles, The University of California Press, 196–255.

Mossman, M. J. (1990), 'Women Lawyers in Twentieth Century Canada: Rethinking the Image of "Portia"', in R. Graycar (ed.), *Dissenting Opinions: Feminist Explorations in Law and Society*, Sydney, Allen and Unwin.

Murray, G. (1987), 'Women Lawyers in New Zealand: Some Questions about the Politics of Equality', *International Journal of the Sociology of Law*, 15, 4, 439–457.

Olsen, F. (1990), 'Feminism and Critical Legal Theory: An American Perspective', *International Journal of the Sociology of Law*, 18, 199–215.

Podmore, D., and A. Spencer (1982), 'Women Lawyers in England: The Experience of Inequality', *Work and Occupations*, 9, 337–361.

Polan, D. (1982), 'Toward a Theory of Law and Patriarchy', in D. Kairys (ed.), *The Politics of Law: A Progressive Critique*, New York, Pantheon Books, 294–303.

Rifkin, J. (1980), 'Toward a Theory of Law and Patriarchy', *Harvard Women's Law Journal*, 3, 1, 83–95.

Roach, Sharyn L. (1986), 'The Recruitment of Men and Women Lawyers to In-House Legal Departments: The Inter-play of Environmental, Organisational and Individual Properties', Unpublished Ph.D. dissertation, University of Connecticut.

——— (1990), 'Men and Women Lawyers in In-House Legal Departments: Recruitment and Career Patterns,' *Gender & Society* 4, 2, 207–219.

Smigel, E. O. (1964), *The Wall Street Lawyer*, New York, The Free Press.

Sokoloff, N. (1988), 'Evaluating Gains and Losses by Black and White Women and Men in the Professions, 1960–1980', *Social Problems*, 35, 1, 36–53.

Spangler, E. (1986), *Professionals for Hire*, New Haven, CT, Yale University Press.

Thornton, M. (1986), 'Feminist Jurisprudence: Illusion or Reality?', *Australian Journal of Law and Society*, 3, 5–29.

Treiman, D. J., and K. Terrell (1975), 'Sex and the Process of Status Attainment', *American Sociological Review*, 40, 174–200.

U.S. Bureau of the Census (1990), *Statistical Abstract of the United States: 1990* (110th edition), Washington, DC, U.S. Government Printing Office.

Wharton, A. S. (1991), 'Structure and Agency in Socialist-Feminist Theory', *Gender & Society*, 5, 3, 373–389.

Wrong, D. (1961), 'The Oversocialized Conception of Man in Modern Sociology', *American Sociological Review*, 26, 2, 183–193.

CHAPTER 23

INVISIBLE NO MORE:
A SOCIAL HISTORY OF
WOMEN IN U.S. POLICING

DOROTHY MOSES SCHULZ

ABSTRACT

In this chapter Schulz traces the rich history of the evolution of women police in the United States. Beginning with nineteenth-century jail and prison matrons, the reader is exposed to the gradual development of the policing role for women. This role moves from the upper-middle-class moral reformers (outside the male police structure), whose main job was the social control of uneducated, poor, and immigrant women and children, to the contemporary crimefighter attempting to be equal in job and status within the male police hierarchy.

With the hindsight of historical study, Schulz concludes that women's genuine acceptance in police work by male peers and police executives has always been, at best, marginal. Each step in the long road to full officer status has been small and hard-won. Equality in pay, assignments, and promotional opportunities is still not secure for women, as Chapters 24 (by Martin) and 25 (by Gomez-Preston and Trescott) report.

Schulz concludes by noting that some see women's role in police work in the future as going beyond equal and gender-neutral to encompass, as in earlier times, a female perspective and female leadership that will shape the very nature of policing. What sorts of changes would a "women's perspective" bring to police work? Would it be more collaborative with the community? Would it be focused less on enforcement and more on social work? How would the community respond to the special styles of policing that a women's perspective might produce? Would women really change the police mission if they had a strong voice in policy development? Or as Anleu pointed out in Chapter 22, would the gender and racial segmentation in policing continue to restrict both the areas in which women participate and the "voices" with which different groups of women speak in this highly male-dominated occupation?

U.S. policewomen officially came into existence in 1910, but their roots are in the early decades of the nineteenth century—the jail and prison matron era. This era began in the 1820s, when volunteer Quaker women, following the example set by British Quakers, entered locked institutions to provide religious and secular training for women inmates. These volunteers, soon joined by other upper-middle-class women, wanted to reform the morals of the inmates and train them for respectable jobs, primarily as domestics in Christian homes. As the reformers became aware of the poor conditions under which these "fallen women" served their prison terms, they attributed a large portion of the neglect to the fact that the inmates were supervised by men. Foremost among their concerns was the sexual vulnerability of the inmates, who were frequently impregnated while in prison by either male inmates or male keepers.

Efforts by the volunteers to create better living conditions and a moral environment for the women they termed their "less fortunate sisters" evolved into a new profession for women—prison matron. These matrons were part of a general benevolent movement of the time, which brought religious, middle-class women into contact with poor women through charitable efforts and sought to create a sense of female solidarity across class lines. Clarice Feinman, who has traced the history of women in corrections, observed that these women reformers believed that women criminals could be saved only if they were removed from the corrupting influences of cities and men.[1] Prisons were therefore set in the countryside and staffed with women only. At the same time that these women reformers were attempting to improve conditions for women inmates, they were also creating a new profession for those who would follow them as paid matrons in these prisons. For almost 50 years, from the 1820s to the 1870s, this remained the only position in corrections open to women. Despite what appears to have been a revolution in women's roles, a second look negates this view, for by reinforcing women's traditional role as the caregiver to other women, these early matrons stayed within the then acceptable sexual boundaries even while ensuring new careers for themselves.[2]

At the end of the Civil War another generation of women expanded this philosophy of "women's sphere," taking it far beyond jail and prison walls into other public sector areas. Women's sphere, the "special responsibility to alleviate harsh conditions," developed from women's traditional, maternal role but allowed activist women to develop a concept of municipal housekeeping that eventually encompassed virtually all activities that placed government or voluntary agencies in contact with women or children. Since women at this time were believed to be morally superior to men, these women argued that it was only proper that they be responsible for the protection of other women in need of moral guidance.[3]

The care of those in police custody became an area of special concern. At a time when components of what today constitutes the criminal justice system were less distinct, the handling of sentenced inmates and those awaiting court appearances was ill-defined. Additionally, police stations frequently functioned as homeless shelters, and many of those who sought refuge were women and their children. The women were almost always poor and frequently intoxicated, two conditions that made them vulnerable to advances by the men responsible for their care.

Using as their model the prison matrons, these post–Civil War women activists

This article was written expressly for inclusion in this text.

demanded and won an expanded role for women caring for women and children in police custody. That their tactics and arguments were similar to those of the women who came before them was to be expected. Their social characteristics were virtually identical with those of the women in whose path they followed. They, too, were primarily socially prominent or politically well-connected upper-middle-class women of native-born families. Many had been abolitionists prior to the Civil War, and now they turned their attention to religious, temperance, and benevolent associations. By the 1880s these women succeeded in creating another new profession for women—police matron.

Police matrons brought custodial care into police stations throughout the nation. They represented another phase of women's involvement in the criminal justice system— their first entry into the police portion of the system. Within a short period of time, police matrons began to perform more than strictly custodial roles. They interviewed accused women and made sentencing recommendations, duties today assigned to probation officers. By the early years of the twentieth century they had ushered in the policewoman era, the second phase of women in policing.

This period is often defined as having begun in 1910, when Alice Stebbins Wells became the first woman in the United States to be called a policewoman. In reality it overlapped the matron movement and was not a new phenomenon but a continuation of women's professionalization within the police environment. Although the women who lobbied for police matrons and policewomen had little work experience outside their own homes and lacked the right to vote, in the period from 1880 to 1910 they created two new professions in the public sector for women. Because in some cities it took "as many" as three years for them to achieve their aims, they frequently voiced frustration.

Within this context, both the matrons' and the policewomen's movements provide insights into how women from a variety of organizations were able to join together and win the support of like-minded men to achieve goals and employment opportunities for women in fields that had previously been closed to them. These movements also indicate how firmly intertwined policewomen were with social purity and early female reform traditions. Social purity (a term generally relating to sexual morality, eradication of prostitution, and control of venereal diseases) was a major national concern for much of the nineteenth and early twentieth centuries. It led to the creation of numerous organizations whose primary purpose was to control vice and sexual activity outside of marriage by women and young people. Many leaders of these social purity organizations were vocal advocates for and allies of policewomen.

Wells, just as the few women who came before her and the many who came after her (sometimes women who had been matrons), conceived her police role in order to fulfill her vision of women helping other women. These women police embodied the concept of the policewoman-as-social worker. During this period, when social work was developing as a profession, it attracted to its ranks a class of women who, under the guise of helping others, actually were as much social controllers as social workers.

The prevention and protection theories these policewomen espoused gave them the opportunity to intervene in the lives of the women and children they claimed to be saving from a life of crime and delinquency. Although this philosophy of moral and social control gave way in the post-Depression era to a more middle-class, female careerist outlook, it was not until the modern, women-on-patrol period (which began somewhat tentatively in 1968 and wholeheartedly in 1972) that the path set by early policewomen was seriously altered. Thus, the history of the policewomen's movement is also a history of intervention by upper-middle-class women into the lives of poor women and children.

These upper-middle-class, educated policewomen used social work, not law enforcement, as their frame of reference. Their allies and peers were female (and male) social workers, feminists, temperance leaders, and members of women's civic clubs, not male police officers or chiefs. The women formed two professional organizations that fostered high entry standards and ongoing training far in excess of male requirements or interest in these areas. The International Association of Policewomen (IAP), which existed from 1915 to 1932, was modeled after and affiliated with the National Conference of Charities and Correction (NCCC—later the National Conference of Social Work [NCSW]). IAP leaders scheduled annual and regional meetings in conjunction with social workers' meetings. The International Association of Women Police (IAWP), formed in 1956 as a reincarnation of the IAP, was not as closely aligned with the social work establishment but continued to have a strong social service and women's sphere orientation well after policewomen had expanded their roles within policing.

Rooted in a value system that stressed the moral superiority of women over men and the differences between men and women, early policewomen were eager to act as municipal mothers to those whose lifestyles they believed needed discipline. Some were actually called "city mothers." In attempting to serve their female and juvenile clients in a professional, nonthreatening atmosphere, they tried to separate themselves physically from policemen and elements of the police world they viewed as hampering their mission. They stressed the need for offices away from police stations, which they viewed as inhospitable to their efforts to prevent crime and delinquency among women and juve-

niles. Although they felt they needed the legal authority the title "police" represented, policewomen did not view themselves as female versions of policemen, a concept they disparagingly termed "little men." Nor did they view policemen—usually of a lower class and education level than theirs—as their equals, although they did stress the need for cooperation with male personnel.

Their view of themselves was, therefore, based on both gender and class, and they consciously sought a peripheral, rather than an integrated, role in policing. The concept of equality of assignment with their male colleagues did not enter their world. It was inconceivable to them, just as it was to policemen. They also eschewed the most obvious trappings of policing. They were vehemently opposed to uniforms, and most chose not to carry firearms even if permitted to do so. The women's willingness to accept assignments men did not want made their presence less threatening to policemen and senior officers, but support from within the police environment was usually unenthusiastic, reluctant, and grudging.

The few African-American policewomen were even further segregated—very much a minority within a minority. Hired to work specifically with African-American women and juveniles, they shared many of the characteristics of their white sisters. They, too, were usually better educated than the average African-American man or woman, and they were often teachers, social workers, or ministers' wives with status in their communities.

The specialized roles filled by early white and African-American policewomen were not forced on them by the male police establishment but were the roles they sought. Understanding women's traditional place in policing puts recent studies into a historical perspective, because it shows that women's acceptance by male peers has always been marginal. From the first day women entered police stations, their presence was imposed on male police executives by outside forces. It was a rare municipal government official or police chief who sought to hire policewomen. Demands for women in the police environment almost always came from outsiders.

If early policewomen, who numbered about 125 employed in about 30 cities in the years from 1910 to 1917, sought neither the trappings of police nor interaction with male officers, the obvious question is, Why did they want to be police rather than purely social workers operating out of municipal or voluntary agencies? The answer lies in the class and ethnic distinctions in the United States that were partially responsible for the movement. Although these policewomen saw themselves as benevolent helpers, their assistance was not always perceived as such. Their views on prostitution, sexual morality, dance halls, penny arcades, curfews for minors, and temperance were rarely shared by those to whom they offered their "preventive help." While policewomen were overwhelmingly college-educated, native-born, upper-middle-class women, those on whom they sought to bestow their benevolence were usually uneducated, poor, and immigrant. Despite the rhetoric of the policewomen, what they viewed as benevolence was viewed by their clients as coercive social control and placed them squarely within the group Anthony Platt has called "the child savers."

Platt coined the term "child savers" to describe a group of juvenile justice system reformers who viewed themselves as "disinterested" and who "regarded their cause as a matter of conscience and morality, serving no particular class or political interests." Just as the policewomen did, these reformers saw themselves as "altruists and humanitarians dedicated to rescuing those . . . less fortunately placed in the social order." But, as Platt has observed, they went beyond this—by highlighting certain behaviors, they "invented new categories of youthful misbehavior which had been hitherto unappreciated" and not viewed as criminal or requiring correction.[4] Just as the child savers diminished the civil liberties and privacy of youths by calling for civic supervision of their activities, so, too, did policewomen bring under municipal control behavior by women and children that had previously not been viewed as requiring the attention or intervention of the police.

Because of their class distance from those they sought to save, child savers and policewomen had different definitions of morality and delinquency than those on whom they imposed their standards of behavior. Their presence in poor, immigrant neighborhoods was often unwelcome and unappreciated, as they tried to force their values on others in a maternal, yet coercive manner.

Reinforcing their class and nativist orientation, policewomen turned for support during World War I to the social purity and social hygiene agencies created to combat prostitution and liquor law violations in and around cities with military installations. Efforts by these agencies—whether voluntary or governmental—resulted in severe limitations on women's mobility and in the majority of instances placed legal and moral blame on women, rather than on the military men who sought their companionship.

Moral reform sentiments continued in the post–World War I period, providing additional allies for the growing numbers of policewomen, particularly among the Progressives, a label given by historians to various well-educated and often well-to-do individuals who joined together during the late nineteenth and early twentieth centuries to advance social and political reform. By the end of the war, the number of policewomen had doubled to about 300 working in more than 200 cities.[5]

Despite increased numbers of policewomen, there were no demands for greater integration into the police environment. In fact, the postwar era, a time when workplace gender segregation was the norm, brought about greater segregation. Women actively sought women's bureaus, some of which operated virtually as independent agencies. They processed all matters pertaining to women and children, sometimes including pre- and postsentencing incarceration for morality offenses. Demands for women's bureaus were a continuation of the ideology of women's sphere, but a new element entered the debate.

When these highly educated and motivated policewomen compared their careers with those of women in correctional facilities, settlement houses, and similar institutions, it was obvious that they lagged behind in achieving policy-making roles. These other women held managerial titles and supervised other women. Yet policewomen, despite their self-segregation within police departments, were not sufficiently independent to warrant their own rank structure. Intertwined with the advocacy of women's bureaus was their recognition that only greater segregation could justify an independent rank structure similar to that in specialized bureaus elsewhere in the police department. Not coincidentally, policewomen and their supporters not only demanded women's bureaus—they demanded that women be in charge of them. Thus, women's bureaus met the two major goals of post–World War I policewomen. They more fully defined women's specialized roles, and they created a mechanism for women to rise through the ranks, if not to the very top, then at least to the middle of the police hierarchy.

Many of the gains—both numerical and bureaucratic—made by policewomen during and after World War I were eradicated by the Depression. Although by 1929 there were close to 600 policewomen serving in 150 to 175 cities,[6] between 1929 and 1931 the number of departments employing policewomen decreased. Additionally, the 1930s spotlighted for the first time the image of the policeman as crimefighter, an image diametrically opposed to how social-work-oriented policewomen saw themselves. By 1940 there were no more than 500 policewomen, the vast majority working in the largest cities.

World War II renewed the nation's concerns with morality and delinquency, and policewomen were able to regain their World War I momentum and allies. Although World War II did not create new roles for policewomen, the women hired were not temporary replacements for men fighting the war but permanent additions to their police departments. Unlike the women personified by Rosie the Riveter, a woman hired to fill a man's industrial job during World War II, policewomen were hired for traditional policewomen's jobs, not to replace policemen who had gone to war. Because policewomen's gender-specific roles in law enforcement were not altered by the war, neither was their employment dependent on the continued absence of men. Therefore, policewomen were not faced with layoffs when the soldiers returned. While Rosie the Riveter is an enduring image from the war years, she represents a highly specialized form of women's entry into previously male occupations and had no parallel in policewomen's history.

Concerns with morality and juvenile delinquency intensified in the postwar years, allowing women to increase their wartime gains. Women's assignments also began to diversify. Policewomen often were teamed with male officers on undercover assignments and more frequently investigated other than morality-based crimes. They were issued uniforms (which were usually based on female military garb and which they rarely wore) and were trained in the use of and expected to carry their firearms. The 1950 U.S. Census reported more than 2,500 publicly employed policewomen, slightly more than 1 percent of all police and detectives and a considerable increase since 1940, when 1,775 women were counted in public and private agencies combined.

The post–World War II period and the decade of the 1950s are vital to policewomen's history not only because women's assignments and responsibilities expanded but also because a different type of woman was brought into policing. Often military veterans and no longer aligned with the social work establishment, the women entering police departments in this period were middle-class careerists, not upper-middle-class feminists and child savers. Although still better educated and higher in class orientation than their male peers, these women were less different from policemen than their predecessors had been. Their goal of upward mobility through civil service and through attainment of rank resembled the goals of policemen and underlined their differences from the first generation of policewomen. This began a trend that was accentuated in the late 1970s, when the requirements for women to become police officers were lowered to the same requirements as for men, rather than qualifications for both men and women being raised to the level they had been for policewomen.

The 1950s are normally viewed as a quiet time in the expansion of women's roles, but these "second generation" policewomen made professional gains. Factors inside and outside police departments led many of the women hired during and after the war to become dissatisfied with the philosophy of women's sphere.

Externally, societal changes pertaining to women's self-image convinced them that occupational segregation was hampering their chances for lateral or upward mobility. Since these women had entered policing to take advantage of its career opportunities rather than to impose their morality on others, their concerns were as much for their own professional development as for societal benefit. In 1956 they reestablished the International Association of Policewomen, changing its name to the International Association of Women Police (IAWP), and began to develop a group consciousness distinct from that of social workers.

Internally, larger numbers and a greater range of assignments, combined with differences in their educational and class orientation, brought policewomen into closer contact with policemen. They saw that even men who were not in traditional uniform patrol had greater career range. Men were eligible for transfer to any bureau. More important, they were eligible for civil service promotion that could increase their status and their incomes. By the 1960s, these women demanded and won similar promotional opportunities.

In 1961, two New York City policewomen sued the New York City Police Department after they were barred from taking a promotion test for sergeant. The case took more than two years to be decided, but they won. Three years later, they were promoted to sergeant; in 1967 both were promoted again, becoming the department's first female lieutenants.[7]

In the years during and soon after this and similar lawsuits, employment law changed considerably as a result of major forces in society, particularly the civil rights and women's movements. This provided new impetus for women and minorities to seek expanded roles in policing. Once again, internal and external factors came to alter the perceptions of policewomen. In 1963 Congress passed the Equal Pay Act, prohibiting unequal pay for equal work. Although the 1964 Omnibus Civil Rights Law's Title VII, prohibiting discrimination based on sex, race, color, religion, or national origin, pertained only to private employers, not government agencies, it began a string of laws and cases limiting employers' control over employment selection.

In 1969 President Richard Nixon issued Executive Order 11478, which declared that the federal government could not use sex as a qualification for hiring, forcing a number of federal law enforcement agencies to begin hiring women agents. In 1971, the Supreme Court ruled in *Griggs v. Duke Power Company* that preemployment tests had to be job-related, and in 1972 Congress passed the Revenue Sharing Act, which prohibited discriminatory use of revenue-sharing funds. Also in 1972, Congress, through the Equal Employment Opportunity Act, extended the provisions of the Civil Rights Act to government employment—including police departments.

The Law Enforcement Assistance Administration (LEAA), a Justice Department agency created under the Omnibus Crime Control and Safe Streets Act of 1968, also pushed police departments to accept equal employment. Forty percent of the funds for the improvement of law enforcement dispensed by LEAA went to local governments, and the Crime Control Act of 1973, which amended the 1968 act, specified that LEAA grantees were prohibited from discriminating in employment practices. This meant that departments that discriminated against women risked losing the federal grants that many were using to upgrade training, equipment, and facilities. In reality, no department met this fate. Yet because LEAA funds were important to job expansion in policing, combined with the new guidelines of the federal government, more positions became available to women and minorities than ever before.

With new promotional rights and newly acquired court and legislative support, more aggressive and less social-service-oriented policewomen in the 1960s moved into areas of the police department that their foremothers would never have dreamed of entering. Although their demands for greater equality were spurred at least in part by the women's movement, this was the first time in their

history that women police officers were not assisted by other professional women; instead, they were aided by new allies—federal legislation and the courts.

Yet in 1960, IAWP President Lois Lundell Higgins, reviewing the golden anniversary of women in the police service, confidently echoed earlier policewomen in the belief that if they were here to stay, it was only because they did not try to compete with men in "work that has been and always will be predominantly a man's job." Women would continue to succeed, she predicted, because "they have brought to their work talents that are peculiarly feminine—usually a highly developed interest in human relationships—and have accentuated, rather than subordinated, their femininity."[8]

Speakers at annual IAWP meetings until the 1970s were more likely to be social work professionals or women's bureau directors than policewomen on patrol or in other nontraditional assignments. But since the 1980s IAWP meetings have acquired the trappings of law enforcement, including firearms competitions and awards that frequently honor bravery under gunfire. While the IAP could exist from 1915 to 1932 with few leadership changes and still reflect the views of its members, by the time the IAWP was formed, change was coming too rapidly for the association to keep pace, forcing it to follow, rather than lead, its members. Many leaders remained at least partially committed to the older, social work ideal; they no longer represented the younger, more law-enforcement-oriented women. Also, since many leaders were in appointed ranks in their police departments, they could not risk taking positions that contradicted the wishes of their chiefs. Ironically, their vulnerable positions were often the result of the very policies they espoused.

Less than ten years after Higgins made her prediction, Indianapolis in 1968 assigned

Betty Blankenship and Elizabeth Coffal to patrol. They became the first policewomen to wear uniforms, strap gun belts to their waists, drive a marked patrol car, and answer general-purpose police calls for service on an equal basis with policemen. Although they eventually returned to traditional policewomen's duties, they were the forerunners of a break with the past. Thus began the demise of the mothering concept. The women who followed them were no longer policewomen in the traditional sense of women social workers in the police environment. They were police officers, women with a law enforcement concept similar to that of their male peers. As crimefighters, they now enforced the law, maintained order, and provided for the public's safety, just as men did.

In the six decades (1910 to 1968) from Alice Stebbins Wells to Betty Blankenship and Elizabeth Coffal, a revolution had occurred. Demands by policewomen no longer reflected their historical feminist, upper-middle-class, educated roots. Modern women, hired under the same rules as men, rejected the constraints of women's sphere and sought equality with male peers. Recent discussion over whether uniform patrol is as much service as crimefighting may have aided these women in breaking down male police resistance to placing them on patrol, but their primary focus is not the components of patrol but the opportunity it presents for equal treatment from and within the police hierarchy, including assignment and promotional equality.

For the first time, the majority of women now enter criminal justice professions for the same reasons as men. In this regard, they are similar to other women who have in the past 20 years entered male fields on an equal basis with male colleagues. They do not seek to change their chosen professions; rather, they wish to benefit from the financial or status rewards these fields offer. Today's women became police officers for the tangible rewards of pay, promotions, and pensions. Their attitudes and goals are similar to those of the men with whom they train and ride in patrol cars, and against whom they compete for assignment and promotion. Although not aligned with traditional women's advocacy groups, today's women police officers are part of a broader social movement which they unwittingly may have helped to create but from which they, too, profited.

Equality, though, has brought new issues for study. As of 1993, only four women have been appointed police chiefs in major cities. Elizabeth Watson, an 18-year veteran of the Houston Police Department, was appointed chief in February 1990. Although a new mayor chose not to retain her two years later and she was forced to return to the rank of assistant chief, by the end of 1992 she was heading to Austin, Texas, as chief. Other women serving as large-city chiefs in early 1993 included Elaine S. Hedtke in Tucson, Arizona; Leslie Martinez in Portsmouth, Virginia; and Mary F. Rabadeau in Elizabeth, New Jersey.[9]

The proportionately small number of women moving up the ranks is of concern to many women officers, as well as to researchers studying their career patterns and paths. Achieving rank in paramilitary organizations that depend overwhelmingly on periodic civil service testing as the means of upward mobility is a slow progression. The process for women has been further slowed, according to some researchers, indicating that women are not availing themselves of promotional opportunities because of personal reasons and also because systemic discrimination against them still exists. The personal reasons women list include not wanting to give up positions with daylight hours owing to family and child-care requirements. Systemic reasons include lack of assignment to high-profile units, seniority beyond the minimal eligibility requirements (often keyed to veteran status), negative (possibly biased) supervisory evaluations, and general attitudes of male coworkers that psychologically discourage ambition.[10]

These systemic reasons belie the legal equality women have achieved and highlight issues pertaining to the subtle and not so subtle discrimination women face as they compete with men on terms defined by and for men.

Recently, these barriers to real equality have spawned new debates. No longer concerned with whether women provide police service in the same way men do, or whether women will somehow change (i.e., soften and humanize) U.S. policing, a growing number of feminist criminologists have argued that women should not have to become "little men" to succeed in policing. As feminists rethink the meaning of equality and pose new theories of its effect on women in the workplace, their views could lessen the demands on women police officers to conform to male definitions of a "good cop," but such views could also provide ammunition for opponents of equality who continue to believe that women's place in policing should be determined by gender—by women's sphere.

Previous feminists writing about women's roles in the criminal justice system (particularly Dorothy Bracey, Clarice Feinman, and Barbara Raffel Price) criticized any vestiges of women's sphere. They advocated gender-neutral policing as the only way women could achieve equality, as well as supervisory and policy-making positions, within the police world.[11] While not in agreement with all the prevailing definitions of success in the police environment, these observers believed that women would be unable to advance professionally by stressing only their differences from, rather than their similarities to, the men who make up the overwhelming majority of police. In this belief they reflected the views of many women officers, who came to believe

that "equal" meant "the same as" rather than "different but just as good as."

Those staking out the new feminist criminology disagree; they do not view gender neutrality positively. Kathleen Daly and Meda Chesney-Lind, discussing postfeminist consciousness, believe that feminists who "sought to achieve equality with men in the public sphere . . . omitted more subtle questions of equality and difference now being raised." Although they are referring to offenders when they observe that "feminist legal scholars are more skeptical of a legal equality model because the very structure of law continues to assume that men's lives are the norm," they could just as easily be discussing women's experiences in the police environment.[12]

Addressing policing directly, Nanci Koser Wilson believes that "not only should there be female police; but there should also be room for women's perspective on what policing should be. Not only should there be female detectives; but women's style of detective work . . . should receive attention." She echoes an earlier view when she states that "women were not introduced to policing . . . to mimic policemen or become stilted versions of men."[13]

If this postfeminist view begins to predominate, we may see the day when Lois Lundell Higgins's 1960 prediction that women will succeed by accentuating, rather than subordinating, their femininity will again prove correct!

NOTES

1. Clarice Feinman, *Women in the Criminal Justice System* (New York: Praeger Publishers, 1980), 27.
2. Ibid., 108–109.
3. Lori D. Ginzberg, *Women and the World of Benevolence: Morality, Politics, and Class in the Nineteenth-Century United States* (New Haven: Yale University Press, 1990), 17, 37; Ann Firor

Scott (ed.), *The American Woman: Who Was She?* (Englewood Cliffs, N.J.: Prentice-Hall, 1971), 88. For a detailed look at how women used the concept of women's sphere to enter policing and eventually expand their roles, see Dorothy M. Schulz, *From Social Worker to Crimefighter: A History of Women in United States Policing* (Ann Arbor, Mich.: University Microfilms International, 1992).

4. Anthony M. Platt, *The Child Savers: The Invention of Delinquency* (Chicago: The University of Chicago Press, 1969), 3–4.

5. *The Woman Citizen,* May 3, 1919, 1055; Peter Horne, *Women in Law Enforcement,* 2d ed. (Springfield, Ill.: Charles C Thomas, 1980), 29.

6. Edith Rockwood and Augusta J. Street, *Social Protective Work of Public Agencies: With Special Emphasis on the Policewoman* (Washington, D.C.: Committee on Social Hygiene—National League of Women Voters, 1932), 10.

7. *Shpritzer v. Lang,* 32 Misc. 2d 693, 1961, modified and affirmed, 234 NYS 2d 1962; Felicia Shpritzer, interview with author, Nov. 21, 1991.

8. Lois Lundell Higgins, "Golden Anniversary of Women in Police Service," *Law and Order,* August 1960, 4.

9. Barbara Hustedt Crook, "Cosmo Talks to Elizabeth Watson: Houston's Pioneering Police Chief," *Cosmopolitan,* October 1990, 116+. On Feb. 17, 1992, Mayor Bob Lanier replaced Chief Watson with a male former member of the Houston PD. Lanier stated that despite "generally a positive impression" of Watson, he preferred to begin a new administration with a new police chief. See Roberto Suro, "Houston Mayor Removes Female Police Chief," *The New York Times,* Feb. 18, 1992, A20:1–6. See also "A Few More Glass Ceilings Are Shattered," *Law Enforcement News,* Jan. 15/31, 1993, 18:1–3.

10. Comments typical of the concern over promotional patterns are from Susan Ehrlich Martin, *Women on the Move? A Report on the Status of Women in Policing* (Washington, D.C.: Police Foundation, 1989), 1, 3–4, and Cynthia G. Sulton and Roi D. Townsey, *A Progress Report on Women in Policing* (Washington, D.C.: Police Foundation, 1981), 4–5.

11. See Feinman, *Women in the Criminal Justice System,* 121 pp.; Barbara Raffel Price and Susan Gavin, "A Century of Women Policing," in Donald O. Schultz (ed.), *Modern Police Administration* (Houston: Gulf Publishing Co., 1979), 109–122; Dorothy Bracey, "Women in Criminal Justice: The Decade after the Equal Employment Opportunity Legislation," in William A. Jones, Jr. (ed.), *Criminal Justice Administration: Linking Practice and Research* (New York: Marcel Dekker, 1983), 57–78; and Edith Linn and Barbara Raffel Price, "The Evolving Role of Women in American Policing," in *The Ambivalent Force: Perspectives on the Police,* 3d ed. Abraham S. Blumberg and Elaine Niederhoffer (eds.), (New York: Holt, Rinehart and Winston, 1985), 69–80.

12. Kathleen Daly and Meda Chesney-Lind, "Feminism and Criminology," *Justice Quarterly* 5, no. 4 (December 1988): 509, 524.

13. Nanci Koser Wilson, "Feminist Pedagogy in Criminology," *Journal of Criminal Justice Education* 2, no. 1 (Spring 1991): 91.

CHAPTER 24

THE INTERACTIVE EFFECTS OF RACE AND SEX ON WOMEN POLICE OFFICERS

SUSAN E. MARTIN

ABSTRACT

On the basis of a national survey of police personnel practices sent to 446 police departments and case studies in five large municipal agencies, Martin discusses both sexism and racism, which daily affect women police officers.* The national study, conducted by the Police Foundation, determined that women have increased from 4 percent in 1978 (when the original Police Foundation study was conducted) to almost 9 percent in 1986 and that minority (primarily black) women make up a disproportionately large share of women police—a full 40 percent. Growth in supervisory positions held by women has not occurred to any meaningful extent in spite of the 5 percent increase in the number of entry-level women officers. In 1978, 1 percent of police supervisors were women (20 percent of whom were minorities), while in 1986 just over 3 percent of all supervisors were women (30 percent of whom were minorities). But most of the supervisors, departments reported, were at the first level above police officer, the sergeant level; the higher supervisory ranks of captain and above were virtually without women.

While minority women have been drawn to police work largely because of its attractive pay scale and job security, compared with opportunities in the private sector, they face both racism and sexism as they perform police work. This chapter describes the ways these two socially structured biases work in undermining job success and in creating harmful work stress. In addition to the long-standing

---

*See two reports by Susan E. Martin: "Women on the Move?: A Report on the Status of Women in Policing," *Women & Criminal Justice*, 1(1):21–40 (1989); *Women on the Move: The Status of Women in Policing*, Police Foundation, Washington, D.C., 1990.

organizational discrimination and personal prejudices of a white male police institution, Martin shows how racism separates white women from black women officers and how sexism divides black men from black women officers. Thus, Martin is able to explore the interactive, rather than additive, effects of racism and sexism for black women. By focusing on black women as the pivotal group, she can define both commonalities and differences between women officers in their experiences of sexism and between black men and women officers in the face of racism in work organizations long dominated by white men. An example of the strength and courage of one black female police officer's response to intense levels of discrimination and prejudice can be seen in Chapter 25, "Over the Edge: One Police Woman's Story of Emotional and Sexual Harassment."

Although not discussed in this chapter, Martin's earlier groundbreaking research described how women police in the late 1970s coped with a hostile, male environment in police work.* She claimed that they adapted to the stress of being token women by becoming either *police*women or police*women*. That is, in the first instance, they assumed a tough, law enforcement personality and emulated the male police model. Alternatively, women stressed their femininity and lack of ability or inclination to engage in male types of behavior involving physical prowess or risk. While today women police are less likely to feel quite so alone or be the only woman in their department or precinct, they are still under considerable pressure from sexual harassment and are expected to meet the standards established by and for men. Data given in this chapter on promotion suggest that very few women are meeting with success in the judgment of their male superiors. Martin's findings reinforce a Morash and Greene study which found that the evaluation of police officers is based on male performance norms with little attention to whether existing male-defined standards produce high-quality policing.[†]

In your experience, do women and men police exhibit different or similar work styles? Why do women function the way they do? Do all women function the same? How do race, ethnicity, class, and sexual orientation affect women's (and men's) policing? Would performing differently lead to better policing? What would be the impact on different groups of women and their careers if they did police work differently, given the white-male-dominated nature of law enforcement?

---

*Susan E. Martin. 1980. *Breaking and Entering: Policewomen on Patrol.* Berkeley: University of California Press.
[†]Merry Morash and J. Greene. 1988. "Evaluating Women on Patrol: A Critique of Contemporary Wisdom," *Evaluation Review.* 10:230–255.

For many years, women and minority men faced discriminatory selection criteria that virtually excluded them from police jobs. The Equal Employment Opportunity Act of 1972 prohibited discrimination by public employers on the basis of race, color, religion, sex, or national origin. Eliminating racist and sexist employment practices in police departments, however, has been a slow and difficult process.

This chapter examines the increasing proportions of women and minorities in urban police departments since 1978, then explores the interactive effect of race and gender on the experience of women officers, particularly Black women. It looks at the ways in which racism has created cleavages among women officers, while sexism divides Black men and women, thus imposing a double burden on Black women.

INTRODUCTION: DISCRIMINATION, LEGAL CHANGES, AND THE INTERSECTION OF RACE AND SEX

Like many other work organizations, during the 1970s large municipal police agencies faced lawsuits alleging race and sex discrimination in selection, promotion, and other employment practices. A number of the lawsuits were initiated separately by Blacks and women, then consolidated by the courts (Sullivan 1988). As a result, many departments were forced to alter discriminatory selection criteria related to education, age, height, weight, use of arrest records, and agility tests (see Sulton and Townsey 1981). Others did so voluntarily or under the threat of litigation.

By the end of 1986, 15 percent of the departments in cities serving populations over 50,000 were operating under court orders or consent decrees, and 42 percent had adopted voluntary affirmative action plans; only four percent of municipal agencies still had minimum height and weight standards as entry criteria (Fyfe 1987).

Although modifications in the selection criteria opened the door to the station house to minority men and all women, the actual integration of those formerly excluded groups still is not complete. The barriers to acceptance and equality in policing faced by Black men and all women overlap to some extent.

They have in common, for example, the fact that they are subjected to the problems related to their status as "tokens." Kanter (1977) observed that by virtue of their numerical rarity, "tokens" are subjected to different treatment by dominants. Due to their visibility, tokens face extra performance pressures, exclusion, and stereotypic treatment by those around them.

At the same time, white men reacted differently to the entrance of women and Black men into policing. One major difference is the stereotypic roles into which various minority groups are cast. Women of both races often are cast into the sexually-defined roles of "mother," "pet," or "seductress," or are labeled "bitches" for failure to comply with the stereotypes (Kanter 1977). Stereotypes of Blacks, particularly males, on the other hand, emphasize their devalued social (not sexual) status.

Women who enter previously male-dominated occupations face a variety of organizational and interpersonal barriers (Epstein 1983; Kanter 1977; Martin 1980; Reskin and Roos 1990; Swerdlow 1989; Williams 1989; Wolshok 1981; Zimmer 1986), which in turn affect their work-related behavior. Reskin (1988) argues that men respond to women's intrusion into their occupational spheres by adopting three possible patterns of sex differentiation: allocating jobs and tasks according to sex; treating women paternalistically; and sexualizing women or the workplace. Gutek (1985) explained the treatment of women in the workplace as a result of "spill over" of sex

This research was completed when the author was a project director at the Police Foundation and was supported in part with funding from the Ford Foundation. It is a revised version of a paper presented at the American Sociological Association Meetings, San Francisco, August 1989.

Source: Susan E. Martin, "The Interactive Effects of Race and Sex on Women Police Officers," in Roslyn Muraskin (ed.), *The Justice Professional*, vol. 6, no. 1, winter 1992, pp. 155–172.

role behavior, because workers are unable to completely separate their work and sex roles. Women in male-dominated occupations are treated as women because their constellation of statuses are inconsistent: those associated with the female sex role become salient, and males treat their female co-workers on the job as they treat women in other roles. The result is a variety of dilemmas and conflicts because sex role norms of appropriate "feminine" behavior conflict with occupational role definitions of appropriate behavior.

Focusing on policing, Martin (1980) observed that the integration of women into police patrol as co-workers:

> . . . threatens to compromise the work, the way of life, the social status, and the self-image of the men in one of the most stereotypically masculine occupations in society.

Consequently, the men's resistance to the incursion of women has included overt discrimination in selection, assignments, and evaluations; exclusion from the informal culture; different standards on evaluations; and harassment including sexual harassment.

Race, too, affects an individual's occupational and economic opportunities. Racial inequality is built into the social structure of the U.S. and, despite civil rights laws and substantial changes over the past 30 years, discrimination against Blacks persists in hiring, pay, promotion, assignment, and the conditions of work.

Until quite recently, the number of Black police officers was very limited. Black officers were denied scout car assignments or relegated to cars marked "colored police," allowed to arrest only other minority citizens, and denied choice assignments and promotions (Leinen 1984; Sullivan 1988). In the past 30 years, the growing representation of Black officers has been accompanied by substantial progress in eliminating institutional discrimination in policing. Nevertheless, problems remain in the hiring and promotion of Black officers. These arise in part because some Blacks do not do as well on traditional measures such as written tests. Consequently, Black officers' potential to achieve leadership positions has been hindered and charges of discrimination and reverse discrimination have led to tensions within many agencies.

Understanding of how employment discrimination and efforts to eliminate it have affected various disadvantaged groups has been hampered because studies have focused either on the effects of race or sex discrimination, ignoring those persons with both disadvantaged race and gender status—minority women. To what extent have they experienced "double jeopardy" (Beale 1970), the positive effect of the double negative (Epstein 1973), or a double bind (Reid 1984) as a result of their unique combination of ethnic and gender statuses?

Research on the perspectives of minority women is limited. As Hooks (1981) noted, most studies of "Blacks" have generalized from data on Black men; examinations of "women" have been universalized to all women on the basis of white women's experience. Black women have been regarded as deviant cases (Gilkes 1981) or they have been invisible "others," objects lacking full human subjectivity (Collins 1986).

Several studies have drawn parallels and identified differences in the dynamics of racism and sexism and their effects (Hacker 1951 and 1975; Feagin and Feagin 1978). These have sometimes been useful as pedagogical tools but, as King (1988: 45) stated:

> . . . we learn very little about Black women from this analogy . . . because (t)he scope, both institutionally and culturally, and the intensity of the physical and psychological impact of racism is qualitatively different from that of sexism.

Recent feminist critiques have undermined the assumption that the effects of racism and sexism are additive (Dill 1983; Palmer 1983; Smith and Stewart 1983; King 1988; Hurtado 1989). Instead, they have sought to develop an interactive model to explore the manner and conditions under which women of color respond to "the interlocking nature of oppression" (Collins 1986: 519) on the basis of their unique combination of race, sex, and class. How does their situation at the intersection of racism and sexism affect their perspectives and behavior within a racist and sexist occupational structure?

Dugger (1988: 442) asserted that to understand the race-specific effects of differences in sex role attitudes one must consider how the dynamics of race have differentially structured Black and white women's experience of gender. Smith and Stewart (1983) point out that differences in the relationships between white men and Black and white women probably affect the way each group of women experiences discrimination. White women have frequent and intimate contact with white men and the potential for increased power by association with or through the influence of a powerful male. But white women's influence is diminished because they have internalized an image of helplessness and accepted exclusion from selected white male arenas. In contrast, racism has often produced physical separation of Blacks and whites and has rested on an element of fear based on white hostility and physical intimidation.

These differences in the relational position of white and Black women with respect to the source of privilege, white men, has led Hurtado (1980: 845) to distinguish between white women's "subordination through seduction" resting on socialization to docility, passivity, and internalized social controls, and Black women's "subordination through rejection" arising from physical separation and a lack of intimate interaction with white men.

Black and white women also historically have differed in their class and occupational

experiences. By examining the experiences of Black and white men and women in a single occupation—police work—it is possible to control for these differences while examining the intersection of race and sex. Policing is one of the few occupations in which there is sufficient heterogeneity of personnel to do so.

A full interactive model of the effects of race and sex would consider "the commonalities that bind and the differences that divide the four groups" (Smith and Stewart, 1983:8). Instead, this paper focuses on Black women as the pivotal group in defining the commonalities and differences between women officers in their experiences of sexism and Black officers in the face of racism in work organizations long dominated by white men. It thus attempts to understand how the interaction of racism and sexism modify the forms and impacts of each.

METHODOLOGY

The data reported in this paper are part of a study that assessed the status of women in policing through both a national survey and case studies in five large municipal agencies (Martin 1990). The survey findings are based on responses to questionnaires sent to 446 municipal departments serving populations over 50,000 in 1986 and a similar survey conducted by the Police Foundation using the same sample in 1978 (Sulton and Townsey, 1981).

The case studies conducted in five agencies explored departmental policies and procedures for integrating women into policing and officers' perspectives on changes in the status of women officers over the past two decades. In three of the agencies (Detroit, Washington, D.C., and Birmingham) the proportion of women officers and supervisors was above the municipal department mean; in two others (Chicago and Phoenix) women's representation was at or below the mean for women. The departments also varied with respect to region, agency size, minority representation, and affirmative action policy. Detroit, Chicago, and Birmingham were operating under court order or consent decree; Washington and Phoenix had voluntary affirmative action plans in effect.

In each agency, about 30 female and 20 male officers and mid-level supervisors were randomly selected for an interview to be conducted during on-duty time. Approximately 25 of these persons actually were interviewed in each agency, depending on the contingencies of scheduling, vacation leave, and their willingness to participate. The interviews were semi-structured, lasted about two and a half hours, and examined respondents' experience of job discrimination (including sexual harassment) and perception of departmental policies regarding the integration of women. Interviews also were conducted with about eight high ranking policy makers in each department regarding the development, implementation, and effectiveness of departmental policies and procedures for integrating women into policing.

INCREASES IN THE PROPORTIONS OF WOMEN AND MINORITIES IN POLICING: 1978–1986

Between 1978 and 1986 the proportion of women in policing increased from 4.2 to 8.8 percent of municipal officers; during the same period the proportion of minority officers in large and moderate sized urban departments rose from 13.8 to 22.5 percent of the sworn personnel, as shown in Table 1. Thus the representation of minorities in policing now approaches their representation in the urban population (Sullivan, 1988),[1] but women still are greatly under-represented in policing.

Focusing on the representation of various minority groups by sex, Table 2 indicates that minority women make up only 3.5 percent of all officers, but comprise 40 percent of all female officers, whereas minority males make up only 21 percent of the men. The table also shows that most minority officers of both sexes are Black, but that Black women comprise a much larger fraction of the female officers (31 percent) than Black men comprise of the male officers (12.5 percent).

Women have made more modest gains in obtaining promotions to supervisory ranks. In 1978 they comprised only 1 percent of all supervisors; by the end of 1986 they made up 3.3 percent of those sworn personnel with the rank of sergeant or higher. Twenty-nine percent of the female supervisors are minority women.

---

[1]In 1985, Blacks made up 12.1% of the American population; Hispanics 6.4%. Because both minority groups tend to live in cities rather than suburban or rural areas, however, they probably remain somewhat underrepresented in urban police agencies. In contrast, women represent 52% of the population and 44% of the labor force.

TABLE 1

Mean Percentage of Police in Municipal Departments in 1978 and 1986 by Ethnicity and Sex

Ethnicity	1978			1986		
	Male	Female	Total	Male	Female	Total
White	83.6	2.6	86.2	72.2	5.3	77.5
Non-white	12.2	1.6	13.8	19.0	3.5	22.5
Total	95.8	4.2	100%	91.2	8.8	100%

TABLE 2
1986 Mean Percentage of Municipal Police Officers
by Sex and Ethnicity

Ethnicity	Male (N = 145,296)	Female (N = 13,979)	Total personnel (N = 159,275)
White	79.1	60.2	77.5
Black	12.5	30.7	14.1
Hispanic	6.5	7.5	6.5
Other	1.9	1.6	1.9
Total	100%	100%	100%

WOMEN OFFICERS' PERCEPTIONS OF DISCRIMINATION

Interviews with 35 white and 31 Black women in the five case study departments indicate that most believe that they have been the victim on job-related discrimination.[2] At the same time, there were significant differences among the women's experiences and perceptions of discrimination on the basis of race and length of police experience.

Sixty-eight percent of the Black women and 80 percent of the white women reported at least one incident involving either race or sex discrimination. White women were more likely to report sex discrimination (77 percent) than Black women (55 percent). Fifty-two percent of the Black women and 20 percent of the white women reported racial discrimination. Thirty-nine percent of the Black women and 17 percent of the white women reported being victim of both race and sex discrimination. Thus while most women officers have been faced with sexism, Black women also have had to deal with racism, which in many instances is more salient in their consciousness.

Black women were as likely as whites (36 percent versus 38 percent) to report benefitting from being Black or female. The benefits were primarily desirable assignments and promotions under court-imposed promotion quotas. The white women were much more likely than the Black women, however, to assert that despite the fact that they had benefitted from them, they opposed affirmative action procedures.

How long they have been police officers also affected the women's perceptions of discrimination. The newer women were far less likely to assert that they have been the victim of discrimination than those with longer police experience. Eighty-eight percent of the women who became officers before 1975, and 79 percent of those who joined between 1975 and 1980 stated that they had been subjected to discrimination on the basis of their race or sex; only 20 percent of the women who became officers in 1985 or 1986 claimed they had faced discrimination.

The apparent decrease in sex discrimination has several possible explanations. The newer women may be less sensitive to discrimination, although many noted (unlike women of the earlier cohorts) that their academy training had included information on the department's EEO policy and grievance procedures, including those related to sexual harassment. It is possible that with more time

---

[2]The survey data often grouped Black, Hispanic, Native American, and Asian women as "minority women." The remainder of the paper, however, focuses exclusively on Black women because the interviews included very few respondents from those other minority groups.

and police experience the newer women may also face discrimination. Alternatively, there may have been a real change.

Both male and female respondents agreed that women today are better accepted in policing, although what they meant by "accepted" varied widely. Women now are routinely assigned to the patrol and to virtually all specialized units. Men are accustomed to working with them. Departmental policies, backed up by a few highly visible disciplinary actions, may have sent a clear message that the discrimination and harassment no longer will be tolerated as they were when women first went onto patrol. These changes, coupled with the effects of promotions of women and minorities to supervisory positions, may have resulted in a reduction in "rational bias" discrimination. Such discrimination occurs when mid-level supervisors respond to perceived cues from superiors suggesting that a show of bias would be rewarded by others or, in the absence of such cues, discriminate based on beliefs concerning the preferences of their bosses (Larwood et al. 1988).

THE INTERSECTION OF RACE AND SEX: BLACK WOMEN OFFICERS AND DISCRIMINATION

How do Black women officers experience and deal with sexism and racism? To what extent are power, opportunities, and numbers—those variables identified by Kanter (1977) as keys to understanding work-related contingencies and occupational performance—different for Black and white women in policing?

Black men and all females are disadvantaged vis-a-vis white males, who have excluded them from positions of power in police departments. Black females, however, appear to be at the greatest disadvantage. White men often have retained control of Black women by disrupting their potential alliances with Black men and white women

through a divide and conquer strategy that rested on the racism of white females and sexism of Black males. Furthermore, even when Black females unified with either of these groups, they have less power to share or confer on them and so face the constant threat of being betrayed or undermined by that group in its quest for advantage.

The manipulation of racism and sexism to the detriment of Black women was strikingly illustrated on the organizational level by the legal struggle over promotion procedures in the Chicago police department, as each group protected its own interest. That agency's hiring and promotion process came under supervision of the federal courts as a result of *US vs. City of Chicago*. In 1973, after a finding that the sergeant's promotional exam was discriminatory, the judge imposed quotas for promotions. Black women initially were called from the promotion list as Blacks, without distinctions between males and females. When the white women realized the Black women were being promoted ahead of them, however, they filed a claim asserting that all females should be treated as one single minority group. The judge ruled that Black women could not be given double benefits and asked the lawyer from the Afro-American League, which was representing all Blacks, if Black women could be counted as women not Blacks for the purpose of the quota.

The lawyer agreed, without consulting the women. Perhaps he recognized that this change would increase the number of positions for which Blacks were eligible. A less benign interpretation of his actions, however, views them as knowingly undercutting the Black women by removing them from competition with Black men in order to increase the latter's promotion opportunities. For the Black women, however, this meant having to compete with the white women whose test scores were better than theirs while those of Black men were not.

The Black women subsequently brought a lawsuit protesting that decision. The judge agreed that they had a valid complaint but refused to grant it because it was deemed "not timely." As one Black woman observed, "Nobody was looking out for our interests."

The differences in the cultural images and job-related experiences of Black and white women in general have been repeated in their reception as police officers. Historically white women were "put on a pedestal" and spared from doing physical labor in exchange for accepting white men's domination and control of their sexuality. Black women had no pedestal. Most worked outside their own homes, often for white women. White women accepted their difference from Black women, and adopted a sense of superiority although, in reality, they were economically and psychologically dependent on white men.

When women initially were assigned to patrol, the white men who dominated policing treated Black and white women according to those traditional patterns. Male and female respondents stated that the first groups of white women assigned to patrol, particularly those that were physically attractive or were attached to influential white men, were "protected" from street assignments; Black women were not. One woman noted:

> White women were put on a pedestal, treated like wives. . . . A lot of white women got jobs doing typing for commanders and downtown assignments. They're high priced secretaries.

In addition, on street patrol white women were more likely to be protected. Being able to count on fellow officers for back up in dangerous situations is a major element in the willingness of an officer to take police action. Providing back up to others, particularly when they call for assistance, is a central norm of police work (Westley 1970). At the same time, officers may support, control, or sanction others by their willingness to "slide

in," adding to the police presence, even when it is not assigned by a dispatcher, and by the speed with which they respond to a call for assistance.

The white patrolmen tended to be protective of white women and the latter often acquiesced by letting them take control of situations because they wanted acceptance and back up. Male protectiveness still persists and creates a dilemma for women. As a male supervisor explained:

> You can't get the men to stop being protective, being the first through the door, backing up women more than they would a man, not letting women take risks. . . . Then the men complain the women lack courage.

Black women also observed that they had been told to remain "back covers" by male partners and most did so. Yet even when they deferred and accepted a passive role, they could not count on being protected as females. A Black woman asserted:

> Black women don't expect to be nice to (white men) because white males won't protect us on the street.

Black men also tended to be protective of women but Black women could not count on their support and assistance. First, they were fewer in number and, therefore, less available as back up when needed. Second, they were sometimes pressured by the white men not to back the women up. Third, some Black men were as strongly opposed to women on patrol as the white men and behaved accordingly.

Martin (1980) observed that a lack of support from other officers resulted in two divergent responses: a more cautious approach to policing and, alternatively, greater self reliance. Some women of both races reacted to male protectiveness by seeking to act independently, despite the punitive reaction of the men. This reaction included refusal to share job knowledge or teach women the skills they routinely imparted to new men and exposing them to greater danger by denying them back up, putting them alone on "killer" footbeats, and "keying out" their radio transmissions (by obscuring them with static). The women's work was closely monitored, they were punished for trivial errors by supervisors, and assigned to the station despite requests to remain on the street (then subjected to criticism for not being "streetwise"). In addition, their personal identity was undercut by being labeled "dykes" and "bitches."

Black women faced racist expectations that compounded gender-based handicaps. It was assumed that they knew less but had to produce more than others to prove their capabilities. A Black woman explained:

> A male could goof off all day and nobody'd say a thing. But especially a Black woman . . . has to work twice as hard.

Women in positions of authority often faced additional challenges which appear to have been compounded for Black females. For example, a Black female detective observed that precinct supervisors often call the burglary unit for information and advice but white males argue with the advice she gives. Another Black female detective observed that the unique effect of her race and sex status produced ambiguity with respect to the nature of the discrimination she faced:

> Sometimes I couldn't tell if what I faced was racial or sexual or both 'cause the Black female is the last one on the totem pole in the department.

A Black female supervisor had a white male subordinate who deliberately violated procedures. She noted that when that man transferred another supervisor had problems with him,

> . . . so it wasn't a female thing . . . but at the time I couldn't be sure. . . . I felt he was rebelling against me because I was a female

lieutenant and a Black lieutenant. I had a double whammy on me as female and Black.

Facing the "double whammy," however, emboldened several Black female supervisors to challenge the system of discrimination they perceived. One Black female supervisor reported that the men in her squad stopped producing, which made her look bad. When she confronted a Black officer about the low productivity, he stated that the white men had pressured the Blacks into embarrassing their female supervisor by threatening not to back them up. The supervisor, invoking racial solidarity, noted that there were more Blacks than whites in the squad and urged the Black men to stop letting themselves be dominated by whites.

Another Black female sergeant directly challenged the systematic discrimination she observed in performance evaluation scores. She noted that Blacks were receiving lower service ratings from their sergeants regardless of the work they were producing and that all the Black women had gotten evaluations about 20 points lower than the white females. To verify her view that these ratings were discriminatory, she kept a log of all activities for the unit for six months. The next rating period, again the whites and another Black (male) sergeant rated Blacks lower than the whites; she rated the females and Blacks higher. The lieutenant demanded an explanation and initially refused to approve her ratings. She countered:

> I told him that I was appalled at the blatant discrimination of my peers. . . . I said I'd kept a six month log on all officers and, based on this documentation, I challenged how sergeants rated their subordinates. . . . I said that if the rating were not changed I would file a grievance and let the records speak for themselves. The lieutenant sat back in his chair and said that in his 15 years as a lieutenant he'd never had a Black officer challenge him. He wondered how long it would take for a Black to speak up. He

added it took guts but the service ratings would be changed.

RELATIONS BETWEEN BLACK WOMEN AND BLACK MEN

A number of Black women observed the dilemmas they faced in dealing with Black men. When one Black woman was promoted to command staff, instead of congratulating her, the Black men suggested that she had taken "their" promotion. Elaborating on the competition theme, one woman observed:

> The white commanders put white women on desk jobs for years. As soon as Black females got desk assignments, however, the Black guys complained (while they'd been silent about white women getting those jobs). They seem to feel the Black women are in competition with them.

Independence as well as competition may cause problems for Black women in their relations with Black men. One Black woman asserted, "if you speak up or show you can think for yourself . . . you have problems from Black men." Her point was illustrated by an incident related by a Black female lieutenant. She stated that she hung up on a white lieutenant who was verbally abusive. The man then complained about her to their (Black) commander who called and asked her why she could not be nicer to the lieutenant. She responded that she had been disrespected as acting commander of her unit, then added:

> I told the commander that the only thing that I hate more than a white man trying to run over me is a Black man clearing the way.

Sexuality also sometimes affects the relationship between Black male and female officers. One Black woman stated:

> The worst harassment I got came from a Black male lieutenant. . . . He created rules that only applied to me. . . . It was outright harassment he didn't even try to cover up. It was partly sex-

ual; he said he'd have me. . . . The only reason I didn't sue is 'cause the lieutenant's Black. I guess that makes me a racist but I looked at the overall problem it would have caused and how it would be played up in the press and didn't do it. If he'd have been anything else I'd have sued his butt.

Another related an instance in which resistance to a Black male partner had life-threatening consequences:

> I had a partner who tried to pry into my private life. He called me stuck up when I wouldn't answer his questions. . . . When he put his hand on my arm, I slapped him. After that he wouldn't get out of the car on runs.

A third woman observed:

> The Black men have assumed they could make sexual approaches to Black women they would hesitate making to whites.

"GETTING UNITY IS LIKE PULLING TEETH:" RELATIONS AMONG WOMEN OFFICERS

All respondents agreed that there is little unity among women. Factors keeping women from acting as a unified political force include divergent occupational role and sex role perspectives, racism, and men's success in applying a "divide and conquer" strategy so that women do not see it in their best interest to organize.

For women officers, sex role norms of appropriate "female" behavior conflict with occupational role definitions of behavior appropriate for a police officer. This leads to interactional dilemmas in their routine interactions with male officers who expect to treat fellow officers as peers but tend to treat female officers as females. Among the dilemmas are when they should act "like a cop," how to still act "like a woman," and how to respond to the sex role stereotypes into which they are cast (Martin 1980).

Faced with these dilemmas, as well as openly discriminatory treatment and the problems of being highly visible tokens, women officers' responses fall into two broad patterns of behavior which transcend racial lines, further dividing them. One group of women, characterized as adopting a deprofessionalized police*women* occupational style, tend to accept the stereotypic sex roles of "pet" or "seductress," emphasize "being a lady" on and off the job, welcome or tolerate the "protection" of males, display little initiative or aggressiveness on street patrol, and seek non-patrol assignments and personal acceptance. The other group, characterized as *police*women, identify with the policemen's culture and seek to gain acceptance by being more professional, aggressive, loyal, street-oriented, and macho than the men (Martin 1980). In resisting traditional sex role stereotypes, however, they face defeminizing labels such as "dyke" or "bitch" as punishment for outproducing the men.

Most female officers, in fact, have sought a balance between these types. They assert that they have been able to maintain their femininity and succeed as officers, gaining individual acceptance as "just me." Nevertheless, men continue to treat women officers as sexual targets and mistrust them as patrol officers and women officers often are their own worst critics. Respondents were particularly outspoken about those women that behave "like clinging vines" or "act mannish" on the job and those that "act like sluts" or "try to make their way around the department on knee pads" because each of these behaviors contributes to negative stereotyping that "rubs off on us."

Some women belong to state or national women's law enforcement organizations. Women's efforts to organize within their own agencies, however, have been short-lived or sporadic. Chicago is the only case study department in which there is an active

women officers' organization, the Coalition of Law Enforcement Officers (CLEO). Formally open to all officers, CLEO was formed in 1989 to address the concerns of Black women officers through educational growth and support activities. A white supervisor, admiring CLEO's success, said:

> White women won't be organized. (At the CLEO meeting) they were talking about daycare! . . . White women have the housewife syndrome; many Black women are single, used to running family, and are more assertive. . . . Black women have much more consciousness of abuse; white women are less aware of abuse as women.

Illustrating this point, one white woman said, "there was nothing we could do for each other." Another asserted:

> Had we organized as a group, it would have hampered our acceptance. We went out as individuals and fit in as individuals and that was the best thing we did for acceptance. If we'd set ourselves apart, it would have turned people off.

Black women were less openly critical of other women and less likely to espouse an individualistic strategy for gaining acceptance. Nevertheless, they too demonstrated divergent approaches for organizational survival.

Racism compounds the divisions. Several Blacks asserted that white women are as racist as white men; others recounted incidents of racism involving women. Some of these were individual; others more organized, as illustrated by the white women's legal action in *U.S. v. Chicago.*

Many of the women fear joining a women's group since the men perceive it both as a direct threat to their power, and as implicitly joining "them" (the other racial group), which is treated as an act of racial disloyalty. For women of both races, acceptance by male officers is more important than that of other women. Women usually work with men and depend on them for back up, making their support a matter of life and death. Men have more experience, "muscle," and are available in greater numbers than women officers. In addition, social activities, including dating and marriages, occur along racial lines. This permits men of each race to influence women's on-duty behavior by threatening social isolation.

Both white and Black men have used racism to control "their" women and prevent a unified effort to address sex discrimination. When a white female rejected the sexual advances of a white male, he started the rumor that she only slept with Blacks, using both racism and sexism to doubly discredit the woman both as "promiscuous" and "disloyal." A Black female supervisor observed:

> They keep us competing, fat versus thin, old versus young, and women seem to fall for it. Getting unity is like pulling teeth. . . . The women say (when I try to counsel them), "she doesn't want to help us" and while the women are feuding, the men are moving up.

White women can gain more from their alliance with white males than Black women can get from cooperation with Black men because white men have more power over the departmental power structure. But white men also have more to lose and other potential allies, so they have less incentive to share power with white women and are able to extract compliance with sex role stereotypes and sexual favors as the price for cooperation.

For Black women a close alliance with Black men offers social benefits and support in fighting racial discrimination. But Black men also sometimes are reluctant to share their limited power, and find they can get rewards from the white men by displaying male solidarity against the incursion of women into work long defined as "masculine."

CONCLUSIONS

Between 1978 and 1986, minority representation in policing increased substantially, but the proportion of women police officers grew more modestly. Women still comprise less than 10 percent of the sworn police officers in municipal departments, with minority (primarily Black) women making up only 4 percent of all officers. Nevertheless, minority women constitute 16 percent of minority personnel whereas white women comprise only 7 percent of the white police.

As tokens who threaten the men's work, informal work culture, and occupational self image, female police officers have faced a number of barriers to their integration and acceptance in policing. Although overt discrimination against women officers has diminished, discrimination and sexual harassment continue. For Black women, the problems they face as women are compounded by patterns of racism, leaving them vulnerable as targets for all groups' displaced frustrations and hostilities. White men's ability to "divide and conquer" has sometimes encouraged Black men to harass the women in order to gain acceptance as "one of the boys." In such instances, Black women are a safer target than white women, some of whom had personal access to powerful white men. At the same time, they played on white women's racism and fear of isolation to inhibit them from uniting with Black women.

Women have coped with their situation by adopting individualistic strategies to gain acceptance, acquiescing to stereotypic roles and accepting the protection and support of the men, or by strictly adhering to police work norms. For white women this included embracing the racial bias of the dominant white males. Although white and Black women have occasionally supported each other in fighting sex discrimination, white women have avoided unifying as a group or allying with the politically weak Black women. Black women have tended to ally politically with Black men and focus their political efforts on fighting racism on the job.

In conclusion, the experiences of Black and white women in police work appear to have differed in ways that are both race-specific and context-related. Although both groups of women officers frequently have encountered sexism, for Black women the additional burden of racism has increased performance pressures, limited their access to power, and resulted in uncertain alliances. Some Black women have benefitted from affirmative action programs. Others have developed remarkable strength and self reliance, enabling them to act independently. Nevertheless, these women have had a difficult struggle, having to perform with fewer informal supports and reduced margin for error.

REFERENCES

Beale, F., 1970. "Double Jeopardy: To Be Black and Female," pp. 90–100 in T. Cade (ed.), *The Black Woman: An Anthology.* New York: New American Library.

Collins, P. H., 1986. "Learning from the Outsider Within: The Sociological Significance of Black Feminist Thought." *Social Problems* 33:514–532.

Dill, B., 1983. "Race, Class and Gender: Prospects for an All-Inclusive Sisterhood," *Feminist Studies* 9:131–150.

Dugger, K., 1988. "Social Location and Gender-Role Attitudes: A Comparison of Black and White Women." *Gender and Society* 2:425–448.

Epstein, C. F., 1973. "The Positive Effects of the Multiple Negative: Explaining the Success of Black Professional Women." *American Journal of Sociology* 78:912–935.

Epstein, C. F., 1983. *Women in Law.* Garden City: Anchor Books.

Feagin, J., and C. B. Feagin, 1978. *Discrimination American Style: Institutional Racism and Sexism.* Englewood Cliffs: Prentice-Hall.

Fyfe, J., 1987. *Police Personnel Practices, 1986.* (Baseline Data Report Vol. 18, Number 6). Washington, D.C.: International City Management Association.

Gilkes, C. T., 1981. "From Slavery to Social Welfare: Racism and the Control of Black Women," pp. 288–300 in A. Swerdlow and H. Lessing (eds.), *Class, Race and Sex: The Dynamics of Control.* Boston: G. K. Hall.

Gutek, B. A., 1985. *Sex and the Workplace: The Impact of Sexual Behavior and Harassment on Women and Organizations.* San Francisco, CA: Jossy-Bass.

Hacker, H., 1951. "Women as a Minority Group." *Social Forces* 30:60–69.

Hacker, H., 1975. "Class and Race Differences in Gender Roles," in L. Duberman (ed.), *Gender and Sex in Society.* New York: Praeger.

Hooks, B., 1981. *Ain't I a Woman: Black Women and Feminism.* Boston, MA: South End Press.

Hurtado, A., 1980. "Relating to Privilege: Seduction and Rejection in the Subordination of White Women and Women of Color." *Signs* 14:833–855.

Kanter, R. M., 1977. *Men and Women of the Organization.* New York: Basic Books.

King, D., 1988. "Multiple Jeopardy, Multiple Consciousness: The Context of a Black Feminist Ideology." *Signs* 14:42–72.

Larwood, L., E. Szwajkowski, and S. Rose, 1988. "Sex and Race Discrimination Resulting from Manager-Client Relationships: Applying the Rational Bias Theory of Managerial Discrimination." *Sex Roles* 18:9–29.

Leinen, S., 1984. *Black Police: White Society.* New York: New York University Press.

Martin, S. E., 1980. *"Breaking and Entering": Policewomen on Patrol.* Berkeley, CA: University of California Press.

Martin, S. E., 1990. *On the Move: The Status of Women in Policing.* Washington, D.C.: Police Foundation.

Milton, C., 1972. *Women in Policing.* Washington, D.C.: Police Foundation.

Palmer, P., 1983. "White Women/Black Women: The Dualism of Female Identity and Experience in the United States." *Feminist Studies* 9:151–171.

Reid, P. T., 1984. "Feminism versus Minority Group Identity: Not for Black Women Only." *Sex Roles* 10:247–255.

Reskin, B., 1988. "Bringing the Men Back In: Sex Differentiation and the Devaluation of Women's Work." *Gender and Society* 2:58–81.

Reskin, B., and P. Roos, 1990. *Job Queues, Gender Queues*. Philadelphia, PA: Temple University Press.

Smith A., and A. J. Stewart, 1983. "Approaches to Studying Racism and Sexism in Black Women's Lives." *Journal of Social Issues* 39:1–13.

Sullivan, F. A., 1988. "Minority Officers: Current Issues," pp. 331–346 in R. Dunham and G. Alpert (eds.), *Critical Issues in Policing: Contemporary Readings*. Prospect Heights, IL: Waveland Press.

Sulton, C., and R. Townsey, 1981. *A Progress Report on Women in Policing*. Washington, D.C.: Police Foundation.

Swerdlow, M., 1989. "Men's Accommodations to Women Entering a Nontraditional Occupation: A Case of Rapid Transit Operatives." *Gender and Society* 3:373–387.

Westley, W., 1970. *Violence and the Police*. Boston, MIT Press.

Williams, C. L., 1989. *Gender Differences at Work: Women and Men in Nontraditional Occupations*. Berkeley, CA: University of California Press.

Wolshok, M. L., 1981. *Blue Collar Women: Pioneers on the Female Frontier*. Garden City, NY: Doubleday.

Zimmer, L., 1986. *Women Guarding Men*. Chicago: University of Chicago Press.

CHAPTER 25

OVER THE EDGE: ONE POLICE WOMAN'S STORY OF EMOTIONAL AND SEXUAL HARASSMENT

CHERYL GOMEZ-PRESTON / JACQUELINE TRESCOTT

ABSTRACT

This chapter provides a graphic, frightening description of sexual harassment at work in an urban police department. (Recall MacKinnon's more theoretical discussion of sexual harassment in Chapter 18.) The victim, Cheryl Gomez-Preston, is a black female police officer from Detroit. In Chapter 24, Martin's study described the double burden of racism and sexism in policing. While this victim of sexual harassment was eventually vindicated by the courts, she was nearly driven to madness and suicide by the experience.

What are the institutional forces that can lead to a competent black women officer being treated this way? Notice that the harassment was perpetrated by both black and white officers. This would indicate, as Martin stated earlier, that both sexism and racism were at work. In addition, the unique way in which Gomez-Preston was violated because she was a black woman married to a physician exposes the race/gender/class bias involved in this case of sexual harassment. A major objective of the tormentors appeared to be either to dominate the victim or to force her to resign.

On the basis of material presented in previous chapters, give an account of the dynamics of sexual/racial harassment in the workplace. What changes would have to occur both in the larger society and in law enforcement—a particularly white-male-dominated arena—to prevent such harassment? What are the hazards for the community policed by a police department that engages in harassment of its own officers?

When Cheryl Gomez-Preston left home at 17, she wasn't sure what she was looking for. But five years later, when she joined the Detroit Police Force at 22, she was sure she'd finally found it. She'd decided she wanted to be a cop. Police officers were strong, independent, tough. They stuck together, cared for one another, protected one another—just like family.

Gomez-Preston's childhood had been chaotic. Before she was 5 years old, she had been shuttled between her grandmother's and mother's houses so much that she wasn't sure where her real home was. Some of the men in her family were alcohol- and drug-addicted—most were "losers," in her mind. And when she was 12, she found out that the man she had grown to love as a father wasn't really her father at all; her mother had never told her that she had been married before.

Gomez-Preston became a good cop, a tough cop—she was one of the first female officers assigned to work the streets—and for five glorious years she was a member in good standing of the Detroit police-force family. But then her "family" turned on her. And before long her living nightmare began.

In 1984, Cheryl Gomez-Preston filed a lawsuit against the Detroit Police Department for sexual harassment: She now describes the experience she went through as emotional rape. In April 1987, a jury initially awarded her $675,000, delivering one of the largest sexual-harassment verdicts in favor of a law-enforcement officer up to that time. After all the legal procedures are exhausted, she hopes to receive at least $500,000. Now 35, Gomez-Preston lives in Philadelphia with her husband and two children. She is still angry and

confused, but she is healing. The following, in her own words, is her story.

This might sound crazy, but a television show, Honey West, which came out in the mid-1960's, was probably the reason I joined the police force. Honey was actually a private investigator, but that was close enough. I saw how strong she was, how self-confident and independent. Everything that I wasn't. So I enrolled in the police academy.

The academy was hard, but I never thought about quitting. You were challenged, stripped of your pride and self-esteem and then rebuilt to be part of the system. If you didn't have the personality and characteristics to be a police officer, if you didn't have what it took, you dropped out or were asked to leave. But I had it.

I was very lonely during that period. Only one member of my family, my grandfather, who had once dreamed of becoming a cop himself, really gave me any support. But in an odd way the negative attitudes of the rest of my family inspired me. I used to constantly hear that I was going to be like my biological father, who was Puerto Rican. I now call myself Gomez-Preston to honor that heritage, but at the time I was ashamed. They used to tell me that I would wind up being nothing. I was told I was the worst of two ethnic groups, Black and Puerto Rican. They said I was a loser.

I couldn't let them be right. I had to prove something to myself; I had started questioning my own ability. The police department became a way for me to prove myself. It became more than a dream—it was my existence—but I didn't have any illusions. I knew when I started that I was going to have a rough time; we were told that. Initially the female officers did have some problems with some of the men because a lot of them didn't want to work with us. Oh boy, talk about the epitome of macho! When a woman comes on the job, she steps on some men's toes, espe-

Source: Cheryl Gomez-Preston and Jacqueline Trescott, "Over the Edge: One Woman's Story of Emotional and Sexual Harassment," Essence Magazine, vol. 20, March 1990, pp. 60–62, 120, 122, 125.

cially if she is an intelligent, attractive woman and can handle the job. But I loved it, I lived it, I ate it up. My reason for living was to be a Detroit police officer. I literally grew up and was raised by the Detroit Police Department. This was the family relationship that I really didn't have, this was it.

There were bad times and good times, but the problems were ones shared by many officers. When you come on the force, you have no rights, and you basically have to take your licks, keep on, pick yourself up and dust yourself off when you fall. On my first permanent assignment, two Black male officers took me under their wing. They protected me. If I made a mistake, they showed me the right way to do things. They didn't make fun of me. They told me not to be embarrassed about mistakes, that everybody makes them. That was so important in building my confidence. I made a lot of arrests, and I guess my supervisors were amused by my aggressiveness. I gained a lot of respect quickly.

I'll never forget the time a suspect on the street called me a bitch. One of the officers I was with knocked a tooth out of his mouth. He didn't wait for me to respond and defend myself. I also remember the time I was working with a white sergeant, and we went to confront a gunman in a barricaded situation. When we got there, the gunman started shooting and the sergeant knocked me down to the ground. I protected them, too. I would have given my life for these officers. I would have.

When I was single everything was fine; for five years it was fine, and then I got married. Bennett, the man I married, was someone I had known since elementary school. Almost since high school he'd wanted to be a doctor, and now he was in medical school. He was working in a hospital when I saw him; I was there on police business. We started going out and ended up getting married in 1979. But after Bennett and I married, I noticed a change in my colleagues' attitudes. At first it

wasn't bad, I guess they figured that it was okay because he was just in school, but after he graduated and started his residency, things really began to change.

In 1982 I was transferred to the largest precinct in the city, which had a reputation for racial tension. I didn't think much of it then. I had begun to run into some problems in my old precinct, petty things, but I had been able to handle them with no problem. When I got into this new precinct, however, the general consensus was that I didn't need the job. Some of the officers began to ask me nasty, mean questions; some even called my husband's hospital to find out if he was black. Then the threats started coming. I started receiving written racial epithets like "nigger bitch" and "rich bitch" scribbled on bits of paper. And the hostility got worse: Notes that said things like "Die, bitch" and "Go back to Africa" were sent to me.

I was devastated. My first response was to seek help from an authority figure. I went to the commanding officer, a Black man, and showed the death threats to him. His attitude was very casual: This is the mentality of the white boys over here, he told me. He showed me a porno magazine opened to the centerfold, a picture of a naked woman with "Kiss Ass, Nigger" written on her genital area. "See this," he said, "this was on another officer's locker." That officer was Black, too. Here I was, standing there looking at this commanding officer, and he was making excuses. I started feeling uneasy.

Then he started questioning me about my marriage, asking me if I was happily married. He caught me off guard. He told me he liked me, and that he was interested in having a relationship. I asked myself, What have I gotten myself into? I told him I was happily married, and I left it at that.

But in the station I was beginning to feel more and more isolated. Other problems started, all involving my family. One day an officer called the hospital where my husband worked and asked if he was actually a doctor. Another time officers went to my home and saw the housekeeper my mother had hired to help me with the children's laundry. They decided I was just too comfortable, too snooty. So five years into my career, everything was starting to crumble. And one cold January night, things really came to a head.

It was about three o'clock in the morning. It wasn't snowing, but it was bitterly cold, and the wind was blowing. I was the only woman on the street. I wasn't wearing my protective gear; I just didn't have my bulletproof vest on. Did the other officers know that? I don't know, but they knew so much about me I have to wonder. I will never forget what happened.

A patrol car was chasing a man who had just tried to shoot somebody while committing an armed robbery. I was the type of police officer who would always go and back up someone, even if I didn't know him—this was my family. My partner and I were driving parallel to the chase, and I had my door open because I was starting to prepare some paperwork on what was happening. When the other officers began to chase the suspect on foot, I jumped out and joined them. There were about six other officers.

I was concentrating so hard on catching the man, I didn't notice when we turned and ran into an alley. The alley wasn't lit, but there was light coming in from the street lamps. All of a sudden the suspect stopped and turned. I looked over my shoulder for my backup, but there was no one there.

I'll never forget the look on the suspect's face. He was scared. He wanted to escape. He knew I was standing in the way of his freedom. I remember knowing he was going to shoot me. He started fumbling around the waist of his pants, trying to find his gun. When I saw him do that, I started thinking about my kids, remembering that I had two

babies at home (my daughter was 2 then, my son was just 8 months). I wasn't ready to die. I pulled my gun and fired two shots and he fell to the ground. Within 15 to 20 seconds, officers came from wherever they'd been. No one said anything; there was nothing to say.

It was obvious to me then that these people didn't care about me. I had been given no backup, and good backup can be the decisive factor in a life-and-death situation. I had been made vulnerable. They were serious with their death threats. I didn't report the incident in any official way, but I talked to a friend on the force, a Black sergeant who had warned me to be careful because some officers might not be there when I needed them. He told me I had to get out.

Soon the whole thing became a nightmare I couldn't awake from. My so-called friends on the force started pulling away from me; it just wasn't very smart to be associated with me. My situation was like a time bomb waiting to explode.

Though he hadn't been helpful, I thought maybe I should talk to the commander again. After all, I hadn't been backed up the way a good cop was supposed to be supported. I could have been killed. But he had another disgusting ultimatum: He was willing to help me if I slept with him. I told him I didn't feel I should have to compromise myself sexually in order to get help from him. I asked him what kind of man he was. He said some of my co-workers were jealous of the fact that my husband was a doctor. He said if he couldn't screw me one way, he would screw me another way.

My nerves were starting to unravel at home now too. My husband couldn't comprehend what was happening to me. He kept telling me to quit, but it wasn't as easy as that. I wasn't a quitter. I was a cop, and cops don't whine and cry. Cops don't quit. I just stopped telling him about a lot of things that were going on. I think that's why there can be such a high incidence of alcohol and drug abuse among police officers; so many of them can't share their pain.

Everything that was happening at work was starting to affect my marriage. My husband and I were not getting along. I felt like a caged animal. I wasn't able to deal with my children. The small things that you share with your kids, the rich, precious moments, those were stolen from me. I was having to force myself to get up and go to work. Every night I would go in and look at my children, because I didn't know if I was going to make it back home.

Finally it was so bad at work that I decided I had to get out one way or another. I was keeping notes and documenting everything that happened, but I was more and more depressed. I was starting to come apart. I went in one day, and I was so desperate I took a typewriter and dropped it on my right foot. I remember thinking it was just going to take a second and then I'd be out of there. I felt a broken foot was a small price to pay for leaving with my life. I broke my foot and was relieved of duty for six weeks. It was during this time that I decided to make a formal complaint of sexual harassment against the commanding officer. I made my report to the internal-affairs division—the body of officers who police the police. Everything was supposed to be kept confidential, but it wasn't. I'm almost certain that before I got out of the elevator, the word was out. I was transferred back to my original precinct.

But by the time I got back to work at that precinct—the place where I'd been assigned after I'd come out of the academy—people had turned against me and things were beginning to take a physical toll anyway. I was having crying spells. I started losing my hair, and my menstrual cycle stopped. I had bouts of depression. I got to the point where I would come home and stay locked up in my room. I started having chest pains.

One day at work everything seemed to collapse at once. The pains in my chest began, and I thought I was dying. I told the supervisor on the desk that I thought I was having a heart attack. He told me to go change into my uniform. I was so out of it I actually changed, then I walked back up to the front desk. Right in front of all who were there, the desk supervisor started yelling at me. He told me there was nothing wrong with me and that I was trying to pawn off my problems onto the police department. I became incoherent. I didn't hear what he was saying; all I saw was his mouth moving. I unbuckled my holster and pulled my gun out. The only thought in my mind was that I had had enough. I just wanted to make him stop, and the only way I could see to do it at that point was to make his mouth stop moving. I poised my gun to shoot when one of the officers grabbed me and stopped me.

I had hit the bottom. I began to feel I had nothing to live for. I had begun to have blackout spells, so I stopped driving. One day in the grocery store after buying an item, I dropped my purse and then, out of confusion, gave the cashier a wad of money. I asked her to take the amount she needed. I cried all the way home. My husband was on call at the hospital that day. The children were with my mother.

When I got home, I thought I knew a way out. Kneeling on the floor next to my bed, I reached beneath my mattress, searching for my off-duty handgun. My face was drenched with tears, and I could hear myself sobbing as I placed the gun at my temple. Raising my head up I saw my reflection in the mirror, and I continued watching as I slowly began to pull the trigger. Scenes from my life flashed before me. Then I saw pictures of my children. I focused on them. I kept seeing my two beautiful babies who still loved and needed me. Right then, I realized that everything, all the trauma, all the pain, was no longer just my problem but belonged to my entire family. I needed help.

Within a couple of weeks of that terrible day, I checked into a hospital. I stayed there for six weeks, and during that time I made some important discoveries. With the help of counseling, I began to understand that I wasn't crazy, but that what I had been through was enough to drive anyone over the edge. Just to know that I was not alone in what I was experiencing emotionally and physically was a relief. I had had so many people telling me I was crazy I had begun to believe it.

I began to find me—and I liked what I found. I found some direction. I began to realize that I was human, not a tough supercop who couldn't cry, but a person filled with rage. And I began to understand that what had happened to me had an official name—sexual harassment—and that I had the right to be angry. I found out that I wasn't alone; this had happened to other people.

For two years I was off the force on disability. I was not emotionally able to go back into the police environment. During this two-year period I had no income. My husband only earned about $19,000 as a resident, and we had a mortgage and other bills to pay. We had been very dependent on my $30,000-a-year salary. We lost all our credit. My mother had

to take care of the children because we had no money to buy groceries. We had utilities turned off. We lived on milk and peanut butter and jelly sandwiches.

Finally I decided to sue the Detroit Police Department. They had tried to kill me spiritually, and I couldn't let them get away with that. I had to get them back. I couldn't kill them with a gun, so I had to use the courts. I found a lawyer courageous enough to take on the department, and we began litigation. On May 5, 1984, I sued the department. In April 1987, I won my case.

What did I learn from all of this? I learned the value of a real family, not an imagined one. Bennett was there for me—taking care of me and our kids when I wasn't functioning. He was always in my corner, loving and supporting me the best way he could. My mother was there for me in ways she wasn't—and couldn't be—when I was a child. I learned that I'm a fighter. I'm fighting now with ASH, the Association for the Sexually Harassed, the organization I founded to help other women and men whose lives have been devastated by sexual harassment. When I lecture across the country, I try to empower other victims in ways in which I wasn't empowered. Finally, I've learned how strong I am. And I know now that no one, no matter how powerful, will ever try to kill my spirit again.

CHAPTER 26

WOMEN IN CONFLICT: AN ANALYSIS OF WOMEN CORRECTIONAL OFFICERS

JOANNE BELKNAP

ABSTRACT

Having studied correctional officers in a large metropolitan jail, Belknap is able to provide a rich description of their work world. As a result, this study of 35 women correctional officers supports most prior research on the conflicts these women face on the job. Evidence of sexual harassment (offensive sexual comments or behaviors) and gender harassment (nonsexual "put-downs" of women)—a distinction rarely made by other writers—is described. The women confirmed the existence of sexual harassment but tended to minimize it, reporting it as less significant than gender harassment. And as with earlier studies,* male officers were found to be more hostile than male inmates to women guards.

Belknap also describes gender differences in job performance. The major work style distinction was identified as better communication skills of women and a greater inclination to use force by men. The reasons for these differences are found in women's prior experiences and socialization (gender model), as well as the organizational structure of the jail and the correctional occupation (job model). Although the women believe that factors related to the gender model are more influential, they understand that they are discriminated against because they are too frequently assigned to work exclusively with female inmates, which limits their job mobility prospects. Thus, although most of the women believed that men and women are equal, they felt that men and women perform the corrections job differently and that women are less likely to advance.

---

*See Nancy C. Jurik, "Striking a Balance: Female Correctional Officers, Gender Role Stereotypes, and Male Prisoners," *Sociological Inquiry*, 58(3):291–304 (1988); Lynn E. Zimmer, *Women Guarding Men*, University of Chicago Press, Chicago, 1986.

The two most common reasons the women chose correctional work were that they wanted to use corrections as a stepping-stone to police or patrol work* or they were attracted to the salary and benefits. Corrections is a major employer of black women, just as Martin (Chapter 24 herein) found among police officers.

Most women in corrections feel that the work environment needs to be altered in order for them to be fully accepted by their male peers. Sadly, the women are pessimistic about this happening. Is their pessimism warranted? Given that some improvement in reducing gender and race bias in the courts has been reported by Schafran (Chapter 20 herein), could we expect similar changes in the future in corrections? Or are there structural conditions in corrections and policing which are different from those in legal institutions and which make reform more difficult?

---

*This was more prevalent among the "older" women, who were probably "forced" to choose corrections because they were barred from police work earlier in their careers. In addition, the same phenomenon has been observed in studies of men who work in departments with dual law enforcement and corrections functions.

A STATEMENT OF THE PROBLEM

Resistance to women working in traditionally male jobs may be most evident when we examine women who work in the criminal justice system. Wilson (1982:360) believes that "the link between masculinity and criminal justice is so tightly bound that we may say it is true not merely that only men can be crime fighters, but even that to be a crime fighter means to be a man." Perhaps no jobs embody the idea of machismo more than those which are designed to control offenders, especially male offenders. Thus it is not surprising that

An earlier version of this paper was presented at the 1990 annual meeting of the Academy of Criminal Justice Sciences.

The author would like to thank Julie Jodarski for help in coding the qualitative data and for entering the quantitative data into the computer, and Kelly McCann and Barbara Volker for assistance in coding the qualitative data. The author is indebted to Lynn Zimmer for her careful review of this manuscript.

women correctional officers (COs) assigned to institutions for men have faced strong opposition from male COs.

Legal pressure, particularly Title VII of the Civil Rights Act, has been the major impetus for hiring women COs in men's prisons since the 1970s (Flynn, 1982: 324; Jurik, 1985: 377; Morton, 1981: 10; Zimmer, 1989). This development has led to increased research on women in corrections to ascertain whether gender role differences exist among correctional staff members, and to determine the reasons for any of these differences. Two explanatory models, the *gender model* and the *job model*, have been suggested (Jurik and Halemba, 1984: 553–554; Zimmer, 1986: 12–13). The *gender model* concerns what women bring to the job in terms of attitudes, prior experiences, and preferred modes of interaction, and how these factors affect women's occupational experiences (Zimmer, 1986: 12). For example, "gender models suggest that women place greater importance than do men on relationships with others in their work environment" (Jurik and Halemba,

1984: 554). The *job model*, on the other hand, suggests that gender differences on the job are influenced more strongly by the organizational structure of the occupation and the institution. For example, restricting women officers to work only with female inmates reduces their job and shift assignments and reinforces their male co-workers' belief that they are unable to "do the job." Most observers recognize the importance of both models because it is likely that they operate simultaneously to promote gender differences among correctional staff members (Jurik, 1985: 376; Jurik and Halemba, 1984: 552; Zimmer, 1986: 13). One model, however, may be more important than the other, and we could obtain a clearer understanding of women COs by determining whether this is the case.

The goal of this study is to test specific findings from prior research regarding women COs: reasons for choosing corrections, their attitudes about gender equality inside and outside work, their preferred working environments, their perceptions of occupational opportunities and obstacles, the conflicts they experience on the job, and their beliefs concerning gender differences among COs. In addition, the study attempts to determine the source and the degree of support for the gender model and the job model. Although a number of studies on women COs have been published in the last few years (e.g., Crouch and Alpert, 1982; Jurik, 1985, 1988; Jurik and Halemba, 1984; Kerle, 1985; Kissel and Katsampes, 1980; Peterson, 1982; Pollock, 1986; Simpson and White, 1985; Zupan, 1986), the current study was influenced most strongly by Zimmer's (1986, 1987) ethnographic research on women COs working in men's prisons. Zimmer's research was conducted in New York state and in Rhode Island in 1980, when women first started to work in men's prisons there. Therefore her research design was exploratory, and "the

important research questions were allowed to emerge during the research process" (1986: 212). Her data were collected primarily from open-ended interviews with 70 women COs as well as from a number of inmates, administrators, and male COs.

METHOD

Although Zimmer's (1986) study was necessarily inductive because of the paucity of knowledge on women COs working with male inmates, the current research, in many respects, is the next logical step. This study is not ethnographic, but in some sense it is a replication of Zimmer's (1986, 1987) work. Structured interviews designed on the basis of Zimmer's findings were conducted on women COs working in a jail. None of the prior studies used representative samples, largely because such samples are very difficult to acquire. Thus it is useful and necessary to replicate research on women COs in different places and times.

This research not only is deductive, but also differs in a number of ways from Zimmer's (1986, 1987) and several other researchers' studies (Jurik, 1985, 1988; Jurik and Halemba, 1985; Peterson, 1982; Pollock, 1986; Simpson and White, 1984). First, the site of this study is a jail instead of a prison. Prisons tend to house inmates of a single sex, whereas jails often house both male and female inmates. The inmate population also tends to differ in that jail inmates usually receive shorter sentences than prison inmates. In addition, women COs are a recent phenomenon in male prisons (only since the late 1970s and early 1980s), but women have been working for many years in jails with female inmates. Finally, considerable changes have taken place in corrections since Zimmer conducted her study, and it is possible that the views of women COs held by their male co-workers, the administrators, and the women themselves may have changed.

The sample of women COs was drawn from a large midwestern metropolitan jail under the jurisdiction of a county sheriff. The jail houses approximately 1,200 male inmates and 100 female inmates. There are approximately 550 correctional personnel, of whom 400 are line officers. At the time of this study (1988) the personnel included 36 female line officers, two female sergeants, one female lieutenant, and one female captain. Thirty-five of the 40 women COs in the jail were interviewed for this study.[1]

I constructed a structured interview format from Zimmer's (1986, 1987) work and pilot-tested it on one woman sergeant from the selected jail site. With the exception of the final question, in which I asked the women to specify which of Zimmer's (1986) occupational styles defined them most accurately, the questions were open-ended. I conducted all of the interviews in the jail, in a private office provided by the administration. Interviews were conducted during each shift (approximately four times per shift) over the course of three weeks in March 1988. I asked each participant identical questions, but the interviews ranged in length from 25 to 95 minutes. Although a few of the women seemed to be suspicious of being interviewed, most appeared to be pleased that someone was interested in their experiences as women in the jail. Because the officers seemed to be very uncomfortable with the idea of tape-recording the interviews, I conducted the interviews in shorthand and transcribed them later.

The typed, qualitative data were coded by four people. All four coders worked to develop categories to responses; two of these coders determined the final categories into which the data were quantified. When disagreements in coding arose, the coders met to agree on the final coding. Because of the small sample size, the quantitative analysis consists primarily of frequencies. Where possible, I conducted cross-tabulations regarding race (white or black), age (under 40 or 40 and over), and experience (under six years or six years or more). Although the tables do not include this analysis (whose findings were largely nonsignificant), relationships of $p \leq .10$ are incorporated into the text. In addition, the text includes some frequency results related to factors listed in the tables but not included in the tables, to expand further on the reasons some women gave for their responses.

FINDINGS

Tables 1 through 7 summarize the findings from this study. Table 1 describes the sample, which was 57 percent white, 91 percent line officers, and divided equally between shifts. The officers ranged in age from 22 to 63 years; the greatest population (32%) were in their thirties. Experience in working in the jail ranged from six months to 25 years; the majority (57%) had worked there between one and eight years. Not surprisingly, the officers' ages and years of experience were related positively and significantly ($x^2 = 9.29$, $p = .002$). Sixty-two percent of the women were assigned to work fairly exclusively with female inmates.

Reasons and Support for Entering Corrections

People choose occupations for a number of reasons, despite prevailing attitudes suggesting that they are not "right" for the job. Many reasons have been offered to explain why women have had limited opportunities in corrections, most notably the conviction that corrections is a "man's" job. Nonetheless,

TABLE 1
Demographics*

Characteristic	N	%
Race		
White	20	57.1
Black	15	42.9
Age		
22–29	8	23.5
30–39	11	32.4
40–49	9	26.5
50–59	3	8.8
60–63	3	8.8
Rank		
Line officer	32	91.4
Sergeant	1	2.9
Lieutenant	1	2.9
Captain	1	2.9
Shift		
First	13	37.1
Second	12	34.3
Third	10	28.6
Experience		
<1 year	5	14.3
1–3 years	8	22.9
4–8 years	12	34.3
9–12 years	4	11.4
13–15 years	3	8.6
16–20 years	2	5.7
>20 years	1	2.9
Job detail of line officers		
Female floor	20	62.5
Medical control room	5	15.6
Central base control	4	12.5
Intake	2	6.2
Recreation department	1	3.1

*Percentages may not total 100.0 because of rounding.

many women choose to work in this field. Thus it may be expected that one aspect of women's working in a traditionally male job is the need for support. Accordingly, this section will examine the factors that influenced the women to choose corrections and their perceptions of support from friends and families.

Choosing a Career in Corrections   The two most common reasons why women chose to become correctional officers were that they wanted to become police or patrol officers (40%) or were attracted to the money and benefits (40%; Table 2).[2] Women recruits were told that working in corrections was the most promising path into police work, although only one woman was known to have advanced to "the road" (road patrol). White women (55%) were more likely than black women (20%) to choose corrections because of their desire to become police officers ($x^2 = 4.38$, p = .04). More experienced ("early") women officers also were more likely than less experienced officers to have chosen corrections as a means of becoming a police offi-

TABLE 2
Reasons and Support for Entering Corrections*

Characteristic	N	%
Reasons for choosing this job*		
To become police/road officer	14	(40.0)
Needed money/job	14	(40.0)
Advancement opportunities	8	(22.9)
Challenge/interesting	8	(22.9)
Had worked other CJ job	8	(22.9)
Help people/work with people	6	(17.1)
Other	7	(20.0)
Have you received support from your family and friends?		
Yes	19	(54.3)
No	12	(34.3)
Mixed	4	(11.4)
Do you have any relatives who are COs?		
Yes	3	(8.6)
No	32	(91.4)

*Officers could provide more than one response.

cer or in relation to the desire to do so (x^2 = 2.76, p = .10). Probably this was the case because women today can pursue careers in policing more easily, whereas "older" women were "forced" to choose corrections because they were barred from police work.

The responses for choosing an occupation in corrections were quite varied.

> I wanted to go into law enforcement since I was a little person, and this was a start. (CO 4)

> I was a young widow with four children who needed a full-time job. It was in the paper, so I applied. (CO 7)

> When I was in high school I wanted to be a police officer, in the sixties, but women were meter maids or worked with juvies. There were always police officers in our family: my uncle, my brother. . . . Instead of becoming a police officer, I got married, and when my family was old enough I was too old to be a street officer, so this was the closest I could get. (CO 8)

The next most frequently given reasons (23% each) for becoming COs included advancement opportunities, the belief that the job would be interesting or challenging, and previous work in another criminal justice job before moving into this one.

These data both support and refute findings from prior research. As in Zimmer's (1986) study, none of the women in the current study had aspired to become COs; two of the primary reasons for choosing corrections were financial and the lack of other opportunities. These findings are also consistent with Jurik and Halemba's (1984: 557) study, in which the second and third most frequently stated reasons why women entered corrections were (respectively) that they viewed it as an entry-level position for other jobs in the department and because of the salary.

The current study, however, also differed from the above studies in significant ways. First, only two of the 70 women in Zimmer's (1986: 40–44) study had aspired to be police

officers. It is unclear why wanting to become a police officer was a primary motive in this study but not in Zimmer's. Perhaps the sample in the current study consisted of more "older" women whose opportunities for entering law enforcement were more limited when they first began to work at the jail. Also, in contrast to the current research, Jurik and Halemba (1984: 557) found that interest in human services or inmate rehabilitation was women's most frequently reported reason for choosing corrections. In this study, only 17 percent of the women reported choosing corrections because they wanted to help people or work with people. It would be useful to examine this motivation in future studies because it appeared to be relatively unimportant in Zimmer's (1986) work and in the current study, but was most important in Jurik and Halemba's (1984) study.

Support from Friends and Families
Although 54 percent of the women claimed unconditional support from their families and friends for their career choice, 11 percent reported mixed support and 34 percent reported no support. Six of the women (17%) reported that the level of support from their families had changed over time: four of the women received more support as their families and friends adjusted to their working in corrections, but two received *less* support than previously. The degree of support varied a great deal among the women.

> I never told my children I got the job until I picked up my uniform. They like it and still say, "Gee, Mom! I can't believe you turned out to be a cop!" (CO 13)

> My family wouldn't be caught dead working here and they hope I quit before I die [laughs]. (CO 19)

> All seem to be supportive. Some can't understand how I can put up with it, but they're supportive. (CO 21)

Women with male relatives in corrections (nine percent of the sample) seemed to report more support from friends and families, although these results may have occurred by chance because of the small numbers. These findings are consistent with Zimmer's (1986: 41–42) findings that women COs face considerable opposition from friends and relatives, although the women in this study seemed to find a little less opposition than did Zimmer's respondents (1986).

Attitudes and Perceptions about Gender Equality Regarding Opportunities, Expectations, and Training

One would think that women entering traditionally male jobs would hold feminist values, but research on women COs and policewomen has not borne out this idea (Martin, 1980; Zimmer, 1986). Zimmer (1986: 43), in fact, found that as a group, women officers tended to have rather conservative sex-role attitudes. It is useful to examine nontraditional women workers' attitudes about gender inequality on the job. Specifically, does women COs' job training differ from that of the men? How do women's advancement opportunities compare with the men's? Table 3 presents the findings concerning these questions on perceptions of gender equality.

Belief in Gender Equality Although 62 percent of the women COs were assigned to work almost exclusively with women inmates, 94 percent believed that men and women are equal and should receive equal opportunities (Table 3). When asked whether male and female officers could be used interchangeably, 71 percent said "yes," 23 percent believed they were interchangeable with some qualifications, and only six percent believed they were not interchangeable.

TABLE 3

Attitudes and Perceptions about Gender Equality Regarding Opportunities, Expectations, and Training*

Question	N	%
Are men and women equal overall, and should they receive equal job opportunities?		
Yes	33	(94.3)
No	2	(5.7)
Can male and female officers be utilized interchangeably?		
Yes	25	(71.4)
No	2	(5.7)
With some qualifications	8	(22.9)
Are female officers at a disadvantage in enforcing jail rules?		
Yes	6	(17.1)
No	28	(80.0)
Unsure	1	(2.9)
Is a different quality of work expected of female COs?		
Yes	19	(54.3)
No	16	(45.7)
How do your advancement opportunities compare with male officers?		
Poorly	31	(88.6)
No difference	1	(2.9)
Unsure	3	(8.6)
Was your job training similar to the male COs'?		
Similar	22	(62.9)
Not similar	8	(22.9)
N/A because no job training for either sex	5	(14.3)

*Percentages may not total 100.0% because of rounding.

[Do you believe male and female officers can be used interchangeably?] Yes, without a doubt. Some people believe there's a need for females only where we hold females. I can handle the males as well as anybody. You can ask any of the male inmates and they'll tell you what a bitch I am. (CO 1)

I would have a problem putting female officers on male housing units on high-security floors. On the other hand, maybe the females wouldn't be as threatening to them. I know the male officers run their mouths and end up starting half the fights. (CO 32)

This study seemed to show rather definitive support for gender equality. The current findings are consistent with prior research claiming that although women COs have an overall high degree of confidence in handling male inmates, they feel some discomfort and confusion regarding certain duties, usually those associated with inmates' privacy (Kissel and Katsampes, 1980: 226; Peterson, 1982: 455).

Advancement Opportunities When asked about their advancement opportunities, 89 percent of the officers believed that they compared poorly with males, one officer believed that there was no difference, and three (9%) were unsure how they compared.

Forty men get promoted before a female because you are only promoted if there is a position open for a female. (CO 3)

We're limited to one floor. . . . We can't work in the kitchen because they don't think we can handle all those male inmates. They don't utilize women as much as they could. There's not much opportunity to prove yourself if you're on the same post month after month. (CO 5)

The point of these comments is similar to Chapman et al.'s (1980: xvi) finding of a "strong perception that women receive less than equal consideration" in hiring and promotion. This perception might be a result of the organizational barrier and the double-edged sword of sex stereotyping in job assignments. Nallin (1981: 21) attributes wom-

en's lack of upward mobility in corrections to the small numbers of women in corrections, their limited range of duties, and their lack of mentors. Similarly, Kerle (1985: 314) found that women jailers' promotion opportunities were affected seriously by their relegation to work only with female inmates. Thus (through no fault of their own) they lacked the experience of working with male inmates and were not considered qualified to become supervisors. Jurik and Halemba (1984: 559), however, found that male and female COs did not differ significantly in their views of promotional opportunities.

Perceptions of Gender Differences in Work Expectations Table 3 also examines the officers' perceptions of gender differences in work expectations. Eighty percent of the women believed that female officers are *not* at a disadvantage in enforcing jail rules against inmates, whereas 17 percent believed that females suffer a disadvantage. One officer claimed that she was unsure because she had never worked with male inmates.[3] Fifty-four percent of the officers believed that a different quality of work was expected of the female officers, but 46 percent did not think so. Younger officers (74%) were more likely than older officers (33%) to believe that a higher quality of work was expected of women officers ($x^2 = 5.54$, $p = .02$); perhaps more *was* expected of the younger women than of the older.

Since we have female supervisors, they expect more, and more is expected of them as women through administration. (CO 5)

They expect us to be better, every way you can think of . . . how clean is the shift, how you write up reports, how quickly you turn in reports, your officers, etc. They can excuse or overlook a male officer making a mistake, but not the females. (CO 7)

Job Training   Pollock (1986: 3) states that the guard subculture is crucial in the socialization of new officers, especially in regard to handling inmates. This point appears to be relevant whether or not the institutions include formal training in addition to on-the-job training. Zimmer (1987: 422) believes that one reason why women COs receive inadequate socialization during their on-the-job training is that the men who train women do not want them there. In the current study, 23 percent of the women claimed that their job training in the academy was different from that received by the men, while 63 percent claimed it was similar. (Fourteen percent had been hired at a time when neither sex received formal training.) At any rate, although the formal academy training is important, all new recruits (as well as seasoned officers) experience the power of the on-the-job subculture. In fact, Van Maanen's (1973) study of police recruits found that the "war stories" exchanged during formal academy training and the influence of the field training officer were powerful enough to override many of the formal training ideologies and goals.

The experiences of the women COs in this study included the following:

> I got thrown out on the cell block. They had a class, but they were desperate for females so I didn't go through the classes for male officers. (CO 9)

> I was the only female in the academy. I got no preferential treatment. It was harder because I took a lot of ribbing for being the only female. (CO 4)

Sex Preferences for Inmates, Officers, and Supervisors

Considerable research on women correctional officers has addressed the acceptance of the women by male inmates and male coworkers. Some research also has questioned these COs on their perceptions and preferences as to the ideal working environment. This section addresses the women COs' preferences for the sex of the inmates, officers, and supervisors with whom they work (see Table 4).

Preference for Inmates   Although the majority of the women (43%) stated no preference for working with male or female inmates, 34 percent preferred male inmates and 14 percent preferred female inmates. (Three officers, or nine percent, had worked only with female inmates, so they claimed that they had no basis for determining a preference.) Thirty-one percent reported that they received more respect or cooperation from male inmates; 17 percent reported that female inmates were easier to handle and to understand. These findings are consistent with Pollock's (1986) findings: 72 percent of women officers preferred male inmates, 11 percent preferred women inmates, and 16 percent had no preference (N = 18). Pollock (1986: 97–98)

TABLE 4
Sex Preferences for Inmates, Officers, and Supervisors*

Characteristic	N	%
Preference for inmates		
None	15	(42.9)
Male	12	(34.3)
Female	5	(14.3)
No basis for a decision	3	(8.6)
Preference for officers		
None	19	(54.3)
Male	10	(28.6)
Female	6	(17.1)
Preference for supervisors		
None	20	(57.1)
Male	9	(25.7)
Female	3	(8.6)
No basis for a decision	3	(8.6)

*Percentages may not total 100.0% because of rounding.

reported that women officers believed male inmates treated them with more respect than did women inmates, and that male inmates were more likely than women inmates to "appreciate them as women," thus making their jobs "more enjoyable."

Some respondents explained why women inmates appear to be more manipulative.

A lot of the officers think that women inmates are more manipulating than the males. But that's just not true. Women inmates have more needs than men: they need more toilet paper, tampons, things like that. So they're put in a situation where they have to be manipulating to get their everyday needs. It's just not fair. (CO 16)

Males have a whole psych ward, females only one section of the female floor for psychs, no rubber room or special effects for women mentals [psych patients] . . . women have to deal with that on their own. (CO 3)

Thus what appear to be differences between male and female inmates' behavior may in fact be sexist perceptions on the part of COs.

Preference for Officers   In this study, 54 percent of the women preferred working with male and female officers equally, 28 percent preferred males, and 17 percent preferred females. Twenty-three percent reported that male officers are less "catty," "petty," or "jealous," while three women (9%) reported that female officers are more responsible or caring.

Preference for Supervisors   Fifty-seven percent of the officers had no preference regarding the sex of their supervisors, 26 percent preferred males, and nine percent preferred females. Nine percent had worked only with female supervisors and so had no basis for a decision. Three of the women (9%) reported that women supervisors were too "picky" or expected too much; four (11%) reported that women supervisors were "jealous" or vindictive. One woman preferred women supervi-

sors because she believed they were more sensitive and easier to get along with. The women supervisors seemed to be forced to walk a fine line between not giving women COs preferential treatment and allowing them more responsibilities and opportunities than the male supervisors typically allowed women.

Sexual and Gender Harassment

Gender harassment refers to nonsexual "putdowns" of women, whereas sexual harassment refers to offensive sexual comments or behaviors. Comments that women are incapable of performing a job or are less intelligent than men are examples of gender harassment. Sexual harassment, on the other hand, includes behaviors such as whistling, pressuring women for sex, and comments on their bodies. Although most women experience sexual and gender harassment, it may be most apparent for women working in traditionally male jobs. Nallin (1981: 20) questions why "masculine" traits are viewed as more appropriate in handling inmates than "more neutral, less sex-typed terms. . . . Firmness, fairness, determination and concern are equally applicable to the correctional setting." Several studies on policewomen and women COs have found that women who perform their jobs adequately are especially likely to have their "femaleness" questioned by male co-workers (Baunach and Rafter, 1982: 350; Martin, 1980: 93; Zimmer, 1986: 57–58). Researchers also report that many male co-workers fear that they must protect or do the work of what they perceive as their intrinsically inept female co-workers (see Martin, 1980: 191; Zimmer, 1986: 54). Thus it appears that women are punished with sexual and gender harassment for both superior and inferior performance.

Sexual Harassment   Thirty-one percent of the women reported that sexual harassment had been an issue for them while working in the jail (Table 5). In this study white women (45%) were more likely than black women (13%) to report sexual harassment (Yates' corrected $x^2 = 2.65$, p = .10), and younger women (47%) were more likely to do so than older women (13%; Yates' corrected $x^2 = 3.01$, p = .08). Seventy-seven percent claimed that male inmates and officers were likely to comment on their appearance, but 29 percent volunteered that they did not find this offensive. Again, the responses varied.

> It could be [offensive] if I allowed it, but I don't. I have a good rapport with the males. We kid, we joke, and some [joking] is sexual, but it's good-natured. . . . They know I'm married. None of it has ever been serious. (CO 8)

> One supervisor is worse than anybody I've dealt with. Basically, he even goes as far as putting his hands on you and saying he'll give you a ride in his van. I've almost decked him. If he touched my chest I would. A lot of other women have had the same problems with him. (CO 12)

> A lot of officers can be cruel. After I pass them they say, "There goes fat ass." If I hear them I turn around and smile because they want to upset you. . . . I consider the source, and it isn't too much better than the inmates. (CO 13)

> I had that coming in here just now. . . . They said, "We were watching you in the [security] camera, and sizing you up." [She does hand movements imitating men cupping her buttocks.] The worst part is that they mean it as a compliment, but of course it comes out wrong. We get these comments on a regular basis. (CO 5)

The findings of this study contrast with Zimmer's (1986: 43) finding that all women interviewed described at least one incident of sexual harassment. This discrepancy may exist because Zimmer did not ask women whether sexual harassment was an issue; she asked them to describe experiences and concluded from those descriptions that every woman suffered from what might be termed as sexual harassment. It is likely that many of the women in the current study experienced sexual harassment, but when asked whether it was "an issue," they stated that it was not.

TABLE 5
Sexual and Gender Harassment

Question	N	%
Has sexual harassment been an issue for you on this job?		
Yes	11	(31.4)
No	24	(68.6)
Are male inmates and officers likely comment on your appearance?		
Yes	27	(77.1)
No	8	(22.9)
Are women as a group "put-down" by male officers?		
Yes	27	(77.1)
No	8	(22.9)
Are women COs seen as one group behaving the same way?		
Yes	20	(57.1)
No	15	(42.9)
Who do you feel you have to prove yourself to more, inmates or male officers?		
Inmates	6	(17.1)
Officers	15	(42.9)
Both	3	(8.6)
Neither	11	(31.4)
Do women COs stand out and receive more scrutiny than male COs?		
Yes	24	(68.6)
No	11	(31.4)
Are the differences between men and women exaggerated making it more difficult to blend in?		
Yes	23	(65.7)
No	12	(34.3)

That is, many of the officers gave the impression that they experienced what is typically defined as sexual harassment, but they tried to ignore and minimize it. Another aspect of sexual harassment prevalent in this and other studies is that of rumors linking the women COs sexually with other officers or inmates (Peterson, 1982: 454).

Gender Harassment Seventy-seven percent of the respondents believed that women as a group tend to be "put-down" by male officers, and 57 percent believed that all women COs are seen as a single group of people who behave in the same way. White women (90%) were more likely than black women (60%) to report that women as a group are put-down (Yates' corrected $x^2 = 2.84$, p = .09).

> [Are women as a group put-down by male officers?] No more so than anywhere else. No more here than in social groups, where men think they're the dominant force or personality. (CO 16)

When asked whether they had to "prove" themselves more to male inmates or to male officers, 31 percent claimed (usually defiantly) that they did not have to prove themselves to anybody. Forty-three percent claimed that they had to prove themselves more to male officers, 17 percent stated that they had to prove themselves more to male inmates, and nine percent believed that they had equal difficulty in proving themselves to male inmates and male officers. Sixty-nine percent of the women believed that women COs receive more scrutiny than male officers, and 66 percent claimed that the differences between men and women make it more difficult to blend in.

> Women are more criticized because there are so few of us. It's easy to lose one bad man, but women stick out. If we make a mistake they say we should be home with diapers, Susie Homemaker. With a guy it's just that he got into the wrong job. (CO 20)

Perceptions about Gender Differences in Behavior and Effectiveness

Pollock (1986: 88) found that "men and women performed the CO role somewhat differently." Even so, women need to be judged by how effective they are, not by whether their approaches are similar to men's. When asked about their perceptions of their behavior at work (Table 6), 71 percent of the women in the current study believed that men and women officers use different means to accomplish the same goals. Twenty-six percent

TABLE 6
Perceptions about Gender Differences in Behavior*

Question	N	%
Do male and female officers use similar or different means to accomplish the same goals?		
Similar	10	(28.6)
Different	25	(71.4)
Do women bring different abilities, skills, and life experiences to the job?		
Yes	32	(91.4)
No	3	(8.6)
Do male and female COs perform the job differently?		
Yes	23	(67.6)
No	11	(32.4)
Ways in which women perform differently from men*		
Less likely to use force/more likely to try to talk it out	10	(29.4)
More likely to enforce rules	3	(8.8)
More in control/efficient	7	(20.6)
Are women COs as effective as male COs?		
Yes	28	(80.0)
Depends on individual/situation	7	(20.0)

*Officers could provide more than one response.

reported that women have to work harder to prove themselves and that this effort changes how they do the job. Thirty-four percent claimed that men are more forceful than women, and two officers (6%) reported that women have more respect than men for the inmates.

> Women tend to do a better job in defusing a situation than men do. (CO 25)

Ninety-one percent believed that women bring different abilities, skills, and life experiences to the job.

> In intake I've been called everything from a dyke to crazy. . . . I don't take a lot of it personally. They've already fought a lot so when they get to me I whisper so they have to stop yelling to hear me. . . . They calm down. (CO 14)

> Women are more compassionate to the inmates than the males because they have children and the inmates act like children. (CO 32)

> The majority of males are extremely lacking in communication skills, which is why they revert to force. They either don't or are afraid that they don't have the verbal and communication skills. (CO 34)

Sixty-eight percent of the women believed that men and women perform the job differently. The most frequently stated difference was that women are less likely to use force and more likely to try to talk issues out with inmates (30%); 21 percent reported that women are more in control and more efficient than male officers; and nine percent stated that women officers are more likely to enforce the jail rules. When asked whether women are as effective officers as the men, 80 percent believed they are; the remaining 20 percent stated that one must look at the individual and the situation, not the officer's sex.

> Females, we'll try to talk a situation down, trying not to use foul language. We even wake them up with "Good morning, ladies. . . ." On male floors it's "OK you motherfuckers, get out of bed." I tell them [male officers], "When you work with me, don't do that again." If you wake them up nice, most are usually pretty cool through the day. (CO 12)

> I am more strict than the male officers, and a lot of times the males will try to talk me out of an action I've taken. (CO 1)

These findings are consistent with prior research. Kissel and Katsampes (1980: 225) found "that the overwhelming majority of female staff . . . felt satisfied with their performance and felt they did as good a job as the males on the staff." Pollock (1986: 90) found that both male and female COs view women COs as more receptive to inmates' problems and more likely to try to "draw them out." These findings also support Zimmer's (1987: 421) contention that women are more likely than men officers to develop friendly relationships with the inmates to generate voluntary compliance, and that the women's nurturing role "is in direct contrast to the macho, competitive role typical of the male guards." In contrast to respondents in the current study, however, Zimmer's (1987: 421) male inmates reported that women COs were more likely than men COs to overlook petty rule infractions. The difference between the findings may be that in this study only women officers were questioned, not male officers and inmates. In general, these women believe that gender differences exist in performing the CO job, particularly that women's behavior toward inmates is more respectful. It also appears that women's actions are devalued in comparison to the men's more aggressive approaches.

The Gender Model versus the Job Model

Table 7 reports the respondents' perceptions of the importance of societal structure (the gender model) versus organizational struc-

TABLE 7
Perceptions of the Influence of Society and the Jail Structure on Differences in Male and Female COs' Job Performance and Self-Classification of Officers into Zimmer's Styles

Question	N	%
Are there ways in which your conditioning as a female, such as how you were raised, affects how you perform your job?		
Yes	24	(68.6)
No	11	(31.4)
Are there ways in which the job is structured which affect differently how male and female COs do the job?		
Yes	18	(51.4)
No	17	(48.6)
Do the differences between men and women working in the jail result more from gender differences between men and women in society (outside the jail) or more from how the job is structured (inside the jail)?		
Society	15	(42.9)
Job structure	13	(37.1)
Equal combination of both	6	(17.1)
Other	1	(2.9)
Which of Zimmer's styles most describes you?		
Institutional	17	(48.6)
Modified	0	(0.0)
Inventive	18	(51.4)

ture (the job model) in explaining differences between male and female correctional officers. Almost 70 percent of the women believed that the manner in which females are conditioned and raised affects how they perform their jobs. Somewhat fewer (51%) believed that the manner in which the job is structured affects how men and women perform the job. Thirty-five percent of the women claimed that this difference was due

largely to women officers being restricted to "the female floor" (working exclusively with women inmates). This response implies that the women, overall, believed that the gender model is a better explanation of gender differences between officers, but that the job model also plays an important role.

> We're segregated and put in pansy jobs and away from male inmates, so it blows your confidence when put on male floors. On the male floors I get tried and tested. If more females were on the male posts, the male inmates would be more used to us. (CO 1)

> In this [women's floor] setting everything is routine. The men get the opportunity to move around more. Females, they look at their job as more routine and thus use less effort. (CO 10)

When asked directly whether they thought the differences between the male and the female officers resulted more from gender differences in society (the gender model) or from how the job is structured (the job model), 43 percent stated that society played a stronger role, 37 percent said they thought the job structure was more dominant, and 17 percent said that society and the job structure played equal roles in determining gender differences. Thus the emphasis on support for the gender model diminished somewhat when respondents were asked to compare the two influences directly. These findings are in contrast with Jurik and Halemba's (1984: 563–64) report of support for the job model, in that women COs' attitudes were more a function of their position in the organizational structure and of working conditions than of gender model characteristics.

Finally, the officers were given a description of each of Zimmer's (1986) women correctional officer styles (institutional, modified, and inventive) and were asked to classify themselves. The *institutional role* describes officers who follow institutional rules closely, downplay the importance of female status, maintain professional distances from inmates and professional relationships with fellow officers, and resent attempts to block their access to prison jobs (1986: 111–22). Officers adopting the *modified role* believe that women cannot perform the job on an equal basis with men, fear inmates and avoid direct contact with them, oppose "women libbers," and rely on male officers to back them up (1986: 122–129). Finally, the *inventive role* comprises officers who view women's status as a distinct advantage, often work in direct contact jobs with male inmates, expect and receive support from male inmates, believe their intuition, communication skills, and abilities with inmates compensate for their disadvantage in physical strength, integrate counseling into their jobs, and receive considerable opposition from male officers (1986: 129–37).

Zimmer (1986) developed these roles after she collected her data, and "assigned" the women to them. This research differs from Zimmer's in that I asked the women which role described them most accurately. (Obviously the women's actual behavior may differ from how they believe they behave.) Seventeen (48.6%) of the women viewed themselves as following the institutional style most closely (as opposed to 11 percent of Zimmer's sample), and 18 (51.4%) viewed themselves as closest to the inventive style (compared to 46 percent of Zimmer's sample). None of the officers chose the modified style, whereas Zimmer assigned 43 percent of her sample to this category. The reason may be that it was difficult to describe the modified style in a manner that seemed as positive as the others. It is also likely that if the interviewer had "assigned" the roles (on the basis of more in-depth information on the individuals in the study), some of the assignments would have differed from the women's perceptions of themselves. Only one woman claimed that none of Zimmer's styles described her.

CONCLUSIONS

This study supports most of the previous research regarding the conflict that these women face at work. Women in this department chose to work in the jail mainly because of the desire to become police/road patrol officers and for financial reasons. Most of the women (66%) reported at least some support from their friends or families for their choice of occupation.

The women expressed a degree of consensus regarding their perceptions of gender inequality in work expectations and opportunities. Most agreed that men and women were equal and that male and female officers could be used interchangeably. The majority also believed that their advancement opportunities compared unfavorably with those of the male officers.

Although most of the respondents had no preference for working with either male or female inmates, officers, or supervisors, they favored working with males when they had a choice. This preference was most pronounced (34%) regarding inmates' sex. A couple of the officers reported that even women officers may be sexist in evaluating inmates' behavior: what may be called "manipulating" in a female inmate is "assertiveness" in a male inmate. Furthermore, it appeared that the women supervisors were under pressure not to be perceived as "giving in" to female officers, while at the same time they may have been trying to help them.

This research showed considerable evidence of sexual harassment, although it seemed that many of the women tended to minimize it. I found more examples of gender harassment than for sexual harassment. The officers tended to believe that women as a group were lumped together, and were viewed as a single group of people who acted in the same way, and that women stood out and received more scrutiny than their male counterparts. Although one-third of the respondents did not believe that they had to prove themselves to male inmates or officers, those who did so were more likely to feel that they had to prove themselves to male officers than to male inmates.

This research also showed a great deal of evidence for the contention that women and men do the CO's job differently. Most significant were the beliefs that men are more forceful than women and that women are better communicators than men. The women believed overwhelmingly that they were doing the job as effectively as the men, or better.

These women reported that both the job model and the gender model are at work in establishing gender differences in jail work. Even so they appeared to believe that the factors related to the gender model are more influential than those related to the job model. The respondents also believed that they view the CO's role differently from their male coworkers on the basis of their experiences outside the jail. Regarding the job model, this study found that the organizational barrier cited most frequently as influencing gender differences in job performance was the practice of assigning most of the women to work exclusively with female inmates.

Finally, the participants seemed for the most part to enjoy their jobs and to feel that they performed well, but they believed that they were not appreciated. These women also felt that the restrictions they faced in their working environment fostered in them a lack of commitment to the job. Therefore this research reveals that most of the women COs in the jail perceive organizational and attitudinal changes as necessary to create an adequate working environment, but consider it unlikely that such changes will occur.

NOTES

1. Forty women, including the pilot-tested individual, were working in nonclerical jobs in the institution. Four COs, all of whom were ranked as officers, chose not to take part in the study. Two were younger white women (aged 25 to 35), one was a younger black woman (aged 25 to 35), and one was an older black woman (aged 40 to 50). The pilot-tested individual was a white sergeant (aged 25 to 35). It is difficult to determine whether these women's participation would have changed the findings appreciably, but the sample seems to represent the women working in the jail adequately.

2. The women could state as many reasons for choosing corrections as they wished.

3. Although some of the other officers also had not worked with male inmates, apparently they were willing to speculate.

REFERENCES

Baunach, P. J., and N. H. Rafter (1982) "Sex-Role Operations: Strategies for Women Working in the Criminal Justice System." In N. H. Rafter and E. A. Stanko (eds.), *Judge, Lawyer, Victim, Thief.* Stoughton, Massachusetts: Northeastern University Press, pp. 341–58.

Chapman, J. R., E. K. Minor, P. Rieker, T. L. Mills, and M. Bottum (1980) *Women Employed in Corrections.* Washington, D.C.: Center for Women Policy Studies.

Crouch, B., and G. P. Alpert (1982) "Sex and Occupational Socialization among Prison Guards." *Criminal Justice and Behavior* 9 (2): 159–76.

Flynn, E. E. (1982) "Women as Criminal Justice Professionals: A Challenge to Tradition." In N. H. Rafter and E. A. Stanko (eds.), *Judge, Lawyer, Victim, Thief.* Stoughton, Massachusetts: Northeastern University Press, pp. 305–40.

Jurik, N. C. (1985) "An Officer and a Lady: Organizational Barriers to Women Working as Correctional Officers in Men's Prisons." *Social Problems* 32 (4): 375–88.

——— (1988) "Striking a Balance: Female Correctional Officers, Gender Role Stereotypes, and

Male Prisoners." *Sociological Inquiry* 58 (3): 291–304.

Jurik, N. C., and G. J. Halemba (1984) "Gender, Working Conditions and the Job Satisfaction of Women in a Non-Traditional Occupation: Female Correctional Officers in Men's Prisons." *Sociological Quarterly* 25 (Autumn): 551–66.

Kerle, K. E. (1985) "The American Woman County Jail Officer." In I. L. Moyer (ed.), *The Changing Roles of Women in the Criminal Justice System.* Prospect Heights, IL: Waveland, pp. 301–17.

Kissel, P. J., and P. L. Katsampes (1980) "The Impact of Women Corrections Officers on the Functioning of Institutions Housing Male Inmates." *Journal of Offender Counseling, Services and Rehabilitation* 4 (3): 213–31.

Martin, S. E. (1980) *Breaking and Entering: Police-women on Patrol.* Berkeley: University of California Press.

Morton, J. B. (1981) "Women in Correctional Employment: Where Are They Now and Where Are They Headed?" *Women in Corrections*, Series 1, No. 1 (February): 7–16.

Nallin, J. A. (1981) "Female Correctional Administrators: Sugar and Spice Are Nice but a Backbone of Steel Is Essential." *Women in Corrections*, Series 1, No. 1 (February): 17–26.

Peterson, C. B. (1982) "Doing Time with the Boys: An Analysis of Women Correctional Officers in All-Male Facilities." In B. R. Price and N. J. Sokoloff (eds.), *The Criminal Justice System and Women.* New York: Clark Boardman, pp. 437–560.

Pollock, J. M. (1986) *Sex and Supervision: Guarding Male and Female Inmates.* New York: Greenwood.

Simpson, S., and M. F. White (1985) "The Female Guard in the All-Male Prison." In I. L. Moyer (ed.), *The Changing Roles of Women in the Criminal Justice System.* Prospect Heights, IL: Waveland, pp. 276–300.

Van Maanen, J. (1973) "Observations on the Making of a Policeman." *Human Organization* 32: 407–18.

Wilson, N. K. (1982) "Women in the Criminal Justice Professions: An Analysis of Status Conflict." In N. H. Rafter and E. A. Stanko (eds.), *Judge, Lawyer, Victim, Thief.* Stoughton, Massachusetts: Northeastern University Press, pp. 359–74.

Zimmer, L. E. (1986) *Women Guarding Men.* Chicago: University of Chicago Press.

——— (1987) "How Women Reshape the Prison Guard Role." *Gender and Society* 1 (4): 415–31.

——— (1989) "Solving Women's Employment Problems in Corrections: Shifting the Burden to Administrators." *Women & Criminal Justice* 1 (1): 55–80.

Zupan, L. L. (1986) "Gender-Related Differences in Correctional Officers' Perceptions and Attitudes." *Journal of Criminal Justice* 14: 349–61.

CHAPTER 27

AFFIRMATIVE ACTION, MULTICULTURALISM, AND CRIMINOLOGY

NANCI KOSER WILSON / IMOGENE L. MOYER

ABSTRACT

Up until this point in the book, we have been discussing the work world of criminal justice practitioners: judges, lawyers, police officers, and corrections officers. Now we examine criminology faculty—those who educate many current and future practitioners—and the criminology/criminal justice curriculum.* Faculty, of course, define the parameters of what is studied, what questions are asked and how, and what articles and texts students read and evaluate. In short, faculty, by their teaching and research, create and shape the body of knowledge in their discipline.

For Wilson and Moyer two issues are important: first, the number and degree of integration of women and minority faculty (as well as staff and students) from diverse multicultural backgrounds and, second, the question of whether these new scholars simply "fit into" existing approaches in the field or are able to "transform" the curriculum so that it becomes more multiculturally diverse and critical of the status quo in criminal justice.

The authors discuss Title VII of the 1964 Civil Rights Act, as amended in 1972, and its effect on educational institutions. The act precludes discrimination in hiring on the basis of race, religion, national origin, and sex. (This is better known as affirmative action.) This legislation covers police, corrections officers, and public legal professionals, as well as faculty, among others. A key problem, argue Wilson and Moyer, is that affirmative action may achieve one goal (increasing the

---

*Typically, "criminology" refers to the study of crime causation and theory building based on traditional sociological models of crime; "criminal justice" refers to the study of the organized response in our society to problems associated with crime: the structuring of policing, courts, corrections, victim services, and the like.

numbers of women and minorities) without accomplishing the second (trans-forming the curriculum and research agenda to reflect the diversity of multicul-tural approaches in our society). And while some critics argue that affirmative action has led to the hiring of "less qualified" women and minority scholars, Wil-son and Moyer assert that these new scholars are equally valuable to academia but are "differently qualified." The authors question whether excellence can exist in criminology without greater gender and multicultural diversity. However, the reader should be aware that women and people of color will bring many "differ-ent voices," some of which will be similar to that of mainstream white male scholars. Many "different voices" may emerge, or, perhaps, no different voice will be heard.

The chapter ends by noting that criminology is inherently a politically conser-vative discipline that provides services for the existing criminal justice system and typically reproduces conditions of existing social inequality. On the other hand, affirmative action in faculty hiring potentially might transform the curricu-lum into more radical or critical perspectives. What can we expect from criminol-ogy if the efforts in increasing women and minority criminologists and fostering multiculturalism and diversity are successful? What can we learn from past opposition to these efforts that will help us to limit such resistance to change in the future?

THE BACKGROUND OF AFFIRMATIVE ACTION PROGRAMS

Affirmative action seeks to redress past wrongs with positive actions in the present. It may be defined broadly as "public or private actions or programs which provide or seek to provide opportunities or other benefits to per-sons on the basis of, among other things, their membership in a specified group or groups" (Jones 1985:902). Hence such programs are explicitly race-conscious, sex-conscious, or ethnically conscious. They recognize the

An earlier version of this paper, presented at the meet-ings of the American Society of Criminology, was coau-thored with Margaret A. Zahn.

Source: Nanci Koser Wilson and Imogene L. Moyer, "Affirmative Action, Multiculturalism and Politically Correct Criminology," *Journal of Criminal Justice Education* 3(2): 277–291 (1992). Reprinted with permission of the Academy of Criminal Justice Sciences.

presence of discrimination against minorities and/or women, and its effect upon employ-ment, educational, or other types of life chances; and within the philosophical context of a liberal democracy with "equal opportu-nity for all," propose *affirmative* remedies.

Though the term "affirmative action" is quite modern, its philosophical and legal principles are venerable. Jones (1985) traces its history to the English Courts of Chancery and their concept of equity. In America a prototype of governmental response to novel problems of inequity may be found in the National Labor Relations Board. If this board finds unfair labor practices, it may issue a cease and desist order and may take such affirmative action as reinstatement of employees with back pay. Other American forerunners of modern affirmative action programs include the remedies enacted under the Fourteenth Amendment and the

Fair Employment Practices Committee established by President Roosevelt in 1941 (see, generally, Jones 1985).

Today Title VII of the 1964 Civil Rights Act (amended in 1972) is the central federal law on equal opportunity. In a wide variety of employment practices, including hiring and promotion, this law prohibits discrimination on the basis of race, religion, national origin, and sex. As Scollay et al. (1989:241) observe, "Institutions of higher education are explicitly covered by Title VII and have incorporated policies in support of equal employment opportunity as standard elements in their expressed institutional goals."

The critical aspect of modern affirmative action programs is not hiring *quotas* but hiring *goals;* employers need only make a good-faith effort to achieve such goals, usually chosen by themselves. Contrary to popular supposition, the government imposes "no fixed quota, no inflexible timetable, and no hiring of the unqualified" in such programs (Jones 1985:904). Nor do these programs invent preferential hiring; instead they seek to eliminate the preferential hiring of white males by guaranteeing the employment of at least some nonwhite, female employees.

Though affirmative action policies have been in effect in most educational institutions since the 1972 amendment to the Civil Rights Act of 1964, evidence on their impact has been mixed. Most studies focusing on the extent or percentage of change in representation of minorities and women find that gains have been made, but those studies which focus on current status find less substantive change. If percentage of change is used as the measure of impact, impressive gains may be noted. Scollay et al. (1989:243) note that one study using such a method found a 93 percent increase in the number of female college presidents. This statistic, however, obscures the picture: at the end of 1984, only 10 percent

of the 2,800 regionally accredited colleges and universities had female presidents.

Despite these mixed findings, it is clear that affirmative action programs have been at least somewhat successful in meeting their originally announced goal of increasing the representation of women and minorities on university faculties, in student populations, and among administrative staffs. In the meantime, however, the concept of affirmative action has been expanded: it has been brought into service as one of the appropriate and perhaps necessary tools for broadening university curricula.

THE DISCIPLINE OF CRIMINOLOGY IN THE 1990s

Criminology may be described appropriately, at its leadership level, as a politically liberal discipline. Substantial changes occurred, however, once it expanded beyond its original confines in this country as a subspeciality of sociology and developed special degree programs in criminal justice/criminology, mostly under the impetus of funds provided by the Law Enforcement Assistance Administration in the late 1960s and early 1970s. Our discipline now attracts many students, especially on the undergraduate level, who align themselves personally and politically with the most conservative aspects of current criminal justice policy. Because programs in our field have flourished during a particularly conservative period in American history, many (if not most) professors, politically more liberal than their pupils, face resistance in the classroom.

Criminology, then, is hardly a radical discipline with a central focus on questioning current social arrangements or analyzing criminal justice policy from a critical standpoint. (Yet such a critical stance is implied in the transformative program of affirmative action as diversity or as a broadening of perspectives.) Instead we see an odd political mix in this discipline, with its by-now thousands of undergraduate majors in every state in the union. Ripped from sociology, its original politically liberal, socially ameliorative context, criminology now stands on its own as a separate discipline. Its intellectual leadership may be described fairly as "liberal," with a sprinkling of conservatives and a sprinkling of radicals, both from the traditional left and from feminism. Its graduate students probably reflect to a very great extent the political leanings of the faculty in particular institutions; thus they vary somewhat from institution to institution. Some of the 15 doctoral programs in the American Association of Doctoral Programs in Criminology and Criminal Justice are markedly conservative; others are much more liberal or even perhaps slightly leftist. In all these programs, however, a significant portion of the undergraduate student population, which is vitally important to the financial support of the department, leans much more toward the right end of the political spectrum. Also, in colleges offering only a bachelor's degree in criminal justice, and in junior colleges, most criminal justice programs are oriented toward training, with a goal of preparing students for entry-level jobs in the official criminal justice system.

The very topic of study in criminology is a source of political conservatism. Insofar as degree programs and research are viewed as providing a service to the extant criminal justice system, conservatism is built into the discipline. Perspectives whereby the criminal justice system is seen as a source of oppression, particularly of women and minorities, and research that reveals how law and law enforcement in America reproduce existing conditions of inequality, are unwelcome to funding agencies, to many undergraduate students, and to the citizens who provide the tax base for public institutions (in which most criminal justice programs are located).

Further complicating the issue is the belief, embraced perhaps by most faculty members, that criminology is a social science. The very canons of science enshrine objectivity and political neutrality. Very likely, most of us who teach research methods reinforce the ideal of objectivity for our students. Whether our romance with science and its supposed political neutrality gives to our discipline only an artificial or contrived and distorted notion of "scientific objectivity" is a question that has exercised social scientists' minds from the beginnings of social science. Is there such a thing as a "neutral statement" in social science, especially a social science that is defined by its focus on social problems? Nonetheless, the worship of science, typical of the modern Western world, and the concomitant belief that science can or should be politically neutral, can militate strongly against the critical perspective typical of a "transformative" curriculum. This is so because research and teaching from an ostensibly neutral stance ratify the status quo, whereas such activities undertaken from a transformative standpoint are regarded as too political or as objectionably biased. Committed scholars are seen to be politically committed only if their work challenges the status quo. Thus we hear the comment that female scholars are "too feminist" or that black scholars are "too touchy" about black issues; we do not hear that objective scholars are "too masculinist" or "too accepting of racial supremacy." Rather the former scholars are "narrow" and "biased;" the latter are "balanced."

Within this context, then, what might be the fate of affirmative action programs that seek to increase diversity as well as to achieve the original and more limited goal of fair representation? Available data on the numbers of women and minorities in various aspects of academia are somewhat scarce. We will address this issue first.

THE ACHIEVEMENT OF FAIR REPRESENTATION

Data on Women

At the university level, data on the first goal of affirmative action (fair representation) are available for women at three levels, as graduate students, as faculty members, and as Directors of Criminal Justice Programs. At Criminal Justice doctoral granting institutions the proportion of women in Criminal Justice master's degree programs ranges from 0 to 75 percent with a mean of 47 percent. The proportion of women in Criminal Justice doctoral programs ranges from 0 to 75 percent with a mean of 37 percent (Flanagan, 1990).

Proportions of women criminal justice faculty members at doctoral degree granting institutions range from 0 to 35 percent with a mean of 18 percent (Flanagan, 1990). Only 12 percent of Directors of Criminal Justice Programs were women in 1990 (Note: 1991 *Journal of Criminal Justice Education*).

In professional activities outside the university, data are available on memberships in professional associations and publications. The Eigenberg/Baro survey (1992) suggests that 21.9 percent of the membership in the two national associations in the discipline (American Society of Criminology and the Academy of Criminal Justice Sciences) is female. Academy of Criminal Justice Sciences lists 27.5 percent of the 1991–1993 membership as female (data provided by ACJS secretariat).

As authors, women members of the American Society of Criminology have a lower publication rate (as measured by numbers of pages published) than do men, both in terms of articles and books (Widmayer and Rabe, 1990). The Eigenberg/Baro study (1992) finds that 28.4 percent of those who present papers at professional meetings are women whereas only 16.5 percent of journal authors are female. Women's lower publication record

may be partially explained by their low representation on Journal Editorial Boards. Eigenberg and Baro (1992) report that for their sample of journals (from 1975–1988) 17 percent of the editors, associate editors and editorial board members were women.

Data on Minorities

At the university level we obtained data on minorities as graduate students, faculty members, and Directors of Criminal Justice Programs. At Criminal Justice doctoral granting institutions the proportion of minorities in Criminal Justice master's programs ranges from 0 to 50 percent with a mean of 19 percent. The proportion of minorities in Criminal Justice doctoral programs ranges from 0 to 36 percent with a mean of 16 percent (Flanagan, 1990). These data apply to students enrolled in Fall, 1989. A 1988 survey shows 270 minority students in Criminal Justice master's programs and 36 in doctoral programs (FYI, 1990). Yet in 1993 the *African American Directory of Criminology and Criminal Justice* lists a total of just 21 doctoral students nationwide. Completed PhDs by 1987 indicated a total of 40 African-Americans in Criminology, Criminal Justice, or a closely related field (Garrett and Darlington-Hope, cited in Heard and Bing, 1993).

The proportion of minority representation on Criminal Justice faculties at doctoral granting institutions ranges from 0 to 11 percent with a mean of 5 percent (Flanagan, 1990). The 1993 *African American Directory of Criminology and Criminal Justice* lists a total of 48 faculty members nationwide. The Heard and Bing (1993) survey could locate only 32 African American faculty members in our field. The 1993 *African American Directory of Criminology and Criminal Justice* lists a total of just 7 Directors of Criminal Justice Programs.

Information is quite scarce regarding minority professional activities outside the university. The Academy of Criminal Justice Sciences lists 10.5 percent of the 1991–1993 membership as minority. This includes American Indians, Blacks, Asians, Hispanic, and "other" (data provided by ACJS secretariat). No data are available on minorities as authors of books and articles or as members of journal editorial boards.

These data suggest some progress toward bringing women and minorities into academic criminology. Yet, the further up the hierarchy of influence in our field, the smaller the number of women and minorities. There are more master's than doctoral students, more doctoral students than faculty, more faculty members than directors of programs. There are more publishers than members of editorial boards and journal editors. Our hope is that these women and minorities will move into higher positions in the future and change the structure of the academic enterprise.

Whether the higher proportions of women and minorities at these various stages (the first goal of affirmative action) will transform the discipline (the second goal of affirmative action) and what effect this will have, in turn, on their representation is the issue to which we now turn. What follows is a model suggesting the parameters for inquiry, with particular emphasis on the impact of "affirmative action hires." It attempts to isolate 1) the factors that determine the race and gender composition of hires, 2) the factors that shape a faculty member's orientation on the faculty, and 3) those factors which determine whether or not agents of change will meet with success.

A MODEL FOR UNDERSTANDING THE IMPACT OF AFFIRMATIVE ACTION

The model shown in Figure 1 depicts the process by which the array of factors that impinge upon the success of affirmative action programs (shown in Table 1) have their

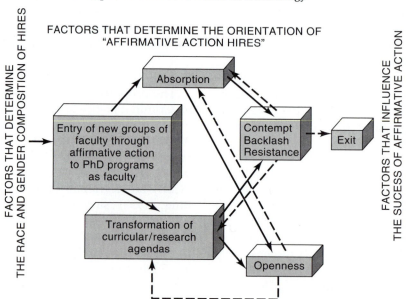

FIGURE 1   The Impact of Affirmative Action on Criminology

effect. As Table 1 illustrates, some of these factors influence the race and gender composition of hires. Others have their effect as factors that determine the orientation on the faculty taken by affirmative action hires: that is, whether they attempt to "just fit in" with the existing program in their department or, alternatively, attempt to transform the curricula and the orientation of the program through their different perspective. The third set of factors consists of those which determine whether affirmative action goals meet with success. As Table 1 shows, some of these factors have their effect in more than one way. For example, the number of female or minority-group members on the faculty and in the

TABLE 1
Factors Accounting for Success of Affirmative Action

1. Larger Culture
   Shape of EEOC and affirmative action statutes
   Vigor of enforcement efforts at the federal and state levels
   Social problems seen as created by minority groups (e.g., abortion, welfare, crack epidemic, crime)
   Level of discomfort with current approaches to problems (e.g., "Burning Bed," "Colors," "Milagro Bean Field Wars")

2. Factors in the University
   Vigor of affirmative action officer
   Existence of black studies, women's studies, Latin studies, international studies programs
   Commitment of the university to broadening the curriculum (gender and racial balancing)
   Political orientation of student population (reactionary, conservative, liberal, radical)
   Presence/absence of student unrest around race/sex issues
   Number/percentage of minority-group/female administrators and faculty members in other departments
   Authority granted to affirmative action officer
   Resources available
   Presence of an active "antipolitically correct" faculty
   Culture of the university town

3. Discipline of Criminology
   Critical mass of blacks/women in available faculty pool (and their ability to withhold labor from rigid institutions)
   Presence of unsolved research problems in the discipline
   Presence of pressure groups in national associations
   Critical mass of publication/research problems defined by minority groups/women that white European males begin to feel they must address (e.g., rape, racial discrimination)

4. The Department
   Reward system for publication (openness to women's and blacks' journals and topics of study)
   Critical mass of female/minority faculty members
   Screening process by search committee (the "good school" syndrome)
   Academic orientation of program
   Commitment of current faculty to affirmative action
   Growth stage of department (new courses needed?)
   Presence of joint research projects on race or gender topics
   Presence of "antipolitically correct" faculty

administrative ranks of a university affects the chances that affirmative action hires will be made in the first place. It also may stimulate faculty members to attempt to transform the curriculum and the research agendas of their own disciplines. Finally, it may affect whether such attempts meet with success.

The model depicts the success of affirmative action in both of its goals—that of fair representation of diverse groups of American citizens, and that of transforming the curricula and the research agendas of academic disciplines to include the varied perspectives of women as well as men, of black and brown citizens as well as white citizens, of Third World peoples as well as Westerners.

One of the more interesting aspects of affirmative action programs is that to some extent, the twin goals of a diverse faculty and a diverse or broad curriculum may be contradictory. This is so because the university curriculum is narrow to begin with: it represents the perspective of white European males. Thus, for instance, a text widely used in art history for years was named simply *History of Art* (Janson 1962). Yet the book focused almost exclusively on the art of white European men. To a very great extent it excluded paintings, sculpture, and architecture of Africa and the East as well as work by women and by people of color. Some faculty members of the "antipolitically correct" persuasion fear that affirmative action will lower standards because such programs seek to include people who have not been trained as thoroughly as themselves in the art, literature, and science of the Western world. Blind to the learning and perspectives of the non-Western, nonmale world, such affirmative action "resisters" see only less qualified rather than differently qualified applicants when they review the vitae of some affirmative action candidates.

This situation creates a real dilemma for affirmative action, because insofar as these "resisters" consider new faculty to "come up to standard," it is quite likely that they do so in part because these "affirmative action hires" conform to existing white, male European standards of university excellence. Yet if the presence of these new hires is to transform the academic world, broadening and enriching the curriculum and the research agendas of the various disciplines through their unique contributions, they must be precisely the sort of scholars who do *not* conform to current standards. (That is, unless they are supermen and superwomen with outstanding traditional qualifications as well as the special qualifications of their own tradition.) At its extreme point, affirmative action may succeed in accomplishing one of its goals (fair representation of diverse groups on the faculty) at the expense of failing in its other goal (achieving a diverse curriculum and research agenda).

Many other factors affect the race and gender composition of a faculty. These include the contours of affirmative action statutes, the vigor of enforcement efforts at the federal and state levels, the commitment of the current faculty to the goals of affirmative action, the vigor of the affirmative action officer at a given university (which includes also the amount of authority given to this person), the presence of a critical mass of minority or female faculty members and administrators at a university, the resources available, the presence of an active "antipolitically correct" group of faculty members, and the culture of the town in which the university is housed. For example, black academicians are loath to move to an area of the country where racial attitudes are less than liberal.

The factors that affect the orientation of a new woman and/or person of color on the faculty are likewise complex. The stance of the "affirmative action hire" may change over time; frequently it does. It seems typical, at least from our personal observations, that many women enter university positions with a "just fit in" approach rather than bringing to the job a self-identification as a woman *for* women. Some of these women become radicalized over time because of contact with a woman's studies program on their campus, and/or as a reaction to encountering contempt or backlash when they attempt to "be one of the boys." On the other hand, because of their very different experiences, American black faculty members frequently enter the university with a strong personal sense of affiliation with black culture. McCombs suggests that to these new recruits "the university appears as a mechanical apparatus that seeks to transform them into being 'university persons' by stripping them of who they are and giving them a new identity tied to a new collective rather than their original one. This new identity tolerates and supports the university that currently exists" (1989:134).

The university may react to "affirmative action recruits" by denying either the individual or the collective identities of these new faculty members or of newly radicalized older faculty members. When only the collective component is affirmed, the faculty member may be expected to pursue only those academic interests related to race or gender or ethnicity and to be an expert in such matters, regardless of training or expertise. "On the other hand, when only the individual component is affirmed, black women [e.g.] are expected not to be actively engaged in research or policy issues related to ethnicity or gender. Moreover, any honest commitment to race and gender issues is viewed with suspicion and devalued" (McCombs 1989:134).

Other factors influencing the orientation of the "affirmative action hire" include the presence or absence of student unrest and agitation around race or gender issues, the amount of support received from fellow faculty members both within and outside one's own department (which itself depends on the

political orientation of that faculty), and the stage of growth of the department.

Factors affecting eventual success in either of the twin goals of affirmative action are highly specific to each discipline because different barriers arise, based on the unique history of the discipline. The political cast of criminology itself has been discussed above. Now we wish to discuss other important determinants of the success of affirmative action within criminology specifically.

FACTORS ACCOUNTING FOR AFFIRMATIVE ACTION SUCCESS IN CRIMINOLOGY AS A DISCIPLINE

When we consider the first goal of affirmative action—that of fair representation of minorities and women on the faculty—specifically in regard to criminology, we note the following. Of first importance is the existence of a critical mass of minority-group members and women in the available faculty pool. This factor in turn depends strongly on the race and gender composition of student populations in the doctoral programs. To date criminology has been more successful in producing white female PhDs than in graduating black doctorates. Thus universities seeking to hire black faculty members persistently face more difficulties than if they seek to add white women to their staff.

Also important in adding women and members of minority groups to university faculties in criminology is the ability of such persons to withhold their labor from institutions with an unfavorable racial or sexual climate. Many white female criminologists now say they will refuse to accept a position on a faculty that includes no other women. This position is more difficult for black scholars because of the smaller number of African-Americans in the discipline. But insofar as some universities have women and blacks on their criminology faculties, job aspirants can withhold their labor from schools with a solidly white, male faculty. Such institutions then increasingly "come under the gun" from their affirmative action officers if those officers are vigorous. The extra push given to affirmative action hiring at universities which are far behind the times then creates new openings, sometimes at premium pay, for minority members and women. Also instrumental in the affirmative action process is the presence of pressure groups in national associations such as American Society of Criminology (ASC) and Academy of Criminal Justice Sciences (ACJS), with the supportive networks they develop for their constituencies of women and/or minorities.

As for the chances that criminology will succeed in the second goal of affirmative action—that of transforming the discipline by broadening and enriching it with perspectives from the worlds of women and of minorities—we may make the following comments.

First, the theories and research studies of criminology consistently have excluded women, especially minority women, and have paid less attention to American blacks than to whites. Although racism and sexism are present in every aspect of American life, a major focus of study in criminology is the criminal justice system, which itself has been a source of oppression for minorities and women. Rape and wife battery serve a political function, as do lynching, the death penalty, and drug wars. The response of the criminal justice system to the inequities created and sustained by these crimes has been less than benign. Criminological studies sometimes reify this reality insofar as they simply describe it without critiquing it.

Further, research based upon so-called universalistic criteria is problematic. Often what is meant is a white, male, European "universality." Here, academic gatekeepers play an important role. In Lynne Spender's (1983) discussion of gatekeeping, she points out that

men have the privilege of choosing the topics and issues that will be considered of fundamental concern to society and to a given discipline. No alternative standards exist to allow for the values and priorities of those who are not white or male. It is not only that men's values are put forward; in addition, women's values are discarded (Spender 1983:4; see also Gilligan 1982). Gatekeepers are in a position to perpetuate their own schemata by exercising sponsorship and patronage towards those who classify the world in ways similar to their own (D. Spender 1981:191).

Publication of journal articles, readers, and monographs is one of the most important resources controlled by academic gatekeepers because it legitimates the researchers and their ideas. When exceptions occur, they often do so in a biased manner. Thus a publication in *Jet, Ebony,* or *Ms.* is not scholarly, but a publication in *The New York Times Magazine* is acceptable. In addition to determining the importance of topics and issues in the discipline, gatekeepers decide how these topics should be defined and investigated; this decision influences generations of future scholars (Cook and Fonow 1984:14). A book on the American prison which focuses exclusively on male prisons is laudable, and its partiality goes unnoticed; a book on women's prisons is considered "narrow." Publication in mainstream journals is essential for "arrival," but scholars who write about African-American, Latin, Native American, or women's issues will find themselves locked out of this avenue to success. Publication in minority or women's journals also is viewed as less important.

In addition to the gatekeeping function of criminological leaders, doctoral programs may be another crucial locus for the transformation of criminology into a more inclusive discipline. Though student unrest at the undergraduate level is a most dramatic source of change, long-term sustainable transformation within the discipline itself will be led and/or stimulated most effectively by the new young scholars whom doctoral programs train. If these scholars are trained appropriately, they will socialize *their* students toward a newer model, as they "fan out" toward teaching careers in colleges with master's and bachelor's degree programs. Classroom lectures and discussion and the textbooks chosen for undergraduate use will become broader, more inclusive, and more critical.

As more faculty members themselves conduct research from a transformative perspective, we begin to see master's theses and doctoral dissertations with a critical perspective on (for instance) wife battery, spousal homicide, and rape; on crime-fighting initiatives in the African, Latin and Native American communities; and on the interface between American welfare policy and crime. As this knowledge builds, and as young minority and female scholars begin to perform gatekeeping roles as journal reviewers and textbook editorial consultants, the newer transformative research will begin to slip even into mainstream journals and textbooks.

A potential exists for backlash, such as the "antipolitically correct" stance, as issues of concern to women, to African Americans, Native Americans and Latin Americans emerge to the point where mainstream scholars are forced to address them in the pages of textbooks and journals. For example, a study of the impact of feminist criminology finds "impressive recent increases in the publication of research on women and crime" but little improvement in coverage in criminology textbooks (Wright 1987:420). Similarly, Hawkins's (1986) work shows lower crime rates for suburban blacks than for suburban whites, but the debate between Wilbanks (1987) and his critics regarding racism in the criminal justice system has been more likely to gain entry into criminology textbooks. In sum, the "trickle-down effect" of transformative research is more evident to date in the pages of journals and research monographs than in textbooks.

CONCLUSION

In this paper we have attempted to outline the array of factors that account for the success or (alternatively) the failure of affirmative action programs in achieving their goals. Insofar as affirmative action programs for university faculty members are successful in recruiting formerly excluded members of American society, they may have two different and sometimes contradictory effects. The new faculty members may become absorbed into the existent culture of criminology (the "just fit in" model), or they may transform the discipline.

A persistent fear is that the process of affirmative action will lower standards—that both the quality of new faculty hires and the quality of students will decline. University of Wisconsin chancellor Donna Shalala notes, "Faculty *assume* minority students are less capable" (Fields 1988:A16). She adds that current faculty members must become convinced that we "can't have first-class universities without diverse student bodies and staff . . . there is no excellence without diversity."

This is the challenge for our discipline and the heart of the debate on politically correct criminology. At odds are opposing viewpoints and the underlying question: Can excellence exist without diversity?

REFERENCES

Bazin, Nancy Topping (1980) "Expanding the Concept of Affirmative Action to Include the Curriculum." *Women's Studies Newsletter* 8(4):9–11.

Berkin, Carol (1991) "'Dangerous Courtesies' Assault Women's History." *Chronicle of Higher Education*, December 11, A44.

Bowers, C. A. (1988) "A Batesonian Perspective on Education and the Bonds of Language: Cultural

Literacy in the Technological Age." *Studies in the Humanities* 15(2):108–29.

Cook, Judith A., and Mary Margaret Fonow (1984) "Am I My Sister's Gatekeeper?: Cautionary Tales from the Academic Hierarchy." Paper presented at the meetings of the Midwest Sociological Society, Chicago.

Edsall, Thomas B., and Mary Edsall (1991) "The Republicans' Racial Wedge Is Flying Back in Their Faces." *Washington Post National Weekly Edition,* December 2–8, 23.

Eigenberg, Helen, and Agnes Baro (1992) "Women and the Publication Process: A Content Analysis of Criminal Justice Journals." *Journal of Criminal Justice Education* 3(2):293–314.

Fields, Cheryl M. (1988) "10 Years after Bakke Ruling, Opinions on Affirmative Action Still Polarized," *Chronicle of Higher Education,* June 29, A14, A15, A16.

Flanagan, Timothy (1990) "Criminal Justice Doctoral Programs in the United States and Canada: Findings from a National Survey." *Journal of Criminal Justice Education* 1(2):195–213.

FYI (1990) "Enrollment in Criminal Justice Graduate Programs, Fall, 1988." *Journal of Criminal Justice Education* 1(1):117–118.

Garrett, Gerald, and Marian Darlington-Hope (1988) "Report of the Affirmative Action Survey Subcommittee." Submitted to the Academy of Criminal Justice Sciences Executive Board, San Francisco.

Gilligan, Carol (1982) *In a Different Voice.* Cambridge, MA: Harvard University Press.

Hawkins, Darnell (1986) *Homicide among Black Americans.* University Press of America.

Heard, Chinita A., and Robert L. Bing (1993) "African-American Faculty and Students on Pre-dominantly White University Campuses." *Journal of Criminal Justice Education* 4(1):1–13.

Janson, H. W. (1962) *History of Art.* Englewood Cliffs, NJ: Prentice-Hall.

Jones, James E., Jr. (1985) "The Genesis and Present Status of Affirmative Action in Employment: Economic, Legal and Political Realities." *Iowa Law Review* 70:901–44.

McCombs, Harriet G. (1989) "The Dynamics and Impact of Affirmative Action Processes on Higher Education, the Curriculum, and Black Women." *Sex Roles* 21(1/2):127–43.

"Note" (1991) *Journal of Criminal Justice Education* 2(1):139.

Scollay, Susan J., Ann P. Tickameyer, Janet L. Bokemeier, and Teresa A. Wood (1989) "The Impact of Affirmative Action in Higher Education: Perceptions from the Front Line." *Review of Higher Education* 12(3):241–63.

Spender, Dale (1981) "The Gatekeepers: A Feminist Critique of Academic Publishing." In Helen Roberts (ed.), *Doing Feminist Research,* pp. 186–202. Boston: Routledge & Kegan Paul.

Spender, Lynne (1983) *Intruders on the Rights of Men.* Boston: Routledge & Kegan Paul.

Widmayer, Alan, and Gary Rabe (1990) "Publication Patterns among American Criminologists: An Analysis of Gender, Regional, and Work Differences." *Journal of Criminal Justice Education* 1(1):99–110.

Wilbanks, William (1987) *The Myth of a Racist Criminal Justice System.* Monterey: Brooks/Cole.

Wright, Richard A. (1987) "Are 'Sisters in Crime' Finally Being Booked? The Coverage of Women and Crime in Journals and Textbooks." *Teaching Sociology* 15:418–22.

CHAPTER 28

THE POLITICS OF RESEARCH AND ACTIVISM: VIOLENCE AGAINST WOMEN

MICHELLE FINE

ABSTRACT

In this final chapter of the section on women practitioners in the criminal justice system, we turn to workers who provide services for women survivors of male crime. The author of this chapter, Fine, points out that these workers are important both because they provide critical services for women crime victims and because many, as activists, have a key role to play in contributing to the research agenda of those who work in this area. The insights of service providers/activists can help guide research on victimization and survival in more realistic and meaningful directions. This should be true for other key areas in criminal justice as well. Specifically, Fine thinks that research on women's victimization, rather than being directed toward the individual victim for answers, should focus on ways in which various institutions (e.g., family, school, employment, the entertainment industry), embedded in a racist, sexist, capitalist society, create a context in which violence against women is perpetuated.

Fine proposes an activist stance for service providers, researchers, and scholars in collaboration with women survivors of male violence whereby they work with and for social movements concerned with changing the system of violence against women. This, she says, will not be easy but is both possible and necessary. She cites several examples of activist-researcher collaboration over the last decade: some activist women have examined the impact of automatic arrest of violent men, which may reduce recidivism of some men but may cause others to become more violent upon release; others have explored strategies for representing in court battered women who have killed their abusers. What do you think of these research agendas? What research questions might you ask that would move the research on violence against women to be more social movement–oriented rather than individual-oriented? How might you reconceptualize research on rape victims or battered women when you are faced with such questions as: Who decides who needs what? And how do you deal with the reality that the answers diverge dramatically by race, class, sexual orientation, age, experience, and politics? Finally, what other areas of research/activism might you consider to be in need of Fine's approach within criminology and criminal justice?

Scene 1. I am in my office, and a colleague enters, quite excited about his new data. He explains:

> We surveyed over 1,000 students on this campus and can predict with a great degree of reliability what individual factors cause young men to be sexually violent with young women— hypersexual socialization, homophobia, and negative attitudes toward women. But here's our problem. We can't predict which women are likely to be attacked by men. Maybe we didn't use the right variables.

I explained that you cannot predict which young women are particularly vulnerable because on a college campus, individual characteristics do not distinguish women about to be victimized from those lucky enough to survive campus life unscathed.

Scene 2. I am in a hospital emergency room with Altamese Thomas. She is a young African-American woman, just gang raped, bruised, but still a bit drunk. I am a young white woman, a rape crisis volunteer, a psychologist, and a feminist. Our conversation goes something like this:

Author's note: An earlier version of this article was presented as a keynote address to the Canadian Research Institute for the Advancement of Women, Quebec, November 1988. This article reflects many conversations with Julie Blackman, Barbara Hart, Susan Ostoff, Lynn Phillips, Susan Schechter, and Jacqui Wade about the possibilities and paradoxes of activist research. They all deserve thanks, but no responsibility for the conclusions reached. Appreciation also to Judith Lorber for rapid and careful editing.

Source: Michelle Fine, "The Politics of Research and Activism: Violence against Women," Gender & Society, vol. 3, no. 4, December 1989, pp. 549–558.

MF (3:00 A.M.): Altamese, the police will be here to speak with you. Are you interested in prosecuting? Do you want to take these guys to court?

AT: No, I don't want to do nothin' but get over this. When I'm pickin' the guy out of some line, who knows who's messin' around with my momma, or my baby. Anyway nobody would believe me. Can I wash now?

MF (3:30 A.M.): Once the exam is over you can wash and brush your teeth. First we need to wait for the doctor for your exam. Wouldn't your friends testify as witnesses?

AT: Where I live, nobody's gonna testify. Not to the police. Anyway, I'm a Baptist and I know God is punishing him right now. He done bad enough and he's suffering.

MF (4:00 A.M.): Maybe if we talked about the rape you would feel better.

AT: You know, I don't remember things. When I was little lots of bad things happened to me, and I forget them. My memory's bad, I don't like to remember bad stuff. I just forget. When I was a young child, my momma told me about rape and robberies. I told her she was wrong. Those things happen in the movies, not here. When I saw such things on the streets I thought they was making a movie. Then one day a lady started bleeding, and I knew it was not a movie.

MF (4:30 A.M.): Do you think maybe you would like to talk with a counselor, in a few days, about some of your feel-ings?

AT: I've been to one of them. It just made it worse. I just kept thinking about my problems too much. You feel better when you're talking, but then you got to go back home, and they're still there. No good just talking when things ain't no better.

MF: Is there anyone you can talk to about this?

AT: Not really. I can't tell my mother, not my brothers either. They would go out and kill the guys. My mother's boyfriend, too. I don't want them going to jail 'cause of me.

MF: You said you sometimes meet with a social worker. Can you talk with your social worker?

AT: She's the one who took away my kids. If they take my baby, I would kill myself. I ain't gonna get myself in trouble, all I got is my baby, and she already thinks I'm a bad mother. But I love my babies and I try hard to take care of them. I just don't under-stand why men have to rape. Why do they have to take, when they could just ask?

MF: How about one of your teachers at college? Can you talk to them?

AT: Those teachers think I'm stupid. Sometimes they call on me, and I don't answer. When you got prob-lems, your mind is on the moon. He calls on you, and you don't know what he's saying. They treat you like a dog, and you act like a dog.

MF: (5:30 A.M.): Soon you will get to leave here and go home, where you'll feel safe.

AT: It ain't safe there. I live in the projects with my baby. I can't go back there now. It feels safer here . . . I hurt so much.

MF: (7:00 A.M.): Can I call you next week just to see how you're doing?

AT: Sure.

All that I knew, as feminist, psychologist, and as volunteer counselor, was rendered ir-relevant by this exchange. My personal and professional ways of coping could not apply smoothly to the material conditions of Alta-mese's life. Even 2 hours into our conver-sation, I still did not quite understand it. Then I thought about how a more traditional psy-chologist might have seen her: learned help-lessness, external locus of control, resistant to the mental health system, cynical about insti-tutions of criminal justice, perhaps depressed. What Altamese offered was a realistic ap-praisal of the slim likelihood that a poor African-American woman would get a hear-ing in the mental health or "justice" systems. Critical of social inequities, she was ambiva-lent about men, cops, sexuality, and the state. And she was tolerant of me. Before me was a woman who was taking control of an uncon-trollable life.

THE INDIVIDUALISTIC RESEARCH BIAS

This essay offers a critique of the individu-alistic research bias that my colleague un-wittingly voiced in his research on date rape, that could have easily perverted the story Altamese had to tell about stranger rape, and that threads through much scholarship on violence against women. While many pro-gressive and feminist researchers have come to understand most poignantly the power of injustice through the lives and words of *individuals* like Altamese, the individualistic research bias that extracts women (and men) from their social contexts has inadvertently invaded the study of violence against women, yielding unfortunate consequences for social theory and social movements.

To focus on the individual, while it may be practically useful given our access to women but not their domestic contexts, contributes to a discourse that finally blames individual survivors, for the source of social inequity is sought inside their bodies and minds. Not only does such an approach decontextualize a woman from her political, social, and personal worlds, but it systematically renders oblique the structures of patriarchy, racism, classism and advanced capitalism that have sculpted what appear to be the "conditions" or "choices" of her life.

The individualistic research bias not only fails to undermine prevailing ideologies that hold individuals—especially women—responsible for their own misery but usually grants these ideologies scientific legitimacy. Women who claim they have been violently attacked by men are typically suspect. Social science research that focuses on qualities of such a woman's life may unwittingly reinforce the belief that she is the locus of her social ills. Changing *her* then appears to be the best solution to institutionalized violence against women.

Finally, individualistic research is situated in a most problematic relationship to social movements. In the case of violence against women, such research not only fails to advance the cause of the battered women's, anti-rape, and anti-sexual harassment movements but often works against them by creating easily assimilated images of women as victims, powerless, unable to fend for themselves, or even masochistic. Such research reinforces hegemonic beliefs that support male violence against women and facilitates secondary institutional victimization by courts, hospitals, schools, therapists, and social agencies. Women who love too much, who are seen as helpless, addicted to violence, or even unaware of their options (as if there were so many), do not lend themselves easily to grass-roots demands for mandatory

arrest laws, privileged consideration in custody battles, acquittal in homicide cases, or even feminist individual and group therapies.

TOWARD A TRANSFORMED RESEARCH AGENDA

If feminists developed activist research projects studying the institutionalization of violence against women, rather than individualistic projects on characteristics of battered women, we would have to reconsider both the research questions we ask and the contexts in which we ask them.

The Questions Asked

Five categories of questions come to mind that feminist activist researchers may want to address over the coming years. These questions seek to understand the politics of gender, power, and violence inside distinct contexts: women's diverse consciousness, intimate relationships, feminist agencies, the battered women's movement, and the institutional structures that sustain violence against women.

On Transforming Consciousness We know a lot about how women feel about male violence, experience it, and make sense of it (see Blackman 1989; Browne 1986; Fine and Gordon 1989; Schechter 1985; Walker 1988). But analyses of women's political consciousness, in which gender braids with class, race, disability, sexual orientation, and community, still remain wanting. That is, we do not know much about how women's consciousness flows over historic and personal time—through self-blame, "ignoring," "tolerating," moral outrage, collective action, legal remedy, flight, or violent revenge. Such shifts in consciousness and resistance need to be understood longitudinally, and not only for different groups of women in differing social contexts but also for the women and men who sit on juries deciding the fates of battered women accused of murder, and those who become psychotherapists, provide health care, and serve as policymakers who legislate, render legal judgments, and determine which research and service projects will be funded.

An example of research on the micropolitics of social consciousness can be found in a study in progress in women's responses to the term *battered woman*. Susan Schechter, Lynn Phillips and I have been interviewing diverse groups of women survivors of male violence about their self-descriptions. We are learning, perhaps ironically, that women who have been abused often distance themselves from precisely those labels feminists use to heighten public recognition of how gendered domestic violence is. One young woman recently commented:

> Not me. I'm not a battered woman. Battered women have bruises all over their bodies. Two broken legs. And he's not a batterer, not like I seen them. No, he just hits me too much.

By popularizing the category *battered woman* and by portraying her usually as powerless and innocent, activists have staked out important but problematic political territory. We need to understand the consequences, for women themselves, of this political act of naming. Adult and adolescent women who feel that they do not fit the category—because they do not feel helpless, they hit back, or they are ambivalent about their lover or the relationship—may resist the category upon which activists rely. We need to know how survivors and nonabused women interpret such politically charged categories and what kinds of homegrown categories they carve to capture and preserve their own experiences.

On Women's Relationships   A second scene for activist research concerns the politics of intimacy, selfishness, and separation in women's personal relationships. Women's lives are situated inside relationships—for better or worse. Given this aspect of women's social realities, it is important to understand how women manage to do *for self*, while still doing *for others*.

An analysis of narratives authored by students at the University of Pennsylvania on their experiences of sexual harassment reveal subtle nuances in how young women translate abuse within existing relationships. Linda Brodkey and I found the young women to be not at all reluctant to name the harassment per se but extremely resistant to naming a faculty member as responsible, that is, getting him in trouble formally or informally, especially when his career or marriage might be threatened (Brodkey and Fine 1989). Battered women are often similarly situated, with even more to lose, in the ambivalence of their relationships. Research is needed to understand how women who remain inside abusive relations, temporarily or permanently, can imagine doing something for themselves. Research on the disrupting politics of women's "selfishness" is clearly on the horizon.

On Battered Women's Shelters   A third scene for activist research involves battered women's shelters. Women who work in or with shelters know the struggles and pains that saturate those sites. Trying to pick up the pieces of a race-, class-, and gender-stratified society, in which housing and health care are inadequate, in which options to violent homes are few, the staff of shelters are beleaguered and frustrated. Feminist researchers need to be inside those shelters, conducting research that enables paid workers and volunteers to feel empowered, to have a grounded sense of their import, and to experience a sense of success in work with little gratification.

In the mid-1980s, the Hilton Foundation solicited an evaluation proposal to assess qualitatively their network of shelters, safe homes, and hotlines in rural Tennessee and to conduct quantitatively a cost-benefit analysis of the effectiveness per woman and child. Jacqui Wade and I competed successfully for the evaluation grant but insisted on the inclusion of another study that would document what it costs per woman and child *not* to provide services.

In our effort to catalog the import of services, we asked the battered women and their children, "What would happen to you/your children if no shelter existed?" They provided rich and tragic responses: broken bones; time off from school; I would be in foster care; my children would be taken away; time missed from work; destroyed furniture; I would have killed him—or he would have killed me.

We next asked the women and staff to define what they thought success meant and what the women needed from the shelters in order to survive. The women in residence offered the following indicators of success: to keep him out as late as possible; to get the kids to bed before he gets violent; to be able to call a friend when he is about to go off; to leave so that he knows that when I come back that I can leave again. In contrast, many shelter workers described success as that imaginary leaving when the woman never returns and is never bothered by him again. Although they knew this to be unattainable in rural Tennessee, anything short of it nevertheless seemed like a failure.

The rural women who had survived violence in their homes and fled, like Altamese Thomas, grappled with the material and psychological realities of poverty, sexism, and classism; with ambivalence surrounding love, hate, and emotional connections; with the tensions of doing "for self" while still being a "good woman." Leaving for good, with no further connections, was an option identified by very few of the survivors. One woman

explained, simply, that on Friday nights every woman in her community gets beaten. "Work's out. The men drink. And we get beat. That's Friday night." Survival meant finding periodic respite.

As a result of our collaborative research with shelter staff and residents, a set of conversations were launched in a few of these settings in which more sensitive and dialectic images of *success* and *empowerment* came to be woven between staff and residents. While tensions were often high between staff and residents, who espoused very different conceptions of womanhood, entitlement, the family, religion, and the appropriate use of violence, the discussions represented an ongoing attempt to fill the yawning cavity that often separates these two groups.

Our research also found that while Hilton's project officer was quite committed to these shelters, safe homes, and hotlines being multiracial, rarely were the residents or the staff racially or ethnically diverse. After much conversation, and with some reservation, we recommended to Hilton that a separate shelter be established to respond to the needs of African-American women and that the staff from that shelter be invited to join the statewide coalition (cf. Matthews 1989). In this case, doing collaborative research meant having the ability to merge agendas between practitioners and ourselves creatively, but also to split voices when necessary.

The Battered Women's Movement   Research is sorely lacking on the politics of social movements against violence against women. Multi-voiced and contradictory though they may be, we have little social history to document their complexity (see Schechter 1985 for a counterexample). An example of a slice of such work comes from Lynn Phillips (1988), who, through interviews with survivors and staff at a series of shelters and agencies in the urban Northeast, has been studying what administrators, staff, and residents mean by the term *empowerment*. She has discovered rich contradictions that typically remain unresolved and therefore confusing at the level of practice.

For some, empowerment seems to mean that the women survivors in residence—women who have been treated terribly for years, who arrive seeking refuge—autonomously identify what they need, which often means safety, sleep, and a television set. But to other staff, these goals seem much too limited and not at all empowering. Some argue that empowerment means launching an autonomous life by pursuing education, paid employment, child care, and housing. And in response to this image, others complain that it sounds too much like the Salvation Army, that is, too moralistic. Phillips's work reminds us that central to the battered women's movement are questions asking: who decides who needs what? And what happens when the answers diverge dramatically by race, class, age, experience, and politics?

Unlike a decade ago, when there seemed to be little space for imagining activist-researcher collaboration, today this space has been opened by practitioners and activists who seek critical analyses of their own work and by researchers who have committed to the practice and politics of feminist scholarship.[1] In particular, activist women have initiated important research on the battered women's movement, seeking to redress racism, homophobia, and residual reluctance to deal with disabled battered women. Some have examined the impact of long-advocated laws and policies, such as automatic arrest, which moves violent men out of their homes and seems to reduce recidivism but may actually intimidate women so that fewer seek help; others have investigated the role of formerly battered and currently battered women in the formulation of movement policies and politics (personal communication from Activist Research Task Force members); and still others have struggled through strategies for representing in court battered women who have killed their abusers (Ostoff 1988).

The Structures of Abuse: Institutionalized Violence against Women The most basic knowledge we need is how social and economic institutions sustain and multiply the kinds of violence women experience (Blackman 1989; Garfield 1989; Kurz 1989; Ostoff 1988; Ritchie 1989; Schechter 1985; Stanko 1985). Only when the dense institutional supports that socialize for male violence, obscure it from public scrutiny, and multiply its effects by doubly victimizing women are revealed, can women's individual psychologies and forms of resistance be fully understood as socially, politically, and institutionally embedded.

REFLECTIONS

Individualistic research on violence against women typically "makes science" of a sweeping and prevailing discourse that holds women responsible for domestic abuse. Such research, at best, positions individual women as the site for remediating such violence. At worst it suggests that these women are themselves the source of the problem. In this article, I have offered alternative images for how feminist scholars might conduct research so as to nurture counterdiscourses that focus popular and policy attention back onto institutions that perpetrate, sustain, and exacerbate violence against women.

---

[1] An activist research network has grown out of the battered women's movement and has begun to investigate questions of ethics, politics, methods, and collaboration. For information about the Activist Research Task Force of the National Coalition against Domestic Violence, contact Pat Kuta and Donna Garske, 1717 Fifth Avenue, San Rafael, CA 94901.

If feminist scholars do move to reinstitutionalize our work on violence against women, we must be sure to collect the diverse voices of women, harmonious and disharmonious, across races, ethnic groups, classes, disabilities, sexualities, communities, and politics, and, together with activists, create forums in which ideas, nodes of agreement, and fault lines of dissension can be aired, studied, resolved, or worked around. In the absence of such collaboration, feminist scholarship will retreat (if unwittingly) toward individualism, to be ignored or, perhaps worse, used against those women whose social contexts we seek to transform.

REFERENCES

Blackman, J. 1989. *Intimate Violence*. New York: Columbia University Press.

Brodkey, L., and M. Fine. 1989. "Presence of Bodies, to Presence of Mind!?" *Journal of Education*, 2.

Browne, A. 1986 *Women Who Kill*. New York: Free Press.

Fine, M., and S. Gordon. 1989. "Feminist Transformations of/Despite Psychology." Pp. 146–174 in *Gender and Thought*, edited by M. Crawford and M. Gentry. New York: Springer Verlag.

Garfield, G. 1989. "Boarder Babies: Institutionalized Violence against Women of Color." Paper presented at the American Psychological Association Annual Meetings, New Orleans, LA, August.

Kurz, D. 1989. "Social Science Perspectives on Wife Abuse: Current Debates and Future Directions." *Gender & Society*, 3:489–506.

Matthews, N. 1989. "Surmounting a Legacy: The Expansion of Racial Diversity in a Local Anti-Rape Movement." *Gender & Society*, 3:519–533.

Ostoff, S. 1988. "Strategies for Justice: Working with Battered Women Who Kill." Paper presented at the American Psychological Association Annual Meetings, Atlanta, GA, August.

Phillips, L. 1988. "Opening Conversation: An Internal Evaluation of the House of Ruth's Shelter Program." Unpublished manuscript.

Ritchie, B. 1989. "Battered Women of Color in the Emergency Room: Institutionalized Violence." Paper presented at the American Psychological Association Annual Meetings, New Orleans, LA, August.

Schechter, S. 1985. *Women and Male Violence*. Boston: South End Press.

Stanko, E. 1985. *Intimate Intrusions; Women's Experience of Male Violence*. London: Routledge & Kegan Paul.

Walker, L. 1988. Respondent, "Justice for Battered Women Who Kill: Theory Research, Service, Activism, Expert Testimony." Panel at the American Psychological Association Annual Meetings, Atlanta, GA, August.

EPILOGUE

This Epilogue on future directions of women and the criminal justice system should be understood as a modest beginning, not a conclusion—much like graduation or commencement. In fact, the single article in this section represents one scholar's creative thinking about traversing different worlds—empirical, intellectual, and political—and provides different visions of studying and transforming the relationship between women and the criminal justice system. The Epilogue suggests directions for feminist research, theory, and activism, all the while warning us of the complexity of the interaction between scholars/researchers from many disciplines, both within and outside criminology, and policy makers, activists, and community groups.

Given the comprehensive nature of this article and its historical analysis of the growth and impact of feminist thought on criminology, some teachers may prefer to use this chapter early in their course. We have included it as our "commencement" chapter in the hope that it will inspire change far beyond that represented in the material in this book.

It gives us great pleasure to close this book with an original chapter by Kathleen Daly, an important feminist criminologist of our time. "Looking Back, Looking Forward: The Promise of Feminist Transformation" develops several themes introduced in the last two chapters in Part Three. In Chapter 27, Wilson and Moyer argued that it was important for criminology to include more women and minority faculty so that these new scholars might transform the curriculum into one more multiculturally diverse and critical of the existing theories and research in criminology. Daly's chapter provides us with a five-stage theory of curricular change (from nonfeminist to transformative) to help us understand the evolution of feminist theory and research and the impact it might have on criminology. Not only does she tell us what stage current thinking seems to be at in criminology, but she suggests that to move to the most developed, inclusive, and diverse stage of feminist thinking will require two tasks: first, we must build a research enterprise committed to thinking in multiple and interactive ways about inequality; second, we must build political and knowledge constituencies by forging partnerships across disciplines, institutions, work sites, and interest groups which will challenge that inequality. Accomplishment of these tasks, she says, is possible through a "class-race-gender" approach to thinking. To use such an approach, criminology must be able to bring in and draw on the feminist, antiracist, and critical literature outside of criminology.

Daly's goal (as is Klein's in the "Afterword" to Chapter 2) is to shift our research viewpoint from that of the controller to include that of the dominated so that the discipline of criminology may be useful to many different as well as disadvantaged groups. This same goal is also expressed by Fine (Chapter 28), who proposes an activist stance for service providers, researchers, and scholars within and outside criminal justice and other service agencies in collaboration with women survivors of male violence and in partnership with social movements aimed at changing the system of violence against women. But Daly goes one step further in the Epilogue. As she urges us to recognize the need for building multiple and progressive partnerships across groups, she also warns of the potential pitfalls of such collaborations.

Finally, Daly suggests that in working on behalf of women in the criminal justice system and in the broader society, academia is an appropriate place to begin. The classroom can become a laboratory for "taking rights" as well as "talking about rights." While this may be personally unsettling, she challenges both teachers and students to take risks. For teachers, this means introducing new material and theories, being prepared to face student criticism and resistance, and helping students to listen to others when they disagree. For scholars, taking risks means "working outside a male-dominated discourse" in criminology; this approach, as Daly describes at the outset of her chapter, entailed considerable risks to her career as a young scholar. For students, taking risks means assuming an active, questioning role in class, going beyond what is formally expected, and confronting a diversity of opinions and ideas. Daly helps all of us who take nonconforming approaches to our teaching and learning to understand that conflicts may erupt in class. This, she says, is a necessary part of a transformative, multicultural feminist scholarship in service to all people.

LOOKING BACK,
LOOKING FORWARD:
THE PROMISE OF FEMINIST
TRANSFORMATION

KATHLEEN DALY

LOOKING BACK

Someone should document how those who were excluded from academia in the past continue to suffer that exclusion. I am referring not simply to constraints on professional advancement but to physical, mental, and emotional problems that result from "not looking the part" or "not measuring up" or simply being "different."

My first few years as an assistant professor interested in feminism, crime, and justice were rough. I began working at an elite institution in 1983; only two other social science faculty members were feminist scholars.[1] Both women left within two years. It took me three years to get one article accepted in a journal. My topic, gender and sentencing, was not thought "significant enough" for the

major journals. I faced an intellectual paralysis in knowing how to frame the question of judicial treatment of men and women defendants. I had to enter into a strange debate about judicial paternalism and chivalry toward women. I could not say what I wanted to say nor begin where I wanted, which was outside a male-dominated discourse (criminology) and within feminist scholarship on gender, work, and family. Scholars who reproduce the field do not face these hurdles: they study all-male samples with theories based on all-male samples; they continue to avoid the vexing questions of gender and masculinity in research on crime and justice. The irony is that they are described as engaged in "general theory." How do they get away with that?

Several years later when I was reviewed for promotion, I was advised that my research and publications were "too narrow." It is hard to understand how research on prisons, prostitution, sentencing, and white-collar crime was "too narrow." Well-known sociologists staked their careers on

Acknowledgments: My thanks to Helen Eigenberg and the editors of this volume, Natalie Sokoloff and Barbara Raffel Price, for their comments on an earlier draft, and to Gregg Barak for source material.

This article was written expressly for inclusion in this text.

just *one* of these areas. Perhaps criminology was narrow. Or perhaps the reviewers were. Surely we have heard this sexist appraisal before: "too narrow" means "your work 'only' deals with gender"[2] (see Wilson and Moyer, Chapter 27 in this volume).

Yes, I am complaining, but not without cause. And yes, I know that other faculty members had it worse. Lives ripped apart by sexual and homophobic harassment. Lives stressed by student and colleague pressures that come from being the token African-American or Mexican-American or gay and lesbian member of the faculty, or being the token white person interested in "minority issues." Lives torn by trying to "balance" male-centered norms of professional achievement with maternity and motherhood. Humiliation and disappointment when achievements are not recognized or credited. These experiences take a toll on our work and ability to make a difference. We discuss them a lot and learn that they are widely shared and structural, not random or individual. I wonder, what will happen to the next generation of students? Will it be different for them?

WHERE WE ARE TODAY

How can we gauge the impact of feminist theory and research on the discipline? McIntosh's (1984) five-stage framework for describing the place of women (and gender) in the curriculum has been applied to sociology and criminology (Andersen, 1988; Goodstein, 1992). Andersen (1988) redefined McIntosh's stage theory to include all women and those men who are members of racial or ethnic minority groups. The five stages are as follows (see Table 1, left side):

Stage 1: All women and minority men are totally excluded from the discipline.
Stage 2: All women and minority men are added to the discipline (otherwise known as "add women and stir" and "add race and stir").
Stage 3: All women and minority men are seen as "problems" or "anomalies" because they do not fit existing ideas; exclusion and invisibility are discussed explicitly.
Stage 4: All women and minority men become the center of research and are studied on their own terms.
Stage 5: A transformed knowledge includes people, with a theoretical focus on multiple relations of class-race-gender.

Curricula Stage Theory

Let us consider how each stage applies to criminology.[3]

Excluding Women and Minority Group Men (Stage 1)   For crime theories, criminologists have long focused on young men, those who grew up in poor or working-class families and who were first-generation immigrants or members of colonized racial and ethnic groups (such as African-, Mexican-, and Native Americans). Unlike many other disciplines, criminology has not excluded minority group men—at least as subjects of crime theories. In fact, a major problem for criminology has been ignoring majority group men as lawbreakers and justice system officials. On the other hand, until recently, all women have been excluded as subjects of crime theories.[4] Why is this the case?

Criminology is part of a larger disciplinary area, deviance and social control, which is organized along lines of gender, class, race/ethnicity, and age. To simplify, deviant groups can be classified as "mad" or "bad." Partly on the basis of behavior and social conditions, and partly on the basis of how behavior is diagnosed and classified, women are more likely to be sorted into the "mad"

TABLE 1
Stages of Curricular Change and Modes of Feminist Production of Knowledge

Stages of curricular change	Modes of feminist production of knowledge
Stage 1: Womanless.	Does not exist.
Stage 2: Add women and stir; add race and stir.	Pre- or nonfeminist stage. Focus on experiences of women or on gender difference, but feminist theory or research is not used to interpret findings.
Stage 3: All women and men members of racial/ethnic minority groups "a problem" or "anomaly."	A. Early feminist critiques of criminology. Research challenges common-sense ideas about women's crime and liberation, raises questions about sources of data on crime, and brings formerly unrecognized victimization to light. B. Critique of feminist inability to deal with "problem or anomaly" of women of color. Critique of inability of criminology to deal with race and ethnic relations. Racial and ethnic differences among women raised as theoretical, research, and political problems.
Stage 4: All women and men members of racial or ethnic groups are the focus.	Feminist questions and debates are central to the research enterprise. May begin outside criminology in raising questions or forming alliances and partnerships with other disciplines or organizations. Theoretical and methodological diversity. Stance of multiple and crosscutting social relations of class-race-gender-age-sexuality.
Stage 5: Fully transformed and inclusive knowledge.	The norm is feminist and inclusive.

group, their deviance less likely viewed as threatening or dangerous.[5] Women's deviance is more often featured in descriptions of mental health rather than crime problems, while men predominate in criminology.

"Adding" Women and Race and Stirring (Stage 2) Scholars today agree that criminology is in Stage 2. Women are no longer invisible, but their presence is infrequent and poorly represented. An analysis of photographs in recent crime and justice textbooks by Eigenberg and Baro (1992: 17–18) found that "males, especially white males, visually dominate images in introductory texts." The authors learned that while white men were predominantly presented in professional roles, minority men were most apt to be portrayed as offenders. White women and women of color were portrayed as victims or "peripheral persons."

Wright (1992) examined criminology textbooks for two time periods: 1956–1965 and 1981–1990. In the earlier time, 2 percent of the books' pages were devoted to women and crime topics; in the more recent period, it was 4 percent (pp. 225–226). With the exception of more pages devoted to rape, there were no significant increases in the coverage of women and crime topics over time.

In reviewing recent criminal justice texts, Wonders and Caulfield (1993) found that none discussed feminist theory. Text coverage given to women was typically 1 to 3 percentage points; the highest was 6 percent. In 7 of 12 texts, there was "no mention of domestic violence or battering in the index or table of contents" (p. 93).

To summarize, analyses of criminology textbooks suggest that minority group men continue to be "visible" (perhaps too visible) as lawbreakers; but a consideration of the impact of race or ethnic relations on crime and justice has not been addressed in criminology. Likewise, statistics may be presented on women as lawbreakers or victims, but the interpretation of statistics and other research is not made with reference to feminist theories.

Stage 2 dominates textbooks because it gives the appearance of incorporating new material or perspectives. A closer look shows incorporation to be a superficial gloss: criminological theory and research are unchanged. Wilson (1991) and Goodstein (1992) worry that criminology will be stuck in Stage 2 unless more transformative energies are deployed. They are concerned that merely "integrating" or "incorporating" new crime and justice information without introducing new theories or perspectives can make things worse. Goodstein (1992: 179) points out that "presenting material on women's lives from a Phase 2 perspective may be more dangerous to students . . . than omitting the material altogether." She notes that presenting new material on women without providing new tools for interpreting that material (the Stage 2 approach) could "lead to considerable victim blaming. [For example], the risk of rape and harassment experienced by female correctional officers might be cited as justification for [limiting their employment] in some correctional facilities" (p. 179).

Women and Minority Men as Anomalies (Stage 3) While criminology texts are at Stage 2, theories and research of some criminologists have moved into Stage 3. This is a first step toward transforming the field. Such efforts can develop in classroom settings when teachers bring in new topics and readings that question traditional criminological

theory and research. When readings and class discussion move from relatively distant topics (such as theories of juvenile crime in the 1950s) to those closer to home (such as abuse in families, rape in college fraternities, race relations in policing), the crime and justice classroom becomes more charged. As students see themselves as subjects of theories of crime, victimization, and justice—not merely as students reading about social problems— they challenge what is missing from those theories. Stage 3 can be imbued with excitement, but it may also be unsettling for students and professors: the class is neither traditional nor completely changed, but it may need to handle a mix of the old and the new. Conflicts in the larger society over class, race or ethnicity, gender, and sexuality may erupt in the classroom among students, as well.

Women and Minority Men at the Center; Transformed Knowledge (Stages 4 and 5) Stages 4 and 5 are more visionary and imagined because we do not yet live in a society in which women and minority group men form part of the knowledge center. Some pioneering theorists and researchers are beginning to map alternative ways of conceptualizing crime, victimization, and justice. Through their efforts, described in the next section, crime and justice curricula may be transformed.

LOOKING FORWARD

Transformation of criminology will occur when feminist and multicultural scholarship on crime and justice is brought more centrally into the discipline. It is important, then, to relate stage theory to these new modes of producing knowledge. Next to each of the McIntosh/Andersen curricula stages shown in Table 1, I identify the corresponding stages in producing feminist knowledge.[6] Stages (or modes) of producing knowledge refer to the theoretical and research tools scholars apply in their work, as described more fully in the next section.

Modes of Feminist Production of Knowledge

Womanless; Pre- or Nonfeminist (Stages 1 and 2) Stage 1 (or womanless) does not exist in feminist knowledge production, and Stage 2 is pre- or nonfeminist. Stage 2 thinking dominates studies of gender differences in rates of lawbreaking or victimization in crime and justice textbooks today. Information may be presented about women or gender differences, but the material is not interpreted with reference to theories of gender.

Challenges to Criminology (Stage 3) The identification by women of "women as a problem or anomaly" for criminology is the first stage of feminist knowledge production. Examples of early feminist critics of crime theories include Heidensohn (1968), Bertrand (1969), Smart (1976), and Klein (Chapter 2 in this volume). They discovered that women were excluded from crime theories; or when women were discussed, their behavior was distorted. Another major "problem or anomaly" for criminology was men's violence against women. This phenomenon was completely ignored by criminology until feminist research brought the experience of victimized women to light (Russell, 1975; Dobash and Dobash, 1979; Browne, 1987, Chapter 13 in this volume).

The identification by women of color of "race as a problem or anomaly" for feminist theory and for criminology came several years later. Authors such as V. Young (1980), Lewis (1981), and Arnold (Chapter 8 in this volume) were concerned that studies of "women" lacked racial specificity. Without careful consideration of racial and ethnic differences, Simpson (1989: 618) wondered if "current theories of female crime, including feminist perspectives, [were] white-female centered." We know that like men, minority group and poor women are disproportionately represented as lawbreakers, in arrest statistics, and in jails or prisons. And as with men's crime, explicit theorizing about the consequences of race and ethnic relations (and economic conditions) for women's crime has not been done. For research on women's victimization, there is greater class and racial or ethnic variation; yet with some exceptions (Williams and Holmes, 1981; Richie, 1985; Ferraro, 1989, Chapter 15 in this volume; Mama, 1989; Matthews, Chapter 12 in this volume; Rasche, Chapter 14 in this volume), we know little about the ways in which diverse groups of women understand and respond to the violence. We do know that minority group women are torn by concerns for their safety and protecting "the race" from further criminalization. Some scholars propose developing a black feminist (or women of color) theoretical framework (Rice, 1990; Stephens, 1993). It is crucial to develop such a framework, but at present, its components have been drawn in sketchy form.

Feminist Questions Are Central (Stage 4) Stage 4 research begins with feminist questions. This means that research on lawbreaking or victimization need not begin with a review and critique of traditional criminological theory and research. Rather, it is possible to begin with a body of feminist theory and research and build on it. For example, Carrington (1990) set out to determine if Chesney-Lind's (1973, 1974) and Hancock's (1981) claims about the "sexualization of female delinquency" were applicable to adolescents in Australia in the 1980s. She finds that the sexualization thesis is no longer accurate empirically, and she suggests that feminist scholars focus on the masculinity of crime, not the sexualization of female delinquency (Carrington, 1990: 15).

Bickle and Peterson (1991) wanted to see if gender-, race-, and family-based sentencing practices described in my research (Daly, 1987, 1989) applied to men and women sentenced for forgery; with some exceptions, they find similar patterns. I wanted to see if a common feminist explanation for women's lawbreaking, which I term "street woman," applied to women convicted in felony court (Daly, 1992a). I learned that the street woman pathway to court was frequent, but there were other life circumstances that brought women to court, including having ended relationships with violent men, angering easily and having fights with others, and having a history of psychological problems.

Feminist research on women's victimization is more developed and matured. Comparative research in several countries has been conducted to determine the role of police and policy responses toward domestic violence (Hanmer, Radford, and Stanko, 1989; Dobash and Dobash, 1992). Much discussion has centered on the impact of different laws and procedural reforms in prosecuting rape (Estrich, 1986) and in defending battered women who kill men who abuse them (*Women's Rights Law Reporter*, 1986; Coker, 1992).

One can also see how authors' analyses have changed over time. The second edition of Campbell's *The Girls in the Gang* (1984/1991) chides feminist researchers for focusing overly much on women's victimization and not enough on women lawbreakers; Campbell also critiques gang researchers for ignoring women and gender relations in gangs. The second edition of Rafter's *Partial Justice* (1985/1990) incorporates feminist legal theory and litigation in changing prison conditions for women. This later edition raises questions about "same" or "different" prison policies for men and women. Reflecting themes in feminist legal theory, Rafter attempts to recast the meaning and practice of equal treatment.

These examples suggest that feminist scholarship in crime and justice borrows from feminist work in the related disciplines of psychology (Gilligan, 1982), philosophy (Spelman, 1989; I. Young, 1990), and law (Smart, 1989). In developing a more autonomous theoretical and research agenda that moves away from traditional criminology concerns, feminist crime and justice scholars are shifting their focus from the "woman question in criminology" to the "criminology question for feminism" (Klein, "Afterword," Chapter 2 in this volume, citing Bertrand, 1991). Such an approach risks cutting feminist theory and research off from mainstream criminology and thus keeping feminist scholarship marginal. That need not happen if review essays, written for mainstream audiences, are published (e.g., Daly and Chesney-Lind, 1988) or if texts incorporate feminist research as a seamless whole (Chesney-Lind and Shelden, 1992) rather than as a separate chapter. Or, as in the case of domestic violence, which has a matured feminist research tradition, scholars can challenge basic assumptions about how violence is measured, and they can bring that critique to a mainstream audience (Dobash, Dobash, Wilson, and Daly, 1992). Although it is hard to imagine what it would be like to live in a world where knowledge norms were inclusive and feminist (Stage 5), one way to get there is by communicative and democratic discussion. By itself, a separatist strategy will fail.

Some feminist scholars see little hope in rehabilitating criminology (Cain, 1990; Smart, 1990); others are optimistic that feminist questions can reform the discipline (Heidensohn, 1987). I think we should recognize the power of criminological discourse, but we do not need to engage with criminology on its terms alone. Thus, I propose we work within and against criminology, in the same way others propose we work within and against the justice system (Dobash and Dobash, 1992: 206).

The ability to enter into research and policy debates with feminist questions in mind is an important achievement. Rudimentary frameworks and debates were established by feminist pioneers in the 1970s and 1980s. Today we are not forced to begin with nonfeminist questions and the paralysis that comes from starting there as I experienced earlier in my career. We can and should begin with feminist theories and with the premise that diverse groups of women and multiple research tools are the ingredients for building feminist knowledge on crime and justice. Two tasks will facilitate the growth and impact of feminist scholarship. The first is building a research enterprise that is committed to thinking multiply and interactively about inequality. The second is building political and knowledge constituencies by forging partnerships across disciplines, institutions, and work sites to challenge that inequality.

The Promise of Class-Race-Gender Analysis: Building a Research Enterprise

It is difficult to know when the phrase "class-race-gender analysis" entered into common usage. I trace its emergence to the experiences of black women during the movement activities of the 1960s and, subsequently, to black feminist scholarship in the late 1970s (Daly, 1993). Today class-race-gender is a frequent and popular buzzword to signal a way that theory and research *ought* to be done. The construct seems to exclude other social relations such as sexuality, age, and ethnicity; but it is possible to stretch its meaning by using it metaphorically.

Class-race-gender announces a way of viewing social inequalities as interrelated and interacting (Combahee River Collective, 1979; Moraga and Anzaldua, 1981; Hooks, 1984; King, 1988; Collins, 1990). Novels and short stories seem to lend themselves to this approach, perhaps because through story-telling, the depth and histories of people's lives can be brought into view (Lorde, 1984; Pratt, 1984; Jordan, 1985). Some feminist law scholars have used storytelling to critique antidiscrimination law (Williams, 1991), as well as reproductive, rape, and domestic violence law (see review by Abrams, 1991). Historians have also used class-race-gender in framing research (e.g., Davis, 1981/1983; Aptheker, 1982; Bynum, 1992).

It may be more difficult to bring a class-race-gender analysis into the social sciences for three reasons. First, while the concept has great appeal, we are just beginning to grasp its full meaning and implications. For example, in a recent edited collection entitled *Race, Class, and Gender in the U.S.: An Integrated Study* (Rothenberg, 1992), one finds many contributors of particular class, gender, racial-ethnic, and religious groups describing their experiences; but the promised "integrated study" does not materialize. Does the collection of many diverse voices constitute a class-race-gender analysis? It may to some, but to me, merely presenting diverse viewpoints alone does not make a class-race-gender analysis. Indeed, such apparent "diversity" may merely be the 1990s version of melting pot pluralism (Vogel, 1991; Platt, 1993). As yet, we lack a theoretical language to trace links and conflicts among multiple crosscutting social relations. Lerner (1990) notes simply that "we have an inadequate conceptual framework for dealing with 'differences'" (quoting from Jaggar and Rothenberg, 1993: 238).

Second, class-race-gender is invoked too narrowly when it could have a broader reach. All men and women, rich and poor, of diverse racial and ethnic backgrounds, and of different sexualities, are socially located in relations of class, race, and gender. However, members on the subordinate side of these relations are "marked." Thus, gender is salient when women, not men, are studied; race, when

African-Americans (or other cultural groups) are the focus; sexuality, when lesbians are researched; and so forth. Thus, women of color, who see themselves on the subordinate side of class, race, and gender relations, may claim a special status as being at the intersection of three relations. Yet, we should see that *all* members of U.S. society are at the intersection of these relations. The difference is that members of socially subordinate groups cannot describe themselves to majority groups or be represented in unmarked ways. At the same time, members of socially subordinate groups may have a more accurate way of seeing social structure from a "bottom-up" or "outsider" perspective, (Rohrlich-Leavitt, Sykes, and Weatherford, 1975; Hartsock, 1984: Chapter 10; Smith, 1987; Collins, 1990). Typically, we find that research on or by black women takes a class-race-gender perspective (e.g., Davis, 1981); but research on or by white women takes a class-and-gender perspective (e.g., Newton, Ryan, and Walkowitz, 1983).[7] We will know that a class-race-gender framework has taken hold when a biography of former President George Bush is subtitled "a class-race-gender analysis," not merely when biographies or research on women of color are.

Third, and perhaps most important for the social sciences, class-race-gender calls attention to the ways in which social research (1) flattens and depoliticizes social relations as "variables" (as Fine discusses in Chapter 28 of this volume) and (2) views social relations as independent and discrete rather than interdependent and multiple. Variable-based analyses and independent effects of these variables are the linchpin of standard quantitative studies in criminology. Yet, as King (1988) finds in analyzing employment patterns, class-race-gender must be examined as multiple and interacting relations (Stage 4), not simply additive (Stage 2). It might be possible to revise the standard quantitative study by using interaction terms, and important insights can come from this approach. For example, Peterson and Hagan (1984) showed that while low-level black drug defendants were treated leniently (as "victims"), the higher-level black dealers were treated harshly (as "villains"). But more than statistical "interaction terms" are involved in taking a class-race-gender approach.

Ultimately, a class-race-gender analysis has the potential to transform sociological theories of inequality. When we consider the nineteenth-century sociological theorists (Marx, Weber, Durkheim), we see they were largely concerned with class relations as the primary axis of power. Neither gender nor race relations were in the picture. As social researchers begin to explore the multiple and crosscutting relations of class-race-gender, we will come to have a more racialized and gendered meaning for class relations, a more racialized meaning of gender and sexuality, and so forth. It is difficult to imagine today what new theories of inequality will be like, since our inherited ways of thinking can act to stymie the imagination.

From Partnerships in Misery to Partnerships for Change

Theories of inequality and analyses of social change are forged by the social worlds we live in and our relationships with others. Thus, Jordan's (1985) observations on how class, race, and gender are sources of connection and fracture are important to heed. She points out that while "race and class and gender [are] real," they cannot be used as automatic proxies for knowing whom you are going to get along with, who will be an ally, or who will betray you:

> So far as I can see, the usual race and class concepts of connection, or gender assumptions of unity, do not apply very well. I doubt that they ever did.

. . . Yes, race and class and gender remain as real as the weather. But what they must mean about the contact between two individuals is less obvious and, like the weather, not predictable.

. . . It occurs to me that much organizational grief could be avoided if people understand that partnership in misery does not necessarily provide for partnership for change: *When we get the monsters off our backs, all of us may want to run in very different directions.*

. . . I am saying that the ultimate connection cannot be the enemy. The ultimate connection must be the need that we find between us. It is not only who you are, in other words, but what we can do for each other that will determine the connection. (pp. 46–47) (emphasis in original)

Jordan's conclusion, "it is not only who you are . . . but what we can do for each other," can be extended to alliances among feminists (or pro-feminists) seeking to describe and change knowledge and practices concerning crime and justice. Many such alliances can be imagined, but I shall focus on four: research partnerships, policy partnerships, research and policy partnerships, and media collaborations.

Research Partnerships Increasingly, one finds that feminists in law schools, schools of public health, medical and nursing schools, and the social sciences are interested in similar problems. The response to state efforts to criminalize drug-using pregnant women is a good example (Humphries et al., Chapter 10 in this volume). Crime and violence are increasingly a part of public health concerns; the Centers for Disease Control now gathers information on causes of violent death. A key partnership should form between those in law schools (including clinical programs) and those in the social sciences. Research is needed on legal interventions that help and on alternative ways of giving legal advice. For example, from interviews with battered women who sought restraining orders, a

colleague and I (Chaudhuri and Daly, 1992) found that battered women appreciated the law student interns more than regular attorneys because they listened to the women's stories. Further, we learned that the process of seeking the restraining order itself could be empowering and positive.

Partnerships that include members of the researched group are ideal. Joan Moore's (1991) collaborative research team of academics and ex-offender gang *veteranos* in studying Mexican-American gangs is exemplary. Mies's (1983) guidelines for feminist research are a model of egalitarian relations, activism, and consciousness-raising. She and others applied the guidelines in documenting the experiences of German women in shelters. The Rights of Women, Family Law Subgroup (1985), is an organization of British law-trained activists and community women who work to change family law. Other case studies of conducting research, which range from the standard to the radical, are presented in Bowles and Klein (1983) and Reinharz (1992). Although collaborative, action-oriented approaches to research may not always be feasible, they remind us that the standard scientific stance—which includes social relations of researcher dominance over those researched, and a professional ethic of "objectivity" and "neutrality"—may not be desirable in conducting research.

Policy Partnerships A common problem all women and racial/ethnic minority group men face is whether policy should be written in gender- or race-"neutral" ways or whether programs and policies ought to be gender- or race-"specific." Again, we see that some groups are marked—set apart—as "different" (e.g., black women differ from white women, or women differ from men), while others are in the neutral or general category (i.e., men and white are neutral, the unmarked standard). Within any public-sector organization, there will be agencies and programs committed to such "general" and "special" categories. The importance of forging partnerships across a historically created organizational divide cannot be stressed too much. Affirmative action programs are only a partial reform in response to the historical exclusion of all women and racial/ethnic minority group men from higher education and employment. Such programs need to work alongside regular personnel policies. Likewise, separate programs and facilities for drug-addicted women need to be developed in tandem with those organized for both men and women. Or as Matthews (Chapter 12 in this volume) suggests, state-imposed racial integration may not be appropriate or effective in counseling programs for rape victims. Workers in justice systems need to recognize that "neutral" versus "special" programming can become a way to divide those who have much in common. It also becomes a way to forestall radical organizational change toward more inclusive policies and programs.

Research and Policy Partnerships Relationships among academics, policymakers, and practitioners in crime and justice would seem obvious. But we need to realize that there are different success criteria in our jobs. For the academic, one criterion is a carefully crafted research study, which will take at least two to five years to complete. For the policymaker, the criteria are reconciling research findings with the political winds, coping with budgetary constraints, and balancing interagency relations; one success criterion is increasing the size of the budget or fending off cuts. And for the activist, one criterion is to get something done—to provide more services or new services, or to change "the system." Because our jobs have different goals and time frames, we will have to blend our notions of "success." This will take time, patience, and an open mind.

In addition to the collaborative efforts noted earlier (e.g., Mies, 1983), the following examples of research and policy partnerships come to mind. Daly, Geballe, and Wheeler (1988), a lawyer and two sociologists, worked together in producing research findings for a class-action suit on behalf of incarcerated women in Connecticut. Activists and researchers joined forces in documenting AIDS outreach workers' relations and roles with high-risk drug users (Broadhead and Fox, 1990). Innovative partnerships can develop when academics, working with prisoners and ex-prisoners, produce journals (e.g., *Journal of Prisoners on Prisons*) or journal articles (Clark and Boudin, 1990).

Media Collaborations Film and media images of women—as victims, lawbreakers, or prisoners—are typically sensationalized, sexist, lesbian-bashing, and just plain wrong (Faith, 1987; Daly, 1992b; Maher and Curtis, Chapter 9 in this volume). Recently I have become more optimistic about the potential of working with journalists. While they labor under the constraints of having to "write a story," some are keen to read and draw from feminist research. The irony is plain: two inches of print in one of the national newspapers will get the word out far more quickly and with greater impact than any number of publications in well-known academic journals. Barak (1988) has named this type of work "newsmaking criminology." The steady diet of headlines about the dangers of predatory street crime and about "monster" crack-using women needs to be countered with *and* replaced by different images of crime and justice drawn from research studies. At the same time, some journalists have produced fine accounts of women prisoners and rape victims (Cooper, 1990, 1992) and responses to battered women and violent men (Hoffman, 1992). Researchers and journalists could benefit by joining forces: researchers might enjoy the freedom of storytelling, and journalists could appreciate some of the rigors of social science methodology.

SOME CONCLUDING THOUGHTS

When I think of social change, one woman's wisdom comes to mind: Sojourner Truth's. Truth was a well-known black woman who was active in both the abolitionist and women's rights movements in the nineteenth century. In an essay about Truth, Harriet Beecher Stowe (1863/1875) asked her, "What do you think of women's rights?" Truth replied:[8]

> Well, honey, I've been to their meetings, and harkened a good deal. They wanted me to speak. So I got up. Says I, "Sisters, I ain't clear what you'd be after. If women want any rights more than they's got, why don't they just *take 'em*, and not be talking about it?" (p. 165) (emphasis in original)

Truth's claim is direct and sensible: *talking about rights* is one thing, but *taking rights* is another. Waiting to be allowed full participation in social life is to take a slow boat to social change. Truth's words are novel, but they raise an uncertain challenge: what does it mean to "take rights"?

For me as a teacher, it means I will take risks in introducing new material and theories in the classroom, I should be prepared to face student critique, and I should help students listen to others when they disagree. As a scholar, it means I must continue to make criminology accountable for its omissions and blind spots, at the same time that I subject my own favored theories to critical review. Students can take rights by taking an active, questioning role in the classroom and by going beyond the expected work for the class. In short, taking rights for students, teachers, and scholars means taking greater responsibility for what is learned, what is taught, what is researched, and how knowledge is

acted on for social change. It means taking risks by being unpopular and nonconforming, and it means holding ourselves and others to more demanding standards of accountability. This is particularly important in the areas of crime and justice because the stakes are so high.

Will it be different for the next generation of students? I hope so. But it won't be easy: every generation confronts new problems. Taking rights may get you in trouble: it's more polite to talk about them. Partnerships in misery, once identified, must be transformed into partnerships for change.

NOTES

1. At the time, there were 140 faculty members in the social sciences, 16 of whom were women (Yale University, 1984).
2. Related criticisms are "your work 'only' deals with women of color," etc.
3. I use stage theory heuristically, which means I do not assume that the history of curricula change or the modes of feminist production of knowledge will necessarily unfold in a linear, progressive way. See Goodstein (1992) for a more detailed application of stage theory to curriculum development.
4. Some exceptions are Lombroso and Ferrero's (1895) and Pollak's (1950) studies of women offenders. Feminist reviews of these and recent works have revealed their flawed and sexist character (Naffine, 1987; Klein, Chapter 2 in this volume).
5. Again, exceptions can be noted. The trials and executions of witches during the fourteenth to the eighteenth centuries in Europe and England reflected a perceived threat to Christian churches of lay healing knowledge and political power. Drawing from several historical sources, Ehrenreich and English (1979: 35) say the estimated numbers of witches killed were "in the millions [with] women making up 85 percent of those executed." A more recent (nineteenth-century) exception is the race-based detection of women and their channeling into reformatories

(largely white) and prisons (largely black) (Rafter, 1990).

6. I will focus here on feminist production of knowledge in criminology because I am most familiar with its themes; it would also be important to trace developments in multicultural knowledge production in criminology.

7. To be fair to these and other authors, there has been a shift in the last decade in the naming conventions used. This is illustrated in the changing subsections in Jaggar and Rothenberg's *Feminist Frameworks*. In the first edition (1978), there were few references to women of color; but in the second (1984), there was a new section titled "Feminism and women of color: The inseparability of gender, class, and race oppression." And in the third edition (1993), the section is now called "Women's subordination through the lens of race, gender, class, and sexuality: Multicultural feminism." Such naming conventions reflect academic fashions and real political-theoretical developments.

8. Stowe used a form of broken English in reporting what Truth said, which I do not use here.

REFERENCES

Abrams, Kathryn (1991). "Hearing the call of stories." *California Law Review* 79 (4): 971–1052.

Andersen, Margaret (1988). "Moving our minds: Studying women of color and reconstructing sociology." *Teaching Sociology* 16 (April): 123–132.

Aptheker, Bettina (1982). *Woman's Legacy: Essays on Race, Sex, and Class in American History*. Amherst: University of Massachusetts Press.

Barak, Gregg (1988). "Newsmaking criminology: Reflections on the media, intellectuals, and crime." *Justice Quarterly* 5 (4): 565–587.

Bertrand, Marie-Andree (1969). "Self-image and delinquency: A contribution to the study of female criminality and women's image." *Acta Criminologia: Etudes sur la Conduite Antisocial* 2 (January): 71–144.

——— (1991). "Advances in feminist epistemology of the social control of women." Paper presented at the Annual Meeting of the American Society of Criminology, November.

Bickle, Gayle S., and Ruth D. Peterson (1991). "The impact of gender-based family roles in criminal sentencing." *Social Problems* 38 (3): 372–394.

Bowles, Gloria, and Renate Duelli Klein (eds.) (1983). *Theories of Women's Studies*. Boston: Routledge & Kegan Paul.

Broadhead, Robert S., and Kathryn J. Fox (1990). "Takin' it to the streets: AIDS outreach as ethnography." *Journal of Contemporary Ethnography* 19 (3): 322–348. (This is a special issue devoted to ethnography and AIDS.)

Browne, Angela (1987). *When Battered Women Kill*. New York: Free Press.

Bynum, Victoria E. (1992). *Unruly Women: The Politics of Social & Sexual Control in the Old South*. Chapel Hill: The University of North Carolina Press.

Cain, Maureen (1990). "Towards transgression: New directions in feminist criminology." *International Journal of the Sociology of Law* 18: 1–18.

Campbell, Anne (1984/1991). *The Girls in the Gang*. New York: Blackwell.

Carrington, Kerry (1990). "Feminist readings of female delinquency." *Law in Context* (special issue on feminism, law, and society) 8 (2): 5–31.

Chaudhuri, Molly, and Kathleen Daly (1992). "Do restraining orders help? Battered women's experience with male violence and legal process." Pp. 227–252 in Eve S. Buzawa and Carl B. Buzawa (eds.). *Domestic Violence: The Changing Criminal Justice Response*. Westport, Conn.: Auburn House.

Chesney-Lind, Meda (1973). "Juvenile enforcement of the female sex role: The family court and the female delinquent." *Issues in Criminology* 8 (2): 51–69.

——— (1974). "Juvenile delinquency: The sexualization of female crime." *Psychology Today* (July): 43–46.

——— and Randall G. Shelden (1992). *Girls, Delinquency, and Juvenile Justice*. Pacific Grove, Calif.: Brooks/Cole Publishing Company.

Clark, Judy, and Kathy Boudin (1990). "Community of women organize themselves to cope with the AIDS crisis: A case study from Bedford Hills correctional facility." *Social Justice* 17 (2): 90–109.

Coker, Donna K. (1992). "Heat of passion and wife killing: Men who batter/men who kill." *Southern*

California Review of Law and Women's Studies 2 (1): 71–130.

Collins, Patricia Hill (1990). *Black Feminist Thought.* London: Unwin Hyman, Inc.

Combahee River Collective (1979). "The Combahee River Collective Statement." Pp. 362–372 in Zillah Eisenstein (ed.). *Capitalist Patriarchy and the Case for Socialist Feminism.* New York: Monthly Review Press.

Cooper, Candace (1990). "Nowhere to turn for rape victims." *San Francisco Examiner,* three-part series, Sept. 16, 17, 18.

———— (1992). "Battered women who kill: Murder or defense." *San Francisco Examiner,* two-part series, Aug. 30, 31.

Daly, Kathleen (1987). "Discrimination in the criminal courts: Family, gender, and the problem of equal treatment." *Social Forces* 66 (1): 152–175.

———— (1989). "Neither conflict nor labeling nor paternalism will suffice: Intersections of race, ethnicity, gender, and family in criminal court decisions." *Crime & Delinquency* 35 (1): 136–168.

———— (1992a). "Women's pathways to felony court: Feminist theories of lawbreaking and problems of representation." *Southern California Review of Law and Women's Studies* 2 (1): 11–52.

———— (1992b). "From the halls of the *New York Times* and Hollywood to the shores of the ASC." Paper presented at the Annual Meeting of the American Society of Criminology, November.

———— (1993). "Class-race-gender: Sloganeering in search of meaning." *Social Justice* 20 (1–2): 56–71.

———— and Meda Chesney-Lind (1988). "Feminism and criminology." *Justice Quarterly* 5 (4): 497–538.

————, Shelley Geballe, and Stanton Wheeler (1988). "Litigation-driven research: A case study of lawyer-social scientist collaboration." *Women's Rights Law Reporter* 10 (4): 221–241.

Davis, Angela Y. (1981/1983). *Women, Race and Class.* New York: Vintage.

Dobash, R. Emerson, and Russell P. Dobash (1979). *Violence against Wives.* New York: The Free Press.

———— and ———— (1992). *Women, Violence, and Social Change.* New York: Routledge.

Dobash, Russell P., R. Emerson Dobash, Margo Wilson, and Martin Daly (1992). "The myth of sexual symmetry in marital violence." *Social Problems* 39 (1): 71–91.

Ehrenreich, Barbara, and Deirdre English (1979). *For Her Own Good: 150 Years of the Experts' Advice to Women.* Garden City, N.Y.: Doubleday Anchor Books.

Eigenberg, Helen, and Agnes Baro (1992). "The invisibility and marginalization of women of color in textbook photographs: A content analysis of introductory criminology and criminal justice texts." Paper presented at the Annual Meeting of the American Society of Criminology, November.

Estrich, Susan (1986). "Rape." *The Yale Law Journal* 95 (6): 1087–1184.

Faith, Karlene (1987). "Media, myths, and masculinization: Images of women in prison." Pp. 181–219 in Ellen Adelberg and Claudia Currie (eds.). *Too Few to Count: Canadian Women in Conflict with the Law.* Vancouver: Press Gang Publishers.

Ferraro, Kathleen J. (1989). "Policing woman battering." *Social Problems* 36 (1): 61–74.

Gilligan, Carol (1982). *In a Different Voice.* Cambridge, Mass.: Harvard University Press.

Goodstein, Lynne (1992). "Feminist perspectives and the criminal justice curriculum." *Journal of Criminal Justice Education* 3 (2): 165–181.

Hancock, Linda (1981). "The myth that females are treated more leniently than males in the juvenile justice system." *Australian and New Zealand Journal of Criminology* 16 (3): 4–14.

Hanmer, Jalna, Jill Radford, and Elizabeth A. Stanko (eds.) (1989). *Women, Policing and Male Violence.* New York: Routledge.

Hartsock, Nancy C. M. (1984). *Money Sex, and Power.* Boston: Northeastern University Press.

Heidensohn, Frances (1968). "The deviance of women: A critique and an enquiry." *British Journal of Sociology* 19 (20): 160–176.

———— (1987). "Women and crime: Questions for criminology." Pp. 16–27 in Pat Carlen and Anne Worrall (eds.). *Gender, Crime and Justice.* Philadelphia: Open University.

Hoffman, Jan (1992). "When men hit women." *New York Times Magazine* (Feb. 16): pp. 21 ff.

hooks, bell (1984). *Feminist Theory: From Margin to Center.* Boston: South End Press.

Jaggar, Alison M., and Paula S. Rothenberg (eds.) (1978, 1984, 1993). *Feminist Frameworks,* 1st, 2d, and 3d eds. New York: McGraw-Hill.

Jordan, June (1985). "Report from the Bahamas." Pp. 39–49 in *On Call: Political Essays*. Boston: South End Press.

Journal of Prisoners on Prisons, P.O. Box 60779, Edmonton, Alberta, Canada, T6G 2S9.

King, Deborah (1988). "Multiple jeopardy, multiple consciousness: The context of a black feminist ideology." *Signs: Journal of Women in Culture and Society* 14 (1): 42–72.

Lerner, Gerda (1990). "Reconceptualizing differences among women." *Journal of Women's History* 1 (3): 106–122. Reprinted in Alison M. Jaggar and Paula S. Rothenberg (eds.) (1993). *Feminist Frameworks*. New York: McGraw-Hill.

Lewis, Diane (1981). "Black women offenders and criminal justice: Some theoretical considerations." Pp. 89–105 in Marguerite Warren (ed.). *Comparing Female and Male Offenders*. Beverly Hills, Calif.: Sage.

Lombroso, Cesare, and W. Ferrero (1895). *The Female Offender*. London: Fisher-Unwin.

Lorde, Audre (1984). *Sister Outsider*. Trumansburg, N.Y.: The Crossing Press.

Mama, Amina (1989). *The Hidden Struggle*. London: The London Race and Housing Research Unit.

McIntosh, Peggy (1984). "Interactive phases of curricular revision." Pp. 25–34 in Bonnie Spanier, Alexander Bloom, and Darlene Boroviak (eds.). *Toward a Balanced Curriculum*. Cambridge, Mass.: Schenkman.

Mies, Maria (1983). "Toward a methodology for feminist research." Pp. 117–139 in Gloria Bowles and Renate Duelli Klein (eds.). *Theories of Women's Studies*. Boston: Routledge & Kegan Paul.

Moore, Joan W. (1991). *Going Down to the Barrio: Homeboys and Homegirls in Change*. Philadelphia: Temple University Press.

Moraga, Cherrie, and Gloria Anzaldua (eds.) (1981). *This Bridge Called My Back: Writings by Radical Women of Color*. New York: Kitchen Table: Women of Color Press (reprint 1983).

Naffine, Ngaire (1987). *Female Crime: The Construction of Women in Criminology*. Boston: Allen Unwin.

Newton, Judith L., Mary P. Ryan, and Judith R. Walkowitz (eds.) (1983). *Sex and Class in Women's History*. Boston: Routledge & Kegan Paul.

Peterson, Ruth D., and John Hagan (1984). "Changing conceptions of race: Towards an account of anomalous findings of sentencing research." *American Sociological Review* 49 (1): 56–70.

Platt, Anthony M. (1993). "Beyond the canon, with great difficulty." *Social Justice* 20 (1–2): 72–81.

Pollak, Otto (1950). *The Criminality of Women*. Philadelphia: University of Pennsylvania Press.

Pratt, Minnie Bruce (1984). "Identity: Skin Blood Heart." Pp. 11–63 in Elly Bulkin, Minnie Bruce Pratt, and Barbara Smith (eds.). *Yours in Struggle*. Ithaca, N.Y.: Firebrand Books.

Rafter, Nicole Hahn (1985/1990). *Partial Justice: Women, Prisons, and Social Control*. New Brunswick, N.J.: Transaction Publishers (2d ed. title and publisher).

Reinharz, Shulamit (1992). *Feminist Methods in Social Research*. New York: Oxford.

Rice, Marcia (1990). "Challenging orthodoxies in feminist theory: A black feminist critique." Pp. 57–69 in Loraine Gelsthorpe and Allison Morris (eds.). *Feminist Perspectives in Criminology*. Philadelphia: Open University Press.

Richie, Beth (1985). "Battered black women: A challenge for the black community." *The Black Scholar* 16 (20): 40–44.

Rights of Women, Family Law Subgroup (1985). "Campaigning around family law: Politics and practice." Pp. 188–206 in Julia Brophy and Carol Smart (eds.). *Women in Law*. Boston: Routledge & Kegan Paul.

Rorhlich-Leavitt, Ruby, Barbara Sykes, and Elizabeth Weatherford (1975). "Aboriginal woman: Male and female anthropological perspectives." Pp. 110–126 in Rayna R. Reiter (ed.). *Toward an Anthropology of Women*. New York: Monthly Review Press.

Rothenberg, Paula S. (ed.) (1992, 2d ed.). *Race, Class, & Gender in the United States: An Integrated Study*. New York: St. Martin's Press.

Russell, Diana (1975). *The Politics of Rape: The Victim's Perspective*. New York: Stein and Day.

Simpson, Sally S. (1989). "Feminist theory, crime, and justice." *Criminology* 27 (4): 605–631.

Smart, Carol (1976). *Women, Crime and Criminology: A Feminist Critique*. Boston: Routledge & Kegan Paul.

——— (1989). *Feminism and the Power of Law*. New York: Routledge.

——— (1990). "Feminist approaches to criminology or postmodern woman meets atavistic man."

Pp. 70–84 in Loraine Gelsthorpe and Allison Morris (eds.). *Feminist Perspectives in Criminology.* Philadelphia: Open University Press.

Smith, Dorothy E. (1987). *The Everyday World as Problematic: A Feminist Sociology.* Boston: Northeastern University Press.

Spelman, Elizabeth V. (1989). *Inessential Woman.* Boston: Beacon Press.

Stephens, Deborah J. (1993). "Crime, victimization, and the black woman." Paper presented at the Annual Meeting of the American Society of Criminology, Oct. 27–30, Phoenix.

Stowe, Harriet Beecher (1863). "Sojourner Truth, the Libyan Sibyl." *Atlantic Monthly* (April). Reprinted in *Narrative of Sojourner Truth.*

Truth, Sojourner (1875). *Narrative of Sojourner Truth, Drawn from her Book of Life.* Published for the author in Boston.

Vogel, Lise (1991). "Telling tales: Historians of our own lives." *Journal of Women's History* (Winter): 89–101.

Williams, Joyce E., and Karen A. Holmes (1981). *The Second Assault: Rape and Public Attitudes.* Westport, Conn.: Greenwood Press.

Williams, Patricia J. (1991). *The Alchemy of Race and Rights—Diary of a Law Professor.* Cambridge, Mass.: Harvard University Press.

Wilson, Nanci Koser (1991). "Feminist pedagogy in criminology." *Journal of Criminal Justice Education* 2 (1): 81–93.

Women's Rights Law Reporter (1986). Special issue: *Women's Self-Defense Law* 9 (3–4).

Wonders, Nancy A., and Susan L. Caulfield (1993). "Women's work?: The contradictory implications of courses on women and the criminal justice system." *Journal of Criminal Justice Education* 4 (1): 79–100.

Wright, Richard A. (1992). "From vamps and tramps to teases and flirts: Stereotypes of women in criminology textbooks, 1956 to 1965 and 1981 to 1990." *Journal of Criminal Justice Education* 3 (2): 223–236.

Yale University (1984). "Report of the Faculty of Arts and Sciences Advisory Committee on the Education of Women," Donald Crothers, Chair, New Haven, Conn.

Young, Iris Marion (1990). *Justice and the Politics of Difference.* Princeton: Princeton University Press.

Young, Vernetta D. (1980). "Women, race, and crime." *Criminology* 18: 26–34.